THIRD EDITION

The Challenge
of Politics

IDEAS AND ISSUES

ALVIN Z. RUBINSTEIN

Professor of Political Science
University of Pennsylvania

GAROLD W. THUMM

Professor of Government
Bates College

PRENTICE-HALL, INC., *Englewood Cliffs, N.J.*

13–125062–0
Library of Congress Catalog Card No.: 77–102128

Printed in the United States of America

Current printing (last digit):

12 11 10 9 8 7 6 5 4 3 2 1

PRENTICE-HALL INTERNATIONAL, INC., *London*
PRENTICE-HALL OF AUSTRALIA, LTD., *Sydney*
PRENTICE-HALL OF CANADA, LTD., *Toronto*
PRENTICE-HALL OF INDIA (PRIVATE) LTD., *New Delhi*
PRENTICE-HALL OF JAPAN, INC., *Tokyo*

to
PHILIP E. JACOB
Inspired Teacher

Preface

This book of readings was brought together to provide the basic substantive material for an introductory course in Political Science which confronts what Leslie Lipson has called *The Great Issues of Politics*.

The course, as we have conducted it, calls on students to examine and grapple with the persistent problems and overriding human aspirations which have dictated the nature of political behavior and the institutions through which such behavior is expressed. The approach is analytical and evaluative. It seeks always to relate political forms and processes to the essential purposes and functions from which they have derived and which they serve. This book is not a survey of theories or theorists, but an exploration of imperatives of conduct. It is the idea of compelling power which commands our attention, and it is the impact of such an idea upon political action which we seek to trace.

The readings were selected with the following objectives in mind: first, to set forth succinctly yet definitively the central questions at issue in the great political controversies; second, to confront, one against the other, the differing responses to these questions which have aroused substantial political commitments; third, to contrast the approaches used by Western and non-Western, democratic and non-democratic societies; and fourth, to show the effects of political ideas upon political institutions and vice versa. Problem to idea; idea to process and institution; and back again, is the "dialectic" of this approach.

There is a further implication of introducing students to political phenomena through the study of key issues of politics. They must transcend narrow bounds of knowledge and find meaningful integration between political and economic and social functions and ideas; and between local and national and international governmental processes;

and between contemporary and previous historical experience. The spread of these readings is therefore purposely extensive.

We hope that these materials will meet the demands of this kind of course. We have focused the readings on the various points of issue, and so organized and related them as to make possible the kind of systematic political analysis which it has been our aim to accomplish.

Preface

TO THE THIRD EDITION

> *"Rarely in history have brutal facts so dominated thought or has such widespread, individual virtue found so dim a collective focus. The fearful question confronts us: Have our problems got beyond our control?"*
> SIR WINSTON CHURCHILL

Almost a decade after we sent the first edition of *The Challenge of Politics* to press we see that man's dilemmas and choices fall as much as ever into the framework of "the Great Issues." Their manifestations, however, have changed drastically: the opposition to the Vietnam war, the racial unrest, the questioning of long-cherished institutions and values, and the impatience of the young with the undemocratic residuals in American society and their demand for a greater voice in the decisions that affect their lives. More than at any time since the end of World War II, there is an implosion of American concerns. Frustrations and disillusionments in foreign affairs have interacted with powerful domestic currents to direct attention from the international to the domestic sphere.

In preparing our revisions we have responded to the reordering of political priorities, and we have expanded our coverage with new analyses of age-old issues. We note that the resurgence of political activism has been accompanied by a reawakened interest in the normative and prescriptive aspects of political science, and by renewed controversy concerning the nature of the discipline.

The new materials have been selected as much for the freshness and clarity with which they are written as for the insights they provide. Though greater attention has been devoted to the American scene, we have also included new essays on non-Western and Communist societies and sharpened the focus on comparative analysis. Instead of emphasizing official documents, speeches, and Constitutions, which are readily available elsewhere, we have given preference to original essays; instead of drawing primarily from the classics, we have turned to contemporary writers; instead of restricting the examination of "Great Issues" to conflicts set in traditional political institutions, we have broadened the coverage to economic, social, and educational settings as well. Forty percent of the selections are new.

To introduce the student to the subject and study of politics and to some of the principal approaches prevalent in the discipline, four new readings have been added to Part 1: W. J. M. Mackenzie sets classical theory and assumptions in a historical-comparative context and offers an overview of the field; Edmond Cahn looks at the concept of the State and its relationship to a democratic society; Heinz Eulau treats the dimensions and contributions of behavioral approaches to the study of politics; and Christian Bay forcefully stresses the moral ends to which politics should be directed. The section on equality has been expanded, particularly as it relates to the American experience. The readings by John F. Kennedy, Herbert J. Gans, Nathan Glazer, and the Kerner Commission reflect the centrality that the issue of racial equality has acquired and the importance of the "Black Revolution" to the future of American society. Other selections deal with developing societies and Czechoslovakia. The section on the sphere and parameters of government has new readings on the role of private organizations in American political life, a recent analysis of power struggles and political developments in Communist China, and a comparison of the American and Soviet political system. The essay by Michael Harrington has a noted American muckraker presenting the case for democratic socialism. John Kenneth Galbraith offers his assessment of the industrial society of the future. As the new additions to Part 4 indicate, we find that the problem of freedom and authority is expressed currently more in varying forms of civil disobedience than in association with a subversive organization having international ties. The readings by T. H. Green, John K. Fairbank, and Yuri P. Frantsev explore the role of the individual in Western and Communist societies; those by Sidney Hook, Martin Luther King, Jr., and Colin Crouch discuss the frontiers of dissent; and the one by D. J. R. Scott deals with political resistance, passive and active, in Soviet history. Part 5 includes new selections on different aspects of the issue of federalism: John Anderson discusses the relationship between the state and federal governments; Walter W. Heller suggests that the federal government search for new ways of improving the financial condition of the states; Pierre Elliott Trudeau offers fresh perspectives on Canadian federalism; and Peter F. Drucker propounds the original idea of "reprivatization," as essential for the efficient functioning of government. Part 6 has been expanded with additional readings on nationalism, U.S. foreign policy, nonalignment, the international system, the Atlantic world, Pan-Africanism, and prospects for world peace.

With these major revisions we have sought to bring contemporary relevance to the treatment of perennial themes. In a word, we see "The Challenge of Politics" still as that of coping with "the Great Issues."

ALVIN Z. RUBINSTEIN
University of Pennsylvania

GAROLD W. THUMM
Bates College

Contents

part one

Man in Society:

The Stuff of Politics

INTRODUCTION, 1

part two

Equality in

The Political Community

INTRODUCTION, 47

part three
The Sphere of Government:
Limited or Unlimited?

INTRODUCTION, 137

part four

Freedom Versus Authority

in the Modern World

INTRODUCTION, 195

part five

The Organization of

The State: Concentration

Or Dispersion of Power

INTRODUCTION, 279

part six

Superstates

And the State System

The Challenge
of Politics

part one

Man in Society:

The Stuff of Politics

INTRODUCTION

Until philosophers are kings, or the kings and princes
of this world have the spirit and power of philosophy,
and political greatness and wisdom meet in one . . .
cities will never have rest from their evils. . . .
— Plato, *The Republic*, V, 473d.

The greatest challenge to man is man. For with his discovery of the key to the energy of the universe he finds himself confronted with what may well be his final challenge. Through technology and science he has made possible his self-destruction. As he has had to control the power of nature for his welfare, so now he must control his own power if he is to survive. The question at the center of his thought is no longer the "why" of his present existence, but the "whether" of his future.

Yet, the "whether" of his future is bound up with the question of the nature of man himself, for his own nature dictates the means he may use to determine his future. In a very real sense, the proper study of politics is the study of man, his ideals and institutions. What is man? Alone, he is unable to create those cultural and technical masterpieces which make civilized life possible—and may make it impossible. In association with his fellow man, he forms a "state"—an organization which enables him to achieve his goals.

But why this association? The reasons may shed light both on the nature of man and the nature and purposes of the state. Whether the

1

state is a product of some fundamental urge in man the "social animal," or a further extension of the functions and authority of the family, or a creation designed to serve some ulterior end of the ruling group, it is one of the most significant institutions in the life of modern man. Through it he seeks protection from enemies without the group, maintenance of order within, and justice everywhere. But what activities are "necessary and proper" to the attainment of these ends? Who is to decide? What procedures are to be followed? What limitations are to be imposed upon the state? Upon its rulers? How can these limitations be enforced?

These questions are never permanently answered; they are subject to continual reinterpretation; they are the "stuff of politics."

Today more than ever before man is torn between an attraction to and a revulsion from politics. His growing "politicization" stems from a number of factors: 1) The development of the state as an increasingly important symbol of his identification with the group; 2) The broadening of democratic and quasi-democratic practices and the popularization of mass participation in governmental activity; 3) The growth of communications with his fellows as a result of technological advances; 4) The search of the individual, in an era of social alienation and depersonalization, for "something to believe in."

At the same time, the reasons for the commensurate revulsion against politics are not hard to find: 1) The sheer "bigness" of government overwhelms the individual and produces a feeling of impotence; 2) The increasing bureaucratization of society discourages his activity and interest; 3) The manipulation of mass media tends to stunt man's critical faculties; 4) Government has failed to meet his social needs and provide ideals he can believe in.

The attraction to and revulsion from politics confront each other at all levels of political life. Despite the drawbacks, politics continues to exert a strong appeal. Is it a desire for personal power? Or an intellectual curiosity concerning the nature of the political process? Or a humanistic concern with improving the way society handles its affairs? Or is it a sense of moral concern and commitment which seeks to end injustice?

Developments in military technology have limited the individual's capacity to shape his survival. Yet, it is only through the political process that man can hope to order his life according to reason and ideals. The allure of pol'tics is strong; the struggle, hard; and the stakes, unique: the future of man.

1. THE TRADITION OF POLITICAL SCIENCE

W. J. M. MACKENZIE

W. J. M. Mackenzie (1909–   ) is professor of government at the University of Glasgow and a leading British student of comparative politics.

I. *THE CLASSIC AUTHORS AND THEIR ROLE*

Given the tradition of law and learning, it is hard to imagine a 'great polity' which does not in some sense include 'political science'. Political science is concerned (among other things) with those who are in power. The legitimation of their authority involves law in the second degree—law about the conditions under which a rule purporting to be a law is in fact a valid rule: it therefore involves men learned in the law. Power rests also on tradition and myth, and the learned men are also custodians of history and precedent, sometimes even adding the role of myth-maker and poet. But one can think of cultures and periods during which the lawyers were no more than 'lions under the throne', and the learned men were no more than panegyrists and propagandists.

There have been perhaps two factors missing in such cases: the element of debate and the element of science. The debate need not be in any sense democratic, it may be no more than debate between the spokesmen of armed bands struggling for a medieval throne. But even such debate implies a forum and an audience; one argues to achieve approval by some entity the approval of which is worth winning. The grounds of such a debate will often be legal, historical, philosophical, theological, and one is tempted to include as political scientist any man who persistently (as it were, professionally) debates issues about political authority with major premises drawn from any of these disciplines.

Modern taste would require also some interest in 'positive' knowledge, some concern with general rules about what actually happens, not about what ought to happen; it would be rather more sympathetic to Machiavelli than to Plato, to Montesquieu than to Hobbes. But the distinction may break down under pressure; it is not very easy to draw conclusions about action from general premises of any kind without including in the argument (openly or tacitly) some propositions about the probable consequences of certain actions in the real world. Indeed, it is by no means certain that in political science one can separate normative propositions from descriptive propositions

From W. J. M. Mackenzie, *Politics and Social Change*. Baltimore, Md.: Penguin Books, Inc., A Pelican Original, copyright 1967. Pp. 40–53. Reprinted by permission of the publisher.

without misunderstanding what is going on. In certain contexts, an apparent statement of fact about political life carries strong recommendations; similarly, a phrase used in a recommendation ('Traitors ought to be executed') could be expanded so as to expose an implied doctrine of cause and effect in political society.

It is therefore not by any means certain that the reference to 'science' is necessary. Perhaps it adds little, in this context, to the idea of open debate and critical appraisal. Certainly the positivist distinction between questions of value and questions of fact does not work very well in analysing political talk; perhaps the reference to debate or dialogue is enough for our purpose here, since 'adversary' argument implies scrutiny of all general statements and their consequences, except in so far as the contestants share unstated presuppositions.

Nevertheless, there is perhaps a working distinction to be drawn between those who spoke and wrote about political authority and obedience in the context of a great philosophical system or world view; and those who wrote as if they sought to be 'naturalists', classifying political phenomena and generalizing from their own observations and those of others. One could place Plato, Augustine, Aquinas, Hobbes, Spinoza, Hegel pretty definitely in the first class; Thucydides, Polybius, Machiavelli, Harrington, Montesquieu, de Tocqueville, Bagehot in the second. But Aristotle stands firmly with a foot in both camps: so does Marx: and anyone who knows their work well can find elements of 'positive science' in the first category, elements of exhortation in the second category.

How did these men fit into the structure of society? They were not of course professionals in the modern sense, men formally certified to have achieved professional standards of competence and thereafter earning a living through fees or a salary. This is a very late phenomenon in politics as in other branches of science and scholarship; indeed, one cause of our present bewilderment is that professionalism has intruded quite suddenly into a subject which was once the province of the gifted amateur. The professionals do not as yet quite know what is expected of them—and society at large has no fixed expectations. Whereas each of the founders shaped a role for himself out of his own experience and situation.

Not surprisingly, a fair number of them were men (like Plato, Machiavelli or Locke) living on the edge of political life but not wholly committed to it. From their experience they drew a practical knowledge of politics and also a sense of its moral and intellectual stresses; one can compare other intellectuals in our own day who experienced personally the muddled and murderous character of ideological war.

The needs that these men satisfied perhaps exist in all political settings. Political authority, in its developed form, is always reinforced by law, myth and rationalization. A minimum function of the political scientist has been to debate as gladiator on one side or another of current political contests: a role distinguishable from propaganda only in settings where the opposition is such as to push the level of debate up to the highest standards of current scholarship. (It is pleasant to read [Jan. 1966] that the Popes have at last forgiven Dante for his championship of the universal empire [*De Monarchia*] against the papal claims.) A great mind, working in an open society, may be incited to take a stand beyond and above current controversies. Plato certainly began to write with a mind full of regret for the young men, his friends, whose lives were wasted in futile attempts at revolution; but the strength of his work is that sometimes he is not merely a spokesman for a lost generation of well-born intellectuals. Sometimes the controversialist becomes myth-maker and metaphysician, and the myth may live longer than the philosophy.

A second role is that of improver, at various levels from that of constitution-maker to that of Organization and Methods man. Bentham tried them all, and also tasted most possible outcomes, from total frustration by bureaucracy to canonization as a lay saint. The man who has established himself as scholar and reasoner has a certain standing which suggests that he will be of use to someone in the process of changing institutions. Even if his wisdom is useless, his reputation may be usable; the constitution-maker is at worst cat's paw, at best mid-wife. Some (like Plato and Bentham) have disagreeable experiences, and emerge with an altered view of human nature; some decide that general reasoning is not of much use without methodical observation, and seek to be empirical rather than philosophical, to separate science from metaphysics.

II. *THEIR STYLES OF ARGUMENT*

On the whole, it seems better to let questions of methodology arise incidentally out of questions of substance: but it is worth adding a little here about the methods of the 'traditional political scientist', who is to be envisaged as a man fully trained in the scholarship of his day, experienced in politics, widely read otherwise, but working alone and writing for an audience of general, not professional, culture. Perhaps not enough has yet been done to analyse the methods of argument used in the classics, but the general outline seems clear enough.

The basic disciplines involved are those of philosophy, law and history, each with its own canon of authority and proof. Till quite recently (it was still there in Mill and Bagehot in the 1860s), there was a strong tie with linguistic disciplines because these were a part of every man's education in 'grammar' and in 'rhetoric'. The notion (a puzzling one) of linguistic correctness could be taken as a matter of course. Persuasion was assumed to have its own rules, at least some of which were to be found in the books of rhetoric (which included a good many sensible reflections on social psychology): and poetry was not something that belonged in another Faculty. Plato was obsessed with the potentialities of the linguistic spell, for good and evil. Mill rejected Bentham's doctrine (James Mill's doctrine too?) that 'pushpin is as good as poetry, the quantities of pleasure being the same'; that is to say, that all pleasures can be measured by the same set of interchangeable units; and Bagehot was by the standards of his day a pretty good literary critic.

In general, scholars primarily oriented to mathematics and physics did not write about politics, but there was no barrier between these sciences and other forms of scholarship. From the beginnings of an intellectual world in the West in the sixth century B.C., gossip about science travelled surprisingly fast. In the West, but not in China and in Islam, there was a gap of perhaps a thousand years in the late Roman Empire and early middle ages; but from the thirteenth century, at least, intellectual news once again circulated quite quickly, and a man could not compete in the world of *savants* unless he was in close touch with current controversies and fashions. Until recently, there was one intellectual world, not two: then for various reasons science and the humanities fell apart. Now there are attempts to bring them together again.

It is not very easy to abstract from this changing background and public but perhaps one can classify traditional arguments under four heads: philosophical, legalistic, analogical and comparative. Some might make a separate category for theological arguments; to me they seem to fall within the first three of these heads.

1. *Philosophy*. It is tempting to label the first with a phrase made popular recently—'over-arching theory'. But we are thinking of periods when metaphysics was taken seriously, either as a matter of deduction from self-evident principles or indirectly (as in Kant) as a statement of the conditions without which there could not be thought and action as we know them. Most of these noble philosophical edifices—Plato's ideas and their shadows; Aristotle's great creature or machine moved by the attraction of god, which is love; the law of nature and its challenger the greatest happiness principle—have now been badly knocked about, and their roofs are gaping.

But it should be noted that they have been knocked about with instruments first forged by the philosophers themselves. 'Once upon a time' no man wrote 'over-arching theory' unless he had had a stiff training in definitions and in Aristotelean logic, a training which is now perhaps given more effectively in economics than in political science. Logical combat was a fairly tough and bruising game, both in Greece and in the Middle Ages, and no author became a classic unless he was dexterous at this formal level. Metaphysics was not a realm for loose thinkers.

2. *Law*. Training in law also gives toughness of logical fibre, and law like philosophy is concerned with first principles and with systematic coherence and consistency. In addition, it is (like theology) concerned with authorities and their interpretation, a trick which makes large tracts of medieval and Renaissance writing repulsive to us, so that we skip the references to the Bible and the Fathers, and miss much of the character of the argument.

As Professor Mitchell notes, in England 'public law is too often regarded as a series of unfortunate exceptions to the desirable generality or universality of the rules of private law, and is not seen as a rational system with its own justification, and perhaps its own philosophy'. As will be seen (in chapters 5 and 16) law in continental Europe is, or has been, inseparably integrated with political science; whereas in England legal argument is applied to politics by analogy, and not as prime mover. Nevertheless, even in England the legal style had great influence.

Hence rather strange legalistic metaphysics of 'contract', 'trust', 'people' and 'nation' in the older books; hence serious attempts at fresh thinking in the years around 1900 by legal scholars of the standing of Gierke, Duguit and Esmein; hence the emergence of Kelsen from the Viennese school of logical positivism and his attempt to exclude that metaphysical creature, the state, from the logic of the law, and to substitute for a supreme entity a supreme legal rule.

This European movement was 'un-English', even more alien than are the philosophical exercises of the American Supreme Court. But it is at least desirable to get the English to understand that it is they who are the 'outsiders' in this. They have never been able to understand what a complete and consistent legal revolution would entail; and this has not been wholly to their advantage, even though it got them round some awkward corners in their history.

3. *Analogy and Homology.* Argument from analogy, on the other hand, is universal. Indeed one view of 'explanation' in general is that it is a matter of arguing from the strange to the familiar and then back again; in fact that 'explanation' is a kind of recognition, an integration of new items into an old pattern. Once this has been achieved the mind can 'rest'; but such satisfaction may or may not have an adequate logical foundation.

There is a technical question about the distinction between analogy and homology. In the latter, one explains a system (a) by using another system (b) which is identical under prescribed mathematical transformations. For instance, a map is usually a simplified projection on a plane surface of natural features on a spherical surface. There are various alternative forms of projection; provided one applies the rules of the relevant projection exactly, moves on the map correspond exactly to movements on the ground. Simulation of motion on an analog computer (for instance the movements of a motor-car's suspension as the car travels) is homologous with that of any car incorporating the factors simulated. In a famous chapter of *Growth and Form*, D'Arcy Thompson studies mathematical transformations of the dimensions of skulls and other bony structures of species in evolution, and claims to detect homologies and also anomalies; the skull of an ape (on this showing) is homologous to that of a man, not merely analogous.

It is difficult to define 'analogy' with equal formality. Probably it would be agreed that the use of analogy is 'heuristic'; that is to say, that likeness between two objects in one strongly marked feature does not logically entitle us to argue from one to the other, but it may suggest fruitful lines of investigation, leading eventually to proof in some other way. Analogy, in fact, is a tricky tool; there are two stages of skill, first to see analogies, secondly to use analogies—and their use can legitimately be rhetorical or poetical, as well as scientific. But according to modern canons of scholarship, an author should not try to use analogy both as poetry and as science at the same time. The 'classics' did this habitually, and some of them (Plato, at least) would defend their method vigorously if they were here to do so. Their case would be that every political writer is a participant in politics, whether he likes it or not, and that if he believes in his case he is under a political obligation to help it to prevail. Political arguments are directed to action: with an able audience only able arguments will prevail; but the test of success in political argument is persuasion, not abstract truth.

Readers will recognize the dictum of Marx, 'Philosophers have previously offered various interpretations of the world. Our business is to change it'. Hence much contemporary argument which remains unresolved: advocacy of commitment on the one hand, of scientific detachment on the other. The argument from analogy (as will be seen in later chapters) is still strong in much contemporary work; and it is never easy to sort out its rhetorical from its scientific content.

There has never been a systematic examination of the analogies traditionally used in political science, but the subject deserves a brief word here, with some reference forward. There are at least five types of analogy which have become traditional.

(*a*) First, analogy with a living creature, plant, beast or man; Burke's oak tree, Hobbes's Leviathan, endless comparisons of different political roles to the different organs of the human body. As will be seen later, the biological analogy between organic system and social system has been pressed hard in recent years. It is powerful largely because it offers the concept of self-regulating whole or system of differentiated parts maintaining itself in an environment; its weakness is that it misses the importance of the great gaps in nature, between solitary creatures and social creatures, between instinct and culture.

(*b*) Secondly, analogy with the life of social animals, above all with the life of bees. Here analogy almost becomes homology: man is not *like* a social animal; he *is* a social animal. But it was an unlucky hit to choose primarily the social insects, who followed quite a different path in the evolution of societies. Indeed, the bee-hive, Virgil's image of the Roman state at peace with itself, has become to us a symbol of Utopia in reverse, 'Brave New World', a possible perversion of human social organization.

It is only rarely that one of the older authors treats human society ecologically, as a social system evolving in an environment, as recent authors have treated the social systems of the apes and other social creatures. But with Montesquieu this concept of the interrelation of society and environment entered a new phase, one in which there was an attempt at systematic comparison and analysis.

(*c*) Medieval thought is so filled with ideas of symmetry and analogy that it is often difficult to know which term of a comparison is to be explained, and which offers the explanation. In the central theme of *The Great Chain of Being,* the whole universe resembles in its structure the gradations of a hierarchical society; each creature, from the throne of Heaven to the inanimate stone, has its place in the universal harmony.

> How could communities,
> Degrees in schools, and brotherhoods in cities,
> Peaceful commerce from dividable shores,
> The primogenity and due of birth,
> Prerogative of age, crowns, sceptres, laurels,
> But by degree, stand in authentic place?
> Take but degree away, untune that string,
> And, hark, what discord follows!

The universe resembles a feudal court more perfect than any real court; the ideal set before a feudal polity is that each member of it should play his part in copying the divine structure of the universe.

(*d*) As feudalism broke up, political debate was invaded by two other analogies: that of the legal system and that of the machine. They have this in common, that they treat the polity as an artefact. One might exclude this possibility by definition, maintaining that institutions created purposively in relation to specified ends should be called 'administrative', not 'political'. Short of this violent remedy, there would be agreement only that the element of manufacture is never the dominant element in a living polity, though most polities bear some marks of the builder's hand. The analogy of purposive creation is a case where a single feature of comparison is allowed to dominate and so to distort.

Social contract is the earlier of the two; it uses analogy between a polity and a legal arrangement created by contract or perhaps by settlement in trust. One advantage of the contract analogy is that it suggests working parts for a model, which admit of combination in various patterns. The model must, by force of analogy, include some pre-existing law to govern legal transactions; one or more transactions under this law, of a nature defined by law; a method of adjudication and rectification where breaches of law are alleged. From these materials contract theories can be tailored to fit almost any set of norms which the author wishes to defend.

The machine analogy is closely associated with the utilitarian doctrine (which is also the Holy Grail of welfare economics) that government is good in so far as it serves the greatest good of the greatest possible number. Enthusiastic utilitarians think of constructing a machine *de novo*, shaping human participants to fit their places in it; more modest utilitarians use the 'greatest good' doctrine merely as a criterion to be invoked in situations which have a relatively clear machine aspect; that is to say, where there is a specified and limited purpose to be achieved, with specified and limited means. This is another case of an analogy strong on one point, hopelessly astray on others. Political society in general is no more like a machine than it is like a contract; but in one point there is a likeness.

In contemporary writing other analogies or metaphors crop up, and these will require some reference later. The machine has now become a homeostatic self-regulatory cybernetic device; and thus glorified, has ascended into the realm of general systems theory, which is dedicated to the search for homologies (not analogies) linking all systems, living or not.

The analogy of language crops up in the repeated references to 'political *style*' and 'administrative *style*'; a metaphor which is illuminating but has not been 'cashed' empirically, perhaps because attempts to quantify style in literature are still fairly new.

Not so with the analogy—or is it homology?—which links together the ideas of individual personality and political culture, of individual character and national character. 'Personality' is now defined operationally as relative consistency in responses to tests by questionnaire and otherwise, which have been standardized so as to produce patterns of reply which are (within limits) reproducible by different observers, using the same or different tests. Character thus defined has some connexion with our ordinary use of the word, and it has been reduced to specific operations. If these operations can be applied to one man they can be applied to many men; and with due precautions the test results can be summed into a single 'index number', or a set of indicators, for 'national character' or 'political culture'. The operations are legitimate, step by step; the problem which remains is to decide what it is they have added to our old personifications of ourselves and others—John Bull, Uncle Sam, the 'frogs', the 'wops', and so on.

4. *Comparative Government*. Perhaps Herodotus is the father of comparative government, in that he used the historical confrontation of Greek cities and Asiatic empires to make a number of points of lasting importance about government under law and the combination of discipline and freedom. A hundred years later, Aristotle set his students to work to collect for him the constitutions of 158 states, mainly Greek cities, but only one of these monographs (that on Athens) has survived, and there is not enough detail in the *Politics* to enable one to see how strictly Aristotle handled the logic of comparison.

Ideally, comparison is a substitute for experiment, particularly useful if experiment is impossible. Collect a number of examples of the category of object to be investigated: Greek city states, federations, smaller European democracies. Analyse them into a number of factors or 'areas' which can be documented in each case, and which bear on the subject to be studied. If the examples are alike in respect of a pretty large proportion of these factors they are 'comparable', and one can proceed to 'experiment' mentally with the small number of factors which remain; factors which lie within a field of special interest to the enquiry, and which show differences in cases clearly alike in other respects. The smaller European democracies, for instance, offer a favourable field for the comparative study of the interaction between party organization and religious organization, because these states are tolerably similar in size, economic development, literacy rate, standard of living, and also in their history of religious divisions. Their party systems too have a good deal in common organizationally. But there are certain sharp differences, and indeed no two party systems are quite alike, although there are certain groups of greater similarity within the main group. Can we discover that party organization varies along with any other factor or factors? For instance, does the electoral system in itself make much difference?

Strictly speaking, there should be two phases in such research: the first is that of hypothesis building, in which there is a search for correlations such as to suggest explanations in general terms (to say 'laws' would be too ambitious); the second phase is one of search for disproof by contrary example. One can thus 'do experiments in one's head', and the now familiar mathematics of factors and correlations helps to analyse such experiments by measuring the relative strength or weakness of the connexion between factors.

But in practice the comparative method has proved hitherto to be no more than another case of argument by example: good rhetoric, bad logic. The excuse would be that the units of political discourse are particularly difficult to handle rigorously. They are not defined for us except in terms of law and history; it is not easy to break down their political and social existence into comparable factors; it is not easy to specify and quantify each factor on a comparable basis; the number of cases is so small that mathematical analysis does not carry us far.

Hence, scepticism about such repertoires of comparisons as Aristotle, Harrington, Montesquieu, de Tocqueville, Lord Bryce, and equal scepticism about the older text-books on comparative government. Most of the traditional generalizations fall down, either because they are based on so few cases that chance is as good an explanation as any for the correlations that occur, or because one can think pretty quickly of a contrary case. The only safe propositions are of a weak kind: that certain forms of proportional representation *tend* to give a better chance to small parties, provided that no other strong factors intervene; that universal suffrage with large electorates *tends* to make direct bribery of individual electors useless; and so on.

III. *THEIR PROBLEMS*

With these tools the 'classics' tackled very large questions at a high level of generality. Not all of them would accept the distinction between normative and positive questions (probably Aristotle would not), but it will serve as a guide.

The grand normative question is—what ought political society to be? What is the good life for man, in general? How is goodness of government related to goodness in general? On what conditions do I owe allegiance to the authority of government? How can I be free, and yet also governed? What is the relation between political rights and political duties?

Some authors (Hobbes and Locke, for instance) have the irritating trick of taking the nature of man in society as given, and of deducing from it (more or less rigorously) rules applicable to men in politics. To be fair, their general argument about man is to be taken as part of the general knowledge of their period. But one feels that one gets fairer play from authors like Plato, Aristotle, Rousseau, Marx, who work out before one's eyes (as it were) a view of society and man together. Their argument is circular rather than deductive, and the systems they build stand mainly by their own interwoven complexity. The evidence cited is generally no more than that of limited analogy and example; if this is taken as criticism, it would be replied that experimental science does not mark the limits of human reason.

Those who set out to establish propositions conducive to prediction and survival had not this excuse, since they set natural science before them as a model; and it is fair to say that they are generally more cautious in the use of evidence. Their problems were those of power and stability, rather than those of right and wrong. What is the nature of political power? What talents must a man cultivate in order to be powerful? How can a state be protected from revolution and from tyranny? What in various contexts are the effects of various constitutional devices? Are there long-term trends (perhaps cyclical) in political development? In what conditions do particular forms of polity flourish? From such generalizations what recommendations can one draw of the 'if . . . then . . .' type?—'if you wanted to secure A, then your best strategy would be to do B'.

Men such as Machiavelli and Montesquieu did pretty well in weaving together knowledge of historical and contemporary events with their own experience of politics. They generally had (it is true) an axe to grind; a good example is that of the Federalists, Jay, Hamilton and Madison, who defended coherently a constitution which might have been attacked as an incoherent compromise, and thus began the process of putting life into legal forms. The bias of the 'classics' is not effectively concealed even by their grand manner, and their scientific standards would not satisfy us in a Ph.D. student. Yet able men in dispute with able critics produced work solid in carpentry and subtle in texture. Perhaps such work must be done afresh in every new polity; afresh, but not better?

2. THE BACKGROUND IN DEMOCRATIC THINKING

EDMOND CAHN

Edmond Cahn (1906–   ) is professor of law at New York University and a specialist in the philosophy of law.

OUTGROWN ALLEGORIES OF THE STATE

For generations we of the world's free nations have been moving into a new realm of being as we instituted representative forms of government and proceeded to extend and universalize the right of suffrage. It is unimportant to say just when the process began; scholars may contend as they please for the date of some event in English or American or perhaps Swiss political history. What really matters is that we have been testing a variety of new

From Edmond Cahn, *The Predicament of Democratic Man*. New York: The Macmillan Company, © by Edmond Cahn, 1961. Pp. 17–23. Reprinted by permission of the publisher.

powers, and find them to be strangely limited. What matters even more is that we have sensed the burden of new moral involvements and know virtually nothing about their limits.

In his late years, Thomas Jefferson, recognizing that representative government had begun something intrinsically novel in human experience, went so far as to recommend our dismissing Aristotle as a preceptor of democratic societies, because like other classical philosophers he had dealt with democracy mainly in the "pure" or direct form which was impracticable beyond the limits of a town. Though the ancients may have had sound ideas on the value of personal liberty, Jefferson thought they could not guide men concerning the structure of a free *representative* government. He concluded, "The full experiment of a government democratical but representative was and is still reserved for us."

As democratic experiments still continue a century and a half after Jefferson, and their moral implications continue to emerge, we cannot escape wondering where they are taking us. We cannot escape asking: When and how far does representative government involve or implicate us in its injuries and wrongs? The question will not brook evasion. There may have been reason for Aristotle and Jefferson to remain silent on the subject, for one of them did not know the modern system of representation and the other saw only its uncertain beginnings. Our situation is quite different; the question of responsibility confronts us in all its ominous vagueness. Again and again during the past century, we have seen some despot or other ruthlessly exploiting this selfsame vagueness to implicate an entire nation in his political crimes—by holding a rigged popular election, a theatrically fraudulent trial, or a plebiscite of pretended ratification. It is the demagogues, above all, who have understood precisely how civic anxiety arises and how it may be manipulated to destroy civil freedoms.

Why the demagogues? I suggest their advantage in detecting and exploiting the citizens' anxieties has a very simple explanation. It is that a typical demagogue employs the same *anthropomorphic* notions of a state as the man in the street. Sometimes he sees the state, in anthropomorphic guise, as though it were a personified leader who will solve the citizens' problems and bear their guilts; sometimes he sees it, in no less anthropomorphic guise, as though it were a primitive tribe whose members they are and whose conquests and crimes they share. In fact, they may not only share the crimes, they may also transmit them to their descendants, for the guilts of the tribe are regarded as hereditary. One way or the other, the anthropomorphic notion of a state either transfers the burden to a demagogic leader or imposes it on persons who are really innocent. As long as men continue to think of the state as some sort of human figure, whether natural or allegorical, or some tribal agglomeration, they will remain unready to understand the moral dimensions of democratic citizenship.

The writings of political philosophers being shot through with anthropomorphism, there is no occasion for wonder that these primitive notions still survive and flourish. Aristotle, who had postulated a state so small that one could see all of it at a single view, understandably went on to argue that the good for a state was the same as the good for a man. A state would include many men, but "many" meant only a few thousands to him. Since the citizens of Athens assembled for action as a tribe or union of tribes, it seemed appropriate for him to assess their state decisions according to the same criteria as their individual decisions.

By like token, during the Middle Ages when society had been reorganized on a feudal, hierarchic basis, it seemed plausible for John of Salisbury, England's earliest political theorist, to compare the state to a human body. The prince, he said, was the head; the priests were the soul and presided over the entire body; the senate was the heart; the judges and governors of provinces were the eyes, ears, and tongue; the soldiers were the armed hand; officials, advocates, and magistrates were the unarmed hand; the prince's attendants were the sides; the fiscal officers were the stomach and intestines; and the husbandmen were the feet, which clung to the soil, supported the body, and needed the care of the head to keep them from stumbling.

The anthropomorphic fallacy went on. In the seventeenth century, a king, claiming to absorb the entire body politic in his own person, declared, "L'état c'est moi." This was the acme of anthropomorphic fiction for a long while, that is, until the next century when the royal title of "sovereign"—which sensible men had long been wont to take as lightly as "your grace" when applied to a duke or "your honor" when applied to a magistrate or "justice" or "peace" when applied to a justice of the peace—this title of "sovereign" was asserted to belong as of right to several million assorted American citizens, at least to those among them who were called "the good people" of the states. Yet, curiously enough, the same theorists who were accustomed to say that the American people were sovereign insisted with like vehemence that the United States Government was sovereign and so too was each of the constituent states. While some few unsophisticated individuals still believed that a "sovereign" should not mean a state but a monarch who ruled over a state, this was charitably ascribed to naïveté or weakness of understanding on their part. Otherwise they would know, as every cartoonist knew, that sovereignty was a term for bespangled and beaming Uncle Sam, for the State of Mississippi in a truculent pose, for the worried British lion with knots in his tail, and for a temporarily thwarted Russian bear. Unfortunately, it is out of such stuff as this that men have fashioned laws and judicial decisions.

If the modern state is not functionally equivalent to a man or a tribe (not to mention a lion, bear, or eagle), is it then to be treated as exempt of moral restraints in its action and administration? How ought one pass judgment on what it does or fails to do? We recognize—or ought to recognize—that a state can rightfully do many things that it would be wrong for a man to do. With complete justice and propriety, it can take our property in taxes, regulate our business affairs, try us in court and incarcerate us, compel us to submit to education, vaccination, and registration, and conscript us to military service. On the other hand, no modern state even claims to be immune to moral standards. None claims a Machiavellian license to disregard all morality and pursue mere naked interest. Certainly, the democratic state cannot. It is neither an ordinary man controlled by a strictly individual morality nor a Renaissance prince controlled by no morality at all. There are moral standards that apply to the state, but we shall not commence to develop them without first understanding why it is that, despite all the cartoons and allegories, a state is not like a man.

To begin with, most people comprehend that a state is not like a man in size or power. Clearly, the difference in size is not a mere matter of geographical expanse, for this might be offset by speed of transportation and communication. The real difference consists rather in the sheer numbers of the citizens, numbers that have passed the hundreds of thousands, the millions, and the tens of millions to teem—beyond imagination—in the hundreds of millions. One cannot cope with quantities of human beings as one copes with quantities of miles.

Contrasted with the resources of a natural person, the overwhelming force available to a state is undeniably impressive. It comprises almost every coercive weapon, beginning at the highest level with the sentimental pressure of patriotism, proceeding more aggressively through various types of economic compulsion, and continuing to the brute plane of fists, clubs, tear gas, prison walls, bullets, and hangmen's ropes. The state has truly redoubtable powers at its call, theoretically more than enough to overcome every kind of delay or obstacle. Yet as we all know, the work of every existing state, even the most absolute, is hourly thwarted in countless ways. Officials may seem to enjoy supreme power but they cannot clear their way of burglars or pickpockets or pimps, sleeping policemen, sclerotic bureaucrats, corrupt administrators, idlers in the public offices, thick-witted oafs in the factories, defiant housewives in the market, or heedless young lovers in the grass. In point of fact, they cannot even monopolize the business of deliberately killing human beings but must share it with jealous husbands, impatient heirs, and professional gangsters.

High officials are often notorious bunglers. There is a story that England lost her American colonies because a minister of state would not postpone a pleasure journey from London to Kent long enough to sign the order which directed Lord Howe to advance up the Hudson Valley and effect a junction with General Burgoyne, marching down from Quebec; and if one finds anything to suspect in the story, it is only the detail that the order had been presented for signature at the office of the right minister. Nevertheless, despite all their limitations and ineptitudes, there is no denying that national states do represent enormous power.

It seems to me that the critical differences between a state and an individual man have less to do with size and power, the physical factors, than with time and function, the biological factors. A human being's moral transactions—at least, most of them—are linked indissolubly with the cycle of his life. He enters into morally significant relations as he is conceived and born, as he is nurtured, disciplined, and educated, as he consorts in friendship, as he lusts and yearns, enters adulthood, business, parenthood, middle age, old age, and the approach to death. He rises, flourishes, and declines; and whether he chooses or not, his moral calculus necessarily involves not only the usual variables of the life stage he happens to occupy at the moment but, in addition, the inevitable and universal constant that continually modifies and ultimately cancels all variables whatever. Death is our only categorical postulate. Whatever beliefs men may have devised to comfort themselves, whatever hopes they may entertain of individual immortality or resurrection, they all face the simple equation between being born and being on the way to die. In this, our morality is bound to be different from a state's, for a state is expected to maintain its existence permanently and indefinitely.

Thomas Jefferson was wise enough to sense that this very attribute of the state, that is, its assumed quality of deathlessness, would pose certain special problems for an aspiring republican society. Throughout his life, the dilemma troubled him. By what title, he asked, could any single generation of a free people assume to bind successor generations to a set of constitutional and legal dispositions? No matter how wise the founding fathers of a nation might have been when they organized its government, the men of the present age always possessed an inalienable right to make their own decisions, rule themselves, and discard outworn institutions. He felt the conviction so strongly that, at the beginning of our government, he proposed that all constitutions, laws, and public debts should expire automatically every nineteen years unless the new generation should deliberately choose to adopt and renew them. Though as a concrete, specific proposal this notion of Jefferson's was quite useless and impractical, there was an important political truth behind it. Jefferson discerned that a state does not conform to the human life cycle; it may renew its youth when a man cannot; it may prosper indefinitely at stages when a man must decline or it may decline and dissolve for causes which would leave a man untouched. Unlike a man's body, the "body politic" cannot be conceived or generated once for all. Its destiny must depend on continual acts of new creation and new revelation.

This insight—that the creating of a state is a continuous and unending process—applies particularly to the variety of functions that a modern state performs. If we should assert in practical terms that a state is whatever it does, then in the light of the history of the past century we should have to conclude that the state is certainly not what it used to be and that it will probably not continue to be what it is, for it performs many functions which we consider indispensable today, though they were left to private hands or simply left undone only a generation ago. There is no possibility of tying the national state down to a fixed list of activities just because we happen to find them familiar in our time. States are continually compelled to grapple with the novel and unfamiliar. Who in the world of political realities could have anticipated that the twentieth century would witness the emergent problems and functions of interplanetary exploration?

In such a time as ours, it seems only reasonable that democratic thinking should graduate from immaturity and discard the crude, outworn anthropomorphic illusions of the past. This would be the first step in developing a philosophy fit for free men.

3. THE NATURE OF POLITICS

ROBERT M. MACIVER

Robert M. MacIver (1882–   ) was professor of political philosophy and sociology at Columbia University. THE WEB OF GOVERNMENT, *published in 1947, was one of his many works on political and social institutions.*

The study of government is very old. The Chinese, the Hindus, the Greeks, and other people wrote many ancient volumes on the subject, with many precepts about the nature of government and many observations about its practices. The theory of government has engrossed leading thinkers throughout modern times. Yet it remains very doubtful whether there exists anything that can properly be called a science of government, if we mean thereby a system of knowledge that either formulates infallible rules, scientifically discoverable, for the guidance of the legislator or establishes invariable connections, exactly determinable, between the measures he proposes and the responsive changes in the social milieu. The difficulty is not only that the myths of government are eternally changing in eternally changing situations, but that neither the myths nor the situations can be reduced to the exactly definable elements postulated by science. The practice of government always confronts new complexities under new conditions which it cannot adequately explore. The myth takes control and drives as far as it can. Government is the organization of men under authority, and their ever-changing myths are themselves sovereign alike over the governors and the governed.

When we speak of a science of government we are not raising doubts concerning the feasibility of political science, as that expression is commonly used. There is an important body of systematic knowledge about the state, about the conditions under which different types of government emerge, about the characteristics of the different types, about the relation of government to the governed in different historical situations, about the modes in which governments carry on their functions according to their kind, and so forth. This body of knowledge may properly be named a science. We do not take sides with the purists who deny the title of "science" to any knowledge that does not present us with eternal laws or that cannot be expressed in quantitative terms. There is really no intelligent issue here. If in their zeal for immutable exactitude these purists are offended when other kinds of knowledge are referred to as sciences, we can call them by some other name—and the knowledge will be just as good and as useful as before. What, however, we are rejecting is the claim that there is a systematic body of knowledge, already in existence or awaiting development, that can serve as a definite guide to the statesman, a science of how to govern, an applied science that does or can do in its field what medicine, say, or engineering does in its field.

Men have often dreamed of a science of government in this sense, and some have even claimed to inaugurate it. From Plato to George Bernard Shaw there have been champions of the view that in the development of this science lies the salvation of mankind. Plato was dominated by one myth-complex, and George Bernard Shaw by another. So it will always be. What then would a full-fledged science of government be? A science of how men *are* governed? We have much on that score, but it is historical description and not systematic knowledge. A science of how men *should* be governed? But the *should* is always expressive of the thinker's own myth-complex, is always subject to his presuppositions, and so lies outside the ambit of science —a fact that in no wise lessens its social importance, since the *it should be* of the mythical is as necessary as the *it is so* of the evidential. A science of how men *can* be governed? Perhaps this seems more hopeful. Machiavelli set the example to the modern world of presenting to the ruler pragmatic principles for his guidance. Men who have had much experience in public affairs, statesmen, diplomats, policy makers, party bosses, the counselors of presidents and of kings have written memoirs in which they have exposed the secrets of political success. Psychologists, publicists, propaganda analysts, have studied the modes of mass response and the devices by which they can be manipulated or evoked. Enlightening as these records are they do not, however, meet the requirements of a science. They are reflections and observations on the art of government rather than the serviceable data for a science of government.

What is the difference? Let us examine, for example, the famous precepts of Machiavelli. Best known of these is his advice to the ruler that he combine cunning and ruthlessness, that he disregard whenever necessary the accepted code of morals but always make a show of observing it. Machiavelli's experience in politics led him to believe that by following this advice a prince could best safeguard his throne. He wrote at a time marked by turbulence and instability. For such times, and for such rulers, the advice might be good, within discretionary limits—but who can assign the limits? Many who have followed Machiavelli's precepts have ended in disaster. Where is the clean-cut nexus that science desiderates? Discretionary precepts for the attainment of particular goals—that is all we are given. That is all we find in the whole series, down to the latest behind-the-scenes writer who informs us that a successful President of the United States must be all things to all men.

Moreover, most of these precepts are concerned not with the larger issues of government but with the much narrower question of how a ruler or a ruling group can gain or retain power; and we cannot reduce the vast business of government to a few precarious techniques for holding on to office. The tasks of government are manifold and comprehensive, emerging from complicated and ever changing conditions. What science prescribes these tasks? The people over whom government is exercised are moved by various conflicting sentiments and impulses, have different needs and different demands from time to time. What science envisages the endless conjunctures to which government must address itself?

Policy making depends on the assessing of alternatives with a view to translating one of them into action. A bill or an executive action is up for consideration. There is then the primary question: will the proposed measure advance the purposes of the government? It must be not only such that the government itself regards it with approval, it must furthermore not entail any untoward consequences such as in the judgment of the government would outweigh the direct advantages. To what reactions will it give rise? There are numerous pros and cons. How weigh the one against the other? At the close of the war, to take an example, there rose the question whether the United States, Great Britain, and Canada should either immediately communicate to their allies in the struggle the secret of the construction of the atomic bomb or should reserve the secret until at least the negotiations for the peace settlement were concluded or until arrangements for a satisfactory system of control over that terrifying agency were completed. This is, for short, a rough and inadequate statement of the alternatives. It was an issue that no government had ever faced before, but in this respect it differed only in degree from every other question that comes before a government, since every situation is for the policy maker a new one. There were many aspects to the situation; many interests would be affected by the decision. There was the major question whether a world system more satisfactory to the holders of the secret would be attainable if the other allies, and one of them in particular, were—or were not—entrusted with the secret. We need not enter into detail. A plausible case could be made for withholding, another for giving. It is so with every issue of policy. Always the situation is many-sided. Always there is a complex set of reactions to be foreseen and assessed. What science can lay down exact rules for that task? What science can postulate explicit and clearly relevant principles to guide the legislator or the minister in the exploration of the alternatives, in the forevision of the consequences, in the practical evaluation of the various considerations that are relevant to his decision?

Let us take again the situation where a particular policy has already been adopted. The New York State legislature has, for example, decided in favor of an antidiscrimination measure. But the framing of the measure, on which its success and efficacy depend, still raises many questions. Should it apply to all forms of employment, including professional employment on all levels? Should it apply not only to employment but also to admission to trade unions, colleges, and so forth? Should it apply to employment units that involve only three or four workers as well as to those that involve hundreds or thousands? What is the test of discrimination? How far can it be made to work in practice? How can evasion be controlled? How can the measure be guarded against the danger that it will create resistance and resentment such as will stimulate in some quarters a stronger spirit of discrimination? How should the board controlling the operation of the act be constituted? What minority groups should be represented in it? What system of inspection and of enforcement should be set up? There are various groups each with its own myth-complex, and their respective susceptibilities and responses must be taken into account. There are no formulas, no clear-cut rules to which we can refer. At every point decisions have to be made that call for experience, knowledge of the intricacies of the situation, the good judgment as well as the good will of the legislator.

We should then be content to think of government rather as an art than as a science. Like every other art it makes use of the appropriate sciences. Among these sciences is social psychology. Analysts of public opinion are learning to measure more accurately the various responses of different groups both to appeals and to situations. From this science, and from others—including economics, which, though still very inadequate, has at least shown the potentiality of becoming systematic knowledge—the practitioners of government can draw much valuable information. But no science can tell men how to govern, as the science of engineering can tell men how to throw a bridge across a river. And for this difference we return to our first argument. The techniques of engineering are relatively independent of the myths of the bridge maker, or of the bridge user, and they are not contingent on the purposes of the company that undertakes to build the bridge or the public authority that sanctions the building of it. But the business of governing is inextricably bound up with the elaborate and ever varying myth-complex that links the governors and the governed.

4. BEHAVIORAL APPROACHES

HEINZ EULAU

Heinz Eulau (1915–   ) is professor of political science at Stanford University and has long been associated with the behavioral movement in his field.

The behavioral persuasion in politics has more than one approach, and there are many voices that speak in its name. But they all have in common a commitment to the study of man as the root of things political, or, to put it more technically, to the individual person as the empirical unit of analysis. Therefore I think it is legitimate to speak of "the behavioral persuasion in

From Heinz Eulau, *The Behavioral Persuasion in Politics.* New York, N. Y.: Random House, Inc., © copyright 1963. Pp. 13–35, excerpts. Reprinted by permission of the publisher.

politics." However these voices do not necessarily speak in harmony. Behavioral researchers on politics differ among themselves in many respects: in their conception of the nature of knowledge and its relation to reality; in their formulation of the theoretical propositions guiding their investigations; in the choice of strategies and tactics of research; in their selection of problems and research sites and, finally, in their appraisal of their own role in relation to the world of politics they are studying. It seems preferable, therefore, to speak of behavioral approaches when it comes to technical matters.

I think that most behavioral researchers agree on at least four major aspects of the behavioral enterprise in politics, aspects that define the stance and style of those who subscribe to the behavioral persuasion. Each aspect involves a set of problems on which behavioral practitioners may differ, but which bind them precisely because they agree that the problems require solutions. First there is the problem of the most adequate theoretical (as against empirical) units of analysis. The second problem is the level of analysis on which political behavior research may be most fruitfully conducted. Third, there is the question of the proper relationship between theory and research. Finally, there is the problem of what methodological requirements should be met. . . .

THEORY AND RESEARCH

No piece of political behavior research is content to describe the universe of politics, no matter how realistic or reliable the description. The goal is the explanation of why people behave politically as they do, and why, as a result, political processes and systems function as they do. There are many methods of explanation. Whatever they are, they require theorizing activity. (I speak of "theorizing activity" rather than "theory" because it frees me from having to say what theory *is*. Any attempt to do so in an essay of this sort would be foolish. My interest is in what, generally, practitioners of the behavioral persuasion in politics *do* when they theorize, not in defining theory.)

What behavioral researchers do when they theorize—by which I mean, very tentatively, when they seek explanations of why people behave politically as they do—differs a good deal from one to the other. At one pole, some would probably say that they are not theorizing at all, but only describing what they see. They deceive themselves, for what they see depends on how they see it, and how they see it depends on images in their minds. These images may be very diffuse and hardly deserve being called theories. But they orient the observer, innocent as he may be of what he is doing and though he may be protesting his theoretical innocence. His work will not get him very far because, paradoxically, his very attempt at *only* describing what he sees is suspect. Did he really see all that could have been seen? What did he leave out? How did he order what he saw? Did this really follow that? On the whole, the overwhelming number of modern behavioral practitioners no longer plead theoretical innocence. More often than not, they seek to make explicit the assumptions and ways of thought that guide their work. This is what I have called theorizing activity, though it does not necessarily entail theory.

At the other pole are the builders of logically consistent, deductive models of political systems, perhaps theories in the sense that "formal truth" is the distinctive content of the theorizing activity in which model builders are engaged. There are not many practitioners of the behavioral persuasion in politics who believe that this is the right time for constructing logically closed, deductive pictures of the political process. I have a great deal of admiration for these efforts, but I must confess to some doubt, not because I question the practicality of formal models or their suggestiveness in research, but because I suspect they are not as theoretically pure as their creators insist. At least I cannot avoid the impression that behind the most formal models there lurk quite explicit images of empirical reality. In other words, just as pure empiricism has theoretical components, so pure theory has empirical components.

In my opinion, this is not a drawback. Out of this duality stems the conviction that, in the present stage of development, theory and research are necessarily interdependent, that theoretical questions must be stated in operational terms for the purpose of fruitful empirical research, and that, in turn, empirical findings should be brought to bear on the theoretical formulation of political problems. This does not deny the possibility of a high road to theorizing about political behavior and a low road. But I am not sure, if there are two roads, which is high and which is low, and I have a hunch that there are many roads in between that are more immediately viable. This is why it seems most feasible to attack the problems of political behavior research on as broad a theoretical front as possible. Whatever the weight given to one or another, it seems quite clear that if the condition of mutual interdependence between theory and research is to be achieved, some theorizing activity must precede empirical work if the latter is to be theoretically relevant, just as empirical considerations must enter theoretical efforts if hypotheses are to be tested by research.

Admittedly, theorizing must be sufficiently independent of operations to give it room in which to breathe. But it cannot be altogether separate from empirical research. One might argue, as some have, that the condition of interdependence is met, and that a theory's operational utility can be appraised, if it can be tested *in principle* by reference to empirical data. This may be a necessary condition, but is not a sufficient one. I cannot see how one can *know* in principle whether theoretical propositions are testable. For theory is not the same thing as knowledge. Whatever the plausibility or validity of theoretical speculations, they are not truths, full, partial, or probable. Theory is not knowledge but a tool on the road to knowledge, just as facts are not knowledge but only the raw materials to be molded, through theorizing activity, into statements acceptable as probably true, or at least not false, because they have been tested in the process of empirical research. It is the theoretician's responsibility not only to assert that his propositions can be tested, but to suggest *how* they can be tested. But not even this makes his propositions empirical, though it may make them empirically relevant.

It is this kind of thinking which produces the characteristic commitment of the behavioral persuasion to theorizing and research as mutually inter-related activities. But if theorizing and research cannot do without each other, they necessarily limit each other. As a result, the behavioral persuasion is characterized by a healthy respect for those problems that research bound by theory and theorizing bound by research entail. On the whole, political behavior research has been limited to relatively modest theoretical proposi-tions. Theorizing activity has been tempered by recognition of obstacles in the collection of data and technical limitations in the treatment of data. Above all, this theorizing of the "middle range," unlike theoretically innocent empiricism or empirically blind model building, has been concerned with viable problems, problems that are operationally manageable and likely to yield returns of a cumulative sort.

The theoretical quest of behavioral research on politics is complicated by having to satisfy two masters. On the one hand, political behavior is only a special case of human behavior. If this is so, any theorizing about political behavior must take account of behavioral theory as it develops in all the social sciences, and the findings of political behavior research cannot contra-dict findings about other aspects of human behavior. From this perspective, there is really no place for an independent general theory of politics. On the other hand, political behavior research is conducted within the large scale institutions and processes of politics. Insofar as there is a special theory of politics on this level of analysis, it must at least be relevant, if not applicable, on the level of the individual. Not much progress has been made as yet along these lines.

Commitment to the interdependence of theory and research and to solving the problem of the relationship between special political and general behav-ioral theory has some interesting consequences for the development of political theory. The behavioral persuasion, in attending to both theory and empirical research, may bring the definitional game that has been played so long in the study of politics to some conclusion. However one defines politics, as the process of allocating values authoritatively, as a competitive struggle for power, as collective decision making for the community, and so on, each definition includes more or less well articulated premises, postulates, or assumptions about politics. One function of behavioral theorizing, certainly, is to lay bare these premises. Another is to clarify the empirical referents of concepts, definitions, and propositions. The notion that politics is an allocative process, for instance, assumes that resources are scarce and may be used in alternate ways. It further assumes that the goals are multiple and that, there-fore, choices must be made among them. This definition also implies that political actors will disagree over what ends are preferable, as well as over how resources are to be allocated in order to achieve agreed on ends.

It is evident that we are not dealing here simply with a primitive definition of politics, but with a model of the political process borrowed from economics. On closer inspection, it also appears that the model makes assumptions about human rationality and about the behavior of rational human beings. And rational behavior is assumed to maximize preferred returns on the investment of resources. It is not accidental, therefore, that the definition of politics as "authoritative allocation of values" is readily translated into an even more formal model of the political process as a chain of inputs and outputs.

In subjecting the model to empirical testing, behavioral research alone can give the theorist some feeling as to what concept or definition is operationally useful and what is not. The specification of the empirical data needed to test a model may reveal which of rival definitions are serviceable and which are expendable. It may show which definitions are empirically, and possibly theoretically, necessary for each other. For instance, I have found in some of my own work on legislative behavior and institutions that a definition of politics as allocation is insufficient unless it is implemented by some definition of politics as conflictual behavior.

Moving simultaneously along both theoretical and empirical paths quickly sensitizes the investigator to what definitions, concepts, or even theories are expendable. For instance, it seems that power, long accepted as the central organizing concept of politics, is rapidly losing ground from the point of view of its operational, if not analytical, utility. Paradoxically, it is losing ground not because it is abused, as it has been by some theoreticians in the past, but because it is used. For as it is used in empirical research, it proves increasingly useless. In recent years, there has been much research interest in community power structures and in power relations in legislative bodies. We now have a large body of research findings as to how, presumably, decisions are made in villages, cities, and metropolitan areas, as well as in legislatures. The more research there is, the more elusive the concept of power shows itself to be.

I am not thinking here of the many methodological and technical difficulties that have been found to stand in the way of operationally defining, identifying, discovering and measuring "power." What I find interesting is that those engaged in power research are increasingly forced to rethink the concept as they face empirical situations that defy its traditional verbal uses. We now find distinctions made between the weight, scope, and domain of power, or between "monolithic" and "polylithic" power. Whether these distinctions and elaborations will save the concept as a theoretically useful one I cannot say. As used to be the case with the concept of "sovereignty" (unlimited and limited, undivided and divided, shared and what not), power is still a concept we cannot do much with apparently, but which we do not dare to do without.

Theorizing depends on the problem to be solved. Some problems are more complex than others, and more may be known about simpler ones. Political behavior involved in the conduct of foreign policies in the international arena is probably more complex than behavior in the domestic legislative process, and the latter is likely to be more complex than a person's behavior in the voting booth. How complexity is handled depends, in turn, on the model used in the analysis of empirical data. Although a simple model is preferable to a complicated one, it is also likely to be empirically more exclusive. On the other hand, an elaborate model or conceptual scheme may make the problem technically unmanageable. Just as the analysis of only two variables that are theoretically linked in rather simple propositions may not explain very much, a comprehensive scheme of a potentially all-inclusive range may defy the practicalities of research. The most feasible alternative is to deal with modest propositions that require simultaneous manipulation of only a few variables, but to do so in a larger conceptual system that, though it cannot be tested directly, serves the very useful purpose of guiding an investigation and giving it theoretical significance.

Considerations of this kind have some further consequences for the development of behavioral theory in connection with problems of varying degrees of complexity. The more complex the empirical problem with which the research is dealing, the more difficult access to relevant behavioral data is likely to be, and the more need there will be for theoretical exploration on high levels of generality. On the other hand, the less complex the empirical problem, the easier the collection of relevant data and the less incentive to theorize. Therefore, theoretical formulations will be very specific and of relatively low generality. This makes plausible the theoretical unevenness of behavioral research in different, substantive areas of political science. In recent years, the behavioral persuasion has generated a considerable body of theoretical work of high generality in the study of international politics, but it has so far produced little *hard* empirical research. On the other hand, empirical studies of electoral behavior are abundant, but this research has been limited to testing very modest propositions of low theoretical generality, and no comprehensive theory of the electoral process has as yet been formulated.

This produces an interesting paradox. It would seem much more reasonable to apply and test theoretical models of high generality in relatively simple research areas about which a good deal is already known and where access to data is relatively easy. For instance, many of the models of international politics could be tested with data drawn from the political life of metropolitan areas. It would also seem more reasonable to cope with behavior in a complex setting by way of more modest theoretical propositions. Some of the work now being done on the national level in underdeveloped areas seems to be of this order. I believe this exchange of complex and simple theoretical formulations between different empirical research fields will be the next major phase in political behavior research, if it has not already begun. Students of international political behavior and large-scale institutional behavior will find it increasingly profitable to deal with propositions that have been found serviceable in studies of voting or problem-solving behavior in small groups. Students of relatively small institutions (such as legislative bodies or courts) and local communities will draw increasingly on the more comprehensive formulations of communication theory, system theory, and other configurative models.

BEHAVIORAL METHODS

The revolution in the behavioral sciences has been predominantly a technological revolution. Compared with developments in the natural sciences, the gimmicks and gadgets of behavioral science remain rather crude. But compared with the tools available to the classical writers, modern behavioral technology represents an enormous advance. It would seem foolish not to apply this new behavioral technology to the problems of politics. Yet, for reasons difficult to pin down, the application of behavioral methods to politics has been halting and circumspect. In some quarters, there has been fierce resistance to increasing our knowledge about politics through behavioral analysis. Why such resistance occurs is a matter of interest to the sociologist of knowledge, and how it might be overcome is a task for the psychoanalyst. The result is that the behavioral persuasion in politics is regarded, by its opponents as well as by its practitioners, as a revolt against the classical tradition in political science. As I suggested earlier, this is a mistake. If the behavioral persuasion revolted against anything, it was against the failure of academic political science to use the modern technology in the study of politics as, I believe, the classical writers would have used it had it been available to them.

Resistance to the application of behavioral methods must be distinguished from some very real difficulties of a methodological sort that the behavioral persuasion faces. . . . I would now like to ask if there are not some "natural limits" to the behavioral analysis of politics, limits that no technological revolution can eradicate. I believe this question can be asked only if one assumes, *a priori,* that there *must* be aspects of political behavior intrinsically immune to scientific analysis. But if one assumes the opposite, that political behavior, like all behavior, can be observed by the methods of behavioral science, the limits appear to be technological ones. Scientific technology knows its present limits; it cannot predict its future limits. As technology advances, the range of phenomena amenable to scientific analysis also expands. Therefore, it is really impossible to say that the data of politics are such that they cannot be harnessed by *any* scientific methods and techniques. The presently available technology has made possible the production and processing of political data, or data relevant to political behavior, that was, until recently, unavailable to political science.

This is not the place to review the areas of political behavior research investigated by the techniques of modern behavioral science nor to present an inventory of research methods. . . . But I do want to emphasize the discovery and amplification of knowledge about politics which the invention of new methods and techniques makes possible.

The development of the probability sample survey as a reliable instrument of data collection is perhaps most noteworthy. It has made public opinion and electoral research a prolific source of political data. Indeed, for a time, the study of political behavior was equated with and restricted to the study of public opinion and voting. But more recently, the extension of systematic surveys to the study of specialized elites and institutionalized groups like legislative bodies or bureaucratic organizations has greatly augmented the store of political data and deepened political analysis. The use of panels of informants, repetitively interviewed in successive waves, has added a longitudinal dimension to behavioral inquiry of politics. Political change can now be observed at the level of the individual actor.

Perhaps equally significant is the invention of metric techniques such as scalogram and factor analysis, and their application not only in survey materials, but also in the treatment of legislative roll-call votes or judicial decisions. Although the individual actor's behavior is known in political action of this kind, it cannot be analyzed meaningfully from the perspective of politics as a collective enterprise unless it can be ordered to reveal underlying regularities and uniformities. Scale analysis, for instance, makes possible the ordering of discrete acts like roll-calls along a single dimension and the classification of actors in terms of their scale positions. It provides for criteria of reliability in such ordering and constitutes an instrument of considerable analytic and predictive power. Similarly, factor analysis of judicial opinions, for instance, makes possible the discovery of the principal components of any set of interrelated decisions. The discovery of regularities and uniformities in judicial behavior made possible by factor analysis gives depth to the study of courts as political institutions.

The analysis of political group behavior has been facilitated by observational techniques recording both form and content of action-in-interaction at the level of the individual. Though few ongoing ("natural") political groups have as yet been subjected to one or another observational technique, it promises rich returns once small groups like legislative committees, administrative bodies, or party councils allow themselves to be systematically studied. The application of sociometric techniques that elicit inter-individual choices among group members has been more immediately useful. These techniques, feasible not only in small but also in middle-sized groups, help in identifying the informal structure of leadership or factions. They make possible the study of group properties such as authority, communication, cohesion, morale, or consensus at the level of the individual. These properties are important not only in explaining the behavior of individuals in groups, but also the actions of a group as a whole.

Through techniques of this kind, then, it is possible to broaden the range of political phenomena that can be made available to behavioral analysis and to refine and systematize political behavior research. However, this is not meant to minimize the difficulties in the way of subjecting political behavior to scientific inquiry. I think that the practitioners of the behavioral persuasion in politics are more sensitive to the problem of a science of politics than those who deny its possibility.

It does not seem very fruitful to specify what a behavioral science of politics might look like "in the end" because science is an ongoing endeavor that has no end. In general, the behavioral persuasion tries to develop rigorous research designs and to apply precise methods of analysis to political behavior problems. In its methodological orientation it is concerned with problems of experimental or *post facto* design, reliability of instruments, and criteria of validation, and other features of scientific procedure. Its function, as I see it, is to produce reliable propositions about politics by reducing error, which involves the invention of appropriate tactics of research, and by measuring error that remains through the application of relevant statistical techniques. As limited as the present success of the behavioral scientific enterprise in politics may be, the alternatives are even less satisfactory.

The discriminating feature of the behavioral persuasion in politics is, above all, its sensitivity to error in its observations of politics and its suspicion of *a priori*, formulated, universal "truths." It proceeds in terms of contingencies and probabilities, rather than in terms of certainties and verities. It represents an attitude of mind, a persuasion as I have called it, that takes nothing for granted and accepts as valid only the results of its inquiries when it would be unreasonable to assume that they can be explained solely by the operation of chance. This is a difficult standard to live by, perhaps more difficult in politics than in other fields of human action. For in politics as in physics and metaphysics, man looks for certainty, but must settle for probability.

5. THE CHEERFUL SCIENCE OF DISMAL POLITICS

CHRISTIAN BAY

Christian Bay (1921–   ) is professor of political science at the University of Alberta at Edmonton and a strong advocate of a normative approach to politics.

Thomas Carlyle in 1850 referred to academic economists as "respectable Professors of the Dismal Science" and thus, as John Kenneth Galbraith has observed, "gave to economics a name that it has never quite escaped because it was never quite undeserved." The economists of Carlyle's day were intent on proving, as are most recognized economists and other social scientists at most times, that there must always be privileged and underprivileged classes, and that the present with all its suffering at the lower end of the social ladder nevertheless constitutes the best of all possible worlds, at least right now and in the foreseeable future.

Respectable professors of politics traditionally have had much the same concerns. If political science has had an easier time escaping the label "dismal," it is perhaps for two main reasons. First, it is in many ways less of a science, still, than economics was even a century ago. Economists have had handy units of measurement to work with; money happens to be quantifiable and yet not unimportant; and with the aid of mathematics economists have been able to figure out prices for almost everything. Political scientists have worked manfully to develop their own quantifiable key concepts, but it seems that they have advanced toward increasing exactness only at the expense of increasing triviality. Thus it may be said that while economists and political

From Christian Bay, "The Cheerful Science of Dismal Politics," in *The Dissenting Academy*, Theodore Roszak, ed. New York: Random House, Inc., © copyright 1968, and Chatto and Windus, Ltd., London. Pp. 208–29, excerpts. Reprinted by permission of Pantheon Books, a division of Random House, Inc.

scientists are equally remote from the comprehension of values in social life, they differ in that political scientists don't even have price tags to work with.

Secondly, if the academic study of politics is less of an exact science, its style is also less gloomy and its image less dismal, because there are strong institutional pressures favoring a more cheerful stance. Every social order is dominated by its privileged classes, whose patriotism celebrates the status quo. While economists are busy explaining the necessity of poverty and, incidentally with increasing effectiveness, seeking to prevent recessions that hit the well-to-do as well as the poor, the central task of political science as a profession apparently is to extol the present order, criticize other existing systems, and debunk radical and utopian political thought. In America in the 1960s, the task is to praise democracy, identifying this particular concept with the existing social order by way of praising pluralism and "free enterprise" in the same breath, and to condemn communism; in fact, all *ideologies* are suspect, and the familiar end-of-ideology literature seeks to conjure them away.

A basic element in this development is the redefinition of "politics." The end of politics, Aristotle tells us, is the highest good attainable by action. For of all creatures, man alone "has any sense of good and evil, of just and unjust, and the like. . . . Justice is the bond of men in states, for the administration of justice, which is the determination of what is just, is the principle of order in political society." Politics, then, is the master science, for its aim embraces the aims of all other scientific pursuits; the study of politics is the study of how best to promote the common good of the political community.

The idealism of Socrates, of Plato, and of Aristotle is a vital part of our intellectual heritage. Innumerable philosophers and intellectuals through the ages have insisted on their right and obligation to keep alive the difference between perceptions of man as he *is* and conceptions of man as he *ought* to be, between existing social institutions and potentially more humane social institutions.

But the modern study of politics stands in stark contrast to this classic conception. Increasingly it becomes identified with the study of existing patterns of political behavior. And for this study the Aristotelian concept of politics is clearly unsuited, focusing as it does on an assumed state of tension between the actual and the ideal, or between existing realities and the optimal common good. It is, rather, formulations like that of Harold D. Lasswell that now seem more pertinent. "Politics," according to Lasswell's boldest and best-known definition, refers to "who gets what, when, how." Other modern behavioralists like to add a "why" to their conception of politics, by way of relating their definitions not only to "power" but to "authority" or "legitimacy" as well. But the latter terms are invariably intended as descriptive rather than normative: "legitimacy" is established by way of opinion surveys and "authority" by way of communication or decision-making as well as survey research. Neither term has anything to do with justice, inherent rightness, or any other normative concept.

Thus, even the study of legitimacy may be just as far removed from a concern with justice or with the needs of man as is the study of power. For the exertion of power in our time relies on the manipulation of political attitudes as much as on coercion. Regardless of political or socioeconomic system, the political leaders and the strata they represent are in control of the bulk of the various media of communication and persuasion. Bayonets are not comfortable to sit on, as Napoleon is said to have remarked; and happily for the powers that be, modern technology makes it possible for almost any present-day regime to establish a comfortable position of "legitimacy," except in revolutionary situations. Hence, a consensual concern with legitimacy *in the empirical sense only* tends, by implication, to make illegitimate for political behavioralists any scientific concern with normatively conceived legitimacy—i.e., the justification of institutions in terms of human needs, justice, freedom, or whatever the conception of the common good may be.

It is not difficult to understand why this capitulation to the status quo has taken place on the part of professional students of politics. "A political science that is mistreated," writes Hans Morgenthau, "is likely to have earned that enmity because it has put its moral commitment to the truth above social convenience and ambition." But a political science that is respected, he continues, helps the powers that be by way of mollifying the conscience of society, justifying existing power relationships, etc. "The relevance of this political science does not lie primarily in the discovery of the truth about politics, but in its contribution to the stability of society."

Conversely, every political philosophy which is concerned with humane ideals and their implications in logically rigorous ways is subversive of every existing order; for it is in the nature of political philosophy, as distinguished from merely linguistic or logical analysis, to contrast existing realities with more ideal alternatives. There is always a strong temptation, then, even for philosophers to adjust to the most basic demands and assumptions of the status quo, for in most societies it is rather uncomfortable to be treated as a subversive. And when political philosophers and other social scientists establish professions and take on public educational employment, the adjustment of basic philosophical assumptions to the postulates of the established order almost inevitably becomes institutionalized. That is, perspectives on the aims of politics or philosophy or social analysis become transformed from a focus on man's needs and potentialities to a focus on systems maintenance; and most individual recruits to the social science professions are spared the agonizing ethical dilemma of choosing between being true to their role as intellectuals and embarking on comfortable careers. Indeed, they are carefully trained *not* to discover this existential dilemma.

It is not only the average academic student of politics, however, who has become theoretically incapacitated for scientific concern with issues of justice or the common good. In their descriptive studies of the political behavior of the supposedly "developed" American and other Western electorates, political scientists have discovered that the public too appears unconcerned with the Public Interest. Quite correctly, they describe most voters as either apathetic or anxiety-ridden, and as rarely able to see their private and group interests in the perspective of their stake in the public interest. The rule, in short, is what I prefer to call "pseudopolitical" rather than "political" behavior.

By "political," I refer to all activity aimed at improving or protecting conditions for the satisfaction of human needs and demands in a given society according to some universalistic scheme of priorities, implicit or explicit. "Pseudopolitical," on the other hand, refers to activity that *resembles* political activity but is exclusively concerned either with alleviating personal neuroses or with promoting private or interest-group advantage, deterred by no articulate or disinterested conception of what would be just or fair to other groups. Thus, pseudopolitics is the counterfeit of politics.

Now, I am in no way opposed to the study of pseudopolitical behavior. The behavioral literature of our profession is an invaluable source of facts about our political and pseudopolitical life; my plea is for more and better behavioral research. What I ask for is a more comprehensive, more humane, more truly *political* framework of theory for the study of pseudopolitical and political behavior. There should be no excuse for jumping from the fact of prevailing pseudopolitical behavior in our competitive, unjust, anxiety-ridden social order to the enormous conclusion that pseudopolitics is "normal" in a "developed society"—that, in other words, we are doomed to a *permanent* eclipse of genuine politics in the modern democratic world, and that no educational liberation from *Time, U.S. News*, and their intellectual equivalents is ever to reach more than a small minority of our electorate.

I plead, further, for the necessity of liberating our political science literature from the following prevailing assumptions: (1) that political research in America must take the present system for granted, leaving out the study of experiments directed toward radical change; (2) that this nation is "politically developed," even though its electorate behaves by and large pseudopolitically, not politically; (3) that it is either impossible or not worthwhile to develop assumptions about national goals (e.g. reduction of suffering, maximization of justice or of freedom) and to study their empirical implications; and (4) that it is either impossible or not worthwhile to develop and apply psychological models of need priorities as a basis for research into their political implications—i.e., to develop a scientific study of politics founded on the study of basic human needs, as distinct from manifest wants and demands.

One would have hoped that our own profession had maintained a Socratic commitment to the defense of genuine politics, particularly in this age of conspicuous, high-powered, systematic propagation of mindless pseudopolitics. But as we have seen, the tendency has been to conform to the powerful demands on us, much as the autonomous spirit of the university has been replaced by the more pliant stance of the "multiversity." We study expressed wants and demands, often the result of indoctrination from the outside, and are unconcerned about inner needs, or prerequisites for social and individual health. We willingly submit to the deception that our corporation-ridden pluralist order is to be called "democratic" and that our laws are to be judged as democratically enacted and therefore legitimate in more than a

descriptive sense of the term. Worst of all, we continue to think of our baili-
wick as the study of means-ends relationships, while conveniently claiming
that ends cannot be studied "scientifically." . . .

What concerns me is that I have yet to find in this literature even a hint
of the possibility that "political development" ought to be defined relative
to *human* development in some sense; certainly there is no such possibility
left open in Pye's work. And this is particularly remarkable in view of the
fact that both Pye and Almond belong to that rare species of political scientist
who are articulate and well read in dynamic psychology. The most plausible
explanation is that Pye, too, has become caught up in the system, i.e., in the
fashion of theorizing about political systems in functional terms, in a normative vacuum in which easy patriotism rather than a more complex and less
professionally rewarding concern with humanity and justice has come to
dictate the underlying value standards.

True, it is hard to do research on genuine human needs as opposed to the
neater categories of expressed wants, demands, and the volumes of noise and
cash displayed by pluralist interest groups. But needs as distinct from conscious wants do exist, as every clinical psychologist and psychiatrist can
testify, and as delinquency experts, penologists, social workers, public health
officials, anthropologists, and sociologists increasingly emphasize in their
work and in their writings. It is time, I submit, that political scientists also
come to recognize this fact and its significance, and in this respect try to
catch up with Plato and Aristotle. I am convinced that our profession will
never help us to advance from our wasteful, cruel, pluralist pseudopolitics in
the direction of justice and humane politics until we replace *political systems*
with concepts of *human need* and *human development* as the ultimate value
frameworks for our political analysis. Almond's functional approach to the
study of input and output processes would by no means become obsolete by
such a change in value perspective. On the contrary, it would become
useful. . . .

"Rationality" has come to be defined in terms of selection of means to
given ends, rarely to the selection of ends. Talcott Parsons offers us one
authoritative definition of the current usage: "An act is rational in so far
as (a) it is oriented to a clearly formulated unambiguous goal, or a set of
values which are clearly formulated and logically consistent; (b) the means
chosen are, according to the best available knowledge, adapted to the realization of the goal." This concept of rationality, which I would call "formal"
rationality, is indispensable to intelligent political inquiry, or indeed almost
any kind of intelligent inquiry.

But I insist that it is not sufficient. Responsible social scientists must also
demand of themselves something more, which may be called *substantive
rationality,* by which I mean the requirement that *ends* should be as rigorously
articulated and tested as are, in political science at its current best, the
proposed means to those ends, or the predictive hypotheses on which statements about means to ends rest.

Granted, the difficulties involved in what I propose are great. Indeed, it
is astonishing how pervasive the notion is, even among gifted critics of our

profession's "pluralistic" abdication of normative responsibility, that there can be no legitimate general purpose for politics. For example, in his fine essay "Tolerance and the Scientific Outlook," Barrington Moore, Jr., writes that one "crucial characteristic of a free society is the absence of a single overriding 'national purpose'. The attempts, never completely successful, to impose such a purpose are the stigma of the modern totalitarian state." Are we to believe this to be true *regardless* of the nature of the proposed purpose, or the means with which it is advocated? Apparently even Moore will not go so far. For in the same essay he tells us that, if men are to live in society, "it may as well be with as little pain as possible." A society is bad and its social order ought to be changed, he argues, to the extent that "unnecessary suffering [is] produced by an historically specific form of government." And he appears to me to set out a fundamental objective for political science when he reflects that it possibly "is not too difficult to determine when the happiness of some people depends on the misery of others. The criterion of minimal suffering implies that such situations ought to be changed when it is possible to do so."

These quotations fail to do justice to Moore's essay, in the sense that they are quite unoriginal. For as a matter of fact, even most of the full-fledged pluralists on occasion come out firmly in opposition to needless suffering. What is remarkable is that none would be so bold as to say that the over-riding purpose of politics ought to be to do away with all avoidable suffering in this world of ours, and that the highest priority for political science should be to study how this can be brought about by means of social organization, including government.

It is precisely this naive view of politics that I adopt here. My position is that the proper purpose of politics is *identical with the proper purpose of medicine; to postpone death and to reduce suffering.* Political science does not prescribe drugs, for its competence is not in human physiology or body chemistry; but it should aim at prescribing the organizational innovations and social experimentation that will allow us to cultivate, in Albert Schweitzer's term, a "reverence for life."

Granted, human well-being is an elusive subject. But human suffering is far less elusive, and so are questions of life or death. Governments cannot, of course, eliminate death, but they can and should see it as their prime obligation to prevent and postpone death whenever and wherever possible. This proposition suggests any number of immediate and obvious tasks. Honorable men in government can work to eliminate capital punishment, for one thing. They can and therefore should institute—as a matter of legal right—full access to the best available medical care, regardless of the patient's ability to pay and regardless of cost to the taxpayers. The government of a truly "developed" society can and therefore should abolish poverty and slums, inferior schools, and other stymieing social institutions in the urban and rural ghettoes. And so on.

In medicine the moral commitment is clear, even if it is not always lived up to: priorities in treatment are determined not by the affluence of the various patients, but by degrees of illness, of suffering, of danger to life.

There is an indisputable consensus among practitioners of medicine, at least in principle, that their commitment is to the cause of postponing death and reducing suffering; this is what their Hippocratic oath is all about, and it is not subject to revocation by the government or by a mindless public opinion which conceivably might demand, say, substandard medical treatment for communists or for ethnic or religious minorities.

There is no Hippocratic oath for politicians; nor would such an oath make any difference, given the pluralist indifference to moral imperatives in our business civilization. And here we discover an important divergence from our medical analogy. While the practice of medicine permits and often requires that first priority be given to those who are the most ill, the practice of modern pluralist politics, or pseudopolitics, almost invariably gives preferential treatment to those who are the most well-off in the sense of being least likely to suffer socioeconomic deprivation of any kind. This is likely to be true to some extent in any stable social order, including a postrevolutionary communist society, on the simple sociological ground that those most privileged with affluence are likely to be disproportionately educated, articulate, and intelligent, statistically speaking, and more likely to know or have access to persons with political influence. Also, they are far more likely to have effective organizations to promote their interests.

It is precisely this state of affairs that makes the need for political scientists of maximal integrity within the academy so pressing. If a commercial society with pluralist political institutions tends to put a premium on unprincipled pragmatism, and to keep rewarding the strong at the expense of the weak, then surely our task as political scientists should not be to blend into the pluralist landscape and offer our services simply as surveyors and landscape architects, thus abandoning the ancient concern with politics as an instrument of the common good. On the contrary, I submit that our primary responsibility should be to gear our inquiry and research to the goal of prescribing the kinds of organizations and institutions that can in fact promote reverence for life.

An intellectual commitment to the study of politics requires the freedom and indeed the obligation to study the fundamental normative issues with an open mind and in the scientific spirit of systematic inquiry. Yet whoever questions the legitimacy of a social order, or the assumptions by which it is habitually justified, is a radical. And radicalism can be uncomfortable and, often enough, inconvenient for career purposes. Liberalism, on the other hand, is a positive advantage nowadays within our universities, much as political conservatism is advantageous in most of the business world. Not only the training of political scientists (who nowadays are apt to refer to their *training* rather than their *education*) but the teaching that goes on at all age levels by and large aims at producing useful, pliable citizens, not free-thinking intellectuals, prone to make their own moral judgments. Every social order seeks to mold and train its young to celebrate the past and present, not to educate them to think freely and responsibly about political ideals for the future.

Nevertheless, as social scientists we must insist on speaking primarily for ourselves. Research on political aims must focus on the aims *we* want. Admittedly, we are prone to be as fallible, as selfish, as vain as the next fellow. But not more so. The comparative shelteredness of the academy and our habits of reading and writing give us at least an *opportunity* denied active politicians and those in many other careers: we *can* think disinterestedly and radically about political aims and their implications without being thrown out of our positions, at least in the better universities.

Unless larger numbers of us soon begin to take advantage of this opportunity, however, and face up to our responsibility as relatively free intellectuals, I see little hope that the social science professions will become anything better than what C. Wright Mills called them: "the utensils of history makers." Unless we learn to cultivate better our powers of substantive as well as formal rationality, and our courage to teach with candor what we know to be true, or just, our present foreign and domestic policies will remain without effective challenge. Where else but in our schools and academies can we hope to develop intelligent, principled champions of the underprivileged and the unborn? . . .

6. THE SOCIAL BASIS OF POLITICS

ARISTOTLE

Aristotle (384–322 B.C.) is known as "The father of political science." The POLITICS *was the first comprehensive study of the political system.*

Observation shows us, first, that every polis (or state) is a species of association, and, secondly, that all associations are instituted for the purpose of attaining some good—for all men do all their acts with a view to achieving something which is, in their view, a good. We may therefore hold . . . that all associations aim at some good; and we may also hold that the particular association which is the most sovereign of all, and includes all the rest, will pursue this aim most, and will thus be directed to the most sovereign of all goods. This most sovereign and inclusive association is the polis, as it is called, or the political association. . . .

If, accordingly, we begin at the beginning, and consider things in the process of their growth, we shall best be able, in this as in other fields, to attain scientific conclusions by the method we employ. First of all, there must necessarily be a union or pairing of those who cannot exist without one another. Male and female must unite for the reproduction of the species—

From Aristotle, *Politics,* translated by Ernest Barker. New York: Oxford University Press, 1958. Published by the Clarendon Press. Pp. 1–7, excerpts.

not from deliberate intention, but from the natural impulse, which exists in animals generally as it also exists in plants, to leave behind them something of the same nature as themselves. Next, there must necessarily be a union of the naturally ruling element with the element which is naturally ruled, for the preservation of both. The element which is able, by virtue of its intelligence, to exercise forethought, is naturally a ruling and master element; the element which is able, by virtue of its bodily power, to do what the other element plans, is a ruled element, which is naturally in a state of slavery; and master and slave have accordingly [as they thus complete one another] a common interest. . . . The female and the slave [we may pause to note] are naturally distinguished from one another. Nature makes nothing in a spirit of stint, as smiths do when they make the Delphic knife to serve a number of purposes: she makes each separate thing for a separate end; and she does so because each instrument has the finest finish when it serves a single purpose and not a variety of purposes. . . .

The first form of association naturally instituted for the satisfaction of daily recurrent needs is thus the family; and the members of the family are accordingly termed by Charondas "associates of the bread-chest," as they are also termed by Epimenides the Cretan "associates of the manger." The next form of association—which is also the *first* to be formed from more households than one, and for the satisfaction of something more than daily recurrent needs—is the village.

The most natural form of the village appears to be that of a colony or offshoot from a family; and some have thus called the members of the village by the name of "sucklings of the same milk," or, again, of "sons and the sons of sons." . . . This, it may be noted, is the reason why each Greek polis was originally ruled—as the peoples of the barbarian world still are—by kings. They were formed of persons who were already monarchically governed; . . . households are always monarchically governed by the eldest of the kin, just as villages, when they are offshoots from the household, are similarly governed in virtue of the kinship between their members. This primitive kinship is that Homer describes [in speaking of the Cyclopes]:

> Each of them ruleth
> Over his children and wives,

a passage which shows that they lived in scattered groups, as indeed men generally did in ancient times. The fact that men generally were governed by kings in ancient times, and that some still continue to be governed in that way, is the reason that leads us all to assert that the gods are also governed by a king. We make the lives of the gods in the likeness of our own—as we also make their shapes. . . .

When we come to the final and perfect association, formed from a number of villages, we have already reached the polis—an association which may be said to have reached the height of full self-sufficiency; or rather . . . we may say that while it *grows* for the sake of mere life . . . it *exists* . . . for the sake of a good life [and is therefore fully self-sufficient]. . . .

From these considerations it is evident that the polis belongs to the class of things that exist by nature, and that man is by nature an animal intended to live in a polis. He who is without a polis, by reason of his own nature and not of some accident, is either a poor sort of being, or a being higher than man: he is like the man of whom Homer wrote in denunciation:

Clanless and lawless and heartless is he. . . .

The reason why man is a being meant for political association, in a higher degree than bees or other gregarious animals can ever associate, is evident. Nature, according to our theory, makes nothing in vain; and man alone of the animals is furnished with the faculty of language. The mere making of sounds serves to indicate pleasure and pain, and is thus a faculty that belongs to animals in general; their nature enables them to attain the point at which they have perceptions of pleasure and pain, and can signify those perceptions to one another. But language serves to declare what is advantageous and what is the reverse, and it therefore serves to declare what is just and what is unjust. It is the peculiarity of man, in comparison with the rest of the animal world, that he alone possesses a perception of good and evil, of the just and the unjust, and of other similar qualities; and it is association in . . . these things which makes a family and a polis.

We may now proceed to add that [though the individual and the family are prior in the order of time] the polis is prior in the order of nature to the family and the individual. The reason for this is that the whole is necessarily prior [in nature] to the part. If the whole body be destroyed, there will not be a foot or a hand, except in that ambiguous sense in which one uses the same word to indicate a different thing, as when one speaks of a "hand" made of stone; for a hand, when destroyed [by the destruction of the whole body], will be no better than a stone "hand." All things derive their essential character from their function and their capacity; and it follows that if they are no longer fit to discharge their function, we ought not to say that they are still the same thing, but only that, by an ambiguity, they still have the same names. . . .

The man who is isolated—who is unable to share in the benefits of political association, or has no need to share because he is already self-sufficient— is no part of the polis, and must therefore be either a beast or a god. [Man is thus intended by nature to be a part of a political whole, and] there is therefore an immanent impulse in all men towards an association of this order. But the man who first *constructed* such an association was none the less the greatest of benefactors. Man, when perfected, is the best of animals; but if he be isolated from law and justice he is the worst of all. Injustice is all the graver when it is armed injustice; and man is furnished from birth with arms [such as, for instance, language] which are intended to serve the purposes of moral prudence and virtue, but which may be used in preference for opposite ends. That is why, if he be without virtue, he is a most unholy and savage being, and worse than all others in the indulgence of lust and gluttony. Justice [which is his salvation] belongs to the polis; for justice, which is the determination of what is just, is an ordering of the political association.

7. THE ORIGIN OF THE STATE

FRIEDRICH ENGELS

Friedrich Engels (1820–1895) was a German socialist leader and a friend and collaborator of Karl Marx. THE ORIGIN OF THE FAMILY, PRIVATE PROPERTY, AND THE STATE, *published in 1894, was intended as part of a longer work which remained unfinished at his death.*

The state is by no means a power forced on society from without; just as little is it "the reality of the ethical idea," "the image and reality of reason," as Hegel maintains. Rather, it is a product of society at a certain stage of development; it is the admission that this society has become entangled in an insoluble contradiction with itself, that it is cleft into irreconcilable antagonisms which it is powerless to dispel. But in order that these antagonisms, classes with conflicting economic interests, might not consume themselves and society in sterile struggle, a power seemingly standing above society became necessary for the purpose of moderating the conflict, of keeping it within the bounds of "order"; and this power, arisen out of society, but placing itself above it, and increasingly alienating itself from it, is the state.

In contradistinction to the old gentile organization, the state, first, divides its subjects *according to territory*. As we have seen, the old gentile associations, built upon and held together by ties of blood, became inadequate, largely because they presupposed that the members were bound to a given territory, a bond which had long ceased to exist. The territory remained, but the people had become mobile. Hence, division according to territory was taken as the point of departure, and citizens were allowed to exercise their public rights and duties wherever they settled, irrespective of gens and tribe. This organization of citizens according to locality is a feature common to all states. That is why it seems natural to us; but we have seen what long and arduous struggles were needed before it could replace, in Athens and Rome, the old organization according to *gentes*.

The second is the establishment of a *public power* which no longer directly coincided with the population organizing itself as an armed force. This special public power is necessary, because a self-acting armed organization of the population has become impossible since the cleavage into classes. The slaves also belonged to the population; the 90,000 citizens of Athens formed only a privileged class as against the 365,000 slaves. The

From Friedrich Engels, *The Origin of the Family, Private Property, and the State,* Selected Works, Vol. II. Moscow: Foreign Language Publishing House, 1955. Pp. 317–21, excerpts.

people's army of the Athenian democracy was an aristocratic public power against the slaves, whom it kept in check; however, a gendarmerie also became necessary to keep the citizens in check, as we related above. This public power exists in every state; it consists not merely of armed people but also of material adjuncts, prisons and institutions of coercion of all kinds, of which gentile society knew nothing. It may be very insignificant, almost infinitesimal, in societies where class antagonisms are still undeveloped and in out-of-the-way places as was the case at certain times and in certain regions in the United States of America. It grows stronger, however, in proportion as class antagonisms within the state become more acute, and as adjacent states become larger and more populated. We have only to look at our present-day Europe, where class struggle and rivalry in conquest have screwed up the public power to such a pitch that it threatens to devour the whole of society and even the state.

In order to maintain this public power, contributions from the citizens become necessary—*taxes*. These were absolutely unknown in gentile society; but we know enough about them today. As civilization advances, these taxes become inadequate; the state makes drafts on the future, contracts loans, *public debts*. Old Europe can tell a tale about these, too.

In possession of the public power and of the right to levy taxes, the officials, as organs of society, now stand *above* society. The free, voluntary respect that was accorded to the organs of the gentile constitution does not satisfy them, even if they could gain it; being the vehicles of a power that is becoming alien to society, respect for them must be enforced by means of exceptional laws by virtue of which they enjoy special sanctity and inviolability. The shabbiest police servant in the civilized state has more "authority" than all the organs of gentile society put together; but the most powerful prince and the greatest statesman, or general, of civilization may well envy the humblest gentile chief for the uncoerced and undisputed respect that is paid to him. The one stands in the midst of society, the other is forced to attempt to represent something outside and above it.

As the state arose from the need to hold class antagonisms in check, but as it arose, at the same time, in the midst of the conflict of these classes, it is, as a rule, the state of the most powerful, economically dominant class, which, through the medium of the state, becomes also the politically dominant class, and thus acquires new means of holding down and exploiting the oppressed class. Thus, the state of antiquity was above all the state of the slave owners for the purpose of holding down the slaves, as the feudal state was the organ of the nobility for holding down the peasant serfs and bondsmen, and the modern representative state is an instrument of exploitation of wage labor by capital. By way of exception, however, periods occur in which the warring classes balance each other so nearly that the state power, as ostensible mediator, acquires, for the moment, a certain degree of independence of both. Such was the absolute monarchy of the seventeenth and eighteenth centuries, which held the balance between the nobility and the class of burghers; such was the Bonapartism of the First, and still more of the Second, French Empire, which played off the proletariat against the bourgeoisie and the bourgeoisie against the proletariat. . . .

In most of the historical states, the rights of citizens are, besides, apportioned according to their wealth, thus directly expressing the fact that the state is an organization of the possessing class for its protection against the nonpossessing class. It was so already in the Athenian and Roman classification according to property. It was so in the medieval feudal state, in which the alignment of political power was in conformity with the amount of land owned. It is seen in the electoral qualifications of the modern representative states. Yet this political recognition of property distinctions is by no means essential. On the contrary, it marks a low state of state development. The highest form of the state, the democratic republic, which under our modern conditions of society is more and more becoming an inevitable necessity, and is the form of state in which alone the last decisive struggle between proletariat and bourgeoisie can be fought out—the democratic republic officially knows nothing any more of property distinctions. In it wealth exercises its power indirectly, but all the more surely. On the one hand, in the form of the direct corruption of officials, of which America provides the classical example; on the other hand, in the form of an alliance between government and Stock Exchange, which becomes the easier to achieve the more the public debt increases and the more joint-stock companies concentrate in their hands not only transport but also production itself, using the Stock Exchange as their center. . . . And lastly, the possessing class rules directly through the medium of universal suffrage. As long as the oppressed class, in our case, therefore, the proletariat, is not yet ripe to emancipate itself, it will in its majority regard the existing order of society as the only one possible and, politically, will form the tail of the capitalist class, its extreme Left wing. To the extent, however, that this class matures for its self-emancipation, it constitutes itself as its own party and elects its own representatives, and not those of the capitalists. Thus, universal suffrage is the gauge of the maturity of the working class. It cannot and never will be anything more in the present-day state; but that is sufficient. On the day the thermometer of universal suffrage registers boiling point among the workers, both they and the capitalists will know what to do.

The state, then, has not existed from all eternity. There have been societies that did without it, that had no conception of the state and state power. At a certain stage of economic development, which was necessarily bound up with the cleavage of society into classes, the state became a necessity owing to this cleavage. We are now rapidly approaching a stage in the development of production at which the existence of these classes not only will have ceased to be a necessity, but will become a positive hindrance to production. They will fall as inevitably as they arose at an earlier stage. Along with them the state will inevitably fall. The society that will organize production on the basis of a free and equal association of the producers will put the whole machinery of state where it will then belong: into the Museum of Antiquities, by the side of the spinning wheel and the bronze axe.

8. THE ETHICS OF POWER

NICCOLÒ MACHIAVELLI

*Niccolò Machiavelli (1469-1527) was an Italian diplomat and phi-
losopher of the Renaissance. He wrote* THE PRINCE *during his enforced
retirement after the collapse of the Republic of Florence he had served.*

And as this part is worthy of note and of imitation by others, I will not
omit mention of it. When he took the Romagna, it had previously been
governed by weak rulers, who had rather despoiled their subjects than governed them, and given them more cause for disunion than for union, so that
the province was a prey to robbery, assaults, and every kind of disorder.
He, therefore, judged it necessary to give them a good government in order
to make them peaceful and obedient to his rule. For this purpose he appointed
Messer Remirro de Orco, a cruel and able man, to whom he gave the fullest
authority. This man, in a short time, was highly successful in rendering the
country orderly and united, whereupon the duke, not deeming such excessive
authority expedient, lest it should become hateful, appointed a civil court
of justice in the center of the province under an excellent president, to which
each city appointed its own advocate. And as he knew that the harshness of
the past had engendered some amount of hatred, in order to purge the minds
of the people and to win them over completely, he resolved to show that if
any cruelty had taken place it was not by his orders, but through the harsh
disposition of his minister. And having found the opportunity he had him
cut in half and placed one morning in the public square at Cesena with a
piece of wood and blood-stained knife by his side. The ferocity of this
spectacle caused the people both satisfaction and amazement. . . .

Reviewing thus all the actions of the duke, I find nothing to blame, on
the contrary, I feel bound, as I have done, to hold him up as an example
to be imitated by all who by fortune and with the arms of others have risen
to power. For with his great courage and high ambition he could not have
acted otherwise, and his designs were only frustrated by the short life of
Alexander and his own illness. Whoever, therefore, deems it necessary in his
new principality to secure himself against enemies, to gain friends, to conquer
by force or fraud, to make himself beloved and feared by the people, followed
and reverenced by the soldiers, to destroy those who can and may injure him,
introduce innovations into old customs, to be severe and kind, magnanimous
and liberal, suppress the old militia, create a new one, maintain the friendship
of kings and princes in such a way that they are glad to benefit him and

From *The Prince* by Niccolò Machiavelli (World's Classics 43), published by the
Oxford University Press. Reprinted by permission of the publisher.

fear to injure him, such a one can find no better example than the actions of this man. . . .

Well committed may be called those [cruelties] (if it is permissible to use the word "well" of evil) which are perpetuated once for the need of securing one's self, and which afterwards are not persisted in, but are exchanged for measures as useful to the subjects as possible. Cruelties ill committed are those which, although at first few, increase rather than diminish with time. Those who follow the former method may remedy in some measure their condition, both with God and man; as did Agathocles. As to the others, it is impossible for them to maintain themselves.

Whence it is to be noted, that in taking a state the conqueror must arrange to commit all his cruelties at once, so as not to have to recur to them every day, and so as to be able, by not making fresh changes, to reassure people and win them over by benefiting them. Whoever acts otherwise, either through timidity or bad counsels, is always obliged to stand with knife in hand, and can never depend on his subjects, because they, owing to continually fresh injuries, are unable to depend upon him. For injuries should be done all together, so that being less tasted, they will give less offense. Benefits should be granted little by little, so that they may be enjoyed. And above all, a prince must live with his subjects in such a way that no accident of good or evil fortune can deflect him from his course; for necessity arising in adverse times, you are not in time with severity, and the good that you do does not profit, as it is judged to be forced upon you, and you will derive no benefit whatever from it. . . .

Beginning now with the first qualities above named, I say that it would be well to be considered liberal; nevertheless liberality such as the world understands it will injure you, because if used virtuously and in the proper way, it will not be known, and you will incur the disgrace of the contrary vice. But one who wishes to obtain the reputation of liberality among men, must not omit every kind of sumptuous display, and to such an extent that a prince of this character will consume by such means all his resources, and will be at least compelled, if he wishes to maintain his name for liberality, to impose heavy taxes on his people, become extortionate, and do everything possible to obtain money. This will make his subjects begin to hate him, and he will be little esteemed being poor, so that having by this liberality injured many and benefited but few, he will feel the first little disturbance and be endangered by every peril. If he recognizes this and wishes to change his system, he incurs at once the charge of niggardliness.

A prince, therefore, not being able to exercise this virtue of liberality without risk if it be known, must not, if he be prudent, object to being called miserly. In the course of time he will be thought more liberal, when it is seen that by his parsimony his revenue is sufficient, that he can defend himself against those who make war on him, and undertake enterprises without burdening his people, so that he is really liberal to all those from whom he ¹oes not take, who are infinite in number, and niggardly to all to whom he does not give, who are few. In our times we have seen nothing great done except by those who have been esteemed niggardly; the others have all been ruined. Pope Julius II, although he had made use of a reputation for liberality in order to attain the papacy, did not seek to retain it afterwards, so that he might be able to wage war. The present King of France has carried on so many wars without imposing an extraordinary tax, because his extra expenses were covered by the parsimony he had so long practiced. The present King of Spain, if he had been thought liberal, would not have engaged in and been successful in so many enterprises.

For these reasons a prince must care little for the reputation of being a miser, if he wishes to avoid robbing his subjects, if he wishes to be able to defend himself, to avoid becoming poor and contemptible, and not to be forced to become rapacious; this niggardliness is one of those vices which enable him to reign. If it is said that Caesar attained the empire through liberality, and that many others have reached the highest position through being liberal or being thought so, I would reply that you are either a prince already or else on the way to becoming one. In the first case, this liberality is harmful; in the second, it is certainly necessary to be considered liberal. Caesar was one of those who wished to attain the mastery over Rome, but if after attaining it he had lived and had not moderated his expenses, he would have destroyed that empire. And should any one reply that there have been many princes, who have done great things with their armies, who have been thought extremely liberal, I would answer by saying that the prince may either spend his own wealth and that of his subjects or the wealth of others. In the first case he must be sparing, but for the rest he must not neglect to be very liberal. The liberality is very necessary to a prince who marches with his armies, and lives by plunder, sack and ransom, and his dealing with the wealth of others, for without it he would not be followed by his soldiers. And you may be very generous indeed with what is not the property of yourself or your subjects, as were Cyrus, Caesar, and Alexander; for spending the wealth of others will not diminish your reputation, but increase it; only spending your own resources will injure you. There is nothing which destroys itself so much as liberality, for by using it you lose the power of using it, and become either poor and despicable, or, to escape poverty, rapacious and hated. And of all things that a prince must guard against, the most important are being despicable or hated, and liberality will lead you to one or the other of these conditions. It is, therefore, wiser to have the name of a miser, which produces disgrace without hatred, than to incur of necessity the name of being rapacious, which produces both disgrace and hatred.

Proceeding to the other qualities before named, I say, that every prince must desire to be considered merciful and not cruel. He must, however, take care not to misuse this mercifulness. Cesare Borgia was considered cruel, but his cruelty had brought order to the Romagna, united it, and reduced it to peace and fealty. If this is considered well, it will be seen that he was really much more merciful than the Florentine people, who, to avoid the name of cruelty, allowed Pistoia to be destroyed. A prince, therefore, must not mind incurring the charge of cruelty for the purpose of keeping his subjects united and faithful; for, with a very few examples, he will be more merciful than those who, from excess of tenderness, allow disorders to arise, from whence spring bloodshed and rapine; for these as a rule injure the whole community, while the executions carried out by the prince injure only individuals. And of all princes, it is impossible for a new prince to escape the reputation of cruelty, new states being always full of dangers. Wherefore Virgil through the mouth of Dido says:

Res dura, et regni novitas me talia cogunt
Moliri, et late fines custode tueri.

Nevertheless, he must be cautious in believing and acting, and must not be afraid of his own shadow, and must proceed in a temperate manner with prudence and humanity, so that too much confidence does not render him incautious, and too much diffidence does not render him intolerant.

From this arises the question whether it is better to be loved more than feared, or feared more than loved. The reply is, that one ought to be both feared and loved, but as it is difficult for the two to go together, it is much safer to be feared than loved, if one of the two has to be wanting. For it may be said of men in general that they are ungrateful, voluble, dissemblers, anxious to avoid danger, and covetous of gain; as long as you benefit them, they are entirely yours; they offer you their blood, their goods, their life, and their children, as I have before said, when the necessity is remote; but when it approaches, they revolt. And the prince who has relied solely on their words, without making other preparations, is ruined; for the friendship which is gained by purchase and not through grandeur and nobility of spirit is bought but not secured, and at a pinch is not to be expended in your service. And men have less scruple in offending one who makes himself loved than one who makes himself feared; for love is held by a chain of obligation which, men being selfish, is broken whenever it serves their purpose; but fear is maintained by a dread of punishment which never fails.

Still, a prince should make himself feared in such a way that if he does not gain love, he at any rate avoids hatred; for fear and the absence of hatred may well go together, and will be always attained by one who abstains from interfering with the property of his citizens and subjects or with their women. And when he is obliged to take the life of any one, let him do so when there is a proper justification and manifest reason for it; but above all he must abstain from taking the property of others, for men forget more easily the death of their father than the loss of their patrimony. Then also pretexts for seizing property are never wanting, and one who begins to live by rapine will always find some reason for taking the goods of others, whereas causes for taking life are rarer and more fleeting. . . .

How laudable it is for a prince to keep good faith and live with integrity, and not with astuteness, everyone knows. Still the experience of our times shows those princes to have done great things who have had little regard for good faith, and have been able by astuteness to confuse men's brains, and who have ultimately overcome those who have made loyalty their foundation.

You must know, then, that there are two methods of fighting, the one by law, the other by force: the first method is that of men, the second of beasts; but as the first method is often insufficient, one must have recourse to the second. It is therefore necessary for a prince to know well how to use both the beast and the man. This was covertly taught to rulers by ancient writers, who relate how Achilles and many others of those ancient princes were given to Chiron the centaur to be brought up and educated under his discipline. The parable of this semianimal, semihuman teacher is meant to indicate that a prince must know how to use both natures, and that one without the other is not durable.

A prince being thus obliged to know well how to act as a beast must imitate the fox and the lion, for the lion cannot protect himself from traps, and the fox cannot defend himself from wolves. One must therefore be a fox to recognize traps, and a lion to frighten wolves. Those that wish to be only lions do not understand this. Therefore, a prudent ruler ought not to keep faith when by so doing it would be against his interest, and when the reasons which made him bind himself no longer exist. If men were all good, this precept would not be a good one; but as they are bad, and would not observe their faith with you, so you are not bound to keep faith with them. Nor have legitimate grounds ever failed a prince who wished to show colorable excuse for the nonfulfullment of his promise. Of this one could furnish an infinite number of modern examples, and show how many times peace has been broken, and how many promises rendered worthless, by the faithfulness of princes, and those that have been best able to imitate the fox have succeeded best. But it is necessary to be able to disguise this character well, and to be a great feigner and dissembler; and men are so simple and so ready to obey present necessities, that one who deceives will always find those who allow themselves to be deceived.

I will only mention one modern instance. Alexander VI did nothing else but deceive men, he thought of nothing else, and found the occasion for it; no man was ever more able to give assurances, or affirmed things with stronger oaths, and no man observed them less; however, he always succeeded in his deceptions, as he well knew this aspect of things.

It is not, therefore, necessary for a prince to have all the above-named qualities, but it is very necessary to seem to have them. I would even be bold to say that to possess them and always to observe them is dangerous, but to appear to possess them is useful. Thus it is well to seem merciful, faithful, humane, sincere, religious, and also to be so; but you must have the mind so disposed that when it is needful to be otherwise you may be able to change to the opposite qualities. And it must be understood that a prince, and especially a new prince, cannot observe all those things which are considered good in men, being often obliged, in order to maintain the state, to act against faith, against charity, against humanity, and against religion. And, therefore, he must have a mind disposed to adapt itself according to the wind, and as the variations of fortune dictate, and, as I said before, not deviate from what is good, if possible, but be able to do evil if constrained.

A prince must take great care that nothing goes out of his mouth which is not full of the above-named five qualities, and, to see and hear him, he should seem to be all mercy, faith, integrity, humanity, and religion. And nothing is more necessary than to seem to have this last quality, for men in general judge more by the eyes than by the hands; for everyone can see, but very few have to feel. Everybody sees what you appear to be, few feel what you are, and those few will not dare to oppose themselves to the many, who have the majesty of the state to defend them; and in the actions of men, and especially of princes, from which there is no appeal, the end justifies the means. Let a prince therefore aim at conquering and maintaining the state, and the means will always be judged honorable and praised by everyone, for the vulgar are always taken by appearances and the issue of the event; and the world consists only of the vulgar, and the few who are not vulgar are isolated when the many have a rallying point in the prince. . . .

part two

Equality in

the Political Community

INTRODUCTION

*. . . All men think justice to be a sort of equality.
. . . Democracy, for example, arises out of the
notion that those who are equal in any respect are
equal in all respects. . . . Oligarchy is based on the
notion that those who are unequal in one respect
are in all respects unequal.*
—Aristotle, *Politics*, III, 12:1 and V, 1:3

At the very basis of society lies the first choice of its citizens: are all men to be equal—the rule of equality—or are some to be "more equal than others"—the rule of privilege? On the answer depends the nature of the fundamental social relations of the society.

The citizens may choose a system in which some are regarded as specially privileged, as peculiarly qualified to rule. If so, which ones? What are the distinguishing characteristics of this elite? Useful criteria must meet three tests: 1) Are the qualities acceptable to those not of the elite? Can they be justified as essential? 2) Are the qualities readily recognizable? 3) Can they be measured? The qualities must be acceptable to those not of the elite, for only so will the authority vested in the privileged be regarded as legitimate by the nonprivileged; they must, therefore, in some way be related to the ability of their possessors to further the ends of the state. The qualities must be recognizable, for the elite must be able to prove its possession of the required characteristics. Finally, they must be measurable, for since most characteristics of mankind are matters of degree, the elite must be able to prove the superior extent of its possession.

On the other hand, the citizens may choose a system based on equality. If so, they face other questions. Above all, what *is* equality? Is it political—equality in ruling or in making public policy? If so, is it an equality subject to qualification? Who determines the qualifications? Or can it be assumed that all men have a potential capacity to rule?

Or do we mean legal equality—equal treatment before the law? Can legal equality be enjoyed by those who do not enjoy political equality? Does the law dispense justice to the privileged and nonprivileged alike? To what extent will differences in other respects affect legal equality?

Is equality economic? If so, how can it be achieved? If achieved, how can it be maintained in the face of differing individual abilities and preferences for types of work and leisure? Can we assume with Plato that a society will be so permeated with "virtue" that every member will voluntarily do his best to serve the interest of the group? Is economic equality to be interpreted as equality of economic opportunity? Or does it imply equality of income, irrespective of the type of work involved? Can there be equality of opportunity between the scion of a family of wealth and social position and the child of the city slum or rural sharecropper? And if there is no equality of opportunity, will not economic inequalities be perpetuated and accumulated?

Or does equality mean social equality? Have all citizens the right to social acceptance based on their own individual merits rather than on the basis of race, religion, or some other group classification? Or is social acceptance an individual matter which is not the legitimate concern of government? On the other hand, can a society expect any of its members to reconcile themselves permanently to an *a priori* inferior social status? If not, can acceptance be promoted without limiting individual freedom of association? Indeed, can social equality be legislated at all?

Societies have differed in their answers to these questions. Even though most modern societies proclaim or affirm their allegiance to the principle of equality, they increasingly entrust effective rule to the few, though in the name of the many. Is this phenomenon the "wave of the future" or a step on the road to a more genuine equality? What kind of equality is compatible with a modern, industrialized, urban civilization? How should the traditional concepts be interpreted to meet the demands of a mass civilization—democratic or totalitarian?

9. THE CLASS BASIS OF POLITICAL POWER

KARL MARX AND FRIEDRICH ENGELS

Karl Marx (1818–1883) was a German economic theorist and the most influential figure in the development of modern socialist theory. THE COMMUNIST MANIFESTO, *written in collaboration with Friedrich Engels, was intended as a declaration of principles of a group of communist exiles.*

The history of all hitherto existing society *is the history of class struggles.*

Freeman and slave, patrician and plebeian, lord and serf, guild master and journeyman, in a word, oppressor and oppressed, stood in constant opposition to one another, carried on an uninterrupted, now hidden, now open fight, a fight that each time ended, either in a revolutionary reconstitution of society at large, or in the common ruin of the contending classes.

In the earlier epochs of history, we find almost everywhere a complicated arrangement of society into various orders, a manifold gradation of social rank. In ancient Rome we have patricians, knights, plebeians, slaves; in the Middle Ages, feudal lords, vassals, guild masters, journeymen, apprentices, serfs; in almost all of these classes, again, subordinate gradations.

The modern bourgeois society that has sprouted from the ruins of feudal society has not done away with class antagonisms. It has but established new classes, new conditions of oppression, new forms of struggle in place of the old ones.

Our epoch, the epoch of the bourgeoisie, possesses, however, this distinctive feature: it has simplified the class antagonisms. Society as a whole is more and more splitting up into two great hostile camps, into two great classes directly facing each other: *Bourgeoisie and Proletariat. . . .*

Modern industry has established the world market, for which the discovery of America paved the way. This market has given an immense development to commerce, to navigation, to communication by land. This development has, in its turn, reacted on the extension of industry; and in proportion as industry, commerce, navigation, railways extended, in the same proportion the bourgeoisie developed, increased its capital, and pushed into the background every class handed down from the Middle Ages.

We see, therefore, *how the modern bourgeoisie is itself the product of a long course of development, of a series of revolutions in the modes of production and exchange.*

Each step in the development of the bourgeoisie was accompanied by a

Karl Marx and Friedrich Engels, *The Communist Manifesto.*

corresponding political advance of that class. An oppressed class under the sway of the feudal nobility, an armed and self-governing association in the medieval commune; here independent urban republic (as in Italy and Germany), there taxable "third estate" of the monarchy (as in France), afterwards, in the period of manufacture proper, serving either the semifeudal of the absolute monarchy as a counterpoise against the nobility, and, in fact, cornerstone of the great monarchies in general, the bourgeoisie has at last, since the establishment of Modern Industry and of the world market, conquered for itself, in the modern representative State, exclusive political sway. The executive of the modern State is but a committee for managing the common affairs of the whole bourgeoisie.

The bourgeoisie, historically, has played a most revolutionary part.

The bourgeoisie, wherever it has got the upper hand, has put an end to all feudal, patriarchal, idyllic relations. It has pitilessly torn asunder the motley feudal ties that bound man to his "natural superiors," and has left remaining no other nexus between man and man than naked self-interest, than callous "cash payment." It has drowned the most heavenly ecstasies of religious fervor, of chivalrous enthusiasm, of philistine sentimentalism, in the icy water of egotistical calculation. It has resolved personal worth into exchange value, and in place of the numberless indefeasible chartered freedoms, has set up that single, unconscionable freedom—Free Trade. In one word, for exploitation, veiled by religious and political illusions, it has substituted naked, shameless, direct, brutal exploitation.

The bourgeoisie has stripped of its halo every occupation hitherto honored and looked up to with reverent awe. It has converted the physician, the lawyer, the priest, the poet, the man of science, into its paid wage laborers.

The bourgeoisie has torn away from the family its sentimental veil, and has reduced the family relation to a mere money relation.

The bourgeoisie has disclosed how it came to pass that the brutal display of vigor in the Middle Ages, which Reactionists so much admire, found its fitting complement in the most slothful indolence. It has been the first to show what man's activity can bring about. It has accomplished wonders far surpassing Egyptian pyramids, Roman aqueducts, and Gothic cathedrals; it has conducted expeditions that put in the shade all former Exoduses of nations and crusades.

The bourgeoisie cannot exist without constantly revolutionizing the instruments of production, and thereby the relations of production, and with them the whole relations of society. Preservation of the old modes of production in unaltered form, was, on the contrary, the first condition of existence for all earlier industrial classes. Constant revolutionizing of production, uninterrupted disturbance of all social conditions, everlasting uncertainty and agitation distinguish the bourgeois epoch from all earlier ones. All fixed, fast-frozen relations, with their train of ancient and venerable prejudices and opinions, are swept away, all new-formed ones become antiquated before they can ossify. All that is solid melts in the air, all that is holy is profaned, and man is at last compelled to face with sober senses, his real conditions of life, and his relations with his kind.

The need of a constantly expanding market for its products chases the bourgeoisie over the whole surface of the globe. It must nestle everywhere, settle everywhere, establish connections everywhere.

The bourgeoisie has through its exploitation of the world market given a cosmopolitan character to production and consumption in every country. . . .

The bourgeoisie, by the rapid improvement of all instruments of production, by the immensely facilitated means of communication, draws all, even the most barbarian, nations into civilization. The cheap prices of its commodities are the heavy artillery with which it batters down all Chinese Walls, with which it forces the barbarians' intensely obstinate hatred of foreigners to capitulate. It compels all nations, on pain of extinction, to adopt the bourgeois mode of production; it compels them to introduce what it calls civilization into their midst, i.e., to become bourgeois themselves. In one word, it creates a world after its own image.

The bourgeoisie has subjected the country to the rule of the towns. It has created enormous cities, has greatly increased the urban population as compared with the rural, and has thus rescued a considerable part of the population from the idiocy of rural life. Just as it has made the country dependent on the towns, so it has made barbarian and semibarbarian countries dependent on the civilized ones, nations of peasants on nations of bourgeois, the East on the West.

The bourgeoisie keeps more and more doing away with the scattered state of the population, of the means of production, and of property. It has agglomerated population, centralized means of production, and has concentrated property in a few hands. The necessary consequence of this was political centralization. Independent, or but loosely connected provinces, with separate interests, laws, governments and systems of taxation, became lumped together into one nation, with one government, one code of laws, one national class-interest, one frontier and one customs-tariff.

The bourgeoisie, during its rule of scarce one hundred years, has created more massive and more colossal productive forces than have all preceding generations together. . . .

We see then: the means of production and of exchange, on whose foundation the bourgeoisie built itself up, were generated in feudal society. At a certain stage in the development of these means of production and of exchange, the conditions under which feudal society produced and exchanged, the feudal organization of agriculture and manufacturing industry, in one word, the feudal relations of property became no longer compatible with the already developed productive forces; they became so many fetters. They had to be burst asunder; they were burst asunder.

Into their place stepped free competition, accompanied by a social and political constitution adapted to it, and by the economical and political sway of the bourgeois class.

A similar movement is going on before our own eyes. Modern bourgeois society with its relations of production, of exchange and of property, a society that has conjured up such gigantic means of production and of exchange, is like the sorcerer who is no longer able to control the powers of the nether world whom he has called up by his spells. For many a decade past the history of industry and commerce is but the history of the revolt of modern productive forces against modern conditions of production, against the property relations that are the conditions for the existence of the bourgeoisie and of its rule. It is enough to mention the commercial crises that by their periodical return put on its trial, each time more threateningly, the existence of the entire bourgeois society. In these crises a great part not only of the existing products, but also of the previously created productive forces, are periodically destroyed. In these crises there breaks out an epidemic that, in all earlier epochs, would have seemed an absurdity—the epidemic of overproduction. Society suddenly finds itself put back into a state of momentary barbarism; it appears as if a famine, a universal war of devastation had cut off the supply of every means of subsistence; industry and commerce seem to be destroyed; and why? Because there is too much civilization, too much means of subsistence, too much industry, too much commerce. The productive forces at the disposal of society no longer tend to further the development of the conditions of bourgeois property; on the contrary, they have become too powerful for these conditions, by which they are fettered, and so soon as they overcome these fetters, they bring disorder into the whole of bourgeois society, endanger the existence of bourgeois property. The conditions of bourgeois society are too narrow to comprise the wealth created by them. And how does the bourgeoisie get over these crises? On the one hand by enforced destruction of a mass of productive forces; on the other, by the conquest of new markets, and by the more thorough exploitation of the old ones. That is to say, by paving the way for more extensive and more destructive crises, and by diminishing the means whereby crises are prevented.

The weapons with which the bourgeoisie felled feudalism to the ground are now turned against the bourgeoisie itself.

But not only has the bourgeoisie forged the weapons that bring death to itself; it has also called into existence the men who are to wield those weapons—the modern working class—the proletarians.

In proportion as the bourgeoisie, i.e., capital, is developed, in the same proportion is the proletariat, the modern working class, developed—a class of laborers, who live only so long as they find work, and who find work only so long as their labor increases capital. These laborers, who must sell themselves piecemeal, are a commodity, like every other article of commerce, and are consequently exposed to all the vicissitudes of competition, to all the fluctuations of the market.

Owing to the extensive use of machinery and to division of labor, the work of the proletarians has lost all individual character, and, consequently, all charm for the workman. He becomes an appendage of the machine, and it is only the most simple, most monotonous, and most easily acquired knack, that is required of him. Hence, the cost of production of a workman is restricted, almost entirely, to the means of subsistence that he requires for his maintenance, and for the propagation of his race. But the price of a commodity, and therefore also of labor, is equal to its cost of production.

In proportion, therefore, as the repulsiveness of the work increases, the wage decreases. Nay more, in proportion as the use of machinery and division of labor increases, in the same proportion the burden of toil also increases, whether by prolongation of the working hours, by increase of the work exacted in a given time or by increased speed of the machinery, etc.

Modern industry has converted the little workshop of the patriarchal master into the great factory of the industrial capitalist. Masses of laborers, crowded into the factory, are organized like soldiers. As privates of the industrial army they are placed under the command of a perfect hierarchy of officers and sergeants. Not only are they slaves of the bourgeois class, and of the bourgeois State; they are daily and hourly enslaved by the machine, by the over-looker, and, above all, by the individual bourgeois manufacturer himself. The more openly this despotism proclaims gain to be its end and aim, the more petty, the more hateful and the more embittering it is. . . .

The lower strata of the middle class—the small tradespeople, shopkeepers, and retired tradesmen generally, the handicraftsmen and peasants—all these sink gradually into the proletariat, partly because their diminutive capital does not suffice for the scale on which Modern Industry is carried on, and is swamped in the competition with the large capitalists, partly because their specialized skill is rendered worthless by new methods of production. Thus the proletariat is recruited from all classes of the population.

The proletariat goes through various stages of development. With its birth begins its struggle with the bourgeoisie. At first the contest is carried on by individual laborers, then by the work-people of a factory, then by the operatives on one trade, in one locality, against the individual bourgeois who directly exploits them. They direct their attacks not against the bourgeois conditions of production, but against the instruments of production themselves; they destroy imported wares that compete with their labor, they smash to pieces machinery, they set factories ablaze, they seek to restore by force the vanished status of the workman of the Middle Ages.

At this stage the laborers still form an incoherent mass scattered over the whole country, and broken up by their mutual competition. If anywhere they united to form more compact bodies, this is not yet the consequence of their own active union, but of the union of the bourgeoisie, which class, in order to attain its own political ends, is compelled to set the whole proletariat in motion, and is moreover yet, for a time, able to do so. At this stage, therefore, the proletarians do not fight their enemies, but the enemies of their enemies, the remnants of absolute monarchy, the landowners, the nonindustrial bourgeois, the petty bourgeoisie. Thus the whole historical movement is concentrated in the hands of the bourgeoisie; every victory so obtained is a victory for the bourgeoisie.

But with the development of industry the proletariat not only increases in number; it becomes concentrated in greater masses, its strength grows, and it feels that strength more. The various interests and conditions of life within the ranks of the proletariat are more and more equalized in proportion, as machinery obliterates all distinctions of labor, and nearly everywhere reduces wages to the same low level. The growing competition among the bourgeois, and the resulting commercial crises, makes the wages of the workers ever more fluctuating. The unceasing improvement of machinery, ever more rapidly developing, makes their livelihood more and more precarious; the collisions between individual workmen and individual bourgeois take more and more the character of collisions between two classes. Thereupon the workers begin to form combinations (Trades' Unions) against the bourgeois; they club together in order to keep up the rate of wages; they found permanent associations in order to make provision beforehand for these occasional revolts. Here and there the contest breaks out into riots.

Now and then the workers are victorious, but only for a time. The real fruit of their battles lies, not in the immediate result, but in the ever-expanding union of the workers. This union is helped on by the improved means of communication that are created by modern industry and that place the workers of different localities in contact with one another. It was just this contact that was needed to centralize the numerous local struggles, all of the same character, into one national struggle between classes. But every class struggle is a political struggle. And that union, to attain which the burghers of the Middle Ages, with their miserable highways, required centuries, the modern proletarians, thanks to railways, achieve in a few years.

This organization of the proletarians into a class, and consequently into a political party, is continually being upset again by the competition between the workers themselves. But it ever rises up again, stronger, firmer, mightier. It compels legislative recognition of particular interests of the workers, by taking advantage of the divisions among the bourgeoisie itself. Thus the ten-hours' bill in England was carried.

Altogether collisions between the classes of the old society further, in many ways, the course of development of the proletariat. The bourgeoisie finds itself involved in a constant battle. At first with the aristocracy; later on, with those portions of the bourgeoisie itself, whose interests have become antagonistic to the progress of industry; at all times, with the bourgeoisie of foreign countries. In all these battles it sees itself compelled to appeal to the proletariat, to ask for its help, and thus, to drag it into the political arena. The bourgeoisie itself, therefore, supplies the proletariat with its own elements of political and general education, in other words, it furnishes the proletariat with weapons for fighting the bourgeoisie.

Further, as we have already seen, entire sections of the ruling classes are, by the advance of industry, precipitated into the proletariat, or are at least threatened in their conditions of existence. These also supply the proletariat with fresh elements of enlightenment and progress.

Finally, in times when the class-struggle nears the decisive hour, the process of dissolution going on within the ruling class, in fact within the whole range of old society, assumes such a violent, glaring character, that a small section of the ruling class cuts itself adrift, and joins the revolutionary class, the class that holds the future in its hands. Just as, therefore, at an earlier period, a section of the nobility went over to the bourgeoisie, so now a portion of the bourgeoisie goes over to the proletariat, and in particular, a portion of

the bourgeois ideologists, who have raised themselves to the level of compre-
hending theoretically the historical movement as a whole.

Of all the classes that stand face to face with the bourgeoisie today, the
proletariat alone is a really revolutionary class. The other classes decay and
finally disappear in the face of modern industry; the proletariat is its special
and essential product. . . .

All preceding classes that got the upper hand, sought to fortify their
already acquired status by subjecting society at large to their conditions of
appropriation. The proletarians cannot become masters of the productive
forces of society, except by abolishing their own previous mode of appropriation. They have nothing of their own to secure and to fortify; their mission
is to destroy all previous securities for, and insurances of, individual property.

All previous historical movements were movements of minorities, or in
the interest of minorities. The proletarian movement is the self-conscious,
independent movement of the immense majority, in the interests of the
immense majority. The proletariat, the lowest stratum of our present society,
cannot stir, cannot raise itself up, without the whole superincumbent strata
of official society being sprung into the air.

Though not in substance, yet in form, the struggle of the proletariat with
the bourgeoisie is at first a national struggle. The proletariat of each country
must, of course, first of all settle matters with its own bourgeoisie.

In depicting the most general phases of the development of the proletariat,
we trace more or less veiled civil war, ranging within existing society, up to
the point where that war breaks out into open revolution, and where the
violent overthrow of the bourgeoisie lays the foundation for the sway of
the proletariat.

*Hitherto, every form of society has been based, as we have already seen,
on the antagonism of oppressing and oppressed classes.* But in order to
oppress a class, certain conditions must be assured to it under which it can,
at least, continue its slavish existence. The serf, in the period of serfdom,
raised himself to membership in the commune, just as the petty bourgeois,
under the yoke of feudal absolutism, managed to develop into a bourgeois.
The modern laborer, on the contrary, instead of rising with the progress of
industry, sinks deeper and deeper below the conditions of existence of his
own class. He becomes a pauper, and pauperism develops more rapidly than
population and wealth. And here it becomes evident, that the bourgeoisie is
unfit any longer to be the ruling class in society, and to impose its conditions
of existence upon society as an overriding law. It is unfit to rule because it
is incompetent to assure an existence to its slave within his slavery, because
it cannot help letting him sink into such a state, that it has to feed him,
instead of being fed by him. Society can no longer live under this bourgeoisie,
in other words, its existence is no longer compatible with society.

The essential condition for the existence, and for the sway of the bourgeois
class, is the formation and augmentation of capital; the condition for capital
is wage labor. Wage labor rests exclusively on competition between the
laborers. The advance of industry, whose involuntary promoter is the bour-

geoisie, replaces the isolation of the laborers, due to competition, by their revolutionary combination, due to association. The development of Modern Industry, therefore, cuts from under its feet the very foundation on which the bourgeoisie produces and appropriates products. What the bourgeoisie, therefore, produces, above all, is its own grave-diggers. Its fall and the victory of the proletariat are equally inevitable.

Position of the Communists in relation to the various existing opposition parties. The Communists fight for the attainment of the immediate aims, for the enforcement of the momentary interests of the working class; but in the movement of the present, they also represent and take care of the future of that movement.

In short, the Communists everywhere support every revolutionary movement against the existing social and political order of things.

In these movements they bring to the front, as the leading question in each, the property question, no matter what its degree of development at the time.

Finally, they labor everywhere for the union and agreement of the democratic parties of all countries.

The Communists disdain to conceal their views and aims. They openly declare that their ends can be attained only by the forcible overthrow of all existing social conditions. Let the ruling classes tremble at a Communistic revolution. The proletarians have nothing to lose but their chains. They have a world to win.

Workingmen of all countries, unite!

10. THE RACIAL STATE

ADOLF HITLER

Adolf Hitler (1889–1945) was leader of the Nazi Party and Chancellor of Germany from 1933–1945. The Party Congresses at Nuremberg were the major political gatherings of the Hitler era in Germany.

Role of the Leader. The individual has as little right to question the action of the political leaders as the soldier to question the orders of his military superiors. And just as the Party demands the subjection of the people to its will, so within the Party itself this same subjection must be an immutable law. There is no possibility of release from obedience to this principle. He

Norman H. Baynes, ed., *The Speeches of Adolf Hitler, April 1922–August 1939,* Vol. 1. New York and London: Oxford University Press, 1942. Pp. 447–48 and 464–71. Reprinted by permission of the publisher.

who will not render this complete obedience cannot look for obedience from others. And if from the bourgeoisie we often hear the objections: "Ah, yes, the Leader, but the Party—that is another matter!" I answer: "No! Gentlemen, the Leader is the Party and the Party is the Leader." As I feel myself to be only a part of this Party, so the Party feels itself to be only a part of me. When I shall close my eyes in death I do not know. But that the Party will live on—that I know, and that over all persons, over weakness and strength it will triumph and will successfully fashion the future of the German nation—that I believe, that I know! For the Party guarantees the stability of the leadership of the people and of the Reich, and through its own stability it guarantees that this leadership shall exercise the authority which it needs.

From this sure foundation there will grow up the Constitution of the new German Reich. This Party as *weltanschaulich* moulder and as political guide of the destiny of Germany has to give the Leader to the nation and therefore to the Reich. The more this principle is proclaimed and observed as the natural and uncontested basis of government the stronger will Germany be. The army as representative and the organizer of the military forces of our people must ever maintain the organized military force of the Reich entrusted to it and in loyalty and obedience must place it at the disposal of the Leader who has been given to the Nation by the Party. For after the Proclamation of the new Leader from time to time he becomes the lord (*Herr*) of the Party, the supreme head of the Reich, and the supreme Commander of the Army.

Race and Political Leadership. In order to understand the diseases from which a people suffers, it is first necessary to understand how a people is built up. Almost all of the peoples of the world are composed today of different racial primary elements (*Grundstoffen*). These original elements are each characterized by different capacities. Only in the primitive functions of life can men be considered as precisely like each other. Beyond these primitive functions they immediately begin to be differentiated in their characters, their dispositions, and capacities. The differences between the individual races, both in part externally and, of course, also in their inner natures, can be quite enormous and in fact are so. The gulf between the lowest creature which can still be styled man and our highest races is greater than that between the lowest type of man and the highest ape.

If on this earth there were not some races which today determine its cultural appearance, it would hardly be possible to speak of any such thing as human civilization (*Kultur*). For this neither climate nor education can be regarded as responsible, but only man himself who was endowed by Providence with this capacity.

But if this cultural capacity is fundamentally inherent in certain races, its full effect is realized only under certain favorable circumstances. Man as an individual, whatever powers he may have in himself, will be incapable of higher achievements unless he can place the powers of many in the service of a single idea, a single conception, a single will and can unite them for a single action.

A glance at Nature shows us that creatures belonging to a pure race, not merely corporeally but in character and capacities, are more or less of equal value. This equality is the greatest hindrance in the way of the formation of any community in work (*Arbeitsgemeinschaft*) ; for since every higher civilization receives its stamp through achievements which are possible only through uniting the forces of human labor, it is thus essential that a number of individuals must sacrifice a part of their individual freedom and must subject themselves to a single will. However much reason may counsel such a course, in reality it would be difficult amongst those who are complete equals to demonstrate the reasons why in the last resort one must be in a position to assert his will as against that of the others.

The two concepts—Command and Obedience—however, exercise quite another and more compelling force when folk of different value come into conflict or association with each other, and then through the action of the stronger section are bound together in pursuit of a common purpose.

The most primitive form of association for a common purpose can already be traced at the moment when man forces his supremacy upon the animals, tears them from the freedom of their former life, and builds them into his own life-process without troubling himself whether his animal-helper consents thereto or not.

But long ago man has proceeded in the same way with his fellowman. The higher race—at first "higher" in the sense of possessing a greater gift for organization—subjects to itself a lower race and thus constitutes a relationship which now embraces races of unequal value. Thus there results the subjection of a number of people under the will often of only a few persons, a subjection based simply on the right of the stronger, a right which, as we see it in Nature, can be regarded as the sole conceivable right because founded on reason. The wild mustang does not take upon itself the yoke imposed by man either voluntarily or joyfully; neither does one people welcome the violence of another.

But, despite this, in the course of a long development this compulsion has very often been converted into a blessing for all parties. Thus were formed those communities which created the essential features of human organization through the welding together of different races. And this organization always demands the subjection of the will and the activity of many under the will and the energy of a single individual. As men come to discover the astonishing results of this concentration of their capacity and labor-force they begin to recognize not merely the expediency but also the necessity of such action. And thus it is that a great and significant Aryan civilization did not arise where Aryans alone were living in racial purity, but always where they formed a vital association with races otherwise constituted, an association founded not on mixture of blood but on the basis of an organic community of purpose. And what was at first undoubtedly felt by the conquered as bitter compulsion later became in spite of this even for them a blessing. Unconsciously in the master-people there grew up ever more clearly and vitally a recognition of the ethical demand that their supremacy must be no arbitrary rule but must be controlled by a noble reasonableness. The capacity to subdue others was not given to them by Providence in order to make the subjects feel that the lordship of their conqueror was a meaningless tyranny, a mere oppression: that capacity was given that through the union of the conqueror's genius with the strength of the conquered they might create for both alike an existence which because it was useful was not degrading to man.

However this process of the formation of a people and a State was begun, its beginning signified the close of humanity's communistic age. For Communism is not a higher stage of development: rather it is the most primitive form of life—the starting-point.

Men of completely similar characteristics, men who are precisely like each other and endowed with the same capacities, will be of necessity also alike in their achievement. This condition is realized in the case of peoples who are throughout of one and the same race. Where these conditions are realized, the individual result of the activity of each will correspond only with the general average of all. . . . In this case it can be a question only of quite primitive values, and the condition for any clear definition of the idea of property is lacking because of the absence of any differentiation in achievement which is essential for the rise of such a concept. Equal achievement carries with it the equal division of the results of that achievement. In such a state Communism is therefore a natural and morally comprehensible ordering of society. But when men of very different values have met together, the result of their achievements will also be different; that is to say that the race which stands higher in the scale of quality will contribute more to the sum total of common work than the race which is lower in the qualitative scale. And in particular men's capacities will lie on different levels. The primitive capacity of the one race will from the first produce values other than those more highly developed or otherwise constituted values produced by the other partner in the common life. As a consequence the administration of the labor-product will necessarily lead to a division which proceeds from a consideration of the character of the achievement; in other words: that which has been created will be administered as property on the same basis as that of its origin. The conception of private property is thus inseparably connected with the conviction that the capacities of men are different alike in character and in value and thus, further, that men themselves are different in character and value.

But one cannot in one sphere of life accept this difference in talent—as giving rise to a moral claim on the result produced by this superiority—and then go on to deny that difference in another sphere. That would be to act illogically. . . . One cannot in fact proceed to maintain that all alike have the same capacity for politics, that is, for the most important sphere in the entire conduct of life.

While it is denied that everyone in a nation is capable of administering a court or a factory or of appointing its administration, yet that they are all capable of administering the State or of appointing its administrators is solemnly certified in the name of democracy.

But here is a direct contradiction: either because of equal capacity all men are equally capable of administering a State, and then the maintenance of the concept of property is not only unjust but simply stupid, or men are in truth not in a position to take into their common administration as common property the sum-total of material and cultural treasure which the nation as a whole has created, and then in that case they are far less in a position to govern the State in common. . . . The State does not owe its existence to all but only to a definite section—the section which formerly created the State and which still supports and maintains it. This view is not unjust or hard: it is simply a statement of the truth. . . . The German people arose in no other way than did almost all of the truly creative civilized peoples (*Kulturvolker*) in the world, of which we have any knowledge. A race, though small in numbers yet with capacities for organization and possessing a creative gift in the sphere of culture, in the course of many centuries spread itself over other peoples, absorbing some, adapting itself to others. All the different elements of which our people is composed naturally brought with them into this alliance their special capacities; but the alliance itself was created solely by a single core which fashioned both people and State. This core-people caused its language to prevail, not, of course, without borrowing from its subjects, and in the end it subdued all for such a length of time to a common destiny that the life of the people which controlled the State became indissolubly united with the life of the other parts which were gradually fused into and on to it. Thus in course of time out of the conquerors and the conquered there was long since created a single community. And that community is our German people of today, and as it is today we love it and cling to it. In the course of its thousand years of history all its very varied characteristics, each of them so different from the other, have become familiar and dear. So great is this community of which we all form a part that we rejoice at every contribution which adds to our wealth. We do not ask to what section of our people we owe our several talents and capacities: each section must guard and foster its special gift. For one cannot only infer from the fact of race that certain capacities will be present, one can also start from the capacities and infer the race. That means, for instance, that it is not necessary first to discover musically gifted persons through the fact of their race in order to entrust to them the encouragement of music, but music discloses the race by discovering the capacity.

And just as in all spheres of life we cannot feel any jealousy when those who are specially born thereto, i.e., endowed from the outset, exercise decisive influence, so it is in the sphere of the political safeguarding of that which in the course of the millennia has become for us a people. Just as the unmusical person will not feel himself injured or insulted because not he, but one who is musically gifted, composes music or conducts an orchestra, so in every other sphere the appointment of qualified persons cannot be regarded as a slight by those who have no capacities in that field. And in fact this does not occur; only a conscious perversion could breed such madness.

Starting from the fact that any created thing can be maintained only by the same force which created it, it follows that the body of a people (*Volks-korper*) can be maintained only by those forces which called it into being and which through their capacity for organization welded it together and solidified it. Thus all who love their people and wish for its maintenance must therefore see to it that that part of the people can bring its political capacities into play which formerly were responsible for the political formation and development of this community.

11. THE BUREAUCRATIC STATE

GAETANO MOSCA

Gaetano Mosca (1858–1931) was an Italian political scientist and professor at the Universities of Turin and Rome. He was a member of the Italian Chamber of Deputies from 1908–1918 and was made Senator for life by royal appointment in 1918.

Among the constant facts and tendencies that are to be found in all political organisms, one is so obvious that it is apparent to the most casual eye. In all societies—from societies that are very meagerly developed and have barely attained the dawnings of civilization, down to the most advanced and powerful societies—two classes of people appear—a class that rules and a class that is ruled. The first class, always the less numerous, performs all political functions, monopolizes power and enjoys the advantages that power brings, whereas the second, the more numerous class, is directed and controlled by the first, in a manner that is now more or less legal, now more or less arbitrary, and violent, and supplies the first, in appearance at least, with material means of subsistence and with the instrumentalities that are essential to the vitality of the political organism. . . .

. . . The man who is at the head of the state would certainly not be able to govern without the support of a numerous class to enforce respect for his orders and to have them carried out; and granting that he can make one individual, or indeed many individuals, in the ruling class feel the weight of his power, he certainly cannot be at odds with the class as a whole or do away with it. Even if that were possible, he would at once be forced to create another class, without the support of which action on his part would be completely paralyzed. On the other hand, granting that the discontent of the masses might succeed in deposing a ruling class, inevitably, as we shall later show, there would have to be another organized minority within the masses themselves to discharge the functions of a ruling class. Otherwise all organization, and the whole social structure, would be destroyed. . . .

Everywhere—in Russia and Poland, in India and medieval Europe—the

From *The Ruling Class* by Gaetano Mosca. Copyright 1939, McGraw-Hill Book Company. Translated by Hannah D. Kahn. Edited and revised by Arthur Livingston. Pp. 50–87 and 404–9, excerpts. Reprinted by permission of the publisher.

ruling warrior classes acquire almost exclusive ownership of the land. Land, as we have seen, is the chief source of production and wealth in countries that are not very far advanced in civilization. But as civilization progresses, revenue from land increases proportionately. With the growth of population there is, at least in certain periods, an increase in rent, in the "Ricardian" sense of the term, largely because great centers of consumption arise—such at all times have been the great capitals and other large cities, ancient and modern. Eventually, if other circumstances permit, a very important social transformation occurs. Wealth rather than military valor comes to be the characteristic feature of the dominant class: the people who rule are the rich rather than the brave.

The condition that in the main is required for this transformation is that social organization shall have concentrated and become perfected to such an extent that the protection offered by public authority is considerably more effective than the protection offered by private force. In other words, private property must be so well protected by the practical and real efficacy of the laws as to render the power of the proprietor himself superfluous. This comes about through a series of gradual alternations in the social structure whereby a type of political organization, which we shall call the "feudal," is transformed into an essentially different type, which we shall term the "bureaucratic state." We are to discuss these types at some length hereafter, but we may say at once that the evolution here referred to is as a rule greatly facilitated by progress in pacific manners and customs and by certain moral habits which societies contract as civilization advances.

Once this transformation has taken place, wealth produces political power just as political power has been producing wealth. In a society already somewhat mature—where, therefore, individual power is curbed by the collective power—if the powerful are as a rule the rich, to be rich is to become powerful. And, in truth, when fighting with the mailed fist is prohibited whereas fighting with pounds and pence is sanctioned, the better posts are inevitably won by those who are better supplied with pounds and pence.

There are, to be sure, states of a very high level of civilization which in theory are organized on the basis of moral principles of such a character that they seem to preclude this overbearing assertiveness on the part of wealth. But this is a case—and there are many such—where theoretical principles can have no more than a limited application in real life. In the United States all powers flow directly or indirectly from popular elections, and suffrage is equal for all men and women in all the states of the Union. What is more, democracy prevails not only in institutions but to a certain extent also in morals. The rich ordinarily feel a certain aversion to entering public life, and the poor a certain aversion to choosing the rich for elective office. But that does not prevent a rich man from being more influential than a poor man, since he can use pressure upon the politicians who control public administration. It does not prevent elections from being carried on to the music of clinking dollars. It does not prevent whole legislatures and considerable numbers of national congressmen from feeling the influence of powerful corporations and great financiers.

In China, too, down to a few years ago, though the government had not accepted the principle of popular elections, it was organized on an essentially equalitarian basis. Academic degrees gave access to public office, and degrees were conferred by examination without any apparent regard for family or wealth. According to some writers, only barbers and certain classes of boatmen, together with their children, were barred from competing for the various grades of the mandarinate. But though the moneyed class in China was less numerous, less wealthy, less powerful than the moneyed class in the United States is at present, it was none the less able to modify the scrupulous application of this system to a very considerable extent. Not only was the indulgence of examiners often bought with money. The government itself sometimes sold the various academic degrees and allowed ignorant persons, often from the lowest social strata, to hold public office.

In all countries of the world those other agencies for exerting social influence—personal publicity, good education, specialized training, high rank in church, public administration, and army—are always readier of access to the rich than to the poor. The rich invariably have a considerably shorter road to travel than the poor, to say nothing of the fact that the stretch of road that the rich are spared is often the roughest and most difficult. . . .

. . . All ruling classes tend to become hereditary in fact if not in law. All political forces seem to possess a quality that in physics used to be called the force of inertia. They have a tendency, that is, to remain at the point and in the state in which they find themselves. Wealth and military valor are easily maintained in certain families by moral tradition and by heredity. Qualification for important office—the habit of, and to an extent the capacity for, dealing with affairs of consequence—is much more readily acquired when one has had a certain familiarity with them from childhood. Even when academic degrees, scientific training, special aptitudes as tested by examinations and competitions, open the way to public office, there is no eliminating the special advantage in favor of certain individuals which the French call the advantage of *positions déjà prises*. In actual fact, though examinations and competitions may theoretically be open to all, the majority never have the resources for meeting the expense of long preparation, and many others are without the connections and kinships that set an individual promptly on the right road, enabling him to avoid the gropings and blunders that are inevitable when one enters an unfamiliar environment without any guidance or support.

The democratic principle of election by broad-based suffrage would seem at first glance to be in conflict with the tendency toward stability which, according to our theory, ruling classes show. But it must be noted that candidates who are successful in democratic elections are almost always the ones who possess the political forces above enumerated, which are very often hereditary. In the English, French, and Italian parliaments we frequently see the sons, grandsons, brothers, nephews, and sons-in-laws of members and deputies, ex-members and ex-deputies.

In the second place, when we see a hereditary caste established in a country and monopolizing political power, we may be sure that such a status *de jure* was preceded by a similar status *de facto*. Before proclaiming their exclusive and hereditary right to power the families or castes in question must have held the scepter of command in a firm grasp, completely monopolizing all the political forces of that country at that period. Otherwise such a claim on their part would only have aroused the bitterest protests and provoked the bitterest struggles. . . .

Before we proceed any further, it might be wise to linger briefly on the two types into which, in our opinion, all political organisms may be classified, the feudal and the bureaucratic.

This classification, it should be noted, is not based upon essentially unchanging criteria. It is not our view that there is any psychological law peculiar to either one of the two types and therefore alien to the other. It seems to us, rather, that the two types are just different manifestations, different phases, of a single constant tendency whereby human societies become less simple, or, if one will, more complicated in political organization, as they grow in size and are perfected in civilization. Level of civilization is, on the whole, more important in this regard than size, since, in actual fact, a literally huge state may once have been feudally organized. At bottom, therefore, a bureaucratic state is just a feudal state that has advanced and developed in organization and so grown more complex; and a feudal state may derive from a once bureaucratized society that has decayed in civilization and reverted to a simpler, more primitive form of political organization, perhaps falling to pieces in the process.

By "feudal state" we mean that type of political organization in which all the executive functions of society—the economic, the judicial, the administrative, the military—are exercised simultaneously by the same individuals, while at the same time the state is made up of small social aggregates, each of which possesses all the organs that are required for self-sufficiency. The Europe of the Middle Ages offers the most familiar example of this type of organization—that is why we have chosen to designate it by the term "feudal"; but as one reads the histories of other peoples or scans the accounts of travelers of our own day one readily perceives that the type is widespread. Just as the medieval baron was simultaneously owner of the land, military commander, judge and administrator of his fief, over which he enjoyed both a pure and a mixed sovereignty, so the Abyssinian *ras* dispensed justice, commanded the soldiery and levied taxes—or rather extorted from the farmer everything over and above the bare necessaries of subsistence. . . .

In the bureaucratic state not all the executive functions need to be concentrated in the bureaucracy and exercised by it. One might even declare that so far in history that has never been the case. The main characteristic of this type of social organization lies, we believe, in the fact that, wherever it exists, the central power conscripts a considerable portion of the social wealth by taxation and uses it first to maintain a military establishment and then to support a more or less extensive number of public services. The greater the number of officials who perform public duties and receive their salaries from the central government or from its local agencies, the more bureaucratic a society becomes.

In a bureaucratic state there is always a greater specialization in the functions of government than in a feudal state. The first and most elementary division of capacities is the withdrawal of administrative and judiciary powers from the military element. The bureaucratic state, furthermore, assures a far greater discipline in all grades of political, administrative and military service. To gain some conception of what this means, one has only to compare a medieval count, hedged about by armed retainers and by vassals who have been attached for centuries to his family and supported by the produce of his lands, with a modern French or Italian prefect or army general, whom a telegram can suddenly shear of authority and even of stipend. The feudal state, therefore, demands great energy and a great sense of statesmanship in the man, or men, who stand on the top rung of the social ladder, if the various social groups, which would otherwise tend to disorganization and autonomy, are to be kept organized, compact and obedient to a single impulse. So true is this that often with death of an influential leader the power of a feudal state itself comes to an end. . . . On the other hand, the personal qualities of the supreme head exert relatively little influence on the destinies of a bureaucratic state. A society that is bureaucratically organized may retain its freedom even if it repudiates an old political formula and adopts a new one, or even if it subjects its social type to very far-reaching modifications. This was the case with the Roman Empire. It survived the adoption of Christianity in the West for a century and a half, and in the East for more than eleven centuries. So our modern nations have nearly all shifted at one time or another from a divine-right formula to parliamentary systems of government.

Bureaucratic organization need not necessarily be centralized, in the sense commonly given to that expression. Often bureaucratization is compatible with a very liberal provincial autonomy, as in China, where the eighteen strictly Chinese provinces preserved broad autonomous privileges and the capital city of each province looked after almost all provincial affairs.

States of European civilization—even the most decentralized of them—are all bureaucratized. As we have already indicated, the chief characteristic of a bureaucratic organization is that its military functions, and other public services in numbers more or less large, are exercised by salaried employees. Whether salaries are paid exclusively by the central government or in part by local bodies more or less under the control of the central government is a detail that is not as important as it is often supposed to be. History is not lacking in cases of very small political organisms which have accomplished miracles of energy in every branch of human activity with the barest rudiments of bureaucratic organization or with practically none at all. The ancient Hellenic cities and the Italian communes of the Middle Ages are examples that flock to mind. But when vast human organisms, spreading over huge territories and comprising millions and millions of individuals, are involved, nothing short of bureaucratic organization seems capable of uniting under a single impulse the immense treasures of economic power and moral and intellectual energy with which a ruling class can in a measure modify conditions within a society and make its influence effective and powerful beyond its own frontiers. Under a feudal organization the authority which a given member of the ruling class exerts over individuals of the subject class, few or many, may be more direct, oppressive, and arbitrary. Under a bureaucratic organization society is influenced less by the given individual leader than by the ruling class as a whole. . . .

The Roman Empire was a highly bureaucratized state, and its sound social organism was able to spread Greco-Roman civilization and the language of Italy over large portions of the ancient world, accomplishing a most difficult task of social assimilation. Another bureaucracy was czarist Russia, which, despite a number of serious internal weaknesses, had great vitality and carried its expansion deep into the remote fastnesses of Asia.

In spite of these examples, and not a few others that might readily occur to one, we should not forget a very important fact to which we have already alluded: namely, the history shows no instance of a great society in which all human activities have been completely bureaucratized. This, perhaps, is one of the many indications of the great complexity of social laws, for a type of political organization may produce good results when applied up to a certain point, but become impracticable and harmful when it is generalized and systematized. Justice is quite generally bureaucratized, and so is public administration. Napoleon I, great bureaucratizer that he was, succeeded in bureaucratizing education and even the Catholic priesthood. We often see bureaucracies building roads, canals, railways and all sorts of public works that facilitate the production of wealth. But production itself we never see entirely bureaucratized. It would seem as though that very important branch of social activity, like so many other branches, lends itself ill to bureaucratized regulation, individual profit being a far more effective spur to the classes engaged in production than any government salary could be.

What is more, we have fairly strong evidence that the extension of bureaucratic control to the production and distribution of wealth as a whole would be fatal. We are not thinking here of the economic evils of protectionism, of governmental control of banking and finance, of the overdevelopment of public works. We are merely pointing to a well-established fact. In a bureaucratic system both the manager of economic production and the individual worker are protected against arbitrary confiscations on the part of the strong and powerful, and all private warfare is sternly suppressed. Human life and property are therefore relatively secure. Under a bureaucratic regime, the producer pays over a fixed quota to the social organization and secures tranquil enjoyment of the rest of his product. This permits an accretion of wealth, public and private, that is unknown to barbarous or primitively organized countries. But the amount of wealth that is absorbed and consumed by the class that fulfills other than economic functions may become too great, either because the demands of the military class, and of other bureaucrats, are excessive, or because the bureaucracy tries to perform too many services, or because of wars and the debts that result from wars. Under these circumstances the taxes that are levied upon the wealth-producing classes become so heavy that the profit that an individual can earn in the field of production is markedly reduced. In that event production itself inevitably falls off. As wealth declines, emigration and higher death rates thin out the poorer classes, and finally the exhaustion of the entire social body ensues. These phenomena are observable whenever a bureaucratic state declines. . . .

Below the highest stratum in the ruling class there is always, even in autocratic systems, another that is much more numerous and comprises all the capacities for leadership in the country. Without such a class any sort of social organization would be impossible. The higher stratum would not in itself be sufficient for leading and directing the activities of the masses. In the last analysis, therefore, the stability of any political organism depends on the level of morality, intelligence and activity that this second stratum has attained; and this soundness is commonly the greater in proportion as a sense of the collective interests of nation or class succeeds in exerting pressure on the individual ambitions or greeds of the members of this class. Any intellectual or moral deficiencies in this second stratum, accordingly, represent a graver danger to the political structure, and one that is harder to repair, than the presence of similar deficiencies in the few dozen persons who control the workings of the state machine. To use a comparison: The strength of any army depends primarily on the intellectual and moral value of the officers who come into direct contact with the soldiers, beginning with the colonel and ending with the second lieutenant. If, by some improbable accident, all the generals and staff officers of an army were to disappear at one stroke, the army would sustain a very serious shock, but it would still be on its feet and the lost leaders could be replaced in a few months' time by promoting the better regimental commanders and raising other officers, from among the more competent, to the staff. But if all the officers who actually lead the soldiers were to disappear the army would dissolve before they could possibly be replaced. The higher stratum in the ruling class corresponds to the generals and staff, the second stratum to the officers who personally lead the soldiers under fire.

In primitive autocratic systems, and in the more ancient ones in general, this second stratum in the ruling class was almost always made up of priests and warriors, the two groups of persons who had the material forces of the society at their disposal, exercised intellectual and moral leadership and, as consequence rather than as cause of that leadership, were economically preeminent. Under social conditions of that sort, it was natural that autocracy in government should be combined with a prevalence of the aristocratic tendency. But as time goes on, in countries where class differentiation rests originally on invasions by foreign peoples, the conquering and conquered races fuse completely. The level of civilization rises. Wealth and culture therefore increase, and technical preparation becomes necessary for the satisfactory performance of public duties. Aristocratic autocracies therefore almost always develop into more or less bureaucratic autocracies. That was the case with the Roman Empire, especially after Diocletian, with the Byzantine Empire, with the Chinese Empire, at least during the last centuries of its existence, with Russia after Peter the Great, with the principal European states in the eighteenth century and, with certain reservations, with Japan after the creation of the Tokugawa shogunate. . . .

Before an autocracy can begin to bureaucratize a great state, the political organization must be so strong that it can regularly levy on the income of private individuals a portion that is large enough to pay the salaries of public officials and defray the expenses of a permanent armed force. But then, as is often the case with social phenomena, a series of actions and reactions follow. Once bureaucratization is well advanced, it in turn enhances the coercive efficiency of the state machine and so enables the ruling class, and especially the leading group in it, to exercise greater and greater influence over the governed masses and to direct the efforts of the governed more and more efficiently toward the purposes that their governors wish to achieve. In other words, a bureaucratized autocracy is a perfected autocracy and it has all the advantages and disadvantages of that perfection.

Among the advantages, one may mention the possibility of assigning the various functions of leadership to specialists and the possibility of opening all doors to talents that are forging upward from the lower strata in society, and therefore of making room for personal merit. So homage is paid to a principle of distributive justice that has always had a grip on the hearts of men and is especially cogent in our time, a feeling that there should be an exact and almost mathematical correspondence between the service an individual renders to society and the position which he comes to hold in the social ranking.

But, as Ferrero well notes, personal merit is one of the things that the passions and interests of men best manage to counterfeit. In autocratic systems, where success depends upon the judgment of one person, or of a few persons, intrigue may be enough to produce the counterfeit semblance of personal merit. In liberal systems, especially when the democratic tendency is also prevalent and the regard and active sympathy of many people are necessary if one is to get on in the world, intrigue has to be coupled with a good dose of charlatanry. At any rate, quite aside from such a prejudicial and, if one will, such an overpessimistic objection, it is certain that the judgment of a person's merits and aptitudes will always be more or less subjective, and that, therefore, each judge will in all good faith give a candidate a higher rating for intellectual and moral qualities which he likes or happens to possess himself. That is one of the chief reasons for the blind conservatism, the utter incapacity to correct one's faults and weaknesses, that is so frequent in exclusively bureaucratic regimes.

The example of China is apt to this point. In China the higher mandarinate was made up of educated persons, but they were educated in the old traditional culture of the country. In the second half of the nineteenth century the mandarinate strenuously opposed a new method of recruiting public employees based on knowledge of European languages and European sciences. In Japan, on the other hand, the men who led the great reform of 1868 grasped the necessity of acquiring European culture at once. These men came almost all from the samurai class. They were educated people, but they were not scholars and scientists by profession.

To avoid distortions in judgments on merit, it is not enough that the higher officials on whom the choice and advancement of the lower functionaries depend should be individuals of great intelligence. They have to be generous and noble of heart. Sometimes the person who is endowed with the rarest and loftiest qualities of mind prefers people of mediocre or second-rate talents. They give him less cause for jealousy and they better supplement his own capacities, for the mediocre man does things that the first-rate one cannot do, or scorns to do. Furthermore, the mediocre man is almost always flattering and smooth: he is without, or at least is better able to dissimulate, a certain youthful cocksureness frequently encountered in men of green age and lively talents—a sort of presumptuousness, real or apparent, other men, even old and experienced ones, either do not see at all or see very tardily.

Suppose, then, that in our distrust of human impartiality we try to replace choice and appointment by superiors with automatic rules of advancement. Such rules can be based only upon the principle of seniority. In this case, unfailingly, the lazy and the diligent, the intelligent and the stupid, get along equally well. The public employee knows perfectly well that it will not help him to do any more or any better than others. He will therefore do the minimum that is indispensable if he is not to lose his position or his promotion. In such circumstances the bureaucratic career tends to become the refuge of the talentless, or of people who absolutely need to have salaried positions in order to provide for their daily wants. If an intelligent man does happen to stray into the bureaucracy, he devotes only a part of his activity and his talent to his office, and often it is not the best part.

Though a bureaucracy may be legally open to all social classes, in fact it will always be recruited from the middle class, in other words from the second stratum of the ruling class. For one thing, those who are born into the second stratum find it easier to secure the education that is required of them, and in their family background they develop a practical sense of the best ways of getting started in the bureaucratic career and of advancing it. How helpful the guidance and influence of a father, of an influential relative or of family friends can be, one can easily imagine. For this reason it can in general be said that in a purely autocratic system, or in systems that combine autocracy and liberalism, the moral level of the bureaucracy is the moral level of the ruling class. That level will be higher when the ruling class has deep-rooted traditions of probity and honor because it has been formed and disciplined over long periods of time, and has devoted itself for many generations to the service of the state, now in civil, now in military capacities. The level will be lower when the ruling class is of more recent date and stems either from rustling, bustling and lucky adventurers, or from families of peasants and shopkeepers who have acquired, at best, the first rudiments of manners and education. Even if such people have developed a certain competence, they are still often without a spark of idealism and retain an inveterate and sordid greed for large, and even for petty, gains.

In cases such as these bureaucratic organization yields its worst results. One notes brazen favoritism in superiors, base servility in subalterns and, in superiors and subalterns both, a tendency to exchange for favors of any sort such influence as their positions put at their disposal. In the more serious cases, bargaining turns into outright sale, and then we get a system of pecuniary corruption which disrupts and paralyzes every state activity once it has become common in the higher and lower grades of the bureaucratic scale.

Another defect common to bureaucracies, even when their moral level is high, is a disposition to believe in their own infallibility. Bureaucrats are by nature exceedingly loath to accept criticisms and suggestion from persons who are not of their calling, and even from those who are.

12. THE IDEALLY BEST POLITY

JOHN STUART MILL

John Stuart Mill (1806–1873) was an English political economist and philosopher. He led the trend in liberal thought from the extreme individualism of the Utilitarians toward greater governmental action.

It has long (perhaps throughout the entire duration of British freedom) been a common form of speech, that if a good despot could be insured, despotic monarchy would be the best form of government. I look upon this as a radical and most pernicious misconception of what good government is, which, until it can be got rid of, will fatally vitiate all our speculations on government.

The supposition is, that absolute power, in the hands of an eminent individual, would insure a virtuous and intelligent performance of all the duties of government.

So extraordinary are the faculties and energies required for performing this task in any supportable manner, that the good despot whom we are supposing can hardly be imagined as consenting to undertake it unless as a refuge from intolerable evils, and a transitional preparation for something beyond. But the argument can do without even this immense item in the account. Suppose the difficulty vanquished. What should we then have? One man of super-human mental activity managing the entire affairs of a mentally passive people. Their passivity is implied in the very idea of absolute power. The nation as a whole, and every individual composing it, are without any potential voice in their own destiny. They exercise no will in respect to their collective interests. All is decided for them by a will not their own, which it is legally a crime for them to disobey. What sort of human beings can be formed under such a regimen? What development can either their thinking or their active faculties attain under it? On matters of pure theory they might perhaps be allowed to speculate, so long as their speculations either did not approach politics, or had not the remotest connection with its practice. On

From John Stuart Mill, *Considerations on Representative Government*. New York: Henry Holt & Company, 1882. Pp. 55–80, excerpts. Reprinted by permission of Holt, Rinehart & Winston, Inc.

practical affairs they could at most be only suffered to suggest; and even under the most moderate of despots, none but persons of already admitted or reputed superiority could hope that their suggestions would be known to, much less regarded by, those who had the management of affairs. A person must have a very unusual taste for intellectual exercise in and for itself who will put himself to the trouble of thought when it is to have no outward effect, or qualify himself for functions which he has no chance of being allowed to exercise. The only sufficient incitement to mental exertion, in any but a few minds in a generation, is the prospect of some practical use to be made of its results.

It does not follow that the nation will be wholly destitute of intellectual power. The common business of life, which must necessarily be performed by each individual or family for themselves, will call forth some amount of intelligence and practical ability within a certain narrow range of ideas. There may be a select class of savants who cultivate science with a view to its physical uses or for the pleasure of the pursuit. There will be a bureaucracy, and persons in training for the bureaucracy, who will be taught at least some empirical maxims of government and public administration. There may be, and often has been a systematic organization of the best mental power in the country in some special direction (commonly military) to promote the grandeur of the despot. But the public at large remain without information and without interest on all the greater matters of practice; or, if they have any knowledge of them, it is but a dilettante knowledge, like that which people have of the mechanical arts who have never handled a tool.

Nor is it only in their intelligence that they suffer. Their moral capacities are equally stunted. Wherever the sphere of action of human beings is artificially circumscribed, their sentiments are narrowed and dwarfed in the same proportion. The food of feeling is action; even domestic affection lives upon voluntary good offices. Let a person have nothing to do for his country, and he will not care for it. It has been said of old that in a despotism there is at most but one patriot, the despot himself; and the saying rests on a just appreciation of the affects of absolute subjection even to a good and wise master.

Religion remains; and here, at least, it may be thought, is an agency that may be relied on for lifting men's eyes and minds above the dust at their feet. But religion, even supposing it to escape perversion for the purposes of despotism, ceases in these circumstances to be a social concern, and narrows into a personal affair between an individual and his Maker, in which the issue at stake is but his private salvation. Religion in this shape is quite consistent with the most selfish and contracted egoism, and identifies the votary as little in feeling with the rest of his kind as sensuality itself.

It is not much to be wondered at if impatient or disappointed reformers, groaning under the impediments opposed to the most salutary public improvements by the ignorance, the indifference, the untractableness, the perverse obstinacy of a people, and the corrupt combinations of selfish private interests, armed with the powerful weapons afforded by free institutions, should at times sigh for a strong hand to bear down all these obstacles, and compel a recalcitrant people to be better governed. But (setting aside the fact that for one despot who now and then reforms an abuse, there are ninety-nine who do nothing but create them) those who look in any direction for the realization of their hopes leave out of the idea of good government its principal element, the improvement of the people themselves. One of the benefits of freedom is that under it the ruler can not pass by the people's minds, and amend their affairs for them without amending them. If it were possible for a people to be well governed in spite of themselves, their good government would last no longer than the freedom of a people usually lasts who have been liberated by foreign arms without their cooperation. It is true, a despot may educate the people, and to do so really would be the best apology for his despotism. But any education which aims at making human beings other than machines, in the long run makes them claim to have the control of their own actions. The leaders of French philosophy in the eighteenth century had been educated by the Jesuits. Even Jesuit education, it seems, was sufficiently real to call forth the appetite for freedom. Whatever invigorates the faculties, in however small a measure, creates an increased desire for their more unimpeded exercise; and a popular education is a failure if it educates the people for any state but that which it will certainly induce them to desire, and most probably to demand.

I am far from condemning, in cases of extreme exigency, the assumption of absolute power in the form of a temporary dictatorship. Free nations have, in times of old, conferred such power by their own choice, as a necessary medicine for diseases of the body politic which could not be got rid of by less violent means. But its acceptance, even for a time strictly limited, can only be excused, if, like Solon or Pittacus, the dictator employs the whole power he assumes in removing the obstacles which debar the nation from the enjoyment of freedom. A good despotism is an altogether false ideal, which practically (except as a means to some temporary purpose) becomes the most senseless and dangerous of chimeras. Evil for evil, a good despotism, in a country at all advanced in civilization, is more noxious than a bad one, for it is far more relaxing and enervating to the thoughts, feelings, and energies of the people. The despotism of Augustus prepared the Romans for Tiberius. If the whole tone of their character had not first been prostrated by nearly two generations of that mild slavery, they would probably have had spirit enough left to rebel against the more odious one.

There is no difficulty in showing that the ideally best form of government is that in which the sovereignty, or supreme controlling power in the last resort, is vested in the entire aggregate of the community, every citizen not only having a voice in the exercise of that ultimate sovereignty, but being, at least occasionally, called on to take an actual part in the government by the personal discharge of some public function, local or general.

Its superiority in reference to present well-being rests upon two principles, of as universal truth and applicability as any general propositions which can be laid down respecting human affairs. The first is, that the rights and interests of every or any person are only secure from being disregarded when the person interested is himself able, and habitually disposed to stand up for them. The second is, that the general prosperity attains a greater height, and is more widely diffused, in proportion to the amount and variety of the personal energies enlisted in promoting it.

Putting these two propositions into a shape more special to their present application—human beings are only secure from evil at the hands of others in proportion as they have the power of being, and are self-protecting; and they only achieve a high degree of success in their struggle with Nature in proportion as they are self-dependent, relying on what they themselves can do, either separately or in concert, rather than on what others do for them.

The former proposition—that each is the only safe guardian of his own rights and interests—is one of those elementary maxims of prudence which every person capable of conducting his own affairs implicitly acts upon wherever he himself is interested.

If we now pass to the influence of the form of government upon character, we shall find the superiority of popular government over every other to be, if possible, still more decided and indisputable.

This question really depends upon a still more fundamental one, viz., which of two common types of character, for the general good of humanity, it is most desirable should predominate—the active or the passive type; that which struggles against evils, or that which endures them; that which bends to circumstances, or that which endeavors to bend circumstances to itself.

The commonplaces of moralists and the general sympathies of mankind are in favor of the passive type. Energetic characters may be admired, but the acquiescent and submissive are those which most men personally prefer. The passiveness of our neighbors increases our own sense of security, and plays into the hands of our willfulness. Passive characters, if we do not happen to need their activity, seem an obstruction to less in our own path. A contented character is not a dangerous rival. Yet nothing is more certain than that improvement in human affairs is wholly the work of the uncontented characters; and, moreover, that it is much easier for an active mind to acquire the virtues of patience, than for a passive one to assume those of energy.

Of the three varieties of mental excellence, intellectual, practical, and moral, there never could be any doubt, in regard to the first two, which side had the advantage.

But, on the point of moral preferability, there seems at first sight to be room for doubt. Contentment is always counted among the moral virtues. But it is a complete error to suppose that contentment is necessarily or naturally attendant on passivity of character; and unless it is, the moral consequences are mischievous. Where there exists a desire for advantages not possessed, the mind which does not potentially possess them by means of its own energies is apt to look with hatred and malice on those who do. The person bestirring himself with hopeful prospects to improve his circumstances is the one who feels goodwill toward others engaged in, or who have succeeded in the same pursuit. And where the majority are so engaged, those who do not attain the object have had the tone given to their feelings by the general habit of the country, and ascribe their failure to want of effort or opportunity, or to their personal ill luck. But those who, while desiring what others possess, put no energy into striving for it, are either incessantly grumbling that fortune does not do for them what they do not attempt to do for themselves, or overflowing with envy and ill will toward those who possess what they would like to have.

Now there can be no kind of doubt that the passive type of character is favored by the government of one or a few, and the active self-helping type by that of the many. Irresponsible rulers need the quiescence of the ruled more than they need any activity but that which they can compel. Submissiveness to the prescriptions of men as necessities of nature is the lesson inculcated by all governments upon those who are wholly without participation in them. The will of superiors, and the law as the will of superiors, must be passively yielded to. But no men are mere instruments or materials in the hands of their rulers who have will, or spirit, or a spring of internal activity in the rest of their proceedings, and any manifestation of these qualities, instead of receiving encouragement from despots, has to get itself forgiven by them.

The maximum of the invigorating effect of freedom upon the character is only obtained when the person acted on either is, or is looking forward to become, a citizen as full privileged as any other. What is still more important than even this matter of feeling is the practical discipline which the character obtains from the occasional demand made upon the citizens to exercise, for a time and in their turn, some social function. It is not sufficiently considered how little there is in most men's ordinary life to give any largeness either to their conceptions or to their sentiments. Their work is a routine; not a labor of love, but of self-interest in the most elementary form, the satisfaction of daily wants; neither the thing done, nor the process of doing it, introduces the mind to thoughts or feelings extending beyond individuals; if instructive books are within their reach, there is no stimulus to read them; and, in most cases, the individual has no access to any person of cultivation much superior to his own. Giving him something to do for the public supplies, in a measure, all these deficiencies. If circumstances allow the amount of public duty assigned him to be considerable, it makes him an educated man.

Still more salutary is the moral part of the instruction afforded by the participation of the private citizen, if even rarely, in public functions. He is called upon, while so engaged, to weigh interests not his own; to be guided, in case of conflicting claims, by another rule than his private partialities; to apply, at every turn, principles and maxims which have for their reason of existence the general good; and he usually finds associated with him in the same work minds more familiarized than his own with these ideas and operations, whose study it will be to supply reasons to his understanding, and stimulation to his feeling for the general good. He is made to feel himself one of the public, and whatever is their interest to be his interest. Where this school of public spirit does not exist, scarcely any sense is entertained that private persons, in no eminent social situation, owe any duties to society except to obey the laws and submit to the government. There is no unselfish sentiment of identification with the public. Every thought and feeling, either of interest or of duty, is absorbed in the individual and in the family. The man never thinks of any collective interest, of any objects to be pursued jointly with others, but only in competition with them, and in some measure at their expense. A neighbor, not being an ally or an associate, since he is never engaged in any common undertaking for the joint benefit, is therefore only a rival. Thus even private morality suffers, while public is actually extinct. Were this the universal and only possible state of things, the utmost aspirations of the lawgiver or the moralist could only stretch to making the bulk of the community a flock of sheep innocently nibbling the grass side by side.

From these accumulated considerations, it is evident that the only government which can fully satisfy all the exigencies of the social state is one in which the whole people participate; that any participation, even in the smallest public function, is useful; that the participation should everywhere be as great as the general degree of improvement of the community will allow; and that nothing less can be ultimately desirable than the admission of all to a share in the sovereign power of the state. But since all can not, in a community exceeding a single small town, participate personally in any way but some very minor portions of the public business, it follows that the ideal type of a perfect government must be representative.

13. THE DERANGEMENT OF THE DEMOCRATIC STATE

WALTER LIPPMANN

Walter Lippmann (1889–   ) is an American journalist and author of many books and articles dealing with public affairs, particularly in the field of foreign policy. He published ESSAYS IN THE PUBLIC PHILOSOPHY *in 1955.*

Internal Revolution in the Democracies. A vigorous critic of democracy, Sir Henry Maine, writing in 1884 just as England was about to adopt general manhood suffrage, observed that "there could be no grosser mistake" than the impression that "Democracy differs from Monarchy in essence." For "the tests of success in the performance of the necessary and natural duties of a government are precisely the same in both cases." These natural and necessary duties have to do with the defense and advancement of the vital interests of the state and with its order, security, and solvency at home.

From Walter Lippmann, *Essays in the Public Philosophy.* Boston: Little, Brown & Company, 1955. Reprinted by permission of Little, Brown & Company and the *Atlantic.* Pp. 8–15 and 54–56, excerpts.

Invariably these duties call for hard decisions. They are hard because the governors of the state must tax, conscript, command, prohibit; they must assert a public interest against private inclination and against what is easy and popular. If they are to do their duty, they must often swim against the tides of private feeling.

The hardness of governing was little realized in the early 1900's. For more than half a century, while democracy was making its historic advance, there had been a remarkable interlude during which the governments rarely had to make hard decisions. . . . Life was secure, liberty was assured, and the way was open to the pursuit of private happiness.

In this long peace, the liberals became habituated to the notion that in a free and progressive society it is a good thing that the government should be weak. For several generations the West had flourished under governments that did not have to prove their strength by making the hard decisions. It had been possible to dream, without being rudely awakened, that in the rivalry of the diverse interests all would somehow come out for the best. The government could normally be neutral and for the most part it could avoid making positive judgments of good and bad and of right and wrong. The public interest could be equaled with that which was revealed in election returns, in sales reports, balance sheets, circulation figures, and statistics of expansion. As long as peace could be taken for granted, the public good could be thought of as being immanent in the aggregate of private transactions. There was no need for a governing power which transcended the particular interests and kept them in order by ruling over them.

All this was only, as we know, a daydream during a brief spell of exceptionally fine weather. The dream ended with the outbreak of the First World War. Then we knew that the Age of Progress had not reformed the human condition of diversity and conflict; it had not mitigated the violence of the struggle for survival and domination. . . .

The strain of the war worked up a menacing popular pressure upon the weak governments. We can, I think, point to 1917 as the year when the pressure became so strong that the institutional framework of the established governments broke under it.

. . . In western Europe and in North America the breakthrough took the form—if I may use the term—of a deep and pervasive infiltration. Behind the façade, which was little changed, the old structure of executive government with the consent of a representative assembly was dismantled—not everywhere and not in all fields, but where it mattered the most—in the making of high policy for war and peace.

The existing governments had exhausted their imperium—their authority to bind and their power to command. With their traditional means they were no longer able to carry on the hyperbolic war; yet they were unable to negotiate peace. They had, therefore, to turn to the people. They had to ask still greater exertions and sacrifices. They obtained them by "democratizing" the conduct and the aims of the war: by pursuing total victory and by promising total peace.

In substance they ceded the executive power of decision over the strategical and the political conditions for concluding the war. In effect they lost control of the war. This revolution appeared to be a cession of power to the representative assemblies, and when it happened it was acclaimed as promising the end of the evils of secret diplomacy and the undemocratic conduct of unpopular wars. In fact, the powers which were ceded by the executive passed through the assemblies, which could not exercise them, to the mass of voters who, though unable also to exercise them, passed them on to the party bosses, the agents of pressure groups, and the magnates of the new media of mass communications.

The consequences were disastrous and revolutionary. The democracies became incapacitated to wage war for rational ends and to make a peace which would be observed or could be enforced.

The Paralysis of Governments. Perhaps, before going any further, I should say that I am a liberal democrat and have no wish to disenfranchise my fellow citizens. My hope is that both liberty and democracy can be preserved before the one destroys the other. Whether this can be done is the question of our time, what with more than half the world denying and despairing of it. Of one thing we may be sure. If it is to be done at all, we must be uninhibited in our examination of our condition. And since our condition is manifestly connected with grave errors in war and peace that have been committed by democratic governments, we must adopt the habit of thinking as plainly about the sovereign people as we do about the politicians they elect. It will not do to think poorly of the politicians and to talk with bated breath about the voters. No more than the kings before them should the people be hedged with divinity. Like all princes and rulers, like all sovereigns, they are ill-served by flattery and adulation. And they are betrayed by the servile hypocrisy which tells them that what is true and what is false, what is right and what is wrong, can be determined by their votes.

If I am right in what I have been saying, there has developed in this century a functional derangement of the relationship between the mass of the people and the government. The people have acquired power which they are incapable of exercising, and the governments they elect have lost powers which they must recover if they are to govern. What then are the true boundaries of the people's power? The answer cannot be simple. But for a rough beginning let us say that the people are able to give and to withhold their consent to being governed—their consent to what the government asks of them, proposes to them, and has done in the conduct of their affairs. They can elect the government. They remove it. They can approve or disapprove its performance. But they cannot administer the government. They cannot themselves perform. They cannot normally initiate and propose the necessary legislation. A mass cannot govern. The people, as Jefferson said, are not "qualified to exercise themselves the Executive Department; but they are qualified to name the person who shall exercise it. . . . They are not qualified to legislate; with us therefore they only choose the legislators."

Where mass opinion dominates the government, there is a morbid derangement of the true functions of power. The derangement brings about the enfeeblement, verging on paralysis, of the capacity to govern. This breakdown in the constitutional order is the cause of the precipitate and catastrophic decline of Western society. It may, if it cannot be arrested and reversed, bring about the fall of the West.

The Enfeebled Executive. In the effort to understand the malady of democratic government I have dwelt upon the underlying duality of functions; governing, that is, the administration of the laws and the initiative in legislating, and representing the living persons who are governed, who must pay, who must work, who must fight and, it may be, die for the acts of the government. I attribute the democratic disaster of the twentieth century to a derangement of these primary functions.

The power of the executive has become enfeebled, often to the verge of impotence, by the pressures of the representative assembly and of mass opinions. This derangement of the government power has forced the democratic states to commit disastrous and, it could be, fatal mistakes. It has also transformed the assemblies in most, perhaps not in all, democratic states from the defenders of local and personal rights into boss-ridden oligarchies, threatening the security, the solvency, and the liberties of the state.

In the traditions of Western society, civilized government is founded on the assumption that the two powers exercising the two functions will be in balance—that they will check, restrain, compensate, complement, inform, and vitalize each one the other.

In this century, the balance of the two powers has been seriously upset. Two great streams of evolution have converged upon the modern democracies to devitalize, to enfeeble, and to eviscerate the executive powers. One is the enormous expansion of public expenditure, chiefly for war and reconstruction; this has augmented the power of the assemblies which vote the appropriations on which the executive depends. The other development which has acted to enfeeble the executive power is the growing incapacity of the large majority of the democratic peoples to believe in intangible realities. This has stripped the government of that imponderable authority which is derived from tradition, immemorial usage, consecration, veneration, prescription, prestige, heredity, hierarchy. . . .

Under the stress and the strain of the great wars of the twentieth century, the executive power has become elaborately dependent upon the assemblies for its enormous expenditures of man and money. The executive has, at the same time, been deprived of very nearly all of his imponderable power: fearing the action of the representative assembly, he is under great temptation to outwit it or bypass it, as did Franklin D. Roosevelt in the period of the Second World War. It is significant, I think, certainly it is at least suggestive, that while nearly all the Western governments have been in deep trouble since the First World War, the constitutional monarchies of Scandinavia, the Low Countries, and the United Kingdom have shown greater capacity to endure, to preserve order with freedom, than the republics of France, Germany, Spain, and Italy. In some measure that may be because in a republic the governing power, being wholly secularized, loses much of its prestige; it is stripped, if one prefers, of all the illusions of intrinsic majesty.

The evaporation of the imponderable powers, a total dependence upon the assemblies and the mass electorates, has upset the balance of powers between the two functions of the state. The executive has lost both its material and its ethereal powers. The assemblies and the mass electorates have acquired the monopoly of effective powers.

This is the internal revolution which has deranged the constitutional system of the liberal democratic states.

The Totalitarian Counterrevolution: Certain of Its Lessons. We can learn something about the kind of incapacity which has brought on disaster for the modern democracies by the nature of the counterrevolutions that have undermined and overthrown so many of them. . . .

Now in all these counterrevolutionary movements there are two common characteristics. One is the separation of the governing power from the large electorate. In the totalitarian states this is done by not holding free elections; in the great number of nontotalitarian but also nondemocratic states, it is done by controlling and rigging the elections.

The other common characteristic of the counterrevolutions is that political power, which is taken away from the electorate, the parties, and the party bosses, is then passed to an elite corps marked off from the mass of the people by special training and by special vows. The totalitarian revolutions generally liquidate the elite of the old regime, and then recruit their own elite of specially trained and specially dedicated and highly disciplined men. Elsewhere, when the liberal democratic system fails, the new rulers are drawn from the older established elites—from the army officers, from the clergy, from the university professors.

It is significant that in the reaction against the practical failure of the democratic states, we find always that the electoral process is shut down to a minimum or shut off entirely, and that the executive function is taken over—more often than not with popular assent—by men with a special training and a special personal commitment to the business of ruling the state. In the enfeebled democracies the politicians have with rare exceptions been men without sure tenure of office. Many of the most important are novices, improvisers, and amateurs. After a counterrevolution has brought them down, their successors are almost certain to be either the elite of the new revolutionary party, or an elite drawn from predemocratic institutions like the army, the church, and the bureaucracy.

In their different ways—which ideologically may be at opposite ends of the world—the postdemocratic rulers are men set apart from the masses of the people. They are not set apart only because they have the power to arrest others and to shoot them. They would not long hold on to that kind of power. They have also an aura of majesty, which causes them to be obeyed. That aura emanates from the popular belief that they have subjected themselves to a code and are under a discipline by which they are dedicated to ends that transcend their personal desires and their own private lives.

A Prognosis. The nature of the counterrevolution reflects a radical deficiency in the modern liberal democratic state. This deficiency is, as I have been saying, the enfeeblement and virtual paralysis of the executive governing functions. The strong medicine of the counterrevolution is needed, on the one hand, to stop the electoral process from encroaching upon and invading the government, and, on the other hand, to invest the government not only with all material power but also with the imponderable force of majesty.

It is possible to govern a state without giving the masses of the people full representation. But it is not possible to go on for long without a government which can and does in fact govern. If, therefore, the people find that they must choose whether they will be represented in an assembly which is incompetent to govern, or whether they will be governed without being represented, there is no doubt at all as to how the issue will be decided. They will choose the authority, which promises to be paternal, in preference to freedom which threatens to be fratricidal. For large communities cannot do without being governed. No ideal of freedom and of democracy will long be allowed to stand in the way of their being governed.

The plight of the modern democracies is serious. They have suffered great disasters in this century and the consequences of these disasters are compounding themselves. The end is not yet clear. The world that is safe for democracy and is safely democratic is shrunken. It is still shrinking. For the disorder which has been incapacitating the democracies in this century is, if anything, becoming more virulent as time goes on.

A continuing practical failure to govern will lead—no one can say in what form and under what banners—to counterrevolutionary measures for the establishment of strong government. The alternative is to withstand and to reverse the descent towards counterrevolution. It is a much harder way. It demands popular assent to radical measures which will restore government strong enough to govern, strong enough to resist the encroachment of the assemblies and of mass opinions, and strong enough to guarantee private liberty against the pressure of the masses.

14. THE COMMON MAN IN POLITICS

A. D. LINDSAY

A. D. Lindsay (1879–1952) was a British philosopher and lecturer on political theory and an active Fabian socialist. For twenty-five years he was Master of Balliol College, Oxford.

The task of the government of a democratic society implies a wisdom and understanding of the complicated life of modern societies very far removed from the simple "horse sense" which is sufficient for the running of small and simple democracies. It is clear that a modern state can do its job only

From A. D. Lindsay, *The Modern Democratic State,* Vol. I. New York: The Oxford University Press, 1943. Pp. 267–79. Reprinted by permission of the publisher.

with a lot of expert help, expert statesmen, expert administrators. We must nowadays go on and say "expert economists and expert scientists." Perhaps we must go further and say "expert sociologists."

That is clear enough. What is not so clear is where the ordinary plain man comes in. What is the justification of submitting the expert work of all these superior people to the control of the ordinary voter? We recognize that the man in the street cannot, in the strict sense of the word, govern a modern state. The ordinary person has not the knowledge, the judgment, or the skill to deal with the intricate problems which modern government involves. The primitive democracy of a Swiss commune or of a New England township in the eighteenth century was quite different. The things which the community had to get done in those simple societies were within the competence of most members of the community and open to the judgment of all. Readers of *Coniston,* that admirable political novel in which the American Winston Churchill describes the corruption of simple New Hampshire democracy by the coming of the boss, will remember the society he depicts—hard-headed, sensible, decent farmers, good judges of men and horses. The selectmen whom they elect to govern them are well known to them all. They have nothing to do about which their electors cannot form a sound and shrewd judgment.

To ignore the immense differences between such a society and the society of the modern democratic state is to court disaster. Where are the simple and familiar issues on which shrewd if unlearned men may judge? Where, perhaps it may be asked, in our great urban populations are the hard-headed, shrewd, independent men to judge soundly on any issues?

We all recognize that expert and technical knowledge must come from specialists—that the ordinary man or woman is not capable of judging the detail of legislative proposals. We say that the public decides upon broad issues. That is what the working of modern democracy is supposed to imply. An election makes clear that the public insists, for example, that something pretty drastic must be done about unemployment, or that the United States should support Great Britain by all measures "short of war," and so on. One party rather than another gets into power because the public broadly approves of its program more than the program of its rivals, and judges well of its capacity to carry out its program. The public is not supposed to have any views as to how that program should be carried out but it is supposed to have decided that it prefers the main lines of one party's program to another's.

What does this imply? Does democracy assume that ordinary men and women are better judges on broad issues than experts or than educated people? We can only take this line if we hold that "broad issues" demand not knowledge or skill or special training but "common sense" or sound judgment and that "common sense" is the possession of the ordinary man.

This is the stumbling-stone of democratic theory. On this subject men seem to hold opposing views which cannot be reconciled. Think of the way in which some people talk with conviction of the mob or the herd or the vulgar. Think of the long tradition of denunciation from Thucydides downwards of the folly and fickleness and weakness of the masses. Think, on the other hand, of the continual appreciation in democratic literature of the good sense and sound judgment of the common man—the often expressed conviction that there is something in the "plain man" or in "the man in the street" which makes his judgment often more worthwhile than that of many superior persons.

There must be something to be said for both sides in such a controversy. It is worthwhile to attempt some disentangling.

Let us begin by noting that there are arguments for democratic control which do not assume that men and women are or ought to be given votes only because of the soundness of their judgment. We may summarize the two arguments in the two statements: "Only the wearer knows where the shoe pinches" and "We count heads to save the trouble of breaking them."

The "Shoes Pinching" Argument. Let us begin with the argument about shoes pinching. If we start with the statement I have described as the authentic note of democracy, "The poorest he that is in England has a life to live as the richest he," if we remember that the end of democratic government is to minister to the common life of society, to remove the disharmonies that trouble it, then clearly a knowledge and understanding of that common life is a large part of the knowledge essential to the statesman. But the common life is the life lived by all members of the society. It cannot be fully known and appreciated from outside. It can only be known by those who live it. Its disharmonies are suffered and felt by individuals. It is their shoes that pinch and they only who can tell where they pinch. No doubt the ordinary voter has the vaguest idea as to what legislative or administrative reform will stop the pinching of his shoes. That is no more his business and no more within his capacity than it is the ordinary customer's business to make shoes. He may think, and often does think, that his shoes are pinching only because of the gross ignorance or perhaps because of the corrupt and evil intentions of his government; he may think the making of governmental shoes which ease his feet to be much simpler business than it is; he may listen too easily to charlatans who promise to make the most beautiful shoes for the lowest possible price.

But for all that, only he, the ordinary man, can tell whether the shoes pinch and where; and without that knowledge the wisest statesman cannot make good laws. It is sadly instructive to find what a gap there always is between the account even the best administrations give of the effect of their regulations and the account you get from those to whom the regulations apply. The official account tells what ought to happen if men and women behaved and felt as decent respectable officials assume that they think and feel. What is actually happening is often quite different.

The argument about shoes pinching is the argument which justifies adult suffrage. If the government needs for its task an understanding of the common life it exists to serve, it must have access to all the aspects of that common life. All classes in society must be able to express their grievances. The qualification for voting is not wisdom or good sense but enough independence of mind to be able to state grievances. This does not seem a difficult qualification, but oppressed people are not always prepared to stand up for themselves or even always to think that there is anything wrong in what happens to them. They do not always accept the teaching of "certain revolutionary maniacs" referred to by the Rev. Mr. Twist "who teach the people that the convenience of man, and not the will of God, has consigned them to labor and privation." They vote as "their betters" or their employers or their bosses tell them. To give more of them votes in a society where these conditions exist is to give more power into the hands of those who can manage and exploit them. So in some societies to give votes to women would only mean to give more power into the hands of the men who could deliver their votes. To be an independent person, to be ready to stand up for your rights, to be able to express your grievances and demand that something should be done about them, demand qualities of character and mind which are not always forthcoming, as organizers and defenders of the downtrodden and oppressed often learn sadly to their cost.

Limitations of This Argument. However weighty this argument about "shoes pinching" may be, it does not seem necessarily to involve the control of government by public opinion. It does involve that government should be sensitive and accessible to public opinion, but that is not necessarily the same thing. The safeguarding of the right of petition has little to do with democracy. It is an old tradition of kingly rule that the humblest member of the public should have access to the king to state his grievances. That is the mark of the good Eastern king from Solomon to Haroun al Rashid. The administration of government always gives opportunities for petty tyranny. The member of parliament who asks a question on behalf of one of his constituents who has a complaint against the administration is fulfilling a very old function which existed in undemocratic days. Why should the argument about shoes pinching imply the control of government by the ordinary voter?

The answer is that experts do not like being told that the shoes they so beautifully make do not fit. They are apt to blame it on the distorted and misshapen toes of the people who have to wear their shoes. Unless there is power behind the expression of grievances, the grievances are apt to be neglected. The very way in which the stories talk about the good king who takes pains to find out what his subjects really think implies that most kings do not do so. Solomons or Harouns al Rashid do not grow on every bush. Contrast the very great care which is officially taken in the army to encourage and listen to complaints with what the men say about it. There may be the most regular machinery by which men can express their grievances, the most frequent opportunities to respond to the question "Any complaints?"; but the rank and file will remain convinced that, if they complain, nothing will be done, but the sergeant-major will have it out of them somehow. Men will continue to talk and think quite differently about getting their grievances redressed through their member of parliament who wants their votes on the one hand and through their superior officer over whom they have no power on the other.

On this theory what happens in parliamentary democracy is that the people vote for a government on the understanding that it will remedy their grievances, deal with what is most manifestly wrong, and that they judge and they alone can judge whether the grievances are remedied. The vote at a general election is primarily a judgment on results: the people say, "Our shoes are still pinching and we shall try another shoemaker, thank you"; or, "Yes, you have made our feet so much more comfortable that we shall let you go on and see if you can do still better." Of course what happens is not so simple as that. The verdict of the electors is not just on results: it is to some extent an assent to this or that proposal for the future; but broadly speaking an election is an expression of approval or disapproval of what has happened. This is of course strictly in accordance with the "where the shoe pinches" theory. It does not imply any more than the theory does that the electorate are particularly intelligent: that their judgment as to what ought to be done is at all out of the ordinary. It does imply that, as the end of government is to promote the free life of all its citizens, all citizens must have their say as to how that free life is actually being hindered and how far the work of government is actually removing those hindrances.

But it will also be clear that this argument has its limitations. It does not mean anything like all the claims made for democratic government. It does not even support the claim that the general public can decide broad issues. It would not, for example, justify the democratic control of foreign policy. Foreign policy involves a judgment as to how the internal life of the country is to be preserved from danger from abroad. If we assume that the democratic voter is only concerned to be allowed to "live his own life," to be freed from hindrances to it, but that he has not the necessary knowledge to know what means should be taken to ensure that end, it follows that the ordinary man or woman has on the argument of "the shoe pinching" no particular competence to control foreign policy. Is he then to leave foreign policy entirely to "his betters"?

No democrat would assent. Let us see why.

What People Are Prepared to Do. Errors in foreign policy may mean that a country is faced with the threat of war which may involve, unless that threat is met in one way or another, the destruction of all in its life which its people hold dear. But there are only two conceivable ways in which a threat of war can be met, and both involve the severest sacrifices falling on the ordinary men and women in the country. One of the ways of course is to meet the threat of war by accepting its challenge and resisting it. The other has never been tried but it is advocated by Mr. Gandhi and extreme pacifists. It is to meet the threat of war by passive resistance. Let us first consider the second.

Passive resistance to invasion which would prevent the invader from destroying the soul of a country demands a heroism and goodness in the population of a kind which no people has ever yet shown. If a sincere pacifist statesman, say Mr. Gandhi in power in India, committed his country to this alternative by making the other alternative impossible, he might produce the most horrible disaster. If his people were not really prepared to act up to his principles, and he had incapacitated them from acting up to their own, the result would be disaster, indeed. No statesman has a right to commit his country to action unless he has reason to believe that the people will respond to the challenge which that action involves.

The same point is obvious when we consider the conditions in which alone a democratic statesman can commit his country to war. If it be true that free men fight better than other men for what they hold dear, it is also true that they fight worse than others for what they do not hold dear. It is possible, as Nazi Germany has shown, for a government to get such control over the minds and wills of a people and to have imposed such discipline upon them that they, the government, can make up their mind about what they intend the nation to do and then make their people ready to undergo almost any sacrifices in obedience to their will. But a democratic people is not disciplined in that way. Its government can never go much beyond what their people are prepared to do. It is therefore quite essential that its government should know what that is. No statesman can pursue a foreign policy of appeasement unless he knows how much his people will stand. No statesman can pursue a policy which may end in resistance to aggression unless he knows for what his people are prepared to fight. The weakness of British foreign policy in the period between the two wars was largely due to the fact that, because of the bad working of the democratic machinery or of faulty leadership or of a combination of both, British statesmen did not have this essential knowledge to guide them in their conduct of foreign policy. Britain found herself in a new position. The development of air power had made her vulnerable as she had never been before. The existence of the League of Nations meant the adoption of a new attitude to foreign policy. The spread of pacifism and semipacifism further confused the issue. Before the last war a foreign minister could say with confidence that the British people would go a very long way to preserve peace but there were certain things which they would not stand, and he could have said what those things were. After the war that could no longer be said, and this had a disastrous effect on the conduct of foreign policy.

This need of knowledge of what people are prepared to do is not confined to foreign policy. In a democratic society at least, laws, if they are to be successful, must rest largely upon consent. The force behind government can do something, but not very much. If laws are to be effectively obeyed, their demands cannot go much beyond what people are prepared to do. Successful lawmaking therefore demands an understanding of the ways and the willingness of ordinary people. That understanding can, to some extent, be got without voting or the ordinary processes of democratic machinery. But in so far as democratic machinery produces the expert representative, it is probably as reliable a way as can be devised of ensuring that this necessary knowledge is in the hands of government and that the government pay attention to it.

It is important to notice that, though "what people are prepared to do" is a matter of fact, it is fact of an odd kind. For anyone who reflects on it knows that what people are prepared to do depends on the varying tone of their societies and that the tone depends on leadership, inspiration, and imponderables of that kind. What people are prepared to do is not a distinct fact, to be discovered in its distinct existence by scientific analysis. Indeed we may say in general about all the argument of these last few pages that we shall go wrong if we think of "the pinching of shoes" and "what people are prepared to do" as distinct facts, existing separately and there to be discovered. They are that to some extent but not altogether. In a small meeting the process of discovering what needs to be done and what people are prepared to do is also a process of getting people prepared to do something. Something of the same is true in the elaborate democratic processes which culminate in men and women recording their votes in the polling booths. They are, or at least ought to be, processes of discussion, discussion carried on in the most multifarious ways as it is in a healthy society, by means of the press, of clubs and societies of all kinds: in public-houses and in W.E.A. classes as well as, indeed more than, at political meetings. The process of discovering the sense of the meeting is also a process of making the sense of the meeting. So to some extent at least with a nation at large.

We shall come back to this point later. Meanwhile let us consider how far towards democracy these two arguments take us. They assert that government needs for its task knowledge which cannot be got by ordinary learning but is provided normally by the democratic machinery. That would not necessarily imply control. If the knowledge could be got in another way, presumably on this argument the democratic machinery would not be necessary. Mass observation may claim to be a scientific process of discovering accurately what is now a rather clumsy by-product of election. There is no reason why Hitler or any other autocrat should not use such a process. It is part of any government's job to know these facts about its people even when its main purpose is to understand how to exploit them to serve its own evil ambitions.

These arguments only imply democracy when we remember that men in power need often to be compelled to serve the true purposes of government. Expert shoemakers, as we saw, do not always like to be told that their shoes are at fault. Men who have control over executive and administrative power easily forget that they are only servants and that their power has only value as an instrument. Hence all the democratic devices to ensure that government shall attend to the purposes for which it exists, shall be made to do something about the grievances and wishes of the ordinary people it is meant to serve. Hence the necessity for responsible government—for arrangements which make the government somehow responsible to the ordinary people as contrasted with the most elaborate arrangements for advising an irresponsible government, for seeing that government has the necessary information without compelling it to act on that information. If the theory of all this were properly put into practice it would mean that the government were given a free hand to deal with means. The purpose of the control exercised by the ordinary voters is to see that those means—the technical skill of the administrative— are used to right ends.

The Wisdom of the Plain Man. This leads to a third argument for democracy where it is assumed that ordinary plain people have a certain wisdom which is denied to the expert, and that therefore they are the best judges of ends if not of means.

This argument can easily be so put as to be absurd. An expert is not necessarily a fool. It may be and often is true that experts are apt to give their minds an almost complete holiday outside their own special sphere. Who does not know the distinguished scientist who thinks that his scientific attainments in one sphere justify his making the most surprising generalizations in matters of which he has no knowledge? But knowledge even in a restricted sphere cannot be a greater handicap to sound judgment than ignorance in all spheres. Yet we are not wrong when we pray to be delivered from the clever ass, and it is on the whole true that for a certain kind of practical wisdom—very important in politics—we do not naturally go to the scientific expert. That does not mean that we go instead to the most ignorant man we can find or to just anyone. We go to someone who has learned wisdom from life.

It is an old story that wisdom in conduct is not learned from books or technical study, but from experience and character. We know what we mean when we talk of men and women of "sound judgment" or of "common sense." We distinguish them from the expert whom we rather distrust. We should defend this attitude by saying that the expert is a specialist: that what is wanted for conduct is all-round experience of people and things. "Sound judgment" or "common sense" are not the products of ignorance. They are produced by experience of a certain kind, by responsibility, by a varied acquaintance with men and things and by an all-round experience. The expert or specialist on the other hand has probably paid for his expert knowledge by having had to undergo a long training which has removed him from the ordinary rough-and-tumble of life. He has probably not had to check his judgments by practical experience. He has perhaps not had to pay for his mistakes. He has become "academic" in the bad sense of that term.

If we think about the men and women whose judgment on practical affairs and on conduct we respect, we should certainly agree that academic education did not seem to be very important in their production. We should say that some of them were learned and some not, some rich, some poor. They have no special training or accomplishment. That is why we contrast the one-sidedness of the expert with the good sense or common sense of the ordinary man and why democrats think that the proposals of the expert should be approved by the ordinary man.

Practical wisdom, the democrat would say, shows itself in the most unexpected places. You must be prepared for it wherever it turns up, and you must not imagine you can, by any training or planning, produce it to order. The democratic leader turns up. He is recognized by his fellows and carries them with him. He has the power of calling out the best in ordinary people. Because he shares the life and experience of ordinary men and women he knows, almost unconsciously, "where the shoe pinches" and "what people are prepared to do," and because he shares the ordinary responsibilities of life, he has an all-round experience and is saved from the narrowness of the specialist. Knowledge of the common life and its possibilities; understanding of the things which produce in it bitterness and thwart men's activities are the wisdom most wanted for politics. The state will be wisely directed if the final control is in the hands of "ordinary" men—men not specialized in their vocation or training—who have "common sense" and "sound judgment." But those men are, in favorable circumstances, the men to whom others listen, and who furnish the real if informal leadership in a community. The great mass of really ordinary people will follow them, and to give power to everybody by means of universal suffrage is to give power to them.

This view still implies a judgment about the mass of ordinary men and women. It implies their power of recognizing "sound judgment" and "common sense" in their fellows; in being able to judge a man and ready to approve the natural leader and reject the charlatan. That they do not always do so is notorious. What is important to discover is whether we can say anything about the conditions favorable to the mass of men and women in society judging men well or ill.

15. THE EROSION OF DEMOCRACY

RUPERT EMERSON

Rupert Emerson (1899–   ) is Professor of Government at Harvard University and author of many books and articles on non-western politics.

. . . What is to be made of the widespread swing away from democratic constitutionalism and the counterassertion of military or strong man rule? One line of approach is to set off from the proposition that each country is a special case and that the reasons for collapse, where it has taken place, are peculiar in each instance to the country concerned. Certainly it is not to be disputed that the circumstances in Pakistan and Burma differed sharply from each other in vital respects and that the kind of military predominance which was established was by no means identical in the two cases. What might be said of the shortcomings of Indonesia's political system could be only partially relevant to the very different situation and problems of the Sudan. Thailand and Vietnam have progressed to where they are by such diverse routes that it would be absurd to assume that they have been moved by wholly similar forces or can be expected to respond in identical fashion to similar political action.

The recognition of this diversity of historical experience and current cir-

From Rupert Emerson, "The Erosion of Democracy," *The Journal of Asian Studies,* Vol. 20, No. 1 (November, 1960). Pp. 1–8, excerpts.

cumstance is of real importance, but it is far from exhausting the matter. The failure of democracy to take root and to flourish except in the case of a small number of Western European peoples and their descendants overseas has been so general as to make it highly implausible that we must in each instance seek out a special set of circumstances. The most likely proposition is that while the particular manifestations vary from country to country the underlying causes have a great measure of identity, not only in the new countries of Asia and Africa but in Latin America and eastern and southeastern Europe as well.

The most familiar approach to the problem of discovering these underlying causes is to attempt to isolate the distinctive attributes characterizing the societies which have pursued democracy with success as contrasted with those in which the pursuit has shortly ended in failure. This line of inquiry has been so often explored as to make it unnecessary to elaborate upon it here. A reasonably high level of literacy, the general spread of education, a degree of prosperity reaching above bare subsistence, a homogeneous and integrated society, the maintenance of peace for a substantial period, and a strong and stable middle class—these are the elements which have most frequently been brought forward as the preconditions for a successful venture into democracy. There can be no doubt that these are in fact attributes which tended to characterize the older and more durable democracies, nor that they are generally lacking in the new countries.

It is sometimes contended that one or more of these attributes may be lacking without presaging the breakdown of democratic institutions. For example, the lack of literacy and formal education is occasionally dismissed as having no real bearing on political intelligence or the ability to participate effectively in democratic processes. No doubt such contentions have their fragment of truth; and certainly the negative proposition cannot be proved that continuing democracy is impossible even when all the suggested attributes are missing. India falls far short of adequacy on every count mentioned and yet its democracy has so far proudly held its head high.

It seems eminently reasonable, however, to suggest that the stresses and strains to which democracy is exposed in the ordinary course of events are multiplied where the new countries depart seriously from the circumstances under which it has survived in the modern West. At the least it can be said that in societies possessing such and such attributes (although we can have no certainty that we have singled out the right ones) democracy has worked, whereas in a number of other and distinguishable situations it has collapsed. But one cannot proceed on to the more dangerous assertion that when these preconditions are satisfied, democracy is a necessary or even a probable result. Without them democracy may be unfeasible, but we have nothing approaching a guarantee that their presence will ensure that it puts in a lasting appearance. Germany and Japan are the two most striking cases of countries which moved far toward meeting the preconditions and yet failed dismally in their prewar incarnations to produce democratic institutions which had the breath of life in them.

The laying down of preconditions of the kind just discussed puts democracy potentially within the grasp of every people, since these are attributes which all may acquire and which are expected to appear automatically as a part of the process of social and economic development. Other preconditions may be suggested, however, which forever bar access to the democratic fraternity or reduce entry into it to a highly improbable accident. If the assertion of race or geography as the decisive factor is dismissed as untenable on the face of it, more can presumably be made of the contention that the Western European peoples proved able to manage democratic systems because of unique elements in their historical background, including their good fortune in becoming the heirs of Greece, Rome, and Christianity. Such things, it may be contended, gave them a kind of preparation essential to democracy but not duplicated elsewhere. This is a piece of historical philosophizing which only time can definitely prove or disprove, if it can be proved at all, but many have an uneasy suspicion that there may be something real to it.

A more concretely identifiable barrier to the successful practice of democracy is that the democratic constitutions which have been newly introduced in Asia and Africa appear to be in no sense a response to popular demand, nor do the great bulk of the people concerned have any familiarity with the sort of political system they are expected to operate. Where the new constitutions are not, as in Malaya, the resultant of negotiations between the imperial authorities and the about-to-be-independent government, they are almost wholly a product of the experience and aspirations of the small Western-trained elite whose goal is not the restoration of the traditional order but as speedy movement as possible into the ranks of modern developed states. I am not contending that these new constitutions have been imposed on the people against their will, but only that the latter effectively had no share in the proceedings and must be assumed to have had only the dimmest awareness of what was being done in their name. This is, of course, in greater or less degree true everywhere. Constitutions are not the work of the masses, nor are revolutions made without leadership; but the democratic systems which grew up in the West were far more nearly the result of a natural evolution within the society itself than those which have been adopted elsewhere as the age of Western imperialism receded.

In the new countries the formal political system has been transformed along Western lines, often including highly complicated modern political gadgetry and all the paraphernalia of the welfare state, while much of the society itself has lingered relatively untouched in its traditional ways. Furthermore, with the rarest of exceptions, the political tradition has not been a democratic one. The established pattern in precolonial as in colonial days was that the few at the top ruled and the mass of the peasantry obeyed, or tried to evade the exactions imposed on them. Government at the local level might be democratic in the sense that a considerable number of people participated in the determination of public affairs, but this participation was in the setting of a close-knit customary community in which each person had his special niche and status. This was an experience by no means easy to transfer to the great impersonal national society based on a one-man, one-vote principle with no special consideration for the status of the elders or the spokesmen of this clan or that. The entire historical experience was such as to establish the belief, accepted on both sides, that an elite should govern and the people accept their inferiority. Save, perhaps, in the village or close to it, government was neither the instrument of the people nor run for their benefit.

To this must be added the fact that in every country there was a shortage of trained manpower when it came to independence, a shortage complicated by the suspicion and hostility which marred relations between political leaders and officials who had served the colonial regime. India, taking over the steel framework of the Indian Civil Service, was better off than others, but grave lacks developed everywhere. To the departure of the Europeans who had held at least the top responsible posts was added the need to man foreign services, expand social welfare and educational systems, establish military forces, promote economic development and bring the economy under national control, and in general manage the complex affairs of societies with an almost incalculable backlog of work to be done if they were to become full-fledged members of the modern world. And that world in the mid-twentieth century was far more intricate, demanding, and intransigent than the one entered by their democratic predecessors in the nineteenth century. Domestically the assumptions of mass welfare and mass participation which had only gradually emerged in the West imposed themselves immediately in an era of immense scientific and technical advance. Internationally a crowded and contentious world, plagued by the cold war and devoid of empty spaces for expansion, forced an endless series of painful decisions. The unilateral and multilateral aid brought by the new concern for development must often have complicated rather than simplified life.

What happened was to be expected and had repeatedly happened in similar circumstances elsewhere, as in Eastern Europe, Latin America, and the Middle East. The borrowed constitutions, representing the political experience of other peoples, increasingly proved unable to provide a framework for effective government. Rather than being overthrown by evil and self-seeking forces, alien or domestic, they appeared merely to collapse under the weight they were supposed to carry. Whatever its ultimate virtues, the democratic system in the setting in which it actually had to operate discredited itself by its performance, inspiring a general disgust with politics, politicians, and parties. In Pakistan and Burma the intervention of the military was widely greeted, not by laments for the loss of political freedom, but by rejoicing that at last a strong man had taken over to clean up the growing mess. . . .

Illiteracy, poverty, lack of political experience, crippling shortages of trained manpower, and age-old assumptions as to the right of an elite to rule—these are all matters which have contributed to the decline of democratic practice; but it is not possible to evade the further questions as to whether liberal democratic constitutions adapted from one or another of the standard Western models must necessarily be seen as the proper form of government for South and Southeast Asian societies now. Few, if any, would dispute that where democracy is living a lusty life, as in India and the Philippines or where it seeks rebirth, as in Korea, it should be given every possible encouragement, in part on the conviction that the continued exercise of democratic rights and responsibilities by itself strengthens the democratic fabric. But what of the countries where only a most meager installment of democracy has been introduced or where the political system has been caught in a downward spiral of inaction, corruption, and self-seeking politicking?

The accusation most frequently levelled at Western-style parliamentary institutions in such circumstances is that they emphasize division and disunity. In particular the parliamentary system is charged with being unable to function effectively where a multiplicity of political parties exists, all the more so where proportional representation emphasizes the plurality of parties. Here Asians point to the example of France as demonstrating the need for a strong executive standing above temporary electoral swings and party feuds. It may be remarked in passing that, as the reverse side of the coin, the parliamentary system has also been accused, not without reason, of legitimizing authoritarian or dictatorial rule where a single centralized party commands an overwhelming parliamentary majority.

The fundamental issue which comes to be involved here does not, however, concern the technicalities of parliamentary government but its underlying assumptions, including decision making by majority vote instead of coming to the sense of the meeting by protracted discussion. To short-circuit lengthy debate it may be said that parliamentary democracy rests upon the premises of liberalism of which the cornerstone is that there should be free expression of all opinions, resulting in wide-open competition in the market place of ideas. The operative guarantee of this conception is the existence of an opposition secure in its right to organize, to speak, to assemble, to put up candidates, and to elect. But, as Raymond Aron has put it, the prime necessity in the new states is to have a working machinery of government: "What is first needed is not an opposition but a majority." In its classic form the parliamentary system, opening the door to full expression of diversity, assumes a solid base of social unity which it would be folly to count upon in the new countries. When the effect of democracy is to give free rein to parties, including the Communists, whose loyalty cannot be assumed and which are perhaps based on sectionalism, religion, caste, or tribe, the desired movement toward integration and ordered advance may be fatally impaired. The liberal society has as part of its essence the right to disagree, whereas what the new countries need is not the provision of secure channels for disagreement but the consolidation of national identity through the positive works of integration and development. What the people as a whole seem to want is not individual but national freedom, not political participation but a share in economic advance in which the government is likely to have to be the prime mover. . . .

A substantial case can be made for the proposition that democracy is by no means necessarily what the doctor ordered for the new countries; but this is far from establishing the succeeding proposition that, in the given circumstances, the doctor can order anything guaranteed to produce better results. The mere imposition of authoritarian rule can by itself give no assurance that the next stage will be better than the last. The leader of the single party or the military ruler may cure some of the ills, such as factional disputes or party corruption, but at the same time demonstrate his incompetence in the sphere of economic development and inflict the evils of dictatorship without adequate recompense. It has been argued that the military in the new countries are likely to present a road to salvation because of their discipline, their national dedication, and their progressive outlook and training. In Pakistan and Burma there is evidence that they have done much to correct the evils of the regimes which preceded them and to start their countries moving ahead again. It may be that they will do so elsewhere. . . .

. . . [But] only an optimist who has departed from the salutary restraints of right reason can believe that the right man with the right entourage is bound to come along at the crucial moment of need in any particular country. The sins and shortcomings of strong men are certainly no less notorious in history than the corruptions and weaknesses of democracies.

One last point of speculation. It is the burden of much of what has been said that, where the preconditions of democracy are lacking, it is not to be assumed that they can be supplied through the practice of democracy itself. Where institutions flounder badly and perhaps degenerate into a game of partisan self-seeking played by the dominant elite, no significant foundations are laid for future democracy and, even worse, the very concept of democracy comes to be discredited.

Is the stouter discipline of a "guided democracy" necessary in order to come back at a later stage to a democracy which would be free in a Western liberal sense? Certainly no all-embracing answer is possible, but the evidence of the past in many countries works against the assumption either that the strong autocrat will gracefully yield power to the democracy whose foundations he has laid—despite the present case of Burma—or that the people themselves will rise up to demand their political rights. None the less, hope for democracy can be found in the social transformation which authoritarian regimes may stimulate. If they are successful in promoting a substantial measure of social and economic development, they will be moving toward the creation of the conditions under which democracy has worked in the West. By far the most important of these conditions is the bringing into being of a populace, or at least of large segments in the populace, which will demand the political participation and freedom to which they have up to now laid little, if any, claim.

Assuming success in economic development, the kind of people will be multiplied who have elsewhere sometimes fought for the managed democratic societies and constitutions; but under Asian circumstances will they be prepared to put up the same fight—and will they win it? Or must one see democracy as a form of government derived from certain phases of European history and fitted to the needs and potentialities of some European peoples, but not possessing either universal applicability or universal value? Despite its present global prestige, democracy, at least in any of its Western guises, may prove to have no rightful place in the Asian environment nor even to be desired by the bulk of the Asian peoples.

16. THE INFLUENCE OF DEMOCRATIC OPINIONS AND SENTIMENTS ON SOCIETY

ALEXIS DE TOCQUEVILLE

Alexis de Tocqueville (1805–1859) was a French aristocrat, a jurist and member of the French parliament. After a visit to the United States, he wrote DEMOCRACY IN AMERICA *as a summary of his observations and the conclusions he drew from them.*

The principle of equality begets two tendencies: the one leads men straight to independence and may suddenly drive them into anarchy; the other conducts them by a longer, more secret, but more certain road to servitude. Nations readily discern the former tendency and are prepared to resist it: they are led away by the latter, without perceiving its drift; hence it is particularly important to point it out.

Personally, far from finding a fault with equality because it inspires a spirit of independence, I praise it primarily for that very reason. I admire it because it lodges in the very depths of each man's mind and heart that indefinable feeling, the instinctive inclination for political independence, and thus prepares the remedy for the ill which it engenders. It is precisely for this reason that I cling to it. . . .

The notion of secondary powers placed between the sovereign and his subjects occurred naturally to the imagination of aristocratic nations, because those communities contained individuals or families raised above the common level and apparently destined to command by their birth, their education, and their wealth. This same notion is naturally wanting in the minds of men in democratic ages, for converse reasons; it can only be introduced artifically, it can only be kept there with difficulty, whereas they conceive, as it were without thinking about the subject, the notion of a single and central power which governs the whole community by its direct influence. Moreover, in politics as well as in philosophy and in religion the intellect of democratic nations is peculiarly open to simple and general notions. Complicated systems are repugnant to it, and its favorite conception is that of a great nation composed of citizens all formed upon one pattern and all governed by a single power.

The very next notion to that of a single and central power which presents itself to the minds of men in the ages of equality is the notion of uniformity

From Alexis de Tocqueville, *Democracy in America,* Vol. II. New York: Alfred A. Knopf, Inc., copyright 1945. Pp. 304–7, 312–13, and 340–45, excerpts. Reprinted by permission of the publisher.

of legislation. As every man sees that he differs but little from those about him, he cannot understand why a rule that is applicable to one man should not be equally applicable to all others. Hence the slightest privileges are repugnant to his reason; the faintest dissimilarities in the political institutions of the same people offend him, and uniformity of legislation appears to him to be the first condition of good government.

I find, on the contrary, that this notion of a uniform rule equally binding on all the members of the community was almost unknown to the human mind in aristocratic ages; either it was never broached, or it was rejected.

These contrary tendencies of opinion ultimately turn on both sides to such blind instincts and ungovernable habits that they still direct the actions of men, in spite of particular exceptions. Notwithstanding the immense variety of conditions in the Middle Ages, a certain number of persons existed at that period in precisely similar circumstances; but this did not prevent the laws then in force from assigning to each of them distinct duties and different rights. On the contrary, at the present time all the powers of government are exerted to impose the same customs and the same laws on populations which have as yet but few points of resemblance.

As the conditions of men become equal among a people, individuals seem of less and society of greater importance; or rather every citizen, being assimilated to all the rest, is lost in the crowd, and nothing stands conspicuous but the great and imposing image of the people at large. This naturally gives the men of democratic periods a lofty opinion of the privileges of society and a very humble notion of the rights of individuals; they are ready to admit that the interests of the former are everything and those of the latter nothing. They are willing to acknowledge that the power which represents the community has far more information and wisdom than any of the members of that community; and that it is the duty, as well as the right, of that power to guide as well as govern each private citizen. . . .

The hatred that men bear to privilege increases in proportion as privileges become fewer and less considerable, so that democratic passions would seem to burn most fiercely just when they have least fuel. I have already given the reason for this phenomenon. When all conditions are unequal, no inequality is so great as to offend the eye, whereas the slightest dissimilarity is odious in the midst of general uniformity; the more complete this uniformity is, the more insupportable the sight of such a difference becomes. Hence it is natural that the love of equality should constantly increase together with equality itself, and that it should grow by what it feeds on.

This never-dying, ever-kindling hatred which sets a democratic people against the smallest privileges is peculiarly favorable to the gradual concentration of all political rights in the hands of the representative of the state alone. The sovereign, being necessarily and incontestably above all the citizens, does not excite their envy, and each of them thinks that he strips his equals of the prerogative that he concedes to the crown. The man of a democratic age is extremely reluctant to obey his neighbor, who is his equal: he refuses to acknowledge superior ability in such a person: he mistrusts his justice and is jealous of his power; he fears and he despises him; and he loves continually to remind him of the common dependence in which both of them stand to the same master.

Every central power, which follows its natural tendencies, courts and encourages the principle of equality; for equality singularly facilitates, extends, and secures the influence of a central power.

In like manner it may be said that every central government worships uniformity; uniformity relieves it from inquiry into an infinity of details, which must be attended to if rules have to be adapted to different men, instead of indiscriminately subjecting all men to the same rule. Thus the government likes what the citizens like and naturally hates what they hate. These common sentiments, which in democratic nations constantly unite the sovereign and every member of the community in one and the same conviction, established a secret and lasting sympathy between them. The faults of the government are pardoned for the sake of its inclinations; public confidence is only reluctantly withdrawn in the midst even of its excesses and its errors, and it is restored at the first call. Democratic nations often hate those in whose hands the central power is vested, but they always love that power itself.

Thus by two separate paths I have reached the same conclusion. I have shown that the principle of equality suggests to men the notion of a sole, uniform, and strong government; I have now shown that the principle of equality imparts to them a taste for it. To governments of this kind the nations of our age are therefore tending. They are drawn thither by the natural inclination of mind and heart; and in order to reach that result, it is enough that they do not check themselves in their course.

I am of the opinion that, in the democratic ages which are opening upon us, individual independence and local liberties will ever be the products of art; that centralization will be the natural government. . . .

It results from the very constitution of democratic nations and from their necessities that the power of government among them must be more uniform, more centralized, more extensive, more searching, and more efficient than in other countries. Society at large is naturally stronger and more active, the individual more subordinate and weak; the former does more, the latter less; and this is inevitably the case.

It is not, therefore, to be expected that the range of private independence will ever be so extensive in democratic countries; nor is this to be desired; for among aristocratic nations the mass is often sacrificed to the individual, and the prosperity of the greater number to the greatness of the few. It is both necessary and desirable that the government of a democratic people should be active and powerful; and our object should not be to render it weak or indolent, but solely to prevent it from abusing its aptitude and its strength.

The circumstance which most contributed to secure the independence of private persons in aristocratic ages was that the supreme power did not affect to take upon itself alone the government and administration of the community. Those functions were necessarily partially left to the members of aristocracy; so that, as the supreme power has always divided, it never weighed with its whole weight and in the same manner on each individual.

Not only did the government not perform everything by its immediate agency, but as most of the agents who discharged its duties derived their power, not from the state, but from the circumstance of their birth, they were not perpetually under its control. The government could not make or unmake them in an instant, at pleasure, or bend them in strict uniformity to its slightest caprice; this was an additional guarantee of private independence.

I readily admit that recourse cannot be had to the same means at the present time, but I discover certain democratic expedients that may be substituted for them. Instead of vesting in the government alone all the administrative powers of which guilds and nobles have been deprived, a portion of them may be entrusted to secondary public bodies temporarily composed of private citizens: thus the liberty of private persons will be more secure, and their equality will not be diminished.

The Americans, who care less for words than the French, still designate by the name of County the largest of their administrative districts; but the duties of the count or lord-lieutenant are in part performed by a provincial assembly.

At a period of equality like our own, it would be unjust and unreasonable to institute hereditary officers; but there is nothing to prevent us from substituting elective public officers to a certain extent. Election is a democratic expedient, which ensures the independence of the public officer in relation to the government as much as hereditary rank can ensure it among aristocratic nations, and even more so.

Aristocratic countries abound in wealthy and influential persons who are competent to provide for themselves and who cannot be easily or secretly oppressed; such persons restrain a government within general habits of moderation and reserve. I am well aware that democratic countries contain no such persons naturally, but something analogous to them may be created by artificial means. I firmly believe that an aristocracy cannot again be founded in the world, but I think that private citizens, by combining together, may constitute bodies of great wealth, influence, and strength, corresponding to the persons of the aristocracy. By this means many of the greatest political advantages of the aristocracy would be obtained without its injustice or its dangers. An association for political, commercial, or manufacturing purposes, or even for those of science and literature, is a powerful and enlightened member of the community, which cannot be disposed of at pleasure or oppressed without remonstrance, and which, by defending its own rights against the encroachments of the government, saves the common liberties of the country.

In periods of aristocracy every man is always bound so closely to many of his fellow citizens that he cannot be assailed without their coming to his assistance. In ages of equality every man naturally stands alone; he has no hereditary friends whose cooperation he may demand, no class upon whose sympathy he may rely; he is easily got rid of, and he is trampled with impunity. At the present time an oppressed member of the community has therefore only one method of self-defense; he may appeal to the whole nation, and if the whole nation is deaf to his complaint, he may appeal to mankind. The only means he has of making this appeal is by the press. Thus the liberty of the press is infinitely more valuable among democratic nations than among all others; it is the only cure for the evils that equality may produce. Equality sets men apart and weakens them; but the press places a powerful weapon within every man's reach, which the weakest and loneliest of them all may use. Equality deprives a man of the support of his connections, but the press enables him to summon all his fellow countrymen and all his fellow men to his assistance. Printing has accelerated the progress of equality, and it is also one of its best correctives.

I think that men living in aristocracies may, strictly speaking, do without the liberty of the press; but such is not the case with those who live in democratic countries. To protect their personal independence I do not trust to great political assemblies, to parliamentary privilege, or to the assertion of popular sovereignty. All these things may, to a certain extent, be reconciled with personal servitude. But that servitude cannot be complete if the press is free; the press is the chief democratic instrument of freedom.

Something analogous may be said of the judicial power. It is a part of the essence of judicial power to attend to private interests and to fix itself with predilection on minute objects submitted to its observation. Another essential quality of judicial power is never to volunteer its assistance to the oppressed, but always to be at the disposal of the humblest of those who solicit it; their complaint, however feeble they may themselves be, will force itself upon the ear of justice and claim redress, for this is inherent in the very constitution of the courts of justice.

A power of this kind is therefore peculiarly adapted to the wants of freedom, at a time when the eye and finger of the government are constantly intruding into the minutest details of human actions, and when private persons are at once too weak to protect themselves and too much isolated for them to reckon upon the assistance of their fellows. The strength of the courts of law has always been the greatest security that can be offered to personal independence; but this is more especially the case in democratic ages. Private rights and interests are in constant danger if the judicial power does not grow more extensive and stronger to keep pace with growing equality of conditions.

Equality awakens in men several propensities extremely dangerous to freedom, to which the attention of the legislator ought constantly to be directed. I shall only remind the reader of the most important among them.

Men living in democratic ages do not readily comprehend the utility of forms: they feel an instinctive contempt for them. I have elsewhere shown for what reasons. Forms excite their contempt and often their hatred; as they commonly aspire to none but easy and present gratifications, they rush onwards to the object of their desires, and the slightest delay exasperates them. This same temper, carried with them into political life, renders them hostile to forms, which perpetually retard or arrest them in some of their projects.

Yet this objection which the men of democracies make to forms is the very thing which renders forms so useful to freedom; for their chief merit is to serve as a barrier between the strong and the weak, the ruler and the people, to retard the one and give the other time to look about him. Forms become more necessary in proportion as the government becomes more active and more powerful, while private persons are becoming more indolent and more feeble. Thus democratic nations naturally stand more in need of forms than other nations, and they naturally respect them less. This deserves most serious attention.

Nothing is more pitiful than the arrogant disdain of most of our contemporaries for questions of form, for the smallest questions of form have acquired in our time an importance which they never had before; many of the greatest interests of mankind depend upon them. I think that if the statesmen of aristocratic ages could sometimes despise forms with impunity and frequently rise above them, the statesmen to whom the government of nations is now confided ought to treat the very least among them with respect and not neglect them without imperious necessity. In aristocracies the observance of forms was superstitious; among us they ought to be kept up with a deliberate and enlightened deference.

Another tendency which is extremely natural to democratic nations and extremely dangerous is that which leads them to despise and undervalue the rights of private persons. The attachment that men feel to a right and the respect that they display for it are generally proportioned to its importance or to the length of time during which they have enjoyed it. The rights of private persons among democratic nations are commonly of small importance, of recent growth, and extremely precarious; the consequence is that they are often sacrificed without regret and almost always violated without remorse.

But it happens that, at the same period and among the same nations in which men conceive a natural contempt for the rights of private persons, the rights of society at large are naturally extended and consolidated; in other words, men become less attached to private rights just when it is most necessary to retain and defend what little remains of them. It is therefore most especially in the present democratic times, that the true friends of liberty and the greatness of man ought constantly to be on the alert to prevent the power of government from lightly sacrificing the private rights of individuals to the general execution of its designs. At such times no citizen is so obscure that it is not very dangerous to allow him to be oppressed; no private rights are so unimportant that they can be surrendered with impunity to the caprices of a government. The reason is plain: if the private right of an individual is violated at a time when the human mind is fully impressed with the importance and the sanctity of such rights, the injury done is confined to the individual whose right is infringed; but to violate such a right at the present day is deeply to corrupt the manners of the nation and to put the whole community in jeopardy, because the very notion of this kind of right constantly tends among us to be impaired and lost.

17. ON REALIZING THE AMERICAN DREAM
JOHN F. KENNEDY

John F. Kennedy (1917–1963) was the thirty-fifth president of the United States.

. . . Following a series of threats and defiant statements, the presence of Alabama Guardsmen was required on the University of Alabama to carry out the final and unequivocal order of the United States District Court of the Northern District of Alabama. That order called for the admission of two clearly qualified young Alabama residents who happened to have been born Negro.

That they were admitted peacefully on the campus is due in good measure to the conduct of the students of the University of Alabama who met their responsibilities in a constructive way.

I hope that every American, regardless of where he lives, will stop and examine his conscience about this and other related incidents. This nation was founded by men of many nations and backgrounds. It was founded on the principle that all men are created equal, and that the rights of every man are diminished when the rights of one man are threatened.

Today we are committed to a worldwide struggle to promote and protect all of those who wish to be free and when Americans are sent to Viet Nam or West Berlin, we do not ask for whites only. It ought to be possible, therefore, for American students of any color to attend any public institution they select without having to be backed up by troops.

It ought to be possible for American consumers of any color to receive equal service in places of public accommodation, such as hotels and restaurants and theaters and retail stores, without being forced to resort to demonstrations in the street, and it ought to be possible for American citizens of any color to register and vote in a free election without interference or fear of reprisal.

It ought to be possible, in short, for every American to enjoy the privilege of being American without regard to his race or his color. In short, every American ought to have the right to be treated as he would wish to be treated, as one would wish his children to be treated. But this is not the case.

The Negro baby born in America today, regardless of the section of the nation in which he is born, has about one half as much chance of completing high school as a white baby born in the same place on the same day, one third as much chance of completing college, one third as much chance of becoming a professional man, twice as much chance of becoming unemployed,

Excerpts from a speech delivered by President John F. Kennedy on June 12, 1963.

about one seventh as much chance of earning $10,000 a year, a life expectancy which is seven years shorter, and the prospects of earning only half as much.

This is not a sectional issue. Difficulties over segregation and discrimination exist in every city, in every state of the Union, producing in many cities a rising tide of discontent that threatens the public safety. Nor is this a partisan issue in a time of domestic crisis. Men of goodwill and generosity should be able to unite regardless of party or politics. This is not even a legal or legislative issue alone. It is better to settle these matters in the courts than in the streets, and new laws are needed at every level, but law alone cannot make men see right.

We are confronted primarily with a moral issue. It is as old as the Scriptures and is as clear as the American Constitution. The heart of the question is whether all Americans are to be afforded equal rights and equal opportunities, whether we are going to treat our fellow Americans as we want to be treated. If an American, because his skin is dark, cannot eat lunch in a restaurant open to the public, if he cannot send his children to the best public school available, if he cannot vote for the public officials who represent him, if, in short, he cannot enjoy the full and free life which all of us want, then who among us would be content to have the color of his skin changed and stand in his place?

Who among us would then be content with the counsels of patience and delay? One hundred years of delay have passed since President Lincoln freed the slaves, yet their heirs, their grandsons are not fully free. They are not yet freed from the bonds of injustice. They are not yet freed from social and economic oppression, and this nation, for all its hopes and all its boasts, will not be fully free until all its citizens are free.

We preach freedom around the world and we mean it, and we cherish our freedom here at home, but are we to say to the world, and much more importantly, to each other that this is a land of the free except for the Negroes; that we have no second-class citizens, except Negroes; that we have no class or caste system, no ghettos, no master race except with respect to Negroes?

Now the time has come for this nation to fulfill its promises. The events in Birmingham and elsewhere have so increased the cries for equality that no city or state or legislative body can prudently choose to ignore them.

The fires of frustration and discord are burning in every city, north and south, where legal remedies are not at hand. Redress is sought in the streets, in demonstrations, parades and protests which create tensions and threaten violence and threaten lives.

We face, therefore, a moral crisis as a country, and as a people. It cannot be met by repressive police action. It cannot be left to increased demonstrations in the streets. It cannot be quieted by token moves or talk. It is a time to act in the Congress, in your state and local legislative body and, above all, in all of our daily lives.

It is not enough to pin the blame on others, to say this is a problem of one section of the country or another, or deplore it. The fact that we face a great change is at hand, and our task, our obligation is to make that revolution, that change, peaceful and constructive for all.

Those who do nothing are inviting shame as well as violence. Those who act boldly are recognizing right as well as reality.

Next week I shall ask the Congress of the United States to act, to make a commitment it has not fully made in this century to the proposition that race has no place in American life or law. The Federal Judiciary has upheld that proposition in a series of forthright cases. The Executive Branch has adopted that proposition in the conduct of its affairs, including the employment of federal personnel, the use of federal facilities and the sale of federally financed housing.

But there are other necessary measures which only the Congress can provide, and they must be provided. . . .

Other features will also be requested, including greater protection for the right to vote. But legislation, I repeat, cannot solve this problem alone. It must be solved in the homes of every American in every community across our country. . . .

My fellow Americans, this is a problem which faces us all—in every city of the North as well as the South. Today there are Negroes unemployed, two or three times as many compared to whites, inadequate in education, moving into the large cities, unable to find work, young people particularly out of work without hope, denied equal rights, denied the opportunity to eat at a restaurant or lunch counter or go to a movie theater, denied the right to a decent education, denied almost today the right to attend a state university although qualified—it seems to me that these are matters which concern us all, not merely President or congressmen or governors, but every citizen of the United States. This is one country. It has become one country because all of us and all the people who came here had an equal chance to develop their talents.

We cannot say to 10 percent of the population that you cannot have that right; that your children can't have the chance to develop whatever talents they have; that the only way they are going to get their rights is to go into the streets and demonstrate.

I think we owe them and we owe ourselves a better country than that.

Therefore, I am asking for your help in making it easier for us to move ahead and prove the kind of equality of treatment which we would want ourselves; to give a chance for every child to be educated to the limit of his talents.

As I have said before, not every child has an equal talent or an equal ability or an equal motivation, but they should have the equal right to develop their talent and their ability and their motivation to make something of themselves.

We have a right to expect that the Negro community will be responsible, will uphold the law, but they have a right to expect that the law will be fair; that the Constitution will be color blind, as Justice Harlan said at the turn of the century.

This is what we are talking about and this is a matter which concerns this country and what it stands for, and in meeting it I ask the support of all of our citizens.

18. THE "EQUALITY" REVOLUTION

HERBERT J. GANS

Herbert J. Gans (1927–   ) is a sociologist-planner on the staff of the Center for Urban Education and the Faculty of Teachers College, Columbia University.

Someday, when historians write about the nineteen-sixties, they may describe them as the years in which America rediscovered the poverty still in its midst and in which social protest, ranging from demonstrations to violent uprisings, reappeared on the American scene. But the historians may also note a curious fact, that the social protest of the sixties has very little to do with poverty. Most of the demonstrators and marchers who followed Martin Luther King were not poor; the college students who have been protesting and sitting-in on campus are well-to-do, and even the participants in the ghetto uprisings of the last few years—although hardly affluent—were not drawn from the poorest sectors of the ghetto.

The social protest of the nineteen-sixties has to do with *inequality*, with the pervasive inequities remaining in American life. So far the demand for greater equality has come largely from the young and the black, but I wish to suggest that in the years to come, America will face a demand for more equality in various aspects of life from many other types of citizens—a demand so pervasive that it might well be described as the "equality revolution."

This demand will take many forms. Some will ask for *equality*, pure and simple; others will press for more *democracy*, for greater participation in and responsiveness by their places of work and their governments; yet others will ask for more *autonomy*, for the freedom to be what they want to be and to choose how they will live. All these demands add up to a desire for greater control over one's life, requiring the reduction of the many inequities—economic, political and social—that now prevent people from determining how they will spend their short time on this earth. . . .

In the past, when most people earned just enough to "get by," they were interested mainly in higher incomes and did not concern themselves with equality or autonomy in their everyday lives. For example, the poor took—and still will take—any jobs they could get because they needed the money to pay for the week's food and the month's rent. Working-class and lower-middle-class people were, and are, only slightly more able to choose; they take whatever job will provide the most comfortable lives for themselves and their families. But in the upper-middle class, the job is expected to offer personal satisfactions, and upper-middle-class people gravitate to the jobs and careers that provide more equality and autonomy. The huge increase in graduate-school enrollments suggests that many college students want the personal freedom available in an academic career; their decreasing interest in business careers indicates that they may be rejecting the autocracy and lack of autonomy found in many large corporations.

Today, as more people approach the kind of economic security already found in the affluent upper-middle class, they are beginning to think about the noneconomic satisfactions of the job and of the rest of life; as a result, aspirations for more equality, democracy and autonomy are rising all over America.

Some manifestations of "the equality revolution" are making headlines today, particularly among students and blacks. Whatever the proximate causes of college protests and uprisings, the students who participate in them agree on two demands: the right to be treated as adults—and therefore as equals—and the right to participate in the governing of their schools. Though the mass media have paid most attention to the more radical advocates of these demands, equality and democracy are sought not just by the Students for a Democratic Society but by an ever-increasing number of liberal and even conservative students as well.

Similar demands for equality and democracy are being voiced by the young people of the ghetto. Only a few years ago, they seemed to want integration, the right to become part of the white community. Today, recognizing that white America offered integration to only a token few and required with it assimilation into the white majority, the young blacks are asking for equality instead. When they say that black is beautiful, they are really saying that black is equal to white; when the ghetto demands control of its institutions, it asks for the right to have the same control that many white neighborhoods have long had.

And although the call for "participatory democracy" is voiced mainly by young people of affluent origins in the New Left, a parallel demand is manifesting itself among the young blue-collar supporters of Governor Wallace. What they are saying, in effect, is that they are tired of being represented by middle-class politicians; they want a President who will allow the working class to participate in the running of the Federal Government and will get rid of the upper-middle-class professionals who have long dominated the formulation of public policies, the people whom the Governor calls "pseudo-intellectuals."

Many other instances of the equality revolution are less visible, and some have not made the headlines. For example, in the last two generations, wives have achieved near equality in the family, at least in the middle class; they now divide the housework with their husbands and share the decision-making about family expenditures and other activities. Today, this revolution is being extended to the sexual relationship. Gone is the day when women were passive vessels for men's sexual demands; they are achieving the right to enjoy sexual intercourse.

Children have also obtained greater equality and democracy. In many American families, adolescents are now free from adult interference in their leisure-time activities and their sexual explorations, and even preteens are asking to be allowed their own "youth culture."

Man's relationship to God and the church is moving toward greater equality, too. The minister is no longer a theological father; in many synagogues and Protestant churches, he has become the servant of his congregation, and the unwillingness of many Catholics to abide by the Pope's dictates on birth control hides other, less publicized, instances of the rejection of dogma that is handed down from on high. The real meaning of the "God is Dead" movement, I believe, is that the old conception of God as the infallible autocrat has been rejected.

In the years to come, the demand for more equality, democracy and autonomy is likely to spread to many other aspects of life. Already, some high-school students are beginning to demand the same rights for which college students are organizing, and recipients of public welfare are joining together to put an end to the autocratic fashion in which their payments are given to them. Public employees are striking for better working conditions as well as for higher wages; teachers are demanding more freedom in the classroom and—in New York—the right to teach where they choose; social workers want more autonomy in aiding their clients, and policemen seek the right to do their jobs as they see fit, immune from what they call "political interference." The right of the individual to determine his job is the hallmark of the professional, and eventually many workers will seek the privileges of professionalism whether or not they are professional in terms of skills.

Eventually, the equality revolution may also come to the large corporations and government agencies in which more and more people are working. One can foresee the day when blue-collar and white-collar workers demand a share of the profits and some voice in the running of the corporations.

Similar changes can be expected in the local community. Although the exodus to suburbia took place primarily because people sought better homes and neighborhoods, they also wanted the ability to obtain greater control over governmental institutions. In the last 20 years, the new suburbanites have overthrown many of the rural political machines that used to run the suburbs, establishing governments that were responsive to their demands for low taxes and the exclusion of poorer newcomers. In the future, this transformation may spread to the cities as well, with decentralized political institutions that respond to the wants of the neighborhood replacing the highly centralized urban machines. New York's current struggle over school decentralization is only a harbinger of things to come.

Consumer behavior will also undergo change. The ever-increasing diversity of consumer goods represents a demand for more cultural democracy on the part of purchasers, and the day may come when some people will establish consumer unions and cooperatives to provide themselves with goods and services not offered by large manufacturers. Television viewers may unite to demand different and perhaps even better TV programs and to support the creation of UHF channels that produce the types of quality and minority programming the big networks cannot offer.

It is even possible that a form of "hippie" culture will become more popular in the future. Although the Haight-Ashbury and East Village hippies have degenerated into an often-suicidal drug culture, there are positive themes in hippiedom that may become more acceptable if the work-week shrinks and affluence becomes more universal; for example: the rejection of the rat race, the belief in self-expression as the main purpose of life, the desire for a more communal form of living and even the idea of drug use as a way to self-understanding. In any case, there is no reason to doubt that many people will want to take advantage of a "square" form of the leisurely hippie existence—now available only to old people and called retirement—while they are still young or middle-aged. This day is far off, and by then marijuana is likely to have achieved equality with liquor as America's major elixir for temporary escape from reality and inhibition.

These observations suggest that the future will bring many kinds of change to America, producing new ideas that question beliefs and values thought to be sacrosanct. Who, for example, imagined a few years ago that the ghetto would reject the traditional goal of integration or that college students would rise up against their faculties and administrations to demand equal rights? Thus, nobody should be surprised if in the next few years adolescents organize for more freedom in their high schools or journalists decide that their editors have too much power over their work.

These demands for change will, of course, be fought bitterly; protests will be met by backlash and new ideas will be resisted by old ideologies.

Today many argue that college students are still children and should not be given a voice in college administration, just as many say that women do not really need orgasms or that men who help their wives at home are becoming effeminate. Undoubtedly, the defenders of out-moded traditions will argue sincerely and with some facts and logic on their side, but processes of social change have little to do with sincerity, facts or logic. When people become dissatisfied with what they have and demand something better they cannot be deterred by facts or logic, and the repression of new ideas and new modes of behavior is effective only in the very short run.

But perhaps the most intense struggle between new ideas and old ideologies will take place over America's political philosophy, for a fundamental change is taking place in the values which guide us as a nation. In a little-noticed portion of the "Moynihan Report," Daniel P. Moynihan pointed out that the civil rights struggle, which had previously emphasized the achievement of liberty, particularly political liberty from Jim Crow laws, would soon shift to the attainment of equality, which would allow the "distribution of achievements among Negroes roughly comparable to that of whites."

Moynihan's prediction was uncannily accurate with respect to the civil rights struggle, and I would argue, as he does, that it will soon extend to many other struggles as well and that the traditional belief in liberty will be complemented and challenged by a newly wide-spread belief in the desirability of equality.

Since America became a nation, the country has been run on the assumption that the greatest value of all is liberty, which gives people the freedom to "do their own thing," particularly to make money, regardless of how much this freedom deprives others of the same liberty or of a decent standard of living. Whether liberty meant the freedom to squander the country's natural resources or just to go into business for oneself without doing harm to anyone else, it was the guiding value of our society.

Today, however, the demand for liberty is often, but not always, the battle cry of the "haves," justifying their right to keep their wealth or position and to get more. Whether liberty is demanded by a Southern advocate of states' rights to keep Negroes in their place or by a property owner who wants to sell his house to any white willing to buy it, liberty has become the ideology of the more fortunate. In the years to come, the "have-nots," whether they lack money or freedom, will demand increasingly the reduction of this form of liberty. Those who ask for more equality are not opposed to liberty *per se*, of course; what they want is sufficient equality so that they, too, can enjoy the liberty now virtually monopolized by the "haves."

The debate over liberty vs. equality is in full swing, and one illuminating example is the current argument about the negative income tax and other forms of guaranteed annual incomes for the underpaid and the poor. The advocates of guaranteed annual incomes want greater equality of income in American society; the opponents fear that the liberty to earn as much as possible will be abrogated. However, neither side frames its case in terms of equality or liberty. The advocates of a guaranteed annual income rely on moral argument, appealing to their fellow Americans to do away with the immorality of poverty. The opponents charge that a guaranteed annual income will sap the incentive to work, although all the evidence now available suggests that professors and other professionals who have long had virtually guaranteed annual incomes have not lost their incentive to work, that what saps incentive is not income but the lack of it.

Being poor makes people apathetic and depressed; a guaranteed income would provide some emotional as well as economic security, raise hopes, increase self-respect and reduce feelings of being left out, thus encouraging poor people to look for decent jobs, improve family living conditions and urge their children to work harder in school. A guaranteed annual income may reduce the incentive to take a dirty and underpaid job, however, and at the bottom of the debate is the fear of those who now have the liberty to avoid taking such jobs that less-fortunate Americans may be given the same liberty.

In the years to come, many other arguments against equality will develop. We have long heard that those who want more equality are radicals or outside agitators, seeking to stir up people thought to be happy with the way things are. This is clearly nonsensical, for even if radicals sometimes lead the drive for more equality, they can succeed only because those who follow them are dissatisfied with the status quo.

Another argument is that the demand for more equality will turn America into a society like Sweden, which is thought to be conformist, boring and suicidal, or even into a gray and regimented society like Russia. But these arguments are nonsensical, too, for there is no evidence that Swedes suffer more from ennui than anyone else, and the suicide rate—high in all Scandinavian countries save Norway—was lower in Sweden at last counting than in traditionalist Austria or Communist Hungary and only slightly higher than the rate in *laissez-faire* West Germany or pastoral Switzerland. And current events in the Communist countries provide considerable evidence that the greater economic equality which some of these countries have achieved does not eliminate the popular desire for freedom and democracy.

But perhaps the most frequently heard argument is that the unequal must do something to earn greater equality. This line of reasoning is taken by those who have had the liberty to achieve their demands and assumes that the same liberty is available to everyone else. This assumption does not hold up, however, for the major problem of the unequal is precisely that they are not allowed to earn equality—that the barriers of racial discrimination, the inability to obtain a good education, the unavailability of good jobs or the power of college presidents and faculties make it impossible for them to be equal. Those who argue for earning equality are really saying that they want to award it to the deserving, like charity. But recent events in the ghettos and on the campuses have shown convincingly that no one awards equality voluntarily; it has to be wrested from the "more equal" by political pressure and even by force.

Many of the changes that make up the equality revolution will not take place for a generation or more, and how many of them ever take place depends on at least three factors: the extent to which the American economy is affluent enough to permit more equality; the extent to which America's political institutions are able to respond to the demands of the unequal, and —perhaps most important—the extent to which working-class and lower-middle-class Americans want more equality, democracy and autonomy in the future.

If the economy is healthy in the years to come, it will be able to "afford" more economic equality while absorbing the costs of such changes as the democratization of the workplace, increased professionalism and more worker autonomy. If automation and the currently rising centralization of American industry result in the disappearance of jobs, however, greater equality will become impossible and people will fight each other for the remaining jobs. This could result in a bitter conflict between the "haves" and the "have-nots" that might even lead to a revolution, bringing about formal equality by governmental edict in a way not altogether different from the Socialist and Communist revolutions of the 20th century. But that conflict between the "haves" and the "have-nots" could also lead to a right-wing revolution in which the "haves," supported by conservatives among the "have-nots," would establish a quasi-totalitarian government that would use force to maintain the existing inequalities.

Although the likelihood of either a left-wing or a right-wing revolution is probably small, even a gradual transformation toward greater equality is not likely to be tranquil. More equality for some means a reduction in privilege for others, and more democracy and autonomy for some means a loss of power for others. Those who have the privilege and the power will not give them up without a struggle and will fight the demand for more equality with all the economic and political resources they can muster. Even today, such demands by only a small part of the black and young population have resulted in a massive backlash appeal for law and order by a large part of the white and older population.

Moreover, whenever important national decisions must be made, American politics has generally been guided by majority rule or majority public opinion, and this has often meant the tyranny of the majority over the minority. As long as the unequal are a minority, the structure of American politics can easily be used to frustrate their demands for change. The inability of the Federal Government to satisfy the demands of the Negro population for greater equality is perhaps the best example. In the future, the political structure must be altered to allow the Government to become more responsive to minority demands, particularly as the pressure for equality grows.

Whether or not such governmental responsiveness will be politically feasible depends in large part on how working-class and lower-middle-class Americans feel about the equality revolution. They are the ruling majority in America, and if they want more equality, democracy and autonomy, these will be achieved—and through peaceful political methods. If the two classes remain primarily interested in obtaining more affluence, however, they will be able to suppress demands for equality by minorities, especially those demands which reduce their own powers and privileges. No one can tell now how these two classes will feel in the future, but there is no doubt that their preferences will determine the outcome of the equality revolution.

Still, whatever happens in the years and decades to come, the equality revolution is under way, and however slowly it proceeds and however bitter the struggle between its supporters and opponents, it will continue. It may succeed, but it could also fail, leaving in its wake a level of social and political conflict unlike any America has ever known.

What I have written so far I have written as a sociologist, trying to predict what will occur in coming generations. But as a citizen, I believe that what will happen ought to happen, that the emerging demand for more equality, democracy and autonomy is desirable. Too many Americans, even among the nonpoor, still lead lives of quiet desperation, and the good life today is the monopoly of only a happy few. I think that the time has come when unbridled liberty as we have defined it traditionally can no longer be America's guiding value, especially if the right to liberty deprives others of a similar liberty. But I believe also that there is no inherent conflict between liberty and equality; that the society we must create should provide enough equality to permit everyone the liberty to control his own life without creating inequality for others, and that this, when it comes, will be the Great Society.

19. SUMMARY OF REPORT

NATIONAL ADVISORY (KERNER) COMMISSION ON CIVIL DISORDERS

INTRODUCTION

The summer of 1967 again brought racial disorders to American cities, and with them shock, fear and bewilderment to the nation.

The worst came during a two-week period in July, first in Newark and then in Detroit. Each set off a chain reaction in neighboring communities.

On July 28, 1967, the President of the United States established this Commission and directed us to answer three basic questions:

What happened?

Why did it happen?

What can be done to prevent it from happening again?

To respond to these questions, we have undertaken a broad range of studies and investigations. We have visited the riot cities; we have heard many witnesses; we have sought the counsel of experts across the country.

This is our basic conclusion: Our nation is moving toward two societies, one black, one white—separate and unequal. . . .

This deepening racial division is not inevitable. The movement apart can be reversed. Choice is still possible. Our principal task is to define that choice and to press for a national resolution.

To pursue our present course will involve the continuing polarization of the American community and, ultimately, the destruction of basic democratic values.

The alternative is not blind repression or capitulation to lawlessness. It is the realization of common opportunities for all within a single society. . . .

The vital needs of the nation must be met; hard choices must be made, and, if necessary, new taxes enacted.

Violence cannot build a better society. Disruption and disorder nourish repression, not justice. They strike at the freedom of every citizen. The community cannot—it will not—tolerate coercion and mob rule.

Violence and destruction must be ended—in the streets of the ghetto and in the lives of people.

Segregation and poverty have created in the racial ghetto a destructive environment totally unknown to most white Americans.

What white Americans have never fully understood—but what the Negro can never forget—is that white society is deeply implicated in the ghetto. White institutions created it, white institutions maintain it, and white society condones it. . . .

From *Report of the National Advisory Commission on Civil Disorders*. Washington, D. C.: U. S. Government Printing Office, 1968. Excerpts.

Certain fundamental matters are clear. Of these, the most fundamental is the racial attitude and behavior of white Americans toward black Americans.

Race prejudice has shaped our history decisively; it now threatens to affect our future.

White racism is essentially responsible for the explosive mixture which has been accumulating in our cities since the end of World War II. Among the ingredients of this mixture are:

Pervasive discrimination and segregation in employment, education and housing, which have resulted in the continuing exclusion of great numbers of Negroes from the benefits of economic progress.

Black in-migration and white exodus, which have produced the massive and growing concentrations of impoverished Negroes in our major cities, creating a growing crisis of deteriorating facilities and services and unmet human needs.

The black ghettos where segregation and poverty converge on the young to destroy opportunity and enforce failure. Crime, drug addiction, dependency on welfare, and bitterness and resentment against society in general and white society in particular are the result.

At the same time, most whites and some Negroes outside the ghetto have prospered to a degree unparalleled in the history of civilization. Through television and other media, this affluence has been flaunted before the eyes of the Negro poor and the jobless ghetto youth.

Yet these facts alone cannot be said to have caused the disorders. Recently, other powerful ingredients have begun to catalyze the mixture:

Frustrated hopes are the residue of the unfulfilled expectations aroused by the great judicial and legislative victories of the Civil Rights Movement and the dramatic struggle for equal rights in the South.

A climate that tends toward approval and encouragement of violence as a form of protest has been created by white terrorism directed against nonviolent protest; by the open defiance of law and federal authority by state and local officials resisting desegregation; and by some protest groups engaging in civil disobedience who turn their backs on nonviolence, go beyond the constitutionally protected rights of petition and free assembly, and resort to violence to attempt to compel alteration of laws and policies with which they disagree.

The frustrations of powerlessness have led some Negroes to the conviction that there is no effective alternative to violence as a means of achieving redress of grievances, and of "moving the system." These frustrations are reflected in alienation and hostility toward the institutions of law and government and the white society which controls them, and in the reach toward racial consciousness and solidarity reflected in the slogan "Black Power."

A new mood has sprung up among Negroes, particularly among the young, in which self-esteem and enhanced racial pride are replacing apathy and submission to "the system."

The police are not merely a "spark" factor. To some Negroes police have come to symbolize white power, white racism and white repression. And the fact is that many police do reflect and express these white attitudes. The atmosphere of hostility and cynicism is reinforced by a widespread belief among Negroes in the existence of police brutality and in a "double standard" of justice and protection—one for Negroes and one for whites.

To this point, we have attempted to identify the prime components of the "explosive mixture." In the chapters that follow we seek to analyze them in the perspective of history. Their meaning, however, is clear:

In the summer of 1967, we have seen in our cities a chain reaction of racial violence. If we are heedless, none of us shall escape the consequences. . . .

Comparing the Immigrant and Negro Experience

In this chapter, we address ourselves to a fundamental question that many white Americans are asking: why have so many Negroes, unlike the European immigrants, been unable to escape from the ghetto and from poverty. We believe the following factors play a part:

The Maturing Economy: When the European immigrants arrived, they gained an economic foothold by providing the unskilled labor needed by industry. Unlike the immigrant, the Negro migrant found little opportunity in the city. The economy, by then matured, had little use for the unskilled labor he had to offer.

The Disability of Race: The structure of discrimination has stringently narrowed opportunities for the Negro and restricted his prospects. European immigrants suffered from discrimination, but never so pervasively.

Entry into the Political System: The immigrants usually settled in rapidly growing cities with powerful and expanding political machines, which traded economic advantages for political support. Ward-level grievance machinery, as well as personal representation, enabled the immigrant to make his voice heard and his power felt.

By the time the Negro arrived, these political machines were no longer so powerful or so well equipped to provide jobs or other favors, and in many cases were unwilling to share their influence with Negroes.

Cultural Factors: Coming from societies with a low standard of living and at a time when job aspirations were low, the immigrants sensed little deprivation in being forced to take the less desirable and poorer-paying jobs. Their large and cohesive families contributed to total income. Their vision of the future—one that led to a life outside of the ghetto—provided the incentive necessary to endure the present.

Although Negro men worked as hard as the immigrants, they were unable to support their families. The entrepreneurial opportunities had vanished. As a result of slavery and long periods of unemployment, the Negro family structure had become matriarchal; the males played a secondary and marginal family role—one which offered little compensation for their hard and unrewarding labor. Above all, segregation denied Negroes access to good jobs and the opportunity to leave the ghetto. For them, the future seemed to lead only to a dead end.

Today, whites tend to exaggerate how well and quickly they escaped from poverty. The fact is that immigrants who came from rural backgrounds, as many Negroes do, are only now, after three generations, finally beginning to move into the middle class.

By contrast, Negroes began concentrating in the city less than two generations ago, and under much less favorable conditions. Although some Negroes have escaped poverty, few have been able to escape the urban ghetto.

WHAT CAN BE DONE?

The Community Response

Our investigation of the 1967 riot cities establishes that virtually every major episode of violence was foreshadowed by an accumulation of unresolved grievances and by wide-spread dissatisfaction among Negroes with the unwillingness or inability of local government to respond.

Overcoming these conditions is essential for community support of law enforcement and civil order. City governments need new and more vital channels of communication to the residents of the ghetto; they need to improve their capacity to respond effectively to community needs before they become community grievances; and they need to provide opportunity for meaningful involvement of ghetto residents in shaping policies and programs which affect the community.

Police and the Community

The abrasive relationship between the police and the minority communities has been a major—and explosive—source of grievance, tension and disorder. The blame must be shared by the total society.

The police are faced with demands for increased protection and service in the ghetto. Yet the aggressive patrol practices thought necessary to meet these demands themselves create tension and hostility. The resulting grievances have been further aggravated by the lack of effective mechanisms for handling complaints against the police. Special programs for bettering police-community relations have been instituted, but these alone are not enough. Police administrators, with the guidance of public officials, and the support of the entire community, must take vigorous action to improve law enforcement and to decrease the potential for disorder. . . .

By 1985, the Negro population in central cities is expected to increase by 72 percent to approximately 20.8 million. Coupled with the continued exodus of white families to the suburbs, this growth will produce majority Negro populations in many of the nation's largest cities.

The future of these cities, and of their burgeoning Negro populations, is grim. Most new employment opportunities are being created in suburbs and outlying areas. This trend will continue unless important changes in public policy are made.

In prospect, therefore, is further deterioration of already inadequate municipal tax bases in the face of increasing demands for public services, and continuing unemployment and poverty among the urban Negro population:

Three choices are open to the nation:

We can maintain present policies, continuing both the proportion of the nation's resources now allocated to programs for the unemployed and the disadvantaged, and the inadequate and failing effort to achieve an integrated society.

We can adopt a policy of "enrichment" aimed at improving dramatically the quality of ghetto life while abandoning integration as a goal.

We can pursue integration by combining ghetto "enrichment" with policies which will encourage Negro movement out of central city areas.

The first choice, continuance of present policies, has ominous consequences for our society. The share of the nation's resources now allocated to programs for the disadvantaged is insufficient to arrest the deterioration of life in central city ghettos. Under such conditions, a rising proportion of Negroes may come to see in the deprivation and segregation they experience, a justification for violent protest, or for extending support to now isolated extremists who advocate civil disruption. Large-scale and continuing violence could result, followed by white retaliation, and, ultimately, the separation of the two communities in a garrison state.

Even if violence does not occur, the consequences are unacceptable. Development of a racially integrated society, extraordinarily difficult today, will be virtually impossible when the present black ghetto population of 12.5 million has grown to almost 21 million.

To continue present policies is to make permanent the division of our country into two societies; one, largely Negro and poor, located in the central cities; the other, predominately white and affluent, located in the suburbs and in outlying areas.

The second choice, ghetto enrichment coupled with abandonment of integration, is also unacceptable. It is another way of choosing a permanently divided country. Moreover, equality cannot be achieved under conditions of nearly complete separation. In a country where the economy, and particularly the resources of employment, are predominantely white, a policy of separation can only relegate Negroes to a permanently inferior economic status.

We believe that the only possible choice for America is the third—a policy which combines ghetto enrichment with programs designed to encourage integration of substantial numbers of Negroes into the society outside the ghetto.

Enrichment must be an important adjunct to integration, for no matter how ambitious or energetic the program, few Negroes now living in central cities can be quickly integrated. In the meantime, large-scale improvement in the equality of ghetto life is essential.

But this can be no more than an interim strategy. Programs must be developed which will permit substantial Negro movement out of the ghettos. The primary goal must be a single society, in which every citizen will be free to live and work according to his capabilities and desires, not his color.

Recommendations For National Action . . .

Employment. Pervasive unemployment and underemployment are the most persistent and serious grievances in minority areas. They are inextricably linked to the problem of civil disorder.

Despite growing federal expenditures for manpower development and training programs, and sustained general economic prosperity and increasing demands for skilled workers, about two million—white and nonwhite—are permanently unemployed. About ten million are underemployed, of whom 6.5 million work full time for wages below the poverty line.

The 500,000 "hard-core" unemployed in the central cities who lack a basic education and are unable to hold a steady job are made up in large part of

Negro males between the ages of 18 and 25. In the riot cities which we surveyed, Negroes were three times as likely as whites to hold unskilled jobs, which are often part time, seasonal, low-paying and "dead end."

Negro males between the ages of 15 and 25 predominated among the rioters. More than 20 percent of the rioters were unemployed, and many who were employed held intermittent, low status, unskilled jobs which they regarded as below their education and ability. . . .

Education. Education in a democratic society must equip children to develop their potential and to participate fully in American life. For the community at large, the schools have discharged this responsibility well. But for many minorities, and particularly for the children of the ghetto, the schools have failed to provide the educational experience which could overcome the effects of discrimination and deprivation.

This failure is one of the persistent sources of grievance and resentment within the Negro community. The hostility of Negro parents and students toward the school system is generating increasing conflict and causing disruption within many city school districts. But the most dramatic evidence of the relationship between educational practices and civil disorders lies in the high incidence of riot participation by ghetto youth who have not completed high school.

The bleak record of public education for ghetto children is growing worse. In the critical skills—verbal and reading ability—Negro students are falling further behind whites with each year of school completed. The high unemployment and underemployment rate of Negro youth is evidence, in part, of the growing educational crisis.

We support integration as the priority education strategy; it is essential to the future of American society. In this last summer's disorders we have seen the consequences of racial isolation at all levels, and of attitudes toward race, on both sides, produced by three centuries of myth, ignorance and bias. It is indispensable that opportunities for interaction between the races be expanded.

We recognize that the growing dominance of pupils from disadvantaged minorities in city school populations will not soon be reversed. No matter how great the effort toward desegregation, many children of the ghetto will not, within their school careers, attend integrated schools.

If existing disadvantages are not to be perpetuated, we must drastically improve the quality of ghetto education. Equality of results with all-white schools must be the goal. . . .

Housing. After more than three decades of fragmented and grossly underfunded federal housing programs, nearly six million substandard housing units remain occupied in the United States.

The housing problem is particularly acute in the minority ghettos. Nearly two-thirds of all non-white families living in the central cities today live in neighborhoods marked with substandard housing and general urban blight. Two major factors are responsible.

First: Many ghetto residents simply cannot pay the rent necessary to support decent housing. In Detroit, for example, over 40 percent of the non-white occupied units in 1960 required rent of over 35 percent of the tenants' income.

Second: Discrimination prevents access to many non-slum areas, particularly the suburbs, where good housing exists. In addition, by creating a "back pressure" in the racial ghettos, it makes it possible for landlords to break up apartments for denser occupancy, and keeps prices and rents of deteriorated ghetto housing higher than they would be in a truly free market.

To date, federal programs have been able to do comparatively little to provide housing for the disadvantaged. In the 31-year history of subsidized federal housing, only about 800,000 units have been constructed, with recent production averaging about 50,000 units a year. By comparison, over a period only three years longer, FHA insurance guarantees have made possible the construction of over ten million middle and upper-income units.

Two points are fundamental to the Commission's recommendations: .

First: Federal housing programs must be given a new thrust aimed at overcoming the prevailing patterns of racial segregation. If this is not done, those programs will continue to concentrate the most impoverished and dependent segments of the population into the central-city ghettos where there is already a critical gap between the needs of the population and the public resources to deal with them.

Second: The private sector must be brought into the production and financing of low and moderate rental housing to supply the capabilities and capital necessary to meet the housing needs of the nation. . . .

20. AMERICA'S RACE PARADOX: THE GAP BETWEEN SOCIAL PROGRESS AND POLITICAL DESPAIR

NATHAN GLAZER

Nathan Glazer (1923–   ), a leading American sociologist and specialist in race relations, is professor at the University of California.

. . . First, let me briefly document the fact that things *are* getting better. We must do this because so many liberal and progressive shapers of opinion, and the vast flock that follows them, are convinced (and *insist*) that the concrete situation of Negro Americans has *not* changed, or has indeed got worse. Sadly enough, social scientists, who should know the facts best, are often among the worst offenders. The writer of that fine study of Negro

From Nathan Glazer, "America's Race Paradox: The Gap between Social Progress and Despair," *Encounter*, October, 1968. Reprinted by permission of the author.

street-corner men, *Tally's Corner,* for example, states casually that "the number of the poor and their problems have grown steadily since World War II. . . ." Social scientists who contend that the economic situation of Negroes is getting worse will point to the rising *absolute* gap between Negro and white incomes and ignore the fact that Negro incomes have come closer to white incomes as a *percentage* of white incomes. By this logic, if we come to a fortunate time when white median incomes are $10,000 and non-white median incomes are $8,000, it could be argued that Negroes are "worse off" than when whites made $5,000 and Negroes $3,500!

In October 1967, the Bureau of Labor Statistics and the Bureau of the Census put out a compendium of statistics on the *Social and Economic Conditions of Negroes in the United States.* Here are some of the major findings:

Income: In 1966, 23% of non-white families had incomes of more than $7,000, against 53% of white families. Ten years before, using dollars of the same value, only 9% of the non-white families had incomes at this level, against 31% of white families.

If we look at the U.S. outside the South, where the Negro situation on all measures is worst, we find in 1966 38% of non-white families with income above $7,000, against 59% of white families at that level.

Occupation: Between 1960 and 1966, the number of non-whites in the better-paying and more secure occupational categories increased faster than whites: a 50% increase for non-whites in professional, technical and managerial work, against a 13% increase for whites; a 48% increase in clerical occupations, against a 19% increase for whites; a 32% increase in sales workers, against a 7% increase for whites; a 45% increase in craftsmen and foremen, against a 10% increase for whites. And during the same time, the proportions of non-whites working as private household workers and labourers dropped.

Education: In 1960 there was a 1–9 years gap in median years of school completed between non-white and white males 25 to 29; by 1966, there was only a .5 years gap.

In 1960, 36% of non-white males 25 to 29 had completed high school, against 63% of white males; by 1966, 53% of non-white males had completed high school, against 73% of white males.

In 1960, 3.9% of Negro males 25 to 34 had completed college, against 15.7% of white males; in 1966, 7.4% of Negro males had completed college, against 17.9% of white males—a 90% increase among non-white college graduates, against a 14% increase in white college graduates.

Housing: Between 1960 and 1966, there was a 25% drop in the number of substandard housing units occupied by non-whites (from 2,263,000 to 1,691,000 units), and a 44% increase in the number of standard units occupied by non-whites—from 2,881,000 to 4,135,000 units.

If we look at political participation—voting, offices held, in effect, political power—we find an equally striking increase. Thus, Negro voter registration in the South increased from 2,164,000 in March 1964 to 3,072,000 in May

1968, while Negro population remained stable. The National Commission on Civil Disorders surveyed twenty cities to find out the extent of Negro political representation. The cities averaged 16% in Negro population; 10% in proportion of elected Negro political representatives. We have to interpret such a figure in the light of the fact that Negroes of voting age are generally a smaller proportion of the total Negro population in most cities than whites of voting age of the white population, since Negroes in cities have a higher proportion of young families and children, whites a higher proportion of the aged.

Even on that sorest point of black-white relations, the police, the Kerner Commission reports progress in one significant respect: there are now substantial numbers of Negroes on many city police forces—Washington 21%, Philadelphia 20, Chicago 17, St. Louis 11, Hartford 11, Newark 10, Atlanta 10, Cleveland 7, New York 5, Detroit 5.

These are simply overall measures. When one considers the large number of programmes devoted to getting Negroes into colleges, into graduate and professional schools, into various corporations, to raise their grades in the Federal Civil Service, to moderate police attitudes—and when one considers the incentives to do all these things to be found in riot and threat of riot, boycott and threat of boycott, one cannot help conclude that the situation of Negroes is changing . . . for "the better."

To be sure, all the figures I have quoted can be disputed. Thus, 14% of Negro males as against only 2% of white males (we have recently become aware) never get counted by the census; and if they were counted, they would undoubtedly depress the Negro figures on income, education, occupation, housing. But as against this, it must be pointed out that we have probably not been counting similar proportions of Negro males of working age in earlier censuses; so the change from one census to another represents real change.

It can be argued that the quality of jobs held by Negroes, even if they are in white-collar and skilled labour categories, is worse than that held by whites; and this too is true. But the changes over time are real, and the quality of jobs has certainly not on the whole decreased. Indeed, it has probably improved. Less Negro professionals today are preachers, more are engineers.

It can be argued that the improvement in the economic and educational and housing condition of the Negro is largely an effect of their migration from the South, and from small town and rural areas, to the North and West, and to big cities; if we were to look at Negroes in the North and West alone, we would not find such marked changes. But the statistics show improvement in every section.

It has been argued that while these overall measures of improvement truly reflect improvement for the Negro middle classes and stable working classes, the lower working classes have relatively declined, and have shown no progress. But an unpublished analysis of income statistics by Dr. Albert Wohlstetter (of the University of Chicago) reveals that the *lower* Negro income groups have improved their position relative to white low-income groups more in recent years than the Negro upper-income groups have improved their position relative to white upper-income groups. In other words, the gap between poor Negroes and poor whites in terms of income is narrower now than in the 1950s. At the same time it is true that other social indicators —*e.g.*, the proportion of broken families and of illegitimacy—continue to reveal worsening conditions.

Finally, one may argue that much of the advance to which I have pointed has taken place since the Viet Nam War expanded in 1965, just as the previous economic advances of the Negro took place during the Korean War, and came to an end when that war came to an end. Between the wars there was relative decline and stagnation.

There is much truth in these last two arguments with the gross statistics of recent improvement. But it is also true that the advances made during wars have not been fully wiped out in the past—it is rather that the rate of change has not kept up. By now the build-up of Negro political power and of national programmes and commitments that guarantee advance is so great and the scale of the advances that have taken place in recent years is so massive, that I cannot believe they will not continue after the war—if, that is, there is not a radical change in the political situation to reverse the social and economic trends of the last eight years.

More striking, however, than the advance itself is the fact that on the basis of our present social statistics we can not single out the Negro as a group in the United States which suffers unique deprivation, *i.e.*, as compared to other ethnic and racial groups which suffer from the effects of poor education, depressed rural backgrounds, and recent migration to urban areas. There has been a division among American social scientists as to how to view Negro Americans in the context of the ethnic and racial history of the United States. One tendency is to emphasize everything that is "unique"—and a great deal is unique: the manner of their arrival (by force, and in chains); the conditions under which they lived for two hundred years (slavery); the conditions under which they have lived for the last hundred years (legal inferiority in a good part of the country); finally, the special role of the Negro Americans in American imagination and in culture (as central participants in shaping it, and as the subjects of some of its major themes). But it is also possible to see Negro Americans as part of a sequence of ethnic and racial groups that have moved into American society and become a part of it.

A new illusion is now abroad in the land. It asserts that all white ethnic groups have rapidly moved into American society, achieving respectable levels of income, good conditions of living, and political power. All racially distinct groups, suffering from the racism of American society, have been held back; and the Negro American, suffering from the special character of chattel slavery, is furthest back. The truth is nothing like this. Some white ethnic groups—such as the Jews—have shown a rapid economic mobility. Others have been much slower to achieve economically. One of these economically-backward white ethnic groups, the Irish, has been politically gifted, and members of the group are to be found disproportionately among elected officials of every level and in almost every part of the country. Others, such as

Italians and Poles, have done poorly both economically *and* politically. Some racially distinct groups—such as the Japanese—have done remarkably well in education and occupation. Most others have done badly. . . .

Almost every ethnic and racial group that has settled in this country has been "nationalistic" and "separatist," and the laws have permitted a level of separatism for many groups that has not yet been quite reached by American Negroes. Many groups have harboured and supported with money (and sometimes with armed volunteers) nationalist leaders interested in freeing or revolutionising their homelands, even when this was a matter of great embarrassment to the U.S.A. Most groups have maintained schools in their own tongue. Most groups have tried desperately to maintain the original home language, religion, and ethnic customs among their children in America. There has been one limit set on the free development of ethnic and racial groups in this country—territorial autonomy. But short of that, subtle and complex adjustments were made to accommodate a wide variety of differences.

The history of the gross prejudice and discrimination which almost all immigrant and racial groups have faced is well known; but we tend to be less aware of these "American adjustments" to accommodate a mixed population of different ethnic and racial groups. Thus, we have developed a pattern of political recognition, through the parties, in which groups of any substantial number get represented, through appointive and elective office. This system has worked well, without any laws requiring quotas, or specifications of "how much" and "what kind." There has been a pattern of economic integration in which groups have developed bases of economic independence. (Undoubtedly the general freedom this country has given to economic enterprises has aided this development.) Unfortunately, the ability to create such an independent economic base is now considerably limited by, among other things, the host of state and social licensing and regulatory requirements, trade union requirements, federal tax and accounting procedures, all of which today make it much harder for the less literate and sophisticated to become successful in business. We have allowed full freedom to religious organisation, and under the protection of religious organisation a wide range of cultural, social, political activities is carried on. We have given freedom to the creation of independent schools. All this has occurred even though a young patchwork nation has had the difficult task of fashioning a single national identity.

Compared with most countries that have tried to create themselves out of a mixed population, there has been a certain genius in the American style of confronting this problem. The principle has been: no formal recognition of the ethnic and racial groups, but every informal recognition of their right and desire to self-development, assimilation or integration at their own chosen rate, to an independent economic base, independent social, religious, and political institutions, and political recognition as part of a united country. The principle has often been broken: laws have been erected against certain groups—most massively in the case of Negroes, but also in the case of American Indians and Orientals; and we have often restricted the free and spontaneous development of various groups through movements of "Americanisation" and forced patriotism. But the most massive and inhumane breaks in these principles have in the end been recognised as "un-American," and wrong: slavery for the Negroes; "separate but equal" facilities for Negroes; public discrimination against Negroes; separate schools for the Chinese; land laws restricting the right of purchase by Japanese; the forced relocation of the Japanese and their loss of property; the immigration laws establishing quotas for peoples and races; attempts of states to ban private schooling. All these have in the end been overcome by courts and legislatures, and the basic principle—no public recognition of race or ethnicity; every private consideration of its reality and meaningfulness—has, in the end, prevailed. . . .

21. EQUAL JUSTICE FOR THE POOR, TOO

ARTHUR J. GOLDBERG

Arthur J. Goldberg (1908–   ) was an Associate Justice of the Supreme Court of the United States.

In theory, all Americans charged with a crime are, so far as the law is concerned, equal before the bar of justice in every American court. This is guaranteed by the "due process" and the "equal protection" clauses to the Constitution, and the inspiration comes from the Bible: "You shall do no injustice in judgment; you shall not be partial to the poor or defer to the great, but in righteousness shall you judge your neighbor." Justices of the Supreme Court and of many state courts take oaths to "do equal justice to the poor and to the rich."

Unfortunately, despite all these guarantees and safeguards, the poor often meet with less than the same justice as the rich (or reasonably well off) in our courts. As Justice Black has stated, "There can be no equal justice where the kind of trial a man gets depends on the amount of money he has." . . .

When the police conduct a roundup of "suspects," they generally do so in poor neighborhoods, rarely in middle-class communities. As a result, more poor than rich are arrested for crimes they did not commit. We do not know how many of these people lose or fail to obtain jobs because of an "arrest record" resulting from guiltless involvement in such episodes. Nor do we know how many poor people are even aware of their rights in such situations: for example, their right to consult an attorney, to sue for false arrest, or to have their arrest records expunged (in jurisdictions which have procedures permitting this). Moreover, psychologists and sociologists tell us that young

From Arthur J. Goldberg, "Equal Justice for the Poor, Too," *New York Times Magazine,* March 15, 1964, pp. 24, 100–103, excerpts. © by The New York Times Company. Reprinted by permission.

people who are close to choosing criminal identities may have this choice confirmed by their repeated treatment as criminal types.

After arrest, the accused who is poor must often await the disposition of his case in jail because of his inability to raise bail, while the accused who can afford bail is free to return to his family and his job. Equally important, he is free during the critical period between arrest and trial to help his attorney with the investigation and preparation of his defense. In a recent case a defendant was imprisoned well over two years between the time he was arrested and the time he was ultimately acquitted on appeal, solely because he could not raise the small amount of money necessary for bail. This is an example of justice denied, of a man imprisoned for no reason other than his poverty.

In preparing for trial the lawyer appointed to represent an accused who is without funds has few, if any, of the investigatory resources available to the prosecution or to an accused with means. He may also be limited in his ability to subpoena necessary witnesses to appear at trial. Under the present federal rule, for example, a defendant with means may automatically obtain all necessary subpoenas by simply paying a fee and designating the desired witness. A defendant who cannot afford to pay the fee, however, must submit a detailed affidavit stating why he needs the witness and indicating the substance of the expected testimony.

Thus, as a price for obtaining the testimony of a witness, the accused without means must do something not required either of the government or of an accused with means: he must disclose his case in advance. This result might indeed be desirable if disclosure were required of all parties to a criminal case. But fundamental fairness and equality would seem to dictate that this should not be exacted alone from an indigent as the price of exercising his Sixth Amendment right to obtain the testimony of necessary witnesses.

After conviction, the defendant's financial condition may have a significant effect on whether he is placed on probation or sent to the penitentiary, on whether and when he is paroled from the penitentiary, and on whether he continues to remain at liberty. Probation and parole frequently depend upon the availability of a job and/or of psychiatric treatment. These conditions can, of course, be met and maintained more easily by one who has means than by one who does not.

The alternative fine/imprisonment penalty still frequently imposed for petty offenses may also be unfair to the defendant without means. The "choice" of paying $100 fine or spending thirty days in jail is really no choice at all to the person who cannot raise $100. The resulting imprisonment is no more or no less than imprisonment for being poor, a doctrine which I trust this nation has long since outgrown. Concern has even been expressed that the most serious penalty of all—death—is imposed with disproportionate frequency on the poor. Warden Lawes, who witnessed the execution of many Sing Sing inmates, remarked: "If a wealthy man, or the son of a wealthy man kills, he is insane or deranged and usually either goes scot free or to an insane asylum. If a poor and friendless man kills, he is a sane man who committed willful murder for which he must die." . . .

The right to counsel at trial and on appeal may prove hollow if appointed counsel is not armed with the tools of advocacy—investigatory resources, expert witnesses, subpoena, trial transcript. If the right to counsel is to be given meaningful content, and if our adversary process is to retain its vitality, the appointed attorney, like the retained attorney, must be permitted to perform as an advocate. . . . If representation is to be as effective for poor as for rich, it follows that services necessary to make this right effective must be supplied at government expense to those unable to afford them. . . .

Our concern, moreover, should not be limited to the very poor alone. . . . I would doubt whether half of the families in this affluent country could today afford an adequate defense if one of their members were accused of a serious crime. Perhaps they could raise sufficient money for bail or even for a trial lawyer, but what about an investigator, a psychiatrist, or an expert in ballistics or handwriting; and what about a complete transcript to prepare an appeal and the prosecution of the appeal itself? . . .

Here, we can learn much from the Scandinavian countries. The services provided there are made available to all accused persons. No test of financial capacity is applied as a condition of receiving them. Far more than the provision of counsel is encompassed within these systems. For example, in preparing the defense, the appointed lawyer may make use of government laboratories and consult with its experts. If the accused is acquitted no effort is made to collect the cost of defense regardless of the defendant's means. If he is convicted some of the countries inquire into his means, and if found financially able he is charged with some or all of the costs of his defense. In at least one country no effort is made to establish the means of the defendant or to charge him with costs even if he is convicted.

Even if we choose not to go as far as the Scandinavian countries, we should certainly consider adopting procedures whereby persons erroneously charged with crime could be reimbursed for their expenditures in defending against the charge. Without such procedures, acquittal may often be almost as ruinous to the defendant and his family as conviction.

At the very least, we should extend our provision of free legal services in criminal cases to include many hard-working people who, although not indigent, cannot, without extraordinary sacrifice, raise sufficient funds to defend themselves or members of their families against a criminal charge.

Whenever the government considers extending a needed service to those accused of crime, the question arises: But what about the victim? We should confront the problem of the victim directly; his burden is not alleviated by denying necessary services to the accused. Many countries throughout the world, recognizing that crime is a community problem, have designed systems for government compensation of victims of crime. Serious consideration of this approach is long overdue here. The victim of a robbery or an assault has been denied the "protection" of the laws in a very real sense, and society should assume some responsibility for making him whole.

These are but a few—indeed a very few—of the areas in which equal justice is lacking. There are many others. It is said that the government cannot be expected to equalize all economic disparities. Of course it cannot, but this does not mean that it should not try to eliminate disparities in certain critical areas like criminal justice. The real question, as put by the Attorney General's Committee on Poverty and the Administration of Federal Criminal Justice, is: "Has government done all that can be reasonably required of it . . . to render the poverty of the litigant an irrelevancy"?

In all candor, we must confess that government in this country—both state and federal—has not done all that can reasonably be required. Equal criminal justice for rich and poor alike is one of the few areas where our country follows rather than leads. If it be true that "the quality of a nation's civilization can be largely measured by the methods it uses in the enforcement of its criminal law," then this situation cannot long be tolerated. We must lead in equality if we are to continue to lead in liberty.

22. THE SOVIET CONCEPT OF EQUALITY

JOSEPH STALIN

Joseph Stalin (1879–1953) ruled the Soviet Union for more than a generation in the tradition of the great tyrants of history. A leading figure in the Bolshevik Revolution of 1917, he emerged victorious from the intra-party struggle for power which followed Lenin's death in 1924, and proceeded to "Stalinize" Soviet society. He ruthlessly eliminated all opposition and was instrumental in transforming the U.S.S.R. from a backward, underdeveloped country into a major industrial-military power.

. . . Every Leninist knows (that is, if he is a real Leninist) that equalization in the sphere of requirements and individual life is a piece of reactionary petty-bourgeois absurdity worthy of a primitive sect of ascetics, but not of a socialist society organized on Marxian lines; for we cannot expect all people to have the same requirements and tastes, and all people to live their individual lives on the same model. And, finally, are not differences in requirements and in individual life still preserved among the workers? Does that mean that the workers are more remote from socialism than the members of the agricultural communes?

These people evidently think that socialism calls for equalization, for leveling the requirements and the individual lives of the members of society.

From Joseph Stalin, *Problems of Leninism.* Moscow: Foreign Languages Publishing House, 1953, pp. 634–38, excerpts, and pp. 463–66.

Needless to say, such an assumption has nothing in common with Marxism, with Leninism. By equality Marxism means, not equalization of individual requirements and individual life, but the abolition of classes, i.e., *a*) the equal emancipation of all working people from exploitation after the capitalists have been overthrown and expropriated; *b*) the equal abolition for all of private property in the means of production after they have been converted into the property of the whole of society; *c*) the equal duty of all to work according to their ability, and the equal right of all working people to receive remuneration according to the amount of work performed (*socialist* society); *d*) the equal duty of all to work according to their ability, and the equal right of all working people to receive remuneration according to their needs (*communist* society). Furthermore, Marxism proceeds from the assumption that people's tastes and requirements are not, and cannot be, identical, equal, in regard to quality or quantity, either in the period of socialism or in the period of communism.

That is the Marxian conception of equality.

Marxism has never recognized, nor does it recognize, any other equality.

To draw from this the conclusion that socialism calls for equalization, for the leveling of the requirements of the members of society, for the leveling of their tastes and of their individual lives—that according to the plans of the Marxists all should wear the same clothes and eat the same dishes in the same quantity—is to deal in vulgarities and to slander Marxism. It is time it was understood that Marxism is an enemy of equalization. Even in the *Manifesto of the Communist Party* Marx and Engels scourged primitive utopian socialism and described it as reactionary because it preached "universal asceticism and social leveling in its crudest form." In his *Anti-Dühring* Engels devoted a whole chapter to a withering criticism of the "radical equalitarian socialism" proposed by Dühring in opposition to Marxian socialism.

The real content of the proletarian demand for equality [said Engels] is the demand for the *abolition of classes*. And demand for equality which goes beyond that of necessity passes into absurdity.

Lenin said the same thing:

Engels was a thousand times right when he wrote that to conceive equality as meaning anything *beyond* the abolition of classes is a stupid and absurd prejudice. Bourgeois professors have tried to make use of the idea of equality to accuse us of wanting to make all men equal to one another. They have tried to accuse the Socialists of this absurdity, which they themselves invented. But in their ignorance they did not know that the Socialists—and precisely the founders of modern scientific socialism, Marx and Engels—said: equality is an empty phrase unless by equality is meant the abolition of classes. We want to abolish classes, and in this respect we stand for equality. But the claim that we want all men equal to one another is an empty phrase and stupid invention of intellectuals. [Lenin's speech "On Deceiving the People With Slogans About Liberty and Equality," *Works*, Vol. XXIV, pp. 293–294.]

Clear, one would think.

Bourgeois writers are fond of depicting Marxian socialism in the shape of the old czarist barracks, where everything is subordinated to the "principle" of equalization. But Marxists cannot be held responsible for the ignorance and stupidity of bourgeois writers. . . .

Now, in the period of intensive reconstruction, when the scale of production has become gigantic and technical equipment has become extremely complex, the heavy turnover of labor power has become the plague of production, which is disorganizing our factories. To "tolerate" the heavy turnover of labor power now would mean disintegrating our industry, it would mean wrecking the opportunities of fulfilling production plans and ruining the opportunities of improving the quality of the articles produced.

What is the cause of the heavy turnover of labor power?

The cause is the wrong structure of wages, the wrong wage scales, the "leftist" practice of wage equalization. In a number of our factories wage scales are drawn up in such a way as to practically wipe out the difference between skilled and unskilled labor, between heavy and light work. The consequence of wage equalization is that the unskilled worker lacks the incentive to become a skilled worker and is thus deprived of the prospect of advancement; as a result he feels himself a "visitor" in the factory, working only temporarily so as to "earn a little" and then go off to "seek his fortune" elsewhere. The consequence of wage equalization is that the skilled worker is obliged to wander from factory to factory until he finds one where his skill is properly appreciated.

Hence, the "general" drift from factory to factory; hence, the heavy turnover of labor power.

In order to put an end to this evil we must abolish wage equalization and discard the old wage scales. In order to put an end to this evil we must draw up wage scales that will take into account the difference between skilled and unskilled labor, between heavy and light work. We cannot tolerate a situation where a rolling-mill hand in a steel mill earns no more than a sweeper. We cannot tolerate a situation where a locomotive driver earns only as much as a copying clerk. Marx and Lenin said that the difference between skilled and unskilled labor would exist even under socialism, even after classes had been abolished; that only under communism would this difference disappear and that, consequently, even under socialism "wages" must be paid according to work performed and not according to needs.

23. CLASS AND PRIVILEGE IN COMMUNIST SOCIETY

MILOVAN DJILAS

Milovan Djilas (1911–   ) was reared in the Communist movement and rose to the vice-presidency of Yugoslavia; he was a close friend of Tito and a national hero. In late 1953 Djilas wrote a series of articles in BOR'BA, *the official organ of the Yugoslav Communist Party. These articles criticized the confining controls of ideology, party, and bureaucracy, and presaged* THE NEW CLASS, *which, in a real sense, is the logical expression of Djilas's disenchantment with communism.*

Everything happened differently in the U.S.S.R. and other Communist countries from what the leaders—even such prominent ones as Lenin, Stalin, Trotsky, and Bukharin—anticipated. They expected that the state would rapidly wither away, that democracy would be strengthened. The reverse happened. They expected a rapid improvement in the standard of living. . . . In every instance, the standard of living has failed to rise in proportion to the rate of industrialization, which was much more rapid. It was believed that the differences between cities and villages, between intellectual and physical labor, would slowly disappear; instead these differences have increased. Communist anticipations in other areas—including their expectations for developments in the non-Communist world—have also failed to materialize.

The greatest illusion was that industrialization and collectivization in the U.S.S.R., and destruction of capitalist ownership, would result in a classless society. In 1936, when the new Constitution was promulgated, Stalin announced that the "exploiting class" had ceased to exist. The capitalist and other classes of ancient origin had in fact been destroyed, but a new class, previously unknown to history, had been formed.

It is understandable that this class, like those before it, should believe that the establishment of its power would result in happiness and freedom for all men. The only difference between this and other classes was that it treated the delay in the realization of its illusions more crudely. It thus affirmed that its power was more complete than the power of any other class before in history, and its class illusions and prejudices were proportionally greater.

This new class, the bureaucracy, or more accurately the political bureaucracy, has all the characteristics of earlier ones as well as some new character-

From Milovan Djilas, *The New Class*. New York: Frederick A. Praeger, Inc., 1957. Pp. 37–40; 44–46; 66–69, excerpts. Reprinted by permission of the publisher.

istics of its own. Its origin had its special characteristics also, even though in essence it was similar to the beginnings of other classes.

Other classes, too, obtained their strength and power by the revolutionary path, destroying the political, social, and other orders they met in their way. However, almost without exception, these classes attained power *after* new economic patterns had taken shape in the old society. The case was the reverse with new classes in the Communist systems. It did not come to power to *complete* a new economic order but to *establish* its own and, in so doing, to establish its power over society.

In earlier epochs the coming to power of some class, some part of a class, or of some party, was the final event resulting from its formation and its development. The reverse was true in the U.S.S.R. There the new class was definitely formed after it attained power. Its consciousness had to develop before its economic and physical powers, because the class had not taken roots in the life of the nation. This class viewed its role in relation to the world from an idealistic point of view. Its practical possibilities were not diminished by this. In spite of its illusions, it represented an objective tendency toward industrialization. Its practical bent emanated from this tendency. The promise of an ideal world increased the faith in the ranks of the new class and sowed illusions among the masses. At the same time it inspired gigantic physical undertakings.

Because this new class had not been formed as a part of the economic and social life before it came to power, it could only be created in an organization of a special type, distinguished by a special discipline based on identical philosophic and ideological views of its members. A unity of belief and iron discipline was necessary to overcome its weaknesses.

The roots of the new class were implanted in a special Party, of the Bolshevik type. Lenin was right in his view that his Party was an exception in the history of human society, although he did not suspect that it would be the beginning of a new class.

To be more precise, the initiators of the new class are not found in the party of the Bolshevik type as a whole but in that stratum of professional revolutionaries who made up its core even before it attained power. It was not by accident that Lenin asserted after the failure of the 1905 revolution that only professional revolutionaries—men whose sole profession was revolutionary work—could build a new Party of the Bolshevik type. It was still less accidental that even Stalin, the future creator of a new class, was the most outstanding example of such a professional revolutionary. The new ruling class has been gradually developing from this very narrow stratum of revolutionaries. These revolutionaries composed its core for a long period. Trotsky noted that in prerevolutionary professional revolutionaries was the origin of the future Stalinist bureaucrat. What he did not detect was the beginning of a new class of owners and exploiters.

This is not to say that the new Party and the new class are identical. The Party, however, is the core of that class, and its base. It is very difficult, perhaps impossible, to define the limits of the new class and to identify its members. The new class may be said to be made up of those who have special privileges and economic preference because of the administrative monopoly they hold.

Since administration is unavoidable in society, necessary administrative functions may be coexistent with parasitic functions in the same person. Not every member of the party is a member of the new class, any more than every artisan or member of the city party was a bourgeois.

In loose terms, as the new class becomes stronger and attains a more perceptible physiognomy, the role of the party diminishes. The core and the basis of the new class is created in the Party and at its top, as well as in the state political organs. The once live, compact Party, full of initiative, is disappearing to become transformed into the traditional oligarchy of the new class, irresistibly drawing into its ranks those who aspire to join the new class and repressing those who have any ideals.

The Party makes the class, but the class grows as a result and uses the Party as a basis. The class grows stronger, while the Party grows weaker; this is the inescapable fate of every Communist Party in power. . . .

If we assume that membership in this bureaucracy or new owning class is predicated on the use of privileges inherent in ownership—in this instance nationalized material goods—then membership in the new Party class, or political bureaucracy, is reflected in a larger income in material goods and privileges than society should normally grant for such functions. In practice, the ownership privileges of the new class manifests itself as an exclusive right, as a Party monopoly, for the political bureaucracy to distribute the national income, to set wages, direct economic development, and dispose of nationalized and other property. This is the way it appears to the ordinary man who considers the Communist functionary as being very rich and as a man who does not have to work.

The ownership of private property has, for many reasons, proved to be unfavorable for the establishment of the new class's authority. Besides, the destruction of private ownership was necessary for the economic transformation of nations. The new class obtains its power, privileges, ideology, and its customs from one specific form of ownership—collective ownership—which the class administers and distributes in the name of the nation and society.

The new class maintains that ownership derives from a designated social relationship. This is the relationship between the monopolists of administration, who constitute a narrow and closed stratum, and the mass of producers (farmers, workers, and intelligentsia) who have no rights. However, this relationship is not valid since the Communist bureaucracy enjoys a monopoly over the distribution of material goods.

Every fundamental change in the social relationship between those who monopolize administration and those who work is inevitably reflected in the ownership relationship. Social and political relations and ownership—the totalitarianism of the government and the monopoly of authority—are being more fully brought into accord in Communism than in any other single system.

To divest Communists of their ownership rights would be to abolish them as a class. To compel them to relinquish their other social powers, so that workers may participate in sharing the profits of their work—which capitalists have had to permit as a result of strikes and parliamentary action—would mean that Communists were being deprived of their monopoly over property, ideology, and government. This would be the beginning of democracy and freedom in Communism, the end of Communist monopolism and totalitarianism. Until this happens, there can be no indication that important, fundamental changes are taking place in Communist systems, at least not in the eyes of men who think seriously about social progress. . . .

In Communism, power and ownership are almost always in the same hands, but this fact is concealed under a legal guise. In classical capitalism, the worker had equality with the capitalist before the law, even though the worker was being exploited and the capitalist was doing the exploiting. In Communism, legally, all are equal with respect to material goods. The formal owner is the nation. In reality, because of monopolistic administration, only the narrowest stratum of administrators enjoys the rights of ownership. Every real demand for freedom in Communism, the kind of demand that hits at the substance of Communism, boils down to a demand for bringing material and property relations into accord with what the law provides.

A demand for freedom—based on the position that capital goods produced by the nation can be managed more efficiently by society than by private monopoly or a private owner, and consequently should actually be in the hands or under control of society exercised through its freely elected representatives—would force the new class either to make concessions to other forces, or to take off the mask and admit its ruling and exploiting characteristics. The type of ownership and exploitation which the new class creates by using its authority and its administrative privileges is such that even the class itself must deny it. Does not the new class emphasize that it uses its authority and administrative functions in the name of the nation as a whole to preserve national property?

This makes the legal position of the new class uncertain and is also the source of the new class's biggest internal difficulties. The contradiction discloses the disharmony between words and actions: While promising to abolish social differences, it must always increase them by acquiring the products of the nation's workshops and granting privileges to its adherents. It must proclaim loudly its dogma that it is fulfilling its historical mission of "final" liberation of mankind from every misery and calamity while it acts in exactly the opposite way.

The contradiction between the new class's real ownership position and its legal position can furnish the basic reason for criticism. This contradiction has within it the ability not only to incite others but also to corrode the class's own ranks, since privileges are actually being enjoyed by only a few. This contradiction, when intensified, holds prospects of real changes in the Communist system, whether the ruling class is in favor of the change or not. The fact that this contradiction is so obvious has been the reason for the changes made by the new class, especially in so-called liberalization and decentralization.

Forced to withdraw and surrender to individual strata, the new class aims at concealing this contradiction and strengthening its own position. Since ownership and authority continue intact, all measures taken by the new class—even those democratically inspired—show a tendency toward strengthening the management of the political bureaucracy. The system turns democratic measures into positive methods for consolidating the position of the ruling classes. Slavery in ancient times in the East inevitably permeated all of society's activities and components, including the family. In the same way, the monopolism and totalitarianism of the ruling class in the Communist system are imposed on all the aspects of social life, even though the political heads are not aiming at this. . . .

This does not mean that the new class cannot make concessions to the people, even though it only considers its own interests. Workers' management, or decentralization, is a concession to the masses. Circumstances may drive the new class, no matter how monopolistic and totalitarian it may be, to retreat before the masses. In 1948, when the conflict took place between Yugoslavia and the U.S.S.R., the Yugoslav leaders were forced to execute some reforms. Even though it might mean a backward step, they set up reforms as soon as they saw themselves in jeopardy. Something similar is happening today in the eastern European countries.

In defending its authority, the ruling class must execute reforms every time it becomes obvious to the people that the class is treating national property as its own. Such reforms are not proclaimed as being what they really are, but rather as part of the "further development of socialism" and "socialist democracy." The groundwork for reforms is laid when the discrepancy mentioned above becomes public. From the historical point of view the new class is forced to fortify its authority and ownership constantly, even though it is running away from the truth. It must constantly demonstrate how it is successfully creating a society of happy people, all of whom enjoy equal rights and have been freed of every type of exploitation. The new class cannot avoid falling continuously into profound internal contradictions; for in spite of its historical origin it is not able to make its ownership lawful, and it cannot renounce ownership without undermining itself. Consequently, it is forced to try to justify its increasing authority, invoking abstract and unreal purposes.

This is a class whose power over men is the most complete known to history. For this reason it is a class with very limited views, views which are false and unsafe. Closely ingrown, and in complete authority, the new class must unrealistically evaluate its own role and that of the people around it.

Having achieved industrialization, the new class can now do nothing more than strengthen its brute force and pillage the people. It ceases to create. Its spiritual heritage is overtaken by darkness.

While the new class accomplished one of its greatest successes in the revolution, its method of control is one of the most shameful pages in human history. Men will marvel at the grandiose ventures it accomplished, and will be ashamed of the means it used to accomplish them.

When the new class leaves the historical scene—and this must happen—
there will be less sorrow over its passing than there was for any other class
before it. Smothering everything except what suited its ego, it has condemned
itself to failure and shameful ruin.

24. 2,000 WORDS: A DECLARATION
FOR DEMOCRATIZATION

LUDVIK VACULIK

*In the spring of 1968, liberalization seemed within reach in Communist
Czechoslovakia. A group of reformers in the Czechoslovak Communist
Party, supported by students, intellectuals, and factory workers, had
succeeded in ousting the old-guard Stalinist and pro-Moscow Communist leadership. The Kremlin, however, fearful over its eroding
influence in the area, and concerned lest the liberalization occasion
similar demands within the Soviet Union, invaded Czechoslovakia on
August 21, 1968, and ended, for the time being, the impetus to reform.*

*Prior to the Soviet invasion, the Czech novelist Ludvik Vaculik,
issued a manifesto, signed by 70 intellectuals and workers, castigating
the Communist Party for its past behavior. His statement intensified
Soviet fears and led the Kremlin to act to nip democratization in
the bud.*

. . . The Communist Party betrayed the great trust the people put in it
after the war. It preferred the glories of office, until it had those and nothing
more. The disappointment was great among Communists as well as non-
Communists. The leadership of the party changed it from a political and
ideological group into a power-hungry organization, attracting egotists,
cowards and crooks.

They influenced the party's operations to such an extent that honest people
could not gain a foothold without debasement, much less make it a modern
political instrument. There were many Communists who fought this deterioration but they could not prevent what happened.

The situation in the party led to a similar situation in the state, resulting
in the linkage of party and state. There was no criticism of the state and
economic organizations. Parliament forgot how to deliberate, the government
forgot how to rule and managers how to manage. Elections had no significance
and the laws lost their value. We could not trust any of our representatives,
and when we could it was impossible to ask them for anything because they

From the manifesto written by Czech novelist Ludvik Vaculik, signed by 70 intellectuals
and workers; published in *Literarni Listy* (Prague), June 27, 1968.

were powerless. What made things even worse was that we could not trust each other.

Personal and collective honor deteriorated. Honesty led nowhere, and it was useless to speak of rewards according to ability. As a result, most citizens lost interest in public affairs. They were concerned only with themselves and with accumulating money. The situation got so bad that now one cannot even rely on money. Relations among people were undermined and joy in work was lost. To sum up, the nation was in a morass that threatened its spiritual health and character.

We are all responsible for the present state of affairs, with the greater responsibility on the Communists among us. But the prime responsibility lies with those who made up the component parts or were the instruments of uncontrolled power, the power of a dogmatic group placed everywhere by the party apparatus, from Prague to the smallest district and community. The apparatus decided what one could or could not do and directed the cooperatives for the cooperative members, the factories for the workers and the national committees for the citizens. No organization was run by its members, not even the Communist party. . . .

The greatest deception of these rulers was that they presented their arbitrariness as the will of the workers. If we believed this, we could now blame the workers for the decline of our economy, for the crimes against innocent people, for the introduction of censorship which made it impossible for all this to be described. The workers would have to be blamed for mistaken investments, for the losses in trade, for the shortage of apartments.

Naturally, no sensible person believes that the workers are guilty of these things. We all know—and each worker knows—that he did not decide anything. Someone else chose the union officials he elected. Power was executed by trained groups of officials loyal to the party and state apparatus. In effect, they took the place of the former ruling class and became the new authority.

In all justice, we can say that some of them [the Communists] did realize what was happening. We know that now because they are redressing wrongs, correcting mistakes, bringing decisions to the membership and the citizens, and limiting the authority and the size of the official apparatus. They no longer support the conservative viewpoint in the party. But there are still many officials opposed to change who exercise the instruments of power, particularly in the districts and in the communities.

Since the beginning of the year we have been in the process of reviving democratization. It began in the Communist party. We must say this. And those non-Communists among us, who, until recently, expected no good to come from the Communists also know it. We must add, however, that this process could not have begun elsewhere. After twenty years, only the Communists had an actual political life; only Communist criticism was in a position to assess things as they were; only the opposition in the Communist Party had the privilege of being in contact with the enemy. . . .

The present effort of the democratic Communists is only an installment in the repayment of the debt the entire party owes the people outside the party, who had no political rights. No gratitude is due to the Communist party, although it should probably be acknowledged that it is honestly striving to use this last opportunity to save its own honor and the nation's. . . .

We turn to you [the Communists] in this moment of hope, which is still under threat. It took several months for many of us to believe that they could speak out and many still do not believe it.

Yet, we have not spoken up. All we have to do is complete what we started out to do—humanize this regime. Otherwise the revenge of the old forces will be cruel. We turn to those who have been waiting. The days immediately ahead of us will determine our future course for many years to come. . . . Consensus can only be found if freedom of expression, which happens to be the only democratic achievement of the year, is permitted. In the forthcoming days we will have to demonstrate our initiative and determination.

Above all, we will oppose views, should they arise, that it is possible to carry out some type of democratic revival without the Communists—or possibly against them. This would be both unjust and unreasonable. The Communists already have functioning organizations, and we should support their progressive wings. They have experienced functionaries and, last but not least, they hold in their hands the decisive levers of control.

The public has the party's action program before it. Above all, the program equalizes some of the greatest imbalances that exist today. No one else has a comparable program. We must demand that local action programs be submitted to each district and community. These long-awaited steps are routine enough but they are what the situation calls for now.

The party is preparing for the congress that will elect a new Central Committee. Let us demand that it be better than the current one. If the party now says that in the future it wants to base its leading position on the confidence of the citizenry and not on force, let us believe this as long as we can believe in the people whom it is sending as delegates to district and regional conferences.

There are some who have recently become upset because they believe that the course of democratization has ended. This derives from the letdown following the first exciting developments—the surprising revelations, resignations from high places and speeches of unprecedented boldness. The struggle has merely become less evident. The battle is now over the formulation of laws and other practical measures. We must give the minister, prosecutors, chairmen and secretaries time to prove themselves. Moreover, one cannot presently expect more of the central political organs, which have already shown, however unwillingly, surprising virtues.

The practical outcome of democracy in the future depends on what happens in the enterprise—it is the economists who hold the cards. We must seek out good managers and see to it that they are put into leading positions. Compared with the highly industrialized countries, we are all badly paid.

We could demand more money. It can be printed but it depreciates in the printing. Instead, let us demand that directors and chairmen explain to us what they want to produce at what price, to whom they want to sell their products and at what price, what the profits are and what part of them is invested in the modernization of production and how much can be distributed.

The newspaper headlines do not reveal the real struggle. On the one hand, the progressives are fighting for democracy and, on the other, the conservatives are fighting to keep their cushy jobs. The workers can intervene in this struggle in a business-like way by choosing the right managers and councils of the enterprises. They will help themselves most if they elect trade union representatives who are capable and honest natural leaders, without regard to party membership.

The central political organs have done all they can up to this point. It is up to us to make new inroads in the districts and communities. Let us demand the resignation of those who have abused their power, who have harmed public property, who have acted dishonestly or cruelly. We must find ways to induce them to leave. Such steps include public criticism, resolutions, demonstrations, collecting funds for their retirement, strikes and boycotts. . . . But we must reject methods which are illegitimate, indecent or gross, since they might prejudice [First Secretary] Alexander Dubcek. We must decry the writing of insulting letters, since they can be exploited by those that receive them. . . .

Many summer vacationers throughout the republic will be interested in learning about a constitutional solution to the Czech-Slovak question. We consider federation as one means of solving the nationality problem, but this is just one of the important steps toward democratization. . . .

Recently there has been great apprehension that foreign forces may interfere with our internal development. Faced with their superior strength, the only thing we can do is humbly hold our own and not start trouble. We assure the government that we will back it, if necessary even with weapons, as long as the government does what we mandate and assures our allies that we will observe our alliance, friendship and trade agreements.

Excited reproaches and unfounded suspicions make the government's position more difficult, without being of any help to us. We can insure a new balance in our system only by improving internal conditions to such an extent that the revival can be carried to a point where we can elect statesmen who will have sufficient courage, honor and political wisdom to defend such conditions. This, by the way, is the problem of governments in all the small countries of the world.

As at the end of the war, we have been given a great chance once again. We have opportunity to take up a common cause, which for all practical purposes we call socialism, and mold it so that it will correspond to the good reputation we once had and the high esteem in which we held ourselves.

With this we conclude our statement—written at the suggestion of scholars —to the workers, farmers, officials, artists, scientists, technicians and all other citizens. . . .

part three

The Sphere of Government: Limited or Unlimited?

INTRODUCTION

"The modern State, with its huge units of organization, is inherently totalitarian, and its natural tendency is toward despotism. These tendencies can only be held in check if we are determined to build the constitutional safeguards of freedom—and personal responsibility."

—R. H. S. Crossman, *Socialism and the New Despotism*

What activities should the state perform? How far does the responsibility of the state for its citizens extend? The state was originally established to provide protection and order. However, it very early assumed corollary functions: for example, it built roads and fortifications, constructed elaborate irrigation systems, and allocated food during periods of famine. At the same time it conducted religious ceremonies and regulated family relationships. These already varied duties of the state, assumed at a relatively primitive stage of development, proliferated with the advent of industrialization and urbanization. As society has become more complex and more interdependent, the relationship between the state and other institutions of society has become critical.

To what extent should the state control the other institutions of society? Should it restrict its activities, leaving to other institutions the responsibility for fulfilling man's goals in the "non-political" areas of life? Or should the state seek to serve as many of the interests of its citizens as possible? Does diversity of religious, economic, ethnic, and cultural institutions enrich a society and make it easier for the individual to satisfy his needs? Or does it rather transform society into a battleground of warring special-interest groups, each seeking to achieve its aims at the expense of the others? And, do such groups tend to weaken the state's performance of its basic functions: protection from enemies without and maintenance of order within? In short, should the state be "pluralist" or "monist"?

If the state is to be "pluralist," how are the inevitable jurisdictional disputes to be resolved? Who is to mediate conflicts between church and church, or between church and state? It is easy to say, "Render therefore unto Caesar the things which are Caesar's, and unto God the things which are God's." But does not he who decides which things are Caesar's and which are God's really have supreme power? Further, can pluralism function effectively in the face of centralizing pressures arising from threats to national survival and increasing demands for public welfare?

If on the other hand the state is to be "monist," how can the sacrifice of traditional individual rights and freedoms on the altar of national security be prevented? What is to be the fate of the democratic ideal of limited government—of the view that "That government governs best which governs least"?

In recent decades these questions have most often been raised by controversies about the relationship between the state and economic institutions: Is the welfare state compatible with political freedom for the individual? Can the state be permitted dominance over the economy without also being permitted to dominate the political process itself? And, on the other hand, if the governors cannot maintain economic power in the face of challenges from other institutions, how can they effectively retain enough political power to govern? Is a highly centralized economy actually the most efficient? Or is there a point beyond which waste becomes endemic, responsiveness to public demands dulled, and innovation stifled?

These questions have confronted both democratic and totalitarian societies. Answers to them have differed fundamentally, not only as between democratic and totalitarian societies, but between various democratic societies and between various totalitarian societies. The question, "What limit, if any, should be placed on the sphere of the state," is yet to be answered.

25. PRIVATE ASSOCIATIONS

GRANT MCCONNELL

*Grant McConnell (1915–   ) is Chairman of the Department of
Political Science at the University of Chicago and a specialist in the
field of interest groups.*

Massive endorsement of the private association as an essential of democracy
is one of the most striking features of American political thought. Freedom
of association has virtually become a fundamental guarantee of the Constitution. The ideas of self-government and self-regulation have entered deeply
into the doctrines of the political order, and they have been institutionalized
to an unheralded degree. The private association, moreover, has been linked
with the values of decentralization and federalism. It has also been pictured
as the source of stability in politics and held up as the medium of the public
interest. Most frequently, however, it has been seen as the guarantor of
liberty. This is the most essential part of the general argument, and any
examination of the doctrine must deal with this claim.

There is no doubt that pluralism belongs in the liberal tradition. The
pluralist attack upon the state's assertion of unlimited power was one of
the most incisive ever made. The defense of the private association against
attempts to suppress it or to subordinate it to the state has almost always
been a defense of liberty itself; the elaboration of this defense by pluralist
writers has provided some of the noblest statements on constitutionalism and
the limits of state action. Pluralist discussions of law carried important
insights on the roots of law in sources other than compulsion. Moreover,
the pluralists for the most part spoke out of a genuine dedication to individual
liberty. Perhaps the most important aspect of pluralist doctrine in the present
context is its adherence to the distinction between the state and society, a
distinction closely related to that between the public and the private spheres
of life.

There can be equally little doubt that the preference of those American
writers who are sometimes classed as pluralists is for liberty. More con-
spicuously, however, the private associations of the United States have fought
with great vigor to protect themselves from government encroachments. The
organizations of business and labor have been the most vociferous in this
regard, but perhaps the churches have made greater contributions; certainly
separation of church and state is a more firmly established principle in
America than in most countries.

From Grant McConnell, *Private Power and American Democracy*. New York: Alfred
A. Knopf, Inc., 1966. Pp. 119–45, excerpts.

When all this has been recognized, however, some very important questions remain. Since the private association has made its claim against the state in the name of liberty, how has the liberty of the individual fared vis-à-vis the private association? If the private association is to maintain the right of self-government and self-regulation, how is it governed itself? What is its conception of government within its own boundaries? These questions were not asked by the pluralists, and only comparatively recently have they been asked by more than a few others. Nevertheless, they are not easily avoidable today. . . .

To the extent that the "iron law of oligarchy" means that leadership is inevitable in organization it is a truism; but there is a much more disturbing implication in the argument. Leaders develop within a different milieu from members. They engage in different activities and come to enjoy a different status. Most important, they acquire different interests. Organization becomes conservative; leaders tend to identify their own interests with those of the organization and seek to preserve the foundations of their own position, thus laying the foundation for conflict of interests between leaders and led. The identity that is commonly assumed to exist among the interests of all within the organization is therefore false. And in contests between leaders and led, the former have virtually all the advantages.

Plainly, this argument is very sweeping. It is also very disturbing, particularly for those drawn to the pluralist belief that the freedom and self-determination of private associations are close to the essence of democracy. If private associations themselves should be undemocratic, as the Michelian thesis would seem to assert, how can they be essential to democracy?

Perhaps the simplest answer offered to this question is that the internal arrangements of the private associations are irrelevant to the question. In the first place, so the argument goes, the private associations as centers of power stand in opposition to the assumption of total power by any all-encompassing tyranny. With such associations in vigorous and separate existence, a sudden *Putsch* or mob action is insufficient to assume complete domination over the nation. Totalitarianism is defeated unless it can either absorb or destroy the private associations; hence, it is argued, private associations preserve democracy against the totalitarian threat.

The contention has much merit if the threat of totalitarianism is considered imminent. Certainly, twentieth-century experience indicates that totalitarianism is an evil greater than almost any other. By comparison with what went on in Hitler's Germany and Stalin's Russia occasional breaches of the democratic ideal inside private associations in America are insignificant. The force of this argument diminishes, however, if the threats of totalitarianism in America appear remote. On a lesser score, this ground for indifference to the internal arrangements of the private associations stands against the pluralist argument that the private associations are schools in democracy for the larger community. If such they are to be, they can hardly be other than models for behavior in the larger arena of national politics.

Another reason sometimes offered for dismissing Michels' charge is that the private associations are mutually countervailing—a modern gloss on the argument of Madison and his colleagues in the Federalist Papers. It tends to merge with the preceding contention that private associations are barriers to totalitarianism, but it goes somewhat further: by opposing each other, private associations supposedly check any overly greedy attempts by particular associations to extend their power. One association protects against another to the extent that in the large community democracy is insured.

This argument is relevant to the fear that one or more associations may exploit the general public. Except under special and unusual circumstances, however, it does not bear on the problem Michels posed. A trade union and a corporation may check each other in the making of decisions affecting the scale of wages and production costs; a high-tariff interest group may find itself confronted by a low-tariff interest group. Yet although each of these contests and the many others commonplace in modern political life may protect the economy and the polity from the extremist policies that might be followed if opposing or countervailing private groups were not active, they do not protect the members of any of these groups when they are threatened by their own organizations. To provide such protection, countervailing organizations would have to exist *inside* the associations, or, alternatively, there would have to be very nearly parallel or rival associations between which members might move without being deprived of the benefits that go with association membership.

In practice, however, private associations tend to be jealous of rivals. They seek to prevent the rise of competitors in the fields they have marked as their own. Often, when such rivals do exist, there is bitter conflict between them, conflict that has as its object the destruction of one or the other. Sometimes, when the conflict cannot be brought to this point, an accommodation takes place and jurisdictional boundaries are agreed upon, so that as a result the condition of monopoly is restored. An entire ethos within the American labor movement holds "dual unionism" to be the worst of sins, but this ethos is not unique to labor; it is found to some degree among farm organizations, veterans' organizations, and others. The appeal made to support this ethos is for unity. The fear is that with two or more organizations in a particular field, competition among them may lead one to appeal to a common foe, with consequent losses to the interests the organizations and their members share. In one degree or another many, if not most, private associations see themselves arrayed against some external enemy and are warring organizations.

If it is unrealistic to look for an escape from the problem through parallel or rival associations, there remains the first alternative: to look inside the associations. This, however, poses the question of how the associations govern themselves. Although the question is plainly relevant in view of the emphasis placed upon the private association as an essential of democracy, it is sometimes suggested that examination of the private association as a form of government is improper, probably because of the fear that such inquiry is a preliminary to suggestions for state regulation. But it can also be objected that the private association is not the same as the state and that the tests applied to public government are not applicable to the government of the private association.

Certainly state and private association are different, but the differences are hard to define. Both are to some extent based on territorial lines. The state, if it is a constitutional state, has, like the private association, limited ends. Both state and association exercise some form of authority. Each makes rules or laws (not infrequently the term "laws" is used by private associations for their own rules). These rules are enforced with penalties of varying degrees of severity, but some organizations' penalties are more severe than many punishments of the states. Fines, suspension, and expulsion, all exacted by private associations, are serious matters where the associations involved control the right to practice a particular trade or profession. This is especially true where, as with medicine, a large investment of money and years in education, training, and experience are also involved. Perhaps (at least for devout communicants) the most awesome penalty of all, excommunication, is enforced by the church, a private association. Of course not all private associations exist in spheres of interest with such degrees of importance. Yet some do, and where they do the problem of authority is substantially the same as it is in the state. . . .

Perhaps first among the general traits of private associations is that emphasized in the word private. The implications of the concept of privacy have never been thoroughly and systematically explored, but it is safe to say that it is fundamental to Western traditions of government. It is closely tied to the idea of constitutionalism, which implies limitations upon the sphere of public government. Most typically, the distinction between *public* and *private* relates to the state and the individual. In the present discussion, however, the tradition of real corporate personality as developed by a long line of pluralist thinkers from Althusius to the early Laski is involved. Most of the pluralists of earlier times combined a deep concern for individual rights with enthusiasm and concern for the corporate personality of the association. If there is irony in their position, it has become apparent only in fairly recent years.

A second distinctive characteristic of these associations is autonomy. Almost all assert a right to be self-determining and self-governing. This may take the form of an appeal to the historical origin of the association in a spontaneous meeting of like-minded individuals. But it is often asserted where such an origin cannot be claimed. Thus the claim of autonomy is hardly less strong among those unions of the old CIO which were the direct creations of organizing campaigns under leadership provided by older unions. The claim and its presumption of rightfulness within the context of American labor ideology was one of the difficulties the CIO encountered when, some years ago, it "tried" several of its component unions for Communist domination and then attempted to destroy them by establishing new organizations to take possession of the convicted organizations' jurisdictions. Autonomy here seemed to reside in the international union rather than the federation, and it was asserted quite as much against the federation as it recently has been asserted by the Teamsters against both federation and public government.

Traditionally the claim to autonomy has involved a hesitancy to utilize public aid, even where this aid could be demonstrated to offer much to the associations' constituencies. Thus, during the long discussion of the merits of unemployment insurance the official (albeit challenged) position of organized labor was that less social security with autonomy for labor's organizations was better than greater social security provided through the medium of public government. The argument that what government might give government might also take away was in part founded on good grounds; it was also a rationalization of the desire for undivided member loyalties. If there was a nice counterpart here to the claims of *laissez faire* from the business organizations, it was also true that in practice the more conservative and consistent position was that of organized labor. Even organized agriculture, traditionally more willing than either organized business or organized labor to resort to public government, has attempted at various times to act autonomously. The Society of Equity sponsored a plan for farmers to withhold their produce from the market until the Equity-declared prices were met. The National Farm Organization has more recently attempted the same tactic. Here was good, if simple, imitation of business practice. It was also an attempt to maintain autonomy. The farm organizations have sought a similar goal with their cooperatives.

An important corollary of autonomy is the association's claim of the right to formulate its own constituency. Nearly every association lays down conditions for membership, affecting both entrance and continued membership. The conditions of eligibility are usually quite explicit, and oaths or pledges are frequently required of new members. Candidates for membership, even when they are solicited by the organizations, must come as suppliants or at least applicants, the formal decision on acceptance being made by the association.

A third important trait of these associations is limited purpose. They do not purport to concern themselves with all aspects of their members' lives. Sometimes their purpose is stated quite specifically, as for example: "To establish through collective bargaining adequate wage standards, shorter hours of work and improvements in the conditions of employment for the workers in the industry"; at other times the object may be quite vague. In either event, it is presumed that the association's objects do not encompass the entire range of the individual constituent's interests or preoccupations. He will have his own privacy, and he will, accordingly, have other loyalties. So a man may be a trade union member of a particular craft; but he may also be a church member, a Legionnaire, and a member of a team in the municipal bowling league, to say nothing of his place within his family or in a political party. The assumption is that no association will encroach on spheres of life other than its own.

A fourth trait, in considerable degree a corollary of some of the characteristics already listed, is homogeneity. Since the autonomous association selects its membership, and since its purposes are limited, within the scope of the association there will be only people of similar characteristics and like minds. Most important, there will be no conflicts of interest or grounds for legitimate conflict within the association; there is thus a presumptive absence of the basic political problem that other democratic societies of larger scope must resolve. If there is no conflict of interest or outlook, the only possible reasons for conflict will be error, personality, or something amounting to treason. The condition of homogeneity is precisely the solution Madison named in his famous argument in the Federalist Number 10, but felt compelled to reject as a solution to the problem of faction in the larger society.

A fifth distinguishing characteristic is the voluntary character of the association. So, although the association may determine its own membership, the individual member also makes a decision to join or not. Typically he must actively request admittance. He is not a member automatically—as he is a citizen by birth in a state—but by virtue of positive choice. Initiation and probationary status serve to emphasize the element of individual choice in joining. Equally important is the individual member's right to resign. Resignation is the individual's ultimate recourse and the element that finally distinguishes the private association from the public body.

The voluntary aspect of private associations has repeatedly been held to place them in a very special relationship to democracy, one often so special that it is described as a necessary condition of democracy. Such a view was cogently argued by the pluralists of several decades ago; more recent writers have repeated the argument forcefully. Thus, V. L. Allen has argued that so long as individuals are free to join and to leave societies of their own choice, the essence of democracy is present even if there is no machinery permitting the members to control the societies.

It should be apparent that these different characteristics of the private association to a very large degree overlap and rest upon each other. The meaning of privacy is impaired without autonomy. Homogeneity cannot be achieved without limitation of purposes, and voluntary choice underlies the entire arrangement. These, indeed, are all aspects of a single perception of the private association. . . .

26. POWER AND POLITICAL DEVELOPMENT IN COMMUNIST CHINA

JOHN M.H. LINDBECK

John M. H. Lindbeck (1915–   ) is Associate Director of the East Asian Research Center at Harvard University. He was born in China and received his early education there. After receiving his Ph.D. from Yale University in 1948, he served in the State Department from 1952 to 1958. He has been affiliated with Harvard University since 1959.

From listening to public discussions and reading newspaper articles about China, one might gain the impression that China's Communist leaders spend much, if not most, of their time thinking about promoting revolutions around the world and plotting to extend their control over China's neighbors. In actual fact, China's leaders are preoccupied with Chinese domestic issues and the country's internal problems and development.

It is true that within the framework of their doctrinal perspectives these men believe there is a close relationship between external and domestic affairs. They believe, for example, that the main forces shaping history—economic and social changes, proletarian revolutions, opposition to imperialism, the expansion of socialism—transcend national boundaries. They see developments in China as part of a larger transnational historic movement. But the "fundamental task" which they set for themselves in the party constitution of 1956 during the period of transition to communism is the "Socialist transformation" of the society and economy and the industrialization of the country. It is their own interests and those of China, as they interpret these, that are foremost in their minds.

China's Communist leaders are specialists in Chinese domestic politics, but amateurs in the field of international politics. However harsh the methods or technically and professionally primitive some of the major programs and policies they have adopted, these men applied themselves with energy to developing and using military force for achieving power within China; to consolidating their control over the country; to modernizing the use of China's human and natural resources; and to overhauling radically China's economic, social, and political systems. If power, organizational skill, and the introduction of radical programs of economic development and social

Statement of John M. H. Lindbeck on "The Political Situation in China Today," *U.S. Policy with Respect to Mainland China. Hearings* before the Committee on Foreign Relations, United States Senate, 89th Congress, second session (March 1966). Washington, D.C.: U.S. Government Printing Office, 1966. Pp. 186–93, excerpts.

modernization are criteria for success, then they have considerable achievements to their credit. . . .

The regime is solidly entrenched in China. By the regime I mean above all the Communist Party, but also the large administrative and economic institutions and mass organizations created by the party and staffed by officials who are party appointees. There is no good evidence, so far as I can see, that the continuity and basic stability of the regime is likely to be jeopardized in the foreseeable future. Even should there be a succession crisis when the present top leaders die, with a sharp struggle for power between competing groups in the party, it is unlikely, I believe, that the authority and control of the regime over the country will be seriously impaired. Contests for power are likely to be confined to groups within the party. The contestants, as influential party officials, will have a vital stake in the survival of the system and of the party as an organization. None of them is likely to seek the support of forces opposed to the regime to win power.

The strength and stability of the regime are a result of several factors. Above all it depends on the unity and efficiency of the Communist Party and the armed forces over which the party exercises particular control. We also must take account of the thoroughness and speed with which the party consolidated its powers after achieving military victory. First, this victory enabled the party to destroy all rival military forces on the China mainland and enabled the Red Army, or the Peoples' Liberation Army, to acquire a monopoly of military power in the country.

Second, political power was consolidated by destroying the party's political opponents and empowering new political groups throughout the country. This meant the liquidation of millions of people, such as village and town leaders, members of landlord families, officials and members of the Nationalist Party and Government groups connected with industrial and commercial enterprises, warlord families and troops, leaders in secret societies, members of criminal gangs, and others. In villages and hamlets, as well as in various enterprises, new men and women selected or endorsed by the party took control. In general, they were drawn from local groups that were dissatisfied with previous conditions and hostile toward established local leaders; thus, they were willing to work for the party. In this process of transferring power to new hands the number of people killed is unknown. During the land reforms of 1950–52 at least a few individuals from each village were singled out as leading enemies of the people. In terms of long-range consequences, the way in which class conflicts were engineered to discredit, to reduce the status, and to penalize those who had economic or social interests which might lead them to oppose the regime was probably more important. This process of identifying and isolating opponents or potential opponents of the party's policies is ongoing.

A third measure adopted by the party was to create new governmental and administrative institutions staffed by the party-approved appointees. Local assemblies were created and governmental councils established, both operating under party supervision. The party linked the operations of these institutions to the mass organizations that it also controlled.

In the fourth place, through its programs of social modernization the regime destroyed the old and created new institutions of property, production, and social relationships. Collective and state farms, nationalized factories, mass organizations, and small discussion groups brought the behavior attitudes and activities of the bulk of the population under the surveillance and direction of the Government and party.

As the party introduced its new and sweeping programs of collectivization and social mobilization, the relationship between the regime and the people underwent a change. Tensions between the regime and major sectors of Chinese society were inevitable. The regime needed control if it was to introduce radical programs of modernization and speed up the economic development of China. Its authority could not rest on broad political support, but only upon effective organization and the use of instruments of persuasion and coercion.

TENSIONS BETWEEN REGIME AND SOCIETY

The basic source of political tensions in China is in the relationship between the regime, or party, and the people. The regime is authoritarian in character, depending principally upon an authoritarian political party to implement its policies. The primary cause of dissatisfaction and resistance to the regime is not, it seems to me, the high concentration of power in the hands of the ruling elite—for despotic power is not unknown to China. Rather it is the nature of some of the policies and programs of the regime, the disruptive pace at which they are introduced, and the intensity with which people are mobilized to implement these programs that generate stress and produce protests.

The range and degree of resistance varies. The party leaders are skilled in trying to limit popular dissatisfactions and keeping them down to manageable proportions. Occasionally, protests have broken through the bounds of control, as they did during the brief hundred flowers period in 1957 when a policy of liberalization of thought and speech to win greater support from intellectuals led instead to a burst of attacks on the party and its policies; or again among farmers during collectivization and communalization when slaughtering of livestock, passivity, and other types of resistance appeared and forced readjustments in the regime's policies and patterns of incentives. During the worst of the post-leap depression, sporadic armed protests occurred. Among the non-Chinese minority groups antagonism to the regime periodically has taken a militant form.

Without going into further details, we seem to see in China a fairly constant process of adjustment taking place between the party and different sectors of the population. The party politicians are responsive to a degree to popular attitudes. They are well aware of the dangers of being alienated from the masses, as the people are called. Where resistance is localized and limited to a small sector of the population, coercive means can be used. But in other, more politically significant cases, the party seeks to use persuasion which is socially, politically, and financially less expensive—rather than physical force to gain compliance or public support. In extreme cases of resistance it has retreated, as from the communes, and reintroduced economic incentives, such as the private plots and free markets, and reinstated the family as a social, housekeeping and child-care unit.

This broad dimension of Chinese politics, the polarization of power between the people and their rulers, finds reflection in the main arena of political activity in China; that is, in the party.

INTRAPARTY POLITICS

We get occasional glimpses of the kinds of political activities that go on within the party. The party is made up of individuals with varying backgrounds, experience, skills, jobs, local connections, and different personal and institutional, as well as class, interests. In a party as large as the Chinese Communist Party, differences between groups and between supporters for different policy alternatives are unavoidable.

Broadly speaking, some groups in the party favor policies and procedures which are at least somewhat responsive to popular desires and needs; others are more inclined to push the pace of social change and economic development and to ignore public opinion. We have seen intraparty struggles between provincial and regional party groups and the top leadership in Peking. Some contests have probably been the result of personal rivalries, others have stemmed from policy differences.

In addition to pulls between central and regional or local interests, there have been differences between functional or institutional components of the party, such as between those members of the party who run the party's own organizations and those who run government and economic ministries. There is some evidence that in the past party members and leaders within the army have tried to obtain a larger slice of China's limited resources in order to promote programs for professionalizing and further modernizing the army, only to be rebuffed by others in the party. This points to the existence of bureaucratic politics within the regime.

Clearly we do not have in Communist China the kind of political activity which occurs in a pluralistic political system in which various groups openly organize to protect and advance their interests. In China, despite the formal existence of nonCommunist parties and organizations, it is not possible for these groups to form coalitions and to establish parties able to enter into active competition with the Communists by mobilizing political support.

But this situation does not lead to the disappearance of politics—the struggle for power and influence and a competition between groups advocating different policy alternatives and program priorities. Politics takes a different form and, above all, is confined, so far as the party can make this possible, to the party itself.

Some of these political developments, or intraparty conflicts, are the result of the changing character of the party and its role and functions in China as a ruling party rather than as a party seeking power.

THE COMMUNIST PARTY

By 1961 the party had 17 million members. Eighty percent of these had joined the party after 1949. When it came to power, the hard core of the party was in the army, whose officers tended for a time to run the government "as the warlord world," to quote the Chinese. After 1949 new recruits to party membership were not warriors but individuals and groups selected by the party leadership through its party-building programs for their usefulness in administration, social, and economic management, and programs of modernization. In the first 7 years of rule, the party took in over 6 million new members. In the 3 years between 1957 and 1961, over 4 million more were recruited. The proportion of army members in the party dropped from about 20 to 6 percent; the number of intellectuals increased from about 5 to 15 percent, or to $2\frac{1}{2}$ million in number; industrial workers, once virtually nonexistent in the party, made up about 15 percent of the membership by 1962. The proportion of peasant members fell from about 80 percent in 1949 to 66 percent in 1961.

After the assumption of power an important change took place in the role of the party and the activities of its members. Instead of being soldiers and administrators of rural base areas providing support for the army, party members became economic planners and factory managers; they were called upon to run railways, banks, courts, educational systems, scientific institutes, in short, to take on the whole gamut of key jobs which needed to be performed in a large and complex society.

Strains developed between the politically reliable old warriors and the newer, better educated members whose abilities promoted them to administrative jobs both in the party and outside. Top party leaders also have shown signs of uneasiness about the lack of revolutionary spirit and commitment of its new professionally and functionally oriented members. Some of them are said to have tried to use the party to advance the interests of nonparty organizations in which they work. Others have shown signs of revisionism and rightism; that is, they have been accused of seeking the good will and support of the people with whom they work by attempting to moderate the pace and direction of the party's policies for transforming China.

The party leaders have made intensive efforts to implant their commitments and values on party members through indoctrination, manual labor, intensified study of Mao's works, and other means. At the same time, the leaders cannot achieve their goals without accepting and using groups with the skills needed for governing the country.

NATURE OF POLITICAL CHANGE

While the men who came to the top in China have stayed on top, vast changes are taking place within the country. I have stressed the changes which have taken place in the party itself, the institution which is the key to their power and control. It is being transformed from an elite corps composed of politically reliable party henchmen and political activists into a complex organization with administrators, well-trained military officers, young intellectuals, scientists, engineers, and other professional specialists. Changes in the party reflect broader changes in the country. These changes are the results in part of programs instituted by the country's rulers. Vast educational programs are bringing new outlooks and skills to millions of people. About 10 percent of the national budget is devoted to this purpose and varying percentages of local budgets. Technological innovations and new attitudes toward science are being actively diffused throughout the country. Industry is growing, albeit slowly in the past few years.

The expectations and needs of new groups and institutions which it has brought into being shape the options and policies of the regime. In addition, the urgency and inescapability of some of the problems it faces determine in certain respects the directions in which the regime must move and the priorities it must adopt. For example, excessive population growth and pressures undoubtedly lay behind Peking's reappraisal in 1961 of once repudiated birth-control programs. Again, the low productivity of agriculture compelled the party to readjust its economic development priorities. . . .

Will the new economic, political, and social institutions imposed by the Communist leaders of China increasingly be accepted and become domesticated? If the country's leaders maintain the relatively moderate and gradualist economic and social policies they have pursued during the past few years, this is likely to be the case. Over 300 million Chinese are children of the post-1949 era. Those 25 years and under have little or no memory of a non-Communist past. On the other hand, the experiences of the period from 1958 to 1962, when China underwent the mad pressures of the great leap, the disorientations of the communes, and economic recession, were undoubtedly traumatic for most Chinese, young and old, but some of the uncertainties and fears of that period are being forgotten with the passage of time. If routinization and continuity of life patterns and social work schedules are encouraged, this too will change the political atmosphere and context in which the regime operates, producing an increased sense of stability and confidence.

I believe that the political situation in China is not static. As in the past, so in the future, there will be important changes. But at present the aging leaders in Peking seem to be uncertain of the directions in which they should move. They want to preserve the fruits of their efforts, but they also seem to realize that the world cannot be remade in a day. They too apparently have learned, or perhaps have been stunned, by the failures of their excessive ambitions. . . .

27. THE AMERICAN AND SOVIET POLITICAL SYSTEMS: A COMPARISON

ZBIGNIEW BRZEZINSKI AND
SAMUEL P. HUNTINGTON

Zbigniew Brzezinski (1928–   ) was born in Poland and received his Ph.D. from Harvard University. He is professor of government and Director of the Research Institute on Communist Affairs at Columbia University. Samuel P. Huntington (1927–   ) is professor of government and member of the faculty of the Center for International Affairs at Harvard University.

The Soviet political system was created to serve as an instrument of communist rule and reform. The American political system was created to provide a loose governmental framework for American society. The peculiar strengths and weaknesses of each system reflect these original intents, in spite of extensive changes since the original inception of the two systems. On the operational level, the Soviet political system appears to be more vigorous, more capable of mobilizing national resources for specific political ends, more likely to be led by skilled practitioners of power. At the same time, the weaknesses of the Soviet system seem potentially more disruptive than those of the American system.

The strengths of the Soviet system flow from the supremacy of its political ideology and institutions over Soviet society and the political leaders' ability to control that society. Conversely, the weaknesses of the Soviet system flow in large part from the disruptive consequences of overconcentrated personal power, from the restrictive impact of official ideology on the country's economy and intellectual life, and from the resulting tensions between the political system and other social forces and institutions. The strengths of the American system, on the other hand, derive primarily from the close unity between society and polity and from the unceasing dynamic adjustments between the two. Its weaknesses, in turn, are due to its subordination to society, which often prevents clear-cut formulation of long-range goals and timely and effective political action.

Soviet ideology gives its leaders a useful conceptual framework for dealing with many contemporary political problems. As an ideology of conflict, it has given them a more effective basis for a strategy of conflict than American statesmen have in their relatively amorphous, compromise-oriented political beliefs and practices. Soviet ideology has helped Soviet leadership combine strategic purposefulness with tactical flexibility. It has provided a basis for Soviet nationalism and thus helped the leaders to subordinate the diverse nationalities in the Soviet Union. It has combined an awareness of the economic basis of politics with stress on the primacy of political action. It has made the Soviet leaders sensitive to the dynamics of class warfare and nationalism in the developing areas. American political beliefs, on the other hand, tend to encourage either moral rigidity and absolutism or purely pragmatic willingness to compromise. They have not furnished the basis for a theory of history, for a definition of long-range goals, or for a delineation of tactics and strategy for reaching those goals.

Yet the doctrinal absolutism of the Soviet leaders has also posed problems for them in handling relations with the new nationalist regimes and with their fellow Communists. Their dogmatism has caused them to underestimate nationalist feelings in the new states. Furthermore, a systematic doctrine can be weakened by schisms in a way in which amorphous political beliefs cannot. Contradictions among American political beliefs do not imperil America's relations with its allies. The United States and its allies, sharing values and interests, are normally able to resolve or live with their conflicts over immediate issues. Among communist states, with their common ideology, differences over policy can rapidly lead to charges of deviationism and heresy.

The goals of the Soviet political system in terms of politization, participation, and the elimination of dissent are far more extensive than those of the American system. Inevitably, the Soviet system has enjoyed only partial success in the pursuit of these goals. Society can never be totally subjected to politics. The Soviet system, however, although it falls short of its proclaimed goals, has created a more effective system of control and mobilization and maintained it for a longer period of time than has any other comparable political system. It has developed elaborate methods for the indoctrination and direct politization of its citizens. In the United States, the relative absence of tension between political system and society means that political socialization is simply a by-product of the general process of education into society. Efforts at direct politization are unnecessary; the energies which in the Soviet Union are devoted to such efforts can be applied to other purposes in the United States.

The intense demands which the Soviet system imposes on its citizens contribute to a high rate of individual alienation in the form of corruption, delinquency, fascination with "bourgeois" morals, and the like. At the same time, the official ideology often prevents recognition of these social problems and constructive solutions for them. Individual alienation of this sort exists in the United States, but because of the more limited scope of politics it is less of a problem for the political system. Mass alienation, on the other hand, is much more of a potential danger in the United States than in the Soviet Union and can give rise to protest movements which may constrict or shake established political institutions. Popular agitation in the Soviet Union is seldom a threat to the regime, and in fact the regime uses mass social orthodoxy as one of the weapons to curb deviationist tendencies among the intellectual elite. The Soviet system, however, has yet to define the tolerable limits of orthodox dissent which can be permitted in its society. As a result, creative initiative tends to be stifled.

Unlike their American counterparts, most Soviet leaders combine bureaucratic and political experience. The Soviet Union is led by professional political leaders recruited entirely from within the bureaucracy of the Communist Party. Their skills and ambitions are focused entirely on the exercise of political power. Wielding it skillfully against domestic or external enemies is the key to personal success. The United States is led by a coalition of electoral politicians, part-time political leaders drawn from the social-economic "Establishment," and top civil servants. Withdrawal from part-time or full-time politics may actually be more profitable to a leader, and many fluctuate between a political and a private career because of high-level lateral access into politics from nonpolitical occupations. Thus the Soviets heed more closely Machiavelli's injunction (in which we substitute the word "politics" for the original "war") that "a prince should . . . have no other aim or thought, nor take up any other thing for his study; but politics and its organization and discipline, for that is the only art that is necessary to one who commands. . . . The chief cause of the loss of states is the contempt of this art. . . ."

The Soviet leadership is thus more cohesive, more uniform in experience, and probably more single-mindedly accustomed to thinking in terms of power. At the same time, it is likely to resist innovation, to be more bureaucratically conservative, and to crush all dissent to the point that internal unity can be harmful to the system.

The structure of American leadership is better adapted than the Soviet structure for avoiding leadership crises and promoting regular reassessment of policy. The institutionalized office of the Presidency provides executive continuity at the top, even though a great deal depends on the special talents and personality of the man who fills it. Although the personality of the leader may determine the difference between an energetic, assertive administration and a passive one that allows other political institutions to dominate the scene, nonetheless the state is always led by a legitimate leader, accepted as such by the political system and society as a whole. The transfer of power in America is smooth and quick. This is not the case in the Soviet Union. There legitimacy follows the seizure and consolidation of power by a leader. Until he emerges from the succession struggle, legitimacy rests vaguely in the ruling Communist Party, precluding the claim to power of anyone outside it but not preventing bitter and destructive conflicts within.

In the American system, the top echelons of the executive branch are changed periodically, even if somewhat abruptly. In the Soviet Union, the change is more gradual, accelerating only during power changes. This means that newcomers to the Soviet national leadership are absorbed into the prevailing outlook, and new initiatives must overcome the inherent resistance of set patterns. In the United States, there are periods of "learning" as a new administration, composed in part of political "rookies," takes over, but there is also more room for initial experimentation and re-evaluation. During periods of stability, the higher professional quality of the Soviet leadership is probably a more important asset than the greater structural elasticity of the American system. On the other hand, it is easier to remedy the absence of professionalism than to reform a major structural defect. In fact, a new professionalism is emerging in the United States, while there is still no evidence that workable provisions for a smooth and effective succession have been devised in the Soviet Union.

In the Soviet Union only rarely do the top leaders of the Party have to bargain extensively with the leaders of social forces and specialized bureaucracies. The leaders virtually monopolize initiation and decision on major policy issues. Through the Party apparat, they mobilize support for their policies and supervise their execution. In the United States, the major functions of the policy-making process—initiation, persuasion, decision, and implementation—are dispersed among many more groups than in the Soviet Union. These groups assert their right to participate in decision-making not only because they wield autonomous economic or social power but in some cases because they possess special knowledge. The compartmentalization of expertise in the Soviet Union means that specialists have highly focused interests, and their views are judged on political grounds by professional politicians. This ensures the application of more politically relevant criteria in decision-making, whereas in America the criteria are often confused. As a result, consensus-building takes much time and energy in the American system.

The concentration of power over policy in the Soviet Union means that its leaders are more frequently able to make clear-cut choices among major alternatives than American political leaders, whose choices are almost invariably marginal or ambiguous. The Soviet leadership is also better able to coordinate policies in various areas, and, because of the greater scarcity of resources, the need for such coordination is far greater in the Soviet Union than in the United States. The concentration of the responsibility for initiating policy in the top leadership means that the Soviet system may be slow in responding to gradually developing policy problems. In the American system the agitation of the affected groups is likely to bring the problem to the attention of the top leadership more quickly. Once the problem is recognized by the Soviet leaders, however, their concentrated power enables them, if they wish, to deal with it vigorously and to reverse, if necessary, earlier policies. Policy innovations invariably are slow in the United States.

All the strong points of the Soviet system—in ideology, in leadership, in policy-making—would be impossible to duplicate in a society which protects the liberty of the individual. One should not be oblivious to the costs of the system to the Soviet citizen. On the other hand, despite the optimistic assertions of Western liberals, the absence of liberty in the Soviet Union does enable the Soviet political system to be strong in ways which are denied to Western liberal democracies.

Whatever their specific political weaknesses, neither system appears likely to suffer a major breakdown. The danger of a crisis or stalemate, however, is not completely absent from the American scene. The most probable source of crisis would be a conflict between the liberal and internationalist forces of the Administration and the "Establishment" on the one hand and the conservative, fundamentalist, and nationalist forces of a popular mass movement and its congressional allies on the other. The American political system moves through compromise. If compromise becomes difficult or impossible, crisis ensues. Compromise does become difficult or impossible when issues that are emotional, symbolic, usually noneconomic arise, primarily in areas such as foreign policy, civil rights, and civil liberties. These issues are peculiarly susceptible to exploitation by demagogues and can become the focus of mass movements of the alienated and discontented. It takes a strong government to score diplomatic, political, and military successes in a cold war. It takes an even stronger one to negotiate détentes, to carry off retreats, and to survive reverses in a cold war. The American government may well be strong enough vis-à-vis its enemies to accomplish the former; it may not be strong enough vis-à-vis its own people to accomplish the latter. The normal and generally healthy play of partisan politics continually restricts an Administration's freedom of action. In times of crisis, restrictions may be supplemented by mass demands for quick victories and simple solutions. For almost two years the Truman Administration found itself boxed into a position where it could neither win the Korean War nor extricate itself from the war. The raw material for McCarthy-like mass movements, capitalizing on popular fears and frustrations, lies beneath the surface in American politics. . . .

Crisis or breakdown is more likely in the Soviet Union than in the United States. Whatever threatens the supremacy of the apparat threatens the Soviet system. Two threats are particularly significant. One comes from the continuing tension between the political leadership in the Party apparat and the social, economic, intellectual, military, and other specialized elites which share in the direction of Soviet society. This tension runs like a thread through the more specific issues of Soviet politics. To what extent are science, art, and literature to develop according to the autonomous initiatives of scientists, artists, and writers and to what extent are they to develop according to the ideology determined by the Party? To what extent are the key positions of political leadership to be pre-empted by apparatchiki and to what extent are they to be shared with industrial managers, military chiefs, scientists, and professional bureaucrats? To what extent are these groups to play a role in policy-making? To what extent are the Party-determined needs for politization to pre-empt the educational and communication processes? The problem of the leadership is to keep the exercise of Party authority between that minimum which is essential to maintain Party supremacy and that maximum beyond which the exercise of control would seriously impair the technical functioning of a modern society. To solve this problem the leadership is attempting to adapt new scientific and technical developments to the purposes of Party control and direction.

The threat to Party supremacy from the demands of other elite groups is one of slow erosion. It is also limited. Ideology cannot replace engineering, physics, military science, or even economics. Nor can engineers, scientists, generals, or economists manage a modern state without becoming politicians. Conceivably, the apparatchiki could be displaced by a military coup d'état or a managerial revolt. The probability of this, however, is very low. It could occur only if the Party apparat were first weakened by an assault not from below but from above, not from the pluralistic tendencies in Soviet society but from the autocratic ones.

The Soviet system requires a supreme political leader. This leader, however, is a potential threat to the supremacy of the Party and its apparat. In Stalin this threat materialized to the point where it almost led to the disruption of the system in the struggle for power after Stalin's death. Every absolute ruler eliminates his peers and encourages "new men." During the Great Purge Stalin eliminated the Old Bolsheviks, the aristocrats of the Communist Party, and replaced them with younger men, the "Class of '38," who were dependent upon Stalin for their position. The last ten years of Stalin's rule saw the steady decline of the Party organs and groups. The competition among various chains of command which at lower levels serves to strengthen Party leadership was extended to the top levels of the Party to weaken that leadership. Zhdanov and Malenkov were encouraged to compete for the number-two spot. Under Beria the MVD developed immense powers. The state bureaucracy was strengthened. Stalin's private police and control agencies were developed. The dictatorship of the Party was replaced by the dictatorship of the dictator. The apparat was undermined by the autocrat.

The effects of personal dictatorship on the Soviet system became clear after the death of Stalin. All the principals in the succession struggle (except Zhukov) were apparatchiki. But the struggle among them was not confined to the apparat. Instead, each apparatchik had his own institutional base of power: Beria in the secret police, Malenkov among some groups of economic administrators, Khrushchev in the Party apparat. At crucial points in the struggle the military played an autonomous role. This struggle was possible only because Stalin had reduced the power of the Party apparat vis-à-vis these other bureaucracies. The victory of Khrushchev between 1953 and 1957 was also the victor of the apparat. It marked the reassertion of the position of the Party as the supreme institution of Soviet society and the drastic reduction in power of the secret police, the industrial managers, and the military. The victory of Khrushchev and the apparat, however, again raised the problem of the relation between the leader and the apparat. In the 1960s some steps were taken which tended to reduce the unity and the power of the apparat. . . .

It is unlikely that the near future will see in the Soviet Union a linkage between social pressure for greater freedom from below with partial, fragmented elite support from above. Yet that has usually been the precondition for politically significant liberalization not only in noncommunist societies but also in communist ones, as the recent histories of Poland and Hungary in 1956 and of Communist China in 1957 show. There is still some disruptive potential from below in Soviet society, particularly among some of the younger intellectuals, the peasants, and the non-Russian nationalities. The new generation of workers, no longer so terrorized, is also anxious for a better deal. These groups could perhaps be stimulated into a violent reaction against the system in the event of a breakdown within the leadership. The millions of former concentration-camp inmates could even provide a hardened spearhead in the event of disturbances. But in such an event the Army would probably step in as a custodian of the Soviet state and would mobilize the intensifying nationalism, particularly of the Great Russians, to preserve the Soviet Union. Events of this sort would depend essentially on unpredictable factors, such as accident, personality, coincidence. Nonetheless, because of the foregoing considerations, a major upheaval is more likely in the Soviet Union than in the United States.

The probabilities of breakdown in the Soviet system or crisis in the American one should not be overrated. The American system of government, a product of the eighteenth century, has functioned successfully without a major breakdown for almost a hundred years. The Soviet system is a product of the twentieth century, but it has functioned successfully without a major breakdown for almost fifty years. Americans are accustomed to thinking of their government as one of the oldest in the world. Despite its twentieth-century origins, the Soviet system also can claim honorable mention in the struggle for survival. Apart from Finland's, it is the only political system to emerge out of the collapse of the Habsburg, Ottoman, Hohenzollern, and Romanov empires in World War I that is still in existence. Since World War I nine countries have essayed major roles in world politics. Of these, France has had four political systems; Germany, Italy, and China three each; Japan and India two each. Only the United States, the United Kingdom, and the Soviet Union have avoided drastic changes in the last forty years.

The Soviet and American governments thus belong to a small club of successful systems. Simply because they *are* able to govern, they have much in common which distinguishes them from the faltering, incomplete, and ineffective systems found in Asia, Africa, and Latin America. The Soviet and American systems are effective, authoritative, and stable, each in its own way. They are endowed with legitimacy by distinct sets of political ideas. They are rooted in homogeneous political cultures. Lacking in aristocratic heritage, they recruit their political leaders from broad strata of the population and have relatively open systems of social mobility. They have both demonstrated an ability to replenish their leadership cadres and to adapt their policies and goals to fundamental changes in their environment. Both systems are dynamic. They are changing—in part spontaneously and in part through purposeful human action. The task that remains is to identify the direction and content of these changes. . . .

28. THE MARKET ECONOMY AND FREEDOM

LUDWIG VON MISES

Ludwig von Mises (1881–   ) was professor of economics at New York University.

The market economy is the social system of the division of labor under private ownership of the means of production. Everybody acts on his own behalf; but everybody's actions aim at the satisfaction of other people's needs as well as at the satisfaction of his own. Everybody in acting serves his fellow citizens. Everybody, on the other hand, is served by his fellow citizens. Everybody is both a means and an end in himself; an ultimate end for himself and a means to other people in their endeavors to attain their own ends.

This system is steered by the market. The market directs the individual's activities into those channels in which he best serves the wants of his fellow men. There is in the operation of the market no compulsion and coercion. The state, the social apparatus of coercion and compulsion, does not interfere with the market and with the citizens' activities directed by the market. It employs its power to beat people into submission solely for the prevention of actions destructive to the preservation and the smooth operation of the market economy. . . . Of his own accord the individual integrates himself into the cooperative system. The market directs him and reveals to him in what way he can best promote his own welfare as well as that of other people. The market is supreme. The market alone puts the whole social system in order and provides it with sense and meaning.

The market is not a place, a thing, or a collective entity. The market is a process, actuated by the interplay of the actions of the various individuals cooperating under the division of labor. The forces determining the—continually changing—state of the market are the value judgments of these individuals and their actions as directed by these value judgments. The state of the market at any instant is the price structure, i.e., the totality of the exchange ratios as established by the interaction of those eager to buy and those eager to sell. There is nothing inhuman or mystical with regard to the market. The market process is entirely a resultant of human actions. Every market phenomenon can be traced back to definite choices of the members of the market society.

The market process is the adjustment of the individual actions of the various members of the market society to the requirements of mutual co-

From Ludwig von Mises, *Human Action—A Treatise on Economics.* New Haven: Yale University Press, 1949. Pp. 258–60, 283–85, and 715–16, excerpts.

operation. The market prices tell the producers what to produce, how to produce, and in what quantity. The market is the focal point to which the activities of the individuals converge. It is the center from which the activities of the individuals radiate.

The market economy must be strictly differentiated from the second thinkable—although not realizable—system of social cooperation under the division of labor: the system of social or governmental ownership of the means of production. This second system is commonly called socialism, communism, planned economy, or state capitalism. The market economy or capitalism, as it is usually called, and the socialist economy preclude one another. There is no mixture of the two systems possible or thinkable; there is no such thing as a mixed economy, a system that would be in part capitalistic and in part socialist. Production is directed either by the market or by the decrees of a production czar or a committee of production czars. . . .

Freedom, as people enjoyed it in the democratic countries of Western civilization in the years of the old liberalism's triumph, was not a product of constitutions, bills of rights, laws, and statutes. Those documents aimed only at safeguarding liberty and freedom, firmly established by the operation of the market economy, against encroachments on the part of officeholders. No government and no civil law can guarantee and bring about freedom otherwise than by supporting and defending the fundamental institutions of the market economy. Government means always coercion and compulsion and is by necessity the opposite of liberty. Government is a guarantor of liberty and is compatible with liberty only if its range is adequately restricted to the preservation of economic freedom. Where there is no market economy, the best-intentioned provisions of constitutions and laws remain a dead letter.

The freedom of man under capitalism is an effect of competition. The worker does not depend on the good graces of an employer. If his employer discharges him, he finds another employer. The consumer is not at the mercy of the shopkeeper. He is free to patronize another shop if he likes. Nobody must kiss other people's hands or fear their disfavor. Interpersonal relations are businesslike. The exchange of goods and services is mutual; it is not a favor to sell or to buy, it is a transaction dictated by selfishness on either side. . . .

. . . In the market economy the individual alone is the supreme arbiter in matters of his satisfaction. Capitalist society has no means of compelling a man to change his occupation or his place of work other than to reward those complying with the wants of the consumers by higher pay. It is precisely this kind of pressure which many people consider as unbearable and hope to see abolished under socialism. They are too dull to realize that the only alternative is to convey to the authorities full power to determine in what branch and at what place a man should work.

In his capacity as a consumer man is no less free. He alone decides what is more and what is less important for him. He chooses how to spend his money according to his own will.

The substitution of economic planning for the market economy removes all freedom and leaves to the individual merely the right to obey. The authority directing all economic matters controls all aspects of a man's life and activities. It is the only employer. All labor becomes compulsory labor because the employee must accept what the chief deigns to offer him. The economic czar determines what and how much of each the consumer may consume. There is no sector of human life in which a decision is left to the individual's value judgments. The authority assigns a definite task to him, trains him for this job, and employs him at the place and in the manner it deems expedient.

As soon as the economic freedom which the market economy grants to its members is removed, all political liberties and bills of rights become humbug. Habeas corpus and trial by jury are a sham if, under the pretext of economic expediency, the authority has full power to relegate every citizen it dislikes to the arctic or to a desert and to assign him "hard labor" for life. Freedom of the press is a mere blind if the authority controls all printing offices and paper plants. And so are all the other rights of men.

A man has freedom as far as he shapes his life according to his own plans. A man whose fate is determined by the plans of a superior authority, in which the exclusive power to plan is vested, is not free in the sense in which this term "free" was used and understood by all people until the semantic revolution of our day brought about a confusion of tongues.

The Delimitation of Governmental Functions. Various schools of thought parading under the pompous names of philosophy of law and political science indulge in futile and empty brooding over the delimitation of the functions of government. Starting from purely arbitrary assumptions concerning allegedly eternal and absolute values and perennial justice, they arrogate to themselves the office of the supreme judge of earthly affairs. They misconstrue their own arbitrary value judgments derived from intuition as the voice of the Almighty or the nature of things.

There is, however, no such thing as natural law and a perennial standard of what is just and what is unjust. Nature is alien to the idea of right and wrong. "Thou shalt not kill" is certainly not part of natural law. The characteristic feature of natural conditions is that one animal is intent upon killing other animals and that many species cannot preserve their own life except by killing others. The notion of right and wrong is a human device, a utilitarian precept designed to make social cooperation under the division of labor possible. All moral rules and human laws are means for the realization of definite ends. There is no method available for the appreciation of their goodness or badness other than to scrutinize their usefulness for the attainment of the ends chosen and aimed at. . . .

The notion of just prices and wage rates always refers and always referred to a definite social order which they considered the best possible order. They recommend the adoption of their ideal scheme and its preservation forever. No further changes are to be tolerated. Any alteration of the best possible state of social affairs can only mean deterioration. The world view of these philosophers does not take into account man's ceaseless striving for improvement of the material conditions of well-being. Historical change and a rise in the general standard of living are notions foreign to them. They call "just" that mode of conduct that is compatible with the undisturbed preservation of their utopia, and everything else unjust.

However, the notion of just prices and wage rates as present to the mind of people other than philosophers is very different. When the nonphilosopher calls a price just, what he means is that the preservation of this price improves or at least does not impair his own revenues and station in society. He calls unjust any price that jeopardizes his own wealth and station. It is "just" that the prices of those goods and services which he sells rise more and more and that the prices of those goods and services he buys drop more and more. To the farmer no price of wheat, however high, appears unjust. To the wage earner no wage rates, however high, appear unfair. But the farmer is quick to denounce every drop in the price of wheat as a violation of divine and human laws, and the wage earners rise in rebellion when their wages drop. Yet the market society has no means of adjusting production to changing conditions other than the operation of the market. By means of price changes it forces people to restrict the production of articles less urgently asked for and to expand the production of those articles for which consumers' demand is more urgent. The absurdity of all endeavors to stablize prices consists precisely in the fact that stabilization would prevent any further improvement and result in rigidity and stagnation. The flexibility of commodity prices and wage rates is the vehicle of adjustment, improvement, and progress. Those who condemn changes in prices and wage rates as unjust, and who ask for the preservation of what they call just, are in fact combating endeavors to make economic conditions more satisfactory.

It is not unjust that there has long prevailed a tendency toward such a determination of the prices of agricultural products that the greater part of the population abandoned farming and moved toward the processing industries. But for this tendency, 90 per cent or more of the population would still be occupied in agriculture and the processing industries would have been stunted in their growth. All strata of the population, including the farmers, would be worse off. If Thomas Aquinas' doctrine of the just price had been put into practice, the thirteenth century's economic conditions would still prevail. Population figures would be much smaller than they are today and the standard of living much lower.

Both varieties of the just-price doctrine, the philosophical and the popular, agree in their condemnation of the prices and wage rates as determined on the unhampered market. But this negativism does not in itself provide any answer to the question of what height the just prices and wage rates should attain. If righteousness is to be elevated to the position of the ultimate standard of economic action, one must unambiguously tell every actor what he should do, what prices he should pay in each concrete case, and one must force—by recourse to an apparatus of violent compulsion and coercion—all those venturing disobedience to comply with these orders. . . .

Whatever freedom individuals can enjoy within the framework of social cooperation is conditional upon the concord of private gain and public weal. Within the orbit in which the individual, in pursuing his own well-being, advances also—or at least does not impair—the well-being of his fellow men, people going their own ways jeopardize neither the preservation of society nor the concerns of other people. A realm of freedom and individual initiative emerges, a realm in which man is allowed to choose and to act of his own accord. This sphere of economic freedom is the basis of all the other freedoms compatible with cooperation under the division of labor. It is the market economy or capitalism with its political corollary (the Marxians would have to say: with its "superstructure"), representative government.

Those who contend that there is a conflict between the acquisitiveness of various individuals or between the acquisitiveness of individuals on the one hand and the commonweal on the other, cannot avoid advocating the suppression of the individuals' rights to choose and to act. They must substitute the supremacy of a central board of production management for the discretion of the citizens. In their scheme of the society there is no room left for private initiative. The authority issues orders and everybody is forced to obey.

The Meaning of Laissez Faire. In eighteenth-century France the saying *laissez faire, laissez passer* was the formula into which some of the champions of the cause of liberty compressed their program. Their aim was the establishment of the unhampered market society. In order to attain this end they advocated the abolition of all laws preventing more industrious and more efficient people from outdoing less industrious and less efficient competitors and restricting the mobility of commodities and of men. It was this that the famous maxim was designed to express.

In our age of passionate longing for government omnipotence the formula laissez faire is in disrepute. Public opinion now considers it a manifestation both of moral depravity and of the utmost ignorance.

As the interventionist sees things, the alternative is "automatic forces" or "conscious planning." It is obvious, he implies, that to rely upon automatic processes is sheer stupidity. No reasonable man can seriously recommend doing nothing and letting things go as they do without interference on the part of purposive action. A plan, by the very fact that it is a display of conscious action, is incomparably superior to the absence of any planning. Laissez faire is said to mean: Let the evils last, do not try to improve the lot of mankind by reasonable action.

This is utterly fallacious talk. The argument advanced for planning is entirely derived from an impermissible interpretation of a metaphor. It has no foundation other than the connotations implied in the term "automatic" which it is customary to apply in a metaphorical sense for the description of the market process. Automatic, says the *Concise Oxford Dictionary*, means "unconscious, unintelligent, merely mechanical." Automatic, says *Webster's Collegiate Dictionary*, means "not subject to the control of the will, . . . performed without active thought and without conscious intention or direction." What a triumph for the champion of planning to play this trump card!

The truth is that the alternative is not between a dead mechanism or a rigid automatism on one hand and conscious planning on the other hand. The alternative is not plan or no plan. The question is whose planning? Should each member of society plan for himself, or should a benevolent government alone plan for them all? The issue is not *automatism versus conscious action;*

it is *autonomous action of each individual versus the exclusive action of the government*. It is *freedom versus government omnipotence*.

Laissez faire does not mean: Let soulless mechanical forces operate. It means: Let each individual choose how he wants to cooperate in the social division of labor; let the consumers determine what the entrepreneurs should produce. Planning means: Let the government alone choose and enforce its rulings by the apparatus of coercion and compulsion.

Under laissez faire, says the planner, it is not those goods which people "really" need that are produced, but those goods from the sale of which the highest returns are expected. It is the objective of planning to direct production toward the satisfaction of the "true" needs. But who is to decide what the "true" needs are?

Thus, for instance, Professor Harold Laski, the former chairman of the British Labor Party, would determine as the objective of the planned direction of investment "that the use of the investor's savings will be in housing rather than in cinemas." It is beside the point whether or not one agrees with the professor's view that better houses are more important than moving pictures. It is a fact that the consumers, in spending part of their money for admission to the movies, have made another choice. If the masses of Great Britain, the same people whose votes swept the Labor Party into power, were to stop patronizing the moving pictures and to spend more for comfortable homes and apartments, profit-seeking business would be forced to invest more in building homes and apartment houses and less in the production of expensive pictures. It is Mr. Laski's desire to defy the wishes of the consumers and to substitute his own will for that of the consumers. He wants to do away with the democracy of the market and to establish the absolute rule of a production czar. He may believe that he is right from a "higher" point of view, and that as a superman he is called upon to impose his own valuations on the masses of inferior men. But then he should be frank enough to say so plainly.

All this passionate praise of the supereminence of government action is but a poor disguise for the individual interventionist's *self-deification*. The great god State is a great god only because it is expected to do exclusively what the individual advocate of interventionism wants to see achieved. . . .

Laissez faire means: Let the common man choose and act; do not force him to yield to a dictator.

29. ECONOMIC CONTROL AND TOTALITARIANISM

FREDERICK A. HAYEK

Frederick A. Hayek (1899–   ) is professor of economics at the University of Freiburg, Germany.

Most planners who have seriously considered the practical aspects of their task have little doubt that a directed economy must be run on more or less dictatorial lines. That the complex system of interrelated activities, if it is to be consciously directed at all, must be directed by a single staff of experts, and that ultimate responsibility and power must rest in the hands of a commander-in-chief whose actions must not be fettered by democratic procedure, is too obvious a consequence of underlying ideas of central planning not to command fairly general assent. The consolation our planners offer us is that this authoritarian direction will apply "only" to economic matters. One of the most prominent economic planners, Stuart Chase, assures us, for instance, that in a planned society "political democracy can remain if it confines itself to all but economic matters." Such assurances are usually accompanied by the suggestion that, by giving up freedom in what are, or ought to be, the less important aspects of our lives, we shall obtain greater freedom in the pursuit of higher values. On this ground people who abhor the idea of a political dictatorship often clamor for a dictator in the economic field.

The arguments used appeal to our best instincts and often attract the finest minds. If planning really did free us from the less important cares and so made it easier to render our existence one of plain living and high thinking, who would wish to belittle such an ideal? If our economic activities really concerned only the inferior or even more sordid sides of life, of course we ought to endeavor by all means to find a way to relieve ourselves from the excessive care for material ends and, leaving them to be cared for by some piece of utilitarian machinery, set our minds free for the higher things of life.

Unfortunately, the assurance people derive from this belief that the power which is exercised over economic life is power over matters of secondary importance only, and which makes them take lightly the threat to the freedom of our economic pursuits, is altogether unwarranted. It is largely a consequence of the erroneous belief that there are purely economic ends separate from the other ends of life. Yet, apart from the pathological case of the miser, there is no such thing. The ultimate ends of the activities of reasonable beings

From Frederick A. Hayek, *The Road to Serfdom*. Chicago: The University of Chicago Press, 1944. Pp. 88–100, excerpts. Reprinted by permission of the publisher.

are never economic. Strictly speaking, there is no "economic motive" but only economic factors conditioning our striving for other ends. What in ordinary language is misleadingly called the "economic motive" means merely the desire for general opportunity, the desire for power to achieve unspecified ends. If we strive for money, it is because it offers us the widest choice in enjoying the fruits of our efforts. Because in modern society it is through the limitation of our money incomes that we are made to feel the restrictions which our relative property still imposes upon us, many have come to hate money as the symbol of these restrictions. But this is to mistake for the cause the medium through which a force makes itself felt. It would be much truer to say that money is one of the greatest instruments of freedom ever invented by man. It is money which in existing society opens an astounding range of choice to the poor man—a range greater than that which not many generations ago was open to the wealthy. We shall better understand the significance of this service of money if we consider what it would really mean if, as so many socialists characteristically propose, the "pecuniary motive" were largely displaced by "noneconomic incentives." If all rewards, instead of being offered in money, were offered in the form of public distinctions or privileges, positions of power over other men, or better housing or better food, opportunities for travel or education, this would merely mean that the recipient would no longer be allowed to choose and that whoever fixed the reward determined not only its size but also the particular form in which it should be enjoyed. . . .

The question raised by economic planning is, therefore, not merely whether we shall be able to satisfy what we regard as our more or less important needs in the way we prefer. It is whether it shall be we who decide what is more, and what is less, important for us, or whether this is to be decided by the planner. Economic planning would not affect merely those of our marginal needs that we have in mind when we speak contemptuously about the merely economic. It would, in effect, mean that we as individuals should no longer be allowed to decide what we regard as marginal.

The authority directing all economic activity would control not merely the part of our lives which is concerned with inferior things; it would control the allocation of the limited means for all our ends. And whoever controls all economic activity controls the means for all our ends and must therefore decide which are to be satisfied and which not. This is really the crux of the matter. Economic control is not merely control of a sector of human life which can be separated from the rest; it is the control of the means for all our ends. And whoever has sole control of the means must also determine which ends are to be served, which values are to be rated higher and which lower—in short, what men should believe and strive for. Central planning means that the economic problem is to be solved by the community instead of by the individual; but this involves that it must also be the community, or rather its representatives, who must decide the relative importance of the different needs.

The so-called economic freedom which the planners promise us means precisely that we are to be relieved of the necessity of solving our own economic problems and that the bitter choices which this often involves are to be made for us. Since under modern conditions we are for almost everything dependent on means which our fellow men provide, economic planning would involve direction of almost the whole of our life. There is hardly an aspect of it, from our primary needs to our relations with our family and friends, from the nature of our work to the use of our leisure, over which the planner would not exercise his "conscience control."

The power of the planner over our private lives would be no less complete if he chose not to exercise it by direct control of our consumption. Although a planned society would probably to some extent employ rationing and similar devices, the power of the planner over our private lives does not depend on this and would be hardly less effective if the consumer were nominally free to spend his income as he pleased. The source of his power over all consumption which in a planned society the authority would possess would be its control over a production.

Our freedom of choice in a competitive society rests on the fact that, if one person refuses to satisfy our wishes, we can turn to another. But if we face a monopolist we are at his mercy. And an authority directing the whole economic system would be the most powerful monopolist conceivable. While we need probably not be afraid that such an authority would exploit this power in the manner in which a private monopolist would do so, while its purpose would presumably not be the extortion of maximum financial gain, it would have complete power to decide what we are to be given and on what terms. It would not only decide what commodities and services were to be available and in what quantities; it would be able to direct their distribution between districts and groups and could, if it wished, discriminate between persons to any degree it liked. If we remember why planning is advocated by most people, can there be much doubt that this power would be used for the ends of which the authority approves and to prevent the pursuits of ends which it disapproves?

The power conferred by the control of production and prices is almost unlimited. In a competitive society the prices we have to pay for a thing, the rate at which we can get one thing for another, depend on the quantities of other things of which by taking one, we deprive the other members of society. This price is not determined by the conscious will of anybody. And if one way of achieving our ends proves too expensive for us, we are free to try other ways. The obstacles in our path are not due to someone's disapproving of our ends but to the fact that the same means are also wanted elsewhere. In a directed economy, where the authority watches over the ends pursued, it is certain that it would use its power to assist some ends and to prevent the realization of others. Not our view, but somebody else's, of what we ought to like or dislike would determine what we should get. And since the authority would have the power to thwart any efforts to elude its guidance, it would control what we consume almost as effectively as if it directly told us how to spend our income.

Not only in our capacity as consumers, however, and not even mainly in that capacity, would the will of the authority shape and "guide" our daily lives. It would do so even more in our position as producers. These two aspects of our lives cannot be separated; and as for most of us the time we spend at our work is a large part of our whole lives, and as our job usually also determines the place where and the people among whom we live, some freedom in choosing our work is, probably, even more important for our happiness than freedom to spend our income during the hours of leisure. . . .

Most planners, it is true, promise that in the new planned world free choice of occupation will be scrupulously preserved or even increased. But there they promise more than they can fulfil. If they want to plan, they must control the entry into the different trades and occupations, or the terms of remuneration, or both. In almost all known instances of planning, the establishment of such controls and restrictions was among the first measures taken. If such control were universally practiced and exercised by a single planning authority, one needs little imagination to see what would become of the "free choice of occupation" promised. The "freedom of choice" would be purely fictitious, a mere promise to practice no discrimination where in the nature of the case discrimination must be practiced, and where all one could hope would be that the selection would be made on what the authority believed to be objective grounds.

There would be little difference if the planning authority confined itself to fixing the terms of employment and tried to regulate numbers by adjusting these terms. By prescribing the remuneration, it would no less effectively bar groups of people from entering many trades than by specifically excluding them. A rather plain girl badly wants to become a saleswoman, a weakly boy who has set his heart on a job where weakness handicaps him, as well as in general the apparently less able or less suitable are not necessarily excluded in a competitive society; if they value the position sufficiently they will frequently be able to get a start by a financial sacrifice and will later make good through qualities which at first are not so obvious. But when the authority fixes the remunerations for a whole category and the selection among the candidates is made by an objective test, the strength of their desire for the job will count for very little. The person whose qualifications are not of the standard type, or whose temperament is not of the ordinary kind, will no longer be able to come to special arrangements with an employer whose dispositions will fit in with his special needs: the person who prefers irregular hours or even a happy-go-lucky existence with a small and perhaps uncertain income to a regular routine will no longer have the choice. Conditions will be without exception what in some measure they inevitably are in a large organization—or rather worse, because there will be no possibility of escape. We shall no longer be free to be rational or efficient only when and where we think it worth while; we shall all have to conform to the standards which the planning authority must fix in order to simplify its task. To make this immense task manageable, it will have to reduce the diversity of human capacities and inclinations to a few categories of readily interchangeable units and deliberately to disregard minor personal differences.

Although the professed aim of planning would be that man should cease to be a mere means, in fact—since it would be impossible to take account in the plan of individual likes and dislikes—the individual would more than ever become a mere means, to be used by the authority in the service of such abstractions as the "social welfare" or the "good of the community."

That in a competitive society most things can be had at a price—though it is often a cruelly high price we have to pay—is a fact the importance of which can hardly be overrated. The alternative is not, however, complete freedom of choice, but orders and prohibitions which must be obeyed and, in the last resort, the favor of the mighty.

It is significant of the confusion prevailing on all these subjects that it should have become a cause for reproach that in a competitive society almost everything can be had at a price. If the people who protest against having the higher values of life brought into the "cash nexus" really mean that we should not be allowed to sacrifice our lesser needs in order to preserve the higher values, and that the choice should be made for us, this demand must be regarded as rather peculiar and scarcely testifies to great respect for the dignity of the individual. That life and health, beauty and virtue, honor and peace of mind, can often be preserved only at considerable material cost, and that somebody must make the choice, is as undeniable as that we all are sometimes not prepared to make the material sacrifices necessary to protect those higher values against all injury.

To take only one example: We could, of course, reduce casualties by automobile accidents to zero if we were willing to bear the cost—if in no other way—by abolishing automobiles. And the same is true of thousands of other instances in which we are constantly risking life and health and all the fine values of the spirit, of ourselves and of our fellow men to further what we at the same time contemptuously describe as our material comfort. Nor can it be otherwise, since all our ends compete for the same means; and we could not strive for anything but these absolute values if they were on no account to be endangered.

That people should wish to be relieved of the bitter choice which hard facts often impose upon them is not surprising. But few want to be relieved through having the choice made for them by others. People just wish that the choice should not be necessary, at all. And they are only too ready to believe that the choice is not really necessary, that it is imposed upon them merely by the particular economic system under which we live. What they resent is, in truth, that there is an economic problem.

In their wishful belief that there is really no longer an economic problem people have been confirmed by irresponsible talk about "potential plenty"—which, if it were a fact, would indeed mean that there is no economic problem which makes the choice inevitable. But although this snare has served socialist propaganda under various names as long as socialism has existed, it is still as palpably untrue as it was when it was first used over a hundred years ago. In all this time not one of the many people who have used it has produced a workable plan of how production could be increased so as to abolish even in western Europe what we regard as poverty—not to speak of the world as a whole. The reader may take it that whoever talks about potential plenty is either dishonest or does not know what he is talking about. Yet it is this false hope as much as anything which drives us along the road to planning.

While the popular movement still profits by this false belief, the claim that a planned economy would produce a substantially larger output than the competitive system is being progressively abandoned by most students of the problem. Even a good many economists with socialist views who have seriously studied the problems of central planning are now content to hope that a planned society will equal the efficiency of a competitive system; they advocate planning no longer because of its superior productivity but because it will enable us to secure a more just and equitable distribution of wealth. This is, indeed, the only argument for planning which can be seriously pressed. It is indisputable that if we want to secure a distribution of wealth which conforms to some predetermined standard, if we want consciously to decide who is to have what, we must plan the whole economic system. But the question remains whether the price we should have to pay for the realization of somebody's ideal of justice is not bound to be more discontent and more oppression than was ever caused by the much-abused free play of economic forces.

We should be seriously deceiving ourselves if for these apprehensions we sought comfort in the consideration that the adoption of central planning would merely mean a return, after a brief spell of a free economy, to the ties and regulations which have governed economic activity through most ages, and that therefore the infringements of personal liberty need not be greater than they were before the age of laissez faire. This is a dangerous illusion. Even during periods of European history when the regimentation of economic life went furthest, it amounted to little more than the creation of a general and semipermanent framework of rules within which the individual preserved a wide free sphere. The apparatus of control then available would not have been adequate to impose more than very general directions. And even where the control was most complete it extended only to those activities of a person through which he took part in the social division of labor. In the much wider sphere in which he then still lived on his own products, he was free to act as he chose.

The situation is now entirely different. During the liberal era the progressive division of labor has created a situation where almost every one of our activities is part of a social process. This is a development which we cannot reverse, since it is only because of it that we can maintain the vastly increased population at anything like present standards. But in consequence, the substitution of central planning for competition would require central direction of a much greater part of our lives than was ever attempted before. It could not stop at what we regard as our economic activities, because we are now for almost every part of our lives dependent on somebody else's economic activities. The passion for the "collective satisfaction of our needs," with which our socialists have so well prepared the way for totalitarianism, and which wants us to take our pleasures as well as our necessities at the appointed time and in the prescribed form, is, of course, partly intended as a means of political education. But it is also the result of the exigencies of planning, which consists essentially in depriving us of choice, in order to give us whatever fits best into the plan and that at a time determined by the plan.

It is often said that political freedom is meaningless without economic freedom. This is true enough, but in a sense almost opposite from that in which the phrase is used by our planners. The economic freedom which is the prerequisite of any other freedom cannot be the freedom from economic care which the socialists promise us and which can be obtained only by relieving the individual at the same time of the necessity and of the power of choice; it must be the freedom of our economic activity which, with the right of choice, inevitably also carries the risk and the responsibility of that right.

30. THE BASIS OF AFRICAN SOCIALISM

JULIUS K. NYERERE

Julius K. Nyerere (1922–   ) is the President of Tanzania.

Socialism—like Democracy—is an attitude of mind. In a socialist society it is the socialist attitude of mind, and not the rigid adherence to a standard political pattern, which is needed to ensure that the people care for each other's welfare.

The purpose of this paper is to examine that attitude. It is not intended to define the institutions which may be required to embody it in a modern society.

In the individual, as in the society, it is an attitude of mind which distinguishes the socialist from the nonsocialist. It has nothing to do with the possession or nonpossession of wealth. Destitute people can be potential capitalists—exploiters of their fellow human beings. A millionaire can equally well be a socialist; he may value his wealth only because it can be used in the service of his fellow men. But the man who uses wealth for the purpose of dominating any of his fellows is a capitalist. So is the man who would if he could! . . .

Apart from the antisocial effects of the accumulation of personal wealth, the very desire to accumulate it must be interpreted as a vote of "no confidence" in the social system. For when a society is so organized that it cares about its individuals, then, provided he is willing to work, no individual within that society should worry about what will happen to him tomorrow if he does not hoard wealth today. Society itself should look after him, or his widow, or his orphans. This is exactly what traditional African society succeeded in doing. Both the "rich" and the "poor" individual were com-

Julius K. Nyerere, *Ujamaa:* The Basis of African Socialism, excerpts. This essay was published in Dar-es-Salaam, Tanganyika, in April 1962.

pletely secure in African society. Natural catastrophe brought famine, but it brought famine to everybody—"poor" or "rich." Nobody starved, either of food or of human dignity, because he lacked personal wealth; he could depend on the wealth possessed by the community of which he was a member. That was socialism. That is socialism. There can be no such thing as acquisitive socialism, for that would be another contradiction in terms. Socialism is essentially distributive. Its concern is to see that those who sow reap a fair share of what they sow. . . .

In traditional African society everybody was a worker. There was no other way of earning a living for the community. Even the Elder, who appeared to be enjoying himself without doing any work and for whom everybody else appeared to be working, had, in fact, worked hard all his younger days. The wealth he now appeared to possess was not his, personally; it was only "his" as the Elder of the group which had produced it. He was its guardian. The wealth itself gave him neither power nor prestige. The respect paid to him by the young was his because he was older than they, and had served his community longer; and the "poor" Elder enjoyed as much respect in our society as the "rich" Elder.

When I say that in traditional African society everybody was a worker, I do not use the word "worker" simply as opposed to "employer" but also as opposed to "loiterer" or "idler." One of the most socialistic achievements of our society was the sense of security it gave to its members, and the universal hospitality on which they could rely. But it is too often forgotten, nowadays, that the basis of this great socialistic achievement was this: that it was taken for granted that every member of society—barring only the children and the infirm—contributed his fair share of effort towards the production of its wealth. Not only was the capitalist, or the landed exploiter, unknown to traditional African society, but we did not have that other form of modern parasite—the loiterer, or idler, who accepts the hospitality of society as his 'right" but gives nothing in return! Capitalistic exploitation was impossible. Loitering was an unthinkable disgrace. . . .

There is no such thing as socialism without work. A society which fails to give its individuals the means to work, or, having given them the means to work, prevents them from getting a fair share of the products of their own sweat and toil, needs putting right. Similarly, an individual who can work—and is provided by society with the means to work—but does not do so, is equally wrong. He has no right to expect anything from society because he contributes nothing to society. . . .

In our traditional African society we were individuals within a community. We took care of the community, and the community took care of us. We neither needed nor wished to exploit our fellow men.

And in rejecting the capitalist attitude of mind which colonialism brought into Africa, we must reject also the capitalist methods which go with it. One of these is the individual ownership of land. To us in Africa, land was always recognized as belonging to the community. Each individual within our society had a right to the use of land, because otherwise he could not earn his living, and one cannot have the right to life without also having the right to some means of maintaining life. But the African's right to land was simply the right to use it; he had no other right to it, nor did it occur to him to try and claim one. . . .

We must not allow the growth of parasites here in Tanganyika. The T.A.N.U. [Tanganyika African National Union] Government must go back to the traditional African custom of land holding. That is to say, a member of society will be entitled to a piece of land *on condition that he uses it.* Unconditional, or "freehold," ownership of land (which leads to speculation and parasitism) must be abolished. We must, as I have said, regain our former attitude of mind—our traditional African socialism—and apply it to the new societies we are building today. . . .

Tanganyika, today, is a poor country. The standard of living of the masses of our people is shamefully low. But if every man and woman in the country takes up the challenge and works to the limit of his or her ability for the good of the whole society, Tanganyika will prosper; and that prosperity will be shared by all her people.

But it must be *shared.* The true socialist may not exploit his fellows. So that if the members of any group within our society are going to argue that, because they happen to be contributing more to the national income than some other groups, they must therefore take for themselves a greater share of the profits of their own industry than they actually need, and if they insist on this in spite of the fact that it would mean reducing their group contribution to the general income and thus slowing down the rate at which the whole community can benefit, then that group is exploiting (or trying to exploit) its fellow human beings. It is displaying a capitalist attitude of mind.

There are bound to be certain groups which, by virtue of the "market value" of their particular industry's products, *will* contribute more to the nation's income than others. But the others may actually be producing goods or services which are of equal, or greater, *intrinsic* value although they do not happen to command such a high *artificial* value. For example, the food produced by the peasant farmer is of greater social value than the diamonds mined at Mwadui. But the mineworkers of Mwadui could claim, quite correctly, that their labor was yielding greater financial profits to the community than that of the farmers. If, however, they went on to demand that they should therefore be given most of that extra profit for themselves, and that no share of it should be spent on helping the farmers, they would be potential capitalists.

This is exactly where the attitude of mind comes in. It is one of the purposes of trade unions to ensure for the workers a fair share of the profits of their labor. But a "fair" share must be fair in relation to the whole society. If it is greater than the country can afford without having to penalize some other section of society, then it is *not* a fair share. Trade union leaders and their followers, as long as they are true socialists, will not need to be coerced by the government into keeping their demands within the limits imposed by the needs of society as a whole. Only if there are potential capitalists amongst them will the socialist government have to step in and prevent them from putting their capitalist ideas into practice! . . .

The foundation, and the objective, of African Socialism is the Extended Family. The true African Socialist does not look on one class of men as his brethren and another as his natural enemies. He does not form an alliance with the "brethren" for the extermination of the "nonbrethren." He rather regards *all* men as his brethren—as members of his ever extending Family. . . . That is why the first article of T.A.N.U.'s creed is: "I believe in Human Brotherhood and the Unity of Africa."

"*UJAMAA,*" then, or "Familyhood," describes our socialism. It is opposed to Capitalism, which seeks to build a happy society on the basis of the Exploitation of Man by Man; and it is equally opposed to doctrinaire socialism which seeks to build its happy society on a philosophy of Inevitable Conflict between Man and Man.

We, in Africa, have no more need of being "converted" to socialism than we have of being "taught" democracy. Both are rooted in our own past—in the traditional society which produced us. Modern African Socialism can draw from its traditional heritage the recognition of "society" as an extension of the basic family unit. But it can no longer confine the idea of the social family within the limits of the tribe, nor, indeed, of the nation. For no true African Socialist can look at a line drawn on a map and say, "The people on this side of that line are my brothers, but those who happen to live on the other side of it can have no claim on me"; every individual on this continent is his brother.

It was in the struggle to break the grip of colonialism that we learned the need for unity. We came to recognize that the same socialist attitude of mind which, in the tribal days, gave to every individual the security that comes of belonging to a widely extended family, must be preserved within the still wider society of the nation. But we should not stop there. Our recognition of the family to which we all belong must be extended yet further—beyond the tribe, the community, the nation, or even the continent—to embrace the whole society of mankind. This is the only logical conclusion for true socialism.

31. SOCIALISM AND CAPITALISM

JOSÉ FIGUERES

José Figueres (1908?–   ) is an eminent Central American statesman and social scientist. He wrote this essay during the period that he served as President of Costa Rica.

In this epoch of cold war with Soviet Russia, it is fashionable in the United States, among uninformed people, to connect the word "socialism" with undemocratic political doctrines.

On the other hand, in England, the Scandinavian countries, and in other

José Figueres, *Cartas a Un Ciudadano*. San Jose, Costa Rica: Imprenta Nacional, 1956. Pp. 109–40, excerpts. Translation by Ignatius DiCola.

places, socialist parties take an active part in present-day politics, enjoying the prestige of being democratic.

On its part, the term "capitalism" has a bad reputation in Latin America, where it is frequently considered a synonym for "colonialism" or "imperialism," and in Europe, where it is frequently the equivalent of a "reactionary" attitude, of exploitation of workers.

In this letter, which I address to the common citizen of Costa Rica, I intend to use these words in their original meaning, as denominations of two different *economic* systems, which should not be tied to the various *political* systems. . . .

Socialism, as an economic doctrine, has nothing to do with political "totalitarianism," that is to say, with despotism. And the theoretical capitalistic system, of absolute freedom of enterprise, should not be connected with colonial exploitation of one people by another. . . .

As you know, Citizen, socialism is an economic system inspired by the ideal that "all things belong to all." Of course, it does not refer to things of *personal use,* such as clothing, house, toothbrush, but solely to productive properties, such as real estate, factories, edifices, railroads, etc. Socialism recommends that all the means of production belong to the entire nation, and that the State administer them. . . .

Capitalism, in the usual meaning of the word, is an economic system of private ownership of land, industry, and other means of production, which permits everyone to produce what he likes, without any planning or aid, to buy and sell as he wishes, to pay the lowest day wages that he can, and to obtain the most advantageous prices which the market will bear, without any sense of responsibility toward his fellow creatures.

Against this economic irresponsibility, the results of which are low production in general and an unjust accumulation for a few, there appeared the idea of socialism, proposing a society diametrically opposed to capitalism.

In practice, neither of the two systems has ruled in any nation in absolute form. Even less in our times. The nations which call themselves socialistic have had to leave in private hands at least the small trade (commerce), which is difficult to administer by a central organization, and a great part of the land, because the custom of property has ingrained itself very deeply among all the peasants (farmers) of the world. On the other hand, the great so-called capitalistic nations, and principally the United States, have organized their industry and commerce more in the form of enterprises, the capital of which belongs to the public who buys "stocks," or of partial titles to property. . . .

The number of stockholders is increasing, so that property is more diffused. At present the very enterprises facilitate the purchase of stocks by their workers. This is a new form of socialization, stimulated precisely by the people who most fear the word "socialism."

There exist, nonetheless, in those nations many thousands of small and medium-size businesses, and private farms. One should be eager to avoid their disappearance. But the State imposes upon them numerous regulations: minimum wages, maximum work day, fixed prices, compulsory insurance, income tax, etc. The State determines the rates, the scope of operation, the schedules, etc. for transportation and other public service enterprises. With all of these "interferences," those businesses are at the service of the community, more than at the service of their owners. There is no such thing as "capitalism."

What has happened is that, while people were discussing in the newspapers such words and phrases as "guided economy" and "free enterprise," "inviolable property" and "social necessity," developments have taken, almost independently, the only possible path: *a combination* of the two systems, capitalist and socialist, which endeavors to integrate the advantages of both, and to minimize the disadvantages of each. To this synthesis of the two historical trends is given now the name of *mixed economy*. . . .

When the modern State intervenes judiciously as a stabilizer in a mixed economy, it forestalls disruptive tendencies, applies remedies in time, and with moderation and skill, and avoids many losses and much suffering. . . .

[But,] the mixed economy, with all its ingenious mechanisms of controls and compensations, does not satisfy fully the socialist mentality, which prefers a simpler formula, such as the fusion of all activities in a single great enterprise, the State. The mixed system gives the impression of being too complicated, insecure, and not very scientific.

Neither does this combination satisfy "liberal" or capitalist thought, which considers it artificial or not very "natural."

Nonetheless, if one takes a good look at it, the system of stimulations cannot be more scientific, nor more natural. What could be more proper than to observe *the natural inclinations*, the tendencies of events, and to place them at the service of man, by means of his intelligence? . . .

Every economic system, every political movement, every social order, has to be judged, in the final analysis, for its spiritual effect upon the men who adopt it; that is to say, for the *human type* which it tends to form, or at least to encourage.

The socialist ideal (which has never been fulfilled, except within small groups), tends to make men less egoistic, more generous, more responsible before society. How? Through an educational process: by making men see that they work in order to serve others, and not merely in order to carry on their own business; by convincing them that the productive effort of each person, his daily contribution to the great economic task, is in reality a *social function*.

In theory, in a completely "free" economy, of pure individual initiative, where anyone can form whatever business he wants, or is empowered to form without the State's help or restraint, man must feel like the hunter who goes out to shoot the deer in uninhabited land, shooting big or small, male or female, all that he encounters during every season.

What we are saying is that a totally capitalistic society (which has never existed), would tend to produce a human type who is oblivious of his fellow man, selfish, greedy for goods or self-gratification, without any sense of social responsibility.

It is necessary to note, however, that the possession of goods, and the exercise of property, in a certain way enhances man, and makes him more responsible, at least before himslf and his family. Accordingly, the capitalist system can also take note of its beneficial effect on the spiritual order. The favorable effects of capitalism emerge plentifully in a mixed economy (such as Costa Rica's, for example), which not only respects property, but also encourages the development of many small farmers.

Let us see now the extent to which the spiritual benefits sought by socialism are realized in a mixed economy where a multitude of private and public enterprises of all types operate, and where the State acts, as need dictates, to stimulate, correct, and stabilize.

It is certain that the intervention of the State has an educational effect. A peasant of the Valle de El General, who once lived in isolation, unknown, almost outside of society, sowing and selling as best he could, did not feel any social responsibility other than that of supporting his family. He was nothing more than Juan Pérez, an individual whose·labor was concerned solely with himself, even though it was an *economic activity* of producing in order to sell.

Juan Pérez is now found and the State opens a highway, because it is as interested as he is in seeing that his beans arrive easily in the capital. The State considers a public servant, and persuades him to produce more beans and less corn this year. The State is interested in supplying him with good seeds, it assures him of the sale of his entire crop at a fixed price, and it advances him money so that he does not fall into the hands of the speculator. If the farmer becomes an employer and hires various farm hands, the State tells him how much he must pay them, and how many hours the work day should be.

Juan Pérez finds himself suddenly converted into a member of society in whom everyone is interested. If a storm comes along which ruins his crop, the loss is considered a national calamity. He starts to realize that he is a servant of others. His work is now not a purely "private" activity, but is in a certain sense "public," since he contributes to feed the population. When he sows beans in order to sell them, that is to say, when he fulfills his *economic activity*, the farmer also serves a social function. In the same sense, the home of the tavern owner is private, but not his tavern. There the public is served, and in that realm, the tavern keeper exercises a social function.

All businesses and agricultural, industrial, or commercial enterprises, big or small, although they enjoy a large degree of autonomy which their "private" character gives them in accordance with the right of property, nonetheless, are subject to a series of laws, controls, inducements, and corrective measures, which confer upon them, in reality, a social function. . . .

If the principle that *economic activity is a social function* is adopted, . . . the laws of the nation, the government's orientation, and the public's education can all be directed toward the attainment of a more just and generous society, which will better be able to fulfill the aspirations of those who compose it.

32. DEMOCRACY AND SOCIALISM: A HOPE

MICHAEL HARRINGTON

Michael Harrington (1928–   ) is a prominent writer on public af-
fairs and a frequent contributor to leading journals of opinion. He
is a member of the national executive committee of the Socialist Party
and chairman of the board of the League for Industrial Democracy.

Either Western man is going to choose a new society—or a new society will
choose, and abolish, him.

It is clear that the contemporary revolution will continue to reshape the
human environment in the most radical way. If anything, time will speed up
even more, for the cybernated technology of today proceeds by geometric
leaps and bounds rather than by arithmetic progression. Short of an atomic
holocaust, which would simply write an end to the whole process, there is no
reason to think that it will slow down. And, as this book has shown, the consequences of this development are not merely material and scientific. They
invade the spirit, the psychology, politics, and every other aspect of life.

In this context, America has for some time been engaged in the wrong
argument. It has been debating as to whether or not the future should be
collective and social, and ignoring the fact that the present is already becoming so. The real issue is not whether, but how, this future will arrive—
unwittingly or consciously chosen.

If the new society imposes itself upon a people who do not notice a revolution, the moment will constitute the decadence of the Western ideal.

The West has marked itself off from other cultures precisely by its confidence in the future. The religious form of this faith is most identified with
St. Augustine, who, breaking with the cyclic theories in which time was a
great wheel turning around itself, asserted the pilgrimage of history toward
the City of God. The secular version of the same hope dates at least from
the Renaissance and culminates in the capitalist and socialist visions of
progress. It was this Faustian restlessness that drove the Western powers to
remake the world during the last several centuries.

Along with this futurism there was the affirmation of the power of reason.
The importance of this commitment cannot be evaded by recourse to a
fashionable irrationalism. Of course, the absolute, unquestioned faith in
reason has been disproved; yes, there were excesses of the Enlightenment

tradition like Comte. But it was the theoretical and practical intelligence which lifted Western man out of the mire and made him, for a while, lord of the earth. Now, if reason has turned out tragically, so has the West. And if men cannot control the products of their own brain, there will be no place to hide, for mystics or for anyone else. Without rational human direction, the accidental revolution is not moving toward a rebirth of poetry but toward an inhuman collectivism. . . .

And yet, there is the possibility that the West will freely choose a new society.

No option which can be taken will solve all human problems. The most happy outcome could even be, as Norman Mailer has suggested, only that suffering will be raised from the level of fate to that of tragedy. For when there are no longer plagues, famines, and natural catastrophes to blame death and evil on, the essential finitude of men could become all the more stark and stripped of its accidental qualities. And, contrary to Marx, in a society where men die from death because they have been born, there could be a religious renaissance as well as a heroic atheism.

The claim put here is minimal. The free choice of the future will not abrogate the human condition. But it will provide the context in which autonomous human beings can grow in depth and understanding, which is all the West has really ever asked.

In order to choose the new society rather than being chosen by it, the West must make this accidental century conscious and truly democratic. And this goal I would call socialism.

There are many arguments against using the word "socialism." Most Americans do not understand it. Communism uses the term as a rhetorical mask for a bureaucratic minority that imposes its private desires upon a social technology. Worse yet, the Communists have attempted to identify socialism with totalitarianism. In the emergent nations, the word "socialism" is used to describe the socialization of poverty for the purposes of accumulating capital. These societies, as the great socialist theorists would have predicted, are far distant from the ideal of the free development of the individual which is of the socialist essence. And even in Western Europe where the Social Democratic parties have maintained the democratic content of socialism, they have often equated their vision with a welfare state more than with a new civilization.

Despite all these semantic and historic drawbacks, the term must be used. With the exception of the United States, socialism is what the most democratic forces in the West call their dream. And even more basically, the nineteenth-century socialists, for all their failures of prediction, were the first to anticipate the present plight and to attempt to resolve it. They were right when they said that the way in which men produce their worldly goods is becoming more and more social. They were right in asserting that this complex, interdependent technology could not be contained within a system of private decision-making. And if there is to be a humane outcome to the contemporary Western adventure, they will have to be made right in their faith that the people can freely and democratically take control of their own lives and society.

And this last idea is the heart of the socialist hope as I define it in this book. From the very beginning, the socialists knew that modern technology could not be made just by dividing it up into tiny parcels of individual ownership. It is of the very nature of that technology to be concentrated and collective. Therefore, the socialists assigned a new and radical meaning to democracy. The people's title to the social means of production would be guaranteed, they said, not through stock certificates, but through votes. The basic economic decisions would be made democratically.

In this context, the nationalization of industry is a technique of socialism, not its definition. It is one extremely important way of abolishing the political and social power that results from concentrated private ownership. It also facilitates directing economic resources to the satisfaction of human needs. When the people "own" the state through political democracy, then public corporations are truly theirs, and nationalization is an instrument of freedom. But there are other ways to forward the democratization of economic and social power. Fiscal and monetary policy, a cooperative sector, and taxes are among them.

In these terms, the one set and undeviating aspect of socialism is its commitment to making the democratic and free choice of the citizens the principle of social and economic life. All other issues—the extent of nationalization, the mode of planning, and the like—have to be empirically tested and measured in the light of how they serve that end. For certainly the old popular definition of socialism as the simple and wholesale nationalization of the economy has not survived the experience of this century, and particularly the Communist experience. At the same time, it has become abundantly clear that the commanding heights of the economy—where decisions affect more of life than most laws of Congresses and Parliaments—cannot be left to private motives.

But it is better to leave this plane of socialist generality and move to the definition of specific examples. In what follows, I am suggesting that the only way the accidental revolution can become socially conscious of itself is through a profound economic and social deepening of democracy. This I call socialism.

Education provides an excellent case in point.

Many of the contemporary arguments against democracy, and particularly those grouped around the idea of mass society, charge that the educational hopes of the nineteenth-century humanists have been utterly disappointed. The disappearance of illiteracy and the spread of universal public education have not, it is said, raised the levels of culture and of thought. On the contrary, this very process threatens to inundate the most serious works of the spirit in a vast flood of written and visual material prepared for the marketplace of mediocrity and semiliteracy. If this is an inevitable result of the combination of communications technology and political democracy, it is a frightening indictment of free institutions. For then, if one were to make the conscious choice of the people the principle of society, that would turn banality—and worse—into the official ideology.

And yet the educational and cultural level of the mass in the advanced societies is a fabricated, not a natural, fact. In the United States in 1964, once again, the Manpower Report, the conclusions of the Senate Subcommittee on Employment and Manpower, and just about every other Government report touching on the subject, told how somewhere between a quarter and a third of the young people had not received sufficient training for the lowest of the decently paying jobs. (To put it roughly, almost a third of the youth were high-school dropouts in an economy that was demanding fourteen years of education for the hope of a serious occupational future.)

At this point, two broad possibilities emerge. On the one hand, the present revolution can continue along on its accidental and creative course. This would divide the society in two: on the one side the janitors, the menials, the underemployed, and the unemployed, numbering in the millions; on the other, all those fortunate enough to have an education. Under such circumstances, there would unquestionably be theorists who would point out the low levels of aesthetic taste to be found in the underclass. The propensity to surly and illogical violence at the bottom of the society would be condemned by the best people. The activity of agitators and the role of extremist political philosophies would be deplored. . . .

The powerful could then point out that such inferiors are not fit to rule and perhaps do not even deserve the franchise.

But there is another possibility. Instead of freeing the people for various, and degrading, forms of underemployment or idleness, the same technology could support the channeling of their energies into education. Indeed, with society liberated from routine and repetitive tasks through cybernation, there will be resources that could make of education a basic industry, a replacement for the automobile assembly line and a most welcome one. (The phrase "basic industry" does not suggest that a school is analogous to a factory. It simply insists that education must become as central to the political economy of the future as mass production was to the past.)

Why not, for example, pay people for going to school? There is already convincing evidence in the United States that such a social investment pays enormous dividends, not simply in the happiness of the participating individual but in the growth of society as a whole. Under the G.I. Bill of Rights, veterans were paid for going to school. This was a bonus in social form (a direct cash payment to individuals would not have had the same effect at all), compensation for having faced death. It also had a pump-priming function in the postwar economy and helped to avoid a return to the Depression thirties.

As a result of the G.I. Bill, the entire United States became more productive. And, if one wants to put it in the parsimonious terms of the conventional wisdom, the increase in tax revenue from this general upgrading far outweighed the expenditure of taxes required to bring it about. But most important of all, the G.I. Bill led to a general cultural gain for society and to the personal growth of those who benefited from it.

It does not require a war to justify such social intelligence.

On another level, the concept of education as a basic industry provides a new definition of work. If, as the coming of the statues of Daedalus promises, the old, traditional occupations are being abolished or transformed, this is an important gain. If the school system is seen as a fundamental investment, then teaching will become a much more important function. And it is relatively automation-proof, like the human care of human beings generally. Moreover, there is no need to restrict teaching to the old categories. There are those who are competent in classics or languages or higher mathematics; and those who can enrich the society with their knowledge of gardening, fishing, photography.

In such a context, older people, whom modern life increasingly segregates as surely as racial minorities, could discover new meanings for their lives. The slums, for example, desperately need nurseries so that the deprivations of poverty which are institutionalized in the tenement home can be combated at an early age. Such a program demands trained teachers, psychologists, doctors, and the like. But it also can make marvelous use of women whose only qualification is their genius with children. Such people can be found in the slums, and part of their liberation from misery can be accomplished through their helping others.

If such an approach were taken, it is absolutely certain that the cultural and educational level of the society can be raised. . . . (a) United States Office of Education study documented the fact that the majority of dropouts were intelligent enough to finish high school and that a significant minority of them could qualify for a college education. This was true even though these young people already had been subjected to the massive miseducation system of the slums, of poverty, and of advertising. Were these terrible disabilities removed, there is no way of estimating how much more talent, and even genius, would be uncovered in the doing.

But in order to embark on such a program requires a vast expansion of the democratic and social principle.

Despite all of the complaints of the fortunate, Western society does not presently grant education the kind of priority it needs. In countries still dominated by the anachronistic search for profit, such a huge allocation of resources to an apparently "unproductive" sector seems unconscionable. The market mechanism, insofar as it works at all, will deliver to the schools just enough funds to train the people actually needed for available work. To understand education as an area for social investment is to realize that the old-fashioned criteria of efficiency no longer apply and that society is now both free and driven to devote itself to higher things. In short, one would have to break with the premises and practices which in 1964 gave General Motors, a planned economy for private profit, more than twice as much income as the federal government allocated for the abolition of poverty.

Such an undertaking would require national planning. It is impossible to structure an educational system without knowing what kind of world the young who are being trained will live in. The absence of such knowledge is unquestionably one of the elements that has made so much of the American vocational education system a waste of time and resources. The intelligent anticipation of occupational needs in the future—and of its leisure possibilities —is a necessity in a modern society. Here again, the old faith in the market, or the new faith in the conscientious corporation, is of little help. . . .

Thus, an increasingly important educational function will be preparation for leisure and not just for work. And this new role will be more difficult to fill than the traditional one. The skill level of a job is quantifiable, and the school system can be measured in terms of how it meets these set requirements. But what are the leisure skills? Here, because the free choice, and even the whim, of the individual is an important element, it is much harder to be specific. Yet answering this challenge could provide some of the most important work of the cybernated age.

To come back to the starting point, all these changes are impossible unless there is a conscious and democratic allocation of resources within the context of national planning. The market will not accomplish such a transformation and neither will the corporation. To achieve it, society has to opt for a conscious social criterion in an area of life already social in fact. The present material eminence of the West more and more derives from the appropriation of the general level of knowledge rather than from the exploitation of the individual's labor. If there is to be a spiritual eminence, it will emerge out of that most revolutionary of the modern means of production, the human mind. . . .

Most of the arguments usually advanced in the United States against what has just been said are fairly weak. One is most definitely not. Before turning to that serious criticism, it is worthwhile to take up two earnestly held, but not very substantial, antisocialisms: the peculiarly American obsession that national economic planning is inherently totalitarian; the more general fear that any attempt to embark upon a socialist course necessarily involves the creation of a dull-witted, unresponsive, and powerful bureaucracy.

It is beyond the scope of this analysis to locate the antiplanning trauma in American history. It will simply be taken as a strange fact. In the midsixties, when Tory businessmen in England, bankers in France, and social Catholics in Italy and Belgium had all recognized the necessity of planning, a good number of Americans still thought the term meant Red Revolution. They did not realize that planning can be used for totalitarian purposes, as in Russia; for corporate ends, as in the huge American firms; for social goals as defined by corporate executives, as in France. As a result, they also did not know that planning could be used to extend and deepen the freedom of the individual. . . .

The second criticism of the socialist proposal is both more general and a bit more compelling. A conscious restructuring of society, it is said, will call into life a huge bureaucracy, and this will limit freedom.

In part, this thought rests upon a familiar and naïve assumption: that the present historical choice is between bureaucracy or no bureaucracy. In point of fact, as Max Weber and Schumpeter and many others realized sometime ago, bureaucracies are a characteristic and inevitable mode of the modern age. They are not imported into nations by outcasts and subversives, but are inexorable deductions from the minute division of labor which is of the essence of contemporary technology. The basic issue is whether it is possible to control these bureaucracies, not whether they should exist. And the argument against socialism on the grounds that it represents a bureaucratic danger is really an argument, often unwitting, in favor of the present private bureaucracies and their egotistical planning institutions. Socialism, I would assert, is not an advocate or creator of bureaucracy—the honors in that regard belong to businessmen—but the one political movement that seeks to represent the claim of the individual as against the bureaucracy by making the latter subject to the democratic will. . . .

This possibility depends upon a democratic populace capable and desirous of determining its needs and making them the guiding principle of the economy and society. And here one comes to the really serious objection against the socialist ideal today: that there is no political and social force really interested in taking hold of the advanced nations—the only places where socialism is now possible—and offering them an alternative view of life. . . .

The fulfillment of this possibility is, of course, a political issue. With so many variables up in the air, it is impossible to set down a program and perspective for the Western nations in this regard. Yet, certain relevant generalizations can be made. In the United States, it is inconceivable that the country can face up to these issues on the basis of politics as usual. The American party system has been structured for some time so as to produce accommodations in the middle of the road and to avoid sharp conflicts. In some ways this trend became particularly marked in the elections of 1964 when Mr. Johnson projected his role as the "President of all the people" against Goldwater extremism. But there is a fateful, and increasingly untrue, assumption underlying such consensus politics in America: that all problems can be solved by conciliation.

If radical options are to intrude in the near future upon all the advanced nations, if the nature of work, the potential of democracy, and the very meaning of economics are in the midst of transformation, then the old wisdom will be inadequate. And what will be required is the appearance of a new party alignment—a new party—in the United States. As of now, there is an American Right and an American Center; but there is not really an American democratic Left. And only the emergence of a democratic Left holds out the possibility of the United States measuring up to its challenge.

For reasons of American history, it is probable that a radical political change will not happen radically. That is to say, if the necessary new party does come, it will not result from the sudden emergence of a full-blown third force, but through the conflict within the present party structure. The potential elements for such a change have already been described: the racial minorities and the poor generally; the labor movement revived; the liberal middle class; both secular and religious humanism. Thus, in looking not to the far distance but the immediate American future, the struggle of the liberal wing of the Democratic Party seems to be the point of departure for any serious hope.

And yet, as all that has been said should make clear, the outcome of this development cannot stop at traditional liberalism. In the process of change, it must become clear that America is having the wrong debate, that the shibboleths about collectivism, balanced budgets, and bureaucracy are without real meaning. For the present premise of most of American politics is that the choice is between a resolute march to the rear in the name of anti-collectivism and a cautious confrontation with the future in the name of a mixed economy. In reality, the past which is the dream of the American Right is beyond recall; and the present which is recognized by American liberalism is much more radical than is imagined. At some point, then, a new political movement must begin to talk of a new political program—the democratic and conscious control of a technology that is already collective and bureaucratic. . . .

33. MAIN LINES OF CHINESE COMMUNIST ECONOMIC POLICY

ARTHUR G. ASHBROOK, JR.

Arthur G. Ashbrook, Jr. (1921–   ) is an economist with the U.S. Government.

The Chinese Communist leadership has consistently backed the production of those goods that would turn China into a modern military and industrial power in the shortest period of time. "What" is to be produced is thus:

1. Only sufficient food, clothing, and other consumer goods to sustain the productive energies and morale of the population at a Spartan level.

2. Sufficient military goods to maintain a large infantry force, a large but obsolescent air arm, a small naval arm, and a growing nuclear capability.

3. As much investment as remaining resources would permit; this investment would encompass a large amount to support the building of arsenals and other military production facilities, a large amount for the expansion of the metallurgical and machinery industries, and a small amount to support the austere consumer objectives.

In all the Communist countries the consumer goods part of the "what" tends to be sacrificed, if necessary, to maintain planned rates of growth in the military and heavy industry sectors. At the same time, as these countries become more urbanized and industrialized, the minimum standards that the consumer will tolerate gradually rise. For Communist China the minimum viable food ration was not provided in the winter of 1960–61 and a quick change in allocation policy was necessary. In 1966 the frenzied campaign of the Red Guards against citified consumption standards has reached the ridiculous stage of destruction of books and phonograph records and the impounding of bourgeois furniture and other household effects. The result is

Published in *An Economic Profile of Mainland China,* Vol. 1. Joint Economic Committee, U.S. Congress. Washington, D.C., 1967. Pp. 41–44, excerpts.

a tangible loss in the stock of consumer durables and a trenchant lesson to all persons not to anticipate the normal rise in living standards that accompanies industrialization. Whether this will be carried to the logical next step—the draconian equalization of housing, clothing, leisure, and all other standards of consumption—remains to be seen.

As between military and heavy industry goods, the Chinese Communist leadership has little room for choice, once the decision to go ahead in the nuclear field has been made. The concentration on nuclear development has preempted the small numbers of highly trained scientists and engineers at the expense of nonnuclear military production, general industrial production, and the teaching of the new generation of scientists and engineers. To the extent choice has been feasible in heavy industry in the post-Leap recovery period, there has been concentration on the expansion of the petroleum and chemical industries.

The Chinese Communist leadership started out quite successfully, . . . with the system of Soviet-style industrialization. The establishment of economic law and order raised China's production possibilities sharply and created the ability to produce enough goods domestically to pay for the 300 Soviet plants. The "how" of production originally was based on the principle of comparative advantage in the form of extensive Soviet assistance, together with rapid but orderly development of domestic Chinese resources. The Great Leap Forward changed the "how" of production for the worse. The pace of development of both the modern and primitive sectors of the economy was speeded up under the slogan of "walking on two legs." The Soviets picked up their blueprints and went home. Nonetheless, there still remained some choice between complete autarchy and partial reliance on the outside world, and in the period 1961–66, China has looked to Japan and Western Europe for a few key elements of industrialization. The Proletarian Cultural Revolution, however, is rabidly xenophobic and could narrow down even this small amount of foreign industrial and technical support.

The Chinese Communist leaders have minced no words about the primary objectives of their economic policy. The question of "for whom" has been settled in favor of the state as a whole and against the individual members of the state. Increases in consumption are made, if at all, only grudgingly. Differentials in pay and living standards are frowned on, that is, material incentives are supposed to be replaced by political motivation; the new Chinese Communist man is not to think of advancing himself materially but of participating in a soul-steeling revolution whose tense glories he will share continuously. This important aspect of "for whom" cannot be put into effect fully. In the recovery period of 1961–65, for instance, the leadership had to bow to the realities of the situation and allow benefits to the rank and file to be at least partially responsive to their productive efforts.

This type of policy toward the "for whom" question earned Khrushchev's jibe of "pantsless communism." In turn, the Chinese Communist leadership professes to scorn the "goulash communism" of the U.S.S.R. as part of the revisionist tendencies of Soviet policy. A curious vestige of former pre-Communist distribution patterns remains in the persons of thousands of former capitalists who have been paid annual interest on their shares in property taken over by the state. The more important of these capitalists live handsomely but discreetly. A second perhaps more important form of inequality in income distribution is the high incomes and perquisites of local party and Government bosses. These bosses are part of a political system of give-and-take, and the existence of local problems of graft and privilege is made clear through periodic purges of the more grasping (or less lucky) violators. A third form of income inequality is incomes accruing from abroad to repatriated Overseas Chinese. A fourth form of income inequality is the high pay and fringe benefits received by top-level scientists and engineers, particularly those trained in the West. Most Communist regimes seem to be forced to tolerate a few apolitical persons in order to keep scientific and military research going. All four of these kinds of inequality in income almost certainly will be reduced if the current Proletarian Cultural Revolution is allowed to run its course. In fact, one aspect of the Red Guards' actions in stripping bourgeois homes is said to be the resentment of the multitudes of poor against these relatively rich families.

In addition to these special high incomes, an important element in assessing the question of "for whom" is the considerable income differentials among rank-and-file families. In the countryside, for example, the fortunes of weather, prices, policies toward private plots, and severities of requisitions vary in the extreme. Some local leaders are said to have protected their local people by secretly retaining large amounts of an extra good harvest. In the cities, differences in the number of workers and their jobs lead to wide differences in family income; stakhanovite workers, for instance, have large fringe benefits. Here again, the Proletarian Cultural Revolution may be expected to lead to a curtailment of these differentials. In contrast, periods of more orderly and rational economic policy are marked by a natural increase in these differentials as a means of rewarding skill and productive effort.

34. THE FUTURE OF THE INDUSTRIAL SYSTEM

JOHN KENNETH GALBRAITH

John Kenneth Galbraith (1908–   ) is professor of economics at Harvard, a former ambassador to India, and author of many books and articles on the nature of modern economic life.

In the latter part of the last century and the early decades of this, no subject was more discussed than the future of capitalism. Economists, men of unspecific wisdom, Chautauqua lecturers, editorial writers, knowledgeable ecclesiastics and socialists contributed their personal revelation. It was taken for granted that the economic system was in a state of development and in time would transform itself into something hopefully better but certainly different. Socialists drew strength from the belief that theirs was the plausible next stage in a natural process of change.

The future of the industrial system, by contrast, is not discussed. The prospect for agriculture is subject to debate—it is assumed to be in course of change. So are the chances for survival for the small entrepreneur or the private medical practitioner. But General Motors, General Electric and U.S. Steel are viewed as an ultimate achievement. One does not wonder where one is going if one is already there.

Yet to suppose that the industrial system is a terminal phenomenon is, *per se,* implausible. It is itself the product, in the last sixty years, of a vast and autonomous transformation. During this time the scale of the individual corporation has grown enormously. The entrepreneurial corporation has declined. The technostructure has developed, removed itself from control by the stockholders and acquired its own internal sources of capital. There has been a large change in its relations with the workers and a yet larger one in its relations with the state. It would be strange were such a manifestation of social dynamics to be now at an end. So to suggest is to deny one of the philosophical tenets of the system itself, one that is solemnly articulated on all occasions of business ritual—conventions, stockholders' meetings, board meetings, executive committee meetings, management development conferences, budget conferences, product review meetings, senior officer retreats and dealer relations workshops. It is that change is the law of economic life.

The future of the industrial system is not discussed partly because of the power it exercises over belief. It has succeeded, tacitly, in excluding the no-

From John Kenneth Galbraith, *The New Industrial State.* Boston: Houghton Mifflin Company and London: Hamish Hamilton Ltd., copyright © by John Kenneth Galbraith, 1967. Pp. 388–99. Reprinted by permission of the publishers.

tion that it is a transitory, which would be to say that it is a somehow imperfect, phenomenon. More important, perhaps, to consider the future would be to fix attention on where it has already arrived. Among the least enchanting words in the business lexicon are planning, government control, state support and socialism. To consider the likelihood of these in the future would be to bring home the appalling extent to which they are already a fact. And it would not be ignored that these grievous things have arrived, at a minimum with the acquiescence and, at a maximum, on the demand, of the system itself.

2

Such reflection on the future would also emphasize the convergent tendencies of industrial societies, however different their popular or ideological billing; the convergence being to a roughly similar design for organization and planning. A word in review may be worthwhile. Convergence begins with modern large-scale production, with heavy requirements of capital, sophisticated technology and, as a prime consequence, elaborate organization. These require control of prices and, so far as possible, of what is bought at those prices. This is to say that planning must replace the market. In the Soviet-type economies, the control of prices is a function of the state. The management of demand (eased by the knowledge that their people will mostly want what Americans and Western Europeans already have) is partly by according preference to the alert and early-rising who are first to the store; partly, as in the case of houseroom, by direct allocation to the recipient; and partly, as in the case of automobiles, by making patience (as well as political position or need) a test of eligibility. With us this management is accomplished less formally by the corporations, their advertising agencies, salesmen, dealers and retailers. But these, obviously, are differences in method rather than purpose. Large-scale industrialism requires, in both cases, that the market and consumer sovereignty be extensively superseded.

Large-scale organization also requires autonomy. The intrusion of an external and uninformed will is damaging. In the non-Soviet systems this means excluding the capitalist from effective power. But the same imperative operates in the socialist economy. There the business firm seeks to minimize or exclude control by the bureaucracy. To gain autonomy for the enterprise is what, in substantial measure, the modern Communist theoretician calls reform. Nothing in our time is more interesting than that the erstwhile capitalist corporation and the erstwhile Communist firm should, under the imperatives of organization, come together as oligarchies of their own members. Ideology is not the relevant force. Large and complex organizations can use diverse knowledge and talent and thus function effectively only if under their own authority. This, it must be stressed once more, is not autonomy that subordinates a firm to the market. It is autonomy that allows the firm authority over its planning.

The industrial system has no inherent capacity for regulating total demand —for insuring a supply of purchasing power sufficient to acquire what it produces. So it relies on the state for this. At full employment there is no mechanism for holding prices and wages stable. This stabilization too is a function of the state. The Soviet-type systems also make a careful calculation of the income that is being provided in relation to the value of the goods available for purchase. Stabilization of wages and prices in general is, of course, a natural consequence of fixing individual prices and wage rates.

Finally, the industrial system must rely on the state for trained and educated manpower, now the decisive factor of production. So it also is under socialist industrialism. A decade ago, following the flight of the first Sputnik, there was great and fashionable concern in the United States for scientific and technical education. Many argued that the Soviet system, with its higher priority for state functions, among which education is prominent, had a natural advantage in this regard.

Thus convergence between the two ostensibly different industrial systems occurs at all fundamental points. This is an exceedingly fortunate thing. In time, and perhaps in less time than may be imagined, it will dispose of the notion of inevitable conflict based on irreconcilable difference. This will not be soon agreed. Marx did not foresee the convergence and he is accorded, with suitable interpretation, the remarkable, even supernatural, power of foreseeing all. Those who speak for the unbridgeable gulf that divides the free world from the Communist world and free enterprise from Communism are protected by an equally ecclesiastical faith that whatever the evolution of free enterprise may be, it cannot conceivably come to resemble socialism. But these positions can survive the evidence only for a time. Only the most committed ideologist or the most fervent propagandist can stand firm against the feeling that an increasing number of people regard him as obsolete. Vanity is a great force for intellectual modernization.

To recognize that industrial systems are convergent in their development will, one imagines, help toward agreement on the common dangers in the weapons competition, on ending it or shifting it to more benign areas. Perhaps nothing casts more light on the future of the industrial system than this, for it implies, in contrast with the present images, that it could have a future.

3

Given the deep dependence of the industrial system on the state and the nature of its motivational relationship to the state, i.e., its identification with public goals and the adaptation of these to its needs, the industrial system will not long be regarded as something apart from government. Rather it will increasingly be seen as part of a much larger complex which embraces both the industrial system and the state. Private enterprise was anciently so characterized because it was subordinate to the market and those in command derived their power from ownership of private property. The modern corporation is no longer subordinate to the market; those who run it no longer depend on property ownership for their authority. They must have autonomy within a framework of goals. But this fully allows them to work in association with the bureaucracy and, indeed, to perform for the bureaucracy tasks that it cannot do, or cannot do as well, for itself. In consequence, so we have seen, for tasks of technical sophistication, there is a close fusion of the industrial system with the state. Members of the technostructure work closely with their public counterparts not only in the development and manufacture of products but in advising them of their needs. Were it not so celebrated in ideology, it would long since have been agreed that the line that now divides public from so-called private organization in miliary procurement, space exploration and atomic energy is so indistinct as to be nearly imperceptible. Men move easily across the line. On retirement, admirals and generals, as well as high civil servants, go more or less automatically to the more closely associated industries. One experienced observer has already called these firms the "semi-nationalized" branch of the economy. It has been noted, "the Market mechanism [is replaced by] . . . the administrative mechanism. For the profit share of private entrepreneurs, it substitutes the fixed fee, a payment in lieu of profits foregone. And for the independent private business unit, it substitutes the integrated hierarchical structure of an organization composed of an agency . . . and its contractors."

The foregoing refers to firms which sell most of their output to the government—to Boeing which (at this writing) sells 65 per cent of its output to the government; General Dynamics which sells a like percentage; Raytheon which sells 70 per cent; Lockheed which sells 81 per cent; and Republic Aviation which sells 100 per cent. But firms which have a smaller proportion of sales to the government are more dependent on it for the regulation of aggregate demand and not much less so for the stabilization of wages and prices, the underwriting of especially expensive technology and the supply of trained and educated manpower.

So comprehensive a relationship cannot be denied or ignored indefinitely. Increasingly it will be recognized that the mature corporation, as it develops, becomes part of the larger administrative complex associated with the state. In time the line between the two will disappear. Men will look back in amusement at the pretense that once caused people to refer to General Dynamics and North American Aviation and A. T. & T. as *private* business.

Though this recognition will not be universally welcomed, it will be healthy. There is always a presumption in social matters in favor of reality as opposed to myth. The autonomy of the technostructure is, to repeat yet again, a functional necessity of the industrial system. But the goals this autonomy serves allow some range of choice. If the mature corporation is recognized to be part of the penumbra of the state, it will be more strongly in the service of social goals. It cannot plead its inherently private character or its subordination to the market as cover for the pursuit of different goals of particular interest to itself. The public agency has an unquestioned tendency to pursue goals that reflect its own interest and convenience and to adapt social objective thereto. But it cannot plead this as a superior right. There may well be danger in this association of public and economic power. But it is less if it is recognized.

Other changes can be imagined. As the public character of the mature corporation comes to be recognized, attention will doubtless focus on the position of the stockholder in this corporation. This is anomalous. He is a passive and functionless figure, remarkable only in his capacity to share, without effort or even without appreciable risk, in the gains from the growth by which the technostructure measures its success. No grant of feudal privilege has ever equaled, for effortless return, that of the grandparent who bought and endowed his descendants with a thousand shares of General Motors or General Electric. The beneficiaries of this foresight have become and remain rich by no exercise of effort or intelligence beyond the decision to do nothing, embracing as it did the decision not to sell. But these matters need not be pursued here. Questions of equity and social justice as between the fortuitously rich have their own special expertise.

4

Most of the individual developments which are leading, if the harshest term may be employed, to the socialization of the mature corporation will be conceded, even by men of the most conservative disposition. The control by the mature corporation over its prices, its influence on consumer behavior, the euthanasia of stockholder power, the regulation by the state of aggregate demand, the effort to stabilize prices and wages, the role of publicly supported research and development, the role of military, space and related procurement, the influence of the firm on these government activities and the modern role of education are, more or less, accepted facts of life.

What is avoided is reflection on the consequences of putting them all together, of seeing them as a system. But it cannot be supposed that the principal beams and buttresses of the industrial system have all been changed and that the structure remains as before. If the parts have changed, so then has the whole. If this associates the mature corporation inextricably with the state, the fact cannot be exorcised by a simple refusal to add.

It will be urged, of course, that the industrial system is not the whole economy. Apart from the world of General Motors, Standard Oil, Ford, General Electric, U.S. Steel, Chrysler, Texaco, Gulf, Western Electric and Du Pont is that of the independent retailer, the farmer, the shoe repairman, the bookmaker, narcotics peddler, pizza merchant and that of the car and dog laundry. Here prices are not controlled. Here the consumer is sovereign. Here pecuniary motivation is unimpaired. Here technology is simple and there is no research or development to make it otherwise. Here there are no government contracts; independence from the state is a reality. None of these entrepreneurs patrol the precincts of the Massachusetts Institute of Technology in search of talent. The existence of all this I concede. And this part of the economic system is not insignificant. It is not, however, the part of the economy with which this book has been concerned. It has been concerned with the world of the large corporation. This too is important; and it is more deeply characteristic of the modern industrial scene than the dog laundry or the small manufacturer with a large idea. One should always cherish his critics and protect them where possible from foolish error. The tendency of the mature corporation in the industrial system to become part of the administrative complex of the state ought not to be refuted by appeal to contrary tendencies outside the industrial system.

Some who dislike the notion that the industrial system merges into the state in its development will be tempted to assault not the tendency but those who adumbrate it. This, it must be urged, is not in keeping with contemporary ethics and manners. Once the bearers of bad tidings were hanged, disemboweled or made subject to some other equally sanguinary mistreatment. Now such reaction is regarded as lacking in delicacy. A doctor can inform even the most petulant client that he has terminal cancer without fear of adverse physical consequences. The aide who must advise a politician that a new poll shows him to be held in all but universal distaste need exercise only decent tact. Those who find unappealing the present intelligence are urged to exercise similar restraint.

They should also be aware of the causes. It is part of the vanity of modern man that he can decide the character of his economic system. His area of decision is, in fact, exceedingly small. He could, conceivably, decide whether or not he wishes to have a high level of industrialization. Thereafter the imperatives of organization, technology and planning operate similarly, and we have seen to a broadly similar result, on all societies. Given the decision to have modern industry, much of what happens is inevitable and the same.

5

The two questions most asked about an economic system are whether it serves man's physical needs and whether it is consistent with his liberty. There is little doubt as to the ability of the industrial system to serve man's needs. As we have seen, it is able to manage them only because it serves them abundantly. It requires a mechanism for making men want what it provides. But this mechanism would not work—wants would not be subject to manipulation—had not these wants been dulled by sufficiency.

The prospects for liberty involve far more interesting questions. It has always been imagined, especially by conservatives, that to associate all, or a large part, of economic activity with the state is to endanger freedom. The individual and his preferences, in one way or another, will be sacrificed to the needs and conveniences of the apparatus created ostensibly to serve him. As the industrial system evolves into a penumbra of the state, the question of its relation to liberty thus arises in urgent form. In recent years, in the Soviet-type economies, there has been an ill-concealed conflict between the state and the intellectuals. In essence, this has been a conflict between those for whom the needs of the government, including above all its needs as economic planner and producer of goods, are pre-eminent and those who assert the high but inconvenient claims of uninhibited intellectual and artistic expression. Is this a warning?

The instinct which warns of dangers in this association of economic and public power is sound. It comes close to being the subject of this book. But conservatives have looked in the wrong direction for the danger. They have feared that the state might reach out and destroy the vigorous, money-making entrepreneur. They have not noticed that, all the while, the successors to the entrepreneur were uniting themselves ever more closely with the state and rejoicing in the result. They were also, and with enthusiasm, accepting abridgement of their freedom. Part of this is implicit in the subordination of individual personality to the needs of organization. Some of it is in the exact pattern of the classical business expectation. The president of Republic Aviation is not much more likely in public to speak critically, or even candidly, of the Air Force than is the head of a Soviet *combinat* of the ministry to which he reports. No modern head of the Ford Motor Company will ever react with the same pristine vigor to the presumed foolishness of Washington as did its founder. No head of Montgomery Ward will ever again breathe defiance of a President as did Sewell Avery. Manners may be involved. But it would also be conceded that "too much is at stake."

The problem, however, is not the freedom of the businessman. Business orators have spoken much about freedom in the past. But it can be laid down as a rule that those who speak most of liberty are least inclined to use it. The high executive who speaks fulsomely of personal freedom carefully submits his speeches on the subject for review and elimination of controversial words, phrases and ideas, as befits a good organization man. The general who tells his troops, and the world, that they are in the forefront of the fight for freedom is a man who has always submitted happily to army discipline. The high State Department official, who adverts feelingly to the values of the free world extravagantly admires the orthodoxy of his own views.

The danger to liberty lies in the subordination of belief to the needs of the industrial system. In this the state and the industrial system will be partners. This threat has already been assessed, as also the means for minimizing it.

6

If we continue to believe that the goals of the industrial system—the expansion of output, the companion increase in consumption, technological advance, the public images that sustain it—are coordinate with life, then all of our lives will be in the service of these goals. What is consistent with these ends we shall have or be allowed; all else will be off limits. Our wants will be managed in accordance with the needs of the industrial system; the policies of the state will be subject to similar influence; education will be adapted to industrial need; the disciplines required by the industrial system will be the conventional morality of the community. All other goals will be made to seem precious, unimportant or antisocial. We will be bound to the ends of the industrial system. The state will add its moral, and perhaps some of its legal, power to their enforcement. What will eventuate, on the whole, will be the benign servitude of the household retainer who is taught to love her mistress and see her interests as her own, and not the compelled servitude of the field hand. But it will not be freedom.

If, on the other hand, the industrial system is only a part, and relatively a diminishing part, of life, there is much less occasion for concern. Aesthetic goals will have pride of place; those who serve them will not be subject to the goals of the industrial system; the industrial system itself will be subordinate to the claims of these dimensions of life. Intellectual preparation will be for its own sake and not for the better service to the industrial system. Men will not be entrapped by the belief that apart from the goals of the industrial system—apart from the production of goods and income by progressively more advanced technical methods—there is nothing important in life.

The foregoing being so, we may, over time, come to see the industrial system in fitting light as an essentially technical arrangement for providing convenient goods and services in adequate volume. Those who rise through its bureaucracy will so see themselves. And the public consequences will be in keeping, for if economic goals are the only goals of the society it is natural that the industrial system should dominate the state and the state should serve its ends. If other goals are strongly asserted, the industrial system will fall into its place as a detached and autonomous arm of the state, but responsive to the larger purposes of the society.

We have seen wherein the chance for salvation lies. The industrial system, in contrast with its economic antecedents, is intellectually demanding. It brings into existence, to serve its intellectual and scientific needs, the community that, hopefully, will reject its monopoly of social purpose.

part four

Freedom versus Authority

in the Modern World

INTRODUCTION

"Man is born free, and everywhere he is in chains."
—Jean-Jacques Rousseau, *The Social Contract*

Rousseau's statement dramatizes the perennial conflict between man's desire for freedom and his need to accept authority. Modern man enjoys cultural and material benefits which he calls "civilization." At the same time, he longs to escape the accompanying confining network of social relationships, institutions, and repressions. Occasionally a Thoreau attempts to escape by seeking isolation, but in the modern world few Thoreaus can find a Walden.

Man's dilemma is that he wants both that which he can have only if he lives alone and that which he can have only if he lives in society. This poses questions: "Are the values he regards most highly those which are inherent in the individual, or those which are produced by society?" and, "How much of one set of values is he willing to surrender in order to secure how much of the other?" How can he reconcile his conflicting aims? If some rights are to be surrendered to the group, how and by whom will they be exercised? Will each man determine for himself what limitations he will accept? Or is he obliged to submit to the dictates of society? If the determination is the province of the rulers, who confers upon them the authority to make such a choice: the rulers themselves—or the ruled? These questions involve the sources of authority in any society and man's relation to authority.

All men desire freedom. But too often man seeks "freedom" without having a clear idea of what he means by the term. What is its nature? Who determines it? Is freedom an absence of governmental restraint? Or is it a positive affirmation of specific rights? Or can freedom be realized by the individual only when he works to fulfill the stated and desired objectives of society? How can these concepts of freedom be reconciled with political reality?

Societies have offered varying interpretations of the meaning of freedom. The Western democracies, and countries governed by elites believing in the essentials of Western concepts of freedom, hold that freedom is not an absolute; rather, it involves a subtle balancing of the rights of the individual against the demands of society, a compromise between private and public interests. But who determines the point of balance between freedom and restraint? Where is the line to be drawn?

Nondemocratic and totalitarian societies, on the other hand, argue that the individual has no rights independent of society; they hold that freedom can be secured only by subordinating the desires of the individual to the needs of society. Freedom is associated with the harnessing of man's anarchic impulses for the good of the group. The rules determine what is "good" for the group. What are the limitations on the exercise of its authority?

What role should the state play in safeguarding individual freedom? What institutional safeguards can be used to promote and protect individual freedom? How far should society go in thwarting the ideas and actions of a minority? Particularly when they conflict with the desires of the majority?

In short, how can freedom be reconciled with authority?

35. THE SCIENTIFIC BASIS OF FASCISM

CORRADO GINI

*Corrado Gini (1884–   ) was a professor of economic policy and
statistics of the Royal University of Rome in the 1920's. He was a
consultant to the Italian Government.*

A few years ago, political scientists would hardly have ventured even to
imagine the existence, among our civilized countries, of a government which
would not hesitate to place limitations upon any of the liberties of the
individual that had been regarded from the beginning of the last century as
a sacred heritage of human individuality; a government which would concentrate the effective control of a great part of public power in the hands
of few, or of a single person, so as to give almost the impression of a
dictatorship; a government which would propose to reform the constitutional
and administrative organization of the state, openly characterizing its action
in doing so as revolutionary; a government, moreover, which would not
shrink from proclaiming itself as representative of the minority of the nation
and which would announce its intention to win the consent of the majority
by the exercise of force. If the Fascist Party, resting on such principles, has
attained to power, and thereafter has succeeded not only in maintaining
itself, but in strengthening its position and in acquiring the support of large
elements even outside of Italy, is not this fact a demonstration that the
premises which the scientific world adopts as the basis of political theory and
political practice are at least incomplete, if not inexact, in so far as they fail
to meet the exigencies of certain situations which can occur in the lives of
nations?

The first, perhaps, of these premises, and the one which appears the most
obvious, is that the government should rest upon the consent of the majority
of the citizens and interpret the will of that majority. Today it would be
difficult to deny that the Fascist government enjoys the support of the great
majority of the Italian population; but there certainly have been periods,
or at least one period, in which that administration did not possess the support
of such a majority.

On the other hand, at times when many could have believed that there
was no basis for doubt on the subject, the head of the administration, and
of the Fascist Party, did not hesitate to declare that he was accumulating
the necessary force in entire confidence of acquiring the consent of the

From Corrado Gini, "The Scientific Basis of Fascism," *Political Science Quarterly,*
Vol. 42 (March, 1927), 99–103, excerpts. By permission of the Academy of Political
Science.

majority little by little in the future. His expression of his confidence in such terms revealed his assumption that he did not possess it at the time. Again, at times when there was more foundation for doubt concerning the extent of the support of the majority, important spokesmen of the Fascist Party proclaimed, amid the applause of the Black Shirts, that the Fascists were disposed to fight and die rather than relinquish power. The impression of objective persons was that those favorable to the Fascist regime constituted, at a given moment, a genuine minority, but a minority ready to die for their chosen cause, while the majority, composed of elements more or less openly opposed to the Fascist regime, did not manifest any comparable interest in the contest.

In this last statement there is, I believe, a basis for criticism of the postulate indicated as the first of those ordinarily set up. That postulate takes for granted—if you examine it carefully—that the majority and the minority which take shape in connection with various questions manifest in the solution of those questions an interest, if not identical with their own magnitude, at least in the same order of magnitude; this, I suggest, is taken for granted not with respect to particular individuals, but with regard to the average of the majority or minority. If we accept the foregoing interpretation as correct, the postulate which we may call that of the right of the majority may be generalized and transformed into the postulate of the paramountcy of interests, according to which the government is to be administered by the part of the population which represents the prevailing interests.

In the ordinary political life of a people, the hypothesis of a corresponding order of magnitude of the interest which the majority and the minority, on the average, manifest in bringing particular questions to solution seems acceptable; and this justifies the adoption of the postulate of the majority as the basis of the ordinary political life of the nation. . . . Even when this hypothesis is not realized, in certain cases there are not lacking correctives which permit the several interests to make themselves effective in proportion to their due weight, regardless of the number of persons who respectively represent them. This circumstance explains why, in practice, the postulate of the majority may serve without grave impairment as a basis for the normal political life of the nation. When, for example, material interests are at stake, the financial elements of importance in the parties at issue assume the leading roles. Their roles may well be decisive because of business relations and interwoven interests, even without any open purchase of votes in the determination of an electoral contest, inasmuch as people who from an abstract point of view would favor one solution, vote in practice against that solution when it might operate to the prejudice of the interests of persons or institutions to which they feel themselves intimately bound.

When, on the other hand, interests are at stake not of a material order, but such as to involve the fundamental principles of public and private life, the force of propaganda may be sufficient to draw the vote of the majority to the party which feels most keenly on the question. But when questions of an ideal character are under discussion, questions which most people regard as fundamental and upon which in any case there is a definite opinion hardly capable of being changed, then neither the force of persuasion nor the bonds of interest will suffice to attract the consent of a majority to a minority group. And this is true, no matter how vital may be the interest of the minority in the question, or how relatively indifferent the majority may be to it. When such is the case, it will be understood how it is that the minority feels itself authorized to impose its program upon the majority. Neither from the moral point of view nor from the political point of view is there anything, as a matter of fact, which can justify a state of affairs wherein one individual whose interests are prejudiced by reason of a given governmental measure or program to the extent, let us say, of ten monetary units, must give way to two individuals each of whom derives, in consequence of the particular program or measure, an advantage to the extent, let us say, of three monetary units. . . .

The existence of a government in the hands of the minority is not, after all, when carefully analyzed, in antithesis to the liberal concept of political life, neither as a *means* in so far as the minority government represents the results of the free action of the citizenry, nor, on the other hand, as a *result*, in so far as the minority government satisfies the prevailing interests. But a more obvious gap existed between the liberal theory and the nationalistic theory which was gradually adopted by the Fascist Party; and this irrecon-cilability was destined to show itself very early. The liberal theory assumes that society consists of an aggregate of individuals who must look after their own interests and it regards the state as an emanation of the individual wills intended to eliminate the conflicts between the interests of individuals. The nationalistic theory, on the contrary, views society as a true and distinct organism of a rank superior to that of the individuals who compose it, an organism endowed with a life of its own and with interests of its own. These interests result from the coordination of the desires for the time being of the current generation together with the interests of all the future generations which are to constitute the future life of the nation. Often enough these are in harmony one with the other, but occasionally the interests of future generations are opposed to those of the present generation, and in any case they may differ notably, if not in direction, at least in intensity. The agency destined to give effect to these higher interests of society is the state, sacrific-ing, wherever necessary, the interests of the individual and operating in opposition to the will of the present generation.

Hence the concept of the government as an agency to which is entrusted a mission of historical character, a mission which summarizes its very reason for existence. It is an agency, not for the changeable wishes of numerical majorities or of major interests, but rather for the effectuation of a program corresponding to the interests of the national organism. In consequence, therefore, there is the tendency to free the administration from the constant control of parliamentary majorities. Once the program of the administration is approved, the administration henceforth derives its authority directly from the program itself and cannot permit others to interfere with it in giving effect to the program. The justification of measures of restraint upon indi-vidual liberties follows from this point of view, although these measures may be opposed to the desire of the majority or, theoretically, of even the entire body of citizens, when such measures of restraint are thought to be necessary in order to give effect to a program identified with the interests of a nation. . . .

One other conclusion may be drawn by many from the foregoing considerations to the effect that, in the last analysis, force is what determines a political party's tenure of power. This conclusion, of course, is in no sense novel. It would not be correct if by "force" we understood merely the physical force derived from muscular strength. But if, on the other hand, we understand "force" in the larger sense to represent the power derived from the intellect no less than from the muscles, and, over and above that derived from the intellect, the force which is derived from the weight of interests and the intensity of feeling, the conclusion I have indicated is hardly to be doubted, I think. Originally electoral contests were assemblies of armed individuals generally aware of one another's equal power and consequently regarding themselves as equal, one to the other; they were willing, therefore, to refrain from struggling, and instead found it more practical to agree beforehand in allowing the victory to rest in the hands of the more numerous group, in the conviction that the latter would have won it in any event if the question were put to the decision of arms and not amicably settled. But where the reality of the situation has advanced far beyond the assumption of equal power, either because of diverse social qualities, for example, such as characterize the relations of white and colored races in the United States, or because of the difference in intensity of feeling and of interests such as characterizes the relations during recent years of the nationalist and Social Democratic parties in Italy—in situations of this sort, there is no legal device or philosophical theory which can prevent the more powerful party from securing the upper hand and actually conquering the place of power, just as there is nothing except some external force which can prevent the body lighter than air from rising, and the body heavier than air from falling to the earth.

36. RULE BY THE PARTY

JOSEPH STALIN

There is a necessity for a new party, a militant party, a revolutionary party, one bold enough to lead the proletarians in the struggle for power, sufficiently experienced to find its bearings amidst the complex conditions of a revolutionary situation, and sufficiently flexible to steer clear of all submerged rocks in the path to its goal.

From Joseph Stalin, *Problems of Leninism*. Moscow: Foreign Languages Publishing House, 1953, pp. 97–99, 100, and 102–108.

Without such a party it is useless even to think of overthrowing imperialism and achieving the dictatorship of the proletariat.

This new party is the party of Leninism.

What are the specific features of this new party?

The Party as the Vanguard of the Working Class. The Party must be, first of all, the *vanguard* of the working class. The Party must absorb all the best elements of the working class, their experience, their revolutionary spirit, their selfless devotion to the cause of the proletariat. But in order that it may really be the vanguard, the Party must be armed with revolutionary theory, with a knowledge of the laws of the movement, with a knowledge of the laws of revolution. Without this it will be incapable of directing the struggle of the proletariat, of leading the proletariat. The Party cannot be a real party if it limits itself to registering what the masses of the working class feel and think, if it drags at the tail of the spontaneous movement, if it is unable to overcome the inertness and the political indifference of the spontaneous movement, if it is unable to rise above the momentary interests of the proletariat, if it is unable to elevate the masses to the understanding of the class interests of the proletariat. The Party must stand at the head of the working class; it must see farther than the working class; it must lead the proletariat, and not follow in the tail of the spontaneous movement. . . . Only a party which realizes that it is the vanguard of the proletariat and is able to elevate the masses to the understanding of the class interests of the proletariat—only such a party can divert the working class from the path of trade unionism and convert it into an independent political force.

The Party is the political leader of the working class.

I have already spoken of the difficulties of the struggle of the working class, of the complicated conditions of the struggle, of strategy and tactics, of reserves and maneuvering, of attack and retreat. These conditions are no less complicated, if not more so, than the conditions of war. Who can see clearly in these conditions, who can give correct guidance to the proletarian millions? No army at war can dispense with an experienced General Staff if it does not want to be doomed to certain defeat. Is it not clear that the proletariat can still less dispense with such a General Staff if it does not want to give itself up to be devoured by its moral enemies? But where is this General Staff? Only the revolutionary party of the proletariat can serve as this General Staff. The working class without a revolutionary party is an army without a General Staff.

The Party is the General Staff of the proletariat.

But the Party cannot be only a *vanguard* detachment. It must at the same time be a detachment of the *class,* part of the class, closely bound up with it by all the fibers of its being. The distinction between the vanguard and the main body of the working class, between Party members and non-Party people, cannot disappear until classes disappear; it will exist as long as the ranks of the proletariat continue to be replenished with newcomers from other classes, as long as the working class as a whole is not in a position to rise to the level of the vanguard. But the Party would cease to be a party if this distinction were widened into a gap, if it shut itself up in its own shell and became divorced from the non-Party masses. The Party cannot lead the class if it is not connected with the non-Party masses, if there is no bond between the Party and the non-Party masses, if these masses do not accept its leadership, if the Party enjoys no moral and political credit among the masses. . . .

The Party as the Organized Detachment of the Working Class. The Party is not only the *vanguard* detachment of the working class. If it desires really to direct the struggle of the class it must at the same time be the *organized* detachment of its class. The Party's tasks under the conditions of capitalism are immense and extremely varied. The Party must direct the struggle of the proletariat under the exceptionally difficult conditions of internal and external development; it must lead the proletariat in the offensive when the situation calls for an offensive; it must lead the proletariat in retreat when the situation calls for retreat in order to ward off the blows of a powerful enemy; it must imbue the millions of unorganized non-Party workers with the spirit of discipline and system in the struggle, with the spirit of organization and endurance. But the Party can fulfill these tasks only if it is itself the embodiment of discipline and organization, if it is itself the *organized* detachment of the proletariat. Without these conditions there can be no talk of the Party really leading the proletarian millions. . . .

The principle of the minority submitting to the majority, the principle of directing Party work from a center, not infrequently gives rise to attacks on the part of wavering elements, to accusations of "bureaucracy," "formalism," etc. It need hardly be proved that systematic work by the Party, as one whole, and the directing of the struggle of the working class would have been impossible if these principles had not been adhered to. Leninism in the organizational question means unswerving application of these principles. Lenin terms the fight against these principles "Russian nihilism" and "aristocratic anarchism," deserving only of being ridiculed and swept aside. . . .

The Party as the Highest Form of Class Organization of the Proletariat. The Party is the organized detachment of the working class. But the Party is not the only organization of the working class. The proletariat has also a number of other organizations, without which it cannot properly wage the struggle against capital: trade unions, cooperative societies, factory organizations, parliamentary groups, non-Party women's associations, the press, cultural and educational organizations, youth leagues, revolutionary fighting organizations (in times of open revolutionary action), Soviets of deputies as the form of state organization (if the proletariat is in power), etc. The overwhelming majority of these organizations are non-Party, and only some of them adhere directly to the Party, or represent its offshoots. All these organizations, under certain conditions, are absolutely necessary for the working class, for without them it would be impossible to consolidate the class positions of the proletariat in the diverse spheres of struggle; for without them it would be impossible to steel the proletariat as the force whose mission it is to replace the bourgeois order by the socialist order. But how can single leadership be exercised with such an abundance of organizations? What guarantee is there that this multiplicity of organizations will not lead to divergency in leadership? It might be argued that each of these organizations carries on its work in its own special field, and that therefore these organizations cannot hinder one another. This, of course, is true. But it is also true that all these organizations should work in one direction for they serve *one* class, the class of the proletarians. The question then arises: who is to determine the line, the general direction, along which the work of all these organizations is to be conducted? Where is that central organization which is not only able, because it has the necessary experience, to work out such a general line, but, in addition, is in a position, because it has sufficient prestige, to induce all these organizations to carry out this line, so as to attain unity of leadership and to preclude the possibility of working at cross purposes?

This organization is the Party of the proletariat.

The Party possesses all the necessary qualifications for this because, in the first place, it is the rallying center of the finest elements in the working class, who have direct connections with the non-Party organizations of the proletariat and very frequently lead them; because, secondly, the Party, as the rallying center of the finest members of the working class, is the best school for training leaders of the working class, capable of directing every form of organization of their class; because, thirdly, the Party, as the best school for training leaders of the working class, is, by reason of its experience and prestige, the only organization capable of centralizing the leadership of the struggle of the proletariat, thus transforming each and every non-Party organization of the working class into an auxiliary body and transmission belt linking the Party with the class.

The Party is the highest form of class organization of the proletariat.

This does not mean, of course, that non-Party organizations, trade unions, cooperative societies, etc., should be officially subordinated to the Party leadership. It only means that the members of the Party who belong to these organizations and are doubtlessly influential in them should do all they can to persuade these non-Party organizations to draw nearer to the Party of the proletariat in their work and to accept voluntarily its political guidance.

That is why Lenin says that the Party is "the *highest* form of proletarian class organization," whose political leadership must extend to every other form of organization of the proletariat. (See Vol. XXV, p. 194.)

That is why the opportunist theory of the "independence" and "neutrality" of the non-Party organizations, which breeds *independent* members of parliament and journalists *isolated* from the Party, narrow-minded trade unionists and cooperative-society officials *grown smug and philistine*, is wholly incompatible with the theory and practice of Leninism.

The Party as the Instrument of the Dictatorship of the Proletariat. The Party is the highest form of organization of the proletariat. The Party is the principle guiding force within the class of the proletarians and among the organizations of that class. But it does not by any means follow from this that the Party can be regarded as an end in itself, as a self-sufficient force. The Party is not only the highest form of class association of the proletarians; it is at the same time an *instrument* in the hands of the proletariat *for* achieving the dictatorship when that has not yet been achieved and *for* consolidating and expanding the dictatorship when it has already been achieved. The Party could not have risen so high in importance and could not have over-shadowed all other forms of organization of the proletariat, if the latter had not been confronted with the problem of power, if the conditions of imperial-ism, the inevitability of wars, and the existence of a crisis had not demanded the concentration of all the forces of the proletariat at one point, the gathering of all the threads of the revolutionary movement in one spot in order to overthrow the bourgeoisie and to achieve the dictatorship of the proletariat. The proletariat needs the Party first of all as its General Staff, which it must have for the successful seizure of power. It need hardly be proved that without a Party capable of rallying around itself the mass organizations of the proletariat, and of centralizing the leadership of the entire movement during the progress of the struggle, the proletariat in Russia could never have established its revolutionary dictatorship.

But the proletariat needs the Party not only to achieve the dictatorship; it needs it still more to maintain the dictatorship, to consolidate and expand it in order to achieve the complete victory of socialism.

"Certainly, almost everyone now realizes," says Lenin, "that the Bolsheviks could not have maintained themselves in power for two-and-a-half months, let alone two-and-a-half years, unless the strictest, truly iron discipline had prevailed in our Party, and unless the latter had been rendered the fullest and unreserved sup-port of the whole mass of the working class, that is, of all its thinking, honest, self-sacrificing and influential elements who are capable of leading or of carrying with them the backward strata." (See Vol. XXV, p. 173.)

Now, what does to "maintain" and "expand" the dictatorship mean? It means imbuing the millions of proletarians with the spirit of discipline and organization; it means creating among the proletarian masses a cementing force and a bulwark against the corrosive influences of the petty-bourgeois elements and petty-bourgeois habits; it means enhancing the organizing work of the proletarians in re-educating and remoulding the petty-bourgeois strata; it means helping the masses of the proletarians to educate themselves as a force capable of abolishing classes and of preparing the conditions for the organization of socialist production. But it is impossible to accomplish all this without a party which is strong by reason of its solidarity and discipline.

"The dictatorship of the proletariat," says Lenin, "is a persistent struggle—bloody and bloodless, violent and peaceful, military and economic, educational and ad-ministrative—against the forces and traditions of the old society. The force of habit of millions and tens of millions is a most terrible force. Without an iron party tempered in the struggle, without a party enjoying the confidence of all that is honest in the given class, without a party capable of watching and influencing the mood of the masses, it is impossible to conduct such a struggle successfully." (See Vol. XXV, p. 190.)

The proletariat needs the Party *for* the purpose of achieving and main-taining the dictatorship. The Party is an instrument of the dictatorship of the proletariat.

But from this it follows that when classes disappear and the dictatorship of the proletariat withers away, the Party will also wither away.

The Party as the Embodiment of Unity of Will, Incompatible with the Existence of Factions. The achievement and maintenance of the dictatorship of the proletariat is impossible without a party which is strong by reason of its solidarity and iron discipline. But iron discipline in the Party is inconceivable without unity of will, without complete and absolute unity of action on the part of all members of the Party. This does not mean, of course, that the possibility of contests of opinion within the Party is thereby precluded. On the contrary, iron discipline does not preclude but presupposes criticism and contest of opinion within the Party. Least of all does it mean that discipline must be "blind." On the contrary, iron discipline does not preclude but presupposes conscious and voluntary submission, for only conscious discipline can be truly iron discipline. But after a contest of opinion has been closed, after criticism has been exhausted and a decision has been arrived at, unity of will and unity of action of all Party members are the necessary conditions without which neither Party unity nor iron discipline in the Party is conceivable.

"In the present epoch of acute civil war," says Lenin, "a Communist Party will be able to perform its duty if it is organized in the most centralized manner, only if iron discipline bordering on military discipline prevails in it, and if its party center is a powerful and authoritative organ, of the Party." (See Vol. XXV, pp. 282–83.)

This is the position in regard to discipline in the Party in the period of struggle preceding the achievement of the dictatorship.

The same, but to an even greater degree, must be said about discipline in the Party after the dictatorship has been achieved.

"Whoever," says Lenin, "weakens ever so little the iron discipline of the party of the proletariat (especially during the time of its dictatorship), actually aids the bourgeoisie against the proletariat." (See Vol. XXV, p. 190.)

But from this it follows that the existence of factions is incompatible either with the Party's unity or with its iron discipline. It need hardly be proved that the existence of factions leads to the existence of a number of centers, and the existence of a number of centers connotes the absence of one common center in the Party, the breaking up of the unity of will, the weakening and disintegration of discipline, the weakening and disintegration of the dictatorship. Of course, the parties of the Second International, which are fighting against the dictatorship of the proletariat and have no desire to lead the proletarians to power, can afford such liberalism as freedom of factions, for they have no need at all for iron discipline. But the parties of the Communist International, whose activities are conditioned by the task of achieving and consolidating the dictatorship of the proletariat, cannot afford to be "liberal" or to permit freedom of factions.

The Party represents unity of will, which precludes all factionalism and division of authority in the Party.

Hence Lenin's warning about the "danger of factionalism from the point of view of Party unity and of effecting the unity of will of the vanguard of the proletariat as the fundamental condition for the success of the dictatorship of the proletariat," which is embodied in the special resolution of the Tenth Congress of our Party "On Party Unity."

Hence Lenin's demand for the "complete elimination of all factionalism" and the "immediate dissolution of all groups, without exception, that had been formed on the basis of various platforms," on pain of unconditional and immediate expulsion from the Party.

37. THE TRUE END OF GOVERNMENT
JOHN LOCKE

John Locke (1632–1704) was an English philosopher whose views expressed the rationalist liberalism of the "Glorious Revolution of 1688."

Of the Ends of Political Society and Government. If man in the state of Nature be so free as has been said, if he be absolute lord of his own person and possessions, equal to the greatest and subject to nobody, why will he part with his freedom, this empire, and subject himself to the dominion and control of any other power? To which it is obvious to answer, that though in the state of Nature he hath such a right, yet the enjoyment of it is very uncertain and constantly exposed to the invasion of others; for all being kings as much as he, every man his equal, and the greater part no strict observers of equity and justice, the enjoyment of property he has in this state is very unsafe, very insecure. This makes him willing to quit this condition which, however free, is full of fears and continual dangers; and it is not without reason that he seeks out and is willing to join in society with others who are already united, or have a mind to unite for the mutual preservation of their lives, liberties, and estates, which I call by the general name—property.

The great and chief end, therefore, of men uniting into commonwealths, and putting themselves under government, is the preservation of their property; to which in the state of Nature there are many things wanting.

Firstly, there wants an established, settled, known law, received and allowed by common consent to be the standard of right and wrong, and the common measure to decide all controversies between them. For though the law of Nature be plain and intelligible to all rational creatures, yet men being biased by their interest, as well as ignorant for want of study of it,

From the book *Two Treatises of Civil Government* by John Locke. Everyman's Library, 1924. Reprinted by permission of E. P. Dutton & Co., Inc. Pp. 179–82, 183–90, and 228–32, excerpts.

are not apt to allow of it as a law binding to them in the application of it to their particular cases.

Secondly, in the state of Nature there wants a known and indifferent judge with authority to determine all differences according to the established law. For everyone in that state being both judge and executioner of the law of Nature, men being partial to themselves, passion and revenge is very apt to carry them too far, and with too much heat in their own cases, as well as negligence and unconcernedness, make them too remiss in other men's.

Thirdly, in the state of Nature there often wants power to back and support the sentence when right, and to give it due execution. They who by any injustice offended will seldom fail where they are able by force to make good their injustice. Such resistance many times makes the punishment dangerous, and frequently destructive to those who attempt it.

Thus mankind, notwithstanding all the privileges of the state of Nature, being but in an ill condition while they remain in it are quickly driven into society. Hence it comes to pass, that we seldom find any number of men live any time together in this state. The inconveniences that they are therein exposed to by the irregular and uncertain exercise of the power every man has of punishing the transgressions of others, make them take sanctuary under the established laws of government, and therein seek the preservation of their property. It is this makes them so willingly give up everyone his single power of punishing to be exercised by such alone as shall be appointed to it amongst them, and by such rules as the community, or those authorized by them to that purpose, shall agree on. And in this we have the original right and rise of both the legislative and executive power as well as of the governments and societies themselves.

For in the state of Nature to omit the liberty he has of innocent delights, a man has two powers. The first is to do whatsoever he thinks fit for the preservation of himself and others within the permission of the law of Nature; by which law, common to them all, he and all the rest of mankind are one community, make up one society distinct from all other creatures, and were it not for the corruption and viciousness of degenerate men, there would be no need of any other, no necessity that men should separate from this great and natural community, and associate into lesser combinations. The other power a man has in the state of Nature is the power to punish the crimes committed against that law. Both these he gives up when he joins in a private, if I may so call it, or particular political society, and incorporates into any commonwealth separate from the rest of mankind.

The first power—viz., of doing whatsoever he thought fit for the preservation of himself and the rest of mankind, he gives up to be regulated by laws made by the society, so far forth as the preservation of himself and the rest of that society shall require; which laws of the society in many things confine the liberty he had by the law of nature.

Secondly, the power of punishing he wholly gives up, and engages his natural force, which he might before employ in the execution of the law of Nature, by his own single authority, as he thought fit, to assist the executive power of the society as the law thereof shall require. For being now in a new state, wherein he is to enjoy many conveniences from the labor, assistance, and society of others in the same community, as well as protection from its whole strength, he is to part also with as much of his natural liberty, in providing for himself, as the good, prosperity, and safety of the society shall require, which is not only necessary but just, since the other members of the society do the like.

But though men when they enter into society give up the equality, liberty, and executive power they had in the state of Nature into the hands of the society, to be so far disposed of by the legislative as the good of the society shall require, yet it being only with an intention in everyone the better to preserve himself, his liberty and property (for no rational creature can be supposed to change his condition with an intention to be worse), the power of the society or legislative constituted by them can never be supposed to extend farther than the common good, but is obliged to secure everyone's property by providing against those three defects above mentioned that made the state of Nature so unsafe and uneasy. And so, whoever has the legislative or supreme power of any commonwealth, is bound to govern by established standing laws, promulgated and known to the people, and not by extemporary decrees, by indifferent and upright judges, who are to decide controversies by those laws; and to employ the force of the community at home only in the execution of such laws, or abroad to prevent or redress foreign injuries and secure the community from inroads and invasion. And all this to be directed to no other end but the peace, safety, and public good of the people.

Of the Extent of the Legislative Power. The great end of men's entering into society being the enjoyment of their properties in peace and safety, and the great instrument and means of that being the laws established in that society, the first and fundamental positive law of all commonwealths is the establishing of the legislative power, as the first and fundamental natural law which is to govern even the legislative. Itself is the preservation of the society and (as far as will consist with the public good) of every person in it. This legislative is not only the supreme power of the commonwealth, but sacred and unalterable in the hands where the community have once placed it. . . .

Though the legislative, whether placed in one or more, whether it be always in being or only by intervals, though it be the supreme power in every commonwealth, yet, first, it is not, nor can possibly be, absolutely arbitrary over the lives and fortunes of the people. For it being but the joint power of every member of the society given up to that person or assembly which is legislator, it can be no more than those persons had in a state of Nature before they entered into society, and gave it up to the community. . . . It is a power that hath no other end but preservation, and therefore can never have a right to destroy, enslave, or designedly to impoverish the subjects; the obligations of the law of Nature cease not in society, but only in many cases are drawn closer, and have, by human laws, known penalties annexed to them to enforce their observation. Thus the law of Nature stands as an eternal rule to all men, legislators as well as others. The rules that they make for other men's actions must, as well as their own and other men's actions, be conformable to the law of Nature—i.e., to the will of God, of which that is a declaration, and the fundamental law of Nature being the preservation of mankind, no human sanction can be good or valid against it.

Secondly, the legislative or supreme authority cannot assume to itself a power to rule by extemporary arbitrary decrees, but is bound to dispense justice and decide the rights of the subject by promulgated standing laws, and known authorized judges. . . .

Absolute arbitrary power, or governing without settled standing laws, can neither of them consist with the ends of society and government, which men would not quit the freedom of the state of Nature for, and tie themselves up under, were it not to preserve their lives, liberties, and fortunes, and by stated rules of right and property to secure their peace and quiet. It cannot be supposed that they should intend, had they a power so to do, to give any one or more an absolute arbitrary power over their persons and estates, and put a force into the magistrate's hand to execute his unlimited will arbitrarily upon them; this were to put themselves into a worse condition than the state of Nature, wherein they had a liberty to defend their right against the injuries of others, and were upon equal terms of force to maintain it, whether invaded by a single man or many in combination. . . .

Thirdly, the supreme power cannot take from any man any part of his property without his own consent. For the preservation of property being the end of government, and that for which men enter into society, it necessarily supposes and requires that the people should have property, without which they must be supposed to lose that by entering into society which was the end for which they entered into it; too gross an absurdity for any man to own. . . .

Fourthly, the legislative cannot transfer the power of making laws to any other hands, for it being but a delegated power from the people, they who have it cannot pass it over to others. The people alone can appoint the form of the commonwealth, which is by constituting the legislative, and appointing in whose hands that shall be. And when the people have said, "We submit, and be governed by laws made by such men, and in such forms," nobody else can say other men shall make laws for them; nor can they be bound by any laws, but such as are enacted by those whom they have chosen and authorized to make laws for them. . . .

When the government is dissolved, the people are at liberty to provide for themselves by erecting a new legislative differing from the other by the change of persons, or form, or both, as they shall find it most for their safety and good. For the society can never, by the fault of another, lose the native and original right it has to preserve itself, which can only be done by a settled legislative and a fair and impartial execution of the laws made by it. But the state of mankind is not so miserable that they are not capable of using this remedy till it be too late to look for any. To tell people they may provide for themselves by erecting a new legislative, when, by oppression, artifice, or being delivered over to a foreign power, their old one is gone, is only to tell them they may expect relief when it is too late, and the evil is past cure. This is, in effect, no more than to bid them first be slaves, and then to take care of their liberty, and, when their chains are on, tell them they may act like free men. This, if barely so, is rather mockery than relief, and men can never be secure from tyranny if there be no means to escape it till they are perfectly under it; and, therefore, it is that they have not only a right to get out of it, but to prevent it.

There is, therefore, secondly, another way whereby governments are dissolved, and that is, when the legislative, or the prince, either of them act contrary to their trust.

For the legislative acts against the trust reposed in them when they endeavor to invade the property of the subject, and to make themselves, or any part of the community, masters or arbitrary disposers of the lives, liberties, or fortunes of the people.

The reason why men enter into society is the preservation of their property; and the end while they choose and authorize a legislative is that there may be laws made, and rules set, as guards and fences to the properties of all the society, to limit the power and moderate the dominion of every part and member of the society. For since it can never be supposed to be the will of the society that the legislative should have a power to destroy that which every one designs to secure by entering into society, and for which the people submitted themselves to legislators of their own making: Whenever the legislators endeavor to take away and destroy the property of the people, or to reduce them to slavery under arbitrary power, they put themselves into a state of war with the people, who are thereupon absolved from any farther obedience, and are left to the common refuge which God hath provided for all men against force and violence. Whensoever, therefore, the legislative shall transgress this fundamental rule of society, and either by ambition, fear, folly, or corruption, endeavor to grasp themselves, or put into the hands of any other, an absolute power over the lives, liberties, and estates of the people, by this breach of trust they forfeit the power the people had put into their hands for quite contrary ends, and it devolves to the people, who have a right to resume their original liberty, and by the establishment of a new legislative (such as they shall think fit), provide for their own safety and security, which is the end for which they are in society. What I have said here concerning the legislative in general holds true also concerning the supreme executor, who having a double trust put in him both to have a part in the legislative and the supreme execution of the law, acts against both, when he goes about to set up his own arbitrary will as the law of the society. He acts also contrary to his trust when he employs the force, treasure, and offices of the society to corrupt the representatives and gain them to his purposes, when he openly pre-engages the electors, and prescribes, to their choice, such whom he has, by solicitation, threats, promises, or otherwise, won to his designs, and employs them to bring in such who have promised beforehand what to vote and what to enact. . . .

To this, perhaps, it will be said that the people being ignorant and always discontented, to lay the foundation of government in the unsteady opinion and uncertain humor of the people, is to expose it to certain ruin; and no government will be able long to subsist if the people may set up a new legislative whenever they take offense at the old one. To this I answer, quite the contrary. People are not so easily got out of their old forms as some are apt to suggest. They are hardly to be prevailed with to amend the acknowledged faults in the frame they have been accustomed to. And if there be any original defects, or adventitious ones introduced by time or corruption, it is not an easy thing to get them changed, even when all the world sees there is an opportunity for it. This slowness and aversion in the people to quit their old constitutions has in the many revolutions that have been seen in this kingdom, in this and former ages, still kept us to, or after some interval of fruitless attempts, still brought us back again to our old legislative of king, lords and commons; and whatever provocations have made the crown be taken from some of our princes' heads, they never carried the people so far as to place it in another line.

But it will be said this hypothesis lays a ferment for frequent rebellion. To which I answer:

First: no more than any other hypothesis. For when the people are made miserable, and find themselves exposed to the ill usage of arbitrary power, cry up their governors as much as you will for sons of Jupiter, let them be sacred and divine, descended or authorized from Heaven; give them out for whom or what you please, the same will happen. The people generally ill treated, and contrary to right, will be ready upon any occasion to ease themselves of a burden that sits heavy upon them. They will wish and seek for the opportunity, which in the change, weakness, and accidents of human affairs, seldom delays long to offer itself. He must have lived but little while in the world, who has not seen examples of this in his time; and he must have read very little who cannot produce examples of it in all sorts of governments in the world.

Secondly: I answer, such revolutions happen not upon every little mismanagement in public affairs. Great mistakes in the ruling part, many wrong and inconvenient laws, and all the slips of human frailty will be borne by the people without mutiny or murmur. But if a long train of abuses, prevarications, and artifices, all tending the same way, make the design visible to the people, and they cannot but feel what they lie under, and see whither they are going, it is not to be wondered that they should then rouse themselves, and endeavor to put the rule into such hands which may secure to them the ends for which government was at first erected, and without which, ancient names and specious forms are so far from being better, that they are much worse than the state of Nature or pure anarchy; the inconveniences being all as great and as near, but the remedy farther off and more difficult.

Thirdly: I answer, that this power in the people of providing for their safety anew by a new legislative when their legislators have acted contrary to their trust by invading their property, is the best fence against rebellion, and the probablest means to hinder it. For rebellion being an opposition, not to persons, but authority, which is founded only in the constitutions and laws of the government: those, whoever they be, who, by force, break through, and, by force, justify their violation of them, are truly and properly rebels. For when men, by entering into society and civil government, have excluded force, and introduced laws for the preservation of property, peace, and unity amongst themselves, those who set up force again in opposition to the laws, do *rebellare*—that is, bring back again the state of war, and are properly rebels, which they who are in power, by the pretense they have to authority, the temptation of force they have in their hands, and the flattery of those about them being likeliest to do, the properest way to prevent the evil is to show them the danger and injustice of it who are under the greatest temptation to run into it.

38. REFLECTIONS ON THE PARTY SYSTEM

SIR ERNEST BARKER

Sir Ernest Barker (1875–1960) was professor of political science at Cambridge University and one of Britain's most distinguished writers in the fields of politics, political theory, and history.

We may . . . define a party as a social formation which has two distinct but complementary functions—first that of serving as a *social reservoir* for the collection of a set of connected political ideas from the area of society; and secondly that of serving as a *political conduit* by which the ideas so collected flow from their social reservoir into the system of the State and turn the wheels of political machinery in that system. So conceived, party performs the service of enabling society to run into the State, and thus of keeping the action of the State constantly and wholesomely responsive to the play of social thought. . . .

What has just been said may lead us to reflect that our system of government, as it stands today, is a system of four factors—party, the electorate, Parliament, and cabinet. What is the relative strength of these factors, and what balance, if we can properly speak of balance, should be expected among them? It has often seemed to the writer that this system of four factors involves the reconciliation of two different and conflicting necessities. One necessity is that each of the factors should think highly of itself and its duty, and act as if everything hung on itself and upon its own decision. That is a condition of efficiency; but it may also lead, if it is not checked, to self-sufficiency and arrogance. The other necessity is that each factor should keep in touch and harmony with the rest, acknowledging that they too have the right and duty to do their work and to be left free to do it effectively. This latter is the sovereign necessity; but the first necessity is only too apt

From Sir Ernest Barker, "Reflections on the Party System," in Sydney D. Bailey, ed., *Political Parties and the Party System in Britain*. New York: Frederick A. Praeger, Inc., 1952, pp. 193–201, excerpts.

to make itself particularly felt. The electorate, feeling its own importance, may claim to impose an "imperative mandate"; Parliament, with a collective pride, may seek to institute a system of parliamentary autocracy for the duration of its term, installing and evicting cabinets at will; a cabinet may attempt to vindicate sovereignty for itself, and may use its majority and its Whips to drill and discipline Parliament; or finally, and this is a danger which in the contemporary world is particularly apparent, a victorious party or combination of parties may claim the last word for a party caucus and for its manipulating managers. But a just and proper system of parliamentary democracy depends not only on a general spirit of give and take in the minds of the people at large: it also depends on a similar spirit, a spirit of balance and accommodation, among the four factors by and through which it works—party, electorate, Parliament, and cabinet; and the greater the ardor of each factor, the more difficult it is to secure such a spirit.

The exaggeration of party is a matter which is closely connected with the number of parties in a country. Here there are three possibilities. One is the system of a single party, which the Communist states of Eastern Europe regard as the basis of a true or popular democracy, based upon the people and acting for the people. Another is the system of multiple parties, common in a number of the states of Western Europe; a system which has, or may claim to have, the advantage of producing a true reflection of the varied currents of social thought, but which has also the disadvantage of making government uneasy and dependent on fluctuating combinations between a number of different parties. A third is the system of two parties, or at any rate two main parties, which is the system generally followed in Anglo-Saxon countries. It may be said that both of the two first possibilities are favorable to the exaggeration of party. A single party prevents that discussion, and that choice, between political alternatives which is a necessary condition of a free electorate: it establishes the open tyranny of one party, whether of the Right or Left. A system of multiple parties may seem to give a large possibility of choice to the electorate; but its ultimate effect may be the secret tyranny of a cabal which unites the leaders of several parties in an interested coalition and controls behind the scenes both the representative body and the nominal government. Nor is that all. If a system of multiple parties is accompanied, as it often is, by the device of proportional representation, it accentuates the ardor of each party, and stimulates all to press for their full pound of flesh and to urge their claims to the uttermost. The third possibility—that of a system of two parties, or at any rate two main parties—also has its defect. It reduces the choice of the electorate to no more than two alternatives: it eliminates shades and nuances, and substitutes in their place two gross averages of opinion: It may even be said to reduce the level of politics to that of football or baseball, with two contending sides each madly cheered and supported by its different partisans. Can a nation ever be one when it splits itself into two?

But whatever may be urged against the system of two parties, there is much to be said in its favor. Life, after all, is largely a matter of choice between two alternatives: there are generally two rival schools in philosophy, two rival views of painting, two rival opinions about music; and why should there not also be two rival views of politics? We have also to reflect that a system of two rival political parties is far from meaning that every voter is attached to one or the other: it leaves room for the floating or unattached voter, who may now give his vote to one and now to another of the two, and can thus bring about those changes and alterations of government which are as valuable and refreshing as changes of the weather. In this respect the system of two parties is more conducive to freedom and change than either of the other systems; for a single party seeks permanently to ensure a total vote for its policy from the whole of the population, and a system of multiple parties tends to enlist every citizen in a permanent and unwavering allegiance to his particular party. In a word, the system of two parties leaves room for a margin of imprecision, or an area of incalculability, which is a safety-valve in the working of a democratic State. . . .

There is a sovereign merit still to be mentioned which belongs to the system of two parties. Each party or side, within itself, is permeated by a force of attraction; but each, in its relation to the other, is equally marked by a force of repulsion. The term Her Majesty's Opposition is one of the most significant and important in British politics. It signifies that a single nation, one in a common allegiance to a common way of life symbolized by its Queen, is none the less also two—two as well as one, and two at the same time that it is one. Her Majesty has her actual advisers, who form the anticabinet. The existence of such an anticabinet, or organized opposition to the acting cabinet, is the salt of the British system of parliamentary democracy. It supplies the constant criticism which is as necessary as constructive creation. It fans the flame of discussion and keeps it bright and clear. It gives the possibility of an alternative government—an actual possibility, actually present and visible —to which the nation can look if it feels the need for a new hand at the helm. The general development of Her Majesty's Opposition, and the general recognition of its function (a recognition which has gone to the length of the parliamentary provision of a salary for its leader), are the clearest signs of the health of the British system of government. But this development, and this recognition, are connected with, and are the results of, the growing tendency towards a clear two-party system. An organized and coherent opposition is only possible under such a system; and an organized and coherent opposition is a necessary condition of healthy democratic discussion and of a proper balance of all the factors and organs of democracy.

Apart from the question of their number, another matter which affects the character of parties is the nature of their composition. Ideally, the cleavage between parties should be vertical, and not horizontal: in other words, party divisions should not follow the strata of class or religious differentiation, but should rather cut down deep through those strata and leave on either side of the cleavage a similar cross section of the nation. Each party will then seek, or at any rate tend, to represent a general view of the national interest, and neither will be committed to a single interest. It may seem, *a priori*, that a single party will include all interests; but in actual practice the single parties of the present century have been based on the interest of a class (the

Fascist on the middle or lower middle class, and the Communist on the proletariat or "toiling masses"), and they have sought to adjust the whole community to the pattern of this particular interest. A system of multiple parties obviously tends to the representation of particular classes or sects; it splits the community not only into Left and Right, but also into different classes, different confessions, and different particular interests. Even a system of two parties may be a system of "two nations," and may split the community into a party of the poor, or the comparatively poor, and a party of the well-to-do. This is not actually the case in Britain, and it need never be the case. The Conservative Party is an all-class party, though more in the composition of its voting mass than in that of its parliamentary representatives, and the Labor Party, though based in the main on the industrial masses, is also a party including members of the professions and other sections of the nation: indeed it is to the interest of both parties, as well as to that of the nation, that they should spread a wide net, for the wider it is, the more their appeal and the greater the number of votes which they are likely to gain. At the same time it must be admitted that the electoral map of Britain, when it registers the result of a general election, has one alarming feature: it shows a clustering of Labor in densely packed areas of urban industry, and a dispersion of the other side over the great rural space of the country. We seem to be drifting into a state of division between the town and the country mouse; and there is peril in that division.

Another question suggested to the mind by any reflection on party systems is the question of the place of doctrine in the life and action of parties. Should a party elaborate a body of doctrine, expressed in a program, and should it seek to make its doctrine a fixed and permanent casing which encompasses and may cramp its life? Or should it rather be wedded to flexibility, and to ideas of progress and evolution; and should it accordingly abjure the expression of a creed, and be content to represent a general tendency and mental temper, with no precise definition in set terms and hard formulations? The question is one which vexes religious confessions as well as political parties; and in both cases there is more to be said for flexibility and evolution than for permanent expressions of doctrine and rigid sets of principle. A single party has a single doctrine or *Weltanschauung,* a single "general line" which all are expected to toe; a system of multiple parties, different as it may seem, may equally be a system of many hard-set doctrines, which harden themselves still more in their opposition and clash. It may be claimed as a merit for a two-party system that a party, seeking to increase the width of its appeal, progressively widens its scope and seeks to transcend old limitations and formulations. But it may also be said to be a demerit of such a system that a party seeks to deny or discredit the progress of the other, and attempts to limit and judge it by some form, or supposed form, of its past, so that the Conservative is condemned to be now what he was, or is supposed to have been, half a century ago, and the Labor candidate is equally condemned as still guilty of his past and outgrown extravangances, and as untaught and untrained by later experience. The chief enemy to the development of the temper and tendency of either party, under a system of two parties, is the refusal of the other party to acknowledge any development. On the other hand, when all is said that can be said in favor of development, the fact remains that there must be something of a hard inner core of steady principle in any party.

39. ONE-PARTY SYSTEM

JULIUS K. NYERERE

At the annual conference of the Tanganyika African National Union (TANU), the ruling political party officially asked the government to give statutory recognition to the one-party system in Tanganyika.

Simultaneously, President Nyerere set forth his views on the subject. He made no apology for supporting the one-party state, nor does he claim to justify his thesis by the "special needs" of an underdeveloped country. He puts forth instead the view that in Tanganyika the one-party state is more democratic.

People who are used to the two-party system cannot imagine democracy without it. They ask: "How can you have democracy with a one-party system?" It will therefore sound to them like heresy when they are told that other people, who also claim to be democrats, are now beginning to ask: "How can you have democracy with a two-party system?"

I must confess that, not so very long ago, I myself would have been content to answer the first of those questions. If I had posed the second it would have been in jest rather than in earnest. Recently, however, I have found myself questioning the democracy of the two-party system very seriously indeed. . . .

I realize that the political theorists are so attached to the pattern of democracy which depends on the existence of opposing parties, that they are likely to have been shocked by my expressing a doubt as to its being so very democratic after all. I am afraid they may be even more shocked by what I am now going to suggest: that, *where there is one party, and that party is identified with the nation as a whole, the foundations of democracy are firmer than they can ever be where you have two or more parties, each representing only a section of the community!*

After all, we do have it on very reliable authority that a house divided against itself cannot stand! So it is surely up to the advocates of the two-party system to defend their own case more convincingly. It is not enough for them simply to insist that it *is* more democratic than a one-party system, and then be horrified when we presume to disagree with them!

From Julius K. Nyerere, "One-Party System." *SPEARHEAD: The Pan-African Review,* Vol. No. 1 (January 1963), 11–22, excerpts.

Now my argument is that a two-party system can be justified only when the parties are divided over some fundamental issue; otherwise it can only encourage the growth of factionalism. Or, to put it another way, the only time when a political group can represent the interests of a section of the community, *without* being a faction, is when that group fights to remove a grievous wrong from society. But then the differences, between this group and those responsible for the wrong it fights, are fundamental; and there can therefore be no question of national unity until the differences have been removed by change. And "change" in that context is an euphemism, because any change in fundamentals is properly termed "revolution." What is more, the reason why the word "revolution" is generally associated with armed insurrection is that the existence of really fundamental differences within any society poses a "civil war" situation, and has often led to bloody revolution. Benjamin Disraeli, who was certainly no advocate of a one-party system, once referred to this situation as tantamount to "Two Nations" within a State. . . .

To return, then, to my argument: in any country which is divided over fundamental issues you have the "civil war" situation we have been talking about. If, on the other hand, you have a two-party system where the differences between the parties are *not* fundamental, then you immediately reduce politics to the level of a football match. A football match may, of course, attract some very able players; it may also be entertaining; but it is still only a game, and only the most ardent fans (who are not usually the most intelligent) take the game very seriously. This, in fact, is not unlike what has happened in many of the so-called democratic countries today, where some of the most intelligent members of society have become disgusted by the hypocrisy of the Party Games called politics, and take no active interest in them. They can see no party whose "line" they could support without reservation and are therefore left with no way of serving their country in the political field, even should they wish to; except, perhaps, by writing a book! For the politics of a country governed by the two-party system are not, and cannot be, *national* politics; they are the politics of *groups*, whose differences, more often than not, are of small concern to the majority of the people. . . .

Let us say that, as a result of your philosophy, you believe an opposition party to be so essential to democracy that you *must* form one. Now if there are no fundamental differences in your society, the only way you can gain support for your opposition party—if you are honest—is to stand before the public and tell them that you want their votes, *not* because you believe the government party's policy to be wrong, *not* because you have a better one to offer, *but simply because democracy requires at least two parties in the parliament.* The trouble is that a completely honest statement like that is not likely to get you very many votes. So what are you to do? According to your belief, democracy demands that you get at least some of your party into Parliament. Complete honesty doesn't seem to be enough to achieve this, so you are faced with the choice of abandoning a little of your honesty or abandoning your idea of democracy. Almost invariably, in such circumstances, it is the former which is sacrificed; and each party is led into conducting its election campaign by the "political" tactics of evasion, distortion, and even downright lies about the other party's motives and intentions. Nor does it stop there. Once in Parliament, as we have seen, members of the opposing parties must still observe the rules of party unity which, in themselves, must inevitably stifle not merely freedom of expression but, indeed, honesty of expression. For a "party line" which requires all members to oppose a rival party's policies must force them, at times, to oppose something which their conscience tells them there is no good reason to oppose. And, since these things happen to some extent in even the best of two-party democracies, it is perhaps not so surprising after all that so many people have come to equate politics with dishonesty or cynicism!

I know that in writing all this as the leader of a one-party government, I may be accused of special pleading. But I could easily counter such an accusation by saying that the defenders of the two-party system might equally well be accused of the same thing. For, in spite of their professed conviction that democratic government *demands* an opposition, I have never heard of a party fighting an election with the object of forming one! On the contrary, each party fights with the hope of winning as many seats as possible. They fail, however, to win them all. And then, having failed, they quite blandly make a virtue of necessity and produce the most high-sounding arguments in praise of their failure! . . .

Another thing which should be remembered is that the defense of any system must take account of its origin. Now the origin of a political system will be found either in history or in theory. That is to say, the evolution of the system must depend either on given historical circumstances without which it would not have developed, or on the practical application of some theory of government conceived as suitable to all conditions and circumstances. So if you want to defend a system which is of purely historical origin, you will find it very difficult if you try to base your defense on political theory. To say, for example, that, given the conditions of such and such a country at such and such a period of its history, the growth of a two-party system was inevitable, even desirable, is one thing. It is quite another thing to say that the *necessary condition* of democratic government is the existence of at least two parties. The first of those statements takes account of the origin of the two-party system; the second does not. . . .

Let me come back, then, to my contention that where there is *one* party— provided it is identified with the nation as a whole—the foundations of democracy can be firmer, and the people can have more opportunity to exercise a real choice, than where you have two or more parties—each representing only a section of the community. In countries which are accustomed to the two-party system it might be difficult to make any drastic change in the method of conducting elections. But what about a country like ours, where the electorate has virtually ruled out the possibility of any interparty conflict? Here, surely, we have a splendid opportunity to give our people a chance of exercising their own choice of leadership through the ballot box. Supposing we accept the fact that there *is* only one party, and stop trying to follow the rules of a multi-party system; then, as long as TANU membership is open to every citizen, we can conduct our elections in a way which is genuinely free and democratic.

I would go further. I would say that we not only have an opportunity to dispense with the disciplines of the two-party system, but that we would be wrong to retain them. I would say that they are not only unnecessary where you have only one party, but that they are bound, in time, to prove fatal to democracy. We have already seen how severely these disciplines must limit freedom of expression in a two-party parliament. This is bad enough, but at least each party can still allow its members to argue freely within their own party meetings. Party loyalty will rally them behind their leaders when they face the rival party in Parliament. (This party loyalty, indeed, is something which feeds on opposition and makes the task of preserving discipline comparatively easy.) In fact, if the only alternative to the two-party system were a one-party system which retained the rules and disciplines of the two-party system it would be better to have even an artificial opposition party, despite all the inconsistencies and limitations of freedom this would involve. For the task of imposing party discipline, of limiting freedom of expression in Parliament, with no rival party to help, would sooner or later involve us in something far worse than the factionalism of which I have accused the two-party enthusiasts. It would become more and more necessary to limit freedom of discussion within the party itself until eventually it was almost entirely suppressed. Why? Because you cannot limit freedom of expression anywhere without a reason. People are not fools. They might accept the "party unity" rules for a time, but the more intelligent members of Parliament would soon begin to ask why they must always support the government in public without argument, since there was no fear of being pushed out of power by a rival party. And what reason could we give them? We should have to convince them, and ourselves, that the "party line" they were compelled to support was so fundamentally right that any deviation from it would be tantamount to a crime against the "people." In other words, we should have to elevate policy decisions to the category of dogma. And once you deal in dogma you cannot allow freedom of opinion. You cannot have dogma without putting contrary ideas on the "index."

This, I believe, is not unlike what has befallen our friends the Communists. They have made their policies a creed, and are finding that dogmatism and freedom of discussion do not easily go together. They are as much afraid of the "other party" as any government in a two-party democracy. In their case the "other party" is only a phantom, but a phantom can be even more frightening than a living rival! And their fear of this phantom has blinded them to the truth that, in a one-party system, party membership must be open to everybody and freedom of expression allowed to every individual. No party which limits its membership to a clique can ever free itself from the fear of overthrow by those it has excluded. It must be constantly on the watch for signs of opposition, and must smother "dangerous" ideas before they have time to spread.

But a national movement which is open to all—which is identified with the whole nation—has nothing to fear from the discontent of any excluded section of society, for there is then no such section. Those forming the government will, of course, be replaced from time to time; this is what elections are for. The leadership of our movement is constantly changing; there is no reason why the leadership of the nation should not also be constantly changing. This would have nothing to do with the overthrowing of a party government by a rival party. And, since such a national movement leaves no room for the growth of discontented elements excluded from its membership, it has nothing to fear from criticism and the free expression of ideas. On the contrary, both the movement itself and the nation have everything to gain from a constant injection of new ideas from within the nation and from outside. It would be both wrong, and certainly unnecessary, to feel we must wait until the leaders are dead before we begin to criticize them!

Any member of the movement (which in this context means any patriotic citizen since it is a national movement we are talking about) would be free to stand as a candidate if he so wished. And in each constituency the voters themselves would be able to make their choice freely from among these candidates; they would no longer be obliged to consider the party label rather than the individual. Of such elections it could truly be said that they were for the purpose of letting the people choose their own representatives. If that is not democracy, I do not know the meaning of the word!

There would be no need to hold one set of elections within the party, and another set afterwards for the public. All elections would be equally open to everybody. In our case, for example, the present distinction between TANU and the TANU government—a distinction which, as a matter of fact, our people do not in the least understand—would vanish. We should simply have leaders chosen by the people themselves to do a job. And such leaders could be removed by the people at any time; there would be no need for a statutory period of so many years to elapse before an unsatisfactory leader could be replaced by them. In this way the government of the country would be truly in the hands of the electorate at all times. It would no longer be a mere matter of their casting votes for or against a "party" at intervals of four or five years. And anybody who continued to occupy a position of leadership under such conditions would do so because the people were satisfied with him; not because he was protected by a law which made it impossible for them to replace him until the next general election.

Furthermore, there would be no need to continue with the present artificial distinction between politicians and civil servants—a distinction desirable only in the context of a multiparty system where the continuity of public administration must not be thrown out of gear at every switch from one "party" government to another. For, once you begin to think in terms of a single national movement instead of a number of rival factional parties, it becomes absurd to exclude a whole group of the most intelligent and able members of the community from participation in the discussion of policy simply because they happen to be civil servants. In a political movement which is identified with the nation, participation in political affairs must be recognized as the right of *every* citizen, in no matter what capacity he may have chosen to serve his country.

Of course, I know that in spite of anything I can say, this idea that a party and its government should be one and the same thing will be another shock to our political "teachers" and those who have accepted their teaching without question. But the distinction between the party and the party government is not, in any case, a logical one. Any party government must necessarily be governed by its party. If it were not, it would not be a party government. And if the party government is governed by the party, then it must obviously be the party which governs the country. In other words, the party in power *is* the government. It must be. If it is not, then it is nonsense to talk about a Labor government, or a Conservative government, or a TANU government, and to say that those governments are carrying out Labor, or Conservative, or TANU policy.

Any government which tries to separate itself from its own party finds there is a perpetual feud between those of its members who are in the legislature and those outside it. And the feud cannot be avoided while this quite illogical distinction is insisted upon. The fact that it *is* insisted upon is, I believe, yet another unconscious evasion of a rational dilemma. It would be very difficult indeed for the advocates of a two-party system to explain how factional rule could be the same thing as democratic rule! So, here again, they beg the question. They simply say that a "party" government is independent of its party! They also claim that a party candidate, once he has been elected to Parliament, should represent *all* his constituents impartially. Quite how the poor fellow is expected to "represent" that section of his constituents whose main interest lies in hoping for the early defeat of his party by their own is not clear! But perhaps it is unfair to probe too deeply into the embarrassments of a democratically minded people handicapped by a factional system. On the other hand, if you are going to tell people to "Vote for Smith—Vote Conservative," or a "Vote for Jones is a Vote for Labor," is it really fair on Smith (or Jones) to turn round directly the elections are over and say that he must now regard himself as a nonpartisan representative of the people (except, of course, in parliamentary debate!)? If the Smiths and Joneses could indeed turn so complete a mental somersault it would be, I suspect, only because of a subconscious recognition on their part that their party labels had about as much political significance as the different-colored jerseys worn by players in a Cup-Tie Final. Try to imagine an eighteenth century Scottish Covenanter politely listening to the problems of a group of Jacobites, and agreeing to "take the matter up" on their behalf, and you will see what I mean!

But an advocate of a one-party system, in which the party is identified with the nation as a national movement, can admit the parallel identity of the government with the movement without any embarrassment at all. And if he happens to be an M.P. he is spared the necessity of turning mental somersaults on every journey between his constituency and the Parliament!

40. THE GENERAL WILL

JEAN-JACQUES ROUSSEAU

Jean-Jacques Rousseau (1712–1778) was a French philosopher who developed the belief in unrestricted and undelegated popular sovereignty which was to become the rationale of radical democracy.

Man is born free; and everywhere he is in chains. One thinks himself the master of others, and still remains a greater slave than they. How did this change come about? I do not know. What can make it legitimate? That question I think I can answer.

The Social Compact. I suppose men to have reached the point at which the obstacles in the way of their preservation in the state of nature show their power of resistance to be greater than the resources at the disposal of each individual for his maintenance in that state. That primitive condition can then subsist no longer; and the human race would perish unless it changed its manner of existence.

But, as men cannot engender new forces, but only unite and direct existing ones, they have no other means of preserving themselves than the formation, by aggregation, of a sum of forces great enough to overcome the resistance. These they have to bring into play by means of a single motive power, and cause to act in concert.

This sum of forces can arise only where several persons come together: but, as the force and liberty of each man are the chief instruments of his self-preservation, how can he pledge them without harming his own interests, and neglecting the care he owes to himself? This difficulty, in its bearing on my present subject, may be stated in the following terms—

"The problem is to find a form of association which will defend and protect with the whole common force the person and goods of each associate, and in which each, while uniting himself with all, may still obey himself alone, and remain as free as before." This is the fundamental problem of which the *Social Contract* provides the solution.

The clauses of this contract are so determined by the nature of the act that the slightest modification would make them vain and ineffective; so that, although they have perhaps never been formally set forth, they are everywhere the same and everywhere tacitly admitted and rcognized, until, on the violation of the social compact, each regains his original rights and resumes

From the book *The Social Contract and Other Discourses* by Jean-Jacques Rousseau, translated by G. D. H. Cole. Everyman's Library, 1913. Reprinted by permission of E. P. Dutton & Co., Inc. Pp. 5, 14–19, 25–27, and 93–94, excerpts.

his natural liberty, while losing the conventional liberty in favor of which he renounced it.

These clauses, properly understood, may be reduced to one—the total alienation of each associate, together with all his rights, to the whole community; for, in the first place, as each gives himself absolutely, the conditions are the same for all; and, this being so, no one has any interest in making them burdensome to others.

Moreover, the alienation being without reserve, the union is as perfect as it can be, and no associate has anything more to demand: for, if the individuals retained certain rights, as there would be no common superior to decide between them and the public, each, being on one point his own judge, would ask to be so on all; the state of nature would thus continue, and the association would necessarily become inoperative or tyrannical.

Finally, each man, in giving himself to all, gives himself to nobody; and as there is no associate over whom he does not acquire the same right as he yields others over himself, he gains an equivalent for everything he loses, and an increase of force for the preservation of what he has.

If then we discard from the social compact what is not of its essence, we shall find that it reduces itself to the following terms—

"Each of us puts his person and all his power in common under the supreme direction of the general will, and, in our corporate capacity, we receive each member as an indivisible part of the whole." At once, in place of the individual personality of each contracting party, this act of association creates a moral and collective body, composed of as many members as the assembly contains votes, and receiving from this act its unity, its common identity, its life and its will. This public person, so formed by the union of all other persons formerly took the name of *city,* and now takes that of *Republic* or *body politic;* it is called by its members *State* when passive, *Sovereign* when active, and *Power* when compared with others like itself. Those who are associated in it take collectively the name of *people,* and severally are called *citizens,* as sharing in the sovereign power, and *subjects,* as being under the laws of the State. But these terms are often confused and taken one for another: it is enough to know how to distinguish them when they are being used with precision. . . .

The Civil State. The passage from the state of nature to the civil state produces a very remarkable change in man, by substituting justice for instinct in his conduct, and giving his actions the morality they had formerly lacked. Then only, when the voice of duty takes the place of physical impulses and right of appetite, does man, who so far had considered only himself, find that he is forced to act on different principles, and to consult his reason before listening to his inclinations. Although, in this state, he deprives himself of some advantages which he got from nature, he gains in return others so great, his faculties are so stimulated and developed, his ideas so extended, his feelings so ennobled, and his whole soul so uplifted, that, did not the abuses of this new condition often degrade him below that which he left, he would be bound to bless continually the happy moment which took him from it for ever, and, instead of a stupid and unimaginative animal, made him an intelligent being and a man.

Let us draw up the whole account in terms easily commensurable. What man loses by the social contract is his natural liberty and an unlimited right to everything he tries to get and succeeds in getting; what he gains is civil liberty and the proprietorship of all he possesses. If we are to avoid mistake in weighing one against the other, we must clearly distinguish natural liberty, which is bounded only by the strength of the individual, from civil liberty, which is limited by the general will; and possession, which is merely the effect of force or the right of the first occupier, from property, which can be founded only on a positive title.

We might, over and above all this, add, to what man acquires in the civil state, moral liberty, which alone makes him truly master of himself; for the mere impulse of appetite is slavery, while obedience to a law which we prescribe to ourselves is liberty. But I have already said too much on this head, and the philosophical meaning of the word liberty does not now concern us. . . .

Whether the General Will Is Fallible. It follows from what has gone before that the general will is always right and tends to the public advantage; but it does not follow that the deliberations of the people are always equally correct. Our will is always for our own good, but we do not always see what that is; the people is never corrupted, but it is often deceived, and on such occasions only does it seem to will what is bad.

There is often a great deal of difference between the will of all and the general will; the latter considers only the common interest, while the former takes private interest into account, and is no more than a sum of particular wills; but take away from these same wills the pluses and minuses that cancel one another, and the general will remains as the sum of the differences.

If, when the people, being furnished with adequate information, held its deliberations, the citizens had no communication one with another, the grand total of the small differences would always give the general will, and the decision would always be good. But when factions arise, and partial associations are formed at the expense of the great association, the will of each of these associations becomes general in relation to its members, while it remains particular in relation to the State: it may then be said that there are no longer as many votes as there are men, but only as many as there are associations. The differences become less numerous and give a less general result. Lastly, when one of these associations is so great as to prevail over all the rest, the result is no longer a sum of small differences, but a single difference; in this case there is no longer a general will, and the opinion which prevails is purely particular.

It is therefore essential, if the general will is to be able to express itself, that there should be no partial society within the State, and that each citizen should think only his own thoughts. . . .

If the State is a moral person whose life is in the union of its members, and if the most important of its cares is the care for its own preservation, it must have a universal and compelling force, in order to move and dispose each part as may be most advantageous to the whole. As nature gives each man absolute power over all his members, the social compact gives the body politic absolute power over all its members also; and it is this power which, under the direction of the general will, bears, as I have said, the name of Sovereignty.

But, besides the public person, we have to consider the private persons composing it, whose life and liberty are naturally independent of it. We are bound then to distinguish clearly between the respective rights of the citizens and the Sovereign, and between the duties the former have to fulfill as subjects, and the natural rights they should enjoy as men.

Each man alienates, I admit, by the social compact, only such part of his powers, goods, and liberty as it is important for the community to control; but it must also be granted that the Sovereign is sole judge of what is important.

Every service a citizen can render the State he ought to render as soon as the Sovereign demands it; but the Sovereign, for its part, cannot impose upon its subjects any fetters that are useless to the community, nor can it even wish to do so; for no more by the law of reason than by the law of nature can anything occur without a cause. . . .

There is but one law which, from its nature, needs unanimous consent. This is the social compact; for civil association is the most voluntary of all acts. Every man being born free and his own master, no one, under any pretext whatsoever, can make any man subject without his consent. To decide that the son of a slave is born a slave is to decide that he is not born a man.

If then there are opponents when the social compact is made, their opposition does not invalidate the contract, but merely prevents them from being included in it. They are foreigners among citizens. When the State is instituted, residence constitutes consent; to dwell within its territory is to submit to the Sovereign.

Apart from this primitive contract, the vote of the majority always binds all the rest. This follows from the contract itself. But it is asked how a man can be both free and forced to conform to wills that are not his own. How are the opponents at once free and subject to laws they have not agreed to?

I retort that the question is wrongly put. The citizen gives his consent to all the laws, including those which are passed in spite of his opposition, and even those which punish him when he dares to break any of them. The constant will of all the members of the State is the general will; by virtue of it they are citizens and free. When in the popular assembly a law is proposed, what the people is asked is not exactly whether it approves or rejects the proposal, but whether it is in conformity with the general will, which is their will. Each man, in giving his vote, states his opinion on that point; and the general will is found by counting votes. When therefore the opinion that is contrary to my own prevails, this proves neither more nor less than that I was mistaken, and that what I thought to be the general will was not so. If my particular opinion had carried the day I should have achieved the opposite of what was my will; and it is in that case that I should not have been free. . . .

41. LIBERAL LEGISLATION AND FREEDOM OF CONTRACT

T. H. GREEN

T. H. Green (1836–1882) was a professor of philosophy at Oxford University. His concept of freedom provided the rationale for "the welfare state."

We shall probably all agree that freedom, rightly understood, is the greatest of blessings; that its attainment is the true end of all our effort as citizens. But when we thus speak of freedom, we should consider carefully what we mean by it. We do not mean merely freedom from restraint or compulsion. We do not mean merely freedom to do as we like irrespectively of what it is that we like. We do not mean a freedom that can be enjoyed by one man or one set of men at the cost of a loss of freedom to others. When we speak of freedom as something to be so highly prized, we mean a positive power or capacity of doing or enjoying something worth doing or enjoying, and that, too, something that we do or enjoy in common with others. We mean by it a power which each man exercises through the help or security given him by his fellow-men, and which he in turn helps to secure for them. When we measure the progress of a society by its growth in freedom, we measure it by the increasing development and exercise on the whole of those powers of contributing to social good with which we believe the members of the society to be endowed; in short, by the greater power on the part of the citizens as a body to make the most and best of themselves. Thus, though of course there can be no freedom among men who act not willingly but under compulsion, yet on the other hand the mere removal of compulsion, the mere enabling a man to do as he likes, is in itself no contribution to true freedom. In one sense no man is so well able to do as he likes as the wandering savage. He has no master. There is no one to say him nay. Yet we do not count him really free, because the freedom of savagery is not strength, but weakness. The actual powers of the noblest savage do not admit of comparison with those of the humblest citizen of a law-abiding state. He is not the slave of man, but he is the slave of nature. Of compulsion by natural necessity he has plenty of experience, though of restraint by society none at all. Nor can he deliver himself from that compulsion except by submitting to this restraint. So to submit is the first step in true freedom, because the first step towards the full exercise of the faculties with which man is endowed. But we rightly refuse to recognise the highest development on the part of an exceptional individual or exceptional class, as an advance towards the true freedom of man, if it is founded on a refusal of the same opportunity to other men. The powers of the human mind have probably never attained such force and keenness, the proof of what society can do for the individual has never been so strikingly exhibited, as among the small groups of men who possessed civil priviliges in the small republics of antiquity. The whole framework of our political ideas, to say nothing of our philosophy, is derived from them. But in them this extraordinary efflorescence of the privileged class was accompanied by the slavery of the multitude. That slavery was the condition on which it depended, and for that reason it was doomed to decay. There is no clearer ordinance of that supreme reason, often dark to us, which governs the course of man's affairs, than that no body of men should in the long run be able to strengthen itself at the cost of others' weakness. The civilisation and freedom of the ancient world were shortlived because they were partial and exceptional. If the ideal of true freedom is the maximum of power for all members of human society alike to make the best of themselves, we are right in refusing to ascribe the glory of freedom to a state in which the apparent elevation of the few is founded on the degradation of the many, and in ranking modern society, founded as it is on free industry, with all its confusion and ignorant licence and waste of effort, above the most splendid of ancient republics.

If I have given a true account of that freedom which forms the goal of social effort, we shall see that freedom of contract, freedom in all the forms of doing what one will with one's own, is valuable only as a means to an end. That end is what I call freedom in the positive sense: in other words, the liberation of the powers of all men equally for contributions to a common good. No one has a right to do what he will with his own in such a way as to contravene this end. It is only through the guarantee which society gives him that he has property at all, or, strictly speaking, any right to his possessions. This guarantee is founded on a sense of common interest. Every one has an interest in securing to every one else the free use and enjoyment and disposal of his possessions, so long as that freedom on the part of one does not interfere with a like freedom on the part of others, because such freedom contributes to that equal development of the faculties of all which is the highest good for all. This is the true and the only justification of rights of property. Rights of property, however, have been and are claimed which cannot be thus justified. We are all now agreed that men cannot rightly be the property of men. The institution of property being only justifiable as a means to the free exercise of the social capabilities of all, there can be no true right to property of a kind which debars one class of men from such free exercise altogether. We condemn slavery no less when it arises out of a voluntary agreement on the part of the enslaved person. A contract by which any one agreed for a certain consideration to become the slave of another we should reckon a void contract. Here, then, is a limitation upon freedom of contract which we all recognise as rightful. No contract is valid in which human persons, willingly or unwillingly, are dealt with as commodities, because such contracts of necessity defeat the end for which alone society enforces contracts at all. . . .

42. FREEDOM AND INDIVIDUALISM IN CHINA

JOHN K. FAIRBANK

John Fairbank (1907–   ) is director of the East Asian Research Center at Harvard University. He is author of numerous books and articles on Chinese thought and institutions.

Even a brief sketch of the historical experience of the Chinese people indicates their cultural differences from the West. Some of these inherited differences have been selected and reinforcd by the new totalitarian rulers.

Chinese tradition is, of course, very broad. It affords examples of a Confucian type of individualism and defiance of state control. Some day these examples may be invoked for democratic purposes, but that time has not yet come.

Today we see these cultural differences affecting the status of the Chinese individual. The old idea of hierarchic order persists. "Enemies" of the new order, as defined by it, are classed as not belonging to "the people" and so are of lowest status. On the other hand, party members form a new elite, and one man is still at the top of the pyramid. The tradition of government supremacy and domination by the official class still keeps ordinary people in their place.

The law, for example, is still an administrative tool used in the interest of the state; it does not protect the individual. This reflects the commonsense argument that the interest of the whole outweighs that of any part or person, and so the individual still has no established doctrine of rights to fall back upon.

As in the old days, the letter of the law remains uncertain and its application arbitrary. The defense of the accused is not assured, the judiciary is not independent, confession is expected and litigation is frowned upon as a way of resolving conflicts. Compared with American society, the law plays a very minor role.

The difference between Chinese and American values and institutions stands out most sharply in the standards for personal conduct. The term for individualism in Chinese (*ko-jen-chu-i*) is a modern phrase invented for a foreign idea, using characters that suggest each-for-himself, a chaotic selfishness rather than a high ideal. Individualism is thus held in as little esteem as it was under the Confucian order.

The difference is that where young people were formerly dominated by

From John K. Fairbank, "U. S. Fighting an Idea in Vietnam," *The Washington Post,* Feb. 27, 1966.

their families, who for example arranged their marriages, now they have largely given up a primary loyalty to family and substituted a loyalty to the Party or "the people." In both cases, the highest ideal is sacrifice for the collective good.

Similarly, the modern term for freedom (*tzu-yu*) is a modern combination of characters suggesting a spontaneous or willful lack of discipline, very close to license and quite contrary to the Chinese ideal of disciplined cooperation.

The cultural gap is shown also by the Chinese attitude toward philanthropy. Giving things to others is of course highly valued where specific relations call for it, as when the individual contributes to the collective welfare of family, clan or community. But the Christian virtue of philanthropy in the abstract, giving to others as a general duty, quite impersonally, runs into a different complex of ideas.

Between individuals, there should be reciprocity in a balanced relationship. To receive without giving in return puts one at a serious disadvantage: one is unable to hold up one's side of the relationship and therefore loses self-respect.

American philanthropy thus hurts Chinese pride. It has strings of conscience attached to it. The Communist spurning of foreign aid and touting of self-sufficiency fits the traditional sense of values. American aid does not.

CRITICS ARE ENEMIES

Cultural differences emerge equally in the area of politics. In the Chinese tradition, government is by persons who command obedience by the example they set of right conduct. When in power, an emperor or a ruling party has a monopoly of leadership which is justified by its performance, particularly by the wisdom of its policies. No abstract distinction is made between the person in power and his policies.

Dissent which attacks policies is felt to be an attack on the policymaker. On this basis, no "loyal opposition" is possible. The Western concept of disputing a power holder's policies while remaining loyal to his institutional status is not intelligible to the Chinese. Critics are seen as enemies, for they discredit those in power and tear down the prestige by which their power is partially maintained. (This idea also crops up in Taiwan.)

Another difference emerges over the idea of self-determination. This commonplace of Western political thinking sanctions the demand of a definable group in a certain area, providing they can work it out, to achieve an independent state by common consent among themselves. This idea runs quite counter to the traditional idea of the Chinese realm that embraces all who are culturally Chinese within a single entity.

Thus the rival Chinese regimes today are at one in regarding Taiwan as part of the mainland. Both want to control both areas. Similarly, they are agreed that Tibet is part of the Chinese realm without regard for self-determination. A supervised plebiscite would seem so humiliating that no Chinese regime would permit it.

Both the Chinese party dictatorships of modern times are also believers in elitism and opponents of the election process, except as a minor device for confirming local popular acquiescence in the regime.

Elections on the mainland are manipulated by the Party. Taiwan has developed a genuine election process at the local level, but the old idea of party "tutelage" is far from dead at the top. Here again, a case can be made for the Chinese practice. Our point is merely its difference from that of the West.

AN ANCIENT DEVICE

Perhaps the most strikingly different political device is that of mutual responsibility, the arrangement whereby a designated group is held responsible in all its members for the conduct of each. This idea goes far back in Chinese history as a device for controlling populous villages.

At first, five-household groups, and later, ten-household groups, were designated by the officials, ten such lower groups forming a unit at a higher level with the process repeated until 1000 households formed a single group. In operation this system means that one member of a household is held accountable for the acts of all other members, one household for the acts of its neighbors and so on up the line.

This motivates mutual surveillance and reciprocal control, with neighbor spying on neighbor and children informing on parents. Communist China uses this ancient device today in its street committees and other groups. It directly denies the Western idea of judging a man by his intentions and condemning him only for his own acts.

Cultural differences lay the powder train for international conflict. China and America can see each other as "backward" and "evil," deserving destruction. We need to objectify such differences, see our own values in perspective and understand if not accept the values of others.

Understanding an opponent's values also helps us deal with him. The old Chinese saying is, "If you know yourself and know your enemy, in a hundred battles you will win a hundred times." . . .

43. THE INDIVIDUAL UNDER COMMUNISM: A SOVIET VIEW

YURI P. FRANTSEV

Yuri P. Frantsev, a Corresponding Member of the U.S.S.R. Academy of Sciences, has written widely on Soviet ideology and politics. He seeks to show that the ideals implicit in Marxism-Leninism are, in fact, being realized in Soviet society and practice.

The individual cannot be absolutely independent of society. Such independence can be only imaginary. All talk about this kind of "freedom" is usually intended to cover up antisocial actions detrimental to the people. Bourgeois tales about "absolute freedom of the individual" are meaningless and harmful. A society which recognises no boundary between permissible and impermissible actions cannot exist. Such freedom would mean abolishing all social activity, all human intercourse and, indeed, society itself. . . .

When Lenin and the Communist Party began their political struggle, they put the question of freedom in specific terms, rejecting the bourgeois ideologists' hypocritical and hazy verbiage about "freedom in general." The question as they posed it was: Freedom *for whom?* Freedom *from what?* In reply to the first question we can say: "We have freedom for all. In our society there are no restrictions on account of sex, nationality or creed. We have achieved real freedom of religion by separating religious organisations from the state and abolishing their links with capital. All citizens enjoy equal rights in the free Soviet land, irrespective of their religion or nationality." As for the question, "What are people free from in the Soviet Union?", our answer is: "They are free from exploitation, from all moral oppression, and consequently their thinking and deeds are free from the age-old shackles created by the economic, political and moral rule of the exploiters."

A summary of the arguments concerning freedom which the advocates of anti-communism trot out shows that most of those arguments come down to defence of individualism. The question is usually of "freedom of the individual", but what is actually meant is freedom of private property. The emphasis is on "free enterprise", or initiative, which modern capitalism is alleged to guarantee. This standard concept may roughly be stated thus: private property brings "economic democracy" and contributes to enterprise and private initiative. As regards "political democracy", it is in keeping with this concept. On the other hand, public property and planned economy

From Yuri P. Frantsev, *Communism and Freedom of the Individual*. Moscow: Foreign Languages Publishing House, n.d., pp. 21–30, excerpts.

are said to stifle private initiative and to lead to "totalitarianism", *étatism,* or tyranny of the state, and to other deadly sins.

But that is perfectly absurd. First of all, the development of private initiative and private enterprise is a thing of the past and not of the present of capitalism. Bourgeois propagandists juggle with the truth by making out the premonopoly period of capitalism to be its modern period. Secondly, enterprise and freedom even at that time were enjoyed only by the few, while the working people lived in poverty and had no rights. Thirdly, it is the socialist system that creates every condition for the continuous development of the initiative and creative activity of all working people and each individual.

Time was when capitalism, which succeeded feudalism, encouraged people to a certain extent to be enterprising and energetic, and bold in displaying initiative. And that explains the creative energy of the Renaissance, the eighteenth century and partly the first half of the last century. But at that time, too, enterprise never involved large sections of the people, never assumed a truly mass scale. For every person who "got on in the world" and was able to exploit others there were hundreds and thousands of "ill-starred" people who barely made both ends meet, and were doomed to work for and enrich others.

"Freedom of the individual" and "free enterprise" today, under monopoly capitalism, are certainly out of the question. "Under *such* capitalism," wrote Lenin, "competition means the incredibly brutal suppression of the enterprise, energy and bold initiative of the *masses* of the population, of its overwhelming majority, of ninety-nine out of every hundred toilers; it also means that competition is replaced by financial fraud, despotism, servility on the upper rungs of the social ladder."

Nowadays, under state-monopoly capitalism, competition means the suppression by a handful of monopolies of the enterprise even of the middle bourgeoisie, who are barred from the big pie. The petty bourgeoisie is bound hand and foot by the monopolies, which keep a stranglehold upon it. As far as the small owners are concerned, free enterprise generally brings them complete ruin, for they cannot compete with the all-powerful monopolies. . . .

The despotism of the monopolies also leaves its imprint on all political activities in the capitalist countries. There is hardly anything left of the limited democracy of the premonopoly period of capitalism. In the United States, for example, public affairs are clearly dominated by the two powerful political corporations known as the Democratic and the Republican parties. Both parties are closely linked with the corresponding groups of monopoly capital. They have wiped out all other political organisations, bourgeois or petty-bourgeois alike. Just as the buyer in the market seized by the monopolies is free to "choose" between the products of the two corporations, so the voter enjoys only a semblance of the right to elect the candidates of one or the other corporation. In the other capitalist countries, the political organisation of society shows similar trends in the imperialist period.

That is why bourgeois politicians are now more anxious than ever to impart a vague, indefinite character to the concept of freedom, to strip it of all substance. And that is why the question which Lenin and the Communists once asked is now even more valid than before. Indeed, freedom from what, and for whom?

The Soviet Union lacks one freedom which the bourgeoisie cherishes above all else: freedom to live at the expense of others, to exploit men and lead a parasitic life. Soviet people concede no one the "right" to declare: "I will work or not as I please." For, speaking plainly, this means: "I will work, or I will live at the expense of others, of those who work." Soviet people abhor the parasite's view of the world and of human relations. We refuse to recognise freedom from work as a legal or moral standard. Any desire to make profit at the expense of others, to elbow out others or infringe their legitimate interests on the pretext of exercising one's alleged individual rights, is abominable bourgeois selfishness and extreme individualism. It is nothing short of the desire to live at the expense of others.

Capitalist society does not and cannot give people freedom from bourgeois relations, which are based on exploitation, on the rule of capital, and run through all spheres of the life of society—economic, political and ideological. The very idea of freedom is reduced to freedom of enterprise for the big owners, for those who own substantial capital.

Socialist society has its own laws, standards and rules which it allows no one to violate. It unrelentingly combats swindlers, parasites, idlers and all dishonest people who would like to live at the expense of others. It considers them to be its enemies.

Now for the "free endeavour" proclaimed by the theoreticians of imperialism. What they advocate is in effect intellectual anarchy, the cult of the lone wolf, of the private individual, as opposed to the community. Some of them represent "free endeavour" as freedom from all principles, as lack of principles raised to the level of a world outlook. But no creative endeavour is possible in the absence of a world outlook, of firm principles. Lack of principles means the degradation and decay of creative endeavour, which thus becomes a meaningless, arbitrary activity. Arbitrary activity is not creative endeavour because the latter cannot exist unless it has meaning and an objective, unless it is inspired by great ideas. The meaning and value of the creative endeavour of the individual are determined by society.

44. ON THE LIBERTY OF THOUGHT AND DISCUSSION

JOHN STUART MILL

John Stuart Mill (1806–1873) was one of Britain's most prominent economists and political theorists. He served one term in Parliament.

The time, it is to be hoped, is gone by, when any defense would be necessary of the "liberty of the press" as one of the securities against corrupt or tyrannical government. No argument, we may suppose, can now be needed, against permitting a legislature or an executive, not identified in interest with the people, to prescribe opinions to them, and determine what doctrines or what arguments they shall be allowed to hear. This aspect of the question, besides, has been so often and so triumphantly enforced by preceding writers, that it needs not be specially insisted on in this place. Though the law of England, on the subject of the press, is as servile to this day as it was in the time of the Tudors, there is little danger of its being actually put in force against political discussion, except during some temporary panic, when fear of insurrection drives ministers and judges from their propriety; and speaking generally, it is not, in constitutional countries, to be apprehended, that the government, whether completely responsible to the people or not, will often attempt to control the expression of opinion, except when in doing so it makes itself the organ of the general intolerance of the public. Let us suppose, therefore, that the government is entirely at one with the people, and never thinks of exerting any power of coercion unless in agreement with what it conceives to be their voice. But I deny the right of the people to exercise such coercion, either by themselves or by their government.

The power itself is illegitimate. The best government has no more title to it than the worst. It is as noxious, or more noxious, when exerted in accordance with public opinion, than when in opposition to it. If all mankind minus one were of one opinion, and only one person were of the contrary opinion, mankind would be no more justified in silencing that one person, than he, if he had the power, would be justified in silencing mankind. Were an opinion a personal possession of no value except to the owner; if to be obstructed in the enjoyment of it were simply a private injury, it would make some difference whether the injury was inflicted only on a few persons or on many. But the peculiar evil of silencing the expression of an opinion is that it is robbing the human race; posterity as well as the existing generation; those who dissent from the opinion, still more than those who hold it.

If the opinion is right, they are deprived of the opportunity of exchanging error for truth: if wrong, they lose, what is almost as great a benefit, the clearer perception and livelier impression of truth, produced by its collision with error.

It is necessary to consider separately these two hypotheses, each of which has a distinct branch of the argument corresponding to it. We can never be sure that the opinion we were endeavoring to stifle is a false opinion; and if we are sure, stifling it would be an evil still.

First: the opinion which it is attempted to suppress by authority may possibly be true. Those who desire to suppress it of course deny its truth; but they are not infallible. They have no authority to decide the question for all mankind, and exclude every other person from the means of judging. To refuse a hearing to an opinion, because they are sure that it is false, is to assume that *their* certainty is the same thing as *absolute* certainty. All silencing of discussion is an assumption of infallibility. Its condemnation may be allowed to rest on this common argument, not the worse for being common.

Unfortunately for the good sense of mankind, the fact of their fallibility is far from carrying the weight in their practical judgment, which is always allowed to it in theory; for while every one well knows himself to be fallible, few think it necessary to take any precautions against their own fallibility, or admit the supposition that any opinion, of which they feel very certain, may be one of the examples of the error to which they acknowledge themselves to be liable. . . .

Let us now pass to the second division of the argument, and dismissing the supposition that any of the received opinions may be false, let us assume them to be true, and examine into the worth of the manner in which they are likely to be held, when their truth is not freely and openly canvassed. However unwillingly a person who has a strong opinion may admit the possibility that his opinion may be false, he ought to be moved by the consideration that however true it may be, if it is not fully, frequently, and fearlessly discussed, it will be held as a dead dogma, not a living truth.

There is a class of persons (happily not quite so numerous as formerly) who think it enough if a person assents undoubtingly to what they think true, though he has no knowledge whatever of the grounds of the opinion, and could not make a tenable defense of it against the most superficial objections. Such persons, if they can once get their creed taught from authority, naturally think that no good, and some harm, comes of its being allowed to be questioned. Where their influence prevails, they make it nearly impossible for the received opinion to be rejected wisely and considerately, though it may still be rejected rashly and ignorantly; for to shut out discussion entirely is seldom possible, and when it once gets in, beliefs, not grounded on conviction are apt to give way before the slightest semblance of an argument. Waiving, however, this possibility—assuming that the true opinion abides in the mind, but abides as a prejudice, a belief independent of, and proof against, argument—this is not the way in which truth ought to be held by a rational being. This is not knowing the truth. Truth, thus held, is but one superstition the more accidentally clinging to the words which enunciate a truth. . . .

Not only the grounds of the opinion are forgotten in the absence of discussion, but too often the meaning of the opinion itself. The words which convey it, cease to suggest ideas, or suggest only a small portion of those they were originally employed to communicate. Instead of a vivid conception and a living belief, there remain only a few phrases retained by rote; or, if any part, the shell and husk only of the meaning is retained, the finer essence being lost. The great chapter in human history which this fact occupies and fills, cannot be too earnestly studied and meditated on.

It is illustrated in the experience of almost all ethical doctrines and religious creeds. They are all full of meaning and vitality to those who originate them, and to the direct disciples of the originators. Their meaning continues to be felt in undiminished strength, and is perhaps brought out into even fuller consciousness, so long as the struggle lasts to give the doctrine of creed an ascendancy over other creeds. At last it either prevails, and becomes the general opinion, or its progress stops; it keeps possession of the ground it has gained, but ceases to spread further. When either of these results has become apparent, controversy on the subject flags, and gradually dies away. The doctrine has taken its place, if not as a received opinion, as one of the admitted sects or divisions of opinion: those who hold it have generally inherited, not adopted it; and conversion from one of these doctrines to another, being now an exceptional fact, occupies little place in the thoughts of their professors. Instead of being, as at first, constantly on the alert either to defend themselves against the world, or to bring the world over to them, they have subsided into acquiescence, and neither listen, when they can help it, to arguments against their creed, nor trouble dissentients (if there be such) with arguments in its favor. From this time may usually be dated the decline in the living power of the doctrine. . . .

It still remains to speak of one of the principal causes which make diversity of opinion advantageous, and will continue to do so until mankind shall have entered a stage of intellectual advancement which at present seems at an incalculable distance. We have hitherto considered only two possibilities: that the received opinion may be false, and some other opinion, consequently, true; or that, the received opinion being true, a conflict with the opposite error is essential to a clear apprehension and deep feeling of its truth. But there is a commoner case than either of these; when the conflicting doctrines, instead of being one true and the other false, share the truth between them; and the nonconforming opinion is needed to supply the remainder of the truth, of which the received doctrine embodies only a part. Popular opinions, on subjects not palpable to sense, are often true, but seldom or never the whole truth. They are part of the truth; sometimes a greater, sometimes a smaller part, but exaggerated, distorted, and disjoined from the truths by which they ought to be accompanied and limited. Heretical opinions, on the other hand, are generally some of these suppressed and neglected truths, bursting the bonds which kept them down, and either seeking reconciliation with the truth contained in the common opinion, or fronting it as enemies, and setting themselves up, with similar exclusiveness, as the whole truth. The latter case is hitherto the most frequent, as, in the human mind, one-sidedness has always been the rule, and many-sidedness the exception. Hence, even in revolutions of opinion, one part of the truth usually sets while another rises. Even progress, which ought to superadd, for the most part only sub-stitutes, one partial and incomplete truth for another; improvement con-sisting chiefly in this, that the new fragment of truth is more wanted, more adapted to the needs of the time, than that which it displaces. Such being the partial character of prevailing opinions, even when resting on a true foundation, every opinion which embodies somewhat of the portion of truth which the common opinion omits, ought to be considered precious, with what-ever amount of error and confusion that truth may be blended. No sober judge of human affairs will feel bound to be indignant because those who force on our notice truths which we should otherwise have overlooked, overlook some of those which we see. Rather, he will think that so long as popular truth is one-sided, it is more desirable than otherwise that unpopular truth should have one-sided asserters too; such being usually the most energetic, and the most likely to compel reluctant attention to the fragment of wisdom which they proclaim as if it were the whole. . . .

In politics, again, it is almost a commonplace, that a party of order or stability, and a party of progress or reform, are both necessary elements of a healthy state of political life; until the one or the other shall have so enlarged its mental grasp as to be a party equally of order and of progress, knowing and distinguishing what is fit to be preserved from what ought to be swept away. Each of these modes of thinking derives its utility from the deficiencies of the other; but it is in a great measure the opposition of the other that keeps each within the limits of reason and sanity. Unless opinions favorable to democracy and to aristocracy, to property and to equality, to cooperation and to competition, to luxury and to abstinence, to sociality and individuality, to liberty and discipline, and all the other standing antagonisms of practical life, are expressed with equal freedom, and enforced and defended with equal talent and energy, there is no chance of both elements obtaining their due; one scale is sure to go up, and the other down. Truth, in the great practical concerns of life, is so much a question of the reconciling and com-bining of opposites, that very few have minds sufficiently capacious and impartial to make the adjustment with an approach to correctness, and it has to be made by the rough process of a struggle between combatants fighting under hostile banners. On any of the great open questions just enumerated, if either of the two opinions has a better claim than the other, not merely to be tolerated, but to be encouraged and countenanced, it is the one which happens at the particular time and place to be in a minority. That is the opinion which, for the time being, represents the neglected interests, the side of human well-being which is in danger of obtaining less than its share.

I am aware that there is not, in this country, any intolerance of differences of opinion on most of these topics. They are adduced to show, by admitted and multiplied examples, the universality of the fact, that only through diversity of opinion is there, in the existing state of human intellect, a chance of fair play to all sides of the truth. When there are persons to be found, who form an exception to the apparent unanimity of the world on any subject, even if the world is in the right, it is always probable that dissentients have something worth hearing to say for themselves, and that truth would lose something by their silence.

45. NEITHER BLIND OBEDIENCE NOR UNCIVIL DISOBEDIENCE

SIDNEY HOOK

Sidney Hook (1902–   ) is professor of philosophy at New York University and author of numerous books and articles in political philosophy, especially on Marxism and civil liberties.

. . . The line between civil and uncivil disobedience is not only an uncertain and wavering one in practice; in some quarters it has become so in theory. A recent prophet of the philosophy of the absurd, in recommending civil disobedience as a form of creative disorder in a democracy, cited as an illustration of it Shays's Rebellion, the 18th-century armed revolt in Massachusetts. And indeed some of the techniques of protesting American involvement in Vietnam have departed so far from traditional ways of civil disobedience as to make it likely that they are inspired by the same confusion between civil and uncivil disobedience.

All this has made focal the perennial problems of the nature and limits of the citizen's obligation to obey the law, of the relation between the authority of conscience and the authority of the state, of the rights and duties of a democratic moral man in an immoral democratic society. The classical writings on these questions have acquired a burning relevance to the political condition of man today. I propose briefly to clarify some of these problems.

To begin with, I wish to stress the point that there is no problem concerning "social protest" as such in a democracy. Our Bill of Rights was adopted not only to make protest possible but to facilitate it. The political logic, the very ethos of any democracy that professes to rest, no matter how indirectly, upon freely given consent *requires* that peaceful social protest be permitted—and not only permitted but *protected* from interference by those opposed to the protest, which means protected by the agencies of law enforcement.

Not social protest but *illegal* social protest constitutes our problem. It

From Sidney Hook, "Neither Blind Obedience Nor Uncivil Disobedience," *New York Times Magazine,* June 5, 1966. © 1966 by The New York Times Company. Reprinted by permission of the publisher.

raises the question of when, if ever, illegal protest is justified in a democratic society. It is of the first importance to bear in mind that we are raising the question as principled democrats in a democratic society. To urge that illegal social protests, motivated by exalted ideals, are sanctified in a democratic society by precedents like the Boston Tea Party, is to lapse into political illiteracy. For such actions occurred in societies in which those affected by unjust laws had no power peacefully to change them.

Further, many actions dubbed civilly disobedient by local authorities are strictly speaking not such at all. An action launched in violation of a local law or ordinance, and undertaken to test it, on the ground that the law itself violates state or Federal law, or launched in violation of a state law in the sincerely held belief that the state law outrages the Constitution, the supreme law of the land, is not civilly disobedient.

In large measure the sympathy with which the original sit-ins were received —especially the Freedom Rides, marches and demonstrations that flouted local Southern laws—was due to the conviction that they were constitutionally justified, in accordance with the heritage of freedom enshrined in the amendments, and enjoyed in other regions of the country. Practically everything the marchers did was sanctioned by the phrase of the First Amendment which upholds "the right of the people peaceably to assemble and to petition the Government for a redress of grievances." Actions of this kind may be wise or unwise, timely or untimely, but they are not civilly disobedient.

They become civilly disobedient when they are in deliberate violation of laws that have been enacted and sustained by the highest legislative and judicial bodies of the nation; e.g., tax laws, conscription laws, laws forbidding segregation in education, and discrimination in public accommodations and employment. Another class of examples consists of illegal social protest against local and state laws that clearly do not conflict with Federal law.

Once we grasp the proper issue, the question is asked with deceptive clarity: "Are we under an obligation in a democratic community *always* to obey an unjust law?"—to which Abraham Lincoln is supposed to have made the classic answer in an eloquent address on "The Perpetuation of Our Political Institutions," calling for absolute and religious obedience until the unjust law is repealed.

I said that this question is asked with deceptive clarity because Lincoln, judging by his other writings and the pragmatic cast of his basic philosophy, could never have subscribed to this absolutism or meant what he seemed literally to have said. Not only are we under no moral obligation *always* to obey unjust laws, we are under no moral obligation *always* to obey a just law. One can put it more strongly: sometimes it may be necessary in the interests of the greater good to violate a just or sensible law. A man who refused to violate a sensible traffic law in order to avoid a probably fatal accident would be a moral idiot. There are other values in the world besides legality or even justice, and sometimes they may be of overriding concern and weight. Everyone can imagine some situation in which the violation of some existing law is the lesser moral evil, but this does not invalidate recognition of our obligation to obey just laws.

Now, of course, there is a difference between disobeying a law which in general one approves of but whose application in a specific case seems wrong, and disobeying a law in *protest* against the injustice of the law itself. In the latter case, the disobedience is open and public; in the former, not. But if the grounds of disobedience in both cases are moral considerations, there is only a difference in degree between them. The rejection, therefore, of legal absolutism or the fetishism of legality—that one is never justified in violating any law in any circumstances—is a matter of common sense.

The implications drawn from this moral commonplace, however, by some ritualistic liberals are clearly absurd. For they have substituted for the absolutism of law something very close to the absolutism of individual conscience. Properly rejecting the view that the law must be obeyed in all circumstances no matter how unjust, they have taken the view that the law is to be obeyed only when the individual deems it just or when it does not outrage his conscience.

Fantastic comparisons are made between those who do not act on the dictates of their conscience and those who accepted and obeyed Hitler's laws. These comparisons completely disregard the systems of law involved, the presence or absence of legal alternatives of dissenting action, the differences in the behavior commanded, in degrees of complicity of guilt, in the moral costs and personal consequences of compliance, and other relevant matters.

It is commendable to recognize the primacy of morality to law but unless we recognize the centrality of intelligence to morality, we stumble with blind self-righteousness into moral disaster. Because, Kant to the contrary notwithstanding, it is not wrong sometimes to lie to save a human life; because it is not wrong sometimes to kill in defense to prevent many from being killed, it does not follow that the moral principles "Do not lie!" and "Do not kill!" are invalid. When more than one valid principle bears on a problem of moral experience, the very fact of their conflict means that not all of them can hold unqualifiedly. One of them must be denied.

But the point is that such negation or violation entails upon us the obligation of justifying it—and moral justification is a matter of reasons not of conscience. The burden of proof rests on the person violating the rule. Normally, we don't have to justify telling the truth. We do have to justify not telling the truth. Similarly with respect to the moral obligation of a democrat who breaches his political obligation to obey the laws of a democratic community. The resort to conscience is not enough. There must always be reasonable justification.

This is all the more true because just as we can, if challenged, give powerful reasons for the moral principle of truth-telling, so we can offer logically coercive grounds for the obligation of a democrat to obey the laws of a democracy. The grounds are many and they can be amplified beyond the passing mention we give them here. It is a matter of fairness, of social utility, of peace, of ordered progress, or redeeming an implicit commitment. But there is one point which has a particular relevance to the claims of those who counterpose to legal absolutism, the absolutism of conscience. There is the tendency, an empirically observable tendency, for public disobedience to law to spread from those who occupy high moral ground to those who dwell on low ground with consequent growth of disorder and insecurity. Disobedience in resisting fancied denial of free speech is followed by legal disobedience in behalf of filthy speech. Defiance of court orders in industrial disputes in which workers are unjustly victimized is followed by defiance of court orders in which the public is chiefly victimized.

Conscience by itself is not the measure of high or low moral ground. This is the work of reason. And where it functions properly the democratic process permits this resort to reason. If the man of conscience loses in the court of reason, why should he assume that the decision or the law is mistaken rather than the deliverances of his conscience?

The voice of conscience may sound loud and clear. But it may conflict not only with the law but with another man's conscience. Every conscientious objector to a law knows that at least one man's conscience is wrong, viz., the conscience of the man who asserts that *his* conscience tells him that he must not tolerate conscientious objectors. From this, if he is reasonable, the conscientious objector should conclude that when he hears the voice of conscience, he is hearing not the voice of God but the voice of a finite, limited man in this time and in this place, that conscience is neither a special nor an infallible organ of apprehending moral truth, that conscience without conscientiousness, conscience which does not cap the process of critical reflective morality, is likely to be a prejudice masquerading as a First Principle or a Mandate from Heaven.

The mark of an enlightened democracy is, as far as its security allows, to respect the religious commitment of a citizen who believes, on grounds of conscience or any other ground, that his relation to God involves duties superior to those arising from any human relation. It, therefore, exempts him from his duty as a citizen to protect his country.

But the mark of the genuine conscientious objector in a democracy is to respect the democratic process. He does not use his exemption as a political weapon to coerce where he has failed to convince or persuade. Having failed to influence national policy by rational means *within* the law, in the political processes open to him in a free society, he cannot justifiably try to defeat that policy by resorting to obstructive techniques *outside* the law—and still remain a democrat.

It is one thing on grounds of conscience or religion to plead exemption from the duty of serving one's country when drafted. It is quite another to adopt harassing techniques to prevent others from volunteering or responding to the call of duty. It is one thing to oppose American involvement in Vietnam by teach-ins, petitions, electoral activity. It is quite another to attempt to stop troop trains; to take possession of the premises of draft boards where policies are not made; to urge recruits to sabotage their assignments and to feign illness in order to win discharge.

The first class of actions falls within the sphere of legitimate social protest; the second class is implicitly insurrectionary since it is directed against the authority of a democratic government which it seeks to overthrow not by argument and discussion but by resistance—albeit passive resistance.

Nonetheless, since we have rejected legal absolutism we must face the possibility that individuals on ethical grounds may in protest refuse to obey some law they regard as uncommonly immoral or uncommonly foolish. If they profess to be democrats, their behavior must scrupulously respect the following conditions:

It must be nonviolent—peaceful not only in form but in actuality. After all, the protesters are seeking to dramatize a great evil that the community allegedly has been unable to overcome because of complacency or moral weakness. They must therefore avoid the guilt of imposing hardship or harm on others who in the nature of the case can hardly be responsible for the situation under protest.

Second, resort to civil disobedience is never morally legitimate where other methods of remedying the evil complained of are available. Existing grievance procedures should be used. No grievance procedures were available to the Southern Negroes. The courts often shared the prejudices of the community and offered little relief, often not even minimal protection. But such procedures *are* available in the areas of industry and education. For example, where charges against students are being heard, such procedures may result in the dismissal of the charges, not the students. Or the faculty on appeal may decide to suspend the rules rather than the students. To jump the gun to civil disobedience in by-passing these procedures is tell-tale evidence that those who are calling the shots are after other game than preserving the rights of students.

Third, those who resort to civil disobedience are duty bound to accept the legal sanctions and punishments imposed by the laws. Attempts to evade and escape them really involve not only a betrayal of the community—Socrates' argument in the Crito is especially valid where democratic political premises obtain—they erode the moral foundations of civil disobedience itself. The rationale of the protesters is the hope that the pain and hurt and indignity they voluntarily accept will stir their fellow citizens to compassion, open their minds to second thoughts, and move them to undertake the necessary healing action. But when we observe the heroics of defiance being followed by the dialects of legal evasion, we question the sincerity of the action.

Fourth, civil disobedience is unjustified if a major moral issue is not clearly at stake. Differences about negotiable details that can easily be settled with a little patience should not be fanned into a blaze of illegal opposition.

Fifth, where intelligent men of goodwill and character differ on large and complex moral issues, discussion and agitation are more appropriate than civilly disobedient action. E.g., those who feel strongly about animal rights and regard the consumption of animal flesh as morally evil would have a just cause for civil disobedience if their freedom to obtain other food was threatened. But they would have no moral right to resort to similar action to prevent their fellow-citizens from consuming meat. (Similarly, with fluoridation.)

Sixth, where civil disobedience is undertaken, there must be some rhyme and reason in the time, place and targets selected. If one is convinced, as I am not, that the Board of Education in New York City is remiss in its policy of desegregation, what is the point of dumping garbage on bridges to produce traffic jams that seriously discomfort commuters who have not the remotest connection with educational policies in New York? Such action can only obstruct the progress of desegregation in the communities of Long Island. Gandhi, who inspired the civil-disobedience movement in the 20th century, was a better technician than many who invoke his name but ignore his teachings. When he organized his campaign against the salt tax, he marched with his followers to the sea to make salt. He did not hold up food trains or tie up traffic.

Finally, there is such a thing as historical timing. Democrats who resort to civil disobedience must ask themselves whether the cumulative consequences of their action may in the existing climate of opinion undermine the peace and order on which the effective exercise of other human rights depend. This is a cost which one may be willing to pay but which must be taken into the reckoning.

All of these considerations are cautionary, not categorical. We have ruled out only two positions—blind obedience to any and all laws in a democracy, and unreflective violation of laws at the behest of individual consciences. Between these two obviously unacceptable extremes, there is a spectrum of views which shade into one another. Intelligent persons can differ on their application to specific situations. These differences will reflect different assessments of the historical mood of a culture, of the proper timing of protest and acquiescence, and of what the most desirable emphasis and direction of our teaching should be in order to extend "the blessings of liberty" as we preserve "domestic tranquillity."

Without essaying the role of a prophet, here is my reading of the needs of the present. It seems to me that the Civil Rights Act of 1964 and the Voting Acts of 1965 mark a watershed in the history of social and civil protest in the U.S. Upon their enforcement a great many things we hold dear depend, especially those causes in behalf of which in the last decade so many movements of social protest were launched. . . .

46. DENNIS v. UNITED STATES

. . . The obvious purpose of the statute is to protect existing government, not from change by peaceable, lawful, and constitutional means, but from change by violence, revolution and terrorism. That it is within the power of the Congress to protect the government of the United States from armed rebellion is a proposition which requires little discussion. Whatever theoretical merit there may be to the argument that there is a "right" to rebellion against dictatorial governments is without force where the existing structure of the government provides for peaceful and orderly change. We reject any principle

341 U.S. 494 (1951).

of governmental helplessness in the face of preparation for revolution, which principle, carried to its logical conclusion, must lead to anarchy. No one could conceive that it is not within the power of Congress to prohibit acts intended to overthrow the government by force and violence. The question with which we are concerned here is not whether Congress has such *power,* but whether the *means* which it has employed conflict with the First and Fifth Amendments to the Constitution.

One of the bases for the contention that the means which Congress has employed are invalid takes the form of an attack on the face of the statute on the grounds that by its term it prohibits academic discussion of the merits of Marxism-Leninism, that it stifles ideas and is contrary to all concepts of a free speech and a free press. . . .

The very language of the Smith Act negates the interpretation which petitioners would have us impose on that Act. It is directed at advocacy, not discussion. Thus, the trial judge properly charged the jury that they could not convict if they found that petitioners did "no more than pursue peaceful studies and discussions or teaching and advocacy in the realm of ideas." He further charged that it was not unlawful to "conduct in an American college and university a course explaining the philosophical theories set forth in the books which have been placed in evidence." Such a charge is in strict accord with the statutory language, and illustrates the meaning to be placed on those words. Congress did not intend to eradicate the free discussion of political theories, to destroy the traditional rights of Americans to discuss and evaluate ideas without fear of governmental sanction. Rather Congress was concerned with the very kind of activity in which the evidence showed these petitioners engaged. . . .

We pointed out in *Douds, supra,* that the basis of the First Amendment is the hypothesis that speech can rebut speech, propaganda will answer propaganda, free debate of ideas will result in the wisest governmental policies. It is for this reason that this Court has recognized the inherent value of free discourse. An analysis of the leading cases in this Court which have involved direct limitations on speech, however, will demonstrate that both the majority of the Court and the dissenters in particular cases have recognized that this is not an unlimited, unqualified right, but that the societal value of speech must, on occasion, be subordinated to other values and considerations.

No important case involving free speech was decided by this Court prior to *Schenck v. United States.* . . . Writing for a unanimous Court, Justice Holmes stated that the "question in every case is whether the words used are used in such circumstances and are of such a nature as to create a clear and present danger that they will bring about the substantive evils that Congress has a right to prevent."

The rule we deduce . . . is that where an offense is specified by a statute in nonspeech or nonpress terms, a conviction relying upon speech or press as evidence of violation may be sustained only when the speech or publication created a "clear and present danger" of attempting or accomplishing the prohibited crime, e.g., interference with enlistment. . . . Speech is not an absolute, above and beyond control by the legislature when its judgment, subject to review here, is that certain kinds of speech are so undesirable as to warrant criminal sanction. Nothing is more certain in modern society than the principle that there are no absolutes, that a name, a phrase, a standard has meaning only when associated with the considerations which gave birth to the nomenclature. To those who would paralyze our government in the face of impending threat by encasing it in a semantic strait jacket we must reply that all concepts are relative.

In this case we are squarely presented with the application of the "clear and present danger" test, and must decide what that phrase imports. We first note that many of the cases in which this Court has reversed convictions by use of this or similar tests have been based on the fact that the interest which the State was attempting to protect was itself too insubstantial to warrant restriction of speech. . . .

Overthrow of the government by force and violence is certainly a substantial enough interest for the government to limit speech. Indeed, this is the ultimate value of any society, for if a society cannot protect its very structure from armed internal attack, it must follow that no subordinate value can be protected. If, then, this interest may be protected, the literal problem which is presented is what has been meant by the use of the phrase "clear and present danger" of the utterances bringing about the evil within the power of Congress to punish.

Obviously, the words cannot mean that before the government may act, it must wait until the *putsch* is about to be executed, the plans have been laid and the signal is awaited. If government is aware that a group aiming at its overthrow is attempting to indoctrinate its members and to commit them to a course whereby they will strike when the leaders feel the circumstances permit, action by the government is required. The argument that there is no need for government to concern itself, for government is strong, it possesses ample powers to put down a rebellion, it may defeat the revolution with ease needs no answer. For that is not the question. Certainly an attempt to overthrow the government by force, even though doomed from the outset because of inadequate numbers or power of the revolutionists, is a sufficient evil for Congress to prevent. The damage which such attempts create both physically and politically to a nation makes it impossible to measure the validity in terms of the probability of success, or the immediacy of a successful attempt.

In the instant case the trial judge charged the jury that they would not convict unless they found that petitioners intended to overthrow the government "as speedily as circumstances would permit." This does not mean, and could not properly mean, that they would not strike until there was certainty of success. What was meant was that the revolutionists would strike when they thought the time was ripe. We must therefore reject the contention that success or probability of success is the criterion.

Chief Judge Learned Hand, writing for the majority below, interpreted the phrase as follows: "In each case (courts) must ask whether the gravity of the 'evil' discounted by its improbability, justifies such invasion of free speech as is necessary to avoid the danger." We adopt this statement of the rule. As articulated by Chief Justice Hand, it is as succinct and inclusive as any other we might devise at this time. It takes into consideration those factors which we deem relevant, and relates their significances. More we cannot expect from words.

Likewise, we are in accord with the court below, which affirmed the trial court's finding that the requisite danger existed. The mere fact that from the period 1945 to 1948 petitioners' activities did not result in an attempt to overthrow the government by force and violence is of course no answer to the fact that there was a group that was ready to make the attempt. The formation by petitioners of such a highly organized conspiracy, with rigidly disciplined members subject to call when the leaders, these petitioners, felt that the time had come for action, coupled with the inflammable nature of world conditions, similar uprisings in other countries, and the touch-and-go nature of our relations with countries with whom petitioners were in the very least ideologically attuned, convince us that their convictions were justified on this score. And this analysis disposes of the contention that a conspiracy to advocate, as distinguished from the advocacy itself, cannot be constitutionally restrained, because it comprises only the preparation. It is the existence of the conspiracy which creates the danger. If the ingredients of the reaction are present, we cannot bind the government to wait until the catalyst is added. . . .

Petitioners intended to overthrow the government of the United States as speedily as the circumstances would permit. Their conspiracy to organize the Communist Party and to teach and advocate the overthrow of the government of the United States by force and violence created a "clear and present danger" of an attempt to overthrow the government by force and violence. They were properly and constitutionally convicted for violation of the Smith Act. The judgments of conviction are

Affirmed.

. . . Mr. JUSTICE FRANKFURTER, concurring in affirmance of the judgment.

The First Amendment categorically demands that "Congress shall make no law respecting an establishment of religion, or prohibiting the free exercise thereof; or abridging the freedom of speech, or of the press; or the right of the people peaceably to assemble, and to petition the government for a redress of grievances." The right of a man to think what he pleases, to write what he thinks, and to have his thoughts made available for others to hear or read has an engaging ring of universality. The Smith Act and this conviction under it no doubt restrict the exercise of free speech and assembly. Does that, without more, dispose of the matter?

Absolute rules would inevitably lead to absolute exceptions, and such exceptions would eventually corrode the rules. The demands of free speech in a democratic society as well as the interest in national security are better served by candid and informed weighing of the competing interests, within the confines of the judicial process, than by announcing dogmas too inflexible for the non-Euclidian problems to be solved.

But how are competing interests to be assessed? Since they are not subject to quantitative ascertainment, the issue necessarily resolves itself into asking, who is to make the adjustment?—who is to balance the relevant factors and ascertain which interest is in the circumstances to prevail? Full responsibility for the choice cannot be given to the courts. Courts are not representative bodies. They are not designed to be a good reflex of a democratic society. Their judgment is best informed, and therefore most dependable, within narrow limits. Their essential quality is detachment, founded on independence. History teaches that the independence of the judiciary is jeopardized when courts become embroiled in the passions of the day and assume primary responsibility in choosing between competing political, economic and social pressures.

Primary responsibility for adjusting the interests which compete in the situation before us of necessity belongs to the Congress. The nature of the power to be exercised by this Court has been delineated in decisions not charged with the emotional appeal of situations such as that now before us. We are to set aside the judgment of those whose duty it is to legislate only if there is no reasonable basis for it.

First.—Free-speech cases are not an exception to the principle that we are not legislators, that direct policy-making is not our province. How best to reconcile competing interests is the business of legislatures, and the balance they strike is a judgment not to be displaced by ours, but to be respected unless outside the pale of fair judgment. . . .

Second.—A survey of the relevant decisions indicates that the results which we have reached are on the whole those that would ensue from careful weighing of conflicting interests. The complex issues presented by regulation of speech in public places, by picketing, and by legislation prohibiting advocacy of crime have been resolved by scrutiny of many factors besides the imminence and gravity of the evil threatened.

The matter has been well summarized by a reflective student of the Court's work. "The truth is that the clear-and-present-danger test is an oversimplified judgment unless it takes account also of a number of other factors: the relative seriousness of the danger in comparison with the value of the occasion for speech or political activity; the availability of more moderate controls than those which the state has imposed; and perhaps the specific intent with which the speech or activity is launched. No matter how rapidly we utter the phrase 'clear and present danger,' or how closely we hyphenate the words, they are not a substitute for the weighing of values. They tend to convey a delusion of certitude when what is most certain is the complexity of the strands in the web of freedoms which the judge must disentangle." . . .

Third.—Not every type of speech occupies the same position on the scale of values. There is no substantial public interest in permitting certain kinds of utterances: "the lewd and obscene, the profane, the libelous, and the insulting or 'fighting' words—those which by their very utterance inflict injury or tend to incite an immediate breach of the peace." We have frequently indicated that the interest in protecting speech depends on the circumstances of the occasion. It is pertinent to the decision before us to consider where on the scale of values we have in the past placed the type of speech now claiming constitutional immunity.

The defendants have been convicted of conspiring to organize a party of persons who advocate the overthrow of the government by force and violence. The jury has found that the object of the conspiracy is advocacy as "a rule or principle of action," "by language reasonably and ordinarily calculated to incite persons to such action," and with the intent to cause the overthrow "as speedily as circumstances would permit."

On any scale of values which we have hitherto recognized, speech of this sort ranks low.

Throughout our decisions there has recurred a distinction between the statement of an idea which may prompt its hearers to take unlawful action, and advocacy that such action be taken. The distinction has its root in the conception of the common law that a person who procures another to do an act is responsible for that act as though he had done it himself. . . . We frequently have distinguished protected forms of expression from statements which "incite to violence and crime and threaten the overthrow of organized government by unlawful means."

The object of the conspiracy before us is clear enough that the chance of error in saying that the defendants conspired to advocate rather than to express ideas is slight. MR. JUSTICE DOUGLAS quite properly points out that the conspiracy before us is not a conspiracy to overthrow the government. But it would be equally wrong to treat it as a seminar in political theory.

These general considerations underlie decision of the case before us.

On the one hand is the interest in security. The Communist Party was not designed by these defendants as an ordinary political party. For the circumstances of its organization, its aims and methods, and the relation of the defendants to its organization and aims we are concluded by the jury's verdict. The jury found that the Party rejects the basic premise of our political system—that change is to be brought about by nonviolent constitutional process. The jury found that the Party advocates the theory that there is a duty and necessity to overthrow the government by force and violence. It found that the Party entertains and promotes this view, not as a prophetic insight or as a bit of unworldly speculation, but as a program for winning adherents and as a policy to be translated into action. . . .

It is not for us to decide how we would adjust the clash of interests which this case presents were the primary responsibility for reconciling it ours. Congress has determined that the danger created by advocacy of overthrow justifies the ensuing restriction on freedom of speech. The determination was made after due deliberation, and the seriousness of the congressional purpose is attested by the volume of legislation passed to effectuate the same ends.

All the Court says is that Congress was not forbidden by the Constitution to pass this enactment and a prosecution under it may be brought against a conspiracy such as the one before us. . . .

Mr. JUSTICE DOUGLAS, dissenting.

If this were a case where those who claimed protection under the First

Amendment were teaching the techniques of sabotage, the assassination of the President, the filching of documents from public files, the planting of bombs, the art of street warfare, and the like, I would have no doubts. The freedom to speak is not absolute; the teaching of methods of terror and other seditious conduct should be beyond the pale along with obscenity and immorality. This case was argued as if those were the facts. The argument imported much seditious conduct into the record. That is easy and it has popular appeal, for the activities of Communists in plotting and scheming against the free world are common knowledge.

But the fact is that no such evidence was introduced at the trial. There is a statute which makes a seditious conspiracy unlawful. Petitioners, however, were not charged with a "conspiracy to overthrow" the government. They were charged with a conspiracy to form a party and groups and assemblies of people who teach and advocate the overthrow of our government by force or violence and with a conspiracy to advocate and teach its overthrow by force and violence. It may well be that indoctrination in the techniques of terror to destroy the government would be indictable under either statute. But the teaching which is condemned here is of a different character.

So far as the present record is concerned, what petitioners did was to organize people to teach and themselves teach the Marxist-Leninist doctrine contained chiefly in four books: *Foundations of Leninism* by Stalin (1924), *The Communist Manifesto* by Marx and Engels (1848), *State and Revolution* by Lenin (1917), *History of the Communist Party of the Soviet Union* (B) (1939).

Those books are to the Soviet Communism what *Mein Kampf* was to Nazism. If they are understood, the ugliness of Communism is revealed, its deceit and cunning are exposed, the nature of its activities becomes apparent, and the chances of its success less likely. That is not, of course, the reason why petitioners chose these books for their classrooms. They are fervent Communists to whom these volumes are gospel. They preached the creed with the hope that some day it would be acted upon.

The opinion of the Court does not outlaw these texts nor condemn them to the fire, as the Communists do literature offensive to their creed. But if the books themselves are not outlawed, if they can lawfully remain on library shelves, by what reasoning does their use in a classroom become a crime? It would not be a crime under the Act to introduce these books to a class, though that would be teaching what the creed of violent overthrow of the government is. The Act, as construed, requires the element of intent—that those who teach the creed believe in it. That is to make freedom of speech turn not on *what is said*, but on the *intent* with which it is said. Once we start down that road we enter territory dangerous to the liberties of every citizen. . . .

Free speech has occupied an exalted position because of the high service it has given our society. Its protection is essential to the very existence of a democracy. The airing of ideas releases pressures which otherwise might become destructive. When ideas compete in the market for acceptance, full and free discussion exposes the false and they gain few adherents. Full and free discussion even of ideas we hate encourages the testing of our own prejudices and preconceptions. Full and free discussion keeps a society from becoming stagnant and unprepared for the stresses and strains that work to tear all civilizations apart.

Full and free discussion has indeed been the first article of our faith. We have founded our political system on it. It has been the safeguard of every religious, political, philosophical, economic, and racial group amongst us. We have counted on it to keep us from embracing what is cheap and false; we have trusted the common sense of our people to choose the doctrine true to our genius and to reject the rest. This has been the one single outstanding tenet that has made our institutions the symbol of freedom and equality. We have deemed it more costly to liberty to suppress a despised minority than to let them vent their spleen. We have above all else feared the political censor. We have wanted a land where our people can be exposed to all the diverse creeds and cultures of the world.

There comes a time when even speech loses its constitutional immunity. Speech innocuous one year may at another time fan such destructive flames that it must be halted in the interests of the safety of the Republic. That is the meaning of the clear and present danger test. When conditions are so critical that there will be no time to avoid the evil that the speech threatens, it is time to call a halt. Otherwise, free speech which is the strength of the nation will be the cause of its destruction.

Yet free speech is the rule, not the exception. The restraint to be constitutional must be based on more than fear, on more than passionate opposition against the speech, on more than a revolted dislike for its contents. . . .

Communism in the world scene is no bogey-man; but Communists as a political faction or party in this country plainly is. Communism has been so thoroughly exposed in this country that it has been crippled as a political force. Free speech has destroyed it as an effective political party. It is inconceivable that those who went up and down this country preaching the doctrine of revolution which petitioners espouse would have any success. In days of trouble and confusion when bread lines were long, when the unemployed walked the streets, when people were starving, the advocates of a short-cut by revolution might have a chance to gain adherents. But today there are no such conditions. The country is not in despair; the people know Soviet Communism; the doctrine of Soviet revolution is exposed in all of its ugliness and the American people want none of it.

How it can be said that there is a clear and present danger that this advocacy will succeed is, therefore, a mystery. Some nations less resilient than the United States, where illiteracy is high and where democratic traditions are only budding, might have to take drastic steps and jail these men for merely speaking the creed. But in America they are miserable merchants of unwanted ideas; their wares remain unsold. The fact that their ideas are abhorrent does not make them powerful. . . .

The First Amendment provides that "Congress shall make no law . . . abridging the freedom of speech." The Constitution provides no exception. This does not mean, however, that the nation need hold its hand until it is in such weakened condition that there is no time to protect itself from incitement to revolution. Seditious conduct can always be punished. But the command of the First Amendment is so clear that we should not allow Congress to call a halt to free speech except in the extreme case of peril from the speech itself.

The First Amendment makes confidence in the common sense of our people and in their maturity of judgment the great postulate of our democracy. Its philosophy is that violence is rarely, if ever, stopped by denying civil liberties to those advocating resort to force. The First Amendment reflects the philosophy of Jefferson "that it is time enough for the rightful purposes of civil government for its officers to interfere when principles break out into overt acts against peace and good order." The political censor has no place in our public debates. Unless and until extreme and necessitous circumstances are shown our aim should be to keep speech unfettered and to allow the processes of law to be invoked only when the provocateurs among us move from speech to action. . . .

47. DECLARATION OF INDEPENDENCE

THOMAS JEFFERSON ET AL.

When, in the Course of human events, it becomes necessary for one people to dissolve the political bonds which have connected them with another, and to assume, among the Powers of the earth the separate and equal station to which the Laws of Nature and of Nature's God entitle them, a decent respect to the opinions of mankind requires that they should declare the causes which impel them to the separation.

We hold these truths to be self-evident, that all men are created equal, that they are endowed by their Creator with certain unalienable Rights, that among these are Life, Liberty, and the pursuit of Happiness. That to secure these rights, Governments are instituted among Men, deriving their just Powers from the consent of the governed. That whenever any Form of Government becomes destructive of these ends, it is the Right of the People to alter or to abolish it, and to institute new Government, laying its foundation on such Principles, and organizing its Powers in such form as to them shall seem most likely to effect their Safety and Happiness. Prudence, indeed, will dictate that Governments long established should not be changed for light and transient causes; and accordingly all experience hath shewn, that mankind are more disposed to suffer, while evils are sufferable, than to right themselves by abolishing the forms to which they are accustomed. But when a long train of abuses and usurpations, pursuing invariably the same Object evinces a design to reduce them under absolute Despotism, it is their right, it is their duty, to throw off such Government, and to provide new Guards for their future Security. Such has been the patient sufferance of these Colonies; and such is now the necessity which constrains them to alter their former Systems of Government. . . .

ON REBELLION

THOMAS JEFFERSON

The British ministry have so long hired their gazetteers to repeat and model into every form lies about our being in anarchy, that the world has at length believed them, the English nation has believed them, the ministers themselves have come to believe them, and what is more wonderful, we have believed them ourselves. Yet where does this anarchy exist? Where did it ever exist, except in the single instance of Massachusetts? And can history produce an instance of rebellion so honorably conducted? I say nothing of its motives. They were founded in ignorance, not wickedness. God forbid we should ever be twenty years without such a rebellion. The people cannot be all, and always, well informed. The part which is wrong will be discontented in proportion to the importance of the facts they misconceive. If they remain quiet under such misconceptions it is a lethargy, the forerunner of death to the public liberty. We have had thirteen states independent for eleven years. There has been one rebellion. That comes to one rebellion in a century and a half, for each state. What country before ever existed a century and a half without a rebellion? And what country can preserve its liberties if their rulers are not warned from time to time that their people preserve the spirit of resistance? Let them take arms. The remedy is to set them right as to facts, pardon and pacify them. What signify a few lives lost in a century or two? The tree of liberty must be refreshed from time to time with the blood of Patriots and tyrants. It is its natural manure.

Letter to Col. W. S. Smith.

48. LETTER FROM BIRMINGHAM CITY JAIL

MARTIN LUTHER KING, JR.

Martin Luther King, Jr., (1929–1968) was educated at Morehouse College, Crozer Theological Seminary, and Boston University, at which he received his Ph.D. He was president of the Southern Christian Leadership Conference at the time of his assassination.

. . . You may well ask, "Why direct action? Why sit-ins, marches, etc.? Isn't negotiation a better path?" You are exactly right in your call for negotiation. Indeed, this is the purpose of direct action. Nonviolent direct action seeks to create such a crisis and establish such creative tension that a community that has constantly refused to negotiate is forced to confront the issue. It seeks so to dramatize the issue that it can no longer be ignored.

I just referred to the creation of tension as a part of the work of the nonviolent resister. This may sound rather shocking. But I must confess that I am not afraid of the word tension. I have earnestly worked and preached against violent tension, but there is a type of constructive nonviolent tension that is necessary for growth. Just as Socrates felt that it was necessary to create a tension in the mind so that individuals could rise from the bondage of myths and half-truths to the unfettered realm of creative analysis and objective appraisal, we must see the need of having nonviolent gadflies to create the kind of tension in society that will help men rise from the dark depths of prejudice and racism to the majestic heights of understanding and brotherhood. So the purpose of the direct action is to create a situation so crisis-packed that it will inevitably open the door to negotiation. We, therefore, concur with you in your call for negotiation. Too long has our beloved Southland been bogged down in the tragic attempt to live in monologue rather than dialogue. . . .

My friends, I must say to you that we have not made a single gain in civil rights without determined legal and nonviolent pressure. History is the long and tragic story of the fact that privileged groups seldom give up their privileges voluntarily. Individuals may see the moral light and voluntarily give up their unjust posture; but as Reinhold Niebuhr has reminded us, groups are more immoral than individuals.

We know through painful experience that freedom is never voluntarily given by the oppressor; it must be demanded by the oppressed. Frankly I have never yet engaged in a direct action movement that was "well timed," according to the timetable of those who have not suffered unduly from the disease of segregation. For years now I have heard the word "Wait!" It rings in the ear of every Negro with a piercing familiarity. This "wait" has almost always meant "never." It has been a tranquilizing Thalidomide, relieving the emotional stress for a moment, only to give birth to an ill-formed infant of frustration. We must come to see with the distinguished jurist of yesterday that "justice too long delayed is justice denied." We have waited for more than 340 years for our constitutional and God-given rights. The nations of Asia and Africa are moving with jet-like speed toward the goal of political independence, and we still creep at horse-and-buggy pace toward the gaining of a cup of coffee at a lunch counter. . . .

You express a great deal of anxiety over our willingness to break laws. This is certainly a legitimate concern. Since we so diligently urge people to obey the Supreme Court's decision of 1954 outlawing segregation in the public schools, it is rather strange and paradoxical to find us consciously breaking laws. One may well ask, "How can you advocate breaking some laws and obeying others?" The answer is found in the fact that there are two types of laws: There are *just* laws and there are *unjust* laws. I would be the first to advocate obeying just laws. One has not only a legal but a moral responsibility to obey just laws. Conversely, one has a moral responsibility to disobey unjust laws. I would agree with Saint Augustine that "An unjust law is no law at all."

Now what is the difference between the two? How does one determine when a law is just or unjust? A just law is a man-made code that squares with the moral law or the law of God. An unjust law is a mode that is out of harmony with the moral law. To put it in the terms of Saint Thomas Aquinas, an unjust law is a human law that is not rooted in eternal and natural law. Any law that uplifts human personality is just. Any law that degrades human personality is unjust.

All segregation statutes are unjust because segregation distorts the soul and damages the personality. It gives the segregator a false sense of superiority and the segregated a false sense of inferiority. To use the words of Martin Buber, the great Jewish philosopher, segregation substitutes an "I-it" relationship for the "I-thou" relationship, and ends up relegating persons to the status of things. So segregation is not only politically, economically, and sociologically unsound, but it is morally wrong and sinful. Paul Tillich has said that sin is separation. Isn't segregation an existential expression of man's tragic separation, an expression of his awful estrangement, his terrible sinfulness? So I can urge men to obey the 1954 decision of the Supreme Court because it is morally right, and I can urge them to disobey segregation ordinances because they are morally wrong.

Let me give another example of just and unjust laws. An unjust law is a code that a majority inflicts on a minority that is not binding on itself. This is *difference* made legal. On the other hand a just law is a code that a majority compels a minority to follow that it is willing to follow itself. This is *sameness* made legal.

Let me give another explanation. An unjust law is a code inflicted upon a minority which that minority had no part in enacting or creating because it did not have the unhampered right to vote. Who can say the Legislature of Alabama which set up the segregation laws was democratically elected? Throughout the state of Alabama all types of conniving methods are used to prevent Negroes from becoming registered voters and there are some counties without a single Negro registered to vote despite the fact that the Negro constitutes a majority of the population. Can any law set up in such a state be considered democratically structured?

These are just a few examples of unjust and just laws. There are some instances when a law is just on its face but unjust in its application. For instance, I was arrested Friday on a charge of parading without a permit. Now there is nothing wrong with an ordinance which requires a permit for a parade, but when the ordinance is used to preserve segregation and to deny citizens the First Amendment privilege of peaceful assembly and peaceful protest, then it becomes unjust.

I hope you can see the distinction I am trying to point out. In no sense do I advocate evading or defying the law as the rabid segregationist would do. This would lead to anarchy. One who breaks an unjust law must do it *openly, lovingly* (not hatefully as the white mothers did in New Orleans when they were seen on television screaming "nigger, nigger, nigger") and with a willingness to accept the penalty. I submit that an individual who breaks a law that conscience tells him is unjust, and willingly accepts the penalty by staying in jail to arouse the conscience of the community over its injustice, is in reality expressing the very highest respect for law. . . .

I had hoped that the white moderate would understand that law and order exist for the purpose of establishing justice, and that when they fail to do this they become the dangerously structured dams that block the flow of social progress. I had hoped that the white moderate would understand that the present tension in the South is merely a necessary phase of the transition from an obnoxious negative peace, where the Negro passively accepted his unjust plight, to a substance-filled positive peace, where all men will respect the dignity and worth of human personality.

Actually, we who engage in nonviolent direct action are not the creators of tension. We merely bring to the surface the hidden tension that is already alive. We bring it out in the open where it can be seen and dealt with. Like a boil that can never be cured as long as it is covered up but must be opened with all its pus-flowing ugliness to the natural medicines of air and light, injustice must likewise be exposed, with all of the tension its exposing creates, to the light of human conscience and the air of national opinion before it can be cured.

In your statement you asserted that our actions, even though peaceful, must be condemned because they precipitate violence. But can this assertion be logically made? Isn't this like condemning the robbed man because his possession of money precipitated the evil act of robbery? Isn't this like condemning Socrates because his unswerving commitment to truth and his philosophical delvings precipitated the misguided popular mind to make him drink the hemlock? Isn't this like condemning Jesus because His unique God consciousness and never-ceasing devotion to His will precipitated the evil act of crucifixion? We must come to see, as Federal courts have consistently affirmed, that it is immoral to urge an individual to withdraw his efforts to gain his basic constitutional rights because the quest precipitates violence. Society must protect the robbed and punish the robber. . . .

I have tried to stand between these two forces saying that we need not follow the "do-nothingism" of the complacent or the hatred and despair of the black nationalist. There is the more excellent way of love and nonviolent protest. I'm grateful to God that, through the Negro church, the dimension of nonviolence entered our struggle. If this philosophy had not emerged I am convinced that by now many streets of the South would be flowing with floods of blood. And I am further convinced that if our white brothers dismiss us as "rabble rousers" and "outside agitators"—those of us who are working through the channels of nonviolent direct action—and refuse to support our nonviolent efforts, millions of Negroes, out of frustration and despair, will seek solace and security in black nationalist ideologies, a development that will lead inevitably to a frightening racial nightmare.

Oppressed people cannot remain oppressed forever. The urge for freedom will eventually come. This is what has happened to the American Negro. Something within has reminded him of his birthright of freedom; something without has reminded him that he can gain it. Consciously and unconsciously, he has been swept in by what the Germans call the *Zeitgeist,* and with his black brothers of Africa, and his brown and yellow brothers of Asia, South America, and the Caribbean, he is moving with a sense of cosmic urgency toward the promised land of racial justice. Recognizing this vital urge that has engulfed the Negro community, one should readily understand public demonstrations.

The Negro has many pent-up resentments and latent frustrations. He has to get them out. So let him march sometime; let him have his prayer pilgrimages to the city hall; understand why he must have sit-ins and freedom rides. If his repressed emotions do not come out in these nonviolent ways, they will come out in ominous expressions of violence. This is not a threat; it is a fact of history. So I have not said to my people, "Get rid of your discontent." But I have tried to say that this normal and healthy discontent can be channeled through the creative outlet of nonviolent direct action. Now this approach is being dismissed as extremist. I must admit that I was initially disappointed in being so categorized.

But as I continued to think about the matter I gradually gained a bit of satisfaction from being considered an extremist. Was not Jesus an extremist in love—"Love your enemies, bless them that curse you, pray for them that despitefully use you." Was not Amos an extremist for justice—"Let justice roll down like waters and righteousness like a mighty stream." Was not Paul an extremist for the Gospel of Jesus Christ—"I bear in my body the marks of the Lord Jesus." Was not Martin Luther an extremist—"Here I stand; I can do none other so help me God." Was not John Bunyan an extremist— "I will stay in jail to the end of my days before I make a butchery of my conscience." Was not Abraham Lincoln an extremist—"This nation cannot survive half slave and half free." Was not Thomas Jefferson an extremist— "We hold these truths to be self evident that all men are created equal."

So the question is not whether we will be extremist but what kind of extremist will we be. Will we be extremists for hate or will we be extremists for love? Will we be extremists for the preservation of injustice or will we be extremists for the cause of justice? In that dramatic scene on Calvary's hill three men were crucified. We must never forget that all three were crucified for the same crime—the crime of extremism. Two were extremists for immorality, and thus fell below their environment. The other, Jesus Christ, was an extremist for love, truth and goodness, and thereby rose above His environment. So, after all, maybe the South, the nation, and the world are in dire need of creative extremists. . . .

In spite of my shattered dreams of the past, I came to Birmingham with the hope that the white religious leadership of this community would see the justice of our cause and, with deep moral concern, serve as the channel through which our just grievances could get to the power structure. I had hoped that each of you would understand. But again I have been disappointed.

I have heard numerous religious leaders of the South call upon their worshippers to comply with a desegregation decision because it is the law, but I have longed to hear white ministers say, follow this decree because integration is morally right and the Negro is your brother. In the midst of blatant injustices inflicted upon the Negro, I have watched white churches stand on the sideline and merely mouth pious irrelevancies and sanctimonious trivialities. In the midst of a mighty struggle to rid our nation of racial and economic injustice, I have heard so many ministers say, "Those are social issues with which the Gospel has no real concern," and I have watched so many churches commit themselves to a completely other-worldly religion which made a strange distinction between body and soul, the sacred and the secular. . . .

I hope the Church as a whole will meet the challenge of this decisive hour. But even if the Church does not come to the aid of justice, I have no despair about the future. I have no fear about the outcome of our struggle in Birmingham, even if our motives are presently misunderstood. We will reach the goal of freedom in Birmingham and all over the nation, because the goal of America is freedom. Abused and scorned though we may be, our destiny is tied up with the destiny of America.

Before the pilgrims landed at Plymouth, we were here. Before the pen of Jefferson etched across the pages of history the majestic words of the Declaration of Independence, we were here. For more than two centuries our foreparents labored in this country without wages; they made cotton "king"; and they built the homes of their masters in the midst of brutal injustice and shameful humiliation—and yet out of a bottomless vitality they continued to thrive and develop. If the inexpressible cruelties of slavery could not stop us, the opposition we now face will surely fail. We will win our freedom because the sacred heritage of our nation and the eternal will of God are embodied in our echoing demands. . . .

49. STUDENTS AND REVOLUTION: THE CHILIASTIC URGE

COLIN CROUCH

Colin Crouch is a graduate student in sociology at the London School of Economics, where he was recently President of the Student Union.

The student revolt is worthy of some attention for three main reasons. First, the fact that it has encouraged a questioning and self-examination within the universities may provide an opportunity for those of more moderate temper than the revolutionaries themselves to achieve reforms that would otherwise be ignored. Second, and in contrast, if it continues to cause disruption, it could lead to the universities resorting to more authoritarian discipline in order to keep going, while at the same time providing a chance for those of the political right who would welcome an excuse to strike at university autonomy generally, with the net result of destroying what are in reality among the more liberal institutions in our society. Third, and on a wider scale, the issues raised by the more serious among the student ideologues and other philosophers of the New Left do touch on the crucial questions of human society and organization that should be demanding our attention. . . .

Leopold Labedz . . . sums up the position very well when he says of the New Left: 'They express the present-day crisis of rationality, and represent the return to the Messianic hopes of earlier ages.' The religious note here is particularly important, as we shall see later. In thanking the left for turning our attention to these fundamental questions of social order, and possibly away from more detailed and smaller questions that otherwise occupy the attention of social scientists, it is as well to remember that it is by no means profitable to become obsessed with these great issues. To believe that all is potentially challengeable is a vital and valuable element of the scientific approach; but to believe that all should be perennially challenged is little more than a recipe for chaos and neurosis. It is perhaps on this point that the far left have made impossible any reconciliation, almost any dialogue, between themselves and the rest of academic and political society. Total questioning and permanent revolution are just not possible positions for anyone who believes it is necessary that the world carry out its day-to-day activities. The only possible points of existence for the total radical are in the ivory tower of the university and in the chaos and crisis of revolutionary activity itself. It is because of his dread of isolation in the former that he must desperately, phrenetically, seek to create the latter. Opportunies for serious revolutionary activity being somewhat limited in Britain, this often

From Colin Crouch, "The Chiliastic Urge," *Survey*, No. 69 (October, 1968), excerpts.

involves resorting to the *ersatz* revolution of the protest march and violent demonstration.

But the fundamental questions are there nevertheless. To distinguish just a few of them which should and do occupy our attention: first, how can the Hobbesian problem of order be resolved while at the same time one assigns as strong an imperative to the demands of democracy as to those of order? Second, is it possible to maintain the individual liberty and potentiality for materialist advance that modern industrial society (as a *Gesellschaft*) has provided us, while at the same time keeping something of the warmth and feeling of 'belonging' that we assume characterizes the 'true' community or *Gemeinschaft*? Third, how does the individual reconcile the instinctive moral urge to act when he perceives evil with the incredible complexities of so many modern problems and the extremely limited prospect of any one individual being able to make more than a slight dent or superficial scratch in their surface? Finally, how applicable is the ideal of rationalism in the resolution of social problems when the possibility of objectivity has been severely questioned by the findings of the sociology and psychology of knowledge?

Of course, to identify these key problem areas in such a way is not to imply that they are necessarily capable of resolution, nor even that the reconciliation of the contradictions they pose is either urgent or necessary. It is entirely possible to live a full, intelligent and constructive life without ever even thinking of these questions. One of the great mercies of the complexity, scale and impersonality of modern society which so grieves and enrages the New Left is that massive contradictory elements can coexist quite happily for most of the time without any fearful consequences for the equilibrium of everyday life. It is a fallacy resulting from the mechanistic analogy which sees contradictions within societies as being the seeds of their destruction.

Furthermore, to suggest that the New Left, including the student left, is making an interesting commentary on fundamental questions is not to suggest that every young hooligan who goes berserk in Grosvenor Square is doing so because of a deep philosophical concern. Nevertheless, there is a philosophical concern at the root of the New Left, and it is undeniably one of the most lively and vital schools of political thought, at least among the young, of the present time. It is rare to find a politically sensitive young person at our universities who has not been in some way affected by it, and there are a good many who have come to share many of its assumptions about our society.

As Labedz shows . . . it is somewhat difficult to speak of the left's assumptions as a collective whole, because the movement is fundamentally divided on many crucial issues. One can see a divide between the followers of Marcuse's élitism and those who continue to place all their hopes in the traditional proletariat. There are those who will say of the Soviet Union and eastern Europe, 'at least they have abolished private ownership', while others regard the societies of the communist world as even more intolerable than those of 'neo-capitalism'. There is fierce debate over whether Hungary in

1956 and Czechoslovakia in 1968 have seen movements of a revanchist bourgeoisie or of a progressive force of liberation. There are those who find their Mecca in Peking or Havana, and those who suspect all leaders, whether revolutionary, reformist or reactionary, of corruption and megalomania. There are the apostles of violence, whether of the black, student or working-class varieties, and there are are those who continue to believe in the possibility of a solution to all our ills by an infinite extension of tolerance and abandonment of human striving and ambition, possibly aided by the relaxing and enervating properties of marijuana and LSD.

But behind all this understandable confusion of analysis and prescription it is possible to identify common themes that make it possible to talk of the New Left as a whole. Viewing it for present purposes in terms of the fundamental issues of human organization and activity mentioned above, there is a common assumption, which flirts dangerously with anarchism, that the problems of order and democracy can be resolved by the overthrow of those tendencies in society which make for material and political inequality, and by the achievement of the society of true consent through the removal of the forces and ideologies of conflict and competition, which are seen as holding in check the forces of an essentially pure human nature. Similarly, the resolution of the demand for individuality with that for community is seen through the creation of a participative society; community is assured through the possibility of direct and immediate participation, through simple and democratic organizational forms, in all decisions which will affect one's life, while individuality is assured through the equality of the participation and the ending of a society which demands conflict between men. The problem of action in a complex world is resolved through the philosophy of revolution, demanding total change and raising the prospect of a massive and powerful movement with which the individual can identify and in whose all-embracing whole he can sink his personal efforts.

The problem of rationality is seen with an acute awareness of the socially based nature of knowledge, linked with a view of that social background as being the victim of a huge class conspiracy. Thus rational action and debate in the existing world is meaningless. Only when the conspiracy has been overthrown can rational discussion acquire value again. As pointed out by Labedz, several people, including myself, have accused the left of a determined anti-rationalism. This charge is justified, but it should be remembered that their view often results from an initial *over*-dependence on and awareness of rationality. It is often the horror felt by the young mind at the extent of irrational inequality, arbitrary use of power, and socially sanctioned injustice that can be seen in so many areas of life, which leads to the conclusion that to attempt to follow a rationalist credo will simply result in being duped and misled. It is interesting to compare them with an earlier devotee of complete rationalism, Vilfredo Pareto, who was led by his observation of the absence of such criteria in human affairs to a position of almost total cynicism, the political implications of which proved the very opposite of those of the New Left.

Thus the philosophy of the left comprises themes which can seem very attractive to the sensitive young person, aware of social evils, distressed by the apparent failure of social democracy and reformist methods (through the Labour Party) to achieve rapid change, and sharing the increasingly widespread perplexity at what is felt to be an inability to become involved, to participate, in the serious business of life.

The left is able, through its philosophy of the participative revolution aiming to create the participative society, to provide a resolution to these problems that few other groups can offer. Disillusioned equally by Soviet communism and social democracy, many young people of the left are finding these new theories, or rather these new approaches to old theories, extremely attractive. . . .

The yearning for involvement, for community, for immediacy and concreteness is not confined to the New Left, although they are the most extreme and determined in their demands. And, whatever one's feelings about their ways of proceeding, it is impossible to deny that they are striking meaningful chords with their ideas. Essentially, I believe . . . these are the chords of the religious experience.

It is through his religion that the sensitive soul has traditionally found an overall sense of the cosmic whole in time and space, has attempted to ascribe a movement, a purpose, to that cosmos, and has sought to locate himself and involve himself within its all-embracing plan. To the exceptionally religious, it is also important that there be a peer group with whom this sense can be translated into everyday life through the mechanism of community. There is much in the ideology of the New Left which fits the requirements of religion. Formerly it could probably be found too in the ideology of the old communist left, but awareness of the reality of the communist world has disqualified it, and the search for a new faith was inevitable.

The religious urge is real, and the question of its role and means of satisfaction in a world which regards itself as 'secularized' is problematic. It is the problem which haunts the whole work of Emile Durkheim, through his studies of the implications for community of the division of labour and the industrial revolution, the elementary forms of the religious life, and the results of the lack of its assurances and constraints in the problem of suicide.

It is also important in the background of the work of the other great founding father of sociology, Max Weber. To quote from Labedz's article: '. . . The chiliastic urge has proved so enduring in the history of humanity that it was unlikely that it would disappear for good. In his time Weber thought that there inevitably would be "rationalization" of society because of "routinization of charisma" and functional bureaucratic necessities. . . .' But Weber was aware of the limits of rationalism. Methodologically, he showed his awareness of the importance of the subjective in his concept of *Verstehen*. And, hostile though he may have been to many aspects of it, he was brought up in the Germanic Hegelian school. Weber was probably aware of the difficulties of reducing all to rationalist, impersonal procedures—that difficulty which J. S. Mill describes in his autobiography when he speaks of how depressing it was actually to live purely according to utilitarian criteria.

Weber was aware of man's need for a feeling of direction, vocation (*Beruf*) in his life. The fascinating thing about the *Beruf* which Weber studied in most detail—that of individualist Protestantism—is that here is a faith, a creed, which reconciles rationalism, for all its impersonality, with the deeper emotional need for fulfilment and vocation, by making a vocation out of rationalist activity, or of activity based on rationalist criteria. The conjunction was by no means a perfect one, but it is a crucially important phenomenon. Even if the Protestant ethic in its earliest forms became changed, its influence and essentials have influenced later developments. In some respects, social democracy can be seen as the individualist ethic with a social conscience.

And it is precisely all this which is now being questioned so seriously. In many ways it is the old spirit of the Protestant ethic which is under the most heavy attack of all in several modern developments. First there is its inevitable association with early *laissez faire* capitalism and its cruelties and now generally discarded theories. At a more extreme level, the popularity of hallucinogenic drugs—with their attendant desire to lose individuality and the everyday world, to distort sense perception, to assert the very reverse of a 'hard work' ideology—is an explicit rejection of everything rationalist individualism stands for. The popularity of Eastern philosophies outside the Judaic-Christian tradition, particularly those philosophies which are non-rationalist and contemplative (hence not active, individualist, ambitious), marks a dissatisfaction with the norms of the rationalist and liberal-individualist tradition in the forms in which it has appeared over the past two centuries. The renewed attack on rationalism from the sociology of knowledge has already been mentioned above, as has the horror expressed by many new radicals at the ideas of planning, calculation and cautiousness.

There is a new desire for romance, excitement, which is becoming elevated into a political virtue. At the present time it is difficult to predict its future or the appropriate response to it of those still loyal to the rationalist creed. In particular, it is extremely difficult to establish alternative responses to the religious urge, and the associated problem of community. It is this question, rather than their own more immediate concerns, which is the most important issue raised by the student revolt.

50. THE RISE OF MODERN DICTATORSHIPS

SIGMUND NEUMANN

Dr. Neumann (1904–1962) was professor of government and social science at Wesleyan University.

Until most recent times the concept of dictatorship as a temporary emergency rule prevailed. In this sense, it is compatible with democratic government. In emergencies democracies may in fact be compelled to suspend temporarily their dependency on the consent of the governed. If in the process they can preserve their constitutional fiber and an open road to normalcy, they do not lose their essential nature.

Since the end of the first World War, however, dictatorship has seemed to convey a very different meaning. It is often identified with autocracy or absolutism. Misleading as such a definition may be, it rightly connotes the aspiration of modern dictatorships to *permanence*. It is not the Romans' six-month rule but at least the "millennium" that the modern dictator aims to establish. The design of modern dictatorship is essentially different from that of its nominal antecedents. Present-day autocracies are not just departures from the democratic norm. They claim to present a system of government outliving their dictatorial creator and extending their sway into a *totalitarian rule* over practically every sphere of human interest and activity. It is this quasi-institutional and totalitarian character, this virtually limitless extension in time and space, that holds out the challenge to democracy.

Modern democracy has not only to meet this challenge, but also to recognize in this dictatorial growth its own quandary; in spite of the fact that dictatorships today represent the opposite of what democracies stand for, they are in many respects the direct outgrowth of our present system with its discords. Resulting from the recent rise of mass democracy and the threatening breakdown of institutions, two elements of crisis loom for modern government. The same elements constitute the historic premises of the new despots. Their primary claim is leadership in the mass state and substitution for shattered institutions. This twofold premise, indeed, determines important social features and at the same time fundamental discrepancies inherent in modern dictatorial rule.

In the sense of this premise present-day dictators are children of a democratic era, much as they seem to despise it. In fact, this democratic background constitutes the basic difference between the absolutism of the *ancien*

From Sigmund Neumann, *Permanent Revolution*. New York: Harper & Row, Publishers, 1942, pp. 2–6 and 36–43. Reprinted by permission.

régime preceding the French Revolution and that of modern tyrannies. Predemocratic autocracies had a comparatively easy task to fulfill. They hardly had to stifle the voice of the people. Control of court factions and of aristocratic intrigues was all that mattered. Then democratic revolutions awakened a mute populace. Since that time every recurrence of autocracy arising in a nation which has gone through a democratic experience (transient though it may have been) has had to answer the queries of people who still remember a predictatorial past. To overcome this historic memory and at the same time to respect and to counteract it, a proper "public opinion" becomes a necessity.

The new tyrannies whose historic hour strikes in the age of mass democracy are "popular dictatorships." Avowedly they exemplify the antithesis of democracy but at bottom they show a pseudodemocratic basis. Their "legal" seizure of power, their pretense to elections, their constant craving for popular acclaim—all these intricate schemes of a quasidemocratic existence are preconditional for the very survival of the new dictatorships. This fact is among the important explanations of the predominant place yielded to propaganda in the daily life of modern totalitarianism.

Important as these propaganda techniques are, these new dictatorships are, however, not simply the result of an unscrupulous and technically perfected system of propaganda. These propaganda techniques undoubtedly reveal most significant symptoms, but they should not be mistaken for the essence and basic impulse of these movements. Propaganda to be effective must answer real needs and desires. This must be especially true of political movements as successful as modern dictatorships are. Justified or not, grievances toward the existing order generate the seekers of change whose greatest strength is often simply their enemy's weakness. Negative characteristics far more than any positive creed serve as a point of departure for a concrete definition of modern dictatorships. They are antiparliamentarian and anticapitalistic, anti-Semitic and anti-Western, antirational and antiindividualistic. They arise as movements of protest; and even if they do not reach beyond this stage of negative criticism, this sheer negativism represents a focal point of crisis elements in modern society. Like all the various types of historic dictatorship, they are children of a crisis, in this case a totalitarian crisis reaching into all ways of life and sweeping over the whole planet.

The impetus and extent of this social and political upheaval largely depend on cultural standards and political traditions in the different nations. Hence scientific observers of the spread of dictatorial rule in Europe have often regarded the educational standards of the different nations as a key to explain its expansion. Countries, so they said, where the percentage of illiteracy is high are likely to become dictatorships. This rule seemed to apply well to Russia, Poland, Italy, Spain, and the Balkans; but when Germany joined the autocracies, the weakness of this argument became manifest. If, however, one looks at the standard of what might be called political illiteracy, their explanation would have been more convincing. In none of these countries had the tradition of self-government and of free institutions been strong and lasting. Beyond this, it is a fact that the political system of the central and eastern European countries was changed suddenly and without adequate preparation from the more or less benevolent paternalism of semiabsolute governments to the independent responsibilities of free democratic institutions. There was no time to build up new traditions and to adjust the institutions to so rapid a social development.

Notwithstanding national deviations in political maturity, a lack of adaptation between social structure and body politic seems to be a characteristic problem of all modern nations, with the possible exception of England. The rise of modern political democracy coincided with the sweeping social changes of modern industrialism and urbanization, with the breakdown of a fixed social order, of basic religious concepts, and of old institutions. The impact of these great social disturbances on political institutions became especially manifest with the change from liberal democracy, i.e., the rule of the classes of property and culture, to mass democracy. Steady extension of the electorate throughout the nineteenth and twentieth centuries made the problem of leadership in a mass state the crucial issue of modern government. With the sudden rise of the mass state the historic hour of the *demagogue* seemed to have arrived—demagogue in the classical sense of the word, the "leader of the people."

The modern dictator is even more indicative of the breakdown of accepted institutions. When an economic system becomes questionable, when a social order is shattered, when religious ties are loosened, people look for new authorities, for substitutes. The cry for the "leader" is the result of the weakening or nonexistence of political institutions, of a ruling class, and an accepted code of values. Wherever these institutions and their governing elements are strong enough not only to preserve but also to adjust the society in its evolutionary development, the danger of the demagogue does not arise. This is the great test for the strength of institutions. When they fail, demagogues arise. They are the *substitute for institutions* in time of transition. Here, if anywhere, lies the historic justification of this new personal rule of the modern dictator. It may fill a gap between two social orders. This was the historic function of the absolute monarchy which helped to develop modern capitalistic society. But the new dictatorship is differentiated from the earlier absolutism by its other historic element: its origin in the age of mass democracy.

All these crisis elements in the age of democracy—its changing social basis, the breakdown of social institutions, the shattering of the predominant system of values—have already been perceived by observers in prewar Europe, such as Tocqueville and Burckhardt, Dostoevski and Kierkegaard, Nietzsche and Sorel. Indeed the war only hastened and accentuated this process. Yet, though it may not have created anything essentially new in the web of time, it gave new impulses, broadened the attack, focused the issues. Thus were prepared the national climate and the international scene most suitable for the unfolding of dynamic totalitarianism. . . .

Modern dictatorships—as the three case studies on their origin in Russia, Italy, and Germany amply prove—are conditioned by national characteristics and historic circumstances, by ideological foundations and social alignments and not least by personality factors. Manifold as their national variations may be, there are, however, a number of common features which typify modern dictatorship and indeed constitute a part of its definition.

Five basic patterns stand out, almost invariably discernible in the gamut of modern dictatorships and visible in all strata of their existence: the promise of security, action instead of program, quasi-democratic foundations, war psychology, and the leadership principle.

Strange as it seems, the basic appeal of dynamic dictatorship is its *promise of stability*. The masses longing for rest are ready to surrender much of their liberty in return for economic security. Thus the rising demagogues promise that every man will be a king and all classes will find security. This necessarily produces a vague and contradictory program—land and corn prices at a premium for the farmers, high wages and low food costs for the industrial workers. This contingency is one of the reasons why most modern dictatorships cannot be defined in terms of their economic and social programs. Even the one-party state represents a multiple, though hidden, party system. The socio-economic program of modern dictatorship is necessarily vague.

In reality, it is not the promise of economic prosperity that is the real backbone of modern dictatorships. It is the guarantee of security in a far more comprehensive sense. The breakdown of economic security in the period of inflation and depression means not only an end to all economic stability, but also the breakdown of the whole set of values of the middle class. With the loss of money, the burgher's training, occupation, standard of living, and the future of his children are no longer guaranteed, and herewith the whole world of the middle class breaks down. This crash is reflected also by the institutions which the middle class had built and backed in the nineteenth century.

It was the middle class that once succeeded in transforming the uncertainties of an absolute monarchy into the rational order of law. The middle class had been the founder of the state of law, warning its sons that "wherever law ends, tyranny begins." Yet the same institutions that the fathers had erected and worshiped are being destroyed by the sons. It is the disillusioned son of a liberal civilization who leads the antibourgeois revolution. The most ardent pamphlets against bourgeois civilization are written by burghers who fell short of their aim. There is always a secret yearning for this lost world that sounds through their accusations. Even the leaders of this revolt against rational civilization—Nietzsche, Sorel, Pareto—are children of the same world of values in which they lived. Their so-called anti-intellectual radicalism is a sudden turn from an overstepping of rational thinking and not at all a genuine response born out of a superabundant life. It is the last stage of a hyperrationalism which at last turns into its negation. This artificial activism born out of despair of a rational order often leads to a self-destruction of this intelligentsia—to a *Trahison des Clercs*.

This cry for a new society of order and permanence has a peculiar character. It is strangely mixed with antibourgeois dynamics, if not revolutionary attitudes. In the beginning of this new credo stands the formula *action instead of program*. The belief in rational programs is shaken because they have not given the ardently desired security. Now people join the movement not because they believe in its program, but because they trust the leader who promises them heroic action. Now they cheer the leader who prides himself on having no program for tomorrow, when he will decide the people's fate. To have no program becomes a virtue. This blank check for the leader means the burgher's liberation from any further political thought. It relieves him of any responsibility.

Such comfort was especially welcome to a generation overstrained by war and postwar experiences, overtired and longing for rest. The rise of dictatorships found its complement in a renunciation of politics by the masses. In these postwar years sport had become popular with the European people as never before. It was a refuge long before dictators discovered the usefulness and propaganda value of Olympics to demonstrate the efficiency and glamour of a totalitarian state. It might almost be said that politics itself was judged like a football match or a bullfight. Let the best man win. Success became the only measuring rod and no moral code could affect it. The right of the stronger nation was accepted. That was the way of legalizing revolutions and consequently of causing their *fait accompli* to be accepted in international politics. Thus a bourgeois society became reconciled to dynamic postwar politics.

All modern demagogues, however, have instinctively felt the necessity of building *quasi-democratic foundations* underneath their dictatorial rule. Their "legal" seizure of power, their all-embracing propaganda machine, their effective policy of *panem et circenses* give daily evidence of this intrinsic feature of post-democratic autocracy. Yet it should be understood that their concept of democracy, if it may be called that, is militant in character. Such a turn may be the simplest way of arriving at some kind of democratic organization especially appropriate to nations with intrinsically military traditions and without the long political training of the Anglo-Saxon people. The nation is seen as an army. Its life is a constant battle. Its citizens are political soldiers. The "new democracy" is nothing but the introduction of the military vision into political life.

In fact these dictatorships were born in the World War and this is their fourth common feature—they are borne along by *war psychology*. Lamartine in his Manifesto to Europe (1848) had said, "War is nearly always a dictatorship. Soldiers forget institutions for men." This is even more true in modern warfare. There are no longer any frontiers. Air raids and hunger blockades affect civilians as well. The civilians' morale is a deciding factor in the outcome of modern warfare; and since it is a war of all groups—men, women, and children alike—the whole nation must be organized. The idea of the totalitarian state was born in the last World War, which became a totalitarian war. In wartime all opposition and discussion must cease. Personal liberty no longer exists. As a matter of fact, the best argument for this sort of suppression is the country's peril. Thus, the claim to absolutist control by the dictatorial parties in postwar Europe has always been based on a real or presumed danger from abroad. War is a dictatorship's beginning, its demand, its test. Therefore modern dictatorship focuses its machinery for propaganda on building up a fighting spirit. No actual warfare is needed in order to create this warlike atmosphere and reaction. As soon as it is aroused, it works automatically and reaches ever-widening circles. Alarmed neighbors naturally respond by gathering their forces against menacing aggression. The dictator in return calls for even stronger power to counter threatening encirclement. When the League of Nations proclaimed its sanctions in the Italo-Ethiopian War, it was a godsend to Mussolini's power: it strengthened the control and prestige of Fascist dictatorship.

This predominant militancy of the dictatorial parties undoubtedly made them especially attractive to the armed forces. In spite of obvious reservations, raised particularly among the higher military caste, against the irrational and unruly elements in these dynamic dictatorships, their continuous call to arms promised dominant position and prestige to the soldierly profession. No wonder that in many lands army circles took a friendly view of rising Fascism, not without flattering themselves that they could easily control these irregulars in the end. This sympathy or at least responsive reserve toward the revolutionary upstart assured their successful *coup d'état*. It was good strategy, therefore, for the new dictatorships to establish the best relations possible with the military.

The warlike temper of modern totalitarianism, however, was not meant only for home consumption in order to win over a restless populace and the military cadres of the nation. The consequences of this militancy for international politics are so obvious and so often told in the daily news that there is no need for further proof. "War" is in fact inseparable from the meaning of Fascism. In one of his few outspoken programmatic declarations Mussolini stated: "And, above all, Fascism believes neither in the possibility nor the utility of perpetual peace. . . . War alone brings up to its highest tension all human energy and puts the stamp of nobility upon the peoples who have the courage to meet it."

This driving force of militant dictatorships is raised to high-pitched intensity by a quasi-religious missionarism. Every revolution which claims to be more than a mere change of government and which pretends to create a new social order must also stir up neighboring countries and awaken in them a spirit of deep unrest. The idea of the great mission is indissolubly mixed with national ambitions. Such a combination characterized the ideas of the French Revolution. It also holds true of the modern ideologies of the Third International, the revival of the Roman Empire, and the Nazis' "New Order."

A dynamic foreign policy is essential for totalitarian dictatorship. . . . It is obvious what an important role national frustration has played in the rise of modern dictatorships. Their design is to liberate the country from national humiliation. This holds even more true in internal affairs. Here the claim to power is based upon the necessary destruction of the nation's, or the classes', archenemy; and when power is won, the *permanent revolution*—even if renounced in foreign affairs, at least at times, for tactical reasons—has to go on in internal politics. Opposition groups have to be seized, the party has to be regularly purged, trials and expulsions have to take place. All this means stamina to a dictatorship, and even the most peaceful work of daily life must show the touch of warlike activity. There are a thousand battles going on: the battle of grain, the battle for raw materials, the fight for joy after work, the battle of the birth rate. And they are all merely preparations for the supreme battle for world power. . . .

Politics itself has been defined . . . in terms of the irreducible category of Friend and Foe. Fully militarized social relationships have been basically conceived on the battlefield. No concept of civil government is left. Militancy reflects all activities of modern dictatorship. It becomes its organizing principle. It shapes its party structure and its *wehrwirtschaft*, its totalitarian control and its revolutionary missionarism. It is the "permanent revolution" in foreign affairs and in internal politics that makes possible the strange mixture of dictatorship's promise of stability and at the same time the belief in revolutionary action. Victorious dynamics become the only security of a war society.

There is, finally, the *leadership principle*, perhaps the most dangerous element of modern dictatorship. "Power corrupts, absolute power corrupts absolutely," in the words of Lord Acton. Says Goering in his *Germany Reborn:* "We National Socialists believe that in political affairs Adolf Hitler is infallible, just as the Roman Catholic believes that in religious matters the Pope is infallible. His will is my law. . . ."

It is characteristic of the leader that he is responsible not to those below him but only to those above him, and therefore is finally responsible only to a supreme Führer or Duce who is responsible not to any man "but to God and the nation."

This twofold justification of political authority reverts to the two premises of modern demagoguery: its character of a substitute and its democratic element. How important the democratic or pseudodemocratic responsibility to the nation is regarded even by the leader state has been indicated above. Modern dictatorship assumes the place of a religion for people who have lost their faith in transcendental power. It ministers to the human yearning for worship. This explains the subsequent and deadly conflict of a totalitarian state with religious authorities. At the same time such a revival of the divine right theory serves as a useful device for shifting final responsibility to an agency deprived of efficient means of control and coercion. It fortifies dictatorship. It transcends human power to combat, thus removing it from the realm of human criticism. It makes the dictator a superman, a demigod.

The leader epitomizes the dictatorial system. He is its beginning, its moving spirit, its fate. The analysis of his power and position, therefore, will lead to the core of modern totalitarianism.

51. RESISTANCE AND OPPOSITION IN THE SOVIET UNION

D. J. R. SCOTT

D. J. R. Scott, who teaches at the University of Glasgow, is the author of SOVIET POLITICAL INSTITUTIONS.

The picture of its political life which the Soviet Union seeks to present to the world is one of quite incredible consensus, in which not only do all leaders, from the heads of the party and government to the members of village soviets, emerge from the taking of thought together without ever the need for a contested election, but complex problems in the determination of values and priorities equally readily suggest, and win support for, their own solutions. Differences of opinion are recognised, and since the death of Stalin have with increasing frequency been expressed in the press, where issues are raised for public discussion; but they are not expected to be pushed to the acrimonious conclusions familiar in other societies. In so far as this is not mere deception—and it is improbable that it is—it represents a sense of the way things ought to be, the way the prophets and founders thought they would be once the poison of the class conflict was cast out and the state, in its internal aspects at least, could begin to wither away.

Much of the explanation of the system as given by outside observers, while emphasising that the process of rational decision-making has proved infinitely more difficult than the founders assumed, suggests that a knocking together of heads may be an effective substitute for this meeting of minds, and that at least the securing of compliance may present little more difficulty than is reflected in the official picture, though the means differ.

In fact it is hardly necessary to prove that resistance and opposition exist, in the Soviet Union as elsewhere. If the question of who was to exercise power had not been a subject of dispute there need hardly have been the purges which poisoned Soviet life in the thirties and have not yet worked themselves out of the body politic. If peasant resistance had ended with the proclamation of the completion of full collectivisation, there can be little doubt, in view of the open statements of a succession of Soviet leaders at all levels, that private plots would long since have been discarded and that the collective farm members—whether or not transformed into state-farm workers—would now be living in agrogorods. If the worker could be relied on to forget that he is also a consumer and to respond to the symbolic incentives offered him, much tedious debate and reversals of policy about the balance of the economy could have been avoided. Politics being the activity of finding courses of

From D. J. R. Scott, "Resistance and Opposition," *Survey*, No. 64 (July, 1967), excerpts.

action which will pass for the will of the organisation to which they are applied, resistance or opposition—the obstacles through which they must pass—must always be a factor in the calculations of those who practice that activity as their craft.

If it appears otherwise it is perhaps because the associations of the words we use mislead us. Resistance, in an age still under the influence in its thought of the legends of the Second World War, suggests a military activity rather than a permanent fact of social life. There is probably no-one who would suggest that in the thinking of Soviet political leaders the possibility of armed resistance now plays any significant part, but it can safely be assumed that, there as elsewhere, courses of action are chosen because they seem likely to raise fewer human difficulties than some other methods of attaining similar ends, and some actions are avoided altogether because they seem likely to raise too many. . . .

Almost all aspiring Russian reformers looked to a single model and source of inspiration, whether to the Russian village or to western Europe. Lenin, though distinctively and, to both contemporaries and successors, disconcertingly eclectic in his vision of how to bring about the Marxian socialist revolution in a society clearly lacking the prescribed preconditions, was even less disposed than most to concede that the location of power and the ends to which it might be used could be a matter of indifference. The harnessing of peasant discontent to the work of disruption, the assumption of what remained of the imperial apparatus of administration, and even the retreat to the NEP —whether or not he envisaged it as a long-term measure or as the temporary expedient which it proved to be—were not surrenders of power to rival claimants but temporary alliances requiring the unfettered control of the enlightened to ensure that they did not get out of hand.

The Bolsheviks' pre-revolutionary vision of the governmental system which it would fall to them to operate, if the inevitable should occur in their lifetime, was fragmentary and not very different from that of other revolutionary factions. The bias of their creed suggested—perhaps more forcibly than with other schools because of the assumptions which they brought from study of the conditions of the industrialised countries—that whatever machinery they might set up or inherit would be predominantely concerned with issues of economic development. . . .

It was less clear before the event what instruments their party would be able to bend to its purpose. The development by the party itself of a complete professional administration of its own, both at the centre and at the several lower levels of administration, might perhaps have been foreseen, but the extent to which, in most fields of operative management, it would duplicate rather than replace or direct, the administrative and ministerial networks, probably could not. The further ramification of a system of checking and rechecking, from the first far reaching, and the concentration of power in the hands of a purely coercive apparatus, traditionally Russian in aspect rather than traditionally Marxist, and responsible, in effect, to the secretary-general alone, would probably have caused concern among the founders. Certainly few of the men of 1917 had conceived of the extinction of such intra-party democracy as there was, whatever might happen outside its ranks. Seen from that viewpoint in time, it is unlikely that the dismantlement of much of this coercive apparatus since 1953 would seem to have gone anything like far enough, even though such of the veterans as have survived to receive re-habilitation and decorations in the post-Stalin period have no doubt been reasonably sincere in expressing their satisfaction with the changes since the passing of the tyrant at whose hands so many of them suffered so much. Whether Lenin, whose policies can be seen to have set the regime well on its way to Stalinism, would have approved of its continuing so long, must be a matter of conjecture and communist conscience-searching, but it seems likely that his authoritarian predilections would have inclined him to see reasons for it.

One of the more paradoxical changes of the Stalin period was the adoption of the traditional outward forms of parliamentarism by direct elections in territorial constituencies, though with pseudo-revolutionary features—covering party manipulation—in the form of nomination. Since this replaced election-up of legislatures from the local soviets, it removed the institutional basis for the claim—still made in the written constitution—that the Soviet Union is a state founded on soviets. The post-Stalin period has seen no attempt to revert to original revolutionary practice in this respect, and there seems to be no advantage which might motivate such a reversion. On the other hand there seems to be no prospect of the forms of election being allowed to function as they do in countries of parliamentary tradition—as means of selection rather than of public affirmation of support. The resem-blance to practice in non-communist countries extends rather to form than to function. Some publicity has lately been given to the fact of meetings of the standing committees of the houses of the legislatures, emphasising the supposed value of their work, though little concrete information on what in fact passes in their deliberations. Given reasonable specialisation of functions, access to information, and leave freely to criticise, these could be as effective a control on the government and its ministries as any likely to be devised, despite the marked disparity of standing between the members and the ministers. But although the post-Khrushchev restoration of the full structure of specialised industrial ministries has been accompanied by an increase in the number of committees of the Supreme Soviet, the signs are not very favourable; given the state's economic preoccupations it is unpromising that each house has only one committee for all industry—apart from the building and building-materials industries, commerce, and the service industries—and that legislative bills are still apparently the concern of a separate single committee in each house. Nor has any hint of disagreement emerged from such bodies, either into the press or into speeches in the subsequent meetings of the chambers to which they report. . . .

In general, it seems probable that rule in the Soviet Union will continue to be exercised by a web of interacting committees appointed by, or under the sanction of, a co-optative elite, and a large number of unconsolidated and imperfectly co-ordinated administrative services (including a rather higher proportion than in most other systems with primarily inspectorial functions, and with most of the others engaged in some degree of mutual supervision), similarly appointed, chiefly on the basis of specialist qualifications. The influence of the system's surviving image of itself as a system of government by public meeting of the uninstructed but spontaneously well disposed, with little need of detailed information or specialised skills, will probably continue to bias this selection slightly in the direction of a preference for skills in the public presentation of policies and performance, and, especially in the party elite itself, some weight will continue to be given to erudition in the largely otiose doctrines of Marxism and to the ability to explain and justify actions in its terms.

It seems to be a reasonable charge against this system that it has not produced the self-critical flexibility required of a regime seeking in a period of rapidly changing technology to optimise the use of scarce resources, even when it is in a position substantially to ignore the wayward desires of the ultimate consumer. To what extent this deficiency is inherent in the formal structure it is perhaps impossible to say. It may well be that the pretensions of the socialist state, the claim to know what is good for a whole society of diversely natured and diversely circumstanced individuals (in the sense of being, by some test, what they want, or, by some moral criteria, what they ought to have), are beyond the capacity of any conceivable central decision-making apparatus; in the case of the Soviet Union the legacy of mutual suspicion and universal insincerity must also be allowed for. Soviet humbug, not necessarily more pervasive than that of other societies, but different, has been inimical to the evolution of the more obviously functional operations of an effective opposition.

Probably the most productive service of a group of potential office-holders outside the official machine is the fashioning of informed and original alternative policies. Originality is more likely to arise from such a source than from the established holders of power, burdened as they are by day-to-day assignments and limited by the loyalties and assumptions of habitual interaction. But this service is less to be looked for in a world of complex systems and integrated programmes than when the business of government consisted characteristically of the solution of discrete problems, and when consequently the cost of not having an opposition of traditional type was less. Even so, the solid crust of official thought is probably enriched by the activity of unofficial earthworms.

Apart from promoting ideas, a tolerated anti-establishment can make itself useful by the promotion of men, the development of leadership talent immediately available for high office, by channels which inhibit originality less than the normal career pattern of the system. An opposition of the British type can, of course, carry this service further by providing a complete alternative management, available both for office and as a standard against which the rising men of the incumbent faction can be measured. The more diverse opposition structure most characteristically found in the United States can similarily both evolve an alternative chief executive and designate, from among members of his faction with experience of high office, leading members for his administration. In the absence of such machinery, the Soviet Union faces a recurrent succession problem and a persistent tendency for incoming office-holders to establish their claim to the newcomer's presumption of innocence by personal recriminations against their predecessors.

Further, it is a function of organised opposition to give coherence and credibility to discontent. Even where no alternative policy can be formulated from outside the organisation, this activity can serve to confront the official holders of power with the dysfunctional aspects of some of their operations in the form of protest which they cannot easily dismiss as factious or insubstantial. The socialist state, as a firm dealing in everything from pepper to total defence systems and the exploration of outer space, is not very like the traditional liberal state, as preventer and adjuster of disputes among natural and corporate persons conceived of as ordinarily capable of furthering their own best interests and entitled to do so; nor is it, as a claimant to sovereignty within the limits of what it judges its subjects will stand, very like the traditional competitive firm, informed and constrained by the indications of the market and by the coercive power of a supposedly impartial arbiter between its claims and those of rivals. It is unlikely to be faced with the example of any other organisation so undeniably comparable to itself in circumstance and purpose that it is obliged to take it as a measure of its own performance. It has no external owners able to claim as of right a voice in its decision-making; as a rule it has little opportunity of extending the range of recruitment of its managerial talent, and though it can often call on advice from outside, it has little reason to suppose it disinterested. If it sometimes loses touch with the economic realities of the world within which it operates, it is hardly surprising.

Perhaps the function of an opposition most readily accepted by established authority, entitling it to raise a suitably deferential voice, and even to some encouragement in doing so, is to vent frustrations which otherwise might become dangerous. The difficulty is to find an opposition group which will content itself with this role and can so operate without losing its support.

The Soviet Union looks to the outside world, as from the first it always has done, for many of the useful services of an opposition. The countries officially styled capitalist, and especially the United States, provide a stimulating threat and a justification for the siege regime, as well as offering a standard for the comparison of achievements. Khrushchev may have been unwise to be so free with target dates for surpassing various indices of American economic success, since in the short term for which he was playing this was a game he had little chance of winning; but in their more guarded way his predecessors and successors have been obliged to use the same index. As a source of ideas, whether in industrial design, methods of management, scientific discovery, or in less tangible fields, the practice of other countries has been studied with conspicuous thoroughness and imitated—usually with equally conspicuous lack of acknowledgement—in any respect judged consistent with the priorities set by authority and with the security of the regime. In this there has been no fundamental break in policy since the days of Lenin himself; with increased achievements the constraints of planning priorities have become less rigid, but the constraints of security seem in no material respect to have been relaxed.

The internal oppositions most overtly institutionalised have, by intention, been allowed least effective influence. The nationalities, granted recognition in one of the two equally empowered chambers of the Supreme Soviet, have gained thereby a standing reminder to authority that they are there, but otherwise nothing in a system in which no vote in either house—or, as far as available evidence runs, in any other publicly elected body at any level of the administrative system—has ever been less than unanimous and in entirely predictable accord with the line of the government and party. The shifts of population since the revolution have reduced many of the national communities to minorities in the territories bearing their names, and the domination throughout the Union of a party recognising no federal limitations on its unity has confined them everywhere to a culture 'national in form and socialist in content', with the party determining what is form and what content.

The trade unions, though consistently maintained as representatives of the special interest of labour, and latterly again recognised as having a place of importance in management, have throughout been so operated as to exclude them from expressing on any matter of importance any distinctive sectional view on behalf of the interest which they are supposed to represent. As representatives of the personnel management function, however, their officers do seem to have operated as a useful partial opposition, not against the purposes of the regime as a whole but against the short-term and narrowly production-oriented actions of plant managers and their less august superiors; in this way they have probably served to direct higher authority to consideration of imbalance in its own thinking, even though they could not compel correction. Among their routine functions appears to have been pressure for keeping labour regulations in some accordance with the realities of practice.

The most fundamental clash of interests which the beneficiaries of the revolution found themselves committed to resolving, that between the peasant *narod* and the urban way of life, was of interest to them almost exclusively as a means of disrupting the previous order. The peasants were excluded as an institutionalised opposition, in the sense of a permanent foreordained loser in a continuing dialogue of government (and from the first it was evident that no opposition could hope for better terms) by their unwillingness to participate according to Bolshevik rules, and by the certainty that for a long time they would be in a majority and under temptation to draw inconvenient conclusions from that fact. Now that a large part of the peasant population has moved to the towns and the rulers have come to accept that certain material inducements, even to peasants, are productive in terms of output from the economy as a whole (with the ideologically suspect private plots providing a more diversified urban diet than the coercive management of agriculture seems able to yield), the width of the gap between the two nations is narrowed to what seem bridgeable proportions. . . .

A more credible opposition than the peasants is Russia's other traditional centre of disaffection, the intelligentsia. They, too, have an official standing in Russo-Marxist theory, and in the constitution, though from ideological scruples they are designated not, like the workers and collective farm members, as a class but as a class stratum. Terminologically, at least, Soviet rule has tamed the disruptive force of former times; the intelligentsia is no more than a sociological residual category for all who cannot, for one reason or another, conveniently be assigned to one of the approved classes. The superfluous man is superfluous no longer, and, whether as regularly employed technical or other specialist, clerk, or educator, or in the formally more autonomous position of the artist or litterateur, he has his place in the scheme of things and enjoys the guidance of the party in his contribution to the building of communism. In the last resort, as we have been reminded by the Sinyavsky-Daniel trial, the regime will not hesitate to force him into line by stiff penalties. Latterly there has been a marked change observable in the journals of the specialised professional and other organisations, including those of the trade unions and the Komsomol. While continuing to echo the sentiments expressed in the leading organs of the general press, and commonly in the same words, they have begun to carry much more genuine controversy as well, often, it seems, stemming from consciously special viewpoints. In this some of the literary journals are among the boldest. Of course, the increased freedom to publicise ideas not fully received in official circles is used somewhat circumspectly by the standards of some other countries. Total suppression of the more objectively verifiable ideas of the scientist or technologist, at least, is now difficult and unlikely; appeal to an informed public can be expected to mobilise some influential support, and with the present wider dispersion of power at the top there are probably more points at which the level of influence can be effectively applied. But if authority, in the last resort, will have none of it, the *intelligent* is still in no position to gang up to force it.

An element in society unknown to the constitution, or to Marxist theory as a distinct class or stratum, but in significant ways distinct from other professional groups and peculiarly difficult to prevent from ganging up, is the military. The Soviet regime has always been careful to ensure, by political penetration and indoctrination, that the esprit de corps of the services is not turned in the wrong direction. In the post-Stalin period this interest, like others, has shown a new-self-confidence and occasional traces of self-assertiveness, but it has been given no reason to suppose that it will be allowed to get away with very much. . . .

To most who have endured through the Stalin years of purgatory, the resilience of the society built by the Bolsheviks to their Marxist plans on their recalcitrant Russian site must seem impressive. To them, as to those of socialist disposition elsewhere, and especially to the more recently emergent countries, it must suggest that by command and determination, even without a regeneration of man, a significantly higher standard of living can still be delivered and an even more considerable figure cut in the world. Few perhaps are conscious of the lack of safeguards in the system for the evolution of more rational leadership in the future, or for its provision with better information. Those who are may well, and with reason, question whether, given their commitment to socialist purposes, with its probably inherent disposition to give less weight to individual aspirations towards liberty than to attaining a materially more abundant life, any other country's experience would be of much use to them. Yet it might be suggested that, given the limitations of man's knowledge and the complexity of the events he seeks to control, some of the forms and responsibilities of freedom might usefully be accepted as means to material abundance itself. Human resistance will in any case limit and bias action, but unless some care is taken to give it due regard, it may act too unpredictably and too late.

part five

The Organization of the State: Concentration or Dispersion of Power

INTRODUCTION

"The accumulation of all powers, legislative, executive, and judiciary, in the same hands, whether of one, a few, or many, and whether hereditary, self-appointed, or elective, may justly be pronounced the very definition of tyranny."
—James Madison, *The Federalist*, No. 47.

Should power be concentrated or should it be dispersed? The answer to this question depends upon the assumptions which a given society chooses to accept, and these, in turn, affect the methods by which common objectives are sought. If the desire is for a government capable of quick and decisive action, then centralization will be favored; on the other hand, if there is fear of abuse of power and a desire to curb the leaders, then an institutionalized dispersion of power will be sought.

The concentration of power in a centralized authority is the pattern of twentieth century political life. Both democratic and authoritarian societies have moved in this direction to solve the complex problems facing them as a result of burgeoning populations, urbanization, industrialization, and the pressures for security and welfare. In the United States, for example, the federal power has grown in the past three decades in areas long regarded as the province of the state governments, e.g., education, unemployment benefits, and housing. The trend toward centralization is also noticeable within state governments.

Concentration of power, then, at all levels of government (and within each level there is the strong move toward enhancing the power of the executive), is one of the realities of American life.

Why is this centralization and concentration taking place?

There is no simple explanation. Sociologically, the trend can be explained in terms of modern society's quest for unity. Technological, urbanized, mass culture breeds disorganization and alienation of the individual from tradition and old value patterns. At the same time, these factors militate toward a unifying institution and ideal—the state. As state administrators assume responsibility for broader areas of social welfare, there is a commensurate attempt to arrogate unto themselves additional power. This situation provides a milieu within which the lust for power by an individual can reach levels of fulfillment hitherto unknown for the middle-grade administrator. Politically, government must possess power more than adequate to cope with the problems created by the rise of giant corporations, unions, and influential pressure groups. If government is to serve the public interest, it must be able to deal with the sum of forces making up the industrial, agricultural, and commercial sectors of the economy. In time of crisis, the central government requires extraordinary powers to provide for the defense of the country. And we now live in an age of perennial crisis.

Against these positive arguments for centralization and concentration, one must weigh the dangers which strengthen the position of advocates of federalism and dispersion of power: Centralization tends to discourage that initiative and active participation at the lower levels of government and society which are the creative life springs of democracy; centralization and concentration of power do not necessarily make for efficient government; the imposition of uniformity in situations characterized by diversity is potentially dangerous to the development of society, for it encourages authoritarian solutions; finally, history shows that these characteristics are fundamentally antithetical to republican and democratic societies.

Advocates of dispersion invariably favor a separation of powers, federalism, or some variant of both. They seek to divide the powers of government between two or more independent groups of rulers, so that no one group can act without the concurrence of the others. They then hope that not all of them will decide to become tyrants at the same time, or that their conflicting aims will cause them to neutralize each other. But the advocate of dispersion and decentralization finds his position affected by the conditions of modern industrialization. Can a government of divided powers deal effectively with an interdependent, integrated economy? Is the large unit of government more effective than the smaller? How can an enlarged bureaucracy be made responsible to the public?

The problems remain at all levels: national, local, and international. Basically, does an industrial society call for increased centralization in government in order to cope with national economic, educational, and social problems? If so, should the executive branch of government be the recipient of the further concentration of power? How can we strengthen popular controls over the activities of the bureaucracy and make it responsive to public opinion? How can we prevent centralization and concentration from promoting that public apathy and political lack of interest so destructive to a functioning democracy?

52. THE FEDERALIST NO. 47

JAMES MADISON

The accumulation of all powers, legislative, executive, and judiciary, in the same hands, whether of one, a few, or many, and whether hereditary, self-appointed, or elective, may justly be pronounced the very definition of tyranny. Were the Federal Constitution, therefore, really chargeable with the accumulation of power, or with a mixture of powers, having a dangerous tendency to such an accumulation, no further arguments would be necessary to inspire a universal reprobation of the system. I persuade myself, however, that it will be made apparent to everyone, that the charge cannot be supported, and that the maxim on which it relies has been totally misconceived and misapplied. In order to form correct ideas on this important subject, it will be proper to investigate the sense in which the preservation of liberty requires that the three great departments of power should be separate and distinct.

The oracle who is always consulted and cited on this subject is the celebrated Montesquieu. If he be not the author of this invaluable precept in the science of politics, he has the merit at least of displaying and recommending it most effectually to the attention of mankind. Let us endeavor, in the first place, to ascertain his meaning on this point.

The British Constitution was to Montesquieu what Homer has been to the didactic writers on epic poetry. As the latter have considered the work of the immortal bard as the perfect model from which the principles and rules of the epic art were to be drawn, and by which all similar works were to be judged, so this great political critic appears to have viewed the Constitution of England as the standard, or to use his own expression, as the mirror of political liberty; and to have delivered, in the form of elementary truths, the several characteristic principles of that particular system. That we may be sure, then, not to mistake his meaning in this case, let us recur to the source from which the maxim was drawn.

On the slightest view of the British Constitution, we must perceive that the legislative, executive, and judiciary departments are by no means totally separate and distinct from each other. The executive magistrate forms an integral part of the legislative authority. He alone has the prerogative of making treaties with foreign sovereigns, which, when made, have, under certain limitations, the force of legislative acts. All the members of the judiciary department are appointed by him, can be removed by him on the address of the two Houses of Parliament, and form, when he pleases to consult them, one of his constitutional councils. One branch of the legislative department forms also a great constitutional council to the executive chief, as, on another hand, it is the sole depositary of judicial power in cases of

The Federalist Papers.

impeachment, and is invested with the supreme appellate jurisdiction in all other cases. The judges, again, are so far connected with the legislative department as often to attend and participate in its deliberations, though not admitted to a legislative vote.

From these facts, by which Montesquieu was guided, it may clearly be inferred that, in saying "There can be no liberty where the legislative and executive powers are united in the same person, or body of magistrates," or, "if the power of judging be not separated from the legislative and executive powers," he did not mean that these departments ought to have no *partial agency* in, or no *control* over, the acts of each other. His meaning, as his own words import, and still more conclusively as illustrated by the example in his eye, can amount to no more than this, that where the *whole* power of one department is exercised by the same hands which possess the *whole* power of another department, the fundamental principles of a free constitution are subverted. This would have been the case in the constitution examined by him if the king, who is the sole executive magistrate, had possessed also the complete legislative power, or the supreme administration of justice; or if the entire legislative body had possessed the supreme judiciary, or the supreme executive authority. This, however, is not among the vices of that constitution. The magistrate in whom the whole executive power resides cannot of himself make a law, though he can put a negative on every law; nor administer justice in person, though he has the appointment of those who do administer it. The judges can exercise no executive prerogative, though they are shoots from the executive stock; nor any legislative function, though they may be advised with by the legislative councils. The entire legislature can perform no judiciary act, though by the joint act of two of its branches the judges may be removed from their offices, and though one of its branches is possessed of the judicial power in the last resort. The entire legislature, again, can exercise no executive prerogative, though one of its branches constitutes the supreme executive magistracy, and another, on the impeachment of a third, can try and condemn all the subordinate officers in the executive department.

The reasons on which Montesquieu grounds his maxims are a further demonstration of his meaning. "When the legislative and executive powers are united in the same person or body," says he, "there can be no liberty, because apprehensions may arise lest *the same* monarch or senate should *enact* tyrannical laws to *execute* them in a tyrannical manner." Again: "Were the power of judging joined with the legislative, the life and liberty of the subject would be exposed to arbitrary control, for *the judge* would then be *the legislator*. Were it joined to the executive power, *the judge* might behave with all the violence of an *oppressor*." Some of these reasons are more fully explained in other passages; but briefly stated as they are here, they sufficiently establish the meaning which we have put on this celebrated maxim of this celebrated author.

THE FEDERALIST NO. 48

JAMES MADISON

In a government where numerous and extensive prerogatives are placed in the hands of an hereditary monarch, the executive department is very justly regarded as the source of danger, and watched with all the jealousy which a zeal for liberty ought to inspire. In a democracy, where a multitude of people exercise in person the legislative functions, and are continually exposed, by their incapacity for regular deliberation and concerted measures, to the ambitious intrigues of their executive magistrates, tyranny may well be apprehended, on some favorable emergency, to start up in the same quarter. But in a representative republic, where the executive magistracy is carefully limited, both in the extent and the duration of its power; and where the legislative power is exercised by an assembly, which is inspired, by a supposed influence over the people, with an intrepid confidence in its own strength; which is sufficiently numerous to feel all the passions which actuate a multitude, yet not so numerous as to be incapable of pursuing the objects of its passions, by means which reason prescribes; it is against the enterprising ambition of this department that the people ought to indulge all their jealousy and exhaust all their precautions.

The legislative department derives a superiority in our governments from other circumstances. Its constitutional powers being at once more extensive, and less susceptible of precise limits, it can, with the greater facility, mask, under complicated and indirect measures, the encroachments which it makes on the coordinate departments. It is not unfrequently a question of real nicety in legislative bodies, whether the operation of a particular measure will, or will not, extend beyond the legislative sphere. On the other side, the executive power being restrained within a narrower compass, and being more simple in its nature, and the judiciary being described by landmarks still less uncertain, projects of usurpation by either of these departments would immediately betray and defeat themselves. Nor is this all: as the legislative department alone has access to the pockets of the people, and has in some constitutions full discretion, and an all-prevailing influence, over the pecuniary rewards of those who fill the other departments, a dependence is thus created in the latter, which gives still greater facility to encroachments of the former.

THE FEDERALIST NO. 51

HAMILTON OR MADISON

To the People of the State of New York:

To what expedient, then, shall we finally resort, for maintaining in practice the necessary partition of power among the several departments, as laid down in the Constitution? The only answer that can be given is, that as all these exterior provisions are found to be inadequate, the defect must be supplied, by so contriving the interior structure of the government as that its several constituent parts may, by their mutual relations, be the means of keeping each other in their proper places. Without presuming to undertake a full development of this important idea, I will hazard a few general observations, which may perhaps place it in a clearer light, and enable us to form a more correct judgment of the principles and structure of the government planned by the convention.

In order to lay a due foundation for that separate and distinct exercise of the different powers of government, which to a certain extent is admitted on all hands to be essential to the preservation of liberty, it is evident that each department should have a will of its own; and consequently should be so constituted that the members of each should have as little agency as possible in the appointment of the members of the others. Were this principle rigorously adhered to, it would require that all the appointments for the supreme executive, legislative, and judiciary magistracies should be drawn from the same fountain of authority, the people, through channels having no communication whatever with one another. Perhaps such a plan of constructing the several departments would be less difficult in practice than it may in contemplation appear. Some difficulties, however, and some additional expense would attend the execution of it. Some deviations, therefore, from the principle must be admitted. In the constitution of the judiciary department in particular, it might be inexpedient to insist rigorously on the principle: first, because peculiar qualifications being essential in the members, the primary consideration ought to be to select that mode of choice which best secures these qualifications; secondly, because the permanent tenure by which the appointments are held in that department, must soon destroy all sense of dependence on the authority conferring them.

It is equally evident, that the members of each department should be as little dependent as possible on those of the others, for the emoluments annexed to their offices. Were the executive magistrate, or the judges, not independent of the legislature in this particular, their independence in every other would be merely nominal.

But the great security against a gradual concentration of the several powers in the same department, consists in giving to those who administer each department the necessary constitutional means and personal motives to resist encroachments of the others. The provision for defense must in this, as in all other cases, be made commensurate to the danger of attack. Ambition must be made to counteract ambition. The interest of the man must be connected with the constitutional rights of the place. It may be a reflection on human nature, that such devices should be necessary to control the abuses of government. But what is government itself, but the greatest of all reflections on human nature? If angels were to govern men, neither external nor internal controls on government would be necessary. In framing a government which is to be administered by men over men, the great difficulty lies in this: you must first enable the government to control the governed; and in the next place oblige it to control itself. A dependence on the people is, no doubt, the primary control on the government; but experience has taught mankind the necessity of auxiliary precautions.

This policy of supplying, by opposite and rival interests, the defect of better motives, might be traced through the whole system of human affairs, private as well as public. We see it particularly displayed in all the subordinate distributions of power, where the constant aim is to divide and arrange the several offices in such a manner as that each may be a check on the other— that the private interest of every individual may be a sentinel over the public rights. These inventions of prudence cannot be less requisite in the distribution of the supreme powers of the State.

But it is not possible to give to each department an equal power of self-defense. In republican government, the legislative authority necessarily predominates. The remedy for this inconvenience is to divide the legislature into different branches; and to render them, by different modes of election and different principles of action, as little connected with each other as the nature of their common functions and their common dependence on the society will admit. It may even be necessary to guard against dangerous encroachments by still further precautions. As the weight of the legislative authority requires that it should be thus divided, the weakness of the executive may require, on the other hand, that it should be fortified. An absolute negative on the legislature appears, at first view, to be the natural defense with which the executive magistrate should be armed. But perhaps it would be neither altogether safe nor alone sufficient. On ordinary occasions it might not be exerted with the requisite firmness, and on extraordinary occasions it might be perfidiously abused. May not this defect of an absolute negative be supplied by some qualified connection between the weaker department and the weaker branch of the stronger department, by which the latter may be led to support the constitutional rights of the former, without being too much detached from the rights of its own department?

If the principles on which these observations are founded be just, as I persuade myself they are, and they be applied as a criterion to the several State constitutions, and to the Federal Constitution, it will be found that if the latter does not perfectly correspond with them, the former are infinitely less able to bear such a test.

53. THE OBSOLESCENCE OF
THE SEPARATION OF POWERS

HAROLD J. LASKI

Harold J. Laski (1893–1950) was professor of history and political theory at the London School of Economics and an intellectual leader of the Labor Party; he was Chairman of its Executive Committee for a time.

Since the time of Aristotle, it has been generally agreed that political power is divisible into three broad categories. There is, first, the legislative power. It enacts the general rules of the society. It lays down the principles by which the members of the society must set their course. There is, secondly, the executive power. It seeks to apply those rules to particular situations; where, for instance, an Old Age Pension Law has been enacted, it pays out the specified sum to those entitled to receive it. There is, thirdly, the judicial power. This determines the manner in which the work of the executive has been fulfilled. It sees to it that the exercise of executive authority conforms to the general rules laid down by the legislature; it may, as in *Ex parte O'Brien,* declare that the particular order issued is, in fact, ultra vires. It settles also the relationship between private citizens, on the one hand, and between citizens and government upon the other, where these give rise to problems which do not admit of solution by agreement.

It may be admitted at the outset that these categories are of art and not of nature. It is perfectly possible to conceive of all these functions being performed by a single body, or even in the name of a single person; and in the modern democratic state the distinction between them cannot, in fact, be consistently maintained. Legislatures often perform executive acts, as when the Senate of the United States confirms the nominations of the President. They perform judicial duties also; the House of Lords is a Court to pass upon impeachments authorized by the House of Commons. Executive bodies, especially in recent times, perform acts it is difficult to distinguish from legislation, on the one hand, and judicial functions on the other; of which the provisional order system in England, and the power of the Ministry of Health in *Arlidge v. Local Government Board* are sufficient examples. The judiciary, moreover, is constantly acting as an executive. The English judges issue rules under the Judicature Acts. They act also as a legislature when they give expression to that part of the law not formally enacted by statute; and it is a striking fact that the responsibility of the French State

From Harold J. Laski, *A Grammar of Politics.* New Haven: Yale University Press, 1929, pp. 295–305, excerpts. Reprinted by permission.

has been largely created by the jurisprudence of the Conseil d'Etat. There exist, moreover, in every State powers like that of declaring war and making treaties, of recognizing governments already de facto as de jure, of the veto of legislation by an executive authority, which it is no easy matter to classify with any precision. Little, indeed, is gained by the formal attempt—the effort, for instance, to make the judicial power merely a species of executive authority—to distinguish between the different types of function here outlined. For rules formulated to govern particular cases become, if they work satisfactorily, general rules; and general rules, in their turn, are made obsolete by the manner, or the result, of their application.

It may yet be fairly argued that, in every State, some distinction between the three powers is essential to the maintenance of freedom.

It is not, I think, possible so to define the area of each of these three authorities that each remains independent and supreme in its allotted territory. The separation of powers does not mean the equal balance of powers. If it is, broadly speaking, the business of the executive to carry out those principles of general policy enacted by the legislature, it must retain the confidence of the latter body; and such confidence implies the power to compel subordination of the executive to its will. The legislature, that is to say, can directly secure, as a matter of right, that the substance of executive acts is suffused with what it deems to be its purposes. So, too, though more indirectly, with the judiciary. The legislature ought not to dictate to any judiciary the nature of the results it should attain in a particular case; but it is entitled, within the limits hereafter discussed, to provide by statute against the recurrence of a decision of which it is in disagreement with the principles. So, also, when a particular decision, as in the Free Church of Scotland case, is likely to result in injustice, a legislative compromise is not an unfair solution of the problems raised. In general, therefore, the powers both of executive and judiciary find their limits in the declared will of the legislative organ.

The case is different in the relationship of executive and judiciary. It is the business of the judge to be the taskmaster of the executive. He has to see that its interpretation of its powers is never so elastic that it either arrogates novelty to itself or bears unequally upon the body of citizens. To such ends as these, it follows that every executive act should be open to scrutiny in the courts; and the decision of the judiciary should always be binding upon the executive unless the legislature otherwise resolves. There should never be the power in an executive body which enables it to escape the scrutiny of men less tempted than itself to identify will with authority. What Professor Dicey has called the rule of law is, with all its implications, fundamental. It means that the State must be put on an equality with all other bodies, that it must answer for its acts; it means, also, that no mysterious prerogative should intervene to prevent the attainment of justice. The power of the judiciary over the executive is, therefore, if contingent, nevertheless essential. The one limitation of substance is that the courts cannot act propriis motibus. There must be complaint before decision, and the complaint must come from the citizen body. But when the complaint is proved, the executive should have no authority to transcend the judicial will. Remedy, if remedy be required, is the business of the legislature.

This separation of functions need not imply, though it has been taken to imply, a complete separation of personnel. Montesquieu's mistaken view of the relation between executive and legislature in England, consecrated as it was by Blackstone, led to the theory that no bridges ought to be built between the organs which represent these various powers. But, as Duguit has pointed out, the execution of any order involves the assistance of all ultimate authorities in the State; and the attempt, as in the American Constitution, rigidly to separate the three powers, has only meant the building of an extra-constitutional relationship between them. The use of patronage, on the one hand, and the peculiar structure of parties, on the other, has effected by means open to serious question a conjunction between executive and legislature which needs, in any case, to be made. Much the best method of obtaining it is to make the executive, as in England and France, a committee of the legislature. Thereby a variety of ends are served. The executive can only stay in office so long as it retains the confidence of the legislature. A flexibility in its policy is thus assured which prevents that deadlock in action which occurs whenever the American President is at odds with Congress, and that even when his own party is in power. The presence of the executive in the legislature enables it to explain its policy in the one way that ensures adequate attention and organized criticism. It is not attention and criticism in a vacuum. It is attention from, and criticism by, those who are eager to replace the executive if it proves unconvincing. It thus makes for responsibility. It prevents a legislature which has no direct interest in administration from drifting into capricious statutes. It arrests that executive degeneration which is bound to set in when the policy of a ministry is not its own. It secures an essential coordination between bodies whose creative interplay is the condition of effective government.

Nor is that all. The executive as a committee of the legislature has an opportunity to drive a stream of tendency through affairs. That is an urgent task. The modern legislature is, of necessity, too large to be left to direct itself; either it loses its center of equipoise in a mass of statutes unrelated to the posture of affairs, or it gives rise to an interest as against the executive which sets one striving against the other in an effort to win credit from the electorate. The value of an executive which forces the legislature either to accept or to reject its measures is that the latter's efforts are then canalized into something like an organized policy. The play of ideas is not prohibited, but it is limited to the measures upon which men are prepared to risk their political existence. The executive is not made to administer measures it believes mistaken; the policy adopted is one for which it is prepared to make itself responsible. Or, alternatively, a different executive comes into view.

This relationship, moreover, presents a simple means whereby persons fitted to be members of an executive may make known their ability. Certainly whatever may have been the defects of the House of Commons, what has been called its selective function has been amazingly well done. It has proved character as well as talent. It has measured the hinterland between oratorical quality and administrative insight with much shrewdness. I know of no alternative method that in any degree approaches it. Certainly the choice of men for high executive office, as during the war, on the ground of great business capacity, or position in the trade union world, was generally, a sorry failure. The average American President represents, at the best, a leap in the dark; his average cabinet rarely represents anything at all. But the average member of an English cabinet has been tried and tested over a long period in the public view. He has the "feel" of his task long before he comes to that task. He has spent his earlier career in contact with the operations he is now to direct. To give the executive, by this means, the initiative in law-making, and to build its life upon the successful use of that initiative in the legislature, is an elementary induction from historic experience.

Nothing in this implies the mastery of the legislature by the executive. Under the system, indeed, there have developed experiences so different as those of Great Britain and France. What, rather, is involved is the coordination of knowledge, so that each aspect of the governmental adventure is used to enrich the other. The position of the judiciary is different. Its whole purpose is impartiality. It is deliberately set aside from the normal process of conflict out of which law emerges. For its object is, above all, to protect the body of citizens from executive encroachment. To make it in any sense subordinate to the executive is to make impossible the performance of the most urgent function within its province. That is why most political systems have set themselves to protect the independence of judges. The federal judiciary in America, the bench in England, can only be removed by a special and difficult procedure; and it is noteworthy that in the American States, where election of judges usually prevails, a much less high standard of competence prevails. It is, I think, clear that the proper performance of the judicial function implies, first of all, that no judge shall be removed except for physical reasons or for corruption. The executive may dislike his pronouncements. His decisions may be unpopular with the people. Unless he is in a position to know that no penalty follows from doing the right as he sees right, he is bound to be the creature of the passing phases of public opinion. It implies, secondly, the rule of law. That rule may be enforced through special tribunals, where technical problems, as in the fixation of gas rates in America, are in issue; but there must be no organ of the executive exempt from judicial inspection. And, clearly, where the executive itself exercises quasi-judicial functions the judiciary should have such power of scrutiny as will enable it to see that the rules adopted by the executive are such as are likely to result in justice. Executive discretion is an impossible rule unless it is conceived in terms of judicial standards.

I have assumed, in this discussion, that while the judiciary may control the acts of the executive, it ought not to control legislative acts. This raises certain complex considerations which need some further analysis. It is obvious that there are two cases in which the work of a legislature is inevitably subject to the scrutiny of the courts. (1) Where the Constitution is written and the powers of the legislature are defined by it, the authority of the legislature is confined to what the courts hold to be within the competence of its powers. (2) In any federal State, even when the central legislature is left unhampered by such restrictions as those represented by the Fourteenth Amendment to the American Constitution, the question of the area of competence of the different elements of the Federation, is also a judicial matter.

Outside of Great Britain, it has been usual in most States to define with some exactitude the powers of a legislative assembly and, as in the United States, to attach to the definition of those powers a system of limitations embodied in a Bill of Rights. We have had experience of a written constitution in England under the Commonwealth; but no attempt has been made since that time to differentiate between constitutional and ordinary legislation. As a result, Parliament can, as a matter of strict law, abolish the Habeas Corpus Act as easily as it changes the laws relating to the liquor traffic. What prevents such an attempt is the tradition which gives to statutes like Habeas Corpus a majesty of a peculiarly impressive kind. Certainly the absence of this differentiation makes for a flexibility that has enormous advantages in a period of great social change. It means that new ideas can make their way without being compelled to pass through the complicated sieve devised to protect ideas deemed fundamental by an earlier period. If England wishes to abolish child labor, that change can be directly effected; but the will of the American Congress is thwarted by the Supreme Court. The English system clearly prevents the judiciary from deciding upon the desirability of legislation the principles of which were unknown, naturally enough, to the generation by which the Constitution was made. And it is obvious that the more the courts can be saved from passing upon such desirability, the more likely they are to retain the respect of citizens.

For it must not be forgotten that much legislation held unconstitutional by the Supreme Court is, in fact, so held not upon principles of strict legal theory, but upon a view of what is reasonable. The substance of reasonableness does not dwell in the clouds, but is built almost entirely upon the habits and contacts of those estimating it. A few men may be detached enough to project themselves beyond the special circle of their limited experience; most, certainly, will be content to be imprisoned therein without any sense of that captivity. Mr. Justice Braxfield had never a shadow of doubt that the Scottish radicals were criminal, not because of overt acts logically construable as crime, but because men in his own environment did not hold those opinions. Mr. Justice Grantham tried election petitions in the simple belief that a decision in favor of the Tory candidate fulfilled the requirements of justice. The remarks of American judges in the political trials of the last ten years have been more frequently like those of counsel determined to secure a conviction than of men anxious to arrive at an impartial verdict on the facts. To entrust the judge with the power to override the will of the legislature is broadly to make him the decisive factor in the State.

In that sense, a written Constitution in which the legislature is so vigorously controlled seems to me a great mistake. For the Constitution will always reflect the spirit of the time at which it was made. The judge will, on the average, be better acquainted with that spirit, more bound to the ideas it reflects, than he will be with a later and more novel, ideology. His views on the advisability, say, of economic legislation are no more likely to be right than those of the legislature, and there seems, therefore, no common sense in allowing his views to prevail.

But, equally, there seems no good reason why a legislature should be able to enforce its will on subjects of great magnitude without control of some kind. There are notions so fundamental that it is necessary in every State to give them special protection. Freedom of speech ought not to be interfered with as easily as the licensing laws. *Ex post facto* laws and bills of attainder are, I think without exception, vicious both in principle and result. . . . Legislation which aims at the disfranchisement of a special class or creed is an outrage upon the whole thesis of citizenship. Powers such as these ought never to be within the compass of a legislature except under severe restrictions as to their exercise.

54. TOWARD A "NEW FEDERALISM"

RICHARD M. NIXON

Richard M. Nixon is the thirty-seventh President of the United States. During his political career he also served in the House of Representatives and as Vice-President (1953–1960).

We confronted the fact that state and local governments were being crushed in a fiscal vise, squeezed by rising costs, rising demands for services and exhaustion of revenue sources.

We confronted the fact that in the past five years the Federal Government alone spent more than a quarter of a trillion dollars on social programs—more than $250-billion. Yet far from solving our problems, these expenditures had reaped a harvest of dissatisfaction, frustration and bitter division.

Never in human history has so much been spent by so many for such a negative result. The cost of the lesson has been high, but we have learned that it is not only what we spend that matters; it is the way we spend it.

Beyond this, we confronted a collapse of confidence in government itself, a mounting distrust of all authority that stemmed in large measure from the increasing inability of government to deliver its services or to keep its promises.

As Professor Peter Drucker has written, "There is mounting evidence that government is big rather than strong; that it is fat and flabby rather than powerful; that it costs a great deal but does not achieve much.

From Richard M. Nixon, speech outlining his ideas on the "new federalism," delivered before the National Governors' Conference, September 1, 1969, excerpts.

"There is mounting evidence also that the citizen less and less believes in government and is increasingly disenchanted with it. Indeed, government is sick—and just at the time when we need a strong, healthy and vigorous government."

The problem has not been a lack of good intentions and not merely a lack of money. Methods inherited from the thirties proved out of date in the sixties; structures put together in the thirties broke down under the load of the sixties.

Overly centralized, over-bureaucratized, the Federal Government became unresponsive as well as inefficient.

In the space of only 10 years, state and local expenditures rose by two and a half times—from $44-billion in 1958 to $108-billion in 1968.

States alone have had to seek more than 200 tax rate increases in the past eight years.

We have to devise a new way to make our revenue system meet the needs of the seventies—to put the money where the problems are and to get a dollar's worth of return for a dollar spent.

Our new strategy for the seventies begins with the reform of the Government:

1. Overhauling its structure.

2. Pruning out those programs that have failed or that have outlived their time.

3. Ensuring that its delivery systems actually deliver the intended service to the intended beneficiaries.

4. Gearing its programs to the concept of social investment.

5. Focusing its activities not only on tomorrow, but on the day after tomorrow.

This must be a cooperative venture among governments at all levels, because it centers on what I have called the "new federalism"—in which power, funds and authority are channeled increasingly to those governments closest to the people.

The essence of the new federalism is to help regain control of our national destiny by returning a greater share of control to state and local authorities.

This in turn requires constant attention to raising the quality of government at all levels. . . .

We have proposed the first major reform of welfare in the history of welfare. . . .

We have proposed the first major restructuring of food programs for the needy in the history of food programs. . . .

We have declared the first five years of a child's life to be a period of special and specific Federal concern. . . .

We have proposed the first major reform of the income tax system in nearly two decades, to remove millions of the poor from the tax rolls entirely, to close loopholes that have allowed many of the rich to escape taxation and to make the entire structure more balanced and more equitable.

We have proposed the most fundamental reform of the unemployment insurance system in the history of unemployment insurance.

We have proposed the first reform in the fiscal structure of federalism since the nineteen thirties. In proposing to begin the sharing of Federal tax revenues with the states—to be spent as the states see fit—we are putting our money where our principles are.

We have proposed, for the first time in history, a comprehensive and effective delegation of Federal programs to state and local management.

We have begun the first overall reform of the organization of the Federal Government since the Hoover Commission. . . .

For the first time, machinery has been created to raise the problems of the cities and the problems of the environment to the level of formal, inter-departmental, Cabinet-level concern with the creation of the Urban Affairs Council and the Council on Environmental Quality.

55. MERITS OF THE FEDERAL SYSTEM

JAMES BRYCE

James Bryce, Viscount (1838–1922) was a noted professor of law at Oxford and a Liberal Party Member of Parliament. He was especially interested in the relationship between law and history. In 1870 he made the first of a series of visits to the United States which culminated in the publication in 1888 of THE AMERICAN COMMONWEALTH.

I do not propose to discuss in this chapter the advantages of federalism in general, for to do this we should have to wander off to other times and countries, to talk of Achaia and the Hanseatic League and the Swiss Confederation. I shall comment on those merits only which the experience of the American union illustrates.

There are two distinct lines of argument by which their federal system was recommended to the framers of the Constitution, and upon which it is still held forth for imitation to other countries. These lines have been so generally confounded that it is well to present them in a precise form.

The first set of arguments point to federalism proper, and are the following:

1. That federalism furnishes the means of uniting commonwealths into one nation under one national government without extinguishing their separate administrations, legislatures, and local patriotisms. As the Americans of 1787 would probably have preferred complete state independence to the fusion of their states into a unified government, federalism was the only resource. So when the new Germanic Empire, which is really a federation, was estab-

From James Bryce, *The American Commonwealth*, Vol. I. New York: The Macmillan Company, 1891, pp. 342–49.

lished in 1871, Bavaria and Würtemberg could not have been brought under a national government save by a federal scheme. Similar suggestions, as everyone knows, have been made for resettling the relations of Ireland to Great Britain, and of the self-governing British colonies to the United Kingdom. There are causes and conditions which dispose nations living under a loosely compacted government, or under a number of almost independent governments, to form a closer union in a federal form. There are other causes and conditions which dispose the subjects of one government, or sections of these subjects to desire to make their governmental union less close by substituting a system of a federal character. In both sets of cases, the centripetal or centrifugal forces spring from the local position, the history, the sentiments, the economic needs of those among whom the problem arises; and that which is good for one people or political body is not necessarily good for another. Federalism may be an equally legitimate resource where it is adopted for the sake of tightening or of loosening a pre-existing bond.

2. That federalism supplies the best means of developing a new and vast country. It permits an expansion whose extent, and whose rate and manner of progress, cannot be foreseen to proceed with more variety of methods, more adaptation of laws and administration to the circumstances of each part of the territory, and altogether in a more truly natural and spontaneous way, than can be expected under a centralized government, which is disposed to apply its settled system through all its dominions. Thus the special needs of a new region are met by the inhabitants in the way they find best: its special evils are cured by special remedies, perhaps more drastic than an old country demands, perhaps more lax than an old country would tolerate; while at the same time the spirit of self-reliance among those who build up these new communities is stimulated and respected.

3. That it prevents the rise of a despotic central government, absorbing other powers, and menacing the private liberties of the citizen. This may now seem to have been an idle fear, so far as America was concerned. It was, however, a very real fear among the great-grandfathers of the present Americans, and nearly led to the rejection even of so undespotic an instrument as the Federal Constitution of 1789. Congress (or the President, as the case may be) is still sometimes described as a tyrant by the party which does not control it, simply because it is a central government: and the states are represented as bulwarks against its encroachments.

The second set of arguments relate to and recommend not so much federalism as local self-government. I state them briefly because they are familiar.

4. Self-government stimulates the interest of people in the affairs of their neighborhood, sustains local political life, educates the citizen in his daily round of civic duty, teaches him that perpetual vigilance and the sacrifice of his own time and labor are the price that must be paid for individual liberty and collective prosperity.

5. Self-government secures the good administration of local affairs by giving the inhabitants of each locality due means of overseeing the conduct of their business.

That these two sets of grounds are distinct appears from the fact that the sort of local interest which local self-government evokes is quite a different thing from the interest men feel in the affairs of a large body like an American state. So, too, the control over its own affairs of a township, or even a small county, where everybody can know what is going on, is quite different from the control exercisable over the affairs of a commonwealth with a million people. Local self-government may exist in a unified country like England, and may be wanting in a federal country like Germany. And in America itself, while some states, like those of New England, possessed an admirably complete system of local government, others, such as Virginia, the old champion of state sovereignty, were imperfectly provided with it. Nevertheless, through both sets of arguments there runs the general principle, applicable in every part and branch of government, that, where other things are equal, the more power is given to the units which compose the nation, be they large or small, and the less to the nation, as a whole and to its central authority, so much the fuller will be the liberties and so much greater the energy of the individuals who compose the people. This principle, though it had not been then formulated in the way men formulate it now, was heartily embraced by the Americans. Perhaps it was because they agreed in taking it as an axiom that they seldom referred to it in the subsequent controversies regarding state rights. These controversies proceeded on the basis of the Constitution as a law rather than on considerations of general political theory. A European reader of the history of the first seventy years of the United States is surprised how little is said, through the interminable discussions regarding the relation of the federal government to the states, on the respective advantages of centralization or localization of powers as a matter of historical experience and general expediency.

Three further benefits to be expected from a federal system may be mentioned, benefits which seem to have been unnoticed or little regarded by those who established it in America.

6. Federalism enables a people to try experiments in legislation and administration which could not be safely tried in a large centralized country. A comparatively small commonwealth like an American state easily makes and unmakes its laws; mistakes are not serious, for they are soon corrected; other states profit by the experience of a law or a method which has worked well or ill in the state that has tried it.

7. Federalism, if it diminishes the collective force of a nation, diminishes also the risks to which its size and the diversities of its parts expose it. A nation so divided is like a ship built with watertight compartments. When a leak is sprung in one compartment, the cargo stowed there may be damaged, but the other compartments remain dry and keep the ship afloat. So if social discord or an economic crisis has produced disorders or foolish legislation in one member of the federal body, the mischief may stop at the state frontier instead of spreading through and tainting the nation at large.

8. Federalism, by creating many local legislatures with wide powers, relieves the national legislature of a part of that large mass of functions which might

otherwise prove too heavy for it. Thus business is more promptly dispatched, and the great central council of the nation has time to deliberate on those questions which most nearly touch the whole country.

All of these arguments recommending federalism have proved valid in American experience.

To create a nation while preserving the states was the main reason for the grant of powers which the national government received; an all-sufficient reason, and one which holds good today. The several states have changed greatly since 1789, but they are still commonwealths whose wide authority and jurisdiction practical men are agreed in desiring to maintain.

Not much was said in the Convention of 1787 regarding the best methods of extending government over the unsettled territories lying beyond the Allegheny mountains. It was, however, assumed that they would develop as the older colonies had developed, and in point of fact each district, when it became sufficiently populous, was formed into a self-governing state, the less populous divisions still remaining in the status of semi-self-governing Territories. Although many blunders have been committed in the process of development, especially in the reckless contraction of debt and the wasteful disposal of the public lands, greater evils might have resulted had the creation of local institutions and the control of new communities been left to the central government. Congress would have been not less improvident than the state governments, for it would have been less closely watched. The opportunities for robbery would have been irresistible, the growth of order and civilization probably slower. It deserves to be noticed that, in granting self-government to all those of her colonies whose population is of English race, England has practically adopted the same plan as the United States have done with their western territory. The results have been generally satisfactory, although England, like America, has found that her colonists are disposed to treat the aboriginal inhabitants, whose lands they covet and whose persons they hate, with a harshness and injustice which the mother country would gladly check.

The arguments which set forth the advantages of local self-government were far more applicable to the states of 1787 than to those of 1887. Virginia, then the largest state, had only a half million free inhabitants, less than the present population of Chicago or Liverpool. Massachusetts had 450,000, Pennsylvania 400,000, New York 300,000; while Georgia, Rhode Island, and Delaware had (even counting slaves) less than 200,000 between them. These were communities to which the expression "local self-government" might be applied, for, although the population was scattered, the numbers were small enough for the citizens to have a personal knowledge of their leading men, and a personal interest (especially as a large proportion were landowners) in the economy and prudence with which common affairs were managed. Now, however, when of the forty-two states twenty-two have more than a million inhabitants, and four have more than three million, the newer states, being, moreover, larger in area than most of the older ones, the stake of each citizen is relatively smaller, and generally too small to sustain his activity in politics, and the party chiefs of the state are known to him only by the newspapers or by their occasional visits on a stumping tour.

All that can be claimed for the federal system under this head of the argument is that it provides the machinery for a better control of the taxes raised and expended in a given region of the country, and a better oversight of the public works undertaken there than would be possible were everything left to the central government. As regards the educative effect of numerous and frequent elections, a European observer is apt to think that elections in America are too many and come too frequently. Overtaxing the attention of the citizen and frittering away his interests, they leave him at the mercy of knots of selfish adventurers. Of this, however, more will be said in a subsequent chapter.

The utility of the state system in localizing disorders or discontents, and the opportunities it affords for trying easily and safely experiments which ought to be tried in legislation and administration, constitute benefits to be set off against the risk, referred to in the last preceding chapters, that evils may continue in a district, may work injustice to a minority and invite imitation by other states, which the wholesome stringency of the central government might have suppressed. Europeans are startled by the audacity with which Americans apply the doctrine of laissez aller; Americans declare that their method is not only the most consistent but in the end the most curative.

A more unqualified approval may be given to the division of legislative powers. The existence of the state legislatures relieves Congress of a burden too heavy for its shoulders; for although it has far less foreign policy to discuss than the Parliaments of England, France, or Italy, and although the separations of the executive from the legislative department gives it less responsibility for the ordinary conduct of the administration than devolves on those chambers, it could not possibly, were its competence as large as theirs, deal with the multiform and increasing demands of the different parts of the union. There is great diversity in the material conditions of different parts of the country, and at present the people, particularly in the West, are eager to have their difficulties handled, their economic and social needs satisfied, by the state and the law. Having only a limited field of legislation left to it, Congress may be thought to enjoy better opportunities than the overtasked English Parliament of cultivating that field well. Nevertheless, as has been shown in a previous chapter, its public legislation is scanty, and its private legislation careless and wasteful.

These merits of the federal system of government which I have enumerated are the counterpart and consequences of that limitation of the central authority whose dangers were indicated in the last chapter. They are, if one may reverse the French phrase, the qualities of federalism's defects. The problem which all federalized nations have to solve is how to secure an efficient central government and preserve national unity, while allowing free scope for the diversities, and free play to the authorities, of the members of the federation. It is, to adopt that favorite astronomical metaphor which no American panegyrist of the Constitution omits, to keep the centrifugal and centripetal forces in equilibrium, so that neither the planet states shall fly off into space, nor the sun of the central government draw them into its consuming fires. The characteristic merit of the American Constitution lies in the method by which it has solved this problem. It has given the national government a direct authority over all citizens, irrespective of the state governments, and has therefore been able safely to leave wide powers in the hands of those governments. And by placing the Constitution above both the national and the state governments, it has referred the arbitrament of disputes between them to an independent body, charged with the interpretation of the Constitution, a body which is to be deemed not so much a third authority in the government as the living voice of the Constitution, the unfolder of the mind of the people whose will stands expressed in that supreme instrument.

The application of these two principles, unknown to, or at any rate little used by, any previous federation, has contributed more than anything else to the stability of the American system, and to the reverence which its citizens feel for it, a reverence which is the best security for its permanence. Yet even these devices would not have succeeded but for the presence of a mass of moral and material influences stronger than any political devices, which have maintained the equilibrium of centrifugal and centripetal forces. On the one hand there has been the love of local independence and self-government; on the other, the sense of community in blood, in language, in habits and ideas, a common pride in the national history and the national flag.

Quid leges sine moribus? The student of institutions, as well as the lawyer, is apt to overrate the effect of mechanical contrivances in politics. I admit that in America they have had one excellent result; they have formed a legal habit in the mind of the nation. But the true value of a political contrivance resides not in its ingenuity but in its adaptation to the temper and circumstances of the people for whom it is designed, in its power of using, fostering, and giving a legal form to those forces of sentiment and interest which it finds in being. So it has been with the American system. Just as the passions which the question of slavery evoked strained the federal fabric, disclosing unforeseen weaknesses, so the love of the union, the sense of the material and social benefits involved in its preservation, appeared in unexpected strength, and manned with zealous defenders the ramparts of the sovereign Constitution. It is this need of determining the suitability of the machinery, for the workmen and its probable influence upon them, as well as the capacity of the workmen for using and their willingness to use the machinery, which makes it so difficult to predict the operation of a political contrivance, or when it has succeeded in one country, to advise its imitation in another. The growing strength of the national government in the United States is largely due to sentimental forces that were weak a century ago, and to a development of internal communications which was then undreamt of. And the devices which we admire in the Constitution might prove unworkable among a people less patriotic and self-reliant, less law-loving and law-abiding, than are the English of America.

56. TWO FACES OF FEDERALISM

ROBERT M. HUTCHINS

Robert M. Hutchins (1899–   ) is president of the Fund for the Republic and of the Center for the Study of Democratic Institutions.

I. The usual emphasis of the phrase "limited government" is on the restriction of the sphere of the state. This restriction is justified either by the incompetence of the state and its consequent lack of jurisdiction, as in religious matters, or by a preference for private as against public action, as in economic matters.

The restrictive connotation of the phrase "limited government" is not the only possible one. A constitution that directs the community to work toward certain objects in certain ways limits the government in the sense that the constitution inhibits the pursuit of other objects or the use of the other means. In this sense any written constitution limits the government, for it is inconceivable that the framers would content themselves with the gratuitous remark that the people could pursue any objects by any methods that appealed to them.

The first way of talking about limited government, which emphasizes restrictions on government, is supported in the name of individual freedom, which is thought to result from immunities against government. . . .

In this view the role of the state is to "secure," that is, to defend and not to interfere with those basic rights which existed before the state, and any other rights that the individual acquires later. For the further protection of the freedom of the individual against government many centers of power that may compete with government are desirable. But freedom may demand protection against them, too. Freedom occurs in the interstices among these centers and in the regions they are prohibited from entering. Only a pluralistic society can be free.

The second way of talking about limited government, which emphasizes limitation to certain means and ends, is supported in the name of political liberty. This is liberty under law. If the laws are just in their object, adoption, and execution, the society is free. Democracy is the most completely just form of government because democracy calls for the consent and participation of the people in the passage of the laws and the processes of their execution.

In this view, neither democracy nor freedom requires the existence of independent or quasi-independent centers of power. Their existence is a matter of expediency. The state, after considering whether or not laws should

From Robert M. Hutchins, *Two Faces of Federalism.* Santa Barbara, California: Center for the Study of Democratic Institutions, 1961, pp. 5–20, excerpts.

be passed governing institutions, might decide that it was best not to have any governing some, or to have the laws that did govern them restricted to such matters as their property and their public conduct.

It will be observed that such conclusions are not dictated by lack of power, interest, or competence on the part of the state. Nor do they result from any limitations inherent in the nature of law. These limitations are simply that law must be just, general, enforceable, and confined to the regulations of external acts. The pluralistic organization of society would not be required by justice or freedom; it would rest on the judgment, politically and democratically arrived at that this organization was the most advantageous at the time. The reciprocal range of public and private action might vary with the circumstances. . . .

The argument presents two faces of federalism, if I may be permitted to extend the word beyond its ordinary meaning to refer to the theory by which a political community organizes its component parts and the groups within it. The first face is that attractive to those who are primarily concerned with protection. This is to be obtained through constitutional declarations affirming the citizen's rights and through constitutional restrictions on governmental power. These limitations develop and follow from the major premise of minimal government. This face of federalism shows us government balancing government and branch of government checking branch of government. The scope of government is such as to leave a wide field to voluntary associations, which act as a restraint on government and on one another. The mutual frustration of the centers of power is the guarantee of individual freedom.

Another face of federalism is seen by those who are primarily concerned with achievement. When something has to be done, a judgment has to be made about who shall do it. All hands agree on the value of individual and group effort, spontaneity, and experimental activity. Hence the first question will be whether the people can do for themselves what ought to be done. If the obstacles to the action of individuals and groups will prevent what ought to be done from being done, or done as well, then there is no objection in principle to having the government do it. Objections must run to the current, but presumably corrigible, defects of governmental machinery.

Both faces of federalism have been visible throughout American history, and we need them both. No sensible person would want to do without protection; none, no matter what he says, wants to have government limited to a police function. One purpose of this paper is to suggest that though there are two, and two equally necessary, faces of federalism, we often create difficulties for ourselves by talking as though there were only one, the first. It is probably fair to say that, though the first has dominated our way of talking, the second has described our way of acting. . . .

Those who remind their fellow countrymen of the second face of federalism must admit that it is disordered and obscure because it has been formed . . . by the exigencies of history rather than by theory and design. They can argue, however, that the time for the construction of theory and design is at hand and that the doctrine of liberty under law provides the basis for the undertaking. This theory might run as follows: the root of present error lies in the distinction between society and state; this distinction is in fact and theory negligible; the political community is and should be charged with the responsibility for the common good; the conflicting claims of individuals and groups cannot be fought out among the competitors with government acting as a referee; decisions must be made and policies formulated by the political process; although associations may be formed for purposes contributing to the common good, the political community is entitled to hold these associations to their purposes.

In accordance with this theory, the principle of federalism, instead of being a means by which government is paralyzed so that the individual may be free, would become a rule by which functions were allocated to governments, corporations, associations, and individuals. The process of allocation would be constitutional and political; that is, according to law. This theory would be a theory of limited government.

Those who look with favor upon the first face of federalism and who are primarily concerned with protection from arbitrary power must concede that in the present circumstances the power of government and the range of law are being and must be greatly extended. Those who look with favor upon the second face of federalism and who seek social achievement must concede that the record of governmental performance is not reassuring. The purification of the political process and the understanding of law, to say nothing of the development of theory, must accompany any proposals to make this face of federalism predominant. To permit the present government of this country to set and enforce standards for universities and churches, for example, would be to risk the life and purpose of these institutions. The question is whether the corruption of government and politics is inevitable or whether intelligence and resolution can prevent it.

The difficulties in taking either of the two positions outlined above have led some European thinkers to take a third, which is, in effect, to abandon politics—and federalism. The position involves the abandonment of democracy and of any democratic notion that participation in politics is desirable for the individual or the community to which he belongs. It involves a vast extension of the realm of privacy, the determined defense of that realm against all outsiders, and a retreat as complete as possible into that realm on the part of the citizen, who would emerge from it only at periodic intervals to express his general satisfaction or dissatisfaction at the polls. The government would be in the hands of an elite, on the principle that the world is now so complicated and precarious that the people cannot understand it and cannot be trusted with it. What they can understand and manage is their private interests. They can understand the degree to which the government, the main function of which is to keep order, succeeds in doing so without interference with those interests.

Apart from the practical difficulties of drawing a line between public and private, as evidenced by such a question as the incidence of taxation for the common defense, and apart from theoretical problems to be mentioned in a moment, this program has some attractions. It promises protection to individual freedom against government and its bureaucracy. It purports to meet the problems of war and technological change by putting them in competent hands. It retains the notion of government by consent. The government would presumably be for the people and, in a sense, of the people.

But it would not be by the people. Admitting that the people in any "indirect" democracy or republic do not literally perform all the acts of government, we can still see that there is a difference between a form of government in which the people participate only to the extent of throwing the rascals out and one in which the interaction among the people, their elected representatives, and the administration determines the substance and direction of public policy. Democracy appears to require this participation of the people and to be in part defined by it.

The view that we are now discussing amounts to saying that democracy should not be attempted in the modern world. The difficulties that democracy is having everywhere lend some credence to this opinion. The supporters of democracy must base their answer on the proposition that it is the most just form of government, since justice requires self-government, and that it is in any event the most desirable, since it rests on the wisdom of the people, which extends to a vision of the common good, and a better vision than any man or group of men is likely to have. If a form of government is demonstrably more just than any other, it should not be abandoned; every effort should be made to achieve the closest approximation of it that is possible in the historic circumstances of time and place. If a people does not appear to be capable of self-government, the aim of self-government should not be given up. The first priority is to do everything possible to develop the wisdom of the people through communication, education, and law. The problem is not to figure out alternatives to democracy, but to make it work. Only interim alternatives can be considered: those which are explicitly regarded as milestones along the way.

57. CREATIVE FEDERALISM: THE STATE ROLE

JOHN ANDERSON, JR.

John Anderson, Jr. (1917–   ) is president of the Citizens' Conference on State Legislatures. A former governor of Kansas, he was chairman of the National Governors' Conference and has been a member of the Advisory Commission on Intergovernmental Relations.

The subject "creative federalism" might well be viewed as a problem of the future of our form of government. There have been many changes in the

From John Anderson, Jr., "Creative Federalism: The State Role," in Donald E. Nicoll, ed., *Creative Federalism.* Washington, D. C.: Graduate School Press, U. S. Department of Agriculture, 1967. Excerpts.

past three decades—some brought about by the very necessary expansion of federal functions to meet the requirements of foreign policy, of national defense, and of certain domestic problems. Other Federal programs have been brought about because State and local governments have failed to meet the needs of the times. We need, at this point in history, to lay aside most of the extremism of partisan politics of the past and to consider these problems as objectively as possible—to consider them in terms of the total structure of government which we want and which will work in a society as complicated as ours. It seems to us that the central problem has to do with maintaining, and hopefully enhancing, *representative* government—that government which is as close to the people as is *realistically* feasible. This, of course, is an extremely complicated problem.

Certainly, since 1932, the role of State government has declined in relation to the role of the Federal Government. In this connection, it is important to differentiate between the public image or impression of the decline of the States and what has actually occurred. State governments *still* play a very basic and important role in governing our daily lives, most of our laws, and most of our court proceedings. State government lays the ground rules for city school districts, counties, and other forms of local government. It still provides most of the support for state colleges and universities, penal institutions, and mental institutions. State legislators and administrators implement and play varying roles in some Federal assistance programs. The bread and butter role of basic laws and basic services is continuing.

Part of the problem in objectively viewing the role of the States relative to the Federal Government is that new Federal programs, even small ones, get publicity and glamour. In recent years, state taxes and appropriations have increased at a faster rate than those of the Federal Government. *Time* magazine reported not long ago that ". . . state and local taxes are growing by 9% a year, or almost twice as fast as the national income. Of the 47 state legislatures in session last year, 32 approved tax increases. . . ."

In addition to the continuing basic service role of the States, very recently a considerable concern has been expressed throughout the country that State governments be revitalized to do their share in meeting the problems of our time. The organization which I now represent, the Citizens Conference on State Legislatures, is one manifestation of that movement. Although the proportions of the current movement to improve State governments and State legislatures should not be exaggerated, it does seem to represent a new and healthier view of the problem. The emphasis is *not* on *States rights,* but on *States responsibilities.* The emphasis is not on federal encroachment but on the inevitability of the Federal Government filling the void if State and local governments abdicate their responsibilities. The emphasis is not on creeping socialism and the dangers of federal bureaucracy but on the need for *representative* government *realistically* close to the people.

In connection with the need to change our perspective on these matters and these problems, let me mention two situations which have adversely affected the image of State government in recent history, both of which, we hope, are past. The rural domination of State legislatures has had the effect, some in practice and more in impression, that State government is opposed to and in conflict with and unsympathetic toward the problems of metropolitan areas. Reapportionment should change this considerably. More tragically, because of the special problems in the South, the interests of the States have come to be identified as opposed to civil rights. We trust that this situation is on its way to resolution.

Among other problems, it seems that State legislatures have not served as effectively as they should as agencies for increasing understanding between, and developing the mutual interests of, rural and urban sections of the population. As farming becomes more professionalized, as urbanites splash into the countryside for recreation, as metropolitan regions spread along interstate highways—with these developments—rural-urban conflict should decline. But what should be stressed is that city interests and city dwellers, including suburbanites, have not been sufficiently interested in statewide problems. Too often their view of State government and State legislatures seems to be confined to their own special interests—efforts to get kick-backs from state revenue (some of which they may deserve) or efforts to get the State, in effect, to leave them alone. When some thorough opinion surveys of public attitudes toward legislatures are made, I suspect we shall find that rural and small-town people of comparable education have greater knowledge about State government, that they are more likely to know their legislators, and that they are better informed about the operations of the legislature than their urban counterparts.

The role our large cities once served in sociopolitical assimilation is being met less and less effectively. Until or unless effective metropolitan government is developed (including the unlikely prospect that its boundaries could be expanded rapidly enough to keep up with the spread of the metropolitan regions), State legislatures also need to serve as a meeting place, as a place of negotiation, and as a place for developing understanding among suburbanites and city dwellers, among socioeconomic classes, and among racial and ethnic groups.

There are many signs which point to some revitalization of State government and of the public image of State government: reapportionment, the resolution of the civil rights crisis, the clear-cut evidence that an anti-Federal program cannot bring victory to a major political party! In connection with this, one might add that the Federal Government appears to have been given nearly all of the new programs that it can reasonably manage in the near future. In other words, it occurs to us that the climate of public opinion now may be opportune for a very different and more realistic appraisal of the federal system and the role of the States. . . .

In connection with the problem of State governments living up to their responsibilities, a few things might be added. Much of the failure of the States in recent decades can be attributed to a lack of revenue. Governors and legislators tend to attribute this to the Federal Government's having pre-empted the income tax and other healthy sources of revenue. This is debatable, of course, because the States have a priority to most of the same sources that the Federal Government employs, including the income tax. The States have been very timid, in part because they have felt competitive with one another, in keeping taxes low. There has been the notion that industry is attracted by low taxes. More recently, we have begun to recognize that industry may want services—good schools and cultural institutions for their employees and well-developed universities for research purposes.

Many States, according to their constitutions, require public referenda to institute or increase certain kinds of taxes. Imagine what the Federal Government might be faced with if such a public vote were required. At any rate, there is need for a very thorough study of the entire revenue structure of all units of government, including the Federal Government, State governments, cities, and public school systems.

Having thoroughly confessed the sins and shortcomings of the States and mentioned some positive, although not yet extensive, efforts to do something about them, let me also mention a few bones we have to pick with the federal establishment and its operation.

First, we who have worked in State government feel that the States should be consulted more in advance about Federal programs which affect them. We are constantly placed in a position, in order to get our proper take of the Federal pool for individual States, of having to enact matching programs in accordance with provisions established by the Federal Government. At the very least we should like to be treated as junior partners.

Some of this may check back to a failure in communication between governors, state legislators, and the U.S. Senators and Congressmen from the States. There is also need to step up communication between the president's office and the governor's. Incidentally, in all of this, State legislatures tend to be left out entirely.

Second, in connection with the problems of *representative* government, there is a trend which needs to be recognized and evaluated. This is the trend for the President and governors to use committees and commissions of elites and other special interest groups to form policy. Congressmen and legislators, the officially elected representatives of the people, are then expected to ratify such policy. I mention this as a trend that we ought to be alert to and consider the implications of. If continued and accelerated, does this mean governments by elites and special interest groups? If continued, does it undermine the officially elected representatives of the people?

Third, let me mention another matter of considerable importance to States and regions. This involves contradictions and confusions among Federal programs. The Federal Government with one hand attempts to assist the poor States and regions in many of its Health, Education and Welfare and other matching programs. But, with the other and stronger arm, the allocation of contracts and grants has the effect of enhancing the wealthier States and regions and of increasing the gap between poor and wealthier States. Although I am not certain as to exactly what proportion of the development of southern California in the past 30 years can be attributed to federal contracts, federal installations, etc., I am confident that it is a major portion. . . .

58. THE FEDERAL SYSTEM

MORTON GRODZINS

Morton Grodzins (1917–1964) was for many years professor of political science at the University of Chicago.

The Sharing of Functions. The American form of government is often, but erroneously, symbolized by a three-layer cake. A far more accurate image is the rainbow or marble cake, characterized by an inseparable mingling of differently colored ingredients, the colors appearing in vertical and diagonal strands and unexpected whirls. As colors are mixed in the marble cake, so functions are mixed in the American federal system. Consider the health officer, styled "sanitarian," of a rural county in a border state. He embodies the whole idea of the marble cake of governments.

The sanitarian is appointed by the state under merit standards established by the federal government. His base salary comes jointly from state and federal funds, the county provides him with an office and office amenities and pays a portion of his expenses, and the largest city in the county also contributes to his salary and office by virtue of his appointment as a city plumbing inspector. It is impossible from moment to moment to tell under which governmental hat the sanitarian operates. His work of inspecting the purity of food is carried out under federal standards; but he is enforcing state laws when inspecting commodities that have not been in interstate commerce; and somewhat perversely he also acts under state authority when inspecting milk coming into the county from producing areas across the state border.

He is a federal officer when impounding impure drugs shipped from a neighboring state; a federal-state officer when distributing typhoid immunization serum; a state officer when enforcing standards of industrial hygiene; a state local officer when inspecting the city's water supply; and (to complete the circle) a local officer when insisting that the city butchers adopt more hygienic methods of handling their garbage. But he cannot and does not think of himself as acting in these separate capacities. All business in the county that concerns public health and sanitation he considers his business. Paid largely from federal funds, he does not find it strange to attend meetings of the city council to give expert advice on matters ranging from rotten apples to rabies control. He is even deputized as a member of both the city and county police forces.

From Morton Grodzins, "The Federal System," in *Goals for Americans,* Report of the President's Commission on National Goals, Englewood Cliffs, N.J.: Prentice-Hall, Inc., 1960, pp. 265–67, 268–71, excerpts.

The sanitarian is an extreme case, but he accurately represents an important aspect of the whole range of governmental activities in the United States. Functions are not neatly parceled out among the many governments. They are shared functions. It is difficult to find any governmental activity which does not involve all three of the so-called "levels" of the federal system. In the most local of local functions—law enforcement or education, for example—the federal and state governments play important roles. In what, *a priori*, may be considered the purest central government activities—the conduct of foreign affairs, for example—the state and local governments have considerable responsibilities, directly and indirectly.

The federal grant programs are only the most obvious example of shared functions. They also most clearly exhibit how sharing serves to disperse governmental powers. The grants utilize the greater wealth-gathering abilities of the central government and establish nationwide standards, yet they are "in aid" of functions carried out under state law, with considerable state and local discretion. The national supervision of such programs is largely a process of mutual accommodation. Leading state and local officials, acting through their professional organizations, are in considerable part responsible for the very standards that national officers try to persuade all state and local officers to accept.

Even in the absence of joint financing, federal-state-local collaboration is the characteristic mode of action. Federal expertise is available to aid in the building of a local jail (which may later be used to house federal prisoners), to improve a local water-purification system, to step up building inspections, to provide standards for state and local personnel in protecting housewives against dishonest butchers' scales, to prevent gas explosions, or to produce a land-use plan. States and localities, on the other hand, take important formal responsibilities in the development of national programs for atomic energy, civil defense, the regulation of commerce, and the protection of purity in foods and drugs; local political weight is always a factor in the operation of even a post office or a military establishment. From abattoir accounting through zoning and zoo administration, any governmental activity is almost certain to involve the influence, if not the formal administration, of all three planes of the federal system. . . .

A Point of History. The American federal system has never been a system of separated governmental activities. There has never been a time when it was possible to put neat labels on discrete "federal," "state," and "local" functions. Even before the Constitution, a statute of 1785, reinforced by the Northwest Ordinance of 1787, gave grants-in-land to the states for public schools. Thus the national government was a prime force in making possible what is now taken to be the most local function of all, primary and secondary education. More important, the nation, before it was fully organized, established by this action a first principle of American federalism: the national government would use its superior resources to initiate and support national programs, principally administered by the states and localities.

The essential unity of state and federal financial systems was again recognized in the earliest constitutional days with the assumption by the federal government of the Revolutionary War debts of the states. Other points of federal-state collaboration during the Federalist period concerned the militia, law enforcement, court practices, the administration of elections, public health measures, pilot laws, and many other matters.

The nineteenth century is widely believed to have been the preeminent period of duality in the American system. Lord Bryce at the end of the century described (in *The American Commonwealth*) the federal and state governments as "distinct and separate in their action." The system, he said, was "like a great factory wherein two sets of machinery are at work, their revolving wheels apparently intermixed, their bands crossing one another, yet each set doing its own work without touching or hampering the other." Great works may contain gross errors. Bryce was wrong. The nineteenth century, like the early days of the republic, was a period principally characterized by intergovernmental collaboration.

Decisions of the Supreme Court are often cited as evidence of nineteenth-century duality. In the early part of the century the Court, heavily weighted with Federalists, was intent upon enlarging the sphere of national authority; in the later years (and to the 1930's) its actions were in the direction of paring down national powers and indeed all governmental authority. Decisions referred to "areas of exclusive competence" exercised by the federal government and the states; to their powers being "separate and distinct"; and to neither being able "to intrude within the jurisdiction of the other."

Judicial rhetoric is not always consistent with judicial action, and the Court did not always adhere to separatist doctrine. Indeed, its rhetoric sometimes indicated a positive view of cooperation. In any case, the Court was rarely, if ever, directly confronted with the issue of cooperation *vs.* separation as such. Rather it was concerned with defining permissible areas of action for the central government and the states; or with saying with respect to a point at issue whether any government could take action. The Marshall Court contributed to intergovernmental cooperation by the very act of permitting federal operations where they had not existed before. Furthermore, even Marshall was willing to allow interstate commerce to be affected by the states in their use of the police power. Later courts also upheld state laws that had an impact on interstate commerce, just as they approved the expansion of the national commerce power, as in statutes providing for the control of telegraphic communication or prohibiting the interstate transportation of lotteries, impure foods and drugs, and prostitutes. Similar room for cooperation was found outside the commerce field, notably in the Court's refusal to interfere with federal grants in land or cash to the states. Although research to clinch the point has not been completed, it is probably true that the Supreme Court from 1800 to 1936 allowed far more federal-state collaboration than it blocked.

Political behavior and administrative action of the nineteenth century provide positive evidence that, throughout the entire era of so-called dual federalism, the many governments in the American federal system continued the close administrative and fiscal collaboration of the earlier period. Governmental activities were not extensive. But relative to what governments did, intergovernmental cooperation during the last century was comparable with that existing today.

Occasional presidential vetoes (from Madison to Buchanan) of cash and land grants are evidence of constitutional and ideological apprehensions about the extensive expansion of federal activities which produced widespread intergovernmental collaboration. In perspective, however, the vetoes are a more important evidence of the continuous search, not least by state officials, for ways and means to involve the central government in a wide variety of joint programs. The search was successful.

Grants-in-land and grants-in-service from the national government were of first importance in virtually all the principal functions undertaken by the states and their local subsidiaries. Land grants were made to the state for, among other purposes, elementary schools, colleges, and special educational institutions; roads, canals, rivers, harbors, and railroads; reclamation of desert and swamp lands; and veterans' welfare. In fact whatever was at the focus of state attention became the recipient of national grants. (Then, as today, national grants established state emphasis as well as followed it.) If Connecticut wished to establish a program for the care and education of the deaf and dumb, federal money in the form of a land grant was found to aid that program. If higher education relating to agriculture became a pressing need, Congress could dip into the public domain and make appropriate grants to states. If the need for swamp drainage and flood control appeared, the federal government could supply both grants-in-land and, from the Army's Corps of Engineers, the services of the only trained engineers then available.

Aid also went in the other direction. The federal government, theoretically in exclusive control of the Indian population, relied continuously (and not always wisely) on the experience and resources of state and local governments. State militias were an all-important ingredient in the nation's armed forces. State governments became unofficial but real partners in federal programs for homesteading, reclamation, tree culture, law enforcement, inland waterways, the nation's internal communications system (including highway and railroad routes), and veterans' aid of various sorts. Administrative contacts were voluminous, and the whole process of interaction was lubricated, then as today, by constituent-conscious members of Congress. . . .

A long, extensive, and continuous experience is therefore the foundation of the present system of shared functions characteristic of the American federal system, what we have called the marble cake of government. It is a misjudgment of our history of our present situation to believe that a neat separation of governmental functions could take place without drastic alterations in our society and system of government. . . .

59. SHOULD THE GOVERNMENT SHARE ITS TAX TAKE?

WALTER W. HELLER

Walter W. Heller (1915–   ) is professor of economics at the University of Minnesota and a former Chairman of the Council of Economic Advisers.

Washington *must* find a way to put a generous share of the huge federal fiscal dividend (the automatic increase in tax revenue associated with income growth) at the disposal of the states and cities. If it fails to do so, federalism will suffer, services will suffer, and the state-local taxpayer will suffer.

Economic growth creates a glaring fiscal gap; it bestows its revenue bounties on the federal government, whose progressive income tax is particularly responsive to growth, and imposes the major part of its burdens on state and local governments. Closing that gap must take priority over any federal tax cuts other than the removal of the 10 per cent surcharge. And even this exception may not be valid. For, as New York Governor Nelson A. Rockefeller has proposed, the revenue generated by the surcharge can easily be segregated from other federal revenue and earmarked for sharing with the states. So perhaps even the taxpayer's "divine right" to get rid of the surcharge may have to give way to the human rights of the poor, the ignorant, the ill, and the black.

For when the state-local taxpayer is beset with—and, indeed, rebelling against—a rising tide of regressive and repressive property, sales, and excise taxes, what sense would it make to weaken or dismantle the progressive and growth-responsive federal income tax? Whether our concern is for justice and efficiency in taxation, or for better balance in our federalism, or, most important, for a more rational system of financing our aching social needs, there is no escape from the logic of putting the power of the federal income tax at the disposal of beleaguered state and local governments. . . .

Far from being just a fiscal problem—a question of meeting fiscal demands from a limited taxable capacity—the issue touches on the very essence of federalism, both in a political and in a socioeconomic sense.

Indeed, it is from the realm of political philosophy—the renewed interest in making state-local government a vital, effective, and reasonably equal partner in a workable federalism—that much of the impetus for more generous levels and new forms of federal assistance has come. . . .

From Walter W. Heller, "Should the Government Share Its Tax Take?" *Saturday Review,* March 22, 1969. Copyright 1969 Saturday Review, Inc. Excerpts.

Moving from the political to the economic, one finds strong additional rationale for new and expanded federal support in the economic—or socio-economic—theory of public expenditures. It is in this theory that our vast programs of federal aid to state and local governments—projected to run at $25 billion in fiscal 1970 (triple the amount in 1960)—are firmly anchored. All too often, they are thought of simply as a piece of political pragmatism growing out of two central fiscal facts: that Washington collects more than two-thirds of the total federal, state, and local tax take; and that nearly two-thirds of government public services (leaving aside defense and social security programs) are provided by state-local government. Throw in the objective of stimulating state-local efforts through matching provisions, and, for many people, the theory of federal grants is complete.

In fact, it is only the beginning. Consider the compelling problems of poverty and race and the related problems of ignorance, disease, squalor, and hard-core unemployment. The roots of these problems are nationwide. And the efforts to overcome them by better education, training, health, welfare, and housing have nationwide effects. Yet, it is precisely these services that we entrust primarily to our circumscribed state and local units.

Clearly, then, many of the problems that the states and localities tackle are not of their own making. And their success or failure in coping with such problems will have huge spillover effects far transcending state and local lines in our mobile and interdependent society. The increasing controversy over the alleged migration of the poor from state to state in search of higher welfare benefits is only one aspect of this. So, quite apart from any fiscal need to run hat in hand to the national government, states and cities have a dignified and reasonable claim on federal funds with which to carry out national responsibilities. Only the federal government can represent the totality of benefits and strike an efficient balance between benefits and costs. Therein lies the compelling economic case for the existing system of ear-marked, conditional grants-in-aid. Such grants will, indeed must, continue to be our major mechanism for transferring funds to the states and localities. . . .

How well does the tax-sharing plan (also called revenue sharing, unconditional grants, and general assistance grants) measure up to the economic and sociopolitical criteria implicit in the foregoing discussion? Let me rate it briefly, and sympathetically, on six counts.

First, it would significantly relieve the immediate pressures on state-local treasuries and, more important, would make state-local revenues grow more rapidly, in response to economic growth. For example, a 2-percentage-point distribution on a straight per capita basis would provide, in 1969, $650 million each for California and New York, $420 million for Pennsylvania, $375 million for Illinois, $140 million each for Mississippi and Wisconsin, $125 million each for Louisiana and Minnesota, and about $65 million each for Arkansas and Colorado.

The striking growth potential of this source of revenue is evident in two facts: 1) had the plan been in effect in 1955, the distribution of 2 per cent of the $125-billion income-tax base in that year would have yielded a state-local tax share of about $2.5 billion; and 2) by 1972, the base should be about $450 billion, yielding a $9-billion annual share.

Second, tax sharing would serve our federalist interest in state-local vitality and independence by providing new financial elbow room, free of political penalty, for creative state and local officials. Unlike the present grants-in-aid, the tax-shared revenue would yield a dependable flow of federal funds in a form that would enlarge, not restrict, their options.

Third, tax sharing would reverse the present regressive trend in our federal-state-local tax system. It seems politically realistic to assume that the slice of federal income tax revenue put aside for the states and cities would absorb funds otherwise destined to go mainly into federal tax cuts and only partly into spending increases. Given the enormous pressures on state-local budgets, on the other hand, tax shares would go primarily into higher state-local expenditures and only in small part into a slowdown of state-local tax increases. Thus, the combination would produce a more aggressive overall fiscal system.

Fourth, tax sharing—especially with the 10 per cent equalization feature—would enable the economically weaker states to upgrade the scope and quality of their services without putting crushingly heavier burdens on their citizens. Per capita sharing itself would have a considerable equalizing effect, distributing $35 per person to all of the states, having drawn $47 per person from the ten richest and $24 per person from the ten poorest states. Setting aside an extra 10 per cent for equalization would boost the allotments of the seventeen poorest states by one-third to one-half. Thus, the national interest in reducing interstate disparities in the level of services would be well served.

Fifth, the plan could readily incorporate a direct stimulus to state and local tax efforts. Indeed, the Douglas Commission (the National Commission on Urban Problems), like many other advocates of tax-sharing plans, would adjust the allotments to take account of relative state-local tax efforts. In addition, they propose a bonus for heavy reliance on individual income taxation.

A more direct stimulant to state and local efforts in the income tax field would be to enact credits against the federal income tax for state income taxes paid. For example, if the taxpayer could credit one-third or two-fifths of his state and local income tax payments directly against his federal tax liability (rather than just treat such taxes as a deduction from taxable income, as at present), it would lead to a far greater use of this fairest and most growth-oriented of all tax sources.

Ideally, income tax credits should be coupled with income tax sharing and federal aid in a balanced program of federal support. But if relentless fiscal facts require a choice, the nod must go to tax sharing because 1) credits provide no interstate income-level equalization; 2) at the outset, at least, much of the federal revenue loss becomes a taxpayer gain rather than state-local gain; and 3) since one-third of the states still lack broad-based income taxes, the credit would touch off cries of "coercion." Nevertheless, it is a splendid device that ought to have clearcut priority over further tax cuts.

Sixth, and finally, per capita revenue sharing would miss its mark it it did not relieve some of the intense fiscal pressures on local, and particularly urban, governments. The principle is easy to state. The formula to carry it out is more difficult to devise. But it can be done. The Douglas Commission has already developed an attractive formula that it describes as "deliberately 'loaded' to favor general purpose governments that are sufficiently large in population to give some prospect of viability as urban units." I would agree with the Commission that it is important not to let "no-strings" federal aid sustain and entrench thousands of small governmental units that ought to wither away—though I still prefer to see the tax-sharing funds routed through the fifty state capitals, rather than short-circuiting them by direct distribution to urban units. . . .

But, of course, opposition goes far beyond crass self-interest. It also grows out of philosophic differences and concern over the alleged shortcomings of tax sharing. There is the obvious issue of federalism versus centralism. A strong contingent in this country feels that the federal government knows best, and that state and local governments cannot be trusted. Others fear that revenue sharing or unrestricted grants will make state-local government more dependent on the federal government—a fear for which I see little or no justification.

On the issues, some would argue that it is better to relieve state-local budgets by taking over certain burdens through income-maintenance programs like the negative income tax; while others feel that too much of the revenue-sharing proceeds would go down the drain in waste and corruption. Here, one must answer in terms of a willingness to take the risks that go with an investment in the renaissance of the states and the cities. Some costs in wasted and diverted funds will undoubtedly be incurred. My assumption is that these costs will be far outweighed by the benefits of greater social stability and a more viable federalism that will flow from the higher and better levels of government services and the stimulus to state-local initiative and responsibility.

In sum, I view tax sharing as an instrument that 1) will fill a major gap in our fiscal federalism; 2) will strengthen the fabric of federalism by infusing funds *and* strength into the state-local enterprise; and 3) will increase our total governmental capacity to cope with the social crisis that confronts us. The sooner Congress gets on with the job of enacting a system of tax sharing, even if it means postponing the end of the 10 per cent surcharge, the better off we shall be.

60. TITO'S HOMEMADE COMMUNISM

ALVIN Z. RUBINSTEIN

Alvin Z. Rubinstein (1927–   ) is professor of political science at the University of Pennsylvania and author of many books and articles on Soviet and East European affairs.

On November 28, 1960, President Tito announced that Yugoslavia would adopt a new constitution in 1962, in which the role of the government in the nation's economy would be curtailed and the power of the worker would be increased. He noted the successes of the past decade and declared that the state should serve only as a coordinator while the citizen acted as "producer and manager." This development is another of a series of steps taken in recent years by the Yugoslav Communist leaders to "democratize" the system.

Yugoslavia is Communist in ideology, but in practice it has been distinguished by elements alien to Soviet Communism: a measure of political toleration unique among Communist systems, a mixed economy distinguished by considerable decentralized authority, and a large degree of cultural freedom. The Yugoslav experiment deserves close attention because it is an outstanding example of the impact of nationalism upon Communism, and because its continued success may well lead underdeveloped countries—many of them seeking to industrialize and modernize their economies within the framework of an authoritarian welfare state—to consider adopting certain Yugoslav policies and practices. An increasing number of these countries have come to the conclusion that Western democracy is a luxury they can ill afford at this stage of their development.

The Differences. In present-day Yugoslavia, freedom to travel exists for foreigner and citizen alike. There are none of the proscriptions on domestic movement so characteristic of the Soviet Union, and few on travel abroad. Everywhere the foreigner is greeted with friendliness, curiosity, and a desire to communicate.

During the past decade Yugoslavia has undergone a series of fundamental transformations. These are perhaps most apparent in the economic sphere, where the regime has established institutions and policies designed to encourage a maximum of local autonomy, democratic procedures, and communal initiative. Yugoslavia has decentralized its industrial sector, granting each enterprise considerable authority to determine its own rate of capital investment, as well as the kind and quantity of goods produced.

Alvin Z. Rubinstein, "Tito's Homemade Communism," *The Reporter,* Vol. 24, No. 2 (Jan. 19, 1961), pp. 42–44, excerpts.

The key institution in this democratization and decentralization program is the workers' council, which combines managerial authority with a countervailing degree of union responsibility in the policy-making process. Each enterprise is run by a workers' council. The council draws up production plans, determines the extent of new investment, and oversees the distribution of profits. Significantly, the councils operate with minimal interference from the federal government. To encourage expanded production and increased productivity, enterprises are permitted to produce the same types of goods and to compete with one another for the available market. If this competition threatens to become disruptive rather than salutary, however, the Federal Executive Council (the key organ of governmental executive power) may intervene and effect a settlement.

Until recently, for example, one Croatian shipping firm had a monopoly on the run to the East Coast of the United States. A Slovenian firm, sensing an opportunity for profit, invested some of its capital in several fast ships and entered into competition. To avoid a prolonged commercial conflict, the government intervened, apportioning the United States runs between the two firms.

Two Yugoslav automobile companies are now competing with each other. The firm having exclusive rights to produce the Fiat 500 and 600 in Yugoslavia is being challenged by a firm which has negotiated the right to produce the French Citroën. The firm producing the Fiats contends that the Yugoslav market cannot absorb both makes at this time and that to permit the production of Citroëns would result in squandering hard currency and an uneconomic utilization of resources. However, the firm seeking to produce Citroëns has apparently convinced the Federal Executive Council that it will not require hard currency and that imported spare parts will be financed by the export of other goods produced by the firm with no concomitant drains on the country's supply of hard currency.

The worker in Yugoslavia is free to choose his occupation, to move from one part of the country to another, and to change jobs. There are ample opportunities for him to improve his skill and status through education and on-the-job training. Unions play an important role in protecting the workers' rights and in obtaining higher wages and better working conditions. They also play an important role in the workers' council of the enterprise. In function they resemble unions in Western Europe more closely than they do Soviet unions.

Another striking feature of the economic system is the prevalence of private enterprise at the artisan and retail level. Though an individual may not own a factory, he may own his own shop or small business. In Belgrade, the wealthiest individuals are reputed to be the operators of private beauty salons. (One can easily distinguish a private shop by the presence of the individual's name under the store sign.) The government no longer seeks to pressure private entrepreneurs into joining state-controlled cooperatives; it hopes in time to gain adherents to the socialized sector by proving its economic advantage.

In agriculture, as a result of decollectivization, the peasantry has accommodated itself to the government. Again, the government hopes to win over the peasants, who own more than seventy-five per cent of the arable land, by demonstrating the advantages of state farms.

These policies seem to have benefited both the regime and the individual without in any way jeopardizing the hegemony of the Communist Party. But the newly expanded availability of consumer goods has led people to work harder and longer. Thus, the tailor in Belgrade who holds down two jobs—one in a government cooperative during the day, the other in his own apartment where he operates a private business in the evening—is not unusual. Increasingly, two jobs are necessary in Yugoslavia to enjoy a reasonably high standard of living.

Rents are relatively inexpensive, but apartments are in short supply. New housing is difficult to obtain. Virtually all new housing is being built by individual industrial and commercial enterprises, and not by the government. Priority for the new apartments is given to the executives and workers employed by the particular organization financing the new construction. The self-employed and those who work in enterprises not having much capital for investment in new housing—for example, the faculty of the University of Belgrade—have little prospect of obtaining new apartments. This may help explain the trend toward small families among the intelligentsia.

Orthodox Art Is Out. In the cultural realm, Yugoslavia enjoys a measure of freedom unparalleled in any other Communist country. There are many publishing houses, each having authority to publish whatever it considers marketable. What this means in practice is that Yugoslav authors may write critically of a wide variety of subjects, but they may not challenge the fundamentals of the socialist system or the concept of Communist Party rule; nor may they criticize President Tito. . . . Though Yugoslav writers have yet to develop a literary tradition of significant social criticism, they are moving slowly in this direction. One negative aspect of this freedom, according to Yugoslav intellectuals, has been the spate of sensational pulp "literature" put on the market.

Western literature is displayed in bookstores and seen regularly on private shelves. Political and economic writings that challenge the fundamentals of the system are not readily available but may be ordered by those engaged in scholarly research.

The "socialist realist" art of the 1945–1950 period, characterized by the regime's insistence upon conformity, orthodoxy, and emulation of Soviet art, is a thing of the past. Yugoslav architects, painters, sculptors, and musicians frequently study in America and Western Europe and are very much a part of contemporary movements. There is only a small market among individuals for their work because people lack the surplus income necessary for patronage. Painters, for example, sell most of their work to cultural institutions, industrial enterprises, and government agencies.

In architecture, Yugoslavs are designing buildings of great beauty, simplicity, and imagination. These can be seen in Belgrade and other large cities. They are especially evident in the provincial cities—in Pristina, for example—

where an even greater willingness to encourage drastic departures from tradition seems apparent.

Rapid strides have been taken to develop an adequate educational system. Eight years of schooling are now compulsory. Anyone completing high school and desiring admission to a university must be accepted. All students are free to choose their areas of specialization; no quotas are established by the government, as in the Soviet Union, prescribing the number of students entering any particular field. Tuition is free and a fourth of the university students also receive further scholarship aid to help defray the cost of books, room, and board. Although the free tuition has created new headaches for the regime, it has opened up new vistas to those of peasant or working-class background.

These developments—in literature, in the arts, and in education—are recent, and therefore, perhaps are not so well established in the system as most Yugoslavs hope and believe. There are encouraging indications, however, that the Yugoslav political elite is convinced of the essential correctness of the present pattern of economic and social organization and does not contemplate any return to a Soviet-type system.

In the political realm, the record is mixed. Yugoslavia remains a one-party state and no opposition to the Communist Party is permitted. But the party has increasingly removed itself from direct involvement in areas irrelevant to national security or the perpetuation of the regime. At the same time, it has encouraged a diffusion of decision-making power in such disparate areas as the workers' councils, the conduct of the universities, and the operation of social and cultural institutions. . . .

The present popularity of the regime rests not only on regard for Tito but on the national unity resulting from Soviet belligerence. Three other postwar developments have contributed to the regime's stability and support.

First, the organization of the state along federal lines has effectively solved Yugoslavia's most serious prewar political problem. The six federal republics—Croatia, Slovenia, Bosnia and Herzegovina, Serbia, Montenegro, and Macedonia—were established along ethnic lines with the specific purpose of reducing, and eventually eliminating, deep-rooted antagonisms among the various nationality groups. The federal solution is designed to prevent any return to the prewar situation when the Serbs dominated the government. It also seeks to give the other nationality groups a more equitable share of governmental representation. The regime's solution of the national question is without doubt its greatest contribution to Yugoslav unity and strength.

A concomitant of the federal solution has been the concept of Yugoslav, as opposed to any particularist, nationalism. With the passage of time a greater sense of national identity may be expected to develop, with its further strengthening of the popular commitment to the present system. To encourage national unity, the federal government seeks, through loans and taxation, to promote the economic development of the more backward areas of the country. It is also a crime to speak disparagingly against any nationality group.

Second, there is widespread acceptance of the objectives of the welfare state, particularly in the fields of education and medicine. The principal problem centers on the rapidity with which these benefits may be extended effectively to other fields and to the entire population. The introduction of free universal education, higher wage levels, socialized medicine, and expanded cultural opportunities have all enhanced the prestige of the regime. No longer is any serious thought given to attaining these objectives outside the framework of the existing system. The reason for this is a direct outcome of a third significant development: the growing political apathy of the younger generation.

Yugoslavs accept, and clearly appreciate, the need to avoid political controversies that might jeopardize the stability and prosperity of the past five years. Years of war and consequent drastic changes have drained people of revolutionary fervor. Aside from a small segment of the party and the intelligentsia, few have any interest in ideological dialogues on the "correct" road to socialism and the organization of society. The present generation is primarily interested in acquiring a higher standard of living and in enjoying Yugoslavia's current prosperity.

It has been said by social scientists that the test of a regime's ultimate character can best be seen in its treatment of its own population. If this is true, then there are signs that the Yugoslav variety of socialism may continue to move ahead slowly, seeking increasingly nonauthoritarian solutions to its complex problems.

61. FEDERALISM AND THE MAKING OF NATIONS

KENNETH C. WHEARE

Kenneth C. Wheare (1907–   ) is rector of Exeter College and Pro-Vice-Chancellor, Oxford University. He is author of many works on political science and allied fields, with special attention to the British Commonwealth.

. . . What is the role which federalism is expected to play in the making of nations? It is, at first sight at any rate, an appropriate form of government to offer to communities or states of distinct or differing nationality who wish to form a common government and to behave as one people for some purposes, but who wish to remain independent and in particular to retain their own nationality in all other respects. Federal government consists in a division

Kenneth C. Wheare, "Federalism and the Making of Nations," in *Federalism, Mature and Emergent,* Arthur W. MacMahon, ed. New York: Russell & Russell, Inc., 1962. Pp. 29–36, 40–41, excerpts.

of the functions of government between an independent common authority for the whole country and independent authorities for the constituent parts of the country. In certain circumstances, then, would not this be an appropriate device for bringing nations together, for preserving them, and at the same time developing over and above their feelings of distinct nationality, a sense of common nationality?

There is no doubt that there have been cases in which federalism has performed this role. But it is important to notice why this has been possible. Though differences of nationality and the desire to supplement them by building a common nationality may be an important argument for choosing a federal form of government, it must not be assumed that it will always be regarded as overwhelming. There may be considerations opposed to federalism which prevail. In the making of the Union of South Africa this was what happened. Many of the important leaders in the movement for closer union, such as Smuts, Botha, and de Villiers, thought that federalism brought complications which were not offset by its merits in giving greater security to differing national loyalties. What appears to have clinched the argument against federalism was that the leaders believed that the regulation of the affairs of the native African—then, as now, an overwhelming majority of the inhabitants of the Union—could be satisfactorily undertaken only by a unitary state. The function that federalism could perform in solving the problem of national differences was subordinated therefore to what were regarded as more pressing problems. Nationality was not ignored entirely. The equality of the two national languages—Dutch and English—was guaranteed in the constitution, and each of the four colonies was allowed to continue as a distinct province in the new Union with its own provincial council and with equal representation in the Senate or upper house of the parliament of the Union. But the provinces were subordinate units; they were not, like the American states, coordinate with the Union.

Then you find cases not where nationalism is too weak to ensure federalism but too strong to permit it. People of differing nationality cannot form a federal union unless they are prepared to accept a government in which those who differ from them in nationality have some share. In many cases, too, some nationalities must expect that, though they may have their own way in their own state or province of the federation, they will be in a minority in the government of the whole federation. A federal union usually implies, too, that those who join it will expect or be expected to develop some common nationality in addition to their distinct nationalities. When people of different nationalities are unwilling to accept these consequences, federal union cannot be made to fit their case. We have had many examples of this in history. When India approached self-government, it was hoped that a federation could be formed in which Hindus, who formed the majority of the population, could be associated with the Moslem minority. Though the Hindus would be in a majority in most of the states of the federation, there would be some states in which the Moslems had a majority—chiefly in the northwest and northeast of India—and in this way it was believed that the distinct cultures of Hindu and Moslem would be preserved and yet reconciled with a United India and an Indian nationalism. But in 1940 the powerful Moslem organization, the Moslem League, declared the Moslems were a separate nation and no mere minority community, and that they must be accorded a separate government whose territory would consist of those areas of India in which Moslems had a majority. So in 1947, when self-government came, it was partition and not federation which occurred, and two new states, India and Pakistan, were created. . . .

The point may be illustrated in another way by looking at the situation in Nigeria. This British dependency of over twenty million Africans contains within a single government three distinct nations—the Moslems of the North, who occupy over three-quarters of the area of the country and comprise over half of the population; the Yoruba-speaking people of the western region who comprise about eighteen per cent of the population; and the Ibo people of the eastern region who make up something like twenty-eight per cent of the population. They are now near to self-government, but the Moslems of the North are most reluctant to be associated with a government in which Ibos and Yorubas are to have an important say. At a conference held in London in August 1953 the first claim of the Moslems was that, if self-government was to come, they must be accorded a separate state. It was only after considerable discussion that they agreed to consider joining in a federation with the peoples of the other two regions. Here is a case where one nation is on the verge of repudiating federation and choosing partition. If the terms of the federation seem to safeguard its national integrity, it will enter into it. Truly to adapt Mr. Calpin's title, there are, as yet, no Nigerians. The most that can be said is that, as an outcome of the conference in London, followed by a further conference in Lagos, the capital of Nigeria, in January and February 1954, the representatives of the three regions are prepared to try to make Nigerians.

One other case where the strength of nationalism rules federalism out is that of Ireland. Though the Republic of Ireland might be ready to form a federation with Ulster, the Ulstermen are unwilling to submit to a government for United Ireland in which they would be in a minority. Partition in Ireland, as in India and indeed as in Palestine, is the consequence of nationalism so strong that there is no basis upon which even a federal union can be founded.

Not only is it necessary that the minority nation should be willing to join in a union if federalism is to become a possibility; it is necessary also that the nation in the majority should be prepared to tolerate the existence of the minority nation. If the majority regard the existence of national states within the federation, even, if they are only minorities in the whole union, as intolerable, then federation is not possible. It may well be that the Afrikaner majority in South Africa today would oppose the notion of transforming the Union from a unitary state into a federation on the ground that Natal, as an English or British enclave, would be a menace to Afrikanerdom. And it would be interesting to know how Englishmen would regard the proposal that the United Kingdom should be transformed into a federation with the autonomous states of Scotland, Wales, Northern Ireland, and England.

One assumption is usually present in any discussion of the use of federalism in making a nation out of differing nationalities. It is taken for granted that the differing nationalities are, in some measure at any rate, territorially segregated. Ideally, of course, it would be best if each area contained its own single nationality exclusively. The federation could then be composed of states none of which contained within its borders any minority group. People do not arrange themselves like that. What is usually regarded as essential, however, is that there should be areas or an area in which each nationality is at least in a majority so that there can be a state or states in the federation to which each nationality can look as to a motherland or national home. If this does not exist, it is difficult to see how federalism in the ordinary sense of a union of territories, with territorial autonomy, can have much relevance to the problem of reconciling differing nationalities.

In practice this is what has usually happened when federalism has been chosen. In Canada not all French Canadians live in Quebec. They are found in substantial numbers in the Maritime Provinces and in Ontario and their numbers there are growing. It is in Quebec, however, that they are in the overwhelming majority and it is through Quebec's existence as an independent unit in the Canadian federation that French Canadian nationality finds its great safeguard in Canada. So also in the twenty-two cantons of Switzerland, where German, French, and Italian nationalities are associated together in a federation, the people are not arranged exclusively in homogenous national cantons. But there is a German-speaking majority in fourteen of the cantons, and a French majority in the three cantons of Vaud, Neuchatel, and Geneva. There is an Italian majority in the canton of Ticino. Each nationality has a part of the federation in which it can enjoy autonomy.

But merely to provide that each nationality shall have its own autonomous area is not usually considered enough. What safeguards are the minority nationalities to receive to ensure that in the conduct of the business of the general government of the whole union their national interests do not suffer? They may be able to preserve their national interests in certain states or provinces where they are in a majority, but this alone provides no guarantee in the general sphere. To meet anxieties of this kind several devices are adopted. Where nationalities differ in say, religion or language or laws, provisions are inserted in the constitution of the federation to safeguard these matters in the federal sphere. In the Canadian constitution the equality of the French and English languages is asserted and certain religious rights in education are preserved. In Switzerland, French, German, and Italian are recognized in the constitution as official languages. It is usual in federations for the second chamber or upper house to be composed of an equal number of representatives from each of the states or cantons and in this way minority nationalities may have their position strengthened. In the lower houses, although representation is in proportion to population, there is usually, as in the case of Quebec for example, a minimum proportion or number of seats guaranteed to minority nations. These safeguards in the working of the general government are just as important as the division of powers itself in a federation in encouraging differing nations to unite together to form a new nation. As a rule they are, if not logically, at any rate practically essential adjuncts to a federal structure where differing nationalities are associated together.

In what has been said up to this point, I have tried to analyze in general terms the sort of situation in which federalism might be of value in making a nation out of a group of communities which are themselves of distinct or differing nationality. It is worthwhile perhaps to look at the way in which, through federation, new nations have been brought into existence. The circumstances differ from case to case and the process is often difficult. There are two or three distinct situations which deserve attention.

First of all there are cases where people of differing nationalities are prepared to join in a federation, but they do not yet feel a sense of common nationality. They say, in effect, "We are not Americans yet but we are prepared to try to become Americans." I believe that this is what happened at the time of the founding of the United States. Samuel E. Morison wrote: "Most citizens of the United States in 1790, if asked their country or nation, would not have answered American but Carolinian, Virginian, Pennsylvanian, New Yorker, or New Englander." "The United States of 1788 were not a nation by any modern standard." It would not be true, of course, to say that there were no Americans at that time. Many of the Founding Fathers were Americans. James Wilson declared in the Convention: "I am both a citizen of Pennsylvania and of the United States." What is certain, however, is that there were many more people who were prepared to become Americans than were Americans already.

When the French joined with the English in 1867 to make the Canadian federation, they were committing themselves to become Canadians in some sense which they could share with the English. It was far from easy to do. Language was against them. The French-Canadian called (and still calls) himself *Canadien* and his English speaking fellow citizens he called *Anglais*. In his language there were and are no Canadians, only *Canadiens* and *Anglais*. The making of a Canadian nation has therefore been a delicate and intricate task. A federation, as John Stuart Mill remarked, binds its people "always to fight on the same side." French Canadians and English Canadians have not always agreed upon which side they would fight or indeed whether they would fight at all. Yet the federation has survived the critical stresses of two wars, and in two of its Prime Ministers, Sir Wilfrid Laurier and Mr. St. Laurent, we have not only two great *Canadiens* but also two great Canadians.

There are other examples where the initiation of a federation has meant that differing nations express an intention of trying to achieve in addition a sense of common nationality but are still far from achieving it. The decision of the Nigerian Conferences in London in August 1953 and in Lagos in January 1954 (already referred to) to attempt a federation meant that the Moslems of the North, the Yoruba of the West, and the Ibo of the East were prepared to try to become Nigerians. So also in April 1953 when representatives of British colonies in the Caribbean decided at a conference in London to support a plan for federation they were undertaking to try to become

West Indians. We may call them West Indians or Caribbeans as we look at them from the outside and they may call themselves that when they talk to outsiders. But most of them are not more than Jamaicans or Trinidadians or Barbadians. . . .

Consider a different sort of situation. There have been many cases where a federation has not been inaugurated until a sense of common nationality had already been fairly strongly developed. The two cases I have in mind are Switzerland and Australia. When the Swiss federation was inaugurated in 1848 the different nationalities in the union had been associated together so long in a looser form of alliance or confederation that they had come to think of themselves not only as German or French or Italian but also as Swiss. Their feeling of being Swiss was no doubt less intense than their feeling of distinct nationality, but it was there. It was possible for them to declare in the preamble to the constitution that they desired not only "to consolidate the alliance of the confederated members," but also to "promote the unity, strength and honor of the Swiss nation." Am I right in concluding that this is something different from "We the people of the United States"? Did not the Founding Fathers choose their words carefully? Could they have said "We the American people" or "We, the American nation"? I believe not.

In Australia the position is hardly free from doubt. The leaders of the federal movement there campaigned for their cause throughout the colonies; the draft constitution was discussed for over ten years and was submitted to the people of the colonies in a referendum. They were persuaded to become Australians and to feel like Australians before they adopted federation. Their sense of Australian nationality was, no doubt, less intense than their feeling of attachment to each separate colony, and there were people who did not feel it at all or felt hostile to it. But it is true to say that there were Australians before there was an Australia.

We can conclude, then, that as a matter of history, federalism has provided a device through which differing nationalities could unite, and, while retaining their own distinct national existence, attempt to create in addition a new sense of common nationality. Nationalism in a federation can be expressed on at least two levels; it is not an exclusive, homogeneous passion.

But of course things do not stand still. What happens to the differing nationalities after the federation has been inaugurated and has worked for a period? In some cases it is clear that the feelings of distinct nationality get weaker and the sense of common nationality gets stronger. In Australia and the United States today I suppose it would be thought exaggerated and unreal to speak of the sentiments which people feel towards their states as national feeling. Some states may evoke a stronger loyalty than others, but generally speaking, though state loyalties exist, Americans now, as a result of history, have one nationality and Australians also. Federation has made of each of these people one nation. . . .

62. NATIONALISM AND FEDERALISM

PIERRE ELLIOTT TRUDEAU

Pierre Elliott Trudeau is Prime Minister of Canada. A complex and controversial figure, he is known as well for his social life as for his political skill. Here he develops his case for Canadian federalism.

Many of the nations which were formed into states over the past century or two included peoples who were set apart geographically (like East and West Pakistan, or Great Britain and Northern Ireland), historically (like the United States or Czechoslovakia), linguistically (like Switzerland or Belgium), racially (like the Soviet Union or Algeria). Half of the aforesaid countries undertook to form the national consensus within the framework of a unitary state; the other half found it expedient to develop a system of government called federalism. The process of consensus-formation is not the same in both cases.

It is obviously impossible, as well as undesirable, to reach unanimity on all things. Even unitary states find it wise to respect elements of diversity, for instance by administrative decentralization as in Great Britain, or by language guarantees as in Belgium; but such limited securities having been given, a consensus is obtained which recognizes the state as the sole source of coercive authority within the national boundaries. The federal state proceeds differently; it deliberately reduces the national consensus to the greatest common denominator between the various groups composing the nation. Coercive authority over the entire territory remains a monopoly of the (central) state, but this authority is limited to certain subjects of jurisdiction; on other subjects, and within well-defined territorial regions, other coercive authorities exist. In other words, the exercise of sovereignty is divided between a central government and regional ones.

Federalism is by its very essence a compromise and a pact. It is a compromise in the sense that when national consensus on *all* things is not desirable or cannot readily obtain, the area of consensus is reduced in order that consensus on *some* things be reached. It is a pact or quasi-treaty in the sense that the terms of that compromise cannot be changed unilaterally. That is not to say that the terms are fixed forever; but only that in changing them, every effort must be made not to destroy the consensus on which the federated nation rests. For what Ernest Renan said about the nation is even truer about

From Pierre Elliott Trudeau, *Federalism and the French Canadians*. New York: St. Martin's Press, 1968. Reprinted by permission of St. Martin's Press and Macmillan & Company, Ltd., and of the University of Toronto Press for use of material from Crepeau & Macpherson, eds., *The Future of Canadian Federalism* (1965). Pp. 191–96.

the federated nation: 'L'existence d'une nation est . . . un plébiscite de tous les jours.' This obviously did not mean that such a plebiscite could or should be held every day, the result of which could only be total anarchy; the real implication is clear: the nation is based on a social contract, the terms of which each new generation of citizens is free to accept tacitly, or to reject openly.

Federalism was an inescapable product of an age which recognized the principle of self-determination. For on the one hand, a sense of national identity and singularity was bound to be generated in a great many groups of people, who would insist on their right to distinct statehood. But on the other hand, the insuperable difficulties of living alone and the practical necessity of sharing the state with neighbouring groups were in many cases such as to make distinct statehood unattractive or unattainable. For those who recognized that the first law of politics is to start from the facts rather than from historical 'might-have-been's', the federal compromise thus became imperative.

But by a paradox I have already noted in regard to the nation-state, the principle of self-determination which makes federalism necessary makes it also rather unstable. If the heavy paste of nationalism is relied upon to keep a unitary nation-state together, much more nationalism would appear to be required in the case of a federal nation-state. Yet if nationalism is encouraged as a rightful doctrine and noble passion, what is to prevent it from being used by some group, region, or province within the nation? If 'nation algérienne' was a valid battle cry against France, how can the Algerian Arabs object to the cry of 'nation kabyle' now being used against them?

The answer, of course, is that no amount of logic can prevent such an escalation. The only way out of the dilemma is to render what is logically defensible actually undesirable. The advantages *to the minority group* of staying integrated in the whole must on balance be greater than the gain to be reaped from separating. This can easily be the case when there is no real alternative for the separatists, either because they are met with force (as in the case of the U.S. Civil War), or because they are met with laughter (as in the case of the *Bretons bretonnisants*). But when there is a real alternative, it is not so easy. And the greater the advantages and possibilities of separatism, the more difficult it is to maintain an unwavering consensus within the whole state.

One way of offsetting the appeal of separatism is by investing tremendous amounts of time, energy, and money in nationalism, *at the federal level*. A national image must be created that will have such an appeal as to make any image of a separatist group unattractive. Resources must be diverted into such things as national flags, anthems, education, arts councils, broadcasting corporations, film boards; the territory must be bound together by a network of railways, highways, airlines; the national culture and the national economy must be protected by taxes and tariffs; ownership of resources and industry by nationals must be made a matter of policy. In short, the whole of the citizenry must be made to feel that it is only within the framework of the federal state that their language, culture, institutions, sacred traditions, and standard of living can be protected from external attack and internal strife.

It is, of course, obvious that a national consensus will be developed in this way only if the nationalism is emotionally acceptable to all important groups within the nation. Only blind men could expect a consensus to be lasting if the national flag or the national image is merely the reflection of one part of the nation, if the sum of values to be protected is not defined so as to include the language or the cultural heritage of some very large and tightly knit minority, if the identity to be arrived at is shattered by a colour-bar. The advantage as well as the peril of federalism is that it permits the development of a regional consensus based on regional values; so federalism is ultimately bound to fail if the nationalism it cultivates is unable to generate a national image which has immensely more appeal than the regional ones.

Moreover, this national consensus—to be lasting—must be a living thing. There is no greater pitfall for federal nations than to take the consensus for granted, as though it were reached once and for all. The compromise of federalism is generally reached under a very particular set of circumstances. As time goes by these circumstances change; the external menace recedes, th economy flourishes, mobility increases, industrialization and urbanization proceed; and also the federated groups grow, sometimes at uneven paces, their cultures mature, sometimes in divergent directions. To meet these changes, the terms of the federative pact must be altered, and this is done as smoothly as possible by administrative practice, by judicial decision, and by constitutional amendment, giving a little more regional autonomy here, a bit more centralization there, but at all times taking great care to preserve the delicate balance upon which the national consensus rests.

Such care must increase in direct proportion to the strength of the alternatives which present themselves to the federated groups. Thus, when a large cohesive minority believes it can transfer its allegiance to a neighbouring state, or make a go of total independence, it will be inclined to dissociate itself from a consensus the terms of which have been altered in its disfavour. On the other hand, such a minority may be tempted to use its bargaining strength to obtain advantages which are so costly to the majority as to reduce to naught the advantages to the latter of remaining federated. Thus, a critical point can be reached in either direction beyond which separatism takes place, or a civil war is fought.

When such a critical point has been reached or is in sight, no amount, however great, of nationalism can save the federation. Any expenditure of emotional appeal (flags, professions of faith, calls to dignity, expressions of brotherly love) at the national level will only serve to justify similar appeals at the regional level, where they are just as likely to be effective. Thus the great moment of truth arrives when it is realized that *in the last resort* the mainspring of federalism cannot be emotion but must be reason.

To be sure, federalism found its greatest development in the time of the nation-states, founded on the principle of self-determination, and cemented together by the emotion of nationalism. Federal states have themselves made use of this nationalism over periods long enough to make its inner contradictions go unnoticed. Thus, in a neighbouring country, Manifest Destiny, the Monroe Doctrine, the Hun, the Red Scourge, the Yellow Peril, and Senator McCarthy have all provided glue for the American Way of Life; but it is apparent that the Cuban 'menace' has not been able to prevent the American Negro from obtaining a renegotiation of the terms of the American national consensus. The Black Muslims were the answer to the argument of the Cuban menace; the only answer to both is the voice of reason.

It is now becoming obvious that federalism has all along been a product of reason in politics. It was born of a decision by pragmatic politicians to face facts as they are, particularly the fact of the heterogeneity of the world's population. It is an attempt to find a rational compromise between the divergent interest-groups which history has thrown together; but it is a compromise based on the will of the people.

Looking at events in retrospect, it would seem that the French Revolution attempted to delineate national territories according to the will of the people, without reference to rationality; the Congress of Vienna claimed to draw state boundaries according to reason, without reference to the will of the people; and federalism arose as an empirical effort to base a country's frontiers on both reason and the will of the people.

I am not heralding the impending advent of reason as the prime mover in politics, for nationalism is too cheap and too powerful a tool to be soon discarded by politicians of all countries; the rising *bourgeoisies* in particular have too large a vested interest in nationalism to let it die out unattended. Nor am I arguing that as important an area of human conduct as politics could or should be governed without any reference to human emotions. But I would like to see emotionalism channelled into a less sterile direction than nationalism. And I am saying that within sufficiently advanced federal countries, the auto-destructiveness of nationalism is bound to become more and more apparent, and reason may yet reveal itself even to ambitious politicians as the more assured road to success. This may also be the trend in unitary states, since they all have to deal with some kind of regionalism or other. Simultaneously in the world of international relations, it is becoming more obvious that the Austinian concept of sovereignty could only be thoroughly applied in a world crippled by the ideology of the nation-state and sustained by the heady stimulant of nationalism. In the world of today, when whole groups of so-called sovereign states are experimenting with rational forms of integration, the exercise of sovereignty will not only be divided within federal states; it will have to be further divided between the states and the communities of states. If this tendency is accentuated the very idea of national sovereignty will recede and, with it, the need for an emotional justification such as nationalism. International law will no longer be explained away as so much 'positive international morality', it will be recognized as true law, a 'coercive order . . . for the promotion of peace'.

Thus there is some hope that in advanced societies, the glue of nationalism will become as obsolete as the divine right of kings; the title of the state to govern and the extent of its authority will be conditional upon rational justification; a people's consensus based on reason will supply the cohesive force that societies require; and politics both within and without the state will follow a much more functional approach to the problems of government. If politicians must bring emotions into the act, let them get emotional about functionalism!

The rise of reason in politics is an advance of law; for is not law an attempt to regulate the conduct of men in society rationally rather than emotionally? It appears then that a political order based on federalism is an order based on law. And there will flow more good than evil from the present tribulations of federalism if they serve to equip lawyers, social scientists, and politicians with the tools required to build societies of men ordered by reason.

Who knows? humanity may yet be spared the ignominy of seeing its destinies guided by some new and broader emotion based, for example, on continentalism. . . .

63. THE SICKNESS OF GOVERNMENT

PETER F. DRUCKER

Peter F. Drucker (1909–   ) is professor of management on the Graduate Faculty of New York University and author of many books and articles on business and industry.

POWER WITHOUT POLICY

Modern government has become ungovernable. There is no government today that can still claim control of its bureaucracy and of its various agencies. Government agencies are all becoming autonomous, ends in themselves, and directed by their own desire for power, their own narrow vision rather than by national policy.

This is a threat to the basic capacity of government to give direction and leadership. Increasingly, policy is fragmented, and execution is governed by the inertia of the large bureaucratic empires, rather than by policy. Bureaucrats keep on doing what their procedures describe. Their tendency, as is only human, is to identify what is in the best interest of the agency with what is right, and what fits administrative convenience with effectiveness. As a result the Welfare State cannot set priorities. It cannot concentrate its tremendous resources—and therefore does not get anything done.

The President of the United States may still be the most powerful ruler—

more powerful than either the prime ministers of parliamentary regimes dependent upon a majority in parliament, or the dictators who can be overthrown by conspiracies against them among the powerful factions within their totalitarian apparatus. And yet even the President of the United States cannot direct national policy any more. The various bureaucracies do much what they want to do. The Anti-Trust Division of the Department of Justice, for instance, has been making its own policies and pursuing its own course these last twenty years, with little concern for what the incumbent President believes or orders. The Soil Conservation Service and the Bureau of Reclamation, the Forestry Service and the Weather Bureau, the Federal Trade Commission and the Army Engineers have similarly become "independent" rather than "autonomous."

Not so long ago, policy control by the political organs of government could be taken for granted. Of course there were "strong" and "weak" presidents as there were "strong" and 'weak" prime ministers. A Franklin Roosevelt or a Winston Churchill could get things done that weaker men could not have accomplished. But this was, people generally believed, because they had the courage of strong convictions, the willingness to lay down bold and effective policies, the ability to mobilize public vision. Today, a "strong" president or a "strong" prime minister is not a man of strong policies; he is the man who knows how to make the lions of the bureaucracy do his bidding. John Kennedy had all the strength of conviction and all the boldness of a "strong" president; this is why he captured the imagination, especially of the young. He had, however, no impact whatever on the bureaucracy. He was a "strong" president in the traditional sense. But he was a singularly ineffectual one. His contemporary, Mr. Khrushchev in Russia, similarly failed to be effective despite his apparent boldness and his popular appeal. By contrast, bureaucratic men who had no policies and no leadership qualities emerge as effective —they somehow know how to make red tape do their bidding. But then, of course, they use it for the one thing red tape is good for, i.e., bundling up yesterday in neat packages.

This growing disparity between apparent power and actual lack of control is perhaps the greatest crisis of government. We are very good at creating administrative agencies. But no sooner are they called into being than they become ends in themselves, acquire their own constituency as well as a "vested right" to grants from the treasury, continuing support by the taxpayer, and immunity to political direction. No sooner, in other words, are they born than they defy public will and public policy. . . .

GOVERNMENT AND MISMANAGEMENT

Government is a poor manager. It is, of necessity, concerned with procedure, just as it is also, of necessity, large and cumbersome. Government is properly conscious that it administers public funds and must account for every penny. It has no choice but to be "bureaucratic"—in the common usage of the term. Every government is, by definition, a "government of paper forms." This means inevitably high cost. For "control" of the last 10 per cent of any phenomenon always costs more than control of the first 90 per cent. If control tries to account for everything, it becomes prohibitively expensive. Yet this is what government is always expected to do. And the reason is not just "bureaucracy" and red tape; it is a much sounder one. A "little dishonesty" in government is a corrosive disease. It rapidly spreads to infect the whole body politic. Yet the temptation to dishonesty is always great. People of modest means and dependent on a salary handle very large public sums. People of modest position dispose of power and award contracts and privileges of tremendous importance to other people—construction jobs, radio channels, air routes, zoning laws, building codes, and so on. To fear corruption in government is not irrational. This means, however, that government "bureaucracy"—and its consequent high costs—cannot be eliminated. Any government that is not a "government of paper forms" degenerates rapidly into a mutual looting society.

The generation that was in love with the state, thirty and forty years ago, believed fondly that government would be economical. Eliminating the "profit motive" was thought to reduce costs. This was poor economics, to begin with. It is worse public administration. The politician's attention does not go to the 90 per cent of money and effort that is devoted to existing programs and activities. They are left to their own devices and to the tender mercies of mediocrity. Politics—rightly—is primarily concerned with "new programs." It is focused on crisis and problems and issues. It is not focused on doing a job. Politics, whatever the form of government, is not congenial to managerial organization and makes government defective in managerial performance.

We have built elaborate safeguards to protect the administrative structure within government against the political process. This is the purpose of every civil service. But although this protects the going machinery from the distortions and pressures of politics, it also protects the incumbents in the agencies from the demands of performance. Of course, we maintain officially that civil-service tenure is compatible with excellence. But if we had to choose, we would probably say that mediocrity in the civil service is a lesser evil than "politics." As far as the judiciary is concerned—where we first created "independence"—this is certainly true. How far it is true in administrative agencies is debatable. A good many people have come to believe that we need some way of rewarding performance and of penalizing nonperformance, even within civil service.

Still, the premium within government will be on not "rocking the boat" in existing agencies, that is on no innovation, no initiative, but rather on doing with proper procedures what has been done before. Within the political process attention will certainly not be paid to the on-going routine work, unless there is the publicized malfunction of a "scandal." As a result, management of the daily work of government will remain neglected. Or be considered a matter of following "procedure" and of filling out forms. By excelling as a manager, no one in politics will ever get to the top, unless at the same time he builds his own political machine, his own political following, his own faction.

We can—and must—greatly improve the efficiency of government. There is little reason these days to insist on "100 per cent audit," for instance. Modern sampling methods based on probability mathematics actually give us better control by inspecting a small percentage of the events. But we need something much more urgently: the clear definition of the results a policy is expected to produce, and the ruthless examination of results against these expectations. This, in turn, demands that we spell out in considerable detail what results are expected rather than content ourselves with promises and manifestos. In the last century, the Auditor General became a central organ of every government. We learned that we needed an independent agency to control the daily process of government and to make sure that money appropriated was spent for what it was intended for, and spent honestly. Now we may have to develop an independent government agency that compares the results of policies against expectations and that, independent of pressures from the executive as well as from the legislature, reports to the public any program that does not deliver.

We may even go further—though only a gross optimist would expect this today. We may build into government an automatic abandonment process. Instead of starting with the assumption that any program, any agency, and any activity is likely to be eternal, we might start out with the opposite assumption: that each is short-lived and temporary. We might, from the beginning, assume that it will come to an end within five or ten years unless specifically renewed. And we may discipline ourselves not to renew any program unless it has the results that it promised when first started. We may, let us hope, eventually build into government the capacity to appraise results and systematically to abandon yesterday's tasks.

Yet such measures will still not convert government into a "doer." They will not alter the main lesson of the last fifty years: *government is not a "doer."*

WHAT GOVERNMENT CAN BE

The purpose of government is to make fundamental decisions, and to make them effectively. The purpose of government is to focus the political energies of society. It is to dramatize issues. It is to present fundamental choices. The purpose of government, in other words, is to govern. This, as we have learned in other institutions, is incompatible with "doing." Any attempt to combine government with "doing" on a large scale paralyzes the decision-making capacity.

There is reason today why soldiers, civil servants, and hospital administrators look to business management for concepts, principles, and practices. For business, during the last thirty years, has had to face, on a much smaller scale, the problem that government now faces: the incompatibility between "governing" and "doing." Business management learned that the two have to be separated, and that the top organ, the decision-maker, has to be detached from "doing." Otherwise he does not make decisions, and the "doing" does not get done either.

In business this goes by the name of "decentralization." The term is misleading. It implies a weakening of the central organ, the top management of a business. The true purpose of decentralization, however, is to make the center, the top management of business, strong and capable of performing the central, the top-management task. The purpose is to make it possible for top management to concentrate on decision-making and direction, to slough off the "doing" to operating managements, each with its own mission and goals, and with its own sphere of action and autonomy.

If this lesson were applied to government, the other institutions of society would then rightly become the "doers." "Decentralization" applied to government would not be just another form of "federalism" in which local rather than central government discharges the "doing" tasks. It would rather be a systematic policy of using the other, *the nongovernmental* institutions of the society—the hospital as well as the university, business as well as labor unions —for the actual "doing," i.e., for performance, operations, execution.

Such a policy might more properly be called "reprivatization." The tasks that flowed to government in the last century, because the family could not discharge them, would be turned over to the new, nongovernmental institutions that have sprung up and grown these last sixty to seventy years.

REPRIVATIZATION

Government would start out by asking the question: "How do these institutions work and what can they do?" It would then ask: "How can political and social objectives be formulated and organized in such a manner as to become opportunities for performance for these institutions?" It would also ask: "And what opportunities for accomplishment of political objectives do the abilities and capacities of these institutions offer to government?"

This would be a very different role for government from that it plays in traditional political theory. In all our theories government is *the* institution. If "reprivatization" were to be applied, however, government would become *one* institution—albeit the central, the top, institution.

Reprivatization would give us a different society from any our *social* theories now assume. In these theories, government does not exist. It is outside of society. Under reprivatization, government would become the central social institution. Political theory and social theory, for the last two hundred and fifty years, have been separate. If we applied to government and to society what we have learned about organization these last fifty years, the two would again come together. The nongovernmental institutions—university, business, and hospital, for instance—would be seen as organs for the accomplishment of results. Government would be seen as society's resource for the determination of major objectives, and as the "conductor" of social diversity.

I have deliberately used the term "conductor." It might not be too fanciful to compare the situation today with the development of music 200 years ago. The dominant musical figure of the early eighteenth century was the great organ virtuoso, especially in the Protestant North. In organ music, as a Buxtehude or a Bach practiced it, one instrument with one performer expressed the total range of music. But as a result, it required almost super-human virtuosity to be a musician.

By the end of the century, the organ virtuoso had disappeared. In his place was the modern orchestra. There, each instrument played only one part, and a conductor up front pulled together all these diverse and divergent instruments into one score and one performance. As a result, what had seemed to be absolute limits to music suddenly disappeared. Even the small orchestra of Haydn could express a musical range far beyond the reach of the greatest organ virtuoso of a generation earlier.

The conductor himself does not play an instrument. He need not even know how to play an instrument. His job is to know the capacity of each instrument: and to evoke optimal performance from each. Instead of "performing," he "conducts." Instead of "doing," he leads.

The next major development in politics, and the one needed to make this middle-aged failure—our tired, overextended, flabby, and impotent government—effective again, might therefore be the reprivatization of the "doing," of the performance of society's tasks. This need not mean "return to private ownership." Indeed what is going on in the Communist satellite countries of Eastern Europe today—especially in Yugoslavia—is reprivatization in which ownership is not involved at all. Instead, autonomous businesses depend on the market for the sale of goods, the supply of labor, and even the supply of capital. That their "ownership" is in the hands of the government is a legal rather than an economic fact—though, of course, an important one. Yet to some Yugoslavs it does not even appear to be incompatible with that ultra-bourgeois institution, a stock exchange.

What matters, in other words, is that institutions not be run by government, but be autonomous. Cooperatives, for instance, are not considered "capitalist" in the Anglo-American countries, although they are "private" in that they are not run by government. And the same applies to "private" hospitals and the "private" universities. On the other hand, the German university has traditionally been almost as autonomous as the American "private" university, even though—as is the case with European universities generally—it is a state institution.

Reprivatization, therefore, may create social structures that are strikingly similar, though the laws in respect to ownership differ greatly from one country to another and from one institution to another. *What they would have in common is a principle of performance rather than a principle of authority.* In all of them the autonomous institution created for the performance of a major social task would be the "doer." Government would become increasingly the decision-maker, the vision-maker. It would try to figure out how to structure a given political objective so as to make it attractive to one of the autonomous institutions. It would, in other words, be the "conductor" that tries to think through what each instrument is best designed to do. And just as we praise a composer for his ability to write "playable" music, which best uses the specific performance characteristic of French horn, violin, or flute, we may come to praise the lawmaker who best structures a particular task so as to make it most congenial for this one or that of the autonomous, self-governing, private institutions of a pluralist society.

THE SPECIAL ROLE OF BUSINESS

Business is likely to be only one—but a very important—institution in such a structure. Whether it be owned by the capitalist, that is, by the investor, or by a cooperative or a government might even become a secondary consideration. For even if owned by government, it would have to be independent of government and autonomous—as the Yugoslavs show—not only in its day-to-day management, but, perhaps more important, in its position in the market, and especially in a competitive capital market.

What makes business particularly appropriate for reprivatization is that it is predominantly an organ of innovation; of all social institutions, it is the only one created for the express purpose of making and managing change. All other institutions were originally created to prevent, or at least to slow down, change. They become innovators only by necessity and most reluctantly.

Specifically, business has two advantages where government has major weaknesses. Business can abandon an activity. Indeed it is forced to do so if it operates in a market—and even more, if it depends on a market for its supply of capital. There is a limit beyond which even the most stubborn businessman cannot argue with the market test, no matter how rich he may be himself. Even Henry Ford had to abandon the Model T when it no longer could be sold. Even his grandson had to abandon the Edsel.

What is more: Of all our institutions, *business is the only one that society will permit to disappear*. It takes a major catastrophe, a war or a great revolution, to allow the disappearance of a university or of a hospital, no matter how superfluous and unproductive they might have become. Again and again, for instance, the Catholic Church in the United States attempts to close down hospitals that have ceased to be useful. In almost every case, a storm of community nostalgia forces the supposedly absolute bishop to retract his decision.

But when the best-known airplane manufacturer in the United States, the Douglas Company, designer and producer of the DC3 was in difficulty in 1967, neither the American public nor American government rushed to its rescue. If a competitor had not bought the company and merged it into his operations, we would have accepted the disappearance of Douglas—with regret, to be sure, and with a good deal of nostalgic rhetoric, but also with the feeling: "It's their own fault, after all."

Precisely because business can make a profit, it *must* run the risk of loss. This risk, in turn, goes back to the second strength of business: alone among all institutions it has a test of performance. No matter how inadequate profitability may be as an indicator, in certain respects, it is a test for all to see. One can argue that this or that obsolete hospital is really needed in the community or that it will one day again be needed. One can argue that even the poorest university is better than none. The alumni or the community always have a "moral duty" to save "dear old Siwash." The consumer, however, is unsentimental. It leaves him singularly unmoved to be told that he has a duty to buy the products of a company because it has been around a long time. The consumer always asks: "And what will the product do for me tomorrow?" If his answer is "nothing," he will see its manufacturer disappear without the slightest regret. And so does the investor.

This is the strength of business as an institution. It is the best reason for keeping it in private ownership. The argument that the capitalist should not be allowed to make profits is a popular one. But the real role of the capitalist is to be expendable. His role is to take risks and to take losses as a result. This role the private investor is much better equipped to discharge than the public one. We want privately owned business precisely because we want institutions that can go bankrupt and can disappear. We want at least one institution that, from the beginning, is adapted to change, one institution that has to prove its right to survival again and again.

If we want a really strong and effective government, therefore, we should want businesses that are not owned by government. We should want businesses in which private investors, motivated by their own self-interest and deciding on the basis of their own best judgment, take the risk of failure. The strongest argument for "private enterprise" is not the function of profit. The strongest argument is the function of loss. Because of it, business is the most adaptable, and the most flexible of the institutions around. Therefore, it is the one best equipped to manage. . . .

TOWARD A NEW POLITICS

We do not face a "withering away of the state." On the contrary, we need a vigorous, a strong, and a very active government. But we do face a choice between big but impotent government and a government that is strong because it confines itself to decision and direction and leaves the "doing" to others. We do not face a "return of laissez-faire" in which the economy is left alone. The economic sphere cannot and will not be considered to lie outside the public domain. But the choices of economy—as well as for all other sectors—are no longer *either* complete governmental indifference or complete governmental control. In all major areas, we have a new choice: an organic diversity in which institutions are used to do what they are best equipped to do. In this society all sectors are "affected with the public interest," whereas in each sector a specific institution, under its own management and dedicated to its own job, emerges as the organ of action and performance.

This is a difficult and complex structure. Such symbiosis between institutions can work only if each disciplines itself to strict concentration on its own sphere and to strict respect for the integrity of the other institutions. Each, to use again the analogy of the orchestra, must be content to play its own part. This will come hardest to government, especially after the last fifty years in which it had been encouraged in the belief of the eighteenth-century organ virtuosos that it could—and should—play all parts simultaneously. But every institution will have to learn the same lesson.

Reprivatization will not weaken government. Indeed, its main purpose is to restore strength to sick government. We cannot go much further along the road on which government has been traveling these last fifty years. All we can get this way is more bureaucracy but not more performance. We can impose higher taxes, but we cannot get dedication, support, and faith on the part of the public. Government can gain greater girth and more weight, but it cannot gain strength or intelligence. All that can happen, if we keep on going the way we have been going, is a worsening sickness of government and growing disenchantment with it. And this is the prescription for tyranny, that is, for a government organized against its own society.

This can happen. It has happened often enough in history. But in a society of pluralist institutions it is not likely to be effective too long. The Communists tried it, and after fifty years have shown—though they have not yet fully learned—that the structure of modern society and its tasks are incompatible with monolithic government. Monolithic government requires absolute dictatorship, which no one has ever been able to prolong much beyond the lifetime of any one dictator.

Ultimately we will need new political theory and probably very new constitutional law. We will need new concepts and new social theory. Whether we will get these and what they will look like, we cannot know today. But we can know that we are disenchanted with government—primarily because it does not perform. We can say that we need, in a pluralist society, a government that can and does govern. This is not a government that "does"; it is not a government that "administers"; it is a government that governs.

part six

Superstates

and the State System

INTRODUCTION

"In a world where there is no security for the small nations, there can be no security for the large nations."

—Jan Masaryk

How large must the state be in order to meet the demands of its citizens for protection and welfare? Aristotle suggested that his *koinonia* (association for the achievement of the good life) could exist only in a city-state so small that its citizens could stand on one wall and see the wall on the other side. Since then, however, man has turned toward ever-larger and more self-sufficient units for the fulfillment of his demands.

Two partially opposing features have marked this search. On the one hand, technological developments have permitted effective governmental control over increasingly large territorial units; concomitantly, these larger units have enabled the state to develop and support a technologically advanced, highly industrialized society. On the other hand, these same technological advances have produced the "nuclear age," with its ever-present possibility of the destruction of the civilization which produced them. The growth of states has in no way decreased the difficulties of maintaining friendly relations between them. Thus, at a time when their very existence is jeopardized, modern states lack the freedom of action and diplomatic maneuver which their predecessors had. Can their problems be solved? Or is the nation-state obsolete? Can the modern state system be made to operate more effectively in the future than it has in the past?

Does collective security offer a solution to the dilemma of the state? Can it overcome the shortcomings inherent in a community of autonomous nation-states? Can the United Nations, as presently constituted, be expected indefinitely to restrain would-be aggressors? If its present organization cannot provide a more effective system than has been demonstrated in the past, can it be strengthened sufficiently to do the job? Or is the United Nations, too, obsolete?

If the nation-state cannot be made adequate, can the "region-state" serve better? Is there a sufficient community of interests and mutual willingness among the peoples of regions to make such a state feasible? Would a "world-state" be preferable? Does mankind share enough interests to permit a "world-state" to be established and maintained? Indeed, is there any type of organization of the international community that offers promise of protection in the larger sense?

Before the international community can develop any new approach to its organization, it must first resolve the issue of nationalism. Nationalism today dominates the world of nation-states. It is particularly strong among the "underdeveloped" states which have recently emerged from colonial status, but it remains strong also among the "mature" states of the industrialized West. How can nationalism be reconciled with any program designed to limit its manifestations? Is it a product of a certain stage of development of the nation-state which can be expected to diminish in intensity with the passage of time? Or can it be controlled only by replacing the nation-state itself with some transcendent loyalty? Illustrations of the problem are found throughout the world.

In Western Europe, while "nationalists" oppose all moves designed to promote European unity, "integrationists" argue that only through unity can Western Europe regain its former position of world influence. These believe a loyalty to a "United States of Europe" must replace traditional nationalistic rivalries and animosities.

The newly independent countries of Asia, Africa, and the Middle East, along with Latin America, regard nationalism as beneficial. These desire economic growth, social change, political power, and a feeling of national identification. To achieve these goals, they look to the state and to nationalism to provide the institution and the concept required. Understandably suspicious of the Great Powers, they are not prepared at this stage of their development to surrender their newly acquired sovereignty to any larger institution or higher goal.

Then, there is the problem of the "ideological conflict" between

Communist and non-Communist states. Are the Communist states irrevocably committed by ideology and interest to hostility toward the non-Communist world? Or can they be induced to enter into cooperative arrangements with non-Communist countries in the interests of international peace and national survival? Is "peaceful coexistence" possible between ideologically opposed systems—and what do we mean by "peaceful coexistence"?

Man must develop a better world order if he is to survive. The challenge is great, the struggle difficult, and the stakes high: the future of man.

64. THE PARADOXES OF NATIONALISM

HANS J. MORGENTHAU

Hans J. Morgenthau (1904–   ) is professor of political science at the University of Chicago and a leading authority on international relations. Born in Germany, he came to the U.S. in 1937.

The Western world faces in the universal triumph of nationalism some extraordinary paradoxes, pregnant with tragic irony. These paradoxes test its political imagination; they challenge its moral judgment; they put in jeopardy not only its own existence, but the survival of civilized life on this planet. Yet it was not the enemy of the West and of civilization that gave the idea of nationalism to the world. That idea, together with Marxism, is the last great original contribution the West has made to the political thought and practice of the world. What has become a threat to civilization, the West has claimed as a condition of civilized life. What has become a source of political anarchy and oppression, the West has offered as the principle of political order and freedom. With what has become a mockery of political morality, the West set out to establish political justice throughout the world.

The idea of nationalism, both in its historic origins and in the political functions it has performed, is intimately connected with the idea of freedom and shares the latter's ambiguity. Nationalism as a political phenomenon must be understood as the aspiration for two freedoms, one collective, the other individual: the freedom of a nation from domination by another nation and the freedom of the individual to join the nation of his choice. . . .

Nationalism, taken by itself, is both in logic and experience a principle of disintegration and fragmentation, which is prevented from issuing in anarchy not by its own logic but by the political power which either puts a halt to its realization at a certain point, as did the peace settlement of 1919, or else uses it for its purposes up to a certain point, as did the unifiers of Germany and Italy in the nineteenth century. There are no inherent limits to the application of the principles of nationalism. If the peoples of Bulgaria, Greece, and Serbia could invoke these principles against Turkey, why could not the people of Macedonia invoke them against Bulgaria, Greece, and Serbia? If it was right for the Czechs and Slovaks to free themselves in the name of nationalism from Austrian rule, it could not be wrong for the Slovaks and Sudeten Germans to free themselves from Czech rule in the name of the self-same principle. . . . Thus yesterday's oppressed cannot help becoming the oppressors of today because they are afraid lest they be again oppressed tomorrow. Hence, the process of national liberation must stop at some point, and that point is determined not by the logic of nationalism, but by configurations of interest and power between the rulers and the ruled and between competing nations.

This paradox of B invoking the principles of nationalism against A and denying them to C—both for the sake of his own survival—is accentuated by the practical impossibility of applying these principles consistently to mixed populations. The individual's rights to his property and pursuit of happiness become incompatible with his right to choose his government according to his national preferences when he is a member of a minority which is inextricably intermingled with the majority controlling the government. Not being able to enjoy both rights simultaneously, he must sacrifice one or the other. The treaties for the protection of minorities, to which Bulgaria, Montenegro, Rumania, and Serbia were subjected in 1878 and Czechoslovakia, Poland, and Rumania in 1919, tried to mitigate the dilemma by protecting certain minorities in the enjoyment of a free national life at least in certain fields, such as language, schools, religion.

However, such attempts were largely frustrated by the fact, which constitutes the second manifestation of the crisis of nationalism in the interwar period, that the conflicts between the new national states and their minorities were more intimately interwoven than ever before with the international conflicts among the new nation-states and the great powers. This had always been the case within certain limits; Russia, for instance, had always supported the Balkan nations against Turkey and the Czechs and Serbs against Austria-Hungary. Yet as in the interwar period the new nation-states competed with each other for power and were at the same time the pawns of the great powers in their struggle for hegemony, the national minorities became to an ever increasing extent, as it were, subpawns whose aspirations and grievances the contestants used to strengthen themselves and their friends and weaken their enemies. . . .

Nationalism, far from creating a just and more viable international order, became the great disruptive and anarchical force of the interwar period. Into the several members of the empires it shattered, nationalism poured the same passions which, first, as lust for power had created these empires and, then, as aspiration for freedom had destroyed them. The endemic disorder thus created cried out for a "new order," which only the strong could make and maintain. Germany and Russia, the new empire builders, saw their opportunity, and in a series of swift and effective strokes, starting in 1938 and ending in 1941, they seized the new nation states of Central and Eastern Europe, endeavoring to melt them down into new structures of empire.

It is another of the paradoxes of nationalism that its defeat on the eve of the Second World War was achieved in the name of the same principle which brought it victory in the aftermath of the First: national self-determination. Germany justified its use of the German minorities of Czechoslovakia and Poland for the destruction of these nation-states with the same principle of national self-determination with which before the Czech, Slovak, and Polish nationalities had justified their attack upon, and destruction of, the Austro-Hungarian Empire. Yet while the words were the same, the passions behind them and the philosophy which roused and justified them were different not only in degree but in kind. The nationalism with which Nazi Germany and the Soviet Union set out to conquer the world has only the name in common with the nationalism of the nineteenth century and the first three decades of the twentieth.

The libertarian goals of the older nationalism were the rightful possession of all nations who wanted to be free; the world had room for as many nationalisms as there were nations that wanted to establish or preserve a state of their own. The international conflicts growing out of this nationalism were of two kinds: conflicts between the nationality and an alien master and conflicts between different nations over the delimitation of their respective boundaries. The issue at stake was either the application of the principles of nationalism or else its interpretation.

The new nationalism has only one thing in common with the old: the nation is the ultimate point of reference for political loyalties and actions. But here the similarity ends. For the old nationalism, the nation is the ultimate goal of political action, the end point of the political development beyond which there are other nationalisms with similar and equally justifiable goals. For the new nationalism, the nation is but the starting point of a universal mission whose ultimate goal reaches to the confines of the political world. While the old nationalism seeks one nation in one state and nothing else, the new one claims for one nation and one state the right to impose its own values and standards of action upon all the other nations.

The new nationalism is in truth a political religion, a nationalistic universalism which identifies the standards and goals of a particular nation with the principles that govern the universe. The few remaining nations of the first rank no longer oppose each other within a framework of shared beliefs and common values which impose effective limitations upon the means and ends of their policies. Rather they oppose each other now as the standard bearer of moral systems, each of them of national origin and each of them claiming to provide universal moral standards which all the other nations ought to accept. The moral code of one nation flings the challenge of its universal claim into the face of another, which reciprocates in kind. . . .

This well-nigh universal commitment to the principles of nationalism revealed a profound difference between the attitude of the Western democracies and that of their totalitarian enemies. That difference was to have far-reaching moral and political consequences. The West had come to see in the principles of nationalism the revelation of universal truth to be lived up to regardless of political consequences. Totalitarianism looked at those principles as political tools to be used if their use promised results, to be discarded otherwise. . . .

Yet when totalitarianism turned the principles of nationalism against the West, the West stood morally and intellectually disarmed. The totalitarian arguments being its own, it could not answer them. The West had welcomed the victory of national self-determination in the aftermath of the First World War on moral and political grounds, and it found itself now incapable, when Hitler used the German minority for the destruction of Czechoslovakia, of defending its interests against its principles. It even lent a helping hand to its defeat and congratulated itself upon its moral consistency. "Self-determination, the professed principle of the Treaty of Versailles, has been invoked by Herr Hitler against its written text, and his appeal has been allowed," wrote the London *Times* on September 28, 1938, commenting upon the Munich settlement.

The Second World War and the cold war following it have both qualitatively and quantitatively magnified the paradoxes of nationalism which the interwar period had brought to the fore, and they have added a new one which has made nationalism altogether obsolete as a principle of political organization. The new fact that has created that new paradox is the feasibility of all-out atomic war.

The justification of the nation-state, as of all political organization, is its ability to perform the functions for the sake of which political organization exists. The most elementary of these functions is the common defense of the life of the citizens and of the values of the civilization in which they live. A political organization which is no longer able to defend these values and even puts them in jeopardy must yield, either through peaceful transformation or violent destruction, to one capable of that defense. Thus, under the impact of the invention of gunpowder and of the first industrial revolution, the feudal order had to yield to the dynastic and the nation-state. Under the technological conditions of the preatomic age, the stronger nation-states could, as it were, erect a wall behind which their citizens could live secure and the weak nation-states were similarly protected by the operation of the balance of power which added the resources of the strong to those of the weak. Thus under normal conditions no nation-state was able to make more than marginal inroads upon the life and civilization of its neighbors.

The feasibility of all-out atomic war has completely destroyed this protective function of the nation-state. No nation-state is capable of protecting its citizens and its civilization against an all-out atomic attack. Its safety rests solely in preventing such an attack from taking place. While in the preatomic age a nation-state could count upon its physical ability to defend itself, in the atomic age it must rely upon its psychological ability to deter those who are physically able to destroy it. The prospective enemy must be induced to refrain from attacking; once he attacks, the victim is doomed.

This psychological mechanism of deterrence operates only on the condition that the prospective atomic aggressor is clearly identified beforehand, that is, that no more than two nations are capable of waging all-out atomic war; for it is only on this condition that deterrence operates with automatic certainty. Today, the Soviet Union knows that if it should attack the United States with atomic weapons, the United States would destroy it, and vice versa; that certainty deters both. Yet the time is close at hand when other nations will have the weapons with which to wage all-out atomic war. When that time has come, nations will have lost even the preventive capacity of psychological deterrence, which they still possess today. For the United States, if then attacked with atomic weapons, will no longer be able to identify the aggressor with certainty and, hence, deter the prospective aggressor with the certainty of retaliations. When this historic moment comes—as it surely must if the present trend is not reversed—the nation-state will connote not life and civilization, but anarchy and universal destruction.

It is in the shadow of this grim reality and grimmer prospect that the inherent paradoxes of nationalism have taken on a novel urgency, threatening to overwhelm the remnants of international order. Balkanization, demoralization, and barbarization on a world-wide scale are the result.

The age which has seen the nation-state become obsolete witnesses the emergence of a multitude of new states fashioned from the fragments of the colonial empires. The number of sovereign states has approximately doubled since the First World War. Many of these new states would not have been viable political, military, and economic entities even in the heyday of the nation-state, deficient as they are in the essential prerequisites of nationhood. They could not have fed, administered, and defended themselves then, nor can they now. The disorder and threats to peace which the dissolution, first, of the Turkish and, then, of the Austro-Hungarian and Western part of the Russian Empires brought in its wake is being spread, in the name of nationalism, to ever wider areas of Africa and Asia. In our age, even the infinitely stronger nation-states of Europe are no longer viable political, military, and economic entities, but must submit either to the support or the conquest of the two remaining nations of the first rank which are significantly not nation-states in the traditional sense but continental states. The tragedy of Hungary and the collapse of the British and French intervention in Egypt in November, 1956, have demonstrated in different ways both the continuing emotional strength of national aspirations and the political and military weakness of the nation-state. Is it then reasonable to expect that these new nations, some of them so artificial as to be even lacking the ethnic and historic foundations of nationhood, will be able to create a viable order among themselves and with their more powerful neighbors?

Only two alternatives appear to be in store for them, perhaps one following the other: Balkanization and a new colonialism. The rivalries which have beset the successor states to the European empires have already appeared among them. Some of the former colonies would like to have colonies of their own. The natural resources of some continue to make them attractive as colonies for stronger nations who need these resources. Their weakness, necessitating continuous support for stronger nations, predestines them as pawns in the power struggles of the latter. Their attractiveness, coupled with weakness, is thus a standing invitation to conquest, conquest by one or the other of them or else from the outside. In any event, the disorder which is taking the place of the old order of empire is likely to call forth, as it did before in Europe, a new order which will be again an order of empire.

It is ironic—and perhaps inevitable—that the great nations of the West should actively promote and support this Balkanization of much of the world, and it is equally ironic—and certainly not inevitable—that they should applaud it. For while they may have no choice but to give up their empires, they cannot afford to look with indifference, let alone with satisfaction, upon the prospect that disorder and violence, exploited by Communism, will spread over ever wider areas of the globe. Here we encounter on a world-wide scale and in the form of anticolonialism that moral perversion which made Great Britain congratulate herself upon having helped Hitler to destroy Czechoslovakia in the name of nationalism. . . .

With characteristic philosophic consistency and lack of political judgment, the West has applied the democratic principles of freedom and equality to the international scene, transforming them in the process from concrete political goals into abstract moral postulates. Yet wherever democracy has succeeded within the nation-state, it was imbedded in a structured social order from which, in turn, it imparted form and direction.

It is this Western dedication to national freedom, not as a concrete political goal but as an eternal verity, which has made the West morally and politically helpless in the face of the anticolonial onslaught of the age. When Japan swept through Asia, carrying the banner of anticolonialism before her, the new colonialism supplanted the old with such immediacy and undisguised exploitation and oppression as to provide a ready target for the West's anticolonial indignation. The anticolonialism of the Soviet Union, Communist China, and the indigenous peoples of Africa and Asia is different and has had a different effect upon the moral consciousness of the West.

While it is for all of them a tool at the service of concrete political goals, used and discarded especially by the Soviet Union and Communist China as the occasion requires, its immediate goal appears to be national liberation and nothing more. What disorders will follow liberation and what new colonialism will follow the disorders is a matter for long-term concern, not for immediate political calculation. Furthermore, the colonialism which the Soviet Union has practiced in Europe since the end of the Second World War is geographically far removed from Africa and Asia, protected from immediate recognition by the "salt-water fallacy" which requires a colony, to be recognized as such, to be separated from the colonial power by some ocean. Finally, in Africa and Asia, as in the European resistance during the Second World War, Communism fights in the forefront of nationalism, making for the time being little of the fact that its nationalism serves the interests of China or the Soviet Union. Thus in a strange and disquieting transformation, nationalism, the moral principle of the West, becomes the most potent weapon in the arsenal of its enemies, and disarmed, before the triumph of its own ideal, the West applauds its own destruction. . . .

"Political imagination" is indeed the key word. If the West cannot think of something better than nationalism, it may well lose the opportunity to think at all. It has been its moral virtue and besetting political sin to look at nationalism as though it were a self-sufficient political principle and could bring freedom, justice, order, and peace simply by being consistently applied. In truth, no political principle carries within itself such a force for good. What good and what evil it will work depends not only upon its own nature, but also upon the configurations of interest and power in which and for the sake of which it is called upon to act.

The West has consistently tended to misunderstand the subtle and complex relationships between these configurations and political principles. Thereby, it has blunted its political will, its political judgment, and its political imagination. It has failed to see that political principles, such as nationalism, must direct, rechannel, even transform these configurations but that they cannot replace them. Yet when their work is done, they must themselves be replaced.

Nationalism has had its day. It was the political principle appropriate to the postfeudal and preatomic age. For the technology of the steam engine, it was indeed in good measure a force for progress. In the atomic age, it must make way for a political principle of larger dimensions, in tune with the world-wide configurations of interest and power of the age.

65. BEYOND THE NATION-STATE

LESTER B. PEARSON

Lester B. Pearson (1897–   ) is with the International Bank for Reconstruction and Development. He was formerly Canada's Secretary of State for External Affairs and Prime Minister.

What is meant by "nationalism"? Few words have come to mean more different things to more people. Nationalism doesn't necessarily mean sovereignty. The word "nation" does not mean state in that sense, though this is the way it is most often used. Indeed, I often use it in that sense, thereby adding to the confusion that I now want to clear up. A nation can, of course, coincide with a state, and often does. But there can be more than one nation inside a sovereign state, and often is. Let's not confuse a nation with a race, either. Race is a far wider concept, which denotes the biological unity of a group with certain physical characteristics. A race can comprise many nations and many states.

Once you begin to look for common factors that determine a nation or nationality, you get into difficulty. Language is not necessarily a common factor: Switzerland has four languages, three of them officially recognized. Size has nothing to do with it: you can have a tiny state that considers itself a nation, or you can have the Union of Soviet Socialist Republics or the United States of America. Clearly, defined boundaries don't make a nation. You can have the boundaries of a nation inside a state, and a national group overflowing state boundaries. How many Chinese settlements are there outside China?

Economic interest is not a determining factor: A nation-state will often cling to a separate existence against its best economic interests. Neither is religion. But if a nation has a common religion, or a common language, that

From Lester B. Pearson, "Beyond the Nation-State," *Saturday Review*, February 15, 1969. Excerpts.

makes the sense of nationalism stronger. Perhaps the most frequently occurring factor is what I will call a common culture, but that word is often so elusive and hard to define that it is not always very helpful as a criterion. By culture I mean common habits, common traditions, common customs, and, above all, a common desire to live together as a separate group, a communal society, with certain well defined loyalties and objectives. Ernest Renan in 1882 described a nation as a "daily plebiscite." It depends, he said, on "the consent, the desire clearly expressed, to continue life as a community." So perhaps we should merely admit that we may not be able to exactly define a nation, but we certainly know one when we see it.

Nationalism is often confused by the presence of ethnic groups within states, but groups that are not nations within the definition I have given the word. Take the United States. It consists of representatives of practically every national culture, every national tradition, in the world. If the United States had encouraged the political growth or the communal cohesiveness of these separate cultures and traditions, they might well have fatally weakened the unity of the state. So the United States has deliberately fostered the idea of "the melting pot," with Americanism being taught and emphasized at the expense of every other tradition. In the United States, with a single language, the educational system can be, and has been, used as a powerful unifying factor. Yet where there is more than one language, education may work in the opposite direction. . . .

If we cannot maintain the existing world political federations, with unity on essential matters but with recognition of differences of culture and tradition and language—and even special constitutional rights—what chance is there in the future of building up a wider international community where these separate racial, national, and even political differences can be merged— not submerged but merged—in the community as a whole? From my own Canadian experience, I believe that cultural and social differences inside sovereign states, as well as cultural influences from outside, can and should strengthen rather than weaken a modern political society in our modern world; that political unity, in other words, does not have to mean either cultural or social uniformity. It would be foolish and futile to insist that such differences should be eliminated in the interest of single sovereign political unity. It would be equally futile and foolish, I hope, in the international field to insist on the complete obliteration of national differences in the interests of international unity. National societies meet a deep need in people's hearts and minds. It's very difficult to become passionate about something that includes everything. So we have to find a way to reconcile the narrower, more intense patriotism with the wider loyalty. I think it can be done. I think it must be done.

Historical experience shows that a state can develop successfully with different national identities. The Scottish people are a national society. You certainly know a Scots group when you see it. They have managed to maintain, and very vigorously, their separateness inside the United Kingdom. They have managed to do more: they have even, some would say, imposed their separateness on other parts of the United Kingdom. Scotland, in that sense, is a nation. So is Wales.

It has been argued that Scotland and Wales would be nations in a more meaningful and satisfying sense if they were able to have more of the local institutions of self-government—if, for instance, they had their own provincial assemblies. That is not for me to say. But surely it is possible in a country such as the United Kingdom to reconcile political unity with national individuality—to maintain a United Kingdom of separate and developing peoples. I certainly hope so for the sake of the bigger international issues we have to solve.

If those who believe in separate nationalities in this cultural sense insist that each nation must then become a separate sovereign state, in the political sense, where do we get? I know that if you encourage the awareness of national separateness in the cultural and social sense, you are bound to create in some peoples' minds the idea that this awareness cannot be carried to its logical conclusion without political independence, too. But if this were accepted in all political societies, where would it get us? Would the *people* of Wales or Scotland be any better off if they had absolute sovereign independence than they would be if there were a Welsh or Scottish province or state inside a United Kingdom where they would have responsibility for their own cultural and certain other forms of development?

Apply this extreme political separatist argument to India, and it would not only be the end of India today, it would be the end of any possibility in the future of uniting the subcontinent of India together in some kind of confederation. Apply the process to the situation in Africa, which is confused enough now: There are at least, I am told, 6,000 separate tribes in Africa, and each can claim to be a nation in this social and cultural sense, with its own tribal loyalty, language, culture, and taboos. . . .

It is interesting to apply the doctrine of nationalism, as I have been describing it, to the Soviet Union. Marxist Leninism, like the Bible, can, of course, be interpreted in any way that is desired by the interpreter at any particular moment. It can mean legally sovereign status for each Soviet Republic. It has in fact meant that Marx's universal brotherhood of the proletariat, which in due course would become the universal brotherhood of all men, has given way to Holy Russia. Indeed, a strong case could be made for the assertion that under Communism the Soviet Union has come closer to being a centralized state than anything that existed before within the same boundaries. Even though there is representation of different national groups in certain central institutions, and even though at every great Soviet display we see the separate cultural groups dancing and marching and singing their special songs in their own languages, there is complete subordination to the center in all political matters. Complete loyalty to the Soviet fatherland is demanded on the part of all its citizens. If such a loyalty is given, it has been brought about in two ways: first, by education, largely through the Communist party; and second, by stirring up the emotions of the great patriotic war against the Nazi aggressor, when every Soviet citizen was imbued with the idea that he was defending the sacred soil, not only of Uzbekistan, Armenia, or Siberia, but of Holy Russia.

Nationalism is often associated with the struggle of unfree peoples for independence. There it can be a very strong and noble emotion. During the struggle for freedom, the new feeling of nationalism and national unity can be stronger even than the old separatist tribal feeling. But after freedom has been achieved, the more restricted loyalties often become strong again. Nationalism is good when it leads to freedom. But it is less good when, after these people become free, it is used for a return to fragmentation; or, at the other extreme, to political or racial arrogance by the new rulers; to the forced and total cultural and linguistic integration of unwilling groups into a centralized state or to forced exclusion of others from that state. There is nothing to be said for these brands of nationalism. They lead to racial discrimination and arrogance, which can only be condemned in any society. We are all descendants of Adam and we are all products of racial miscegenation. Indeed, racial purity depends on where you start to count.

It was only a few years ago that we thought of Nigeria, the most populous of the new African states, as an example of what could be done, in the march to freedom, to reconcile tribal feeling with national development. It was a set-piece which was working well. So we thought; and then the whole thing seemed to be collapsing—because of fierce forces of tribal separation and tribal domination which had not been sufficiently taken into account when the Constitution of the country was drafted. The hopes we had for Nigeria were so high that our present distress over what is happening there must be that much greater. And yet, if we do not have some kind of federal society in many of these new countries, what chance is there for them surviving as free peoples at all—because the fragmentation will go on and on until some tyrant ends it. . . .

How far that family solidarity can be maintained in the second or third generation of leaders, who didn't go to a British school or college, I don't know. Certainly the Commonwealth can't be held together much longer on the "old boy" sentimental basis that has been so effective. It seems that the Commonwealth is being taken less seriously in the world, even among some of its own members. Yet the very difficulties of holding it together now underline the importance of doing so, because the Commonwealth in its varied, multi-racial membership of free states does reflect the world in which we live. It's a pluralistic political association representing every tribe, creed, color, religion, and continent.

It is of great importance to show that this kind of association of small powers and large powers, of former colonial states and former imperial states, can meet and discuss, and at times decide together, even though there are no formal bonds, but some divisions, between them. I would like to think that such associations as the Commonwealth are stages in the development of something more formal and united. But certainly if we tried to make the Commonwealth a more formal association now, with demands on its members, with a constitution binding on them—convert it into some kind of confederation, however loose—it would simply break up. Yet, if we can develop on this new multi-racial basis a new kind of cooperation between free countries, with each desiring to work with and help each other, we may be able to give a new and constructive functional expression to the old family feeling that once was strong. In doing this, we will have modified separate and sovereign nationalities in the interests of a deeper feeling of international unity.

This modification is shown elsewhere in the growth of other and more formal international institutions which illustrate the increasing need for co-operation between states, as well as the growth of world opinion in favor of it. Sovereign states have accepted, even if not always very warmly, the right of such international agencies to conduct ad hoc, or even regular, investigations into their affairs. International inspectors now examine national books. If you want a loan from the World Bank, or if you want some financial assistance from the International Monetary Fund, they will send men around who look into your national accounts and financial policies. If you want their help, you have to accept their criticism. Indeed, decisions that concern currency, that most vital part of national sovereignty, as we know very well now, are no longer solely under national control. This kind of intervention is the price governments pay for the benefits of international assistance and cooperation—especially in the financial and economic sphere. But it would have been unthinkable 100 years ago, except in the case of colonies, or, of course, subordinate states.

International political investigations are more difficult to reconcile with national sovereignty, but on occasions they also have been accepted. Some years ago, the NATO Council agreed to a procedure by which three officials— British, American, and French—were authorized to examine the defense programs and the economic and financial resources of all the member states, and to make recommendations on the contributions of each member to collective defense, so that there would be a fairer sharing of the total burden. That was progress. True, the members accepted the recommendations only when it suited them to do so. This showed that the power of decision still resided, ultimately, in the sovereign nation-state. Yet our NATO experience has also shown that national decisions can be and are strongly influenced by the opinions and recommendations of persons not responsible to one's own government but representing an international organization, and that is quite a change.

In any rational analysis, we can surely now say that sovereign power, exercised through the nation-state, which came into being to protect its citizens against insecurity and war, has failed in this century to give them that protection. The rationale for change has been established. The will to make it has not.

66. THE NATURE OF IMPERIALISM

V. I. LENIN

V. I. Ulianov (Lenin) (1870–1924) was leader of the Bolshevik (Communist) wing of the Russian Social Democratic Party and led it through the Revolution of 1917.

While capitalism remains capitalism, surplus capital will not be used for raising the standard of living of the masses in a given country, for this would mean a decrease in profits for the capitalists; rather, it will be exported abroad to backward countries in order to increase profits. In these backward countries profits are unusually high, for capital is scarce, the price of land is comparatively cheap, wages are low, and raw materials are cheap. The possibility of exporting capital is created by the fact that a number of backward countries are drawn into the system of world capitalism; main railway lines have either been built or are being built there, the basic conditions for the development of industry have been assured, etc. The need to export capital arises from the fact that in a few countries capitalism has become "overripe," and capital cannot find (due to the backward state of agriculture and the impoverishment of the masses) field for "profitable" investment. . . .

The Division of the World Among the Capitalist Combines. The monopolistic corporations of the capitalists, cartels, syndicates, trusts, divide among themselves first of all the internal market, seizing control more or less completely of the production of a given country. But the internal market, under capitalism, is inevitably linked with the foreign market. Capitalism long ago created a world market. As the export of capital increased, and as foreign and colonial relations and "spheres of influence" spread in every possible way by the biggest monopolistic corporations, affairs "naturally" tended toward a global agreement among them, toward the establishment of international cartels. . . .

The capitalists do not divide the world out of personal malice, but because the degree of concentration which has been reached impels them to adopt this course in order to obtain profits; they divide the world according to "capital," and according to "strength," for there can be no other method of division under the system of commodity production and capitalism. Power varies with the degree of economic and political development; in order to understand what is taking place it is necessary to know what questions are solved by such changes in power; whether these changes are "purely" economic or *non*economic (e.g., military) is a question of secondary importance

From V. I. Lenin, "Imperialism, the Highest Stage of Capitalism" in Alvin Z. Rubinstein, *The Foreign Policy of the Soviet Union.* New York: Random House, Inc., 1960. Pp. 13–18, excerpts.

which cannot in the least affect the basic views of the latest epoch of capitalism. To substitute for the question of the *content* of the struggle and agreement among capitalist combines, the question of the form of the struggle and agreement (today peaceful, tomorrow not peaceful, the day after tomorrow again not peaceful) is a peaceful way to descend to the role of sophist.

The epoch of modern capitalism shows us that certain relations are established among combines of capitalists *based* on the economic division of the world; parallel with these relations, and in connection with them, certain relations are established among political alliances, among states, on the basis of the territorial divisions of the world, of the struggle for colonies, and of "the struggle for economic territory."

The basic feature of contemporary capitalism is the domination of monopolist combines by the biggest entrepreneurs. These monopolies are most durable when *all* the sources of raw materials are controlled by one group, and we have seen with what zeal the international capitalist combines exert their effort to make it impossible for their rivals to compete with them; for example, by buying up mineral rights, oil fields, etc. Only possession of colonies provides a complete guarantee of success to the monopolies against all competitors, including the possibility that the competitors will defend themselves by means of a law establishing a state monopoly. The more capitalism develops, the stronger the need for raw materials is felt, the more bitter competition and the hunt for raw materials become throughout the world, the more desperate the struggle for the acquisition of colonies becomes. . . .

Imperialism, as a Particular Stage of Capitalism. Imperialism emerged as a development and direct continuation of the basic characteristics of capitalism in general. But capitalism became capitalist imperialism only at a definite, very high stage of its development, when certain of the basic characteristics of capitalism began to change into their opposites, when the features of a period of transition from capitalism to a higher socio-economic system began to take shape and reveal themselves in all spheres. Economically, the replacement of capitalist free competition by capitalist monopolies is of key importance. Free competition is the fundamental characteristic of capitalism, and of commodity production generally; monopoly is exactly the opposite of free competition, but we have seen the latter being transformed into monopoly before our eyes, creating large-scale industry, squeezing out small-scale industry, replacing large-scale industry by still larger-scale industry, and finally bringing about such a concentration of industry and capital that monopoly has become and is the result. . . . At the same time, the monopolies growing out of free competition do not eliminate it, but exist over it and alongside of it, thereby giving rise to a number of particularly acute and intense antagonisms, frictions, and conflicts. Monopoly is the transition from capitalism to a higher order.

If it were necessary to give the briefest possible definition of imperialism, we should have to say that imperialism is the monopoly stage of capitalism. Such a definition would include, on the one hand, that finance capital is bank capital of the few biggest monopolist banks, merged with the capital of the monopolist combines of industrialists; and on the other hand, that the division of the world is the transition from a colonial policy which has spread without opposition to territories unoccupied by any capitalist power, to a colonial policy of monopolistic possession of the territories of the world.

Imperialism is capitalism in that stage of development in which the domination of monopolies and finance capital has been established, in which the export of capital has acquired outstanding importance, in which the division of the world by the international trusts has started, and in which the partition of all the territory of the earth by the largest capitalist countries has been completed. . . .

The Critique of Capitalism. The question of whether it is possible to change the bases of imperialism by reforms, whether to proceed to a further aggravation and deepening of the contradictions which it engenders, or backwards towards allaying them, is a fundamental question in the critique of imperialism. . . . Let us take India, Indo-China and China. It is well known that these three colonial and semicolonial countries, inhabited by six/seven hundred million souls, are subjected to the exploitation of the finance capital of several imperialist powers: England, France, Japan, the United States, etc. Let use assume that these imperialist countries form alliances against one another in order to protect or expand their possessions, interests, and "spheres of influence" in these Asiatic countries. These will be "interimperialist" or "ultraimperialist" alliances. Let us assume that *all* the imperialist powers conclude an alliance for the "peaceful" partition of these Asiatic countries; this alliance would be "internationally united finance capital." There have been actual examples of such an alliance in the twentieth century, for example, in the relations of the powers with China. We ask, is it "conceivable," assuming the preservation of capitalism, . . . that such alliances would not be short-lived, that they would preclude frictions, conflicts and struggles in any and every possible form?

It is enough to state this question clearly in order to make any reply other than a negative one impossible. For, under capitalism, there can be *no* other conceivable basis for partition of spheres of influence, of interests, of colonies, etc., than a calculation of the *strength* of the participants, their general economic, financial, military, and other strength. But the relative strength of these participants is not changing uniformly, for under capitalism there cannot be an *equal* development of different enterprises, trusts, branches of industry or countries. Half a century ago, Germany was a pitiful nonentity if its strength was compared with that of England; the same was true with Japan as compared with Russia. Is it "conceivable" that in ten or twenty years the relative strength of the imperialist powers will have remained *un*changed? Absolutely inconceivable.

Therefore, "interimperialist" or "ultraimperialist" alliances, given the realities of capitalism, . . . no matter what form these alliances take, whether of one imperialist coalition against another or of a general alliance embracing *all* the imperialist powers, are *inevitably* only "breathing spells" between wars. Peaceful alliances prepare the ground for wars, and in their turn grow out of wars; one is the condition of the other, giving rise to alternating forms of peaceful and nonpeaceful struggle on *one and the same basis,* namely, that of imperialist connections and relationships between world economics and world politics.

67. SOME REFLECTIONS ON COLONIALISM

HANS KOHN

Hans Kohn (1891–   ) is professor emeritus of history at the City College of New York and an internationally known authority on problems of nationalism and imperialism.

Colonialism as a Historical Phenomenon. The meaning and implications of the word colonialism and of the closely connected terms of empire and imperialism have undergone a profound transformation in the last decades. Until the end of the nineteenth century the word empire or imperialism was generally used in a laudatory and not a pejorative meaning. The Roman Empire had been the model for Western political thought for one thousand years. The Americans at the end of the eighteenth century proudly and hopefully spoke of their empire. The French revolutionaries proclaimed the imperial expansion of their leadership. Modern Western civilization was regarded as superior to other more stagnant civilizations, and to bring higher civilization to less developed countries was considered a praiseworthy enterprise, in spite of the fact that like so many human efforts this too was inextricably mingled with all kinds of corruption and greed. Empire and colonialism always implied dominion and power; and power, whether exercised by "native" or "alien" governments, has a potency for abuse as probably no other relationship has. Yet liberal alien governments—and liberalism means primarily restraint upon, and limitations of, governmental authority—will be more easily controlled by public opinion against abuse of power than illiberal "native" governments.

Colonies may be of two different kinds: those of settlement and those of mere dependence. The former ones are more dangerous for the natives. The outstanding example is the United States where the settlement of the vast continent meant the practical extermination of the natives. Where the natives were not exterminated by settlement of immigrants but only driven out or relegated to subordinate positions, as in Aryan India, South Africa, Palestine, and partly in French North Africa, tragic situations have been created,

From Hans Kohn, "Some Reflections on Colonialism," *The Review of Politics,* Vol. 18, No. 3 (July, 1956). University of Notre Dame. Pp. 259–68, excerpts.

factually for the natives, morally for the immigrant settlers where they were inspired by liberal ideals. Such inspiration was lacking among Aryan Indians and South African Boers.

In a much more fortunate position are the colonies where no large-scale immigrant settlement was attempted. There the dependent status has worked on the whole to the advantage of the natives, who have found themselves, or will find themselves at some future time, in control of a vastly improved native land. Such was the case in British India and in Malaya, to quote only two instances.

In those areas, thanks to colonialism, for the first time, capable native cadres for the administration of the country and for all walks of civilized life have come into existence. Many of the new "nations" like India, Indonesia, and Nigeria owe their existence and potential cohesion as nations to the colonial regimes. . . .

Land Empires and Maritime Empires. American thinking about colonialism has been largely influenced by emotional misunderstandings. For obvious reasons the United States felt itself striving for complete political, economic, cultural, and ideological independence from Britain, disregarding the interdependence and affinity existing in all these respects between the two nations which have developed from the same historical roots; the striving for independence led to competition and to overcompensation of existing cultural and political inferiorities by a feeling of moral superiority.

In addition, there existed the widespread though unwarranted assumption, which had its origin in the fifteenth-century age of discoveries, that empires are established by sea powers, whereas expansion into contiguous land masses does not produce empires or colonialism. The then agrarian empire of Rome looked with contempt upon Carthage's maritime empire. But Rome was an empire too. And the United States in its war against Mexico and in its many wars against the various Indian tribes and nations created an empire as truly as did the sea-faring island states of Britain and Japan. Yet the United States, not considering itself an imperial power—even after 1898 when it occupied Pacific and Caribbean territories and established distant naval bases—applied similar criteria of non-"imperialism" to the military conquests and ruthless expansive policies of Russia and China. These land empires were never regarded in the same way as the sea empires.

This American attitude was easily shared by the colonial peoples under British, Dutch, or French rule in Asia. It coincided with the reality which confronted them. As a result, these people did not regard Russia, in spite of her immense land conquests in Asia, as an imperial power comparable to the sea empires. Russia seemed in a different category. This feeling was strengthened by the fact that Russia, through her history and her isolation from Europe until the eighteenth century resembled in its attitude toward authority and government, in its agrarian backwardness, and in the lethargy of its church and its masses, much more the countries of Asia than the dynamic, individualistic, and progressive West. . . .

Capitalism and Colonialism. The American view distinguishing between expansion across land masses and across separating waters was now strengthened among Asian intellectuals by the Leninist theory, that imperialism and colonialism were the product of late and overcapitalized capitalism, seeking new outlets. On the one hand the colonial relationship was regarded as primarily "capitalistic exploitation"; on the other hand a noncapitalistic nation by definition could not be imperialistic or exploiting. Thus the U.S.S.R., in spite of its having subjected so many peoples in Europe and Asia to a process of Russification and absolute control from Moscow, and Communist China, in spite of not liberating Tibet or Sinkiang from its imperial control and trying to restore its control over Korea, Annam, Burma, etc., do not appear as imperialist countries to the Asian nations.

Anticolonialism and Power Struggle. The issue of anticolonialism has been used for some time in the international power struggle, and not only by the U.S.S.R. Anti-imperialism and anticolonialism are widespread among the independent nations of Latin America, which have seen for a long time in the United States the leading imperialist and colonial nation, American imperialism being chiefly though not exclusively "dollar imperialism." Argentina, an independent nation for over a century, very proud of its independence and hardly in danger of imperialist aggression, has used the issue of anticolonialism as a weapon in her struggle against the United States for leadership at least in the southern and middle parts of the Western Hemisphere. The United States has used the issue of anticolonialism in its rivalry with, or dislike of, Britain for very many decades. Now the Soviet Union is using the same issue in her rivalry with, and hatred of, the United States. But there is hardly anything fundamentally new in it except that the Western nations, especially Britain, have by now set many nations in Asia and Africa free, and that it is above all among these nations which are now independent that the issue of anticolonialism is raised.

Is Colonialism a Western "Crime"? It is a widespread propaganda slogan that imperialism introduced wars, poverty, racial and economic exploitation to Asia and Africa. That is not the case. Poverty has existed in Asia and Africa since time immemorial, as it has existed in Europe until the rise of liberalism and capitalism. Poverty in Asia and Africa was for reasons of climate and temperament greater than in Europe. As far as historical memory goes, there has been perpetual warfare in Asia and Africa; one Asian nation or king enslaved other Asian peoples; African tribes enslaved and exterminated other African tribes. Imperialism is no Western invention. For many centuries Asian tribes and empires have endangered Europe. An accident saved Europe, but not Russia, from Mongol domination in the thirteenth century. As recently as 1683 the Turks were at the gates of Vienna, and Turks and Berbers enslaved Christian Europeans.

Western imperialism has had only a brief day in history. Its sun is now setting, and though this sun has been shining over many injustices and cruelties, in no way worse than the normal cruelties in Asia and Africa, it has brought lasting benefits to Asia and Africa, as the imperialism of Alexander the Great and of the Romans did for their empires, and has awakened and vitalized lethargic civilizations. . . .

Colonialism and National Independence. Reduced to its barest outline colonialism is foreign rule imposed upon a nation. Apart from the fact that no nations existed in most cases where colonialism was established often with the connivance of the colonial peoples themselves, it must be emphasized that this phenomenon of "foreign" rule has nothing to do with *European* control of Asia. Within Europe there has been rule of one people over another, or rather of one government over several peoples, and this has been resented as strongly and often, using the very same words as the anticolonialists in Asia do today, who have learned their slogans and their tactics from European nationalist movements. This has nothing to do with race or race superiority, one of the most bewildering myths of the present time. Closely related peoples opposed each other, Norwegians against Danes or Swedes, Croatians against Serbs, Slovaks against Czechs, Ukrainians against Russians, Catalans against Castilians, etc., and more bitterly resented what they regarded as political dominion, economic exploitation and relegation to a status of inferiority.

Nor will Asian aspirations for independence and conflicts resulting from it be solved by the dissolution of the existing Western empires and their replacement either by nation-states or by Asian empires. . . .

. . . The Indian government will probably suppress any attempt for independence on the part of some of the peoples of India with much greater ferocity than the British ever tried. Nor would it be fair to compare the position of the Negro in the United States to that of the outcasts in India. Though the position of the Negro is by far not yet what it should be, it is infinitely better than that of the Indian Untouchables. In the new Asian nations movements for independence continue: the territorial conflicts between India and Pakistan, between Pakistan and Afghanistan, the independence movements of the Karens in Burma and of the South Moluccans in Indonesia, the division between south and north in the Sudan and in Nigeria —these are some examples of continuing unrest after "imperialism" has gone. The Indian element in East Africa and the Chinese in Southeast Asia may create great hardship for the natives, once imperial protection is removed.

The West and Colonialism. If the anticolonial issue is brought up, the Western speakers should not put themselves on the defensive, but state the facts as they are. There have been Mongol, Chinese, Indian, Ottoman empires with their subject peoples as there has been a British empire. Which was "better" history will tell. Much is bad in many colonies, but much is bad in independent countries too. The British colony of Basutoland is much more progressive and salutary for the natives than the independent Union of South Africa which nevertheless claims Basutoland. British Hongkong is an oasis of order and liberty in the Far East, entirely due to British efforts and ideas. In the case of Cyprus the strategic interests of the Turks and their well-founded fears should be taken as much into consideration as French interests and fears in the Saar. There is no reason to assume that the New Guinean Papuas would fare better under the administration of Indonesian rulers, with whom they have no affinity in race, language, or religion, than under Dutch administration. All that does not mean that all colonial countries or all dependencies, whether in Europe or in other continents, should remain in this status. *Change and reforms are due everywhere.* . . . It may well be asked whether the application of the principle of national independence—instead of transformation and reform of supranational empires and political entities—has helped the cause of liberty and peace in Europe. The most important maxim guiding our actions in all parts of the world should be the recognition that gradual reforms are necessary everywhere, that there is no panacea, and that each case must be judged on its own merits, according to its historical setting.

The people of the United States should not only renounce the use of the anticolonial slogans, they should also give up the vain endeavor of competing in promises and panaceas with the Soviets. The Soviet short cuts for achieving economic well-being and social happiness are naturally attractive, and they provide spiritual satisfaction to an intellectual elite which has abandoned its own traditional values and has turned against those of the West. But the Soviet heaven can come only *after* the total revolution which is not reversible. We cannot promise a Utopia like that either for ourselves or for others, and should in all decency stress the fact. Sound progress can come only slowly and by great efforts and self-control. In Asia the moral and social conditions do not exist to make the Asians in any foreseeable future as rich as we are. This fact may be deeply regrettable, but it cannot be attributed to our or to anybody's fault. Yet the only thing which would apparently satisfy the emotional dissatisfaction of some Asian intellectuals seems to be the lowering of our and the British standards to theirs. That we cannot do. We are not free because we are rich; it has been our long and hard developing tradition of individual liberty and responsibility which has made it possible for us to become rich. . . .

68. THE AMERICAN IMPERIAL DISEASE

J. A. LUKACS

J. A. Lukacs is professor of history at Chestnut Hill and La Salle Colleges in Philadelphia. He is the author of A HISTORY OF THE COLD WAR, THE GREAT POWERS AND EASTERN EUROPE, *and the editor of a volume of de Tocqueville's writings.*

In 1898, the march toward an American world empire began with the acquisition of Caribbean and Pacific colonies through the Spanish-American War. Twenty years later, for the first time in history, American armies landed in Europe and American brigades camped within Russia: 1918 was the year of

J. A. Lukacs, "The American Imperial Disease," *The American Scholar,* Vol. 28, No. 2 (Spring 1959). Pp. 141–50, excerpts. Professor Lukacs made some slight changes for this excerpted version of his original article.

the Fourteen Points, when the *George Washington* carried Wilson to an exhausted Europe to the chairmanship of world peace. Little less than another twenty years later Franklin Roosevelt's Quarantine Speech indicated the potentiality of American involvement in a coming Second World War. But while in 1938 there were virtually no American possessions or military bases outside the Western Hemisphere, in 1958, another twenty years later, an American world empire involving five continents and an overwhelming network of American military bases abroad had grown up.

It is almost always a source of wonder to me that Americans do not recognize the immense character of this American world revolution. It is true that the Russians have a world-revolutionary dogma and that the Americans do not (although certain doctrines and procedures of our diplomatic and propaganda services are dogmatic and revolutionary, while the Russians do not always act in accordance with the tenets of Marx or even of Lenin). But the point is that by the middle of the twentieth century American troops are stationed in the Mediterranean, in Central Europe, in Arabia and in the Arctic, while the Russian empire does not extend much beyond the frontiers of the czardom of a hundred years ago. Indeed, ever since the end of the last world war, the Russians have retreated from some of their advanced positions in Asia and in Europe, while we have advanced in leaps rather than within bounds. We now have alliances with peoples far beyond our oceanic frontiers, while the Russians have virtually no binding alliances except with their Communist and satellite neighbors. . . .

It is true that the American people did not want an empire; and it is true that not even their government consciously knew what it was doing as it spun out a network of bases and alliances all around the Soviet Union. But I invite my readers to consider the revolution in the American national attitude during these last ten or fifteen years. I believe that the evidence is striking.

It was fifteen years ago, about 1943, that the primacy of American power became evident. Yet for the next five years the United States refused to consider the stationing of American forces in Europe with any degree of permanence. It nearly refused to accept occupation zones in southern Germany and in Austria. It refused to listen to various Churchillian plans aimed at forestalling Russia in Southern or Central Europe. Even after Yalta, it refused to take positive action against the developing Sovietization of Eastern European states. It refused, beyond mediation, to intervene in the civil war in China. It agreed to set up the supranational United Nations on American soil and to give the Soviet Union three votes to one American vote. It offered to set up a central German government based on national elections. It proposed to give up its monopoly of the atomic bomb in exchange for fair international inspection.

It is true that some of these policies were narrow and some of them foolish; yet there remained within them a residue of American idealism. Consequently, between 1948 and 1952, the American government took energetic action against the potential overflow of Communist tyranny to the unaffected areas of the world. It underwrote the defense of Western Europe. It supported the cause of a united Europe without second thoughts or qualifications. It chose to defend Greece, Berlin, and Korea at the cost of American blood. It established what, in practice, amounted to a generous peace settlement with West Germany and Japan. Most of these policies were neither narrow nor foolish; they were but the hardly avoidable consequences of the earlier mistakes. And throughout the ten years between the North African landing and the death of Stalin, the specter that chilled broadminded Americans as well as the peoples of the free world was that of a resurgent isolationism, a repetition of the post-Wilsonian American disillusionment, the fear that the American people would have had enough and would leave the rest of the free world to its fate.

But now comes the contrast. During the five years between 1953 and 1958, the government of this country has made it clear on a number of important occasions that it would not contemplate the eventual withdrawal of American forces from the middle of Europe even if the Russians, in turn, would remove their troops from some of their East European satellites. More important, during the NATO Conference in December of 1957, the American government indicated that we would not consider such a withdrawal even if some of our own allies desired it. We had agreed to the mutual evacuation of Austria, on our original terms, only after some reluctance. Appearances notwithstanding, we have refused to discuss German unification on the basis of our original proposals that called for a free and neutral Germany. In Europe at least we are among the revisionists and the Russians are among the *status quo* powers, not only ideologically (for in that respect it is natural that we should not acquiesce in the permanent enslavement of Eastern European nations) but also territorially, for we alone among the Great Powers have given tacit support to German ambitions directed against the present western frontiers of Poland (which is, by the way, about the only outstanding territorial issue in Europe). Appearances and alliance texts notwithstanding, for the first time in history our government has chosen Germany and not Britain to be our main European ally. Despite appearances and propaganda, we are now supporting the movement for a united Europe only insofar as such a European union does not attempt to pursue a truly independent role. I am not even speaking of our tergiversations on the atomic armament issues. We have involved ourselves in the corrupting and treacherous maze and mire of Arab politics. We are transforming the United Nations into an instrument which, by reason of numbers, tends more than often to act against the interests of Britain and Europe. It is now an accepted axiom of our government that everything we do must be related to our imperial position vis-à-vis Russia: that we must outproduce, outshout, outeducate, outpropagandize, outbomb, outspy, outfinance, and outdance the Russians whenever and wherever possible. The State Department, openly or surreptitiously, has found it proper to use the money of American taxpayers to erect clandestine radio stations, to finance the tours of American "amateur" athletes, to send bop "musicians" and help "architects" all around the world, while it bribes thousands of American "experts," writers, artists, and scholars to work on dubious "projects" subordinated to the cold war. My quotation marks are not accidental.

And now, when we are literally shooting for the moon, it has been recognized by only a handful of Americans that the Russians have already felt compelled to retreat from those advanced positions that they held at the end of the last war. In Europe, they have withdrawn from the Finnish naval base, from the Danish island of Bornholm, from their strategically valuable portion of eastern Austria; they have grumbled but felt they had to acquiesce in the independence of Yugoslavia and, to some extent, of Poland; and they have at least suggested that, under certain conditions, they might withdraw from parts of Eastern Europe. In Asia they have given up Sinkiang, their naval bases in Dairen, their domain over the Manchurian railroads; they ceded their pre-eminence in North Korea to the Chinese, while even in Outer Mongolia their hold may be weakening. It is a curious and regrettable paradox that although many of these concessions would have been inconceivable under Stalin, it has been since his death that a new American Administration has refused to discuss or even to acknowledge most of them.

Of course, the Russians have not acted in accord with some profound change of heart. They withdrew when they felt that it would be to their advantage in the long run. But what else, I ask, can we expect of them? Here we meet with another State Department shibboleth: the "tactical retreats" of the Soviets, the "zigzag course" advocated by Lenin. But isn't any and every retreat a tactical one? At any rate, in some parts of Europe the Russians now are learning the lesson Talleyrand was supposed to have enunciated—that one can do many things with bayonets (but not sit on them). One can also do many things with party platforms (but not stand on them)— and yet I am still amazed that a plank in Section Nine of the Republican Party Platform of 1956 has never attracted any attention. For this plank called for no less than "the establishment of American bases strategically dispersed all around the world."

Nothing better illustrates the extent of the revolution in American political attitudes, and the absolute anachronism of our accepted political categories, than the thoughtless endorsement of this plank by what is still called by commentators the "conservative" and "traditionally isolation-minded" Republican party of the United States.

Perhaps this is not a revolution in our political attitudes. It is something else. For "politics," in the original, Aristotelian sense of the word, means a concern with one's own community, with a reasonable approach to its affairs. But as I read Gaither Reports, Rockefeller Reports, space-age reports or what-not, it occurs to me that we are no longer talking politics. Our "experts" are talking something else. They are talking Globics (*pron.* Globix).

Globics or politics, I am concerned with the revolutionary transformation of the postulates of our official position. And I am concerned with the effects of all of this on the American people. When I see young Americans, and especially their wives, now so eager to be employed abroad because of the luxurious benefits of this new sort of proconsulship; when I see the glutted American industry growing permanently dependent on military orders in peacetime; when I see our commerce growing dependent on exports for the first time; when I see the increasing inclination of our professional intellectuals to angle for governmental contracts and foreign propaganda assignments; when I see many more evidences of our gradual transformation into an imperial garrison state; when I see that we now have a student generation born twenty years ago which is accustomed to regard these extraordinary world-wide involvements as normal and to be taken for granted—I am, of course, reminded of the Roman Empire. Although I know that history does not necessarily repeat itself, I see the similarities perhaps less with the rising Imperium of Octavian than with the declining Empire of Constantine. In my lifetime I have seen what has happened to great European nations when they had been bitten by the imperial bug and soaked with the arguments of a Chosen People. I am now seeing what this is doing to Russia. I do not like to speculate what the further propagation of the imperialist virus might do to the qualities of the American people.

As I am writing for an American audience, at this point the inevitable American question arises: "What does he want us to do about all this?" My answer is that once Americans begin to think about this disease, they will do something about it. For the correction of the disease depends wholly on the proper recognition of its existence, of its extent, and of its sources. And the source of this disease lies in the peculiar sickness of the modern intellect whose analytical capacities are impaired in the twentieth century. I am struck by the cultivated blindness of our "experts" and, indeed, of many more benevolent and decent Americans who are unable even to recognize the existence of the events that I have attempted to outline. Are Americans no longer able or willing to see the dangers in trying to become the Scoutmasters of the World? What will this do to the soul and body of this great nation? . . .

For the fault lies with those responsible, opinion-making elements in American society—and this includes a thin but broad stratum of people extending from the State Department to college professors in international relations—people who have allowed themselves to rest satisfied with intellectual slogans; who are now profiting from the lucrative opportunities provided by our imperial revolution; who feel comfortable in being listened to and in being on the side of the respectable Christian legions; who, led by certain refugee "experts" of European origin, have attempted during the past ten years to promote a new sort of American *Realpolitik,* an atomic Machiavellianism custom-tailored to American needs; who are talking about the wrong kind of danger abroad as well as at home, against the dying ideology of communism instead of warning us against Russian national ambitions, and against the new dead tendency of American isolationism instead of warning us against radical global "crusades." Hence, there is all this cheap nonsense about "clean bombs" and our "posture of strength," as well as the melancholy, if not frightening implications of the change that I claim to detect in American public and private life in the twelve years during which I have lived among the American people and taught their children: the shift, at the bottom, from the previously often insubstantial and individualistic American overoptimism about human nature, to the present suspicious and fatalistic overpessimism—a shift evident in many fields of American life right now. Because of the strange alchemy of human souls and minds it is very easy to slide from undue illusions to undue cynicism.

But it is not only that I do not want to witness and that I do not want to live in a cynical America. It is that I believe, and not only for spiritual reasons, that a cynical America will be courting surprising and shattering defeat.

Strategically, politically, and culturally, the best hope for these United States is the emergence of a truly independent Europe, and not a "united" Europe tied to American atomic power lines and purse strings. There is evidence to believe that this is exactly what our government and "experts" do not want; it may deprive them of a big share of their self-proposed jobs. Meanwhile, new sets of jobs are being created under such names as "challenge in Africa," "challenge in Asia," etc. But we are forgetting two things about Europe: first, decline and fall are not the same; and, second, that although the nations of Europe may no longer be the main actors, Europe is still the main theater of history.

But the movements of the spirit are still at the bottom of politics. On the one hand, I not only trust but know and feel that surprising reservoirs of chastened American idealism do exist. On the other hand, I see that strange American mixture of narrow fideism and broad fatalism, of outward confidence and inward fear, expressed nowadays in these falsely "realistic" words: An Atomic War With Russia Is Inevitable. But, like "irresistible," the "inevitable" is so often only what people do not wish, or dare, to resist. I do not say that the Russians are already the Publicans—far from that, alas—and not even that we are already the Pharisees. All I say is that if we choose the road of the Pharisee, this Republic, my adopted country, the erstwhile hope of the free world is doomed.

69. PROTRACTED CONFLICT: A NEW LOOK AT COMMUNIST STRATEGY

ROBERT STRAUSZ-HUPÉ

Dr. Strausz-Hupé (1903–   ) is professor of political science at the University of Pennsylvania. He has written extensively on world affairs and is the author of GEOPOLITICS, THE ZONE OF INDIFFERENCE, *and co-author of* INTERNATIONAL POLITICS, PROTRACTED CONFLICT, *and* A FORWARD STRATEGY FOR AMERICA.

In the conflict between the U.S. and U.S.S.R., two alien systems confront one another. This confrontation takes place in space and in time; the contest is over the domination of the earth and, now, its outer space and over the future of human society. It is the climactic phase of the systemic revolution

From Robert Strausz-Hupé, "Protracted Conflict: A New Look at Communist Strategy," *Orbis,* Vol. 2 (Spring 1958). Pp. 13–38, excerpts.

through which the world has been passing ever since 1914. It is thus a power-political as well as a social contest, a war as well as a revolution.

So absorbing has been the search for the ideological consistencies or inconsistencies of Communism that, by comparison, not enough attention has been given to Communism as a method. Communism is a method of conflict in space over a sustained period of time, i.e., of protracted conflict. This neglect of the method as against what Communism really is (or says it is) is due to many causes. Some of these are inherent in the Communist method itself— to deceive the opponent as regards the nature of the method is part of the method; others are inherent in our own society, which is neither revolutionary nor aggressive nor monolithic. Our society does not subordinate all its aspirations to considerations of power; Communist-dominated societies do. And the struggle being what it is, namely a revolutionary one, Communism presses all men and all things into the service of one cause: the overthrow of the existing social order and the establishment of a Communist society. It is only within this context that we can read meaning into Communist strategy and develop the counterstrategies that will bracket the range of the Communist threat and not merely seek to fill the breach opened by the latest Communist thrust. . . .

The conflict between the United States and the Soviet Union now holds the center of the historical stage. Yet, this confrontation is the mere contemporary expression, the vast powers arrayed in each camp notwithstanding, of pervasive conflict that encompasses all lands, all peoples and all levels of society. The United States and the Soviet Union are now the leading protagonists; the struggle which is civil as well as international cleaves all societies. Hence any effective strategy for waging the ubiquitous protracted conflict must be, by necessity, a revolutionary strategy: to wit, a strategy that puts the revolutionary forces-on-the-loose in politics, economics, culture, science, and technology to its own use and denies their exploitation to the enemy. Insofar as Communist strategy has been able to do just that, it has been effective. The Communists have benefited from the errors of their opponents who let themselves be bemused by the Marxist myth of revolution and remained blind to the realities of revolutionary strategy.

Marxist thought is rooted in a concept of dynamic historical change. Marx foresaw, albeit obscurely, the systemic change which was soon to unmake and remake human society. He erred in attributing it exclusively to economic forces; but he perceived clearly that modern techniques would quicken its pace and widen its range. This insight, together with his unerring grasp of the potentialities of political and social conflict latent in the crisis of the old order, is Marx' greatest legacy to the Russian Communists.

The Russian Communists did not create the "revolutionary situation" in Asia; that "situation" had been taking shape for a long time. The Communists, however, were quick to exploit it and "to push what was falling." First hampered by ideological preconceptions, they soon adjusted their sights to political realities: the colonial peoples would forge the political ideas which they had received from the West into instruments for dislodging the Western powers from their imperial holdings. Although the incipient breakdown of the colonial system would be paced by economic and social transformation, the prospect of proletarian revolution held, for the Kremlin, less attraction than the strategic prize: to inflict upon the Western powers, who were, in point of time, the principal opponents of the Soviet Union, heavy losses in political prestige, markets and raw material resources, and to weaken them through the debilitating effects, military, economic and moral, of colonial wars of attrition. . . .

Classic Marxian economics is dead; nowhere is it probably taken less seriously than in Russia. Yet Communism has outlived its intellectual sterility as well as its moral bankruptcy. Communism now draws its vigor from a dialectical theory of total conflict of indefinite duration between world political systems. Although the Communist objective is indeed total victory, its attainment does not necessarily follow upon the same kind of total military conflict which has characterized Western warfare in the twentieth century. The Communist attitude toward war is rooted in the early experience of Soviet Communism. At the outset, Communist power was vastly inferior to that of the capitalist order which it sought to overthrow. The Communists had to fight from an inferior position. Unable to engage a technologically superior West in all-out military warfare at which it excelled, they were forced to resort to methods of conflict which had been used either haphazardly or not at all in the epoch of total wars. Clausewitz' idea of the relativity of peace and war is not an original discovery of Western thought. The interaction and fundamental identity of opposites is the basic premise of such Asian philosophies as, for example, Taoism. Indeed, the most succinct statement of the Communist methods of conflict is contained in Mao Tse-tung's work *On the Protracted War*. Thus the Communist doctrine on protracted conflict is a blend of many intellectual contributions. It has been refined by practice. Not the least of its virtues, from the point of view of the Communists, is its relative obscurity. The West has given it little systematic thought or has misunderstood it.

The salient characteristics of the doctrine of protracted conflict are: the total objective, the carefully controlled methods and the constant shifting of the battleground, weapons systems, and the operational tactics for the purpose of confusing the opponent, keeping him off balance and wearing down his resistance. The doctrine of protracted conflict prescribes a strategy for annihilating the opponent over a period of time by limited operations, by feints and maneuvers, psychological manipulations and diverse forms of violence. But this strategy should not be mistaken for one of limited war in the style of European warfare in the eighteenth century. It does not rule out the final and total knockout punch. In Communist theory, various techniques of political warfare and graduated violence are so coordinated as to form a spectrum that reaches all the way from clandestine distribution of subversive literature to the annihilating blow delivered with every weapon available.

For the Communists, protracted conflict brackets all possible relationships between states and groups—political, economic, and cultural—and some that, from our point of view, signify the exact opposite of conflict. Even within

Communist society itself, unceasing conflict rages: there are always "anti-party" activities that must be combatted and "traitors" that must be rooted out. Were Communism to foreswear conflict, it would cease to be. Were it not for those international tensions, the alleviation of which is the favorite theme of Communist propaganda, Leninism would be as meaningless an ideology as Marxian "science" has been for a long time. The rulers of Soviet Russia have no claim to the allegiance of their people and no justification in their own theory other than their propitiatory role in the unending struggle of Leninist demonology: the "ruling circles" of the capitalist states are determined to destroy "socialism," i.e., Soviet Russia; they may have become too weak now to do so by armed attack, but they keep on plotting the ruin of the "socialist camp"; the fight is not yet won, and the schemings of the "capitalist warmongers" can only be defeated by unflagging, militant vigilance.

In this context, the word negotiation has a meaning that is difficult to reconcile with our understanding of it. Since a global settlement with the "capitalist camp" is inconceivable for the Communists, negotiation on any level—on the "summit" or in the "valley"—is a tactical maneuver that, to be worthwhile, must subvert a new position whence to launch a new attack. This, in itself, is not an argument against "negotiating with Soviet Russia," for there is, in theory at least, no reason why both sides cannot play at the same game. If, however, by "negotiating with Soviet Russia" is meant a diplomatic activity that is to result in a lasting, all-around settlement of the basic issues of peace and war, such as the one achieved by the Congress of Vienna in 1814, then "negotiating with Soviet Russia" leads straight into the baited trap of the Communists.

There is much to be said for a return to traditional diplomacy and against "open covenants, openly arrived at." The Soviets themselves are careful students and skillful practitioners of the established art of diplomacy. They have shown themselves keenly aware of the virtue of self-enforcing agreements and piecemeal settlements of sticky issues; we can do worse than to dust off the manuals of cabinet diplomacy and bargain with the Soviets to mutual advantage. But the limits of negotiation with the Communists are sharply drawn by their own conflict doctrine. To negotiate for a cessation of protracted conflict before the Communist has rejected its operational doctrine and Messianic aspirations would be tantamount to negotiating for surrender. At Brest Litovsk, forty years ago, the Communists, although they yielded, did not capitulate. Then, their writ extended no farther than the suburbs of Leningrad and Moscow. Today, they hold one third of the globe. It is unlikely that Nikita Khrushchev or his successor will do what Leon Trotsky refused to do. Conflict to the bitter end is the stuff from which Communism draws its very sustenance. Negotiation is merely one technique, albeit a highly effective one, prescribed by the doctrine of protracted conflict. . . .

The West can only hope to defeat the Communists by giving battle on its own chosen terrain. It must carry the battle to the vital sectors of Communist defense. To do that it must learn to counter the strategy of protracted conflict—to manage conflict in space and in time.

The development of proper Western attitudes towards protracted conflict will be immensely difficult. The Communists possess a mentality that is much better suited to protracted and controlled conflict than that of the Western peoples. According to Marxist-Leninist theory, history has been always on the side of Communism. The Russian Communists are, by now, convinced that, indeed, it is. They are patient and tenacious in their efforts to win the inevitable victory. They must make certain that they do nothing foolish, nothing that might jeopardize their chances of ultimate success. They are capable not only of accepting but also of exploiting a tactical defeat, if such a defeat leads their opponent to relax his guard and thus to neglect his defenses. Furthermore, a monolithic structure enables the Communist rulers to execute their foreign policies with a unity of purpose and a ruthless efficiency that is unparalleled among modern governments.

The West has neither a doctrine of protracted conflict nor an international conspiratorial apparatus for executing it. What is more, we do not want such a doctrine or such a political apparatus, for it would be a tragic piece of irony if the men of the Free World, in trying to combat the Communists, should become like them.

According to a Roman proverb, one should school oneself in the school of the enemy. Studying the Communist text, should we elaborate a doctrine of protracted conflict of our own which would prescribe the gamut of responses for meeting every conceivable Communist challenge? Some of our "weaknesses" vis-à-vis the Communists are irremediable: we cannot turn ourselves into a conflict society, nor can we assign to the government and, in the last resort, to the police the discipline of our conscience. It is within these limitations—which are the ramparts of civilized self-restraint—that we are forced to cope with Communist perversity.

Pericles long ago was confronted with a similar problem. As the leader of the open society of Athens, locked in an irreconcilable conflict with the garrison state of Sparta, he recognized a relatively simple fact which many of the theorists of war in the nuclear age have overlooked, namely that there are subtle alternatives to the risky and blunt strategy of engaging the enemy in direct and decisive military action. In the protracted conflict known as the Peleponnesian War, Pericles chose to pursue an *extended strategy* which was designed to avoid a showdown battle while wearing down, by a campaign of economic, political, and psychological attrition, the enemy's will to resist. Liddell Hart pointed out that the Periclean plan was simply a war policy aimed at "draining the enemy's endurance in order to convince him that he could not gain a decision." In today's protracted conflict, the United States must maintain and use its power for the same ultimate purpose: to turn the tide of battle against the Communists, to induce them to overextend themselves, to exploit the weakness of their system, to paralyze their will, and to bring about their final collapse. Within the framework of mutual deterrence, both sides can employ the strategy of protracted conflict—and we can do so quite effectively without the dispensation of a jealous and demanding dogma of conflict for conflict's sake. . . .

A psychopolitical offensive, directed against the Communist citadel itself,

offers the West its best chance for winning the battle for its own survival
and for spoiling the Communist strategy for the subversion of the uncommitted world. Although the currents within the uncommitted world are running against the West, the West need not despair of holding its remaining
positions once it has forced the Communists on the psychopolitical defensive
by engaging them on the most favorable terrain, namely the Communists'
own "peace zone." . . .

70. THE PRESSURES BEHIND SOVIET EXPANSIONISM

BARRINGTON MOORE, JR.

*Barrington Moore, Jr. (1913–   ) is lecturer on sociology and Senior
Research Fellow at the Russian Research Center, Harvard University.
He is the author of many books and articles on Soviet society.*

. . . Has Soviet expansion during the past decade been primarily defensive,
and would it come to rest if external threats were removed? Or is the world
now witnessing a special variety of expansionism: Communist imperialism?
The same general questions would have to be answered about the United
States, but the analysis in this study must necessarily be confined to the
Russian side of the equation.

Four considerations enter into the conclusion advanced by many that the
Soviet system contains a number of internal expanionist forces impelling it
to seek one conquest after another. It is often said that, because the U.S.S.R.
is an authoritarian state, its rulers need a continuous series of triumphs in
order to maintain their power. The rulers of a dictatorship, it is claimed,
cannot afford to rest on their laurels. Occasionally this type of argument is
supported by a neo-Freudian chain of reasoning. It is asserted that the
frustrations imposed upon the individual in modern society, especially under
a dictatorship, tend to produce socially destructive impulses that have to be
channeled outward against an external enemy if the society is not to destroy
itself. The second line of argument, at a different level of analysis, emphasizes
the indications of a strong power drive in Stalin's personality. Parallels can
be drawn on this basis between his urge for new worlds to conquer and the
political aspirations of Napoleon, Hitler, and others. A third line of reasoning
points to various indications in Soviet statements and actions of an old-

From Barrington Moore, Jr., *Soviet Politics: The Dilemma of Power.* Cambridge,
Mass.: Harvard University Press. Copyright, 1950, by the President and Fellows of
Harvard College. Pp. 394–401, excerpts. Reprinted by permission of the publisher.

fashioned interest in territorial expansion that shows strong resemblances to traditional czarist policy. The latter argument draws its reasoning from the facts of geography and history, emphasizing traditional Russian interest in warm-water ports, the long drive to the South and East, and similar matters. Under the fourth type of argument, Marxist-Leninist ideology is selected as a separate expansionist force. Persons who hold this view point out the Messianic qualities of Marxist doctrine and the continuous need for struggle and victory that it generates.

Each of these arguments and hypotheses represents some portion of the truth. . . .

Concerning the first point, that authoritarian states tend to be expansionist ones, it is necessary to express reservations and doubts on both general and specific grounds. The connection between the internal organization of a society and its foreign policy is a complex question that cannot yet be answered on the basis of simple formulas. Athens engaged in foreign conquest perhaps more than did warlike Sparta, and the Japanese, despite the militaristic emphasis of their society, lived in isolation for centuries until the time of their forced contacts with the West. To show that the authoritarian structure of any state is a source of expansionist tendencies, one would have to show the way in which these pressures make themselves felt upon those responsible for foreign policy. At this point the argument often breaks down, though there are cases where it can be shown that the rulers have embarked on an adventurous policy to allay internal discontent. But those at the apex of the political pyramid in an authoritarian regime are frequently freer from the pressures of mass discontent than are the responsible policy makers of a Western democracy. They can therefore afford to neglect much longer the dangers of internal hostilities. Furthermore, modern events reveal the weakness of the argument that a warlike policy is the result of hostilities toward outsiders among the individuals who make up the society. In the days of total war it is necessary to use all sorts of force and persuasion, from propaganda to conscription, to make men and women fight. To regard war as primarily the expression of the hostilities of rank-and-file citizens of various states toward one another is to fly in the face of these facts.

In the case of the Soviet Union, the Nazi-Soviet Pact of 1939 shows that the rulers of modern Russia had no difficulty in disregarding the hostilities to Nazism that had been built up during preceding years, and that in this respect they enjoyed greater freedom for prompt adjustment of disputes than did other countries. Both totalitarian partners were able to keep mass hostility under control as long as it suited purposes and plans based on the configuration of international power relationships. . . .

An acceptable modification of the argument that the authoritarian nature of the present Soviet regime is a source of an aggressive and expansionist foreign policy may be found along the following lines. It is probable that a certain amount of hostility toward the outside world is an essential ingredient in the power of the present rulers of Russia. Without the real or imagined threat of potential attack, it would be much more difficult to drive the Russian masses through one set of Five Year Plans after another. Yet it does not seem likely that this hostility is in turn a force that reacts back on the makers of Russian foreign policy. Their power can be more easily maximized by the threat of war than by war itself—a precarious enough situation. Nor is there evidence that mass hostility is in any way cumulative or sufficient to force the Soviet leaders into an aggressive policy. There are a number of devices for draining off internally generated hostility into channels other than those of external expansion. Military and combative sentiments, aroused for specific purposes, can be and have been directed into the socially productive channels of promoting a conquest of the physical environment. . . .

Those who emphasize the continuity of the Russian historical tradition and the importance of Russia's geographical position in the determination of Soviet foreign policy are correct insofar as Russia's place on the globe and her past relations with her neighbors set certain limitations and provide certain readily definable opportunities for Russian foreign policy. In other words, an expansionist Soviet foreign policy can follow only certain well-defined lines of attack. It may have Persia, China, or Germany as its major object of infiltration, but Latin America and the Antarctic are much more remote objectives.

The reappearance of old-fashioned Russian territorial interest in various parts of the globe has been associated with the revival of Russian strength from the low ebb of revolution, intervention, and civil war. It may be suspected that the early idealist statements of the Bolshevik leaders about the abandonment of czarist imperialism were inspired not only by Marxist doctrine but were also made on the grounds that they were the only possible tactics to follow in Russia's weak condition. Now that the proletarian revolution has a territorial base, it is understandable that attempts should be made to combine the interests of the two, and that some of the results should show marked similarities to czarist policy. Furthermore, the possibility may readily be granted that the present rulers of Russia are somewhat influenced by the model of czarist diplomacy. But the driving forces behind any contemporary Soviet expansionism must be found in a contemporary social situation. Historical and geographical factors may limit the expression of an expansionist drive. They cannot be expansionist forces in their own right.

Turning to the ideological factor, it has already been noted that the Messianic energies of Communism can be, and at times in the past have been, very largely directed toward tasks of internal construction. The "creative myth of Leninism," to use Sorel's suggestive term, involves the building of factories in desert wastes and the creation of a more abundant life for the inhabitants of the Soviet Union. One must agree, however, that a creative myth, if it is effective, is usually an article for export as well as for domestic consumption. Those who really believe in socialism usually believe it is necessary for the world as a whole, just as do the more emotional believers in the virtues of democracy and the four freedoms. There remains, however, another important aspect of Soviet doctrine, which sets at least temporary limits to its expansionist qualities. It is a cardinal point in the Leninist-Stalinist doctrine that a retreat made in good order is not a disgrace. The Soviet myth does not have a "victory or death" quality—there is no urge to seek a final dramatic showdown and a *Götterdämmerung* finale. When faced with superior strength, the Soviets have on numerous occasions shown the ability to withdraw with their forces intact. Although the withdrawal may be followed by a renewal of pressures elsewhere, it may be repeated once more if superior forces are again brought to bear.

The foregoing considerations are enough to suggest the complexity of the problem of interpreting the expansionist forces contained in the Soviet system. They should make us wary of dramatically pessimistic conclusions to the effect that the Soviet leaders, propelled by forces beyond their control, are marching to a world holocaust. But they give many more grounds for pessimism than for optimism concerning the probability of preventing a further increase in tension in the power relationships of Moscow and Washington. Even though Soviet expansionism of the past decade may be explained as primarily an adaptation to the changing balance of power, such an explanation by no means precludes the possibility, perhaps even the probability, that the series of adaptations and "defensive" measures taken by the United States and the U.S.S.R. may culminate in war.

The situation in which the two major powers stand at uneasy guard, carefully watching each other's activities and countering one another's strengthenings in all portions of the globe, contains internal forces of its own that could lead to a violent explosion. That it has not done so already is an indication that both sides are still making their political calculations largely in defensive terms, inasmuch as neither antagonist is committed by its own system of values to war for war's sake. . . .

If the prospects of fundamental improvement in American-Russian relations are dim indeed, they are not necessarily hopeless. One of the few warrants for hope is the Communist tradition that retreat from a situation that threatens the power of the leaders is no defeat. If, as seems most likely, neither side is yet actively seeking war, there is still room for the reduction of tension through the familiar devices of highly skilled diplomacy. To succeed, this diplomacy would have to part company with the parochial moralism that has characterized much American negotiation and free itself from the miasma of dogmatic suspicion likely to become chronic on the Russian side. Whether modern diplomats can escape from the pressures engendered by their own societies remains to be seen.

71. MYTH AND ILLUSION IN AMERICAN FOREIGN POLICY

J. W. FULBRIGHT

J. W. Fulbright (1905–   ) is chairman of the Senate Foreign Relations Committee.

There is an inevitable divergence, attributable to the imperfections of the human mind, between the world as it is and the world as men perceive it. As long as our perceptions are reasonably close to objective reality, it is possible for us to act upon our problems in a rational and appropriate manner. But when our perceptions fail to keep pace with events, when we refuse to believe something because it displeases or frightens us, or is simply startlingly unfamiliar, then the gap between fact and perception becomes a chasm and actions become irrelevant and irrational.

There has always—and inevitably—been some divergence between the realities of foreign policy and our ideas about it. This divergence has in certain respects been growing rather than narrowing, and we are handicapped, accordingly, by policies based on old myths rather than current realities. This divergence is, in my opinion, dangerous and unnecessary—dangerous because it can reduce foreign policy to a fraudulent game of imagery and appearances, unnecessary because it can be overcome by the determination of men in high office to dispel prevailing misconceptions by the candid dissemination of unpleasant but inescapable facts. . . .

The master myth of the cold war is that the Communist bloc is a monolith composed of governments which are not really governments at all but organized conspiracies, divided among themselves perhaps in certain matters of tactics, but all equally resolute and implacable in their determination to destroy the free world.

I believe that the Communist world is indeed hostile to the free world in its general and long-term intentions but that the existence of this animosity in principle is far less important for our foreign policy than the great variation in its intensity and character both in time and among the individual members of the Communist bloc. Only if we recognize these variations, ranging from China which poses immediate threats to the free world to Poland and Yugoslavia which pose none, can we hope to act effectively upon the bloc and to turn its internal differences to our own advantage and to the advantage of those bloc countries which wish to maximize their independence. . . .

Senator J. W. Fulbright; speech delivered in the United States Senate on March 25, 1964.

For a start, we can acknowledge the fact that the Soviet Union, though still a most formidable adversary, has ceased to be totally and implacably hostile to the West. It has shown a new willingness to enter mutually advantageous arrangements with the West and, thus far at least, to honor them. It has therefore become possible to divert some of our energies from the prosecution of the cold war to the relaxation of the cold war and to deal with the Soviet Union, for certain purposes, as a normal state with normal and traditional interests.

If we are to do these things effectively, we must distinguish between Communism as an ideology and the power and policy of the Soviet state. It is not Communism as a doctrine, or Communism as it is practiced within the Soviet Union or within any other country, that threatens us. . . .

Insofar as a great nation mobilizes its power and resources for aggressive purposes, that nation, regardless of ideology, makes itself our enemy. Insofar as a nation is content to practice its doctrines within its own frontiers, that nation, however repugnant its ideology, is one with which we have no proper quarrel. . . .

We are to a great extent the victims, and the Soviets the beneficiaries, of our own ideological convictions, and of the curious contradictions which they involve. We consider it a form of subversion of the free world, for example, when the Russians enter trade relations or conclude a consular convention or establish airline connections with a free country in Asia, Africa, or Latin America—and to a certain extent we are right.

On the other hand, when it is proposed that we adopt the same strategy in reverse—by extending commercial credits to Poland or Yugoslavia, or by exchanging ambassadors with a Hungarian regime which has changed considerably in character since the revolution of 1956—then the same patriots who are so alarmed by Soviet activities in the free world charge our policy makers with "giving aid and comfort to the enemy" and with innumerable other categories of idiocy and immorality.

It is time that we resolved this contradiction and separated myth from reality. The myth is that every Communist state is an unmitigated evil and a relentless enemy of the free world; the reality is that some Communist regimes pose a threat to the free world while others pose little or none, and that if we will recognize these distinctions, we ourselves will be able to influence events in the Communist bloc in a way favorable to the security of the free world. . . .

The problem of Cuba is . . . heavily burdened with the dead weight of old myths and prohibitions against "unthinkable thoughts." I think the time is overdue for a candid re-evaluation of our Cuban policy even though it may lead to distasteful conclusions.

There are and have been three options open to the United States with respect to Cuba: first, the removal of the Castro regime by invading and occupying the island; second, an effort to weaken and ultimately bring down the regime by a policy of political and economic boycott, and, finally, acceptance of the Communist regime as a disagreeable reality and annoyance but one which is not likely to be removed in the near future because of the unavailability of acceptable means of removal.

The first option, invasion, has been tried in a half-hearted way and found wanting. It is generally acknowledged that the invasion and occupation of Cuba, besides violating our obligations as a member of the United Nations and of the Organization of American States, would have explosive consequences in Latin America and elsewhere and might precipitate a global war. . . .

The prospects of bringing down the Castro regime by political and economic boycott have never been very good. Even if a general free-world boycott were successfully applied against Cuba, it is unlikely that the Russians would refuse to carry the extra financial burden and thereby permit the only Communist regime in the Western Hemisphere to collapse. . . .

Having ruled out military invasion and blockade, and recognizing the failure of the boycott policy, we are compelled to consider the third of the three options open to us with respect to Cuba: the acceptance of the continued existence of the Castro regime as a distasteful nuisance but not an intolerable danger so long as the nations of the hemisphere are prepared to meet their obligations of collective defense under the Rio Treaty.

In recent years we have become transfixed with Cuba, making it far more important in both our foreign relations and in our domestic life than its size and influence warrant. We have flattered a noisy but minor demagogue by treating him as if he were a Napoleonic menace. . . . It is necessary to weigh the desirability of an objective against the feasibility of its attainment, and when we do this with respect to Cuba, I think we are bound to conclude that Castro is a nuisance but not a grave threat to the United States and that he cannot be gotten rid of except by means that are wholly disproportionate to the objective.

Cuban Communism does pose a grave threat to other Latin-American countries, but this threat can be dealt with by prompt and vigorous use of the established procedures of the Inter-American System against any act of aggression.

I think that we must abandon the myth that Cuban Communism is a transitory menace that is going to collapse or disappear in the immediate future and face up to two basic realities about Cuba: first, that the Castro regime is not on the verge of collapse and is not likely to be overthrown by any policies which we are now pursuing or can reasonably undertake; and second, that the continued existence of the Castro regime, though inimical to our interests and policies, is not an insuperable obstacle to the attainment of our objectives, unless we make it so by permitting it to poison our politics at home and to divert us from more important tasks in the hemisphere. . . .

The Far East is another area of the world in which American policy is handicapped by the divergence of old myths and new realities. Particularly with respect to China, an elaborate vocabulary of make-believe has become compulsory in both official and public discussion . . . we have been unwilling to undertake [a rethinking of our policy toward China] because of the fear of many government officials, undoubtedly well founded, that even the suggestion of new policies toward China or Vietnam would provoke a vehement public outcry.

I do not think that the United States can or should recognize Communist China or acquiesce in its admission to the United Nations under present circumstances. It would be unwise to do so because there is nothing to be gained by it so long as the Peking regime maintains its attitude of implacable hostility toward the United States.

I do not believe, however, that this state of affairs is necessarily permanent. As we have seen in our relations with Germany and Japan, hostility can give way in an astonishingly short time to close friendship; and as we have seen in our relations with China, the reverse can occur with equal speed. It is not impossible that in time our relations with China will change again, if not to friendship then perhaps to "competitive coexistence." It would therefore be an extremely useful thing if we could introduce an element of flexibility, or, more precisely, of the capacity to be flexible, into our relations with Communist China. . . .

In all the issues which I have discussed, American policy has to one degree or another been less effective than it might have been because of our national tendency to equate means with ends and therefore to attach a mythological sanctity to policies and practices which in themselves have no moral content or value except insofar as they contribute to the achievement of some valid national objective.

I believe that we must try to overcome this excessive moralism, which binds us to old myths and blinds us to new realities and, worse still, leads us to regard new and unfamiliar ideas with fear and mistrust. . . . If we are to disabuse ourselves of old myths and to act wisely and creatively upon the new realities of our time, we must think and talk about our problems with perfect freedom, remembering, as Woodrow Wilson said that "the greatest freedom of speech is the greatest safety because, if a man is a fool, the best thing to do is to encourage him to advertise the fact by speaking."

72. WORLD ORDER AND
AMERICAN RESPONSIBILITY

CHARLES W. YOST

*Charles W. Yost (1907–   ) is U. S. Ambassador to the United
Nations. At the time of writing this article he was Senior Fellow on
the permanent staff of the Council on Foreign Relations. He has been
Deputy U. S. Representative to the U. N. (1961–66), and ambassador
to Laos, Syria, and Morocco. He is author of* THE AGE OF TRIUMPH
AND FRUSTRATION *and* THE INSECURITY OF NATIONS.

One lesson of the last fifteen years, most conspicuous in the Viet Nam war,
is that the capacity of even the strongest power to intervene effectively in
other states has been eroded by time, space and history. Apparently the only
state a great power can still attack with impunity is one of its allies. Even
there, as the Soviet Union will no doubt discover, the costs of intervention
will in time heavily outweigh the gains.

Far from encouraging the two superpowers to protect their interests or
their creeds by the exercise of military force, the consequences of intervention
in Viet Nam and Czechoslovakia are likely to make them much more chary
of doing so in the future. Indeed, as far as Americans are concerned, Viet
Nam risks causing them to revert to their post-World War I fantasy of withdrawal and isolation. The dissidence of Czechoslovakia, like that of China,
is another symptom of the disintegration of the communist monolith, which
will limit Russia's freedom of action.

Yet the world in the autumn of 1968, despite all the lessons of the past,
is no less unstable than it was a few years ago. The appetite for ever more
devastating weapons quickens the arms race at all levels and in all latitudes;
détente is interrupted and Europe once more brutally shaken by the misuse
of the Red Army; peace in Viet Nam seems as far off as ever and China as
hostile; the interminable conflict in the Middle East threatens more than ever
before to provoke new confrontations among the great powers.

We can argue about what "responsibilities" the United States or any other
state must assume in face of this situation. What is not open to doubt is
that the United States and the Soviet Union at least, however harshly each
may condemn the other's behavior, have an overriding national interest in
restricting possible occasions for a nuclear war to the absolute minimum, since
both would be likely to become main targets and suffer most. It therefore

From Charles W. Yost, "World Order and American Responsibility," *Foreign Affairs,*
Vol. 47, No. 1 (October, 1968). Pp. 1–13, excerpts. Reprinted by permission of *Foreign
Affairs.*

continues to be in the interests of both, as much if not more than before, to prevent or limit international violence in places where both are directly or indirectly involved and where the violence might escalate into wider hostilities and drag them both in.

To what extent does this mean that the United States has a continuing national interest, over and above an international responsibility, to check violence wherever it occurs? In other words, what is the proper mean between, on the one hand, overinvolvement, compulsive military intervention, "policing the world" and, on the other, abdication of responsibility, neo-isolationism, letting the rest of the world "stew in its own juice"? . . .

What does this actually mean in practice?

It probably means, first, that in case serious international disorder is provoked by communist states, parties or movements, the United States, if it considers that this disorder threatens its own "vital" interests or those of an ally, will have either to work out with the Soviet Union an agreed means of checking or limiting it, or act against it more or less unilaterally with only such help as the state or states directly concerned can supply.

If the Soviet Union has itself either provoked or encouraged the disorder, it will obviously not be willing to coöperate in suppressing it, though it may join in preventing serious escalation. If the disorder has been provoked (after a Viet Nam settlement) by one of the East Asian communist states, particularly China, the Soviets may coöperate in checking it, especially if it violates international agreements they have signed, though their action may be discreet and ambiguous.

The degree to which Soviet leaders themselves will in the future encourage or support "wars of national liberation" will depend primarily on developments inside the Soviet Union. But clearly four factors already restrain them from doing so: (1) the fear that such wars may escalate; (2) the strong objection of most Afro-Asian and Latin American states to communist revolutionary movements inside independent nations; (3) the apprehension that the Chinese might gain most from such wars; (4) the decline of revolutionary fervor inside the Soviet Union and its preoccupation with preserving the status quo inside its own bloc. Indeed the intervention in Czechoslovakia, while it was clearly a victory for the reactionary Stalinists inside the Kremlin, may further inhibit Soviet involvement in "wars of liberation," both by the problems it will create within the bloc and by its impairment of the Soviet posture as a "liberator."

The Soviets will of course be more willing to coöperate in checking or limiting international disorders having no significant communist component. They have done so recently in the Cyprus conflict, the India-Pakistan war of 1965 and, to a limited extent, the post-hostilities phase of the Middle East crisis of 1967. Even in such cases, however, domestic preoccupations or conflicting interests of friends of the United States and the U.S.S.R. will often lead to differing assessments as to just when and how peace-keeping should be conducted and the lengths to which it should be carried.

The conception of Chinese national interests held by its communist leaders may still for some time reflect quite esoteric estimates of the hazards and benefits of wars not directly and immediately involving China. Since 1949, and particularly since 1953, Mao and his principal colleagues have shown remarkable prudence in this respect. For some time, however, they may be expected to encourage international violence in the belief that it will not escalate to a point involving themselves. In this judgment they may sometimes prove wrong.

The present time, when the Chinese régime is momentarily incapable of governing effectively and is hostile both to the United States and the U.S.S.R., is perhaps uniquely favorable for these two to commence more genuine coöperation. The United States should remember that if a more pragmatic régime in Peking emerges from the present turmoil it might resume coöperation with the Soviet Union and again confront the United States with a communist bloc of over one billion people; in the meantime Soviet suppression of "revisionism" in Prague may narrow the gulf between Moscow and Peking. On the other hand, Moscow is aware that if the radical Chinese Communists consolidate their power and successfully continue their nuclear weapons development, they might constitute a much more serious threat.

Nevertheless, competition with the United States has become a way of life for the Soviet leadership; they are obviously trying to close the "missile gap"; they are desperately trying to stave off disintegration or impairment of their East European empire; they are developing a greater capability to intervene with conventional military forces in areas not contiguous to their own territory; they are determined to be recognized as a "world power" on more or less the same level as the United States. To the extent they succeed, their new capabilities will tempt them to make the same mistakes the United States has made in Viet Nam and elsewhere. They have just made a tragic though traditional mistake in Czechoslovakia. Soon the question will arise whether they will perceive any better than the Americans did that their new capabilities, exercised unilaterally, are just as likely to be damaging as to be favorable to their own interests, not to mention the interests of others.

The other side of the coin of the efforts of the Soviets to achieve status and recognition is their recurrent interest (temporarily in abeyance during Viet Nam) in being in conspicuous association with the United States. "Summit meetings," "hot lines" and similar devices emphasize equality of status; they also facilitate common action in areas which have so far been very narrow but which could be widened. The appalling consequences of direct confrontation between them has long been apparent to both sides; the possible consequences of indirect and involuntary confrontation are also gradually becoming apparent. If we are right in estimating that in the coming decade limitation of international violence may be largely dependent on some coöperation between the United States and the U.S.S.R., the former should be no more inhibited in seeking it because of Czechoslovakia than the Soviet Union has been because of Viet Nam. After twenty years of bitter hostility and still unimpaired ideological incompatibility, coöperation will at best be precarious and partial. It still seems so essential, however, that the new American administration should promptly undertake to explore whether it is feasible and how extensive and reliable it might become.

The Soviet leaders should be aware, however, that, if they persist in suppressing all liberalization in Eastern Europe by force, they risk once again so antagonizing American public opinion that all coöperation between the two countries, even that which is much in the interest of both, will for a further period of time be politically out of the question. After all, the cold war was born in Eastern Europe and will have eventually to be buried there.

The main areas requiring urgent examination are: (1) the nuclear arms race and its impending escalation, which poison the relationship between the two states, limit their ability to deal with grave domestic problems and make the whole balance of international order and peace precarious; (2) the security situation in East Asia where, after Viet Nam, the two states may be able to find a limited common interest in preventing the outbreak of further hostilities from which China could profit; (3) the security situation in the Middle East where the aggravation of the Arab-Israeli conflict, the withdrawal of Britain and the increasingly active Soviet policy create a likelihood not only of more local conflict but, unless precautions are taken, of more great-power involvement.

A hazard involved in such far-reaching American-Soviet consultation, and perhaps limited agreement, even for such unexceptionable ends, would be the anxiety created on the one hand in Western Europe and Japan and on the other among the "developing" states that the two superpowers were setting up a dual hegemony to police the world. Unhappily there is little likelihood that they could reach wide enough areas of agreement in the foreseeable future to give substance to such anxiety. A much greater danger would be that their agreement would fall far short even of maintaining basic international security. Nevertheless, the United States should seek at all times to bring its allies and friends into the nexus of negotiation and agreement whenever their interests are involved and they may be willing to participate and share responsibility. If any are excluded from peacekeeping, it should be only because they exclude themselves. It is the regretful thesis of this article, on the basis of the evidence so far at hand, that over the next decade many are likely to do so.

In cases, however, where the United States, the Soviets and whoever else may be willing to share responsibility are agreed that some immediate exercise of peacekeeping force is required, the appropriate instrument will usually be the United Nations. Exercise of force properly authorized and conducted by the United Nations has the sanction of more than 120 member states; it avoids unilateral intervention by either superpower, reaction by the other, or the appearance of dual hegemony by both; it can be carried out through procedures elaborated and accepted over the past twenty years. At the present time any such U.N. peacekeeping would have to be conducted under those procedures; that is to say, it would have to be sanctioned by the Security Council, would also require the consent of the government or governments within whose territory the operation is to take place, would be manned by ad hoc contingents from states other than the United States and the U.S.S.R., and would be supported by funds voluntarily contributed by a minority of U.N. members.

If, over a period of years, the two superpowers and others should decide that it is in their common interest to use the United Nations systematically for peacekeeping, it might be possible gradually to activate the more decisive procedures for the maintenance of international security laid down in the Charter, that is, to revive the Military Staff Committee and to negotiate among member states special agreements providing armed forces and facilities to the United Nations on a regular and permanent basis.

So much for the first alternative by which serious international violence might be curbed over the next decade, namely, by limited coöperation between the United States, the U.S.S.R. and others both inside and outside the United Nations. But what if even sincere and persistent efforts to work out this coöperation prove abortive? What if the legacies of the cold war prove still to dominate thought and policy on both sides?

There will certainly, at the very least, be cases in which the Soviet Union refuses to coöperate in peacekeeping, either because it or one of its friends has provoked the violence, or because it expects to extract some political capital from the conflict, or simply because it does not want to become involved. In these cases—if our conclusion is correct that no other state will be willing to play a significant security role outside Europe and Latin America during the next decade—the only alternative to permitting the violence to proceed unchecked would be unilateral intervention by the United States, assisted only by those closely involved. In the light of our recent experience, when would such unilateral intervention be justified and when would it not?

We have referred to treaty commitments which the United States must respect if it is not to lose all international credit. These commitments are not necessarily for all time. Some, such as those to SEATO and implicitly to CENTO, are in many respects out of date and in need of early review. Those to NATO and the OAS, on the other hand, while evolving, still have solid justification. Under existing circumstances the United States would no doubt have to join in resisting an attack, if requested by the party attacked, on Japan, South Korea, Taiwan, the Philippines, Thailand, Australia, New Zealand and Israel. It would also probably feel obligated to assist, though it is not clear to what degree, certain other states, such as India and Iran, if they were attacked by communist neighbors.

The most important twilight zones, where the United States most needs to clarify its obligations, interests and intentions, would appear to be Southeast Asia and the Middle East. We have already suggested that, after Viet Nam, the United States and the U.S.S.R. jointly endeavor to sort out their interests and commitments in these areas and to work toward stabilization there. While one could not be sanguine about the response, Communist China should certainly also be offered the opportunity to take part in such stabilization. What, however, if this joint reëxamination proves unproductive or, because of the limited influence of the United States and the U.S.S.R. in these areas, inconclusive?

The most decisive lesson of Viet Nam would seem to be that, no matter how much force it may expend, the United States cannot ensure the security of a country whose government is unable to mobilize and maintain sufficient popular support to control domestic insurgency. It can assist by checking external invasion or massive aid to insurgents, but only the local government can suppress the insurgency itself. If indigenous dissidents, whether or not communist, whether or not supported from outside, are able to mobilize and maintain more effective popular support than the government, they will eventually prevail. The United States cannot prevent them even if it so desires and even if it is willing for a time to pour out lives and resources to that end. Under such circumstances, unpalatable as it may be, the United States will have to reconcile itself to the "loss" of the country in question, either to the communists or to other effective insurgents. (Of course the United States should not put itself in the position of always opposing insurgency and supporting the status quo. After all, its principles are revolutionary even if its political action outside its borders cannot often be.)

The problem of violent insurgency, wherever it arises throughout the underdeveloped world, will essentially be solved or not solved by the will and capacity of the government and the élite to meet to a sufficient degree the political and economic imperatives of their evolving society. The role of the United States, to the extent it wishes and is asked, will be to assist these governments and élites to meet these imperatives before armed insurgency has broken out or at least before it has reached unmanageable proportions. If the local government and the élite are unable or unwilling to meet these imperatives, the United States will certainly not be able to do so.

These principles of course apply to the states of Southeast Asia, including the Philippines and Indonesia. The survival of their governments will depend upon their success or lack of it in meeting the above-mentioned imperatives. They can be given, if they wish, military "guarantees" and economic aid, but their fate will be determined by their will, their capacity, their sophisticated concern for the "hearts and minds" of the people.

It seems improbable that China or North Viet Nam will undertake overt aggression against Southeast Asian states (after the end of the present conflict), at least for some time, because of domestic conditions. The United States would be justified, however, in giving new or renewed assurances of support in case of *such* aggression to any Southeast Asian state or group of states that asked for them. Particularly if the outcome in Viet Nam proves to be unfavorable or ambiguous, such assurances might be required to block a rapid exploitation of the "domino theory." Great care should be exercised, however, to ensure that any assurances, other than those having to do with overt invasion, are not open-ended and are strictly dependent on appropriate performance by the recipient government.

One means of reducing unilateral American peacekeeping responsibilities in Southeast Asia after a Viet Nam settlement might be what is loosely called a "neutralization" of the area. The means would be a treaty guaranteeing the independence and territorial integrity of some or all of the states there on condition of their "nonalignment" with any military bloc. Such "neutralization" would, however, hardly be meaningful unless underwritten by Communist China and North Viet Nam, which may or may not be inclined to coöperate. In any case the area's conspicuous vulnerability to communist misbehavior presents a further compelling argument, in addition to many others, that the United States should persistently seek accommodation of its differences with Peking and support all feasible means for drawing China back into the community of nations. The most obvious first means of doing so would be a change of American policy regarding Chinese representation in the United Nations.

In the Middle East the situation is different because the United Nations has long been and still is deeply involved there and because the chief great power concerned, other than the United States, is the Soviet Union rather than China. Moreover, the state in the area to which the United States is most heavily committed, Israel, has shown a remarkable capacity for taking care of itself.

Indeed the chief problem for the United States arising from the Arab-Israeli conflict is not the danger that Israel may be overrun but the fact that the rigidity of both sides perpetuates the conflict and sucks in the two superpowers. The commitment of the United States to one and the U.S.S.R. to the other has long embroiled the United States with the Arabs, and now risks embroiling it with the Soviet Union over interests not really "vital" to either side. In this sense the Middle East could, with even less reason, come to play a disastrous role between the two superpowers similar to that which the Balkans played between the two European alliances before 1914.

In view of the passionate nationalism of most of the states in the area, as well as its fragmentation and the crisscross of rivalries among the countries involved, it is most unlikely that either the Soviet Union or the United States could hope to dominate the area or any significant part of it. New intruders into the Arab world cannot expect, particularly in this day and age, to be any more permanently successful than old ones were. It can hardly be doubted that their aid will be used by their respective clients more in the interests of the clients than of the patrons.

If this analysis is correct, both the United States and the Soviets should firmly forego unilateral military intervention in the area or indeed other competitive measures which could lead to confrontation between them. The traditional involvement of the United Nations creates a convenient cushion, to the extent they use it, between the interests of the two superpowers and their respective friends. Before new disasters occur, the United States, the U.S.S.R. and the Europeans should exert every ounce of leverage they possess to achieve whatever elements of settlement can be extracted from the Security Council resolution of last November. If multilateral peacekeeping fails again in the Middle East, there is little we can do unilaterally that would not entail greater peril than profit to ourselves and our friends.

Only a few words need to be said about the expediency of unilateral American military intervention in areas outside East and Southeast Asia and the Middle East. As far as Latin America is concerned, the machinery of the Organization of American States is available. It would seem to be a sound principle that the United States should not intervene militarily in Latin America without the approval of a substantial majority of the OAS. One can imagine cases of massive intervention by an external power, as the introduction of missiles into Cuba, which might require a response by the United States even in the absence of OAS sanction, but such cases will occur very rarely if at all. In Latin America as elsewhere, the proper emphasis of our policy will be to assist Latin American states, if they wish us to do so, in meeting the political and economic imperatives of modernization and, where necessary, in dealing with incipient insurgency. As in Southeast Asia, if and when insurgency should reach massive proportions in any country and the local government should lose the support of most of its population, it would be beyond the power of the United States to maintain the status quo.

As to Africa, while the state of the continent is in many ways tragic and violence seems almost certain to proliferate, there is little chance that American military intervention would be either attractive or useful. What can be done, the Organization of African Unity and the United Nations will have to do, though neither can do much until the developed states decide that it is contrary to their interests to permit a whole continent to stagnate.

There are at least three potential threats to international security in Africa. One would be an outbreak of violence between the "radical" and "moderate" Arab states on the North African littoral, with one side (as in the Middle East) being backed by the Soviet Union and the other by the United States and some of its European allies. A second would be the outbreak of large-scale racial war in South Africa, Rhodesia and the Portuguese colonies. A third would be a comprehensive and successful Chinese exploitation of retarded development, frustrated expectations, violence and despair. None of these eventualities seems probable within the next few years, but the existence of all of them is further evidence of the need for creating over the next decade more effective multilateral peacekeeping machinery. . . .

73. INDIA'S POLICY OF NONALIGNMENT

JAWAHARLAL NEHRU

Jawaharlal Nehru (1889–1964) was prime minister of India from the founding of the Republic to his death. He was regarded as the leading spokesman for the philosophy of "third world" nonalignment.

When we say our policy is one of non-alignment, obviously we mean non-alignment with military blocs. It is not a negative policy. It is a positive one, a definite one and, I hope, a dynamic one. But, in so far as the military blocs today and the cold war are concerned, we do not align ourselves with either bloc. This in itself is not a policy; it is only part of a policy. Countries talk and act so much in terms of military blocs and the cold war in the world today that one has to lay stress on the fact that we are not parties to the cold war and we are not members of or attached to any military bloc.

The policy itself can only be a policy of acting according to our best judgement, and furthering the principal objectives and ideals that we have. Every country's foreign policy, first of all, is concerned with its own security and with protecting its own progress. Security can be obtained in many ways. The normal idea is that security is protected by armies. That is only partly true; it is equally true that security is protected by policies. A deliberate policy of friendship with other countries goes farther in gaining security than almost anything else.

Apart from this, from the larger point of view of the world also, we have laboured to the best of our ability for world peace. We realize that our influence in such matters can only be limited, because we are not in posession of, nor have we the capacity to possess, weapons like the modern nuclear weapons. Still our influence has not been negligible. This is not because we ourselves are influential, but because we do believe that what we have said in regard to peace has found an echo in people's minds and hearts in all countries. In spite of governmental policies, the people have appreciated what we have said and reacted to it favourably.

Whatever our influence on governments, I can say with some assurance that our influence on peoples generally all over the world in regard to the matter of peace has been very considerable. Any hon. Member who happens to go to any part of the world will always find India's name associated with peace. It is a privilege to be associated with peace, but it brings a great responsibility. We should try to live up to it. In our domestic sphere also

From Jawaharlal Nehru, *India's Foreign Policy: Selected Speeches,* September, 1946–April, 1961. New Delhi, India: Publications Division, Ministry of Information and Broadcasting, 1961. Pp. 79–80.

we should work on lines which are compatible with peace. We cannot obviously have one voice for the world outside and another voice internally.

Our foreign policy has thus this positive aspect of peace. The other positive aspects are an enlargement of freedom in the world, replacement of colonialism by free and independent countries and a larger degree of co-operation among nations. It is completely incorrect to call our policy "Nehru" policy. It is incorrect because all that I have done is to give voice to that policy. I have not originated it. It is a policy inherent in the circumstances of India, inherent in the past thinking of India, inherent in the whole mental outlook of India, inherent in the conditioning of the Indian mind during our struggle for freedom, and inherent in the circumstances of the world today. I come in by the mere accidental fact that during these few years I have represented that policy as Foreign Minister. I am quite convinced that whoever might have been in charge of the foreign affairs of India and whatever party might have been in power in India, they could not have deviated very much from this policy. Some emphasis might have been greater here or there because, as I said, it represents every circumstance that goes towards making the thought of India on these subjects.

I say this because some people in foreign countries imagine that this policy has suddenly grown out of nothing, and that it is merely a policy of sitting on the fence. There is no question of sitting on the fence or trying to woo this person or that person or this country or that country. We want to be friends with all of them. It is said there are only two ways of action in the world today, and that one must take this way or that. I repudiate that attitude of mind. If we accept that there are only two ways, then we certainly have to join the cold war—and if not an actual military bloc, at least a mental military bloc. I just do not see why the possession of great armed might or great financial power should necessarily lead to right decisions or a right mental outlook. The fact that I have got the atom bomb with me does not make me any the more intelligent, wiser or more peaceful than I otherwise might have been. It is a simple fact, but it needs reiteration. I say this with all respect to the great countries. But I am not prepared even as an individual, much less as the Foreign Minister of this country, to give up my right of independent judgement to anybody else in other countries. That is the essence of our policy. . . .

74. STATEMENTS ON THE BALANCE OF POWER

1. DAVID HUME

David Hume (1711–1776) was a leading British philosopher and historian of his day. He was known for his willingness to challenge conventional patterns of thought.

. . . In all the politics of Greece, the anxiety, with regard to the balance of power, is apparent, and is expressly pointed out to us, even by the ancient historians. Thucydides represents the league which was formed against Athens, and which produced the Peloponnesian war, as entirely owing to this principle. And after the decline of Athens, when the Thebans and Lacedemonians disputed for sovereignty, we find that the Athenians (as well as many other republics) always threw themselves into the lighter scale, and endeavored to preserve the balance. They supported Thebes against Sparta, till the great victory gained by Epaminondas at Leuctra; after which they immediately went over to the conquered, from generosity, as they pretended, but in reality from their jealousy of the conquerors. . . .

It is true, the Grecian wars are regarded by historians as wars of emulation rather than of politics; and each state seems to have had more in view the honor of leading the rest, than any well-grounded hopes of authority and dominion. If we consider, indeed, the small number of inhabitants in any one republic, compared to the whole, the great difficulty of forming sieges in those times, and the extraordinary bravery and discipline of every freeman among that noble people; we shall conclude, that the balance of power was, of itself, sufficiently secured in Greece, and need not to have been guarded with that caution which may be requisite in other ages. But whether we ascribe the shifting of sides in all the Grecian republics to *jealous emulation* or *cautious politics,* the effects were alike, and every prevailing power was sure to meet a confederacy against it, and that often composed of its former friends and allies. . . .

From David Hume, "Of the Balance of Power," *Essays and Treatises on Several Subjects.* Edinburgh: Bell & Bradfute, and W. Blackwood, 1817. Pp. 331–32, excerpts.

2. SIR EYRE CROWE

Sir Eyre Crowe (1864–1925) was a British career diplomat. His famous memorandum was written in 1907 for the guidance of his superiors in the Foreign Office.

. . . History shows that the danger threatening the independence of this or that nation has generally arisen, at least in part, out of the momentary predominance of a neighboring state at once militarily powerful, economically efficient, and ambitious to extend its frontiers or spread its influence, the danger being directly proportionate to the degree of its power and efficiency, and to the spontaneity or "inevitableness" of its ambitions. The only check on the abuse of political predominance derived from such a position has always consisted in the opposition of an equally formidable rival, or of a combination of several countries forming leagues of defense. The equilibrium established by such a grouping of forces is technically known as the balance of power. . . .

From Sir Eyre Crowe, "Memorandum," in G. P. Gooch & Harold Temperley, eds., *British Documents on the Origins of the War, 1898–1914,* Vol. III. London: His Majesty's Stationery Office, 1928. P. 403.

75. INTERNATIONAL STRUCTURE, NATIONAL FORCE, AND THE BALANCE OF WORLD POWER
KENNETH N. WALTZ

Kenneth N. Waltz (1924–   ) is professor of politics at Brandeis University and author of a number of books and articles in the field of international affairs.

Balance of power is the hoariest concept in the field of international relations. Elaborated in a variety of analyses and loaded with different meanings, it has often been praised or condemned, but has seldom been wholly rejected. In a fascinating historical account of balance-of-power concepts, Martin

From Kenneth N. Waltz, "International Structure, National Force, and the Balance of World Power," *Journal of International Affairs,* Vol. 21, No. 2 (1967). Pp. 215–31, excerpts.

Wight has distinguished nine meanings of the term. For purposes of theoretical analysis a tenth meaning, cast in causal terms, should be added.

Balance-of-power theory assumes that the desire for survival supplies the basic motivation of states, indicates the responses that the constraints of the system encourage, and describes the expected outcome. Beyond the survival motive, the aims of states may be wondrously varied; they may range from the ambition to conquer the world to the desire merely to be left alone. But the minimum responses of states, which are necessary to the dynamics of balance, derive from the condition of national coexistence where no external guarantee of survival exists. Perception of the peril that lies in unbalanced power encourages the behavior required for the maintenance of a balance-of-power system.

Because of the present narrow concentration of awesome power, the question arises whether the affairs of the world can any longer be conducted or understood according to the balance-of-power concept, the main theoretical prop of those traditionally called realists. Even many who share the realist concern with power question its present relevance. They do so for two reasons.

It is, in the first place, widely accepted that balance-of-power politics requires the presence of three or more states. Political thought is so historically conditioned that the balance of power as it is usually defined merely reflects the experience of the modern era. In Europe for a period of three centuries, from the Treaty of Westphalia to the Second World War, five or more great powers sometimes sought to coexist peacefully and at other times competed for mastery. The idea thus became fixed that a balance of power can exist only where the participants approximate the customary number. But something more than habit is involved. Also mixed into ideas about necessary numbers is the notion that flexibility in the alignment of states is a requirement of balance-of-power politics. The existence of only two states at the summit of power precludes the possibility of international maneuver and national realignment as ways of compensating for changes in the strength of either of them. Excessive concentration of power negates the possibility of playing the politics of balance.

Second, war or the threat of war, another essential means of adjustment, is said to be of only limited utility in the nuclear age. In balances of power, of course, more is placed on the scales than mere military force. Military force has, however, served not only as the *ultima ratio* of international politics but indeed as the first and the constant one. To reduce force to being the *ultima ratio* of politics implies, as Ortega y Gasset once noted, "the previous submission of force to methods of reason." Insufficient social cohesion exists among states and the instruments of international control are too weak to relegate power to the status of simply the *ultima ratio*. Power cannot be separated from the purposes of those who possess it; in international politics power has appeared primarily as the power to do harm. To interdict the use of force by the threat of force, to oppose force with force, to annex territory by force, to influence the policies of other states by the threat or application of force—such uses of force have always been present at least as possibilities in the relations of states. The threat to use military forces and their occasional commitment to battle have helped to regulate the relations of states, and the preponderance of power in the hands of the major states has set them apart from the others. But, it is now often said, nuclear weapons, the "best" weapons of the most powerful states, are the least usable. At the extreme, some commentators assert that military force has become obsolete. Others, more cautious in their claims, believe that the inflated cost of using military force has seriously distorted both the balance between the militarily strong states and the imbalance between the strong and the weak ones. National military power, though not rendered wholly obsolete by nuclear weapons, nevertheless must be heavily discounted. The power of the two nuclear giants, it would seem, is then seriously impaired.

A weird picture of the political world is thus drawn. The constraints of balance-of-power politics still operate: each state by its own efforts fends for its rights and seeks to maintain its existence. At the same time, the operation of balance-of-power politics is strangely truncated; for one essential means of adjustment is absent, and the operation of the other is severely restricted. In the nineteenth-century liberals' vision of a world without power, force was to be banished internationally by the growing perfection of states and their consequent acceptance of each other as equals in dignity. The liberal utopia has reappeared in odd form. The limitation of power—or in extreme formulations, its abolition—is said to derive from the nuclear armament of some states; for nuclear armament makes at once for gross inequality in the power of states and for substantial equality among all states through the inability of the most powerful to use force effectively. Those who love paradox are understandably enchanted. To examine the ground upon which the supposed paradox rests is one of the main aims of this essay.

The first reason for believing that balance-of-power politics has ended is easy to deal with, for only its relevance, not its truth, is in question.

If the balance-of-power game is really played hard it eventuates in two participants, whether states or groupings of them. If two groupings of states have hardened or if the relation of major antagonism in the world is simply between two nations, the balance-of-power model no longer applies, according to the conventional definition. This conclusion is reached by placing heavy emphasis on the process of balancing (by realignments of states) rather than on altering power (which may depend on the efforts of each state). In a two-power world, emphasis must shift from the international process of balancing to the prospect of altering power by the internal efforts of each participant.

Admittedly, the old balance-of-power model cannot be applied without modification to a world in which two states far exceed all others in the force at their disposal. Balance-of-power analysis, however, remains highly useful if the observer shifts his perspective from a concentration upon international maneuver as a mode of adjustment to an examination of national power as a means of control and national effort as a way of compensating for incipient disequilibria of power. With this shift in perspective, balance-of-power politics does not disappear; but the meaning of politics changes in a manner that can only be briefly suggested here.

In a world of three or more powers the possibility of making and breaking alliances exists. The substance of balance-of-power politics is found in the diplomacy by which alliances are made, maintained, or disrupted. Flexibility of alignment then makes for rigidity in national strategies: a state's strategy must satisfy its partner lest that partner defect from the alliance. A comparable situation is found where political parties compete for votes by forming and reforming electoral coalitions of different economic, ethnic, religious, and regional groups. The strategies (or policies) of the parties are made so as to attract and hold voters. If it is to be an electoral success, a party's policy cannot simply be the policy that its leaders may think would be best for the country. Policy must at least partly be made for the sake of party management. Similarly in an alliance of approximately equal states, strategy is at least partly made for the sake of the alliance's cohesion. The alliance diplomacy of Europe in the years before World War I is rich in examples of this. Because the defection or defeat of a major state would have shaken the balance of power, each state was constrained to adjust its strategy and the deployment of its forces to the aims and fears of its partners. This is in sharp contrast to the current situation in NATO, where de Gaulle's disenchantment, for example, can only have mild repercussions. Though concessions to allies will sometimes be made, neither the Soviet Union nor the United States alters its strategy or changes its military dispositions simply to accommodate associated states. Both superpowers can make long-range plans and carry out their policies as best they see fit, for they need not accede to the demands of third parties. That America's strategy is not made for the sake of de Gaulle helps to explain his partial defection.

Disregarding the views of an ally makes sense only if military cooperation is relatively unimportant. This is the case in NATO, which in fact if not in form consists of unilateral guarantees by the United States to its European allies. The United States, with a preponderance of nuclear weapons and as many men in uniform as all of the Western European states combined, may be able to protect her allies; they cannot possibly protect her. Because of the vast differences in the capacities of member states, the approximately equal sharing of burdens found in earlier alliance systems is no longer conceivable. The gross inequality between the two superpowers and the members of their respective alliances makes any realignment of the latter fairly insignificant. The leader's strategy can therefore be flexible. In balance-of-power politics, old style, flexibility of alignment made for rigidity of strategy or the limitation of freedom of decision. In balance-of-power politics, new style, the obverse is true: rigidity of alignment in a two-power world makes for flexibility of strategy or the enlargement of freedom of decision.

Those who discern the demise of balance-of-power politics mistakenly identify the existence of balances of power with a particular mode of adjustment and the political means of effecting it. Balances of power tend to form so long as states desire to maintain their political identities and so long as they must rely on their own devices in striving to do so. With shrinking numbers, political practices and methods will differ; but the number of states required for the existence and perpetuation of balance-of-power politics is simply two or more, not, as is usually averred, some number larger than two. . . .

Only a sketch, intended to be suggestive, can here be offered of the connections between the present structure of the global balance of power, the relations of states, and the use of force internationally.

Unbalanced power is a danger to weak states. It may also be a danger to strong ones. An imbalance of power, by feeding the ambition of some states to extend their control, may tempt them to dangerously adventurous activity. Safety for all states, one may then conclude, depends upon the maintenance of a balance among them. Ideally, in this view, the rough equality of states gives each of them the ability to fend for itself. Equality may then also be viewed as a morally desirable condition. Each of the states within the arena of balance will have at least a modest ability to maintain its integrity. At the same time, inequality violates one's sense of justice and leads to national resentments that are in many ways troublesome. Because inequality is inherent in the state system, however, it cannot be removed. At the pinnacle of power, only a few states coexist as approximate equals; in relation to them, other states are of lesser moment. The bothersome qualities of this inevitable inequality of states should not cause one to overlook its virtues. In an economy, in a polity, or in the world at large, extreme equality is associated with instability. To draw another domestic analogy: where individualism is extreme, where society is atomistic, and where secondary organizations are lacking, government tends either to break down into anarchy or to become highly centralized and despotic. Under conditions of extreme equality, the prospect of oscillation between those two poles was well described by de Tocqueville; it was illustrated by Hobbes; and its avoidance was earnestly sought by the authors of the *Federalist Papers*. In a collection of equals, any impulse ripples through the whole society. Lack of secondary groups with some cohesion and continuity of commitment, for example, turns elections into auctions with each party in its promises tempted to bid up the others. The presence of social and economic groups, which inevitably will not all be equal, makes for less volatility in society.

Such durable propositions of political theory are lost sight of in the argument, frequently made, that the larger the number of consequential states the more stable the structure of world politics will be. Carried to its logical conclusion, the argument must mean that perfect stability would prevail in a world in which many states exist, all of them approximate equals in power.

The analysis of the present essay leads to a different conclusion. The inequality of states, though not a guarantee of international stability, at least makes stability possible. Within the structure of world politics, the relations of states will be as variable and complex as the movements and patterns of bits of glass within a kaleidoscope. It is not very interesting to ask whether destabilizing events will occur and disruptive relations will form, because the answer must always be yes. More interesting are such questions as these:

What is the likely durability of a given political structure, whether international or domestic? How does it affect the relations of states, or of groups and individuals? How do the relations of constituent units and changes within them in turn affect the political structure? Within a state, people use more violence than do governments. In the United States in 1965, 9,814 people were murdered, but only seven were executed. Thus one says (with some exaggeration, since fathers still spank their children) that the state enjoys a monopoly of *legitimate* violence. Too much violence among individuals will jeopardize the political structure. In international relations it is difficult to say that any particular use of violence is illegitimate, but some states have the ability to wield more of it. Because they do, they are able both to moderate others' use of violence and to absorb possibly destabilizing changes that emanate from uses of violence that they do not or cannot control. In the spring of 1966, Secretary McNamara remarked that in the preceding eight years there had been "no less than 164 internationally significant outbreaks of violence. . . ." Of course, not only violence is at issue. To put the point in more general terms, strong structures are able to moderate and absorb destabilizing changes; weak structures succumb to them.

No political structure, whether domestic or international, can guarantee stability. The question that one must ask is not whether a given distribution of power is stable but how stable different distributions of power are likely to be. For a number of reasons, the bipolar world of the past two decades has been highly stable. The two leading states have a common interest in stability: they would at least like to maintain their positions. In one respect, bipolarity is expressed as the reciprocal control of the two strongest states by each other out of their mutual antagonism. What is unpredictable in such a two-party competition is whether one party will try to eliminate the other. Nuclear forces of second-strike capacity induce an added caution. Here again force is useful, and its usefulness is reinforced in proportion as its use is forestalled. Fear of major war induces caution all around; the Soviet Union and the United States wield the means of inducing that caution.

The constraints of duopolistic competition press in one direction: duopolists eye each other warily, and each is very sensitive to the gains of the other. Working in the opposite direction, however, is the existence of the immense difference in power between the two superpowers and the states of middle or lesser rank. This condition of inequality makes it unlikely that any shifts in the alignment of states would very much help or hurt either of the two leading powers. If few changes can damage the vital interests of either of them, then both can be moderate in their responses. Not being dependent upon allies, the United States and the Soviet Union are free to design strategies in accord with their interests. Since the power actually and potentially at the disposal of each of them far exceeds that of their closest competitors, they are able to control in some measure the possibly destabilizing acts of third parties or to absorb their effects. The Americans and Russians, for example, can acquire the means of defending themselves against the nuclear assaults that the Chinese and French may be able to launch by the mid-1970's. Anti-ballistic-missile systems, useful against missiles launched in small number, are themselves anti-proliferation devices. With considerable expectation of success, states with vast economic, scientific, and technological resources can hope to counter the armaments and actions of others and to reduce their destabilizing effects. The extent of the difference in national capabilities makes the bipolar structure resilient. Defection of allies and national shifts of allegiance do not decisively alter the structure. Because they do not, recalcitrant allies may be treated with indifference; they may even be effectively disciplined. Pressure can be applied to moderate the behavior of third states or to check and contain their activities. The Suez venture of Britain and France was stopped by American financial pressure. Chiang Kai-shek has been kept on a leash by denying him the means of invasion. The prospective loss of foreign aid helped to halt warfare between Pakistan and India, as did the Soviet Union's persuasion. In such ways, the wielding of great power can be useful.

The above examples illustrate hierarchical control operating in a way that often goes unnoticed because the means by which control is exercised are not institutionalized. What management there now is in international relations must be provided, singly and occasionally together, by the duopolists at the top. In certain ways, some of them suggested above, the inequality of states in a bipolar world enables the two most powerful states to develop a rich variety of controls and to follow flexible strategies in using them.

A good many statements about the obsolescence of force, the instability of international politics, and the disappearance of the bipolar order are made because no distinction has been clearly and consistently drawn between international structure, on the one hand, and the relations of states on the other. For more than two decades, power has been narrowly concentrated; and force has been used, not orgiastically as in the world wars of this century, but in a controlled way and for conscious political purposes. Power may be present when force is not used, but force is also used openly. A catalogue of examples would be both complex and lengthy. It would contain such items, on the American side of the ledger, as the garrisoning of Berlin, its supply by airlift during the blockade, the stationing of troops in Europe, the establishment of bases in Japan and elsewhere, the waging of war in Korea and Vietnam, and the "quarantine" of Cuba. Seldom if ever has force been more variously, more persistently, and more widely applied; and seldom has it been more consciously used as an instrument of national policy. Since the war we have seen, not the cancellation of force by nuclear stalemate, but instead the political organization and pervasion of power; not the end of balance of power owing to a reduction in the number of major states, but instead the formation and perpetuation of a balance *à deux*.

76. THE NECESSARY PARTNERSHIP: THE ATLANTIC WORLD

J. ROBERT SCHAETZEL

J. Robert Schaetzel (1917–   ), a career Foreign Service Officer, is Ambassador to the European Communities. His last previous assignment was Deputy Assistant Secretary of State for Atlantic Affairs.

If we assume that a continued although sporadic movement toward a united Europe will continue, the question remains whether this is desirable from an American point of view. In considering this matter we should have one thing clearly in mind. What the Europeans do will not necessarily match at all points what we conceive to be in our own interests, nor will American conceptions of European organization dominate their thinking. None the less, we have no excuse for failing to think through the kind of Europe that we hope will develop.

First, in the simplest terms, what we wish for—and need—is a politically stable and economically expanding Europe, able and willing to make an equitable contribution to its own and the Alliance's security. Second, it is our objective that Germany, as the central unsolved problem of World War II, should share as an equal the burdens and responsibilities of the Atlantic world; and that she should play this role within the stabilizing framework which she herself seeks—namely, the institutions of the European Community and of NATO. Third, we want Europe—the only really great-power center of the free world outside the United States—to expand rather than contract its efforts for economic development and security elsewhere in the world. Fourth, we hope that Western Europe will coöperate with us in a common search for ways of enlarging the peaceful contacts between East and West, the object being an evolutionary change in the East toward more normal and mutually beneficial relations between the nations of Eastern Europe and those of the North Atlantic.

There are basically three broad alternative ways in which European and North American relations can be organized. There is first the national-state system. Its most evident appeal is that everyone is used to it. It is a system that permits people to continue to do what comes naturally. For those in the United States who look with apprehension on a united Europe and anticipate that such a Europe might have a mind of its own, the nineteenth-century arrangement of nation-states has the advantage of offering the known rather than the unknown dangers. With the largest European state (Germany)

From J. Robert Schaetzel, "The Necessary Partnership," *Foreign Affairs,* Vol. 44, No. 3 (April, 1966). Pp. 424–33, excerpts. Excerpted by special permission from *Foreign Affairs.* Copyright held by Council on Foreign Relations, Inc., New York.

having a gross national product about 15 percent of that of the United States, there is not much reason for Americans to fear that even the major European states will individually be able to dictate Western policy. In a word, this pattern of Atlantic organization seems to hold the seductive promise of conscious or unconscious American dominance which some see as a kind of American Commonwealth.

The second arrangement is the Atlantic Union or the federated Atlantic Community. In the late 1940s, in the immediate aftermath of a world war that changed all things and for a time made all things seem possible, the goal of a federated Atlantic union attracted considerable attention. Congressional resolutions endorsed the principle. Those who have tirelessly advocated this course do so with the highest of motives. They appreciate the common cultural and political heritage of Europe and America and see clearly the need to organize the great potential strength of the North Atlantic. They urge that Washington take the lead in convening an Atlantic convention, drawing on the historic achievement of the Philadelphia Convention of 1787. They are enthusiastic over the prospect of a twentieth-century conference framing a charter for a North Atlantic federation.

Whatever chance there was for Atlantic Union existed during the dark postwar years. Then a destitute and politically demoralized Europe had few choices and in desperation was ready to explore almost any solution. With new-found strength the United States, freed from the foreign policy restraints of the past, showed a remarkable willingness to innovate and, not least important, had been forced by 1948 to the conclusion that the U.S.S.R. under Stalin was bent on pursuing its crusade for world domination. Yet even in this unique period of ferment and creativity, Atlantic Union never became a matter of serious inter-governmental negotiation. Today, while the goal remains credible and the motivations unassailable, it is hard to discern either popular or governmental support for this approach—especially in Europe. Some advocates of Atlantic federation argue that this approach would appeal to the French Government. But if a central issue in the current intra-European dispute has been French resistance to majority rule among six nations and unwillingness to concede powers to a common executive body, by what jump in logic can one assume French willingness to accept similar political restraints in a larger Atlantic Community, one, moreover, inevitably dominated by the United States?

There are problems common to both the system of national states and Atlantic Union. An overriding issue is the great and growing disparity in power—political, military and economic—between the United States and even the strongest of the European nations. While American dominance in both these systems may seem an attractive advantage to some Americans, the disadvantageous side effects should be recognized. The essential difficulty of a grossly disparate trans-Atlantic relationship is that it forces America to assume the major responsibility for the security of the free world. We have fallen heir to this burden at a time in history when leadership offers none of the real or even the illusory benefits that spurred Europe on in its imperial adventures of the eighteenth and nineteenth centuries. Nor do Americans show any sign of enjoying the isolated splendor of world leadership. Psychologically we are a people who want colleagues and partners.

It is in connection with this point that the disparity of power becomes significant. Given the limited size and capacity of the individual European nations, they are neither willing nor able to play more than supporting roles. And the United States, carrying a large share of the burdens and the costs, cannot realistically share responsibility for policy decisions with reluctant junior associates. The axiom is inverted and becomes "no representation without taxation." A vicious circle sets in. We want European participation, but cannot fully share decisions in the absence of a European contribution commensurate with our own; the Europeans are neither organized to make this contribution nor much interested in doing so. . . .

The third policy choice is the concept of partnership with a uniting Europe. "Partnership" is a confining word. But as used by President Kennedy in 1962 and subsequently by President Johnson, it conveys a sweeping concept —the idea of a united Europe with which the United States could work in close cooperation and on equal terms.

Such a course of policy would by no means be free of problems or uncertainties. The uncertainties of the moment are all too evident, with the Kennedy Round of tariff negotiations, for instance, effectively stalled due to the unresolved Common Market crisis. Even assuming that agreement is reached among the Europeans and a sense of common purpose restored, the way of the Atlantic partners is bound to be difficult. The sheer magnitude and novelty of the task of unifying Europe will preoccupy the Europeans. Caught up in these affairs, their governments will be less inclined, at least in the short run, to give attention even to what they would agree are common problems, or to give an equal priority to urgent international questions.

A degree of "European nationalism" is also inevitable—not aggressive nationalism but an introspective egocentricity, a primary concern with the development of a united Europe. Nor can we expect that European attitudes will be wholly free of anti-Americanism. Just as giant America is one stimulus toward forming a united Europe, so the evolution of Atlantic relations will be colored by envy, resentment and, on occasion, policies that self-consciously set Europe apart from the United States.

However, seen from any distance and in any perspective, the basic interests of the United States and Europe appear to converge rather than conflict. We have few, if any, doctrinal differences. Our complex industrial societies are theoretically and practically interconnected; we struggle with largely identical problems. We may fall into disagreement on solutions, as Americans or Europeans do among themselves. It is hard to visualize conflict among the Atlantic nations arising out of differing ambitions or objectives toward the less developed world. Outside the minds of propagandists and unregenerate Marxists, there is no European or American colonialist impulse. The problem today is precisely the opposite: how to restrain the European—and our own —instinct to withdraw, to find other shoulders to which the security and development burden can be transferred.

Europeans occasionally see hypocrisy in the American advocacy of European unity. If the loss of national sovereignty is good for Europe, why isn't it good for America? One answer is that Americans today are less aware of a need to consider limits on their freedom of national action. Willingness to consider restraints will presumably occur in time of crisis or when Europe is so organized as to make such changes or restraints attractive, necessary or inevitable. There is some evidence that such a stimulus can bring about fundamental change. . . .

In the light of this analysis it is possible to test the three policy alternatives —nationalism, Atlantic union and Atlantic partnership—against the four major interests of the United States.

With regard to the objective of economic growth and a more equitable sharing of the burden of security, neither nationalism nor a loose Atlantic union dominated by the United States is as likely to achieve results as the policy of Atlantic partnership. This conclusion need not be based on political speculation but derives from known attitudes, current contributions of the smaller nations and the diminishing role of the major European states.

With respect to the German problem, both nationalism and the Atlantic-community approach decisively fail. The classical world order of sovereign national states leaves Germany alone once more to seek its own destiny. It was Adenauer's conscious choice in 1950 to place Germany's future within a European community. This has remained the heart of German foreign policy. At the same time Germany has never conceived of European unity outside the context of a strong Atlantic partnership.

As for the problems of the third world—the less developed countries in the Southern Hemisphere—the issue is how to encourage a further sense of European responsibility, and thus greater participation. The current evidence shows a diminishing European interest. Many Europeans today see themselves as playing only a supporting role to the United States. It would seem axiomatic that with a system of nation-states, or a political framework within which the Europeans are merely small components of a loosely organized Atlantic community, this state of mind would continue.

With respect to the complex problem of normalizing relations with the East, it would appear, as Professor Brzezinski has pointed out, that a prosperous, politically stable and unified Western Europe is most apt to induce the kinds of evolutionary changes we seek. Should West European unity fade and the system of nation-states reëmerge, then this present source of magnetic attraction to the East would be lost.

In even this abbreviated analysis it becomes clear that the choice is essentially between a system of national European states and Atlantic partnership. In this context Atlantic union—or federation—runs as a poor third principally because this alternative has so little appeal to the Europeans at the present time. It should be noted, however, that at some point in time interest in Atlantic partnership and in the goal of Atlantic union may very well converge. There is nothing in the concept of Atlantic partnership that precludes an eventual fusing of a united Europe and the United States. . . .

It can be asked whether the sweeping goal of Atlantic partnership is not too ambitious. Today we accept as a matter of course audacity in the pure sciences, but seem reluctant to match it with similar audacity in our political behavior. It is generally argued that great political changes are possible only in times of stress or acute and evident danger. I take issue with this point of view. But if political innovation requires danger as a prod, then we have danger in abundance, even if it appears in ambiguous form. If comprehended, it should produce the stimulus out of which new, creative political ideas should emerge and persevere. One framework within which such ideas should take shape is the embryonic concept of an Atlantic partnership. . . .

77. PAN-AFRICANISM

RUPERT EMERSON

Rupert Emerson (1899–   ) is professor of government and research associate at the Center for International Affairs at Harvard University. He has pioneered in the political study of non-western areas.

The African scramble for independence has led to two major political trends which have at least the superficial look of being contradictory but which may still turn out to be complementary. One is the consolidation of states, and, it may be, of nations, within the frontiers traced on the map of Africa with an imperial flourish by the colonial powers. The other is the unceasing agitation and conferring to secure some sort of African unity which would bring together within a common framework either all the African peoples or such more limited groupings of them as are now prepared to join forces for general or particular purposes. The unanswered, and still unanswerable, question is whether the states which have been emerging in such quantities, with more still to come—29 African Members of the UN at the end of 1961 as against five in 1955—will serve as the building blocks for a greater African union or whether they will jealously guard the separate identity which they have now achieved.

The realist is likely to be tempted to dismiss Pan-Africanism as an idle and romantic dream, unable to make a significant breach in the solid walls of state sovereignty which Africans are in process of erecting. The turn of events may well prove him to be correct, but in the interim the devotion to Pan-Africanism is both widespread and charged with emotion. Nkrumah is far from being alone in his repeated insistence that the independence of par-

Reprinted from Rupert Emerson, "Pan-Africanism," *International Organization,* Vol. 16, No. 2 (Spring, 1962), pp. 275–90, excerpts.

ticular African states takes on its full meaning only if all of Africa is free and if African unity is achieved. This sense of a mutuality of interest in freedom among all African peoples and countries found virtually no counterpart in the corresponding anticolonial drive of the Asian peoples, each of which pursued and enjoyed its independence without significant regard for the others. In the eyes of the believers the case for Africans' unity rests not only on such utilitarian grounds as the need to collaborate and to establish a common front against Africa's enemies but also on the *mystique* of the conviction that Africans are born to share a common destiny. To the special circumstances of Africa which press toward unity the contention is often added that this is an era of global interdependence in which particularist nationalisms have become anachronistic.

SELF-DETERMINATION AND TERRITORIAL INTEGRITY

The present consolidation of African states within the former colonial frontiers runs counter to much of what had been both predicted and desired during the colonial era. It was widely assumed that as soon as Africans came to freedom they would sweep aside the arbitrary boundaries imposed by the imperialists which cut across tribes and overrode the dictates of geography and economics. The continent had been partitioned to meet colonial convenience, but it would now be reshaped to realize its "natural" contours and return to its African essence. The accusation that the colonial powers had arbitrarily divided Africa among themselves rested on indisputable historical evidence; the further accusation, however, that they had broken up preexisting African unity could be established only by a reconstruction of history. The balkanization of Africa is an old-established matter to which European colonialism only added new dimensions. Furthermore, the fact was normally neglected that while the job might on a number of counts have been much better done, the creation of states of a sensible size to live in the modern world could only be accomplished by a lumping together of tribal peoples who had no heritage of common identity.

The characteristic problem confronting anyone who seeks to establish the political shape of Africa south of the Sahara is that there are no "natural" communities or political entities between the smallest and the most typical expression of African community, the tribe, at one extreme, and the whole of the African continent at the other. A number of African kingdoms and empires which reached beyond a single tribe existed in the past, but they appear to have left only a slight imprint, if any, as far as a continuing sense of community is concerned, although the names of Ghana, Mali, and the like still command respect. Such regional groupings as West or East or Central Africa are not infrequently spoken of, but they generally lack clear definition, could be constituted in a number of different guises, and have no identifiable African past. This is not to deny that unions built on such regional foundations may come into being, but, only that, if they do, they will either be new creations or adaptations of cooperative arrangements established under colonial auspices.

The political vehicle to which the Africans south of the Sahara have everywhere entrusted their new found independence is the colonial state, despite the fact that none of these states had any existence prior to their invention by the colonial regimes responsible for them. (This includes Liberia if the Americo-Liberians are substituted for the colonial regime.) In all or most of the countries a great number of the people still have no effective awareness of their "national" stature, as defined by the colonial boundaries, but the political life of the leaders and their followers in the nationalistic movements was led at the level of the colonial territory. As soon as they got down to serious business parties and movements were organized on the basis of the several territories, and the immediate enemy to be overcome was the colonial government, even though at a remote distance behind it there stood the imperial power. During the search for independence each territory had its own party or parties, each concentrating on the political situation of that particular territory and paying relatively little attention to the activities of its neighbors. The one notable exception was in the two big French federations of West and Equatorial Africa, where parties—most notably the *Rassemblement Démocratique Africain* (RDA)—overflowed the lesser territorial boundaries and operated at a federal level in a number of the countries which have since come separately to sovereign independence. In the postwar years when the RDA flourished it was no doubt a relevant item not only that the federations were in existence but also that much of the political life of the territories centered in Paris and in the National Assembly where they were all represented, thus bringing the African leaders into intimate contact with each other. It seems reasonable to assume that the federal and Parisian ties which were thus built up among the leaders were largely responsible for the fact that since independence the former French colonies have made move after move to regain at least some of the unity which was sacrificed as the individual territories began to exercise the autonomy granted them under the *loi cadre* of 1956. In Lockean terms it might be said that the territorial units with which the leaders had mixed their political labor were the ones which retained political existence as colonialism came to an end; and in the French case this concerned both the twelve separate territories and the two federations they had constituted.

In most instances the transition from colonial status to independence was made in amicable agreement with the controlling power, which meant that the new African regimes could take over intact the going concerns, as they have been called, of the colonial administrations. Except for the lack of a foreign office and perhaps of a military establishment, the instrumentalities of government were already in operation and needed only to be nudged over to a new posture. The leading African political figures were often already substantially in charge of the affairs of their countries in the last phase of colonialism, and the africanization of the government services was in varying degrees under way. If new constitutions were generally written, they tended to build on the inherited institutions. The more painful transition in the case of Guinea, where France resented the assertion of independence, and the speedy disintegration of the Congo, where no preparation had been made for independence, only underlined the good fortune of the rest. . . .

Responsible political leaders everywhere are wary of the principle of self-determination, and African political leaders have good reason to be warier than most. For the reasons which have been suggested above, the African state system as a whole and in its parts is fragile. It has neither the sanction of old-established political entities nor well-knit communities to lend stability to its states. The effective units of community are the tribes, but to open the door to African tribal self-determination would be to move toward a balkanization which would verge on anarchy, if it did not wholly achieve it. Furthermore, it is generally true that the present leaders seek a modernization of their societies in which the tribal past would play at best only a ceremonial role. To allow the tribes to take over as the dominant elements in the shaping of Africa would be to expose to ruin much of what these leaders have accomplished and seek to accomplish in the immediate future. The tragic affairs of the Congo, where tribalism partially reasserted itself when the central authority collapsed, stand as a warning as to what may happen.

Given the circumstances of Africa it is eminently comprehensible that there should be a determination on the part of many African statesmen to stand by the existing political structure of the continent even though any one can with ease poke his fingers through the loopholes with which it is riddled. The consolidation and utilization of what presently exists seems a far sounder procedure than an effort to reconstruct the political map of Africa which would run the immediate risk of creating a far worse situation than the one which now exists. . . .

THE SOURCES OF PAN-AFRICANISM

The Pan-Africanism which is being pursued simultaneously with the internal consolidation of the new states has many faces and can take on many guises. The simplest and, all in all, perhaps the most satisfactory version of it is the sense that all Africans have a spiritual affinity with each other and that, having suffered together in the past, they must march together into a new and brighter future. In its fullest realization this would involve the creation of "an African leviathan in the form of a political organisation or association of states," as Nnamdi Azikiwe, Governor-General of Nigeria and one of the pioneer leaders of African nationalism, recently put it in a speech in which he expressed his conviction that such a leviathan was bound to arise. At lesser levels it might involve an almost infinite variety of regional groupings and collaborative arrangements, all partial embodiments of the continent-embracing unity which is the dream of the true Pan-Africanist.

The sources from which Pan-Africanism derives are in part obscure and debatable and in part reasonably clearly written on the record.

How much of the claimed sense of common identity is to be attributed to the feeling that all Africans, despite the unmistakable physical differences among them, are members of the same race? Here, as in most other social-political manifestations of the idea of race, what is important is not the unascertainable biological fact of common physical heritage but the belief that there is such a heritage, at least in the sense of distinguishing Africans from the other peoples of the world.

One complication raised by the racial approach is the question as to whether North Africa, Arab and Berber in composition as against the *Afrique noire* south of the Sahara, forms a part of a single continental Pan-Africa. If blackness of skin be taken as the principal outward criterion of African-ness, the North African peoples evidently belong in a different category, but the general assumption and practice have been to include North Africa in the Pan-African family, despite the fact that it has attachments to the Arab world of the Middle East not shared by sub-Saharan Africans as well as attachments to the broader world of Islam which are shared by only some of the peoples to the south. My own crystal ball suggests that while for some purposes the North African countries will be drawn into continental African groupings, they will continue to have Arabic, Mediterranean, and Muslim affiliations which will keep them from anything approaching total absorption into a conceivable Pan-African union.

Even though Africans generally, having been the principal victims of a prior racialism, repudiate a new racialism asserting itself in a Pan-African guise, it seems very difficult to escape racial conceptions as one of the basic elements in Pan-Africanism. The concept of *Négritude,* expounded by Aimé Césaire, Léopold Senghor, and others, bases itself explicitly on the people of "Negro race" (incidentally leading into the further demographic question as to the relation of African-descended people through the world to a Pan-African or Pan-Negro movement). Nkrumah's conception of the African Personality is less obviously tied to racial moorings but it cannot evade the racialist implications which are inherent in any such idea. Senghor overtly brings these implications to the fore in his asserton that

Négritude is the whole complex of civilised values—cultural, economic, social, and political—which characterize the black peoples, or, more precisely the Negro-African world. . . . the sense of communion, the gift of myth-making, the gift of rhythm, such are the essential elements of Négritude, which you will find indelibly stamped on all the works and activities of the black man.

It is both fruitless and unwise to seek to give to either *Négritude* or African Personality a precise and specific content. Both, like Americanism and other similar concepts, stand as proud symbols of the accomplishments and virtues of a people, to be phrased in large and generous terms. Any effort to define them more closely runs the risk of starting arguments which divide those whom it is sought to unite rather than to bring them together. One key feature of these concepts and of the general trend of African thinking in recent years is that black has become a color to admire and be proud of. The earlier assumption, convenient for the slave owner and white ruler, had been that white represented the superior beings endowed with a high and advanced civilization whereas black stood for the properly servile inferiors who had not progressed beyond the primitive stages of mankind. African nationalism has brought about a transvaluation of values which establishes the African as a person of consequence and the heir of a history and culture, still in process of rediscovery, which have made their contribution to the world. To be black is itself a distinctive bond of unity.

Running through this range of thought and emotion is the conviction that the Africans as a people have been oppressed, exploited, and degraded to a greater extent than any other great mass of mankind in history. No elaborate exposition of the centuries of the slave trade, slavery, and colonialism is needed to point the moral of the African belief that they have been collectively mistreated and that their common identity has been forged in the flames of their common suffering. If all hands have been against them in the past, it is all the more necessary for them now to join forces to ensure that their weakness does not again invite disaster.

In the creation of the conception that the continent forms a single Pan-African whole a large role has been played by the Negroes overseas and particularly those in the West Indies and the United States. Having lost the memory of the particular tribes and regions from which they came and being aware of the anonymous unity which slavery had thrust upon them, it was natural that they should look across the Atlantic and see Africa and their fellow Negro brethren as a whole. Many Negro religious figures, teachers, professional men, and others contributed to the stream which flowed toward Pan-Africanism, but four names can be singled out as peculiarly significant: E. W. Blyden, who was the distinguished nineteenth century precursor of later developments; W. E. B. Du Bois, who fathered a series of Pan-African Congresses; Marcus Garvey, who sought to establish a "universal confraternity" and a "central nation" for the Negro race; and George Padmore, who served as a crystallizing center for Pan-Africanism in London, influencing many Africans, including Kwame Nkrumah.

The considerable number of African leaders who have been educated or have lived abroad must have experienced a similar inclination toward a Pan-African outlook as they were thrown into contact with Africans from many countries and were forced to look at the affairs of their continent through other eyes and from afar.

It seems eminently probable that not only Africa's elements of unity but, perversely, its diversity and heterogeneity as well have had an influence in promoting Pan-Africanism. Precisely the instability of African states within their arbitrary frontiers and the lack of any "natural" stopping points between the tribe and continental Africa in the large lend an attraction to the broader view which it might not otherwise have—and which it may cease to have if and when African states achieve the internal consolidation which they are now seeking. The depth and breadth of an exclusive attachment to the new states is inevitably open to question, and it is reasonable to think that some of the ills from which Africa suffers or which potentially threaten it can be better handled on a collective basis than by some forty separate political entities. Thus Gabriel d'Arboussier, Senegalese Minister of Justice, predicting a Union of West African States by 1965, sees as the decisive weapon in the present evolution of Africa the unity which it has not yet achieved but which is imposed on it by its multiple diversities and internal divisions whether they be tribal, religious, ethnic, or territorial.

In particular, the threat of contingent anarchy contained in the fact that Africa's tribal structure only accidentally coincides with state frontiers might be greatly eased if larger unions of states could be brought into being, thus making possible arrangements by which tribes that straddle boundaries within the union could reestablish some measure of unity. It is, of course, true that in many parts of Africa boundaries are sufficiently porous to enable people to move easily back and forth across them in the interior, but the more states assert their sovereignty the more the boundaries will seal them off from each other, making formal agreements necessary if tribal and other customary links are to be maintained. Thus an East African union, for example, of the kind which has been much discussed recently, could lay the groundwork for a solution or at least an amelioration of the three-way political partition which has been imposed on the Somalis and the Masai and perhaps of the problem of the Kenya coastal strip as well. . . .

AFRICAN HARMONY AND DISCORD

Deep in the heart of every true believer is the conviction that the principle of the natural harmony of interests applies in his domain. For the Pan-African-ist this implies belief in the assumption that, once the affairs of the continent cease to be distorted by the machinations of the colonialist and neocolonialist, African states and peoples will live in harmony with each other. Such a view rests upon the faith that the apparent differences and difficulties between states can be overcome by goodwill since all Africans have common outlooks and desire the unity of their peoples. In actuality the potentialities for conflict among African states are as great as those in other parts of the world; and several of them center on Ghana either because of its ethnic-territorial claims on Togo and the Ivory Coast or because of plots which it is alleged to have concocted against the regimes in other African countries. Three other disputes may be mentioned which seem symptomatic of the kind of troubles which may be coming along as the African states work out their relationships among themselves and establish their own continental balance of power: Morocco's claim to take over Mauritania, the demand of Somalia that the Somali-in-habited portions of Ethiopa and Kenya should be joined to it, and the controversy between Cameroun and Nigeria as to the status of the northern portion of the former British Cameroons. To these must of course be added any number of possible disputes arising from cross-frontier tribal claims, not to mention all the usual subjects which offer fertile fields for disagreement among states.

The suspicions which divide the African states came out clearly in the opening address of Governor-General Azikiwe to the conference of the twenty Monrovia group countries at Lagos on January 25, 1962. Referring with regret to the absence of the Casablanca contingent (it was, incidentally, rumored that Guinea and Mali would have liked to attend), he warned about an ideological difference between the two groups which stemmed from "the conspicuous absence of specific declaration" by the Casablanca states of belief in the fundamental principles enunciated at Monrovia. These were the inalienable right of African states, as at present constituted, to legal equality, to self-determination, to inviolability of their territories from external aggression, and "to safety from internal interference in their internal affairs through subversive activities engineered by supposedly friendly states." He recalled that the United Nations Charter provides such safeguards in general terms, but asked for overt adherence to the Monrovia principles.

Otherwise it can be a matter for speculation whether these principles are capable of becoming spectres to haunt the conscience of those who would rather pay lip service to the Charter of the United Nations, whilst secretly they nurse expansionist ambitions against their smaller and perhaps weaker neighbors.

Another variant of difference between the African states, this time coming from the Casablanca side, was contained in a speech delivered by President Modibo Keita of Mali in June 1961. Here he spoke of his continuing conviction that the countries of Africa can never achieve full independence as long as they remain small and each concentrates on itself alone. Although, he pointed out, the constitution of Mali provides for total or partial abandonment of sovereignty on behalf of a grouping of African states, actual political unification with other states could be undertaken only if there were an identity of views on both international policy and domestic economic policy. Even without such an identity of views, cooperation would be possible with all African states, whatever their political or economic position, but the conditions for a political merger were much more stringent. President Keita had, of course, been one of the central figures in the collapse of the Mali Federation, whose demise could in good part be attributed to sharp disagreements on both foreign and domestic policy between Senegal and Soudan. It might be added that the more recent divorce of Syria from Egypt, shattering the United Arab Republic, was in part attributable to similar differences in outlook and policy between the two countries.

Which way the African future will turn is still a matter for wide-open speculation. It is evident that strong forces are pulling in a number of different directions, that African states are frequently divided among themselves, and that all African leaders express their devotion to the cause of African unity although with varying interpretations and varying degrees of intensity. Most of them would undoubtedly concur in the verdict of Julius Nyerere, principal architect of Tanganyika's independence, that African nationalism is different from other nationalisms of the past in that "the African national State is an instrument for the unification of Africa, and not for dividing Africa, that African nationalism is meaningless, is dangerous, is anachronistic if it is not at the same time pan-Africanism."

How different African nationalism is remains to be seen. Insofar as precedents are relevant it is clear on the historical record that elsewhere the more parochial nationalist forces have almost always won out over the more broadly integrating supernational forces. It remains the fact that the rediscovery of Africa by the Africans is still only in its opening stages. It is a vast continent which has always been internally divided, and the superimposed colonial divisions worked to prevent the different peoples from establishing any real contact with each other. Pan-African gatherings, United Nations caucuses, and a host of other meetings and interstate visits are bringing at least an upper crust of the African peoples in touch with each other, but it will be long before the colonially-determined lines of transport and communications can be so reconstructed as to open up easy intercourse between the countries.

But perhaps the precedents are not relevant. Times have changed and African nations still have an insubstantiality about them which distinguishes them from their fellows around the globe. Of all the questions which may be asked the most significant is as to the depth and universality of the belief that Africans are born to a common destiny.

78. THE PLURAL WORLD

RONALD STEEL

Ronald Steel is a well-known writer on U. S. foreign policy.

A collision between the super-powers can be prevented, but it will require the willingness of both sides not to treat a change in the ideological status quo among the underdeveloped states of Africa and Asia as a threat to their vital interests. Only by putting these states into an ideological isolation can the balance between the great powers be preserved. This will not be easy. Astute leaders in the emerging countries will appeal for their help in the name of communism or anti-communism, and the great powers will be tempted to intervene because they will see the outcome of such insurrections as crucial to their role as global powers.

America and Russia cannot prevent "wars of national liberation" from occurring, any more than they can be sure who will ultimately benefit from them. But because of their common interest in halting the arms race and preventing a great-power confrontation, they must agree not to take advantage of any change in the status quo through military alliances or bases. This is the minimum on which any hope for cooperation rests, for otherwise it will be extremely difficult for either side to resist military intervention. There can be no possibility of eliminating guerrilla wars within the confines of a single country. The best the great powers can hope to achieve is to contain these wars so that they do not imperil the nuclear détente.

To do so, it will be necessary to divorce ideology from the vital questions of national interest. This will mean a retreat from interventionist policies that are essentially global to those based upon spheres of primary and secondary interest. In the vast areas of secondary interest throughout most of the southern hemisphere, the only workable rule of thumb must be that every nation should be allowed to have its own revolution without the intervention of outside forces. Sometimes such revolutions will bring to power regimes we do not like, at other times they will bring to power regimes we favor, but if we have learned anything over the past two decades it should be that no one can predict the course a national revolution will take. Ten years ago we thought Egypt was falling into the hands of the communists; today we look upon her as a bulwark against communist expansion. Today we are obliterating North Vietnam; ten years from now we will probably be building her up as a barrier to China. A policy of keeping hands off civil insurrection does not mean we need stand by in the case of foreign aggression. When the fact of aggression is clear, there are ways of dealing with it, either through the United Nations or in conjunction with other *major* powers.

A general policy of detachment from Third World insurrections will not be easy for many of us to accept, and it may be even more difficult for the Russians, with their messianic view of the communist faith, to accept. Even if we are able to follow a policy more closely based on national interest than on ideological compulsion, the Russians may not go along. Perhaps they will not be able to separate their ideology from their national interest, or refrain from intervening in the chronic disturbances of the southern hemisphere. This is a danger we must be prepared to cope with, although not by indiscriminate interventions of our own. But it is precisely because we want to persuade Moscow that such a policy of restraint in the unsettled areas of the Third World is to its interests as much as to ours, that we must re-evaluate our own diplomacy. This is not to say that world peace is going to be assured by a Russo-American condominium. Even if such a creation were desirable, it is no longer possible. But an accord between the super-powers in the Third World, just as they have reached an unwritten accord in Europe, is essential if the current détente is not to be destroyed by a new arms race and by Russian military interventions to match our own.

If such an accord is to have any meaning, there must be an agreement on the role the United Nations can be expected to play. When the international organization was established at the end of the Second World War, it was assumed that the power of decision would rest with the five great powers— America, Russia, Britain, France, and China. They were given permanent seats on the Security Council and the power to veto any proposals which threatened their national interests. They were expected to use their influnce and their power to enforce agreements and dampen conflicts that threatened the peace. Under Roosevelt's plan, each of the great powers was to attend to its own area, while America, whose global interests overlapped them all, would ensure a favorable world balance through her power over Britain, France, and China. Composed in equal parts of idealism and self-interest, this was the design for the American Century—world peace through world law administered by the Security Council of the United Nations.

The American Century, as it turned out, lasted barely a few months, for agreement among the great powers. With their accord, minor disputes throughout the Third World can be isolated and neutralized. Without their accord, the United Nations cannot hope to be much more than an international debating society. The Security Council must regain some of the authority that has been taken over by the General Assembly, and various regional or functional organizations should be created so that the great powers may delegate peace-keeping tasks that it is inadvisable for them to administer directly. These steps would mean, ironically, a return to the principles envisaged by Franklin Roosevelt, who conceived of the United Nations as an instrument for the maintenance of peace through great-power unanimity. His analysis was essentially correct, even though he could not have predicted the countervailing power that would be exercised by scores of new nations. It is upon the creation of a balance between the demands of the great powers and the rights of the small powers that the future of the United Nations rests.

A re-evaluation of our role in the United Nations is merely part of a long-overdue reassessment of our role in the world. The mantle of empire rides uneasily upon American shoulders. We are not a people meant to maintain foreign garrisons, administer distant colonies, and conduct imperial wars for influence and prestige. This goes too much against the grain of the American character and American institutions. We are not Rome, although we maintain a global empire, and our standards are not those of Metternich, although we have been engaged in suppressing revolutions. America was not meant to maintain a shabby empire with Marines, napalm, and foreign-aid bribes, and the American people have become increasingly uneasy over the global interventions that have been carried out in their name.

Possessed of enormous power—which we have, for the most part, exercised with relative restraint—we have allowed ourselves to become intoxicated with it, to believe that it has given us a mandate to impose our own particular ideas of justice and virtue. Our great power has disturbed our sense of proportion and destroyed many of the old guide lines that once served as limitations. Power has proved to be a terrible dilemma to Americans, inspiring some with an exaggerated sense of mission, disturbing others with a guilty conscience, and perplexing many who seek to use it beneficially, yet who fear the infinite distortions to which any application of power is subject.

In grappling with the phenomenon of our enormous power, we have tended to lose sight of a crucial distinction that governs the use of power. That distinction rests not upon *whether* power should be used, but upon *when* and *how* power should be used—not whether power in itself is evil, but whether power indiscriminately applied may not be self-defeating as well as morally compromising. America is, in a sense, a prisoner of her own great power. She cannot ignore that power any more than she can repudiate it. But she can dissipate it on false or ignoble ends, and she can distort it into an instrument of repression that may betray her own values.

Power is an opportunity, but it is also a burden, for those who exercise it determine the fate of others. Something more than self-assurance of moral purpose is necessary to those who take on such a burden. It is not enough that power be applied for noble ends. History is a compilation of cases in

it could not survive the collapse of great-power unity. Once the cold wa
broke out and the two great powers became bitter adversaries, there coul
be no hope of using the United Nations as an instrument of law enforcemen
The veto ensured that the Security Council could not act contrary to th
interests of any of the great powers, and the inability of the great powei
to agree assured the paralysis of the Security Council. The United State
acting upon the fact that she controlled a majority of the votes in the Genera
Assembly during the first fifteen years of the organization's existence, trie
to break this impasse by circumventing the Security Council. Thus she wa
able to enlist the authority of the United Nations to justify the United State
intervention in Korea. But the enormous expansion of the United Nations
particularly since 1960, caused by the break-up of the European colonia
empires, has diminished American control over the General Assembly. Th
has led to an "agonizing reappraisal" of our attitude toward a forum in whic
a decisive two-thirds vote can now be made up of countries that possess onl
10 per cent of the world's population and pay less than 5 per cent of th
United Nations budget. Ironically, Washington has now taken a more benig
look at the Security Council, which more accurately reflects the real powe
balance in the world, and in which the United States enjoys the right of vet(

The United Nations, therefore, is at a crucial juncture. While in man
ways it is more necessary than ever before—especially to isolate small-scal
conflicts and to provide a framework for economic development—its futur
prospects are dim. Perhaps the United Nations is not greatly important t
the super-powers, for they certainly do not need it to augment their influenc
or protect their vital interests. But it does, for all its pettiness and inade
quacies, provide a vitally needed forum in which the privileged minority i
forced to account for its behavior to the impoverished majority, and it ca
also help the super-powers to avoid direct intervention in areas not really vita
to their own security. "We might profitably ask ourselves," U Thant has said

how much sorrier a state the world would now be if the United Nations had no
existed and acted to soften the conflicts arising among nations. We might also as
ourselves where the world would now be if there were not today's means o
international cooperation to ease the problems of development.

If it is to remain viable, the United Nations cannot lose the support o
the super-powers, for without them it is nothing but a forum of the im
poverished. Thus it must serve, or at least seem to serve, the interests o
the great as well as of the small. The mini-powers would be well advised t(
take this into consideration in pushing "anti-colonial" resolutions througl
the General Assembly. The weakness of the United Nations rests on the very
structure of the organization, which is based upon the legal fiction of equality
for every member state, without, however, the means to enforce order. S
long as such means are lacking, the system merely reinforces what amounts
to international anarchy. The only feasible reform of the United Nations lies
through a return to the original principles of the Charter, itself based upon
the unavoidable truth that the major burden for peace-keeping rests upon

which the most terrible crimes have been committed for the most noble reasons. It is not enough that the exercise of our power should bear the stamp of our virtuous motives. Those who suffer from the application of that power will not appreciate our motives, and we will have to live not with the purity of our motives but with the consequences our power has inflicted.

Power is a tool, and it is also a responsibility. We cannot recapture the innocence of our former isolationism by shutting out a recalcitrant world. The obligations of power are inescapable, and, once having tasted the fruits of power, no nation can easily return to the role of passive observer. But if power is a responsibility, it is also a temptation. In exercising power for causes it deems just, a nation may fall into the error of confounding its responsibility with its ambitions. In so doing it may, even unconsciously, seek to impose its own standards upon other nations in the name of a higher morality. Nations, like individuals, that exert overwhelming power over their neighbors are often given to the abuse of power quite without realizing or intending it.

While great power and a quiet conscience do not normally go together, this need not be an excuse for behavior which would be morally reprehensible if carried out by a small nation. Weak states, too, often have disturbed consciences. Yet the pangs of a disturbed national psyche need not necessarily be relieved by the application of military power wherever frustrations arise. To recognize the anguish of power is useful. But to relieve that anguish by seeking to apply national power everywhere is to plunge from the innocence of isolationism to the arrogance of global interventionism.

The lesson of imperial Britain is a lesson for contemporary America. Like the United States today, Britain stood at the center of a great empire. For most of the nineteenth century she was the strongest power in the world, and the Pax Britannica was imposed for the purpose of managing her empire. It rested upon a balance of power in Europe and upon the acquiescence of the colonized peoples, who were subdued by the superior technology of the imperial nations. Britain was insufferably smug and hypocritical about her empire, engaging in inflated rhetoric about her moral purpose and the "anguish" that such heavy responsibilities inflicted upon the British conscience. Yet for all their cant about the onerous responsibilities of empire, the British did not allow their concern for stability in their distant outposts to involve them in costly wars. They had mercenaries to ensure order, or else they let the inhabitants fight among themselves and then concluded an agreement with the victor. They did not overly trouble themselves with the politics of their wards, they were not seduced by labels, and they did not allow their hypocrisy to interfere with a cold calculation of their national interest.

They marshaled their strength, gauged every crisis according to its impact upon the national interest, and refused to dissipate their resources on involvements that affected them only peripherally. With great pain and under considerable opposition from the hawks of the day, Britain brought her commitments into line with her resources and drew a clear distinction between conflicts that crucially affected her interests and those that did not. Whatever anguish the British may have felt over the power they possessed and the way in which it was applied, they were careful to reserve it for situations which they could hope to control and which were directly related to their national interest.

They were, in short, the opposite of the ancient Athenians, who wasted their substance in foreign wars, sent their fleet to its destruction in the tragic Sicilian campaign, and finally destroyed their own democracy by a policy of military adventurism. In ancient Athens the philosophers gave way to the demagogues, the virtues of the city-state were squandered in the effort to maintain an empire, and the interest of the community was lost in the search for new worlds to conquer. Athens was the opposite of Britain; one sought glory, the other searched for profits; one worried about its world mission, the other about protecting the interests of the nation. Thucydides described the glory and the tragedy of Athens, but it was Palmerston who provided the motto for Britain in declaring, "We have no eternal allies and we have no perpetual enemies. Our interests are eternal and perpetual, and those interests it is our duty to follow." It is the counsel of a man who did not confuse power diplomacy with a higher morality, and who knew the difference between the necessary involvement and the *beau geste.*

The hidden danger of power is that it conceals its own limitations. It is the breeding-ground of self-deception. The words of Edmund Burke to his English countrymen in 1790, when the explosions from revolutionary France seemed ready to shake all imperial Europe, are worth recalling:

Among precautions against ambition it may not be amiss to take one precaution against our *own.* I must fairly say, I dread our *own* power and our *own* ambition. I dread our being too much dreaded. . . . We may say that we shall not abuse this astonishing and hitherto unheard-of power. But every nation will think we shall abuse it. It is impossible but that, sooner or later, this state of things must produce a combination against us which may end in our ruin.

Power, as Burke understood, is an instrument of inflicting evil as well as good, and therefore to be applied only with the greatest reluctance and discrimination when other measures of dissuasion have failed and where the vital interests of the nation are threatened. There are times when this may be so, as it was in Europe during and after the Second World War. In such cases we shall have no alternative but to intervene militarily in defense of our vital interests. But there will be other times, far more numerous, when we shall be tempted to intervene simply because we are powerful and our self-esteem is involved. Those are the cases which are the most difficult, for they involve the highest degree of political self-discipline and the highest qualities of statesmanship. In the delicate balancing of vital interests, discrimination is all. It is here that American policy has often failed, leading the nation into perilous involvements that cannot be satisfactorily resolved and which bring discredit upon ourselves.

If we can gain a sense of perspective about ourselves and what we conceive to be our mission, we may discover that the global quest that has so enchanted us for the past two decades, like the isolationism that came before it, is not a foreign policy but a search for the absolute. Globalism, like isolationism, has been a romantic retreat from the real world. Before the Second World War we thought we were too good for a corrupt world, and so we sought to preserve our moral purity through isolationism. When that failed twice, we then decided to purify the world by transforming it into our own image.

Among the ruins of these two failures we are now faced with the task of adjusting to a world that will not necessarily adopt the virtues we so admire in ourselves but that has its own conflicting values and ambitions, some of which may be the opposite of ours but no less virtuous. "Great as is our strength," a former Secretary of State has written,

we are not omnipotent. We cannot, by fiat, produce the kind of world we want. Even nations which depend greatly upon us do not always follow what we believe to be the right course. For they are independent nations, and not our satellites. Our power and policy are but one significant factor in the world in which we live. In combination with other factors we are able to influence importantly the course of events. But we cannot deal in absolutes.

The words of John Foster Dulles are even more relevant today than when he wrote them in 1957.

Because of his obsession with ideology, Dulles was never able to reconcile his policy with his rhetoric, as he demonstrated at Budapest, or to relate effectively American idealism to the reality of American power. It is an error his successors have compounded. Having turned their back on the old isolationism, and having assumed an exalted sense of world responsibility commensurate with our enormous power, they can see no feasible alternative to a policy of global interventionism. Isolation or intervention: this powerful but essentially false dichotomy has been the hallmark of American postwar diplomacy and the obstacle to the urgently needed reassessment of our role in a revolutionary world.

To turn away from the obsessive globalism that has dominated our foreign policy is not to turn our back on the world. On the contrary, a liberation from globalism will allow us to follow a freer role in world affairs, unhobbled by the obsolete dogmas of the cold war, the self-appointed responsibilities of a world policeman, and the crumbling alliances that inflate our national ego.

What we need are fewer historical compulsions, less Manifest Destiny, more skepticism about the ideals we are promulgating, and a greater realism about the causes in which we have become involved. Above all, we need to develop a sense of proportion about our place in the world, and particularly about ourselves as the pathfinders to the New Jerusalem. America has little to fear from the world, although perhaps a good deal to fear from herself— her obsession with an obsolete ideological struggle, her well-meaning desire to enforce her own conception of virtue upon others, her euphoria of power, and, perhaps most dangerous of all, the unmet, and often unacknowledged, inadequacies of her own society. . . .

79. MAKING THE WORLD ONE

HARVEY WHEELER

Harvey Wheeler is a member of the staff of the Center for the Study of Democratic Institutions.

Among the factors inhibiting the institution of world order, national sovereignty must be given high rank. For example, any effort to expand the jurisdiction of the World Court is met with firm opposition everywhere. The United States adopted the Connally Resolution to prevent the court from exercising jurisdiction over the actions of this country without its express consent. Other countries have followed the same principle when their sovereign integrity was at issue. For example, the developing nations, believing the court to be an instrument of colonialism, refuse to submit disputes to it for adjudication.

At least on this nugatory principle the world is already unified. Soviet ministers, American senators, and African diplomats speak with one voice. They defend their position under the theories of legal sovereignty perfected by nineteenth-century European legal philosophers. This was the jurisprudential tradition that reached from Jean Bodin to John Austin. However, one thing should be clarified immediately: with regard to world order, the critical problem was raised by Hugo Grotius in the seventeenth century, not by Jean Bodin in the sixteenth century.

Sovereignty has both an external and an internal meaning. Grotius's meaning was external, or international. He drew an imaginary juridical boundary line around each of the realms held by the monarchs of Europe and if he found it impervious to laws issuing from the outside, then the ruler was sovereign and his realm possessed sovereignty; that is, it possessed an autonomous corporate personality. But this fact alone had little bearing on what transpired legally *inside* the sovereign realm.

The internal doctrine of sovereignty was first delineated by Jean Bodin and later amplified by such legal philosophers as Thomas Hobbes and John Austin. It meant something quite different from Grotius's concept. It held that internally a proper nation-state ought to be legally monolithic; that is, it should contain an identifiable office or institution with the ultimate authority to resolve internal legal conflicts and with a monopoly of the power required to enforce the law. Internal sovereignty of Bodin's variety possessed much validity. Actual political affairs often revolved around the implications of

From Harvey Wheeler, "Making the World One," *The Center Magazine,* Vol. 1, No. 7 (November, 1968), pp. 34–39. Reprinted by permission of *The Center Magazine,* a publication of the Center for the Study of Democratic Institutions.

internal legal sovereignty, as in the American Civil War. Yet even Bodin and his followers found it necessary to find a place for *political* sovereignty. This was a principle of authority entirely separate from the formal principle of internal legal sovereignty. It made states look dualistic and seriously weakened the argument that each proper state ought to possess a single legal sovereign.

When we speak today of the relation of sovereignty to world order it is necessary to remember that we are applying the international doctrine of Grotius, not the domestic doctrine of Bodin. Eighteenth-century America, for example, struck against Bodin's doctrine in her War of Independence. Parliament had tried to force the Colonies to submit to a legal subordination to England. After the war America created a polity that completely defied any effort to detect where internal Bodinian sovereignty might reside. Other nations that introduced federal systems during the nineteenth century were more fastidious about such problems. Canada, for example, made it clear that supreme authority resided in the Dominion government. Later, on the other hand, the U.S.S.R. was like America; Bodin would have found it difficult to fit either the American or the Soviet system into his scheme.

The same is true of the internal legal orders of today's new nations. Many of them, like Cuba, Yugoslavia, and the United Arab Republic, make no rigid separation between political and legal authority, the two features jurists like Austin rigorously distinguished. And with places like Nigeria and Tanzania the meticulous jurist is further confounded. However, despite such problems regarding the nature of Bodinian internal sovereignty, the new nations are of one mind in upholding their Grotius-style sovereign independence from external encroachment. The monolithic doctrine of internal sovereignty is not at issue when today's nations become exercised over invasions of their sovereignty. It is external sovereignty, the right to conduct one's own affairs independently, that is at issue.

When senators, congressmen, and other public spokesmen denounce world order, they warn against the invasions of sovereignty that they fear will result —interferences with a nation's control over its own internal affairs. These opponents claim that world order would require a nation to give up some of its sovereignty, as if the realm of world order were like the kitty in a poker game which can be built only if each member antes up some of his own money. This is like the old economic fallacy which held that there is only so much money in circulation and if the income of one group is raised, the income of other groups has to be reduced by the same amount.

This was the "wages-fund" theory. In the same way there is a kind of "authority-fund" theory in the minds of the opponents of world order. They believe it is impossible to create any world authority without giving up the same amount of national authority. This is no more true of authority than it is of money. History shows that various groups have often increased their "take" of money when an increase in productivity has occurred. Moreover, it is possible for a wage increase to stimulate an increase in over-all productivity. Something similar is true of political authority. A group of settlers, for example, may join together to create a new village in order to protect themselves from outlaws and to free each individual member from having to maintain his own guard. The creation of a new authority actually expands, rather than detracts from, the power possessed by each member. It is possible, indeed almost inevitable, that world order will be something entirely new. It will not be built out of pieces of sovereignty given up by the member nation-states but, rather, will add something new to the power of each member.

Formerly, it was not too difficult to classify nations, at least on paper. There was something known as the nation-state. It had been born in Europe during the sixteenth and seventeenth centuries. Its power spread over the world during the nineteenth century. By the twentieth century it seemed as if this made-in-Europe type of polity was destined to stamp its image on all corners of the world. The League of Nations and the United Nations were designed with the implicit assumption that its members would be European-type nation-states. This brings us back to the problem of Grotius; namely, the problem of territorial sovereignty. For his conception of the political community was associated with the ownership of real estate.

It is true that real estate has extremely important implications for politics. People live on it and off it. Such territoriality has injected special complications into the problem of sovereignty and now poses a major obstacle for anyone attempting to visualize the legal nature of a future world order. The fact that American federalism linked states together on a territorial basis appears to provide a model for a future world constitution, and it is seductive to regard American federalism as a prototype for unifying the separate states of today's world—a dress rehearsal for world order, as Arthur N. Holcombe called it in a book published shortly after World War II.

Since the present nation-states of the world possess territorial sovereignty, it seems to follow that a world constitution can somehow link these territorial units together in an American-style federal union that might ultimately grow into a "more perfect union." But applying the American model to the world creates more problems than it solves. The conditions existing among nations today are too unlike those of revolutionary America. It is important to remember that the American Colonies had once been unified under the British Crown; they lived under one law, spoke one language, and shared one history. After the Revolution, the problem was not to create union but to re-create one that had existed for a hundred and fifty years before. Moreover, there is considerable merit in the charge that American federalism was basically feudal, a land-based type of politics resting upon the control of estates. New nation-states had been formed by assembling previously autonomous estates and provinces. However, what usually happened in this "feudal" form of federal organization was that parcels of land were unified without their people's ever acquiring a true political being. Two things came to be represented: parcels of land and census counts. But pieces of land and head-counts do not comprise political orders and are not politically real.

There are different kinds of political combinations in which true political communities can be represented: people have professions and functions, they have needs, they have ethnic and cultural traditions, they belong to associations. These are not fortuitous groupings like such geographic entities as Nebraska or Nigeria, which are merely carved out of a land-mass. Likewise, political orders can be unified through non-territorial forms of federalism. Examples range from seventeenth-century Holland to twentieth-century Yugoslavia. The term "polyvalent federalism" is applied to contemporary Yugoslavia because its legislature represents not only regional ethnic units but also economic functions and human needs, all knitted together by an over-all political party that is itself federative. The Yugoslav example provides a much better dress rehearsal for world order than the United States, for territorial federalism like America's requires representative institutions authorized and maintained by those elected from the member-states, and this is impossible in today's world. Yugoslavia demonstrates that several types of non-territorial federal union could be inaugurated on the world level without requiring any prior changes in the institutions of the member-states of the world as they now exist.

Territorial federalism rests on the assumption that each state possesses territorial autonomy and legal sovereignty. If a group of them enters into a compact in which each retains complete autonomy, as in Switzerland, the result is called a confederation. If they form a new, general government, giving it exclusive jurisdiction over some matters but preserving local autonomy for others, it is called a federation. The latter is the American type, sometimes considered dualistic because it provides for two different types of sovereignty: general (federal) sovereignty and state sovereignty. This same dualism can be seen in the non-territorial type of federalism of Yugoslavia. However, the American and the Yugoslav types of federalism are distinguish able. The former is "distributive," the latter is "associative."

Distributive federalism distributes authority between territorial units (states) and the general (federal) government. It declares that it is valid to lay the foundations for authority on a territorial base. Associative federalism, on the other hand, builds a political order by associating functions and needs, rather than by linking together pieces of land.

Distributive federalism has meant at least two different things in American history—one version before the Civil War and something else afterward. I believe that the form of government after the Civil War in this country has been non-federal, because it has provided for all kinds of jurisdictional conflicts to be resolved at a central place; that is, in the general government. Thus, it can be claimed that true federalism existed in America only before the Civil War, for what originally characterized it was the simultaneous maintenance of two different kinds of organized political authority. Federalism basically is a condition of plural loyalty and plural authority, a political order in which there are two or more equally authoritative claims on a citizen's allegiance. This has not been true in America since 1865.

However, there is another kind of dualism to be discovered in the American Constitution. This is based upon the distinction between what might be called the more enduring general principles that express the spirit of the Constitution and the more perishable and transient institutional arrangements that make up a large part of its content. A constitution must provide for both. There is some value in conceiving of a constitution as being divided into two separate sections, comprising two distinct political orders or, in classical language, "two cities." The loftier city, the city of general principles, may be compared to the medieval City of God. It contains the body of highest constitutional ideals. It changes as man's understanding advances. The mundane city changes through advances in the realm of practice. Obviously, each influences the other, but the distinction remains useful and valid.

Translating this to the level of world politics would permit all the nations of the world to be unified in the higher city of fundamental principles and still remain autonomous in the concrete realm of institutional devices. This would not mean that there would be no differences of principle, or of interpretations of principle, between the various members, but that, as in the American experience, these conflicts could take the form of constitutional rather than ideological disputes.

Two separate principles of federal union were incorporated in the Constitution and both might possibly be seen in the governmental institutions that began to appear immediately thereafter. This ambiguity begins with the Preamble and continues to the end of the Bill of Rights. When the Preamble announces its principle of sovereignty by stating: "We the People of the United States . . ." it is unclear whether it is the people as a whole or the people as organized in states who are sovereign. Later on, this ambiguity is maintained in the supremacy clause for the general government, which is counterbalanced by the reserved-powers clause for the states. For more than seventy years these competing federalisms were argued pro and con throughout the land.

Many students regard this as a distressing, or at least an untidy, situation. I find it not only attractive but also wise, for it rests upon the proposition that the dialectic of statesmanship is best generated in a political order so organized that conflicts take the form of disputes over the nature of the Constitution rather than over the competing claims of opposing classes. Constitutional dualism, like most dualisms, stimulates the minds of men to try to resolve the conflict.

Constitutional dualism facilitates the emergence of a high political dialogue on what the political order should be and how it should function. There is no reason why the same result cannot be achieved on the level of world order. It will be objected that the American effort to resolve the dualism failed. Witness the Civil War. Would not the same thing arise from instituting dual constitutionalism on the world level? This is the sort of question that cannot be resolved by arguments from historical evidence. Yet the criticism implies that if the world remains in its present state of ideological conflict, worldwide war can be avoided. It is safe to say that this view is erroneous. Indeed, the Cold War is already a worldwide civil war purportedly based on ideological differences. Any device that can bring the Cold War antagonists into a political order where their ideological disputes can be converted into constitutional disputes can only be an improvement.

But is today's world not divided by the kind of cultural conflict that existed between the North and South in nineteenth-century America? The answer is no. Today's world, taken in the large, is agreed on at least one thing: the elimination of the colonial and slave systems of the past and the institution of modern, industrial systems in their stead. The differences between today's nations are profound but they are differences about means rather than ends, and even these are disappearing. They are becoming much more like the differences between twentieth-century Republicans and Democrats than like those between nineteenth-century New York businessmen and Southern plantation owners. There is a growing similarity, for example, between the economic systems of the U.S.S.R. and the United States. This does not mean they will produce a form of economic union, but it is not necessary to have economic union before there can be a form of political union.

One can begin to conceive of a dynamic political order, either on a national or on a world basis, whose component parts possess very different kinds of governmental systems. This is not difficult to imagine because there is still another virtue in the principle of dualistic federalism. It has to do with the question of revolutionary vs. constitutional change. It is often charged that the great defect of modern constitutionalism is its inability to provide for fundamental changes in social systems. This has meant that change could occur only through revolution. However, successful revolutions usually occur as a result of the gradual creation of a new social order within the confines of the old; the final dramatic act is the installation of the new in place of the old. In the past, this act of substitution had to be violent because constitutions failed to provide for the prior existence side by side of two conflicting social orders. But dual federalism provides precisely this. Thus it may help us, at last, to constitutionalize revolutionary change.

The most serious objection to world order, as we have noted, is the fear that it involves sacrificing some part of one's sovereignty. But the history of federalism shows that an advance toward world order can proceed without creating a unitary world government at all. The Middle Ages had the notion of a "society of peoples." Today there exists a true society of peoples in the world. World order, as described here, could introduce order into that society. The result would not be a state, like the present nation-states. Moreover, it might never become a state. World government might never be the terminus. Instead, it might express itself by using law in new ways. For example, the mechanism for allocating functions among the various peoples of the world might work like Calhoun's nullification scheme: a minority, or any group that found itself threatened, might nullify a proposed plan of action by threatening a veto. This would force a reconsideration of the problem that caused the crisis, and the effort to find a resolution might create a new basis for unification through new forms of law rather than through the governing institutions.

The general proposition is that if there is to be any world order at all, it has to be of a kind that provides for coöperation and integration on the one hand but also firmly defends the disparate and autonomous and unrelated nature of the component parts. This was the dream of the American Constitution. It was to be a form of dual authority that would permit, and even generate, a great deal of governmental experimentation and diversity among the member-states.

This is provided for in the two-city or two-story constitution described earlier. It allows both diversity and plurality in the means for achieving common goals. The result might be no more of a political community than was Christendom. There was never an overriding authority in Christendom to resolve the two-swords controversy. There was no Supreme Court. But out of the conflict came the leading governmental institutions of the nation-state.

What institutions can be devised that would not threaten the sovereign integrity and authority of any one member-nation? The precedents already exist. There is an associative federalism growing up throughout the world in the various international institutions and organizations the members of which are drawn from most of the countries of the world. There is the example of the World Bank, which has assets that nobody owns because only the "world" owns them. There is the proposed internationalization of the ocean beds, of the control of the atmosphere, of the allocation of airline routes, and so on. All of these areas of growing world integration are based upon the building of organizations along functional and associative, rather than territorial, lines. They already represent a kind of world order and therefore of world union. And no nation is any the worse. In fact, the contrary is true.

International policing and international adjudication would not be the immediate consequences of this new type of federal union. Results of this kind do not come in that way. The first step is the creation of a union in the realm of the spirit and in the realm of allegiance. Then, some while after that, union can become possible in the realm of actual operations. This may seem, in a sense, a doctrine of gradualism, but, in truth, it is a doctrine that says: Go slow in order to make haste.

80. THE ILLUSION OF
WORLD GOVERNMENT

REINHOLD NIEBUHR

*Reinhold Niebuhr (1892–   ) is professor emeritus of Applied Chris-
tianity at Union Theological Seminary and a leader of the Liberal Party
in New York. He has written extensively on the relationship of
politics to ethics.*

. . . Virtually all arguments for world government rest upon the simple
presupposition that the desirability of world order proves the attainability of
world government. Our precarious situation is unfortunately no proof, either
of the moral ability of mankind to create a world government by an act of
the will, nor of the political ability of such a government to integrate a world
community in advance of a more gradual growth of the "social tissue" which
every community requires more than government.

Most advocates of world government also assume that nations need merely
follow the alleged example of the individuals of another age who are supposed
to have achieved community by codifying their agreements into law and by
providing an agency of some kind for law enforcement. This assumption
ignores the historic fact that the mutual respect for each other's rights in
particular communities is older than any code of law; and that machinery
for the enforcement of law can be efficacious only when a community as a
whole obeys its laws implicitly, so that coercive enforcement may be limited
to a recalcitrant minority.

The fallacy of world government can be stated in two simple propositions.
The first is that governments are not created by fiat (though sometimes they
can be imposed by tyranny). The second is that governments have only
limited efficacy in integrating a community.

The advocates of world government talk of calling a world constitutional
convention which would set up the machinery of a global constitutional order
and would then call upon the nations to abrogate or abridge their sovereignty
in order that this newly created universal sovereignty could have unchallenged
sway. No such explicit abnegation has ever taken place in the history of the
world. Explicit governmental authority has developed historically from the
implicit authority of patriarchal or matriarchal tribal forms. Governments,
so established, have extended their dominion over weaker neighbors. But the
abridgement of sovereignty has always been indirect rather than direct; or

From Reinhold Niebuhr, "The Illusion of World Government," reprinted with permission from *Bulletin of the Atomic Scientists,* October, 1949. Copyright Educational
Foundation for Nuclear Science, Inc., Chicago, Ill. Pp. 289–92, excerpts.

it has been attained by the superimposition of power. . . . No group of individuals has ever created either government or community out of whole cloth. One reason why the social contract conception of government has a particular plausibility with us is because the United States came closer to a birth by "contract" than any other nation. But the preamble of our Constitution declares that its purpose is to establish a "more perfect union." That is a very telling phrase which presupposes a previous union. This previous union was in fact established on the battlefield in a common struggle against a common foe; it needed only to be made "more perfect." It may be observed in passing that, though the Thirteen Colonies had never enjoyed sovereignty, they did not find it too easy to submit what had only been potential, and not actual, sovereignty to the authority of the Federal Union. We fought a civil war before it was proved that they had, in fact, done this without reservations.

When the question is raised whether the nations of the world would voluntarily first create, and then submit to a supernational authority, the possible reluctance of nations, other than Russia, to take this step is fortunately or unfortunately obscured by the Russian intransigence. The Russians have declared again and again that they would leave the United Nations if the veto power were abolished. This means that Russia, as a prospective minority in a world community is not ready to submit her fate to the will of the majority, even in such a loose organization as the United Nations. It is therefore obvious that she would be even more unwilling to submit her sovereignty to a more highly integrated constitutional order.

The proponents of world government have two answers to the problem posed by Russian intransigence. One is to assert that the Russians never have had the chance to accept or reject a genuinely constitutional world order; and that there are real possibilities of her acceptance of a constitution which is not weighted against her. This answer contains in a nutshell the rationalist illusion implicit in world government theories. . . .

The other answer to the problem of Russian intransigence is a proposed creation of a "world" government without Russia. Thus in the name of "one world" the world would be divided in two. Proponents of world government are always ready with criticisms of the ambiguities in the Charter of the United Nations, without recognizing that those ambiguities correspond to the actual historical situation. The Security Council is, for instance, a bridge of a sort between the segments of a divided world. They would destroy that bridge for the sake of creating a more logical constitutional system. This done, they look forward to one of two possibilities.

One is that Russia, faced with a united opposition, and concluding that she would not have to sacrifice her Communist government but only her ambition to spread Communism, would ultimately capitulate and join the world federation. This abstract approach to political problems is completely oblivious of the dynamism of Communism.

The other course chosen by some advocates of world government is to create such a government without Russia and to divide the world more consistently in the name of the principle of "one" world. If this should lead to a world conflict they believe that the agonies of war will be assuaged for us by our knowledge that we are at least fighting for a principle of ultimate validity. . . .

The ambiguities in the Charter of the United Nations which so outrage the advocates of world government are in fact the consequence of seeking to guarantee two, rather than one, objectives. The one objective is to preserve the unity of one world, even though it be seriously divided, and to provide a meeting ground between East and West where some of the tensions and frictions may be resolved. The other is to preserve the integrity of our way of life against a tyrannical system which we abhor. The Russians, insofar as they are honest devotees of a Marxist dream of world order, are presumably in the same position. Each of us hopes ultimately to create a world order upon the basis of our conception of justice. Neither of us is ready, at the moment, to submit our fate to a world authority without reservation, so long as the possibility remains that such an authority could annul a system of law and justice to which we are deeply committed.

So far we have considered only the difficulties of creating a world government by constitutional fiat. But a much more serious defect in world government theories is to be found in their conception of the relation of government to community. Governments cannot create communities for the simple reason that the authority of government is not primarily the authority of law nor the authority of force, but the authority of the community itself. Laws are obeyed because the community accepts them as corresponding, on the whole, to its conception of justice. This is particularly true of democratically organized communities but it is well to observe that even in traditional, non-democratic communities of the past there was a discernible difference between tyranny and legitimate government. It consisted precisely in the fact that a legitimate government relied primarily upon the implicit consent of the community. . . .

The priority of the community to its laws and its use of force does not mean that both law and force may not have limited efficacy in perfecting the organization and preserving the integrity of the community. Good constitutions provide for the rational arbitrament of many conflicting and competing forces which might otherwise tear the community apart. Preponderant force in one part of the community may also so shape the social forces of the total community that its use need not be perpetual. . . . The analogy in present global terms would be the final unification of the world through the preponderant power of either America or Russia, whichever proved herself victorious in a final global struggle. The analogy teaches us nothing about the possibilities of a constitutional world state. It may teach us that though the perils of international anarchy are very great, they may still be preferable to international tyranny.

The coalescence of communities from city-states to empires in the ancient world, and from feudal entities to nations in the modern period, was frequently accomplished only by the imposition of preponderant power. The fact is particularly significant, since all of these communities could rely upon all sorts of "organic" factors for their force of cohesion which the rudimentary world community lacks. By organic factors, I mean such forces as the power of ethnic kinship, the force of a common history—particularly the memory of joint struggles against a common foe—a common language, a common culture, and a common religion. We do have examples of ethnically and religiously pluralistic nations and empires, but they possess a basic homogeneity of some kind, underlying the differences.

The fact is that even the wisest statecraft cannot create social tissue. It can cut, sew, and redesign social fabric to a limited degree. But the social fabric upon which it works must be "given."

The international community is not totally lacking in social tissue; but it is very scant, compared with that of particular states. Let us briefly assess the various factors in it. Most important as a force of social cohesion in the world community is the increasing economic interdependence of peoples of the world. But it is important to contrast this economic interdependence immediately with the wide disparity in the economic strength of various nations.

A second factor in the social tissue of the world community is the fear of mutual annihilation, heightened in recent years by the new dimension which atomic discoveries have given to mankind's instruments of death. We must not underestimate this fear as a social force, even as we must recognize that some culturally pluralistic communities of past history have achieved some cohesion through the minimal conviction that order is to be preferred to anarchy. But the fear of destruction in itself is less potent than the fear of specific peril from a particular foe. There is no record in history of peoples establishing a common community because they feared each other, though there are many instances when the fear of a common foe acted as the cement of cohesion.

The final and most important factor in the social tissue of the world community is a moral one. Enlightened men in all nations have some sense of obligation to their fellow men, beyond the limits of their nation-state. There is at least an inchoate sense of obligation to the inchoate community of mankind. The desperate necessity for a more integrated world community has undoubtedly increased this sense of obligation, inculcated in the conscience of mankind since the rise of universal, rather than parochial, philosophies and religions. This common moral sense is of tremendous importance for the moral and religious life of mankind; but it does not have as much immediate political relevance as is sometimes supposed. Political cohesion requires common convictions on particular issues of justice; and these are lacking. . . .

In short, the forces which are operating to integrate the world community are limited. To call attention to this fact does not mean that all striving for a higher and wider integration of the world community is vain. That task must and will engage the conscience of mankind for ages to come. But the edifice of government which we build will be sound and useful if its height is proportionate to the strength of the materials from which it is constructed. The immediate political situation requires that we seek not only peace, but also the preservation of a civilization which we hold to be preferable to the universal tyranny with which Soviet aggression threatens us. Success in this double task is the goal; let us not be diverted from it by the pretense that there is a simple alternative. . . .

81. WORLD PEACE THROUGH LAW

CHARLES S. RHYNE

Charles S. Rhyne (1912–   ) is a practicing attorney and former Chairman of the American Bar Association and of its Committee on World Peace Through Law.

I now speak of the No. 1 problem of mankind in the world today: how to achieve and maintain world peace.

As a foundation for my thesis that peace between nations may be achieved and maintained through use of the rule of law in a new world-wide system of courts, it is helpful to recall the rapid forward rush of events in our era of unprecedented change. History teaches that these dramatic new advances are mere promises and preludes to even greater achievements in the future. One who would postulate any plan to solve any problem of our day must therefore also look beyond the present to the new horizons and the new frontiers envisioned by the world in which we now live. . . .

The World Today. Today, when man has learned how to destroy the world, his greatest need is for instrumentalities and institutions which can save mankind from the mass extermination of nuclear war. The sands of time have about run out in the hour-glass of our civilization. Few will dispute that the No. 1 problem of our day is how to achieve and maintain true peace. This situation presents a unique and unparalleled opportunity to lawyers, for it is the rule of law which contains the key to a peaceful world. . . .

The Machinery Now Used Has Not Created Peace. A look at the policy of the United States today reveals that our government is maintaining the current truce through (1) military force, (2) diplomatic negotiations, agreements, and treaties, (3) trade and aid, (4) the United Nations and alliances with friendly nations, and (5) measures designed to offset Communist propaganda. But all of this together has not achieved true peace. . . .

A Universally Comprehensible New Plan: The Rule of Law. To pull the world out of its present drift toward destruction, and to set it on the path of progress toward peace, a dramatic new approach is essential. . . . Settlement of international disputes through law in the courts is such a plan.

"Law" and "courts" are universal terms all men comprehend. All peoples

From Charles S. Rhyne, "World Peace Through World Law," reprinted from *American Bar Association Journal,* Vol. 44 (October, 1958), pp. 937–40 and 997–1001, excerpts.

know the law and courts have proved their worth as a keeper of the peace within nations. They will readily grasp the concept, content, and the value of this plan of going to court instead of to war. They know what law and the courts have done nationally, and if proper leadership is given they can be brought to see what law can do internationally.

Law Is Civilization's Best Concept to Create Peace. An evaluation of the ideas, ideals, and concepts which mankind has developed since the dawn of history leads to the inescapable conclusion that the rule of law offers the best attainable rule to peace. . . . Men know that peace reigns where law prevails. People everywhere experience law's use almost daily in courts in their local communities. Out on the vast new frontier of the international community, disputes previously settled by the bloodbath of war must come to be settled by similar tribunals of justice.

Man has not realized what law can do for him internationally, and that is the reason why law has not been used in this field as it can and must be. The basic ungrasped fact of our time is that the lack of the rule of law in the world community is today the greatest gap in the growing structure of civilization. A community, whether local, national, or international, can become and remain peaceful only so long as it is subject to the rule of law. Down through the ages, people have lived in terror and fear wherever the rule of law has not prevailed within nations. . . .

Existing Court Inadequate. . . . The sine qua non of this plan for peace is a world-wide court system to make law accessible and usable. Within nations we have thousands of courts, local, state, regional, and national. But for the entire world community we have only one court. It is the International Court of Justice. The Court has 15 judges. It has decided 10 cases in the 12 years of its existence. The major nations of the world seemingly ignore its availability and utility.

Our own country—despite the American Bar Association's express opposition to this policy—reserves to itself the right to decide whether complaints filed in the International Court of Justice are within the domestic jurisdiction of the United States. Such a stultifying provision says to the world that we decline to trust the Court to rule correctly on such an issue. This lack of respect by us and other nations with similar reservations, has largely destroyed the prestige and usefulness of the Court. The inaccessibility of the Court also contributes to the failure of nations to use it. It is the present practice of the Court to hold all its hearings at The Hague.

The United States should assume leadership in creating respect and prestige for the Court by removing our reservation on jurisdiction. The Court can itself make its processes more useful and accessible by sitting constantly at the seat of the United Nations in New York. The Court should also announce its willingness to sit all over the world in chambers of three judges. Its charter now authorizes such action by the Court, but it has done nothing to make this provision meaningful. These are things which the United States can do, and which the Court can do, to move the Court forward toward its potential use as a mechanism for peace. But more is needed to make law and the courts serve as they can and must in this vital field.

Applying the lesson of history, we need to go beyond the present structure of the International Court of Justice and create an entirely new and additional world-wide system of courts to make law as an instrumentality for peace accessible to the people throughout the world. A system of circuit courts under the International Court of Justice is needed. Perhaps we should go beyond that and have one judge sitting constantly in a branch of the world court system in each sovereign nation. There could be intermediate courts of appeals on a regional basis with a final appeal to the International Court of Justice. Such a world legal system would parallel in the international community the setup of the federal court system in the United States.

Without the institution of the courts the rule of law cannot be made effective internationally. An international judicial system would throw a blanket of law over the world. Any nation refusing to participate would be automatically branded as outlaw by world public opinion. . . .

Jurisdiction of New World Court System. The jurisdiction of the new world court system should include all disputes between nations whose resolution depends upon facts and the application of the principles of the rule of law. . . .

Enforcement of World Court Judgments. Enforcement of world court decrees and judgments would depend in the first instance, as it does now within nations, upon voluntary compliance. . . . Full faith and credit could be granted also by national courts to the decrees and judgments of world courts, thus permitting enforcements to be sought in such national forums. If enforcement is refused, or prevented, diplomatic and economic sanctions could be imposed. Finally, some kind of world police force has been suggested for use in extreme cases under proper safeguard. The latter idea would certainly require extreme caution, care, and insurance against misuse and abuse, but experience with such a force already indicates it can be useful in proper situations. . . .

Objections to World Peace Through Law. World peace through law is not put forward as a utopian scheme for a perfect world community, and the plan here espoused is limited to use of law in a world court system. But there are those who oppose even this modest beginning toward settlement of conflicts between nations in a civilized manner. The objections can be classified as follows: (1) This plan is an idealistic dream; (2) law has been around from time immemorial but has not stopped wars; (3) the international judiciary might make some wrong decisions; (4) the plan is just too difficult to create and get into operation; (5) such a plan would never work because Russia would not join in it; and (6) the world community needs more than just a judiciary.

To say that peace through law in the courts is an idealistic dream which therefore cannot be realized is to deny the facts of history. America was built on idealism. . . .

Certain it is that law has been around for many years, and granted, it has not stopped wars. The outlawing of war through the Kellogg-Briand Pact did not stop wars because that pact had no institution of a world court system to implement it. The mechanism of law plus the institution of the courts has never been tried in the way herein urged. In this respect, law is like religion. It has not failed; it has never really been tried. Within nations law plus the courts has certainly brought peace. On such a record of accomplishment it is reasonable to believe that such a mechanism can do the same if utilized in the world community.

Certain it is also that the world court system would be manned by human beings and those human beings may sometimes decide contrary to our wishes and even make wrong decisions. Law plus the courts is not a cure-all. . . . But court decisions if contrary to fact and reason are always subject to change, while the millions of gravestones all over the world are mute testimony to the unchangeability of the results of war. A few wrong court decisions do not destroy the value of this plan, any more than a few wrong court decisions destroy the value of the use of law in the courts within nations. Few will deny that it is better to have a few wrong court decisions than millions of deaths in all-out nuclear war.

As to the objection that an effective international judicial system will be too difficult to create and get into operation, twentieth century man has not let difficulties prevent him from accomplishing other seemingly impossible goals. A short time ago the splitting of the atom was looked upon as an unrealizable dream, but now it is a reality. A short time ago the satellite was a fantastic dream, but now it is a reality. Twentieth-century man has developed a technique for concentration of the talents of many people on seemingly insoluble problems so as to achieve a breakthrough. . . .

We must face the fact that despite the interest expressed by Russian lawyers on my recent visit with the American Bar Association delegation to the Soviet Union, Russia will probably not agree to use of the rule of law in a world-wide court system as a mechanism for settlement of international disputes, particularly those in which she is involved. But to let Russia exercise a veto preventing the creation of this world court system would give the Kremlin an unthinkable control over world progress toward peace. The world court system can operate without the Soviet Union. After this court system is established, and as it demonstrates its worth by use outside the Iron Curtain, it will have a tremendous attraction for the neutral and uncommitted nations. These nations want peace so that their social and economic development plans can go forward and will want to join in any system which brings world peace. Russia's propaganda which is now directed so strongly to those nations would have no answer to the liberty, equality, and justice which the world court system offers as contrasted with slaughter on the battlefield. If Russia refuses to use this mechanism, and the free world does use it, Russia's adherence to lawlessness would be crystal-clear to the whole world. Here only actions would count. With the increasing education of the Russian people, and the strong desire for peace which persists in the hearts of men even behind the Iron Curtain, perhaps this plan might even reduce the depth of the Iron Curtain itself. Adherence to this plan by nations seeking freedom from the Russian colonial empire is certainly a very real possibility. The lawyers of Yugoslavia with whom our American bar delegation conferred in Belgrade recently indicated tremendous interest in this idea.

I quickly concede that the world community has been reluctant to make much use of law in the past, and that it needs more than just a new world court system. All I contend for here is that use of law in the courts will aid in preventing war so that the other needs of the world community can be met through other mechanism. . . .